A Servant's Song

Daily Spiritual Meditations

Michael B. Hobbs

Copyright 2008 Michael B. Hobbs. All rights reserved.

No part of this book may be reproduced, stored in a retrieval system, or transmitted by any means without the written permission of the author.

First published by Lulu Publishers July 2008

ISBN: 978-0-557-00611-3

A SERVANT'S SONG
published by Lulu Publishers

All scripture quotations, unless otherwise indicated, are taken from the ***Holy Bible, New International Version***®. NIV®. Copyright © 1973, 1978, 1984 by International Bible Society. Used by permission of Zondervan. All rights reserved.

Other Scripture references are from the following sources:

The King James Version of the Bible (KJV), The KJV is public domain in the United States.

The Message (MSG), Scripture taken from The Message. Copyright © 1993, 1994, 1995, 1996, 2000, 2001, 2002. Used by permission of NavPress Publishing Group.

The New King James Version (NKJV), Scripture taken from the New King James Version. Copyright © 1982 by Thomas Nelson, Inc. Used by permission. All rights reserved.

The New Living Translation (NLT) copyright © 1996, 2004. Used by permission of Tyndale House Publishers, Inc., Wheaton, Illinois 60189. All rights reserved.

J. B. Phillips: The New Testament in Modern English (Phillips), (Revised Edition Phillips). Copyright © J. B. Phillips 1958, 1960, 1972. Used by permission of Macmillan Publishing Co., Inc.

The New Revised Standard Version Bible (NRSV), Scripture taken from the New Revised Standard Version Bible, copyright © 1989 National Council of the Churches of Christ in the United States of America. Used by permission. All rights reserved.

The Bible in Today's English Version (TEV), Scriptures and additional materials quoted are from the *Good News Bible* © 1994 published by the Bible Societies/HarperCollins Publishers Ltd. Used with permission

Cover design by Laurie Dandiford Hobbs

The pictures of the stained-glass windows on the cover were taken in the sanctuary of the First United Methodist Church, Rockingham, North Carolina by Ann Crotts.

Dedicated to my wife,
a servant of God
who lives, serves,
and sings her faith.
And to our children:
Michael, Angela, Lindsay,
Connie, and Eddie
who are gifts of grace
from a loving Father.

Acknowledgments

"No man is an island unto himself." Though John Donne penned those words, I am sure that there have been many before and after him who were well acquainted with the truth they convey. As we make our way through life, there are hundreds, if not thousands, of people who shape, influence, and contribute to what we become. For most of us it will begin with our parents, siblings, and other relatives. Add to that neighbors, Sunday school and school teachers, college professors, ministers, co-workers, and friends with whom we grow up and mature. I am grateful for all those whose lives affected mine for good and helped shape me into the person I have become.

It would be impossible to mention all the many members of congregations that I served who showed me love and granted me the grace to be their pastor. I sought to teach and preach the gospel to them; they blessed me by living it out before me.

I will be forever grateful to Mrs. Bett Lyles, a member of the last church that I served before retiring. She, more than any other person, pushed me to publish this book. She would not let me give up, even when I had decided I would. She has waded through the manuscript several times, but alas, I fear that my typographical and grammatical errors were so many that a few even slipped past her. Thank you, Bett, for your persistence!

I am indebted to my daughter-in-law, Laurie, for her assistance in helping me prepare the manuscript for publication and for the beautiful artwork which graces the cover of this book.

I am deeply grateful to my wife, Gaye. She has been my closest friend, and for me, the best model of what a Christian should be. There is so much of God's grace in her that I am awed by how deep and genuine it is. She truly is the best person I have ever known. If we all sought to diligently nurture and develop our spiritual life as she does hers, how much better our world would be. She is truly a servant who sings the song of our Lord Jesus!

Michael B. Hobbs

Introduction

In some ways, the writing of this book was quite similar to my call to be a minister. For eight long years, I fought that call; I struggled to run from it and sought to live life according to my will, rather than God's. The fallen nature of my humanity beckoned me to take the easy path, the one **most** traveled, and to be content with life as I knew it. I surmised that there were plenty of other people more talented and qualified than I to be ministers. Let God use them. Who am I? What can I possibly do for God that would have any lasting value at all? But the Spirit would not leave me undisturbed in my "contentment." It relentlessly pursued me until I was overwhelmed by His persistence and finally yielded my life in service to my Lord.

I have no idea who or how many will ever read this book; and in reality, that is not my concern—it is God's. In striving with myself over writing this book, I felt the same persistent voice of God come to me again and again—often through the encouragement and insistence of friends and loved ones. "You must put those devotions into a book," they argued. In all candor, I felt reluctant to do that because I honestly didn't feel that what I had to say would make much difference to the world. I guess I must be one of the stones that Jesus said His Father would make cry out if the voice of His people remained silent. Since I feel compelled to cry out, then may my words be heard as the mere *song of a servant*. It is the song that is important, not the servant!

As I type these words I am reminded of the magnificent spiritual autobiography written by E. Stanley Jones—*A Song of Ascents*. In his introduction he writes:

> You can only sing when you have something to sing about. But my "something" is a Someone. My theme is Jesus Christ.... when it comes to Jesus Christ, there are no apologies on my lips, for there are none in my heart. My song about Jesus Christ is not a species of whistling in the dark to keep up my courage, I sing with my total being—with my mind, my emotion, my will—with the consent of all my being. I sing because I can't help it. If I held my peace, the stones—the hard bare facts of life—would cry out. (p.19)

The words in this book flowed out of the lives of many, including my own, as we struggled together to discover God's kingdom and to discern and do His will. That flow carried us from the ecstatic experience of mountain peaks to the life-shaping experiences of deep valleys. It meandered its way through times of health, vitality, and strength and plunged headlong into the uncharted land of sickness, pain, and sorrow. Each incident, each experience shapes and molds us into what we become. But what we become, in no small measure, is determined by how we react to what we experience. We can either sing our song with joy, or we can simply wail into the night. We can use stumbling blocks as stepping stones, or we can be content to wallow in fallen despair and not get up.

Like everyone else, I have had to deal with the "ups" and "downs" of living. I have known the glorious light of joy, peace, and fulfillment and I have also known the darkness of failure, sorrow, and sickness. I have struggled through the trauma of divorce and lived with the recurring reality of cancer. Each experience has taken a toll on my life, but more importantly, each has shaped my spiritual life and drawn me closer to God. From those experiences, which are common to all humanity, I hope the devotions in this book will sing to you a song of hope and encouragement. May they point you toward God and may they help you hear His loving voice more clearly.

Daily devotionals have been favorites of many Christians for years. They are like poetry in the sense that they seek to condense thoughts on a subject into a limited number of words that can be digested in a brief period of time. They serve as mini-sermons or "thought-starters" to engage not just the mind, but also the soul. The daily devotions in this book are a little longer than those in other devotional booklets such as *The Upper Room* or *Our Daily Bread*, which are favorites of many. Still, one can easily read each of these daily devotions in less than five minutes.

While serving as pastor of several different churches, I discovered that the church newsletter offered an excellent opportunity to challenge not only the mind but also the spirit of my people outside the normal Sunday worship service. Having been the recipient of many church newsletters in my life, I was amazed at how few ministers took the opportunity to use the "pastor's space" as a time to draw their congregations deeper in faith. Too often, the "note from the pastor" dealt only with business matters that left the congregant's soul starved for spiritual nourishment.

Most of the articles in this book were written over a period of ten years that spanned portions of pastorates at three different churches. For the most part, they were written to be spiritual food for those whom I was privileged to serve. It never occurred to me as I began writing them that I would one day put them into the form of a daily devotional book. Much to my surprise, many individuals began to ask for copies of some of the articles and others encouraged me to put them in a booklet each year and allow members of the church to purchase them. This I did by photocopying the articles, placing them in loose-leaf binders, and donating all the proceeds to various mission works with which our church happened to be involved.

You will note that the articles are replete not only with scripture but also with scores of illustrations that I gathered over the course of my years as a pastor. Jesus was the master of the parable, which basically is a simple illustration from everyday life that makes a theological statement clearer. People love to hear good stories and I noted over the years during my sermons, that the interest of the people almost always seemed most intense when a story was told to illustrate the point. A good story can touch the emotions and the soul in a way that a spiritual truth, no matter how well defined, cannot. For example, consider this story by and unknown author:

> *Do you know the legend of the Cherokee Indian youth's rite of passage? His father takes him into the forest, blindfolds him and leaves him alone. He is required to sit on a stump the whole night and not remove the blindfold until the rays of the morning sun shine through it.*
>
> *He cannot cry out for help to anyone. Once he survives the night, he is a MAN. He cannot tell the other boys of this experience, because each lad must come into manhood on his own.*
>
> *The boy is naturally terrified. He can hear all kinds of noises. Wild beasts must surely be all around him. Maybe even some human might do him harm. The wind blows the grass and earth, and shakes his stump, but he sits stoically, never removing the blindfold. It is the only way he can become a man!*

Finally, after a horrific night, the sun appears and he removes his blindfold. It was then that he discovered his father sitting on the stump next to him. He had been at watch the entire night, protecting his son from harm.

We are never alone. Even when we don't know it, our Heavenly Father is watching over us, sitting on the stump beside us. When trouble comes all we have to do is reach out to Him.

The illustrations that I chose were intended to make clearer the spiritual issues that reveal themselves in the devotions. The articles, written over the ten year period, are not all in chronological sequence. In compiling them, I arranged them so that they would be timely for special seasons of the Christian year—such as the beginning of a new year, Lent, Easter, July Fourth, Thanksgiving, Advent and Christmas.

Lent includes the forty days preceding Easter (excluding Sundays), and is determined by the date set for Easter. As a result, the season does not cover the same period each year. The earliest possible date for Lent (which always begins with Ash Wednesday) is February 4; the latest it can begin is March 10. Therefore, I placed the Lenten articles in the book beginning on February 15. In so doing, most of the articles, regardless of the year, will fall within the season of Lent. Most of the meditations in that section of the book will direct your thoughts to the passion of Christ, especially the events of Holy Week and specifically to the Cross. Similarly, the days leading up to Christmas in the Advent season will focus on Christ's birth and the people and events that surrounded it.

Every one of these articles has been gone over multiple times; not only to correct typos and grammatical errors, but to modify them so that they would be relative for any person in any congregation. While many were written for the specific needs of the church I happened to be serving at the time, I have tried to reword the articles so that they would be applicable to almost any church.

In 1996, I was diagnosed with cancer (liposarcoma). A massive tumor (six by nine inches) was discovered between my stomach and my spine. As a result of that tumor and its recurrence, I underwent two major operations, chemotherapy, and radiation therapy. The prognosis indicated that the cancer would continue to recur and would have to be surgically removed every two to three years for the rest of my life. Eventually, it would probably become inoperable. Six years after the initial discovery of liposarcoma, I was diagnosed with prostate cancer that required more surgery. I share this information with you for two reasons. First, because several of the articles I wrote during those years mention my battle with cancer. Few things in life cause us to be more aware of our spirituality than those things that threaten our physical life. It is in those moments that we either seek to draw closer to God or we turn away from Him. I chose the former.

Secondly, I perceived it to be important to let you see how one Christian sought to deal with the life-threatening illness of cancer. Will faith make any difference in how we face such news, or will the nature and impact of the illness cause faith to crumble and God to be forsaken? As I once said to my congregation at the threshold of my illness, "I may not always have lived the way I should have for my Lord, but if this illness should result in my death, then I invite you to watch how I die!"

Perhaps you have had or will experience cancer or some other terrible disease in your own life or in the life of one you love. How it ultimately effects you will be determined by how you face it. The articles I wrote concerning my own life-threatening illness were intended to encourage and strengthen not only those who were also dealing with such issues, but also those who loved me and were distraught over the suffering that I endured. If you are interested in those articles, they can be found on pages 40, 41, 51, 89, 104, 128, 148, 149, 152, 161, 173, 181, 190, 362, 420, 449, 501, and 536.

It has been twelve years since my initial diagnosis—I'm still here! My song has not been a complaint or a wail, but a song of praise and celebration—not just because my life has been extended by God's grace, but because God found a way to use my experience of suffering to bring glory to Himself and some sense of comfort to others who shared similar experiences in life.

Life has taught me that it is in our willingness to become a servant that we learn how to sing God's song. Surrendering our will to His gives birth to a melody that not only seems pleasant to the ears but also stirs the soul and sends the spirit soaring to a place it has never known. May God use the simple words in this book to cause your spirit to soar on eagle's wings to heights you've never known.

MBH

Contents

January

Beginning Anew	1
Memories	2
Spiritual Inventory	4
The Someone Song	5
It's Time to Begin	6
God's Epiphany	8
The Runner	9
Love Makes No Demand	11
The Importance of a Relationship	12
A Spiritual Kingdom	13
The Richest Man in the Valley	15
Worship	16
Faith and Adversity	18
Love Leaves No Room	19
Nourishing the Spirit	20
Of Joy and Sorrow	22
The Treasure of the Kingdom	23
Receiving the Bread of Life	25
Are You God's Friend?	26
Do You Live With Jesus?	27
Overcoming Discouragement	29
Growing in the Midst of Sorrow	30
The Poverty of the Soul	32
The Present Moment	33
Loved for Who You Are	34
When Adversity Comes	36
The Mystery of Life	37
On Seeing the One Who Died for Us	39
For God's Glory	40
The Discovery of Joy	41
Freedom From Fear	43

February

Trusting in God	44
Come and Die	46
Grace Awaits You	47
The Church	48
On Measuring Your Life	50
When Trouble Comes	51
On Making Choices	53
Cheap Grace/Costly Grace	54
The Search for Truth	55
Hearing and Believing	57
Abundant Living	58
Solitude With God	60
The Necessity of Accountability	61
Buried Treasure	63
The God of Brokenness	64
The Way of the Cross	65
Lent	67
When a Cross Becomes a Cross	68
The Cross and the Pain of God	70
Sacrifice and the Cross	71
The Cross—Divine/Human Intersection	73
Love, Suffering, and the Cross	74
Reflections on a Crucifix	75
Death on a Cross	77
The Cross	78
The Glory of the Cross	80
The Revelations of Pain	81
The Choice	83
The Great Exchange	85

March

The Heart of God`	86
The Great Intersection	88
It's Springtime Again	89
The Extravagance of Love	91
The Cross Speaks Again	92
Crucified With Christ	94
If Only You Had Known . . .	95
Day of Triumph	96
Six Hours	98
Watch With Me	99
The Depths of Divine Love	101
Center Stage	102
Life's Ups and Downs	104
Resurrection Living	105
People of the Resurrection	106
Grief, Hopelessness, and Easter	108
Between Good Friday and Easter	109
"It" Brought Easter	111
The Unsealing of a Tomb	112
The Day After	114
The Illogic of Faith	115

The State of Your Mind and Soul	117
The Dark Night of the Soul	118
Dealing With Temptation	120
Living Life on the Level of Spirit	121
Love Will Set Us Free	122
The Heavenward Call	124
The Reality of Jesus	125
When You Don't Feel Needed	127
Thankfulness in the Midst of Trouble	128
The True Kingdom	130

April

The Process of Becoming	131
Living in Christ	132
Free From the Fear of Death	134
Faith on a Tombstone	135
The Touch of Faith	137
The Empowering Renovation	138
Because We're Christians	140
Nothing Wasted	141
Is Church Really Important?	142
What Would Jesus Do?	144
Are We Truly the Church?	145
Membership or Discipleship?	147
I Have Learned . . .	148
Faith is Trust	149
Today is Our "If Only" Time	151
Resting in God	152
The Wonder of Love	154
A Living Well or a Swamp?	155
Discovering Our Aliveness	157
Living in Two Worlds	158
The Treasures of Darkness	160
Which Day Are You Living In?	161
Spiritual Living	163
Love and Obedience	164
Does Your Life Matter?	166
The Mountain or Mountain Mover?	167
Abide in Christ	169
The Power of Prayer	170
The Homeland of the Soul	171
Life—A Sacred Trust	173

May

Living Life Faithfully	174
The World We Alone Can See	176
The Great Transformation	177
The Growing of Faith	178
The Great Encounter	180
The Presence of Tribulation	181
Time Alone With God	183
The Storehouse Called Faith	184
The Origin of Faith	186
Necessities for the Spiritual Life	187
The God Who Speaks From Within	189
Choosing a Dwelling Place	190
Peace Like a River	192
Come Aside and Pray	193
Spend Time With Yourself	195
The Value of Pain	196
What a Savior!	198
Love Birthed in Brokenness	199
God's Hidden Image	200
Self-love or Self-loathing?	201
Spiritual Pigmies or Giants	203
The Wonder of Grace	205
What Are You Following?	206
What's Missing?	208
What Are You Living For?	209
Soul Glory	211
Paper Doll Days	212
Faith is a Journey	214
Time for God	215
Paradoxical Living	217
Obedience and the Spirit	218

June

The Healing Balm of Grace	219
The Best of the Past	221
The Battle With Fear	222
The Temporary and the Permanent	224
The Eyes of the Soul	225
The Boomerang Principle	227
The Assurance of Salvation	228
Grace and Assurance	229

A More Beautiful Melody	231
Called to Follow	233
Sing Me a Song	234
Tears in a Bottle	236
Building or Body?	237
The Value of Small Things	239
Adversity—Rock or Stepping Stone?	240
The Bondage of Sin	241
The Poor in Spirit	243
O the Joy of Mourning	244
On Going Home	246
Inheritance Through Humility	247
The Joy of Being Thirsty	249
The Joy of Showing Mercy	250
The Joy of a Pure Heart	252
The Joy of Peacemakers	253
Finding Joy in Persecution	255
Making Friends With Grief	256
Grief Over Material Things	257
Grief When Relationships End	259
Grieving Over Lost Hopes & Dreams	260
Grieving When We Lose Ourselves	262

July

Grieving When We Lose Our Role	263
Grief When the Circle is Broken	265
What Comes First?	266
One Nation Under God	268
Strength in Our Weakness	269
Faith Beyond the Turning Points	271
Are You Donating to Life?	272
What Do You Bring to Church?	274
A Friend Inside	275
Head and Heart	277
People of the Way	278
The Voice in Silence	280
Honest Questions	281
Power in His Presence	283
The Tree of Life	284
I Thirst . . . I Thirst . . . I Thirst!	286
The Jesus Who Disappoints	287
The Simple Truth	289
The Simple Invitation	290
The Peace of God's Presence	292
Let's Hear it for Tears!	293

Yesterday, Tomorrow, and Today	295
Life is Made For Sharing	296
Poverty of the Soul	298
The Clothing of Prayer	299
A Consciousness of God	301
Spiritual Thirst	302
Waiting For God	304
Coming Home	305
When Tears Bring Rainbows	307
The Hidden Place	308

August

The Eternal Treasure	310
The Locked Gate	311
A Sheep's Song	313
Living For Life	314
Does Jesus Care?	315
Love—Evidence of God's Promise	317
The Place to Live	318
In Search of Life	320
All Things Work Together for Good	321
A Living Soul	323
Dependence	324
Another Day	326
Amazing Grace	327
The Darkness of Silence	329
Death—Only a Servant	330
The Pursuit of God	332
The Absence of Joy	333
Is There Any Word From the Lord?	335
Law or Grace	336
Estrangement	338
It's a Small World	339
On Being Remembered	340
Life Through the Eyes of a Child	342
The Fall of a Nation	343
Inner Healing	345
Giving in or Going On	347
Life—Death—Life	348
Faith and Love	350
Oak or Morning Glory?	351
Kindness	353
The Walk of Faith	354

September

The Cross of Servanthood	356
A Living Expression of Grace	357
The Bedrock of Life	359
Hide, Whine, or Serve	360
The Special Place of Peace	362
Guidelines for Living	363
On Being a Christian	365
A Simple Truth	366
Godly Discipline	368
Two Groups in One	369
It's What's at the Center	371
Fear or Faith	373
Life Yet to Be	374
Learning to Listen	376
Emotions	377
God in Today	379
Guilt	380
Hope	382
God's Thoughts	383
The Weight of Regret	385
How Important Are You?	386
Loneliness	388
To Be or Not to Be—the Church	389
The Pain of Rejection	391
Home	392
The Burden of the Day	394
The Wonder of It All	395
The Simplicity of Faith	397
Dealing With Discouragement	398
Hope for Disquieted Souls	400

October

Forgiveness	401
Soul Purging	403
Fear and Love	404
Birth—Death—Birth	406
Inner Sanctuary	407
God's Gift of Yourself	409
Quiet Time	410
Unbendable Truth	412
Non-negotiable Truths	413
Two Worlds	415
At the Heart of It All	416
The Gift of Comfort	418
A Closer Look at Love	419
At the Center	420
The Hiding Place	422
In Search of the Holy	423
A Different Perspective	425
In Search of a Savior	426
Spiritual Hunger	428
Spiritual Laziness	429
Hope for the Broken-hearted	431
The Prayer of Silence	432
Daily Inward Renewal	434
Silk Flowers	435
Refocusing Life	437
Wanted Happiness	438
The Night of Lightless Dark	440
The Hidden Part	441
I Know a Man	443
A Simple Man	444
Are You Listening?	446

November

Are You Wasting Your Life?	447
The Prayer of Relinquishment	449
The Faithful Prayer	450
Reminders of Grace	452
Union With God	453
The Starting Point	454
The Undivided Life	456
Intentional Stillness	457
The Throne Room of Grace	459
The Gate of Forgiveness	460
The Road Less Traveled	462
The Place Called Faith	463
The Pseudo Power of Fear	465
Has the Church Become a Club	466
The Secret	468
Where Are Your Roots	469
The Spirit-Filled Church	470
Which Life Will You Live?	472
Are You Contented?	473
A Single Act of Kindness	475
Discovering the Plan	476
Profoundly Simple	478
The Joy Drought	479

Thanksgiving	481
What Does God Have to Say About It?	482
What Kind of Church Are We?	484
The Melody of Life	485
The Ancient Beauty Within	487
Love Discovered in Pain	488
A Name Above All Names	490

December

The Mystery of Love	492
Spiritual Enlightenment	493
The Hunger for Righteousness	495
God Suffers With us	496
When Peace is Elusive	498
Is Your Savior Your Lord?	499
Voluntary Poverty	501
The Mind Controlled by the Spirit	503
Living in Hope	504
Sound and Sight	506
Darkness and Light	507
The Fullness of Time	508
What Will You Bring?	510
That First Christmas	511
The Fullness of Grace`	512
Christmas and a Hummingbird	514
No Room in the Living Room	516
Journey Toward Destiny	517
Christmas Reminds Us We're Not Alone	518
When Fear Gives Way to Joy	520
What About Joseph?	521
When Christmas Really Comes	523
The Shrinking of God	524
It's a Celebration	526
The Christmas Baby	527
Grace Brings Peace	529
When the Guests Have Gone Home	530
Inner Thoughts Revealed	531
Something to Ponder	533
Fear Not!	534
A Day With God	536

January

Beginning Anew

1   There is something about the human psyche that is drawn to that which is "new." It has a captivating allurement to it that grabs our attention and almost demands that we pay it heed. Each year as we celebrate New Year's Day we are reminded that the old is behind us and the unwritten page of the new year lies fresh ahead. It is uplifting and encouraging; it fills us with hope and expectation. In the secret places of our heart, if we have had an unusually bad year the year before, we hunger for the new one to be better. God's Word is filled with the promise of "new" beginnings. Though the word "new" is found in the Bible 145 times, it is not until you get to the Book of Isaiah (almost three-fourths of the way through the Old Testament) that you discover God beginning to talk about a new order. By the time you reach the New Testament many of the references in it are to the new thing that God is doing in human life.

When we wear out our clothing, our furniture, and our automobiles, we look to replace them with something better. Likewise, when we human beings corrupted the world that God had given us in pristine splendor, He began to declare the need for something better. The first reference to that idea is found in Isaiah 42:8-9, "I am the Lord, that is my name! I will not give my glory to another or my praise to idols. See, the former things have taken place and new things I declare; before they spring into being I announce them to you." And that beautiful promise in Isaiah 43:19: "See, I am doing a new thing! Now it springs up; do you not perceive it? I am making a way in the desert and streams in the wasteland." The chapters of Isaiah from 40-66 are the messianic proclamations that church tradition has acknowledged as prophecies of Jesus. When you read 65:17ff it's as if you have fast-forwarded to the Book of Revelation: "Behold I will create new heavens and a new earth. The former things will not be remembered nor will they come to mind." (Compare to Revelation 21:1ff).

As we reflect back on our lives, serious introspection leads us to hunger for renewal. We see our mistakes, the wrong choices we made, the sins we committed, the hurts we have caused, and we long for second chances and new beginnings. God's Word holds out to us that

January

possibility. "Though your sins are like scarlet they shall be as white as snow, though they are red as crimson they shall be like wool" (Isaiah 1:18). The apostle Paul writes, "If anyone is in Christ, he is a new creation; the old has gone, the new has come!" II Corinthians 5:17).

None of us has the power to undo mistakes of the past. In some cases we can seek to make restitution but we cannot cause the mistake to be undone. That's why God created and offers the reality of forgiveness. It is the nature of forgiveness to bring healing and to restore wholeness. It is the spiritual balm created by God and appropriated by human beings that brings about restoration and new beginnings. Perhaps you need to apply it to your marriage, maybe to a relationship with siblings, children, or parents. Maybe you need to forgive yourself and allow God to give **you** back to you.

Every day you open your eyes on a new day is a new opportunity to begin again. A new year has just begun! Do your best to fill it with goodness, with peace, and with love. May God empower you to do it.

Memories

2 As we begin a new year, many of us will stumble for a few weeks trying to adjust to the changing of the year-date with which we had become familiar. Dates are a human creation, whose main purpose is for establishing markers in time. More important than the date, however, is what we bring with us into the new year. Everyone enters a new year with the twin entities of memories from the past, and hopes and expectations for the future. Many of our memories are pleasant and bring us comforting feelings. Others are filled with sadness because of some loss we have experienced. Whether the memory is good or bad, we do not have the ability to remove it at will. There is, however, a repository for memories that can greatly affect their power over us—it is in surrendering them to God.

There are experiences from our past that have the ability to imprison us. They come in many forms, among which are unrepented sins and resentments concerning hurt or injuries that have been done to us. Sins that go unconfessed and unsurrendered to God are sins that

January

will attach themselves to us like parasites and eat away at the vitality of our physical and spiritual life. Likewise, pent-up anger, resentment, and unforgiveness also have the power to make us become spiritual invalids. That which we hold within does not lie still and dormant, but silently and pervasively spreads throughout our entire being. If the thing held within is good, it enriches our life and makes us a happier, more contented person. If it is bad or negative it detracts from us, sometimes crippling us to the point that we are unable to function in a healthy manner.

I believe that God gives us memories for a purpose—purposes that go beyond the obvious. If we had no memory we could not learn from experience, and experience, as they say, "is the best teacher." Memories are like building blocks. Each one is somehow attached to or at least important to the next one, in order to make sense out of life. Imagine the trauma of trying to live without memories. We see the extreme tragedy of such living in those with Alzheimer's or severe loss of memory. They become non-functional and almost completely dependent on others just to survive.

But beyond the negative impact of memory loss, we find that memories have the ability to make relationships invaluable. Those we love and hold dear are held there by memories of our sense of belonging. Even among those we love, however, we retain a mixture of good and bad memories. Where the memory is built on love, not even the pain caused by those we care deeply about can rob us of the value of the loved one to whom we relate. When painful memories of betrayal or injury are surrendered to the redeeming power of God, that brokenness can be transformed into a bridge to greater closeness. There is no power that heals brokenness more completely or more redemptively than the divine love of God working its power of healing within the heart.

We begin the new year with all that we are—including our memories. Are they healthy or harmful, fulfilling or debilitating? Why not begin the new year by surrendering **all** your memories to the love of God? In His power and presence they can become instruments of goodness and healing. Not a bad way to start the journey into an unknown future!

January

Spiritual Inventory

3 Just as a business needs to take an inventory every so often, Christians would also do well to assess now and then where we stand spiritually in our relationship to God. The beginning of a new year always challenges us to think both about the past and the promise of what is yet to be. When was the last time you took stock of your soul? Is it well with your soul? The author of Genesis wrote, "And the Lord God formed man of the dust of the ground, and breathed into his nostrils the breath of life; and man became a living soul." The human body formed from dust had no life, no soul, until God breathed into it that invisible, physically indiscernible force which causes life to be.

The soul is a mystery. We cannot see it and yet, like the wind, we can see the evidence of its existence. In his book *The Kingdom Within*, John Sanford writes, "The spiritual side of man will always be in distress as long as the soul is not recognized and loved" (p. 154). Peace and serenity spring forth from the soul. They are qualities that we cannot experience by putting something inside us, but by allowing that which God has already planted, to blossom outward.

Most of our entire life is spent concerning ourselves with our physical needs and appetites while almost wholly ignoring the rich treasure within. We hear Jesus' admonition to "take no thought for tomorrow, what you shall eat, and what you shall put on, . . ." but we never comprehend how to apply it to our own lives. When our bodies remind us that they need feeding, by causing us to feel hunger pangs, we begin to seek food to satisfy their craving. But when our souls cry out, we seem incapable of recognizing their voice or message.

"How," you might ask, "do our souls cry out?" They cry out by bringing to our consciousness a realization of an emptiness within; a dissatisfaction with our lives, and an inexplicable hunger that emanates from deep within that is never satisfied. They reveal themselves to us as "spiritual" sadness that results from an absence of the inner presence of God. Our souls speak to us when we feel a stirring within at the sound of some glorious hymn or anthem, or when the Word is proclaimed in power by a servant of our Lord.

January

To consciously choose to spend time in union with God is to feed the soul. If you don't feel close to God then ask yourself how often do you pray and immerse your heart and mind in His word. As a minister, one of the great tragedies I often witness is the number of people who are rapidly approaching the conclusion of their lives without any conscious awareness of the state of their soul. They come to the end of life with a feeling of loneliness and desolation within and do not know how they got there or why.

Just as our bodies are literally part of our mother and father, so our souls are part of the God who breathed life into our being. Failure to recognize that is to ensure that one will die a spiritual orphan. When we establish a loving relationship with our parents our lives are nourished, protected, and loved; we draw strength and wisdom from them. It should be likewise with our souls; and will be when we consciously choose to establish such a relationship with our Heavenly Father. Do you feel like there is something missing in your life? Maybe it's your soul telling you it is malnourished!

The "Someone" Song

4 "And the Word became flesh and lived among us." So says the writer of the Gospel of John (1:14, NRSV). No one can fully comprehend the mystery of the Incarnation. It defies understanding that the creating force behind the universe would choose to reduce Himself to the smallness of a human baby and be pleased to live in a world which we corrupted with our sinfulness. And yet He did! How else could God ever reveal to us the truthfulness of His nature and the depths He would go to in order to make known His love to us?

The book of Genesis tells us that God "spoke" the world into existence. God said, "Let there be light, and there was light." He said, "Let the waters be separated from the dry ground," and they were separated. We human beings can create things by first imagining them and then through the use of our hands and feet we construct them. It defies our ability to understand, how God is so powerful that His simple words create life. And so when we interpret John's prologue about "the Word becoming flesh and dwelling among us," we can now

January

see that what is meant is that the creating power of God, that life-giving, life-sustaining force reduced itself into the smallness of a human being and walked among us. Little wonder then that wherever Jesus went He brought life and wholeness for that was and is the essence of His being.

The good news of the gospel is that the same life-giving power that was exhibited in His flesh now dwells in glory; but comes to us through the power of the Holy Spirit. It is the nature of God to create, to give life. No wonder He would not allow death to be the final victor over His creation, but out of death He continually brings forth life. When winter comes, it appears that everything dies. Grass turns brown, bushes lose their flowers, trees shed their leaves and everything appears dead. But every spring, God announces anew that nothing has the power to stop His creating life-giving power from renewal.

When we sin, we are dead in our relationship to God, neighbor, and self. But when we are transformed by the redeeming power of God we are made to come alive. Life is restored and the harmony of God's will causes our lives to sing. In his spiritual autobiography, *A Song of Ascents,* E. Stanley Jones writes, "When I am in His will, life is not a struggle; it is a Song. . . . You can only sing when you have something to sing about. But my 'something' is a Someone. My theme song is Jesus Christ" (pp. 18-19).

We exist because God has desired for us to exist and He desires us to exist in peace and joy. Until we discover our aliveness within His love, we have yet to truly live. Breathing is not the same as living! True life is experienced when we rest in His will and come to be at peace with the purpose for which we were created. We were created to love and be loved by God. Apart from that love, we exist as hollow, empty lives. In the Incarnation, God revealed to us what human life was meant to be. And the song of life became a "Someone" and we have nothing greater about which to sing!

It's Time to Begin

5 Jesus' method of providing for the continuation of His message was simple. He called together a small group of followers, taught them what they needed to know, and sent them out to do His work. Twelve became seventy, and seventy became 120. From the 120 who were present at Pentecost, an evangelistic explosion took place that enlarged their numbers to over 3,000. The message of the church began in Jerusalem and it spread into Asia Minor, to Rome, and to the rest of the world. There is no power on earth that can stop the "good news" from going forth and accomplishing its purpose, if an individual Christian is committed to letting the Holy Spirit work through him or her. Whether it was Peter, James, John, or Paul the key to the growth of the Christian faith is dependent upon individuals yielding themselves to the purpose of God.

It is true that God could raise up stones that would declare His glory, but He has chosen to do it through ordinary human beings. With the exception of the Apostle Paul, we have no reason to believe that any of the first disciples were well educated or particularly talented. We know that several were common fishermen and one was a reviled tax collector. If you were God, would you have entrusted the message of salvation to fishermen and tax collectors? No? God often surprises us with His choices! Maybe He is looking to you, an ordinary human being, to be one of those who continues the message through the simple witness of your faith.

Every church member needs to pause and ask him or herself, "Why did I become a Christian? Why do I belong to a church? What do I expect the church to be and what is my part in it? Do I care about what becomes of my church, and if I do, what can I do to ensure that the body of Christ continues to flourish?" Do you care about the church to which you belong? With all of its faults and failures (because it is made up of human beings) it is still the body of Christ. Does your presence take away from or add to the effectiveness of the church? When was the last time you asked God to use you for His glory? Or are you even interested in whether He does or not?

Most churches will eventually reach a crossroad, a turning point in their history. Members can either sit on the sidelines and observe a spiritual Hospice take place (make the dying church comfortable and watch over its demise), or they can begin to take positive steps to reinvigorate it and seek to restore it to life. It's time we quit sitting idly by and expecting God to miraculously resurrect our future; we

January

need to start being the instruments of His spiritual renovation. Hey folks, get excited! You've been given the gift of eternal salvation; quit acting like it is an insignificant gift!

We all should approach this year with more hope, more anticipation, and more commitment to the work of our Lord than we ever have. Why not yield yourself to the guidance of the Holy Spirit and begin to believe and expect that God is about to do something great in your midst? Pray, believe, serve! YOU are important to God: you certainly are important to your church.

God's Epiphany

6 Today is Epiphany! How quickly we breezed through the four Sundays of Advent and the two that are in Christmastide. The word Epiphany means, "to make manifest" or "to make known." Epiphany Day always comes on January 6, which is 12 days after Christmas. It is often called Old Christmas. One major theme of Epiphany is the coming of the Magi (three wise men). But on the first Sunday following Epiphany the church celebrates the baptism of our Lord Jesus. Another major emphasis of the season of Epiphany is Jesus' presence at the wedding feast that took place in Cana of Galilee.

Why would men from a foreign land travel hundreds of miles (perhaps even a thousand) just to see a baby, even if He was born to be a king? (By the way, there is nothing in Scripture that says they rode camels!) What is there in human nature that finds itself being drawn to that which is greater than itself? On the human level we see it happen with athletes who are superstars, with celebrities, and singers. There is something about the famous that draws people to them. People will stand in line for hours to see a sports hero and get his or her autograph. Some will swoon when they touch the hand of a famous singer or movie star. If Billy Graham were to come and preach at your church, the pews would overflow. We like to be in the presence of the famous because it gives us a sense of importance. If a celebrity will condescend to speak to us, it makes us feel like we are special. The truth of the matter is that each of us is special whether a celebrity speaks to us or not.

January

The coming of Christ into the world was God's way of saying that every human being matters. No one is unimportant! Not the homeless person sleeping in the doorway, the black child in the ghetto, the Vietnamese woman in the rice paddy, nor the primitive jungle warrior. All humanity finds its importance as it discovers its value in relationship to Jesus Christ. The atoning death on the cross was not just for pious Jews nor for converted Christians, it was for all humanity! And yet, not all humanity can come to understand that truth unless those of us who know Christ are willing to share the good news. Atonement is universal; salvation is not! Christ died for all people; unfortunately, all people do not accept His gift of salvation.

God will always make Himself known to anyone who will come aside to acknowledge Him. Moses turned aside to see a bush that burned, and discovered God. Shepherds left their sheep and sought a baby in a stable and discovered the face of God. Wise men followed a star and lo, the light led them to the very throne of God's grace.

As a new year begins, I hope your path of life will lead you to discover the epiphany of God's presence. We can start our journey fresh and new and begin to marvel at the greatness of God's gifts. You are entitled to receive them because He has declared that all who will simply believe in Him are children of God. His voice is beckoning you, "Come aside, and behold my glory!" Will you come to the light? May His grace ensure that you will!

The Runner

The apostle Paul wrote to Timothy, his beloved son in Christ, words that stir all of us, especially as we near the end of the race of life.

> *I have fought a good fight, I have finished my course, I have kept the faith: Henceforth there is laid up for me a crown of righteousness, which the Lord, the righteous judge, shall give me at that day: and not to me only, but unto all them also that love his appearing.* (II Timothy 4:7-8, KJV)

January

Life is a race that we run in which we aren't in competition with others for the prize. There is a prize to be won, but it is not at the expense of others. Our success or failure is not measured against what someone else did, but how we finished the course.

During the summer Olympic Games of 1992, a British runner named Derek Redman was competing in the 400-meter semi-final event. The gun sounded and eight male athletes exploded out of the starting blocks. Their bodies were lean and their muscles rippled as they swiftly made their way around the oval track. Suddenly, on the far side of the track, Redman jumped straight up in the air and grabbed his right leg. He stumbled forward a few more steps and fell to the ground, his face contorted in excruciating pain. In a few moments, he struggled to rise to his feet and began hopping on one leg around the track, unable to put his weight on what later proved to be a pulled hamstring.

The roaring crowd's attention suddenly became fixated on the wounded runner and the crowded arena became immersed in silence. All at once, out of the massive crowd, there appeared an overweight middle-aged man running toward the injured athlete. At first security guards tried to restrain him but he was able to break free. He grabbed Redman by the arm and placing his arm around his shoulders the two men stumbled toward the finish line. As they drew nearer and nearer, the crowd began to erupt in cheering, reaching deafening proportions as they crossed the finish line. Later, we were to learn that the man who helped Derek complete the race was his father.

As tears flowed down my cheeks I was suddenly reminded of how often we struggle in the race of life. When life overwhelms us, whether we are hurt inwardly or outwardly, when we feel we've given it our best and there's nothing left within us, we discover the strength of God's arm as He lifts us and carries us securely across the finish line. Each of us must face challenges in this life and many will often seem too great to overcome, but it will be in facing those challenges that we finally begin to discover and experience the strength, love, and grace of God.

The apostle Paul reminds us: "Everyone who competes in the games goes into strict training. They do it to get a crown that will not last; but we do it to get a crown that will last forever" (I Corinthians

January

9:25). As Christians we run many races in life, but none is more important or significant than the race toward eternal life. The One who ensures that we will arrive at the finish line, did so from a cross. Strange—how powerfully Derek Redman's father reminded me of that.

Love Makes No Demand

8   I suppose the concept of love has been written about since the first person learned how to express him or herself with words. People, from St. Paul to Elizabeth Barrett Browning, people of every generation and culture have tried vainly to describe its mystical quality. Paul attempted to describe love by defining its nature; Browning struggled to put into words the greatness of its power and effect. Still, the concept of love is far better shown through action than through words. Love as a concept does not minister to us; the act of love does.

Writing in Daily Guideposts, Sue Monk Kidd tells the story of a man who came each day to the hospital where his six-year-old daughter was a patient. Even though she was in a coma, he came each day with a handful of daisies and sat patiently beside her bed. He would talk to her about her dog, her brother, even the weather, while he gently stroked her hair.

Sue, who watched him come so faithfully, wondered how the father could do this day after day, week after week, without ever getting a thank you for the flowers, without his daughter's eager eyes to follow his stories, without a smile to meet his, or a hug, or even the flutter of an eye lash. He gave his love and all he ever got in return was her slow, comatose breathing and the awful stillness.

"It must be hard to keep giving so much love when she's like this," Sue said gently.

"I suppose," he answered," "but I'll keep coming and bringing the flowers and telling these stories even if she's oblivious to it, because, you see, I love her whether or not she loves me back."

In that moment, Sue realized what all of us need to know: that even if we ignore God's gifts and fail to return His smile; even if we

January

are unaware of His presence and don't return His love, still He keeps coming back again and again. God's love is unconditional and eternal; it does not depend upon our returning it. Love gives; it does not demand anything in return.

Could there be a greater portrait of the reality of love than that one which Jesus painted with His life and death? No one gave more than He did and what the world gave Him in return was a cross. Even while He was dying, cruel words of hatred, sarcasm, and taunting were hurled at Him—and still He loved us. Their biting words were answered with soft words of forgiveness. Before Jesus, love really was just a word searching for a way of expressing itself. Divine love was just a concept that more often than not was blurred by the righteous, judgment of God revealed in the Old Testament.

But God sent His only Son to show us His love, so that if we would believe it and accept it, He could give us eternal life. You see, God loves us, even when we don't love Him in return.

The Importance of a Relationship

The Bible teaches us that we are justified in God's sight not by our works but by the relationship we have with His Son. Even the best among us are far from perfect. When we come into the presence of the Holy God, we have entered a place where sin cannot survive. Yet we are able to approach His throne because Jesus made it a throne of grace. It is a throne of grace because of One man, not because of many. Therefore, it is essential that we have a "right" relationship with the One who is worthy to stand in the presence of that which is Holy.

Babe Ruth hit 714 home runs during his illustrious career. He was playing one of his last games for the Boston Braves, against the Cincinnati Reds. The skill and agility that he once possessed had left him. He fumbled the ball, made bad throws, and in one inning alone was responsible for five Cincinnati runs.

As Babe walked off the field he was greeted by boos and catcalls from the fans in the stands. All at once, a young boy jumped over the railing and down onto the playing field. With tears streaking

January

down his cheeks, he ran toward his hero and threw his arms around the legs of this waning legend. Ruth didn't hesitate for a moment. Quickly he picked the boy up and hugged him tightly, set him down on his feet and playfully patted him on the head. Suddenly the booing stopped and a quiet hush fell over the stadium. In those few brief moments, the crowd saw a different kind of hero: a man who in spite of a dismal day on the field could still care about a little boy. Babe was no longer being judged by his accomplishments—neither the past successes nor the present failures—but by the standard of his relationship with a person. (Adapted from Alfred Kolatch in *Guideposts*, August, 1974)

God doesn't judge us by past failures or present successes. He judges us by how we relate to the grace of His Son. Paul writes to the Romans "There is therefore now no condemnation to those who are in Christ Jesus, who do not walk according to the flesh, but according to the Spirit" (Romans 8:1, NKJV). If we relate to God through faith in His Son, then we fall under no condemnation. If we relate to His Son then we will surely have living within us the Spirit of His Son. That makes us "right" before God.

To live in right relationship with God requires that we seek to live in right relationship with other human beings. John challenges us where we live when he writes: "If anyone says, 'I love God,' yet hates his brother, he is a liar. For anyone who does not love his brother, whom he has seen, cannot love God, whom he has not seen" (I John 4:20). So how can we love our fellow human beings who sometimes seem unlovable? Solely through the grace of God.

God asks us to love others—even those who are sometimes unlovable. The task would be impossible were it not for His love within us that not only seeks to reach out to the unlovable, but transforms and empowers us to love in ways, that prior to His grace dwelling in us, we could never do. And it's all because of a relationship—the one we have with God's son.

A Spiritual Kingdom

10 From my point of view, the primary purpose for the existence of the church is to establish and maintain a spiritual relationship with the Living God. The kingdom of God is a

January

spiritual kingdom that establishes itself in the heart and soul of those who believe. The strength or weakness revealed in any congregation will be in direct proportion to its depth of commitment to the Lord Jesus Christ.

Our Lord has revealed a deep spiritual truth in John's Gospel which we would do well to study and heed: He said:

> *I am the true vine, and my Father is the gardener. He cuts off every branch in me that bears no fruit, while every branch that does bear fruit he prunes so that it will be even more fruitful. You are already clean because of the word I have spoken to you. Remain in me, and I will remain in you. No branch can bear fruit by itself; it must remain in the vine. Neither can you bear fruit unless you remain in me. (John 15:1-4)*

We are reminded by our Lord, that apart from Him we can do nothing. If we are disconnected from Him then our lives become fruitless entities hurtling through meaningless space. The universe, from the tiniest speck to the greatest object, from the lowest form of life to the highest (humanity) was created for the purpose of dwelling with and bringing glory to Him who created us. God is the center of life; we are not. When our lives become centered on ourselves then all of life is thrown out of kilter.

We have been given the right to go through life ignoring the power of God in this world and in our lives. But when we do that the inevitable result is a restless lack of peace within. Jesus said to not look for the kingdom of God here or there but look within, for there is where you will discover it. The kingdom He spoke of is not one that can be outwardly observed, dissected, or constructed. Paul said, "The kingdom of God is not a matter of eating and drinking but of righteousness and peace and joy in the Holy Spirit" (Romans 14:17). Peace, joy and righteousness are inner experiences not outward appropriations.

Two characteristics dominated the lives of the early Christians revealed in the Book of Acts and in the writings of the apostles—love and inner peace. They were persecuted, beaten, imprisoned, and martyred but those two qualities never left them. The reason was that they were connected to the Source of love and peace and it transformed their lives. When troubles came they drew from a strength and power that was not their own, but was that of the One who loved them and had already given Himself for them.

We live in a world that constantly demands that we conform, that we turn our eyes away from God and fix them on ourselves or the world. If we follow its beckoning, we will surely never find God's peace and we will discover the reservoir of love within us drying up. Nothing in life will seem right within until we center our lives on God. Unfortunately, that goes against our sinful nature and so we resist doing the very thing that will give us what we yearn for in the depths of our soul but are too blind to see. God's kingdom is a spiritual realm and it is only in that realm that the physical world will find its proper place and its true meaning.

The Richest Man in the Valley

11 A story is told about a rich man named Carl who loved to ride his horse through his vast estate to congratulate himself on his enormous wealth—he had accumulated much. One day on such a ride, he came upon Hans, an old tenant farmer who lived in a poor home with his beloved wife of 40 years, on a corner of Carl's land. Hans was having his meager lunch in the shade of a tree, and was sitting with his head bowed in prayer.

"Humph!" snorted the rich man, Carl, wondering what this poor peasant had to be thankful for in the first place.

"It's remarkable that you should come by today, Sir. I feel I should tell you, I had a strange dream just before awakening this morning."

"And what did you dream?" Carl asked with an amused smile.

Old Hans answered, "There was beauty and peace all around, and yet I could hear a voice saying, 'The richest man in the valley will die tonight.'"

"Dreams!" cried Carl, "Nonsense!" and turned and galloped away. But try as he might, Carl couldn't get the old man's dream out

January

of his head. He knew it was ridiculous; he had felt fine, at least until Hans described his stupid dream. Now he wasn't so sure, so he called his friend and doctor and asked if he would come over that evening to talk.

When the doctor arrived, Carl told him the old man's dream—how the richest man in the valley would die that night. "Sounds like poppycock to me," the doctor said, "but for your peace of mind, let's examine you." A little later, his examination complete, the doctor was full of assurances. "Carl, you're as strong as that horse of yours. There's no way you're going to die tonight." Carl thanked his friend and told him how foolish he felt for being upset by old Hans' dream.

It was about 9 a.m. the next morning when a messenger arrived at Carl's door. "It's old Hans," the messenger said, "He died last night in his sleep" (Printed in *The American Rabbi*, August 1994).

Each of us would do well to examine our lives and determine what there is that makes us wealthy. The Son of God had no where to lay His head, no closet filled with flashy clothes, no huge mortgage to worry Him each day, and no vast "Ponderosa" to ride across and claim as His own. Yet, He was the richest man alive—rich in relationship to His Father, rich in love and adoration heaped on Him by His followers, rich in freedom found in living life in utter simplicity. Jesus was rich in that He had a profound understanding of what it is in life that brings peace to the human heart and joy to the eternal soul.

That which really makes us wealthy is our awareness of God's love and our willingness to live under the guidance of His Spirit. If we do that we will quickly discover that we are walking in the footsteps of One who has gone before us to show us the way. To really be wealthy we have to begin looking at life differently. Are you willing?

Worship

12 The worship of God is at the heart of what we are called to do. We were created for the purpose of bringing glory and praise to Him who created us. Too many of us go through life never discovering the value that can and should be found in the worship of God. Like the air we breathe we take it all too much for granted until it is no longer there.

January

I once heard a story about a Chinese monk who was approached by a man who was seeking the way to eternal life. He asked the priest what he had to do to discover the path to life eternal. The monk took him down to the river, waded out waist deep, grabbed the man and forced him under the water. The man kicked and struggled and almost drowned before the wise old teacher allowed him to rise above the surface. The man coughed and sputtered and struggled to regain his breath. "When you were under the water," the monk said to the half-drowned man, "what was it that you wanted more than anything else in the world?" "Why, I wanted a breath of air," the man exclaimed. "Well," said the monk, "when you want eternal life that much, you will discover it."

Unfortunately, most of us make our way through life paying very little attention to the state of our soul, until we become sick or think we are going to die. But it shouldn't be that way. When the church is what it was meant to be, it guides people along their journey to God and to life everlasting. In an article in the *Circuit Rider Magazine* several years ago, Laurence A. Wagley wrote:

> *If worship is for our pleasure rather than God's praise, the whole purpose of the church is lost. When the main business of the Administrative Board is to balance the budget and the major concern of education is baby sitting, it is not surprising that worship becomes entertainment. The church has lost its identity and worship its sense of the presence of God.*

We should seek to re-discover the glory of God and to journey together along the spiritual path back to Him who created us. There needs to be a hunger within us to grow spiritually. A pastor's role is not to try to impress you with homiletical skills or grammatical flourishes that tickle your ears. The role of a pastor is to lead you in discovering the beauty and power and grace of God and what a difference it makes in life when we live life in peace with Him.

Each of us is like a tiny seed planted in the soil of God's kingdom. We will grow and blossom only as long as we are willing to be nurtured by God's Spirit. That comes only as we yield ourselves to His molding. It will begin with worship and it will culminate in greater

January

worship. In The Book of Revelation, there is a scene that takes place in heaven where a great multitude is gathered in God's presence. One does not need to be a biblical scholar to realize that what takes place in that scene is worship. Songs are sung to God and crowns are thrown at his feet in adoration and in submission. If you don't want to worship God eternally, you might want to reconsider your desire to go to heaven.

Faith and Adversity

13 Faith is a gift from God; we don't accidentally stumble on to it. We don't just decide one day that we will start having it. Paul lists it in I Corinthians 12:9 as one of the "gifts" of God's Spirit. But just as every living thing comes into this world small and then grows, so does faith. I know of no one who has faith who got the full measure of it in one overpowering moment. Like any gift that someone offers us, it becomes ours only when we are willing to accept it and allow it to affect or influence our lives.

God plants faith in our heart and soul. We are like soil that allows a seed to be placed within it. The more we yield to God's Spirit growing within us, the greater becomes the strength of faith. The more we are willing to trust God beyond what our eyes can see and our minds can comprehend, the greater becomes our faith.

One of the great paradoxes of spiritual growth is that our faith often seems to grow the greatest when we are in the midst of adversity. When everything in life is going great our consciousness of a need for God's strength wanes. We unwittingly fall into the trap of feeling all too self-secure. All of us are familiar with the Beatitudes. The King James Version renders one: "Blessed are the poor in spirit, for theirs is the kingdom of heaven." But how much more clearly does William Barclay define it when he gives literal meaning to the Greek words, "O the bliss of the man who has realized his own utter helplessness, and who has put his whole trust in God, for thus alone he can render to God that perfect obedience which will make him a citizen of the kingdom of heaven" (*The Daily Study Bible*, Matthew, Vol. 1, p. 92).

The normal human response to adversity is not only to find no joy in it, but to flee from it at every turn. And yet, it is the struggles,

January

the strains of life that often have the power to multiply our spiritual growth to its greatest degree. In his book *Prescription for Anxiety* (p. 31), Leslie Weatherhead writes,

> *Like all men, I love and prefer the sunny uplands of experience, when health, happiness, and success abound, but I have learned far more about God, life and myself in the darkness of fear and failure than I have ever learned in the sunshine. There are such things as the treasures of darkness. The darkness, thank God, passes. But what one learns in the darkness, one possesses forever.*

In the matter of faith, especially when it is being called on in the midst of some problem, it is far more important that we trust that God is with us, than for us to demand that He give us what we want. The trust we have in God as we face adversity will determine whether we meet the encounter with a spirit of peace or a spirit of fear. The greater our trust in God, the smaller will be our sense of fear of the unknown. Therefore, let us give thanks to God for his presence in adversity. Rather than curse the darkness, let us light a candle.

Love Leaves No Room

14 On November 4, 1995, the world was once more victimized by the power of hate. We recoiled in disbelief at the news that the Prime Minister of Israel, Yitzhak Rabin, had been assassinated by a fanatical Jewish zealot who was enraged that Rabin had signed the Olso Peace Accords. In what has become an all too frequent occurrence, an act of hatred and violence added Rabin's name to the pages of history that are saturated in the blood of those who have been slain because they proclaimed a message of peace—Lincoln, Ghandi, King, and Sadat. Why is it that people would rather live in a world filled with violence than one of tranquility and peace?

At Rabin's funeral, a heart-rending and eloquent eulogy was delivered by his seventeen-year-old granddaughter, Noa Ben-Artiz. She spoke of him in words of love and admiration that could come only from one who had observed his soul and not just the outer man.

January

How touching were her words: "I have no feelings of revenge because my pain and loss are so big, too big." In essence, she was saying that her pain was so great it left no room for revenge.

My mind quickly transported me back in time to the scene of another assassination. A man had died who proclaimed peace more nobly than anyone who had ever lived. There was no violence in Him and His heart was the most tender of human hearts. His death was not so sudden and so there was more than enough time to struggle with anger and hatred toward those who were killing Him. But His immortal words were devoid of biting, slashing invectives—"Father forgive them, for they know not what they do." As I thought of Noa's words, I suddenly realized that He would have said, "There is no revenge in me, for love does not leave room." That is not to denigrate the deeply felt and noble words of Noa, but to simply remind all of us again that the heart of God is so different from our own.

I don't know about you, but I hunger to feel such love for people. Would to God that I had already arrived at such a state of perfect love, but alas, I haven't. Yet each of us is called by God to be a peacemaker. The ritual for the service of Holy Communion that was found in our older Methodist Hymnals used to remind us that we were called "to live in love and charity with our neighbors" and as far as possible to live "in peace with all human beings." But unfortunately, the reality is that like molten magma simmering and bubbling beneath the surface, our lives are filled with anger, resentments, hatred, and ill will and are but a moment away from erupting in fury.

So, how can we ever be any better? Only by a persistent willingness to open our hearts to the scrutiny of the loving heart of God and allow His Spirit to burn away all that keeps us from being what He intended for us to be. How I hope, how I pray that at some point in this life, we can say with utter truthfulness, there is no hatred, prejudice, and violence left in me, for love has left no room.

Nourishing the Spirit

15 No human relationship will grow or survive if it is not intentionally nourished; neither will our relationship with God. Just as in many marital relationships in which sacred

January

vows are quickly taken far too lightly, so does the Christian's relationship with God wane when sacred vows are ignored or broken.

We live in a superficial world—a world in which life is viewed as so mundane and routine that people find little significance in anything. We develop a conscious or perhaps a subconscious cynicism that refuses to allow us to believe that much of anything in life is ultimately important. Human life becomes expendable, momentary pleasure becomes intoxicating, commitment to God and others becomes secondary. We hunger for happiness and self-worth and discover it to be as elusive as trying to hold water in a hand with outstretched fingers. Our lives become as much a fantasy as the TV programs that inspire us to believe that they represent the real world.

When we live life on the superficial level, the spiritual world that most influences us is the demonic, not the holy. For those who refuse to believe there is such a thing as the demonic, Satan's battle is half won. Our society is inundated with the demonic and we seem too blind to see it in our midst. What has more demonic power than the addiction of drugs and alcohol? How many human lives, how many families have been plunged into despair and grief because of the spiritual power of addiction to destroy not just the body but also the very soul from within. How do you explain America's love for violence, its obsession with illicit sex, its love affair with hate and prejudice? It is not by chance that serial killers perpetrate their depravity on individuals and madmen see killing over 180 people in the Federal Building in Oklahoma City as a justifiable act. The inevitable result of living life superficially is that the "golden calf" of human self-centeredness becomes the god who claims the throne.

Jesus said, "There are none so blind as they who will not see." Not only are we surrounded with evil which we cannot comprehend, we have far too much of it residing within our own being. We have grown so comfortable with its presence that we have no desire to have it removed. It has become a comfortable companion that controls us. Paul warned us of its reality and power when he wrote:

> *For our struggle is not against flesh and blood, but against the rulers, against the authorities, against the powers of this dark world and against the spiritual forces of evil in the*

January

heavenly realms. Therefore put on the full armor of God, so that when the day of evil comes, you may be able to stand your ground.... (Ephesians 6:12-13)

The way out of our dilemma is to listen for and respond to the still small voice of God within, calling us to come and seek His presence. Every noble person in history who rose to the level of a saint did so by pursuing the hunger within to know the God who made them. Even now God is speaking to you through these inadequate human words. He says, "Come to me, my child!" What will your answer be?

Of Joy and Sorrow

16 Life is filled with both joy and sorrow. Sometimes it seems the two are closely interlinked. In thinking about the thin line that often separates joy from sorrow, I was reminded of the wisdom of one of my favorite writers, Kahlil Gibran, who was a deeply spiritual Lebanese Christian. In his book *The Prophet* (pp. 29-30*)*, he wrote the following profound thoughts on joy and sorrow:

Then a woman said, speak to us of Joy and Sorrow.
And he answered:
Your joy is your sorrow unmasked.
And the self-same well from which your laughter rises was often times filled with your tears.
And how else can it be?
The deeper that sorrow carves into your being, the more joy you can contain.
Is not the cup that holds your wine the very cup that was burned in the potter's oven?
And is not the lute that soothes your spirit, the very wood that was hollowed with knives?
When you are joyous, look deep into your heart and you shall find it is only that which has given you sorrow that is giving you joy.

January

When you are sorrowful look again in your heart, and you shall see that in truth you are weeping for that which has been your delight.

Some of you say, "Joy is greater than sorrow," and others say, "Nay, sorrow is the greater."

But I say unto you, they are inseparable.

Together they come, and when one sits alone with you at your board, remember that the other is asleep upon your bed.

Verily you are suspended like scales between your sorrow and your joy.

Only when you are empty are you at standstill and balanced.

When the treasure-keeper lifts you to weigh his gold and his silver, needs must your joy or your sorrow rise or fall.

His words have great spiritual depth. We all would do well to ponder their truth until they have touched the intimate part of our soul. Truly, joy cannot be known apart from the reality of sorrow.

The Treasure of the Kingdom

17 What do you understand the kingdom of God to be? The Jews, before Jesus, considered it to be that time in history in which God would establish His reign on earth in a powerful and dramatic way—The Day of the Lord. Jesus talked about it in terms of the reign of God within the human heart. And yet, it is a kingdom that comes through and by the power of Jesus Himself.

In his book *Is the Kingdom of God Realism?* E. Stanley Jones writes, "When Jesus stood before Pilate, He did not say, 'The Kingdom of God,' but 'My Kingdom'—He put Himself and the kingdom together—in Him they had coalesced and were one" (p. 54). It was the incarnation of God in Christ that delivered the kingdom to the world. Only as we dwell in Christ and allow Christ to dwell in us does the kingdom become reality for any of us. In the life of Jesus, the kingdom took tangible form and all the characteristics of the kingdom are revealed in the life and teachings of our Lord.

January

When we speak of redemption, we can only fully understand it as it is revealed in the redemptive suffering act of Jesus. When we think of forgiveness it becomes clear only as we see how Jesus imparted it. When we meditate upon the highest form of love, no love surpasses that which we see revealed in Christ our Lord. Whether it's obedience, compassion, mercy, faithfulness, or any other concept that is noble and virtuous, we find its greatest example exhibited in the life of Jesus. One cannot live life in the Kingdom until one is willing to embrace the life of Him who is the embodiment of the Kingdom.

Jesus told us not to look for the kingdom "here or there", for it is not external, but to look for it within ourselves. We commune with God on a spiritual level and that level will not be discovered apart from our heart and soul. When Jesus said to Pilate, "My kingdom is not of this world," He was not saying that the kingdom could not touch us on this plane of existence, but that the kingdom should not be confused with the establishment of some earthly monarchy to which human beings must pay homage.

We are surrounded by treasure, and just as Jesus described in the parable of the treasure hidden in the field, we are oblivious to it until one day we discover what was there all along. How many of us make our way through life never aware of the gift within our midst? How is that so? It is because we have failed to grasp the value of our spirit. It is through spiritual awakening that we become cognizant of God's reality and presence.

Once more quoting E. Stanley Jones:

The Kingdom of God is not an ideal for which we are to strive and for which we are not made. The Kingdom of God is our nature—our real nature, the way we were made to work. The laws of the Kingdom are the very laws of our own being. When we try to live against the Kingdom of God, we try to live against ourselves, to live against nature. The result? We perish. (p. 65)

The treasure within each of us is that immortal part that has the potential to commune with God, but which we remain content to keep buried deep within. All our lives we have lived with a hidden treasure.

January

May God grant that this very day you will discover the value of what He has placed within you.

Receiving the Bread of Life

18 Some time ago I read an article by Norman Vincent Peal entitled, "What My Father Taught Me About the Church."

Dr. Peale made a statement that captured my attention and caused me to pause and reflect. He said, "Being a minister is just reminding people over and over, and then reminding them again, of what is most important in life."

Undoubtedly, there are many reasons why millions of people get up on Sunday morning to go to church. They get "appropriately" dressed, drive whatever distance is required and walk into a sanctuary somewhere. They go to their established side of the church and sit down on a certain pew that has "unofficially" become their spot. They sing familiar hymns (most of the time), join in the liturgical responses, and repeat again and again the same affirmations of faith. They give their offering, listen to the choir sing an anthem and then grant a minister 15 to 25 minutes of their time as they listen to (or daydream through) a sermon on some religious subject.

What makes so many people be willing to repeat again and again this weekly ritual? Could it be something far more important than one realizes is taking place? We need to be reminded again and again about what is really important in life. If it is true that we do have an eternal soul, then it is essential that preparation be made through life for its eternal well-being. Where true preaching takes place, people are offered the bread of life. Where the bread of life is genuinely offered, the soul can be fed and the spirit can be nourished.

After His resurrection, Jesus' admonition to Peter was, "If you really love me, Peter, then feed my sheep." As if to drive home the importance of that statement, Jesus repeated that command to Peter three times. In essence He was saying that Peter had nothing more significant to do than to commit himself to sharing the "good news" about Jesus and what it meant for their eternal souls. Either God is real or He is not. Either there is an eternal life or there is not. If there is, then we dare not ignore the reality of what that means to us.

January

On one occasion John Wesley's advice to his preachers was, "You may be elegant, you may be winsome, you may be a good financier, yea, you may be in great demand, but if you do not win souls, you are a failure. You are not called to do this or that, but to win souls." Good preaching is more than telling people how to be happy; it is more than giving good moral instruction, it is more than expounding on Biblical history or characters from the Bible. Good preaching should draw a person closer to God and enhance one's awareness that we are spiritual beings as well as physical ones, and that we all stand in need of a Savior. Pastors should care deeply about **all** your needs, but their hearts ought to be caught up in a sincere hunger to nourish your soul, to help you grow spiritually, and to walk with you in and toward God's eternal kingdom.

If in some small way the words that God gives me to share with you can draw you closer to His heart and more securely into His kingdom, then by God's grace, my purpose will have been fulfilled and together, we will have accomplished that to which I have been called.

Are You God's Friend?

19 Are you God's friend? I'm sure that seems like a rather strange question to ask, but it comes to mind after reading John 15:12-15. Listen to the words that Jesus spoke to His disciples less than twenty-four hours before He was to die:

> *No one has greater love than this, to lay down one's life for one's friends.* **You are my friends** *if you do what I command you. I do not call you servants any longer, because the servant does not know what the master is doing; but I have made known to you everything that I have heard from my Father.* (NRSV)

Now one might ask, "What kind of friend is it who **commands** us to do certain things?" Suppose our friend was a doctor, and he diagnosed that we had a certain illness and unless we followed his advice we would die. So he instructs us ("commands us") to take a

January

certain medication for a prescribed period of time and we will become completely well. Does his instruction, bitter though the medicine might seem, make him less of a friend or more of one?

Why did Jesus give us certain commandments to follow? Did He want to burden us with more things to do, or refrain from doing? No, He tells us Himself in John 15:11, "I have said these things to you so that my joy may be in you, and that your joy may be complete." He commands us in order that we might experience joy!

Stubborn creatures that we are, we are insistent upon trying to find joy outside of Him and we always come up short. When Jesus commands us, I picture His face as one with a smile not a scowl. The smile makes all the difference because it reveals a loving heart and the power of one who makes us feel safe and secure in His knowledge.

Robert Louis Stephenson told a story about a ship at sea that was engulfed in a terrible storm. The wind and waves had pushed it dangerously close to rocky shoals; destruction seemed imminent. The passengers were frightened beyond words. Contrary to orders, one of the passengers made his way out on to the deck and struggled to reach the pilothouse. There he found the pilot lashed fast at his post. He held the steering wheel firmly in his hands and inch by inch was turning the ship out to sea, safe from the rocky shoals. The pilot looked down at the passenger and smiled. The man made his way back below deck to the terrified passengers. He comforted them with the simple words, "I have seen the face of the pilot, and he smiled."

When we behold the smile on the Pilot's face we rest in the knowledge that come what may, all will be well. The storms of life may rage around us, but In His love our lives are secure. It is in that love we find truth and freedom and peace—in that love we are declared to be His friends. Friends trust one another with their lives. Do you trust Jesus with yours? If you do, then you are His friend.

Do You Live With Jesus?

20 Jesus did not become incarnate in human flesh and suffer death on a cross in order to establish another religion in the world. Nor did He come for the purpose of simply trying to reform the religious practices of ancient Judaism. Jesus entered this

January

world to convince humanity that it was possible, yes, even essential that we establish and live in a constant relationship of love and praise with the God who called us into being.

Many of us probably don't think much about God during the week, and when our thoughts are finally turned to Him on Sunday, it is more out of our submission to the established habit of attendance than to a real hunger to experience the uniqueness of His presence. Over the years we have made faith far too much about ritual and liturgy and not enough experience of the Living Presence. Jesus was not born in order to become a ritual! We often recite affirmations and responsive readings with all the conviction and enthusiasm that one would experience if we were simply reading words from a dictionary. I am not suggesting there is no value in ritual and liturgies—there is—but I am suggesting that their value is greatly diminished if they do not bring us to a conscious awareness of the presence of God.

The Incarnation by its very definition means "God present with us." When the Incarnation ceases to be a real experience and becomes only a theological concept, then it has been robbed of all its power and significance and simply takes its place on the shelf with the philosophies and tenets of any and all world religions. The Christian faith proclaims that God not only entered the world in the man called Jesus, but He continues to abide in this world with and in us in the form of the Holy Spirit. The Holy Spirit is the evidence of God's presence with us!

That which separated the early Christians from all other "religious people" and which caused many to want to become a part of the church (ecclesia - the "called out.") was the undeniable evidence and power of the Holy Spirit in their lives. Just as Jesus once said "the very stones would cry out" if His presence was not acknowledged, it is impossible for the Spirit-filled Christian to be silent about his or her faith, or to be content to pigeonhole it in a neat little compartment until the appropriate time of the week (Sunday) to take it out and dust it off.

Where religion and faith are genuine, there is no compartmentalization of our faith from what we are each moment we live and breathe. If my faith is not brought with me to work, to school, to play, to whatever I am doing, then it becomes no more than a

January

spiritual placebo that shields me from acknowledging the delusion that I am living.

Jesus lived and died in order that we could live with Him, not so we could just hear and tell wonderful stories about Him. It never occurs to some people that if they don't have any desire to live with Jesus now, why should they want to spend eternity with Him? Do you live each day with the Risen Christ, or do you just hear about Him on Sundays and find yourself content to leave Him there when you depart the church?

Overcoming Discouragement

21 At some point in life, we all have known the heavy weight of discouragement: a time when people, circumstances or events have left us disappointed or disillusioned. Discouragement is an inner feeling that drains us of happiness, energy, and the joy of living. It often debilitates us to the point of wanting to give up, sit down in the middle of our misery, and say as Jonah did under the gourd tree, "It would be better for me to die than to live" (Jonah 4:8).

Since discouragement is an inner feeling, it is therefore a spiritual problem. When we become discouraged, we have allowed something or someone in life to have more power over us than God. Discouragement, left unchallenged, will inevitably drag us into the pit of depression and depression allowed to continue will always blind us to the reality of God's presence. The way out of the maze of discouragement is to turn to God, not so much to ask for solutions but to request that we might simply abide peacefully in His presence. In moments like that we need to cling to Him like a child to its mother or simply like a vine to the trunk of a tree.

B. M. Launderville has written:

> *The vine clings to the oak during the fiercest of storms. Although the violence of nature may uproot the oak, twining tendrils still cling to it. If the vine is on the side of the tree opposite the wind, the great oak is its protection; if it is on the exposed side, the tempest only presses it closer to the trunk. In some of the storms of life, God intervenes and shelters us; while*

January

in others He allows us to be exposed so that we will be pressed more closely to Him. (*Encyclopedia of 7700 Illustrations*, p. 1511)

In discouragement our focus becomes transfixed on our sense of loss, disappointment, or sadness. In other words, we focus our attention and energy almost completely on ourselves. It's like being in quicksand and trying to pull yourself out by grabbing hold of yourself. In times like that we have to reach for something beyond ourselves.

Discouragement is rooted in fear: fear that we won't succeed, we won't be loved or accepted, fear that we will be misunderstood, or that we must deal with something that we cannot control. The answer to fear, according to I John, is "perfect love which casts out fear." The only place we will find perfect love is in the presence of God.

If you are discouraged, go to a place where you have previously felt the strong presence of God (a sanctuary, a lake, a quiet place in the woods) and sit down in the presence of God and let His healing power absorb from you that anguish which seeks to harm you. Even on the cross Jesus found hope by His willingness to surrender into the hands of His loving Father the preciousness of His own spirit.

The way out of discouragement begins with surrender— surrender to the Power that is greater than we are. Just as God causes the sun to rise each morning, so will the divine light of His presence bring new dawn to our every gloomy day.

Growing in the Midst of Sorrow

22 Phillips Brooks, the author of *O Little Town of Bethlehem*, once sought to console a dear friend whose heart was shattered at the death of his wife. His grieving friend still heavy on his heart, Brooks wrote the following letter on November 19, 1891:

My dear Friend,
I have thought much about our meeting last Sunday, and the few words we had together. May I try to tell you again where your comfort lies? It is not in forgetting the happy past. People bring us well-meant but miserable consolation when

January

they tell us what time will do to our grief. We do not want to lose our grief because our grief is bound up with our love and we could not cease to mourn without being robbed of our affection. But if you know—as you do know—that the great and awful change, which has come into your life and brought you such distress, has brought your dear wife the joy of heaven, can you not, in the midst of all your suffering, rejoice for her? And if knowing she is with God, you can be with God, too, and every day claim His protection and try to do His will, may you not still in spirit be very near to her?

She is not dead, but living, and if you are sure what care is holding her, and educating her, you can be very contentedly with her in spirit, and look forward confidently to the day when you shall also go to God and be with her. I know that this does not take away your pain—no one can do that—you do not want any one to do that—not even God, but it can help you to bear it, to be brave and cheerful, to do your duty and to live the Pure, Earnest, Spiritual life which she, in heaven, wishes you to live. . . . My friend, she is yours forever. God never takes away what He has once given. May He make you worthy of her! May He comfort you, and make you strong!

God stands in the gap, not just as the bridge between temporal time and eternity, but between us and the one we love who has gone before us. On the cross Jesus was suspended between heaven and earth. In glory, He is suspended between present and future: interceding with God for us—not just for the forgiveness of our sins, but also to seek healing and consolation for our sorrow.

We are given the gift of memory, so that which we love cannot be stolen from our heart. But possessing that gift means the inescapable reality of pain when we are called upon to give them up. Love immersed in sorrow is love tempered by the fire of pain. That which is tempered is made stronger, and that which is tempered by God's love is made eternally strong. Just as steel glows with burning fury when immersed in the fire, so our hearts burn when they are immersed in sorrow. But just as the heat cools and fades and leaves the steel stronger and more useful than before, so God will not allow our

January

pain to be wasted and our loss to become meaningless. In the midst of sorrow rest in God and allow Him to transform your pain into spiritual strength.

The Poverty of the Soul

23 We find ourselves alive! We breathe, we think, we laugh, we worry, we cry. We feel the warmth of love and the downward pull of loneliness. We sometimes ponder about the reality of God and if He really exists and if He really cares about us. Every day becomes a clone of the day before and we pass our days without much purpose, simply going through the routines that life has imposed on us. We make decisions by default and we commit ourselves to little more than the mundane things that bring us occasional moments of happiness or at least do not cause us to feel pain.

It seems to me that is how many of us live our lives. There appears to be no divine purpose, no mystical compulsion to look within and discover the mystery and miracle of our "aliveness." Part of the problem is that we have made religion a yoke to be borne, rather than an experience in which to be empowered. True religion in its most simple and purest form is the consistent if not constant experience of the loving presence of God. But we have made religion become a duty rather than an awakening; and duty is often performed out of a sense of stoic resolution rather than from joyful surrender born out of a desire to be obedient.

In *A Testament of Devotion*, Thomas Kelly writes, "The deepest need of men is not food and clothing and shelter, important as they are. It is God. We have mistaken the nature of poverty and thought it was economic poverty. No, it is poverty of soul, deprivation of God's recreating, loving peace" (p. 121). There is a "holy center" to life which we have buried under a lifetime of living; and yet, it is not dead: it is only covered up, waiting to be rediscovered.

Too often we seek to commune with God on the outer periphery of half-hearted commitments, motivated by the faint possibility that God might exist and life may indeed be eternal. We must return again to our center, look within our souls and be awed once more by the

January

eternal presence of God within. Jesus said, "the kingdom of God is within you." Therefore we must be willing to come aside from the world's demands and look for God where He is most near— within the soul where spirit communes with spirit.

"Ah", you say, "I am too busy, I don't have time!" Too busy to plumb the mysteries of the purpose and destiny of your life? Too busy to embrace the gifts of peace and tranquility which God sent His Son to give you? Too busy to finally become acquainted with the person God created you to be? We embrace the trivial and reject the eternal; we trade away contentment and flounder in the storms of turmoil.

It will be in the deep silences with God that we will begin to live, not in the noisy spiritual vacuum into which the world seeks to pull us. Fight, Christian! Fight to return to fellowship with your Creator! The struggle is within; that's where the battle must be fought. It is only there that the victory, by God's grace, can be won. And when it is won, the poverty of the soul will be transformed into the glorious, inexhaustible wealth of union with God.

The Present Moment

24 In one of America's greatest dramas, *Our Town*, written by Thornton Wilder, there is a scene in the play in which Emily, who dies at the age of 26, asks to be able to return to her family for a brief visit. She is allowed to choose any day from the past that she would like.

So Emily returns to her home on her twelfth birthday. Her father, back from a business trip, ignores her. He is concerned about his business problems and has no time for little Emily. Her mother, also unaware that Emily will die quite young during childbirth (in just 14 years), is busy cooking and pays no attention to her daughter in the hot kitchen. Poor Emily looks at her mother and father and says, "I can't bear it. Oh Mama, just look at me one minute as though you really saw me. Mama, 14 years have gone by and I'm dead! But just for a moment now we're all together, Mama, just for a moment we're happy. Let's look at one another."

But her father and mother continue to ignore her. They're too busy with life's problems to see her and so she leaves. "I can't! I can't

January

go on. It goes so fast. We don't even have time to look at one another." Emily breaks down sobbing, "Goodbye, goodbye world. Goodbye, Mama and Papa. Oh, earth, you're too wonderful for anybody to realize you! Do any human beings ever realize life while they live it—every, every minute!"

One of the great weaknesses of our humanity is that we don't marvel at the beauty and sacredness of the present moment. We let life fritter away totally oblivious to the value of each precious day. Today is the day we have. Not yesterday and not tomorrow. Why do we spend so much of our lives living in the past or dwelling on the future?

There is a Sanskrit poem that says, "Look to this day! For it is life, the very life of life. In its brief course lie all the verities and realities of your existence. For yesterday is already a dream and tomorrow is only a vision; but today, well lived, makes yesterday a dream of happiness, and every tomorrow a vision of hope" (Source unknown).

Do you suppose that after Jesus ascended to heaven the disciples wished they had treasured more deeply those precious moments of life that they had spent with him for three years? None of us can go back in time and recapture what is already past, but we can discipline ourselves to become conscious of the treasure of the present moment. We still have people around us whom we love and who love us. Are we going to wait until they are gone before we realize their value? The day we're living today cannot be relived tomorrow.

God has given you today! How will you live it—rejoicing, praising, laughing, enjoying, sharing? Or will you dread it, complain about it, and make yourself and others miserable in it? The Psalmist said, "This is the day the Lord has made, let us rejoice and be glad in it." Will you?

Loved for Who You Are

25 When Jesus walked this earth in human form, He did not encounter people who had found the secret to perfect humanity. There were none. No, He found people just like you and me, who had within their souls a gnawing hunger that would

January

not go away and leave them alone. There is within each of us that same hunger that longs for us to be something other than what we are; that desperately wants to throw off the shackles that rob us of peace and distort our vision of the real us that we can become.

We cannot make ourselves good and we cannot create peace within our own hearts. When tossed about on the waves of an angry sea, the lesson the disciples learned was not that they had no power to calm a raging sea, but that they suddenly beheld in Jesus One who had the power to not only command the billowing waves and roaring wind, but even more importantly, had the power to calm and transform the human heart and soul.

We do not love ourselves because we do not have the power to make ourselves become what something within us tells us we need to be. All of our most noble efforts have failed to transform us, and like strangers lost in the wilderness, we continue to trudge around in meaningless circles. BUT, THERE IS HOPE! There really is an answer to what seems insoluble.

Perhaps Kahlil Gibran said it most beautifully and poetically in his *Jesus, the Son of Man,* when he put upon Mary Magdalene's lips these words about herself:

I cried to Him and I said, . . . "I entreat you, come to my house."

Then He stood up and looked at me even as the seasons might look down upon the field, and He smiled. And He said again:

"All men love you for themselves. I love you for yourself."
And then He walked away.

But no other man ever walked the way He walked. Was it a breath born in my garden that moved to the east? Or was it a storm that would shake all things to their foundations?

I knew not, but on that day the sunset of His eyes slew the dragon in me, and I became a woman.

When finally we are able to see ourselves, not just the way we are, but the way God sees that we can be; and when we reach that point of utter surrender and allow the Carpenter of Nazareth to reshape

January

our lives by the power of His crucified love, then we will discover the transforming, life-giving power of the breath of God's love. Then for the first time in our existence peace will cease to be a word and will become an experience.

Do you have any idea what God would have you be? Then gaze into the eyes of Jesus in prayer, and let Him show you the YOU that you were created to be. Let Him show you what it feels like to be loved for who you are.

When Adversity Comes

26 One of the obvious realities of life is that we will not live very long on this earth before we encounter adversity, sorrow, or pain. When things "go wrong" in our lives we can either allow those things to make us grow frustrated and bitter, or we can use them to help us grow stronger. The natural tendency for most of us when trouble comes is to withdraw into an inner shell and feel sorry for ourselves. In doing so, we only prolong our sorrow and delay our recovery.

Unless we believe that God allows adversity for the purpose of destroying us (and I don't!) then we need to realize that God may allow it because He knows that the life immersed in Him will use adversity to rise above the conflict and thus be made all the stronger. The muscles in our body only grow stronger when we force them to strain against some object that challenges them.

In his book *Christ and Human Suffering*, E. Stanley Jones writes:

> When a storm strikes an eagle, he sets his wings in such a way that the air currents send him above the storm by their very fury. The set of the wings does it. The Christian is not spared the pains and sorrows and sicknesses that come upon other people, but he is given an inner set of the spirit by which he rises above these calamities by the very fury of the calamities themselves. (p. 90)

The Apostle Paul wrote, "I have learned in whatsoever state I am, therewith to be content." Note he says that he "learned" how to be

January

content; it did not come to him naturally, but undoubtedly only as he learned the value of a spiritually disciplined life. When trouble comes seek refuge in God's presence, not in self-pity. Be honest with God! Tell Him if you're hurting, are sorrowful, or are depressed. Ask for the power of His presence to lift you like an eagle facing the storm. Remember the verse from Isaiah 40:31: "They that wait upon the Lord shall renew their strength, they shall mount up with wings as eagles, they shall run and not be weary, they shall walk and not faint."

We each have a choice to make in the midst of trouble—we can allow it to overwhelm us and roll us on the ocean bottom of life like a powerful wave; or we can resist it in the Spirit and force it to make us stronger. Joni Eareckson Tada, who at the age of 17 became a quadriplegic in a diving accident, has lived her entire adult life with her horrible affliction. She could have chosen to remain bitter and scream unfair to the world, but she didn't. She learned how to rest in God and she says that she learned to see her life "no longer as a bed of affliction but as an altar of praise." Out of a devastated life she became a world-renowned painter, writer, singer, speaker, advocate, and Christian leader.

There is much in life that we cannot control; what we do have the ability to do, however, is to choose how we will react to the things that happen to us. Attempting to deal with them in our own strength will only sink us into the depths of our weakness. Surrendering them to God's power will ensure that we will, by His grace, rise above whatever comes our way. How are you dealing with the adversities of life—like an eagle or an ostrich?

The Mystery of Life

27 Have you ever pondered your existence and asked yourself questions about the reality of God? Have you ever gazed into a darkened sky that was speckled with twinkling stars and wondered about the greatness of this world in which we live? Have you sat on a sand dune and gazed in awe at the greatness and power of the ocean? Well, so did the Psalmist before you!

When I consider your heavens, the work of your fingers,
the moon and the stars, which you have set in place,

January

What is man that you are mindful of him?
You have made him a little lower than the heavenly beings
And crowned him with glory and honor.   (Psalm 8:3-5)

God formed us out of the mystery of His own mind, and breathed into us that unfathomable reality we call life. He placed us on this earth, held out to us the potential for goodness, and then set out to convince us how deeply He loves us.

Existence! Aliveness! The mystery of life! That imperceptible, indefinable ingredient that causes life to be where none was before. What makes a heart beat? What causes a brain to send electrical pulses throughout the body? When death comes and the heart and brain cease to function, what has gone out of them and where did it go? Naive children that we are, we soak up life and pridefully proclaim our wisdom, boast of the world we have created, and with sinful indifference ignore the Being who gives and sustains life.

We fill our days with busy activities, running to and fro like relentless ants. We work hard, save, build houses, and accumulate material possessions; grow old, sit in soft chairs and wistfully stare out windows wondering what life was all about. We chase the elusive carrot-on-the-string called "happiness", never able to quite catch up with it; and when life has been spent unsuccessfully pursuing it, we sit down in old age in despair because we feel unfulfilled and life seems devoid of meaning. If happiness is to be found, and if happiness means peace, contentment, fulfillment, hope, love, and joy, we will never find it outside a conscious desire to rest in God. We don't look for water in a desert: why do we look for the qualities possessed by God in places that He isn't?

Our problem is that we deny the soul within us and give not time nor attention to the spirit buried deep inside. In order for plants to flourish they must sink their roots into that which can give them life. Cut off from the source of life they wither and fade. Dare we think human life is any different? It just takes us longer to die.

How wonderful it is to behold people who have attained great age and who depart this world with joy and peace. There is no fear in their eyes and there is hope in their heart. They eagerly await the next wondrous experience that God has prepared for them. The Psalmist concluded his pondering of human life and existence in the same place we would do well to conclude—with God. "O Lord, our Lord, how majestic is your name in all the earth!" (Psalm 8:9)

On Seeing the One Who Died For Us

28 Alexander the Great and his army captured a small village. The citizens of the village were brought before Alexander, at which time their future was determined. There appeared before him a young man, his bride, and the bride's mother. As they stood before the general, the young man was asked, "What would you give for your life?" upon which he replied, "I would give all my gold and silver, Sir." Then Alexander asked, "What would you give for the life of your wife?" upon which he replied, "I would give my life, Sir." Alexander said, "Let them go free." As they left, the mother asked the daughter, "Did you see the golden coat Alexander had on?" "No," replied the daughter, "I could only see the one who said, 'I would die for her'."

Those who gathered at the foot of Jesus' cross two thousand years ago were heartbroken as they beheld Him dying on that Roman gibbet. They wept simply because they loved Him and knew they were losing Him, not because they had any comprehension that His death on the cross was really for them. But what if they had fully comprehended that it was for them that He died? What if it were they who were being dragged toward Calvary for the purpose of execution, and Jesus stopped the rushing mob and said, "I will take their place." The soldiers grabbed Him and let the others go free. Up Calvary's slope they carried Him, and when they had fastened Him on the tree they stood it erect so the world could watch Him die.

Can you now see how different the sorrow would be? Whatever emotion one would have felt before would now be intensified a hundredfold. No longer would we grieve just because we were feeling a sense of loss and empathy for His pain; now we would know the deepest sorrow of all—sorrow that is mingled with loss, gratitude, and a sense of unworthiness. Sorrow that is like no other, because when someone dies for us their life has become inextricably intertwined with our own.

January

Once we have come face to face with the reality of Jesus' sacrifice, the certainty that it was for us, and the assurance that we were unworthy of it, then we will view our commitment to God in a totally different light. When we become committed to God, the sorrow will give way to joy, because then we will be confronted with the historical reality of the Resurrection. Yes, Jesus died, but praise God, Jesus also lives!

I am convinced that it is not the fear of God's wrath that ultimately changes us for the better, but the confrontation with His love. For centuries the prophets, from Moses on, warned the Hebrews about God's wrath and judgment, but the people continued on their merry sinful way. Fear of divine punishment subsides with the passing of time. Confrontation with divine love can never be completely forgotten or ignored.

When we really behold One who was not only <u>willing</u> to die, but <u>did</u> die for us, like the woman who stood before Alexander, we will see nothing else but Him who died for us.

For God's Glory

29 From whence comes sickness? Is it by mere chance that we become ill, or does some unseen force impose upon our bodies that foreign organism which depletes us of strength and robs us of the vitality of life? Many attempt to take comfort in their suffering by assuming that God caused the illness to teach them some lesson that could be learned by no other method. They say that it is God's will, therefore I will gladly suffer. Some assume that it is imposed on them because of some great sin, therefore God is punishing them. Oftentimes they will lash out in anger at God and scream that they are being treated unjustly—like Job, they demand an audience with God to plead their case.

To ask God, "Why me?" is to lay at the feet of God the responsibility for one's misfortune. It is to imply that He, if not causing the dilemma, is not doing anything about it. I believe that this is the wrong approach to sickness and misfortune. I have not spent my time in the hospital or since asking, "Why me?" Nor have I demanded that God cure me of this malignant tumor which has taken up residence in

January

my body. My one prayer from the first moment I was told it was there until now has been "God, glorify yourself in this!" Whether I am cleansed of this disease or whether it eventually overcomes this body of flesh and weakness is not my ultimate concern and certainly is not where I spend my prayer time. What I long for is for God to find a way in the midst of my pain and my sickness to bring honor unto Himself.

I am as yielded to His Spirit as I consciously know how to be. There is no fear in my heart; no anxiety in my soul. There is truly a peace that says, "Come what may, just as it has always been, my heart, my soul, my life are sheltered securely in the safety of God's hands." I have no death wish, no relentless hunger to leave this earth; but neither am I bound here. The roots of my eternal soul are already grounded in heaven and when this life ends, whether next week or thirty years from now, it will only blossom in fullness in the presence of God; it will not wither and fade on this earth and cease to be.

The God I served three weeks ago before I was told I had a malignant mass growing in my abdomen is the same God I know today. He loves me no less, He provides me with no less grace and strength. I loved Him then; if anything, I love Him more now.

The writer of Hebrews says that Jesus became man and died on a cross so that "through death He might destroy him that had the power of death, that is, the devil; and deliver them who through fear of death were all their lifetime subject to bondage" (Heb. 2:14, 15). When Jesus died for me the means of my freedom from the fear of death and from death's power were gracious gifts God's Son bestowed upon me without reservation or limitation. I have lived in the absolute freedom of that knowledge and power and it has not failed me for a moment.

Let your one prayer for me be that I might bear witness to His glory and that in my sickness many might find the glory and power of God being revealed through me and be drawn closer to Him who loves them. I ask nothing more!

The Discovery of Joy

30 Do you find joy in living, or do you get up each day feeling unhappy and depressed? Does one day slip into

January

another without any discernible difference? Has your relationship with those closest to you settled into a stagnant pattern of behavior that no longer excites you or brings joy to your heart? If so, then you aren't living life the way God desires for you to experience it! If your life experience is similar to the one described above, the problem is that you have allowed your existence to become centered on yourself. This should not be the way Christians live their days on this earth.

Undoubtedly, there have been moments in your life in which you experienced the exhilaration of being alive. Life seemed good, the future appeared exciting and bright, you made plans that created within yourself a sense of expectation and anticipation. Maybe you had just fallen in love and he or she returned it. You felt your heart would burst with joy! Or maybe you just shared in the birth of a child and you held him or her in your arms and looked with awe into the face of innocence and the miraculous gift of a human life entrusted to you to love, protect, and rear into adulthood. Perhaps you landed that first good job and the possibilities seemed so promising. It could be hundreds of things, but somehow the joy of that experience was so powerful it caused the downside of life to fade into obscurity.

I believe that real joy in life is found in relationships, not in things. It is found in what we experience with God and with other human beings. When life gets reduced to the lowest common denominator, when we are forced to acknowledge what is of ultimate value, most of us will always come to the same answer. What is valuable is loving and being loved by God and by other human beings.

I just spent a week up at our home near Kerr Lake. It is a beautiful place surrounded by trees, singing birds, soft breezes, nature whispering in all of its glory—"Life is good". I could have gotten up each day and said, "Woe is me, my body hurts, my strength is depleted, the course of my life has been forever altered by the 'C' disease." I could have walked around and bemoaned how unfortunate I am and how unfair life has been. But I didn't, simply because I couldn't. I'm no super-saint, no particularly brave person, I'm not even what one would label an optimist. I'm simply one human being who has been richly blessed by God in immeasurable ways. And so I walked out on my deck and I praised God for His goodness, thanked

January

Him for my loving wife and children, praised Him for the avalanche of love and support that we have received from you, and felt so lucky to be alive and in the midst of a serious illness to know a peace in my heart that would not let me go.

It all comes from discovering that I can rest in God, just as you can, and when we rest in God, nothing, nothing, nothing, can take His peace from our soul and His joy from our heart. If you are unhappy with life, turn to God and discover anew that the Being who created you; created you for joy, happiness, and peace. The kingdom of heaven is within you waiting for you to allow it to be born. Joy in living will be found when God becomes the center of your life.

Freedom from Fear

31 Fear is all too much a part of human nature. Generally, we fear that which we do not understand, that which we believe has the power to harm us, or that which we feel has power over us. When we are living life on the level of fear, we are living it in the flesh and not the spirit. Paul writes to the Romans: "You did not receive a spirit of slavery to fall back into fear, but you received a spirit of adoption" (8:15, NRSV). When we begin to live with God on the level of the spiritual, His Spirit incorporates us into His family and sets us free from the bondage of fear.

While indeed there are things in this life which can cause us bodily harm, pain, or sickness, there is nothing which exists that has the power to tear us away from the secure grasp of the hand of God which holds us. The writer of I John says, "There is no fear in love, but perfect love casts out fear; for fear has to do with punishment, and whoever fears has not reached perfection in love" (4:18). God is perfect love and it is His desire that our lives be spared the experience of living in fear. Time and again Jesus would say to someone in the gospels, "Fear not," or "Let not your heart be troubled, neither let it be afraid." I cannot imagine a moment in Jesus' life when He looked into a human face and felt fear. He was too immersed in the Spirit and will of His Father to waste His energy on useless fear.

The only way we can live apart from fear is to live life more fully in the Spirit of God. When we become conscious of God's

February

nearness and of His love for us, then all else fades in comparison. One of the fascinating things about the early Christians and especially those who faced martyrdom was the peace and lack of fear that they revealed. Those who witnessed their deaths were amazed at how they responded to those who were taking their very lives. How did they do it? They were dwelling on a level of the Spirit that would not allow room for fear. While life could be taken from them and suffering may have had to be endured, still nothing could rob them of the presence of the God who loved them and would give them eternal life.

Hidden deep inside each of us is that glorious and mysterious reality that we call the soul. It is there that God communicates most deeply with us and it is there that He desires to dwell. When we consciously choose to open up our soul, to be in union with God, we will discover that our fears will subside. Not only can we rest secure in the knowledge that nothing can ultimately harm us; equally important is the comfort we can take in the reality that if we surrender to God then we no longer have to understand everything, nor do we have to be in control. It's a far greater feeling of security in our heart when we know that God is in control, than when we insist on being the one in charge.

Young people today walk around with shirts that have NO FEAR emblazoned on them. But that statement is a myth, unless they walk in the Spirit of our Lord. The only person who can truly have no fear is the person who dwells in the presence of perfect love—and God is the place of perfect love!

Trusting in God

1 "I need oil," said an ancient monk, so he planted an olive sapling. "Lord," he prayed, "it needs rain that its tender roots may drink and swell. Send gentle showers." And the Lord sent gentle showers. "Lord," prayed the monk, "my tree needs sun. Send sun, I pray Thee." And the sun shone, gilding the dripping clouds. "Now frost, my Lord, to brace its tissues," cried the monk. And behold the little tree stood sparkling with frost, but at evening it died.

Then the monk sought the cell of a brother monk, and told his strange experience. "I, too, planted a little tree," he said, "and see! It

February

thrives well. But I entrust my tree to its God. He who made it knows better what it needs than a man like me. I laid no condition. I fixed not ways or means. 'Lord send what it needs,' I prayed, 'storm or sunshine, wind, rain, or frost. Thou has made it and Thou dost know" (*Streams in the Desert*, p. 98).

When we pray, there will be moments in which we petition God with certain requests—certain needs. The needs we place before God become the seeds of faith that we long to see blossom into healthy reality. But no seed can grow until the hand that plants it lets it go. True, we seek to nurture the seed with water, with tilling, by weeding around it, but ultimately the seed is hidden from our eyes as the ground covers it, and in faith it is entrusted into the Hands of Him who is Life.

How often we make our petitions to God and then try to become the power of life which makes them grow. We cannot, for we are not God. When a loved one is critically ill, it is right that we should pray, but we must pray as the second monk who with profound wisdom realized that God knows more about the "whens" and "hows" of life than we do. With all of our good intentions, with all of our righteous concern, our power is limited and can unwittingly become an encumbrance if we seek to assume the role of God.

That which we bring to God we must be willing to leave with God. Are we afraid that God will not "do it right" without our instructions? How can a physician heal a sick child if the loving parent will not remove his or her arms of love so that the child can be examined? Prayer has always been about trust. When requests are offered on the wings of prayer we come face to face with the meaning of faith. "O, but faith is such a hard concept to grasp!" you say. Only because we make it so! Faith is no more complicated than the person who takes his or her money to a bank, deposits it, then leaves it there with the calm assurance that those to whom it has been entrusted will not only keep it safe, but increase its measure. Do we trust the bank, the post office, the grocery store, the operator of the water purification system more than we do God? In faith we entrust to them many of the most important matters of our life. Why not trust God?

We have a God to whom we can entrust our deepest needs, our most intimate secrets, our greatest fears, and our human frailty. God is

February

the Creator; we are the created. God is the Source of life; we are the result of life. God has the power: "We have this treasure in earthen vessels, that the excellence of the power may be of God and not of us" (II Corinthians 4:7). Trust God—He is trustworthy!

Come and Die

2 In order to get along in this world, whether we realize it or not, we surrender part of ourselves to someone else (though sometimes we do it quite grudgingly!). Most of us work for someone else; pay taxes to the government; give part of ourselves to our families and occasionally, our friends. We give our time to various endeavors and once in a while to a charitable cause.

Then along comes God and He asks for something from us too—only His request is—"I want all of you!" Dietrich Bonhoeffer, the renowned theologian, once wrote, "When Christ calls a man [woman] he bids him come and die." What he meant, of course, was that to follow Christ means you must be willing to die to self. Our ol' human nature resists that like the plague, because at the root of sin is the desire to elevate self. Therefore, most of us will probably go through life resisting to the very end the giving of ourselves totally to the God who made us. Of course, at the very end, we finally say, "Okay, Lord, you can have all of me now! Just take me to heaven to be with You!"

The "self" in us has deceived us in that it has convinced us that to give ourselves completely to God is to make ourselves miserable. The truth is that the more we give ourselves to God, the happier we become. But we want to be the one who controls our happiness and we don't feel inclined to leave that up to anyone else, not even God—especially God, because He will undoubtedly expect us to do or not do a lot of things that we wouldn't choose.

How differently John Wesley (and other giants of the faith) viewed surrender. Wesley passed on to anyone who would embrace it, a beautiful covenant prayer (# 607 in the United Methodist Hymnal). Listen to its power, beauty, and surrender:

February

I am no longer my own, but thine.
    Put me to what thou wilt, rank me with whom thou wilt.
Put me to doing, put me to suffering.
    Let me be employed by thee or laid aside for thee,
        exalted for thee or brought low by thee.
Let me be full, let me be empty.
    Let me have all things, let me have nothing.
I freely and heartily yield all things
    to thy pleasure and disposal.
And now, O glorious and blessed God,
    Father, Son, and Holy Spirit,
        thou art mine, and I am thine. So be it.
And the covenant which I have made on earth,
    let it be ratified in heaven. Amen.

Do you have the courage and conviction to pray that prayer in utter sincerity? It would be life-transforming. And yet that is the kind of faith and commitment I know our Lord desires of each of us. Let us at least try, and in our effort say honestly to God, "Help me, Lord, to become so yielded that Wesley's words can truly become my own!"

Grace Awaits You

3 Do you have all of God's grace that you want? If so, then read no further! Grace is often defined as "unmerited love." In other words, love that is poured upon us even though we are unworthy to receive it. But grace is more than unmerited love; it is the very spiritual energy which transforms us and sustains us. It is that power of God which comes to us and causes us to long to become something better than we are. It is that mystical presence that descends into our souls and makes us conscious of the reality of our spiritual nature.

Grace is the living presence of God within us. It is the life-giving source which gives birth to the kingdom of God within. The kingdom cannot come until grace precedes it, for it is grace that gives it life. Grace is that cleansing balm that sweeps through our darkened souls and washes away the guilt and shame of our sinfulness. It has the power to make us whole and to rescue us from a lifetime of our

February

brokenness. Like the wind, which cannot be seen, it makes itself known by the effect of its presence.

Grace is the only thing that can quench the hunger and thirst that cries out from deep within us. It is the true bread come down from heaven and the living water that forever satisfies. Its origin is the heart of God, its destination is the heart of humanity. It begins in heaven; it descends to earth in order that it might bring heaven to earth, and in so doing carry humanity to heaven. Grace is the doorway to life, the escape from eternal death. It shields and protects, it defends and uplifts. Grace is that which banishes fear and despair. On the wings of grace, peace is borne and joy is ushered in.

It is grace that comes into the heart that has no hope and crushes the head of despair. It gently caresses the soul and like a soothing brook on a scorching afternoon, it bathes the parched spirit in love. Grace lifts the burden of guilt and restores the sense of self-worth. It rips asunder the veil of sin that has blinded us to our worth to God. Grace erects a cross at the center of our lives and from that cross its power emanates outward.

Jesus is God's grace. It is His body and blood which become the essence of all that God's grace can bestow. At Holy Communion our Lord will once again set forth His table. Upon the altar of divine love the body and blood of God's Son will be offered. It will come to you in the form of a tiny piece of bread, and juice in the small confines of a little glass. They will appear to the world as insignificant and meaningless, but to the heart that embraces them in faith, they will become the totality of all that I have described above as grace.

Do you hunger for God's grace? Do you thirst for its quenching power? Then come with humble hearts and outstretched hands and let your souls be fed. Lift up your empty palms and receive the grace of God. Let the mystery of its power enter your body and find its place in your soul. Jesus waits to give you grace. Will you come?

The Church

4 In his powerful book entitled *The Church,* Hans Kung, renowned Catholic theologian writes:

February

> *The Church must constantly reflect upon its real existence in the present with reference to its origins in the past, in order to assure its existence in the future. It stands or falls by its links with its origins in Jesus Christ and its message; it remains permanently dependent, for the ground of its existence, on God's saving act in Jesus Christ, which is valid for all time and so also in the present.* (p. 35)

When we as a body of believers separate ourselves from the words, deeds, and life of the Jesus of history, we by that very act separate ourselves from the Lord of glory who desires to dwell with us in the present. There are eternal truths that have been handed down to us that cannot be altered or improved upon. We cannot fashion a "modern" Jesus who bears little or no resemblance to the historical Jesus and expect to have a living, vibrant faith.

The Church is far more than an ecclesiastical institution that is housed in buildings with steeples on top. Thank God, the true church is also more than the individuals who make up its varied membership rolls. The Church on earth that we know is composed of imperfect human beings who all too often make mistakes in judgment and claim to speak for God when in essence their words and deeds reflect their own view of the world—not God's. As a result, the church has often been the instrument that causes pain and brokenness rather than the body which God envisioned would be a means of grace, healing, and reconciliation. The evidence of the existence of the true church will be where peace, love, harmony, and joy flow forth in abundance in the lives of those who claim Jesus as Lord.

The "true" church is that body which is so surrendered to the living Spirit of Jesus Christ that it truly becomes the embodiment of the divine will of God. To live in God's kingdom is to be willing to do God's will. We were taught by Jesus to pray, "Thy kingdom come, Thy will be done." Yet how blind we seem to be to the inseparable link of those two phrases. One cannot exist without the presence of the other. When members of a Christian congregation truly desire to know and do God's will, then the kingdom will come in fullness. It will be birthed from within and manifest itself outwardly. Its conception will be by the Spirit of God and not the mind or will of human beings.

February

Unfortunately, the church as we know it is too much of a human creation and not enough of a divine creation. While we may have the seeds of the true church in our midst, we have not allowed ourselves to become in fullness what God intended. We cannot willfully and consciously live apart from God's teaching and with any legitimacy call ourselves the church. That's not to suggest that we are capable of doing His will perfectly, but we must long to know and do it as perfectly as we can. Are we willing to make such a commitment?

On Measuring Your Life

5 When you have come to the end of your life how will you measure its value? Will it be by the financial comfort you have achieved? By the possessions you have accumulated? Perhaps by the education and degrees you have attained? Maybe by how productive you were on your job? The most important question will be, "How will God evaluate our lives?" Recently I read a quotation from an unknown author that said:

> *Measure your life by loss instead of gain:*
> *Not by the wine drunk, but in the wine poured forth;*
> *For love's strength stands in love's sacrifice;*
> *And who suffers most, has most to give.*

I had never before thought about measuring the value of my life by what I was willing to give up. As a minister, it's understandable that I would interpret those words in the context of what one is willing to give up in obedience to God's will. It is God's will that we love Him and one another. That is at the heart of our faith. And oftentimes loving God and our neighbor will mean that there will be something in our own life that we must sacrifice in order to express that love. For example, if we are to be obedient to His command to love Him and our neighbor, then that means we must love those around us including those whose skin color may not be like ours. This means that we must be willing to let go of years of prejudice in order to be obedient. We must sacrifice racial bias on the altar of God's love. To take such a stand could very well alienate us from family and friends who desire to

February

hold on to their prejudices. And so we may have to sacrifice their acceptance of us in order to fulfill God's will in our lives.

Who among us can read the Gospel accounts of Jesus' life and not behold the sacrifice God was willing to make for His creation? The central message of the gospel is the cross. It is God sacrificing Himself for the sake of humanity. We are awed by it, drawn by it, bewildered by it! Yet there it stands for all eternity—the love of God impaled on a cross. God's love can be measured by the depth of loss and sacrifice He was willing to endure for our sake. Is there not a message here?

What we have yet to discover is that everything sacrificed for the sake of Christ becomes gain. Read Matthew 19:27-29. It is Jesus' response to Peter's question, "Look, we have left everything and followed You. What then will we have?" And Jesus said, "Everyone who has left houses or brothers or sisters or father or mother or children or fields, for my name's sake, will receive a hundredfold and will inherit eternal life" (NRSV).

The wondrous, marvelous beauty of following Jesus is that there will come a time in which you are no longer interested in what the reward might be, you will follow Him simply because you love Him and know that you are loved by Him. That is reward enough! That is how you can measure your life.

When Trouble Comes

6 To live as a human being is to be assured that your life will be both a mixture of good and bad, health and sickness, joy and sorrow, peace and discord. We tend to view life in terms of positives and negatives. We love the positives and despise the negatives. But the truth is that when we curse the negatives we are cursing the very things that can make us better. Since every life is an accumulation of both good and bad, just maybe we ought to pause and ask if one of the powerful ways God intervenes in our lives and makes us conscious of our human frailty and His divine omniscience is through our encounter with the bad things that befall us.

Most of us have heard the axiom, "It is better to light a candle than to curse the darkness." There is great truth here that we would do

February

well to pursue. When faced with adversity we can embrace it and grow from it or we can resist it, hate it, curse it, complain about it, and learn nothing from it. Jesus' life was filled with adversity, with inner and outer suffering and in each case he turned the adversity to his (and our) advantage. He didn't pursue evil, it pursued Him, but when He encountered it He overcame it by facing it and conquering it with His inner spiritual strength. His suffering on the cross brought the glory of our redemption. His death brought forth the possibility of our resurrection. His ascension into heaven became the pathway to our own eternal life.

Henri Nouwen, in his book *Life of the Beloved*, writes:

> *The deep truth is that our human suffering need not be an obstacle to the joy and peace we so desire, but can become, instead, the means to it. The great secret of the spiritual life, the life of the Beloved Sons and Daughters of God, is that everything we live, be it gladness or sadness, joy or pain, health or illness, can all be part of the journey toward the full realization of our humanity.* (p. 77)

I can attest to the absolute truth of his statement in the recent events of my own life. I have never felt closer to God than I do now. I have never known the peace I feel nor the joy I carry in my heart—all because when sickness and suffering came, I embraced it in faith and surrendered it to God. Instead of complaining and asking why me in the prime of my life, I totally gave it to God, asking only that He bring to Himself glory in my suffering. He did! And the result for me was a happiness in living that I had never known before.

To embrace suffering with joy and confidence is not to be masochistic, but to recognize that God's promise to be with us no matter what, is reason enough to find joy in living. The result of such a response is to discover a freedom in living that is awesome. The fear and uncertainty of life is gone and each new day becomes an adventure, even if that day is one in which we face illness. The evil things of this world will never be overcome through complaining but through grabbing hold to them and forcing them to yield to us all the goodness that we can squeeze from them.

February

On Making Choices

7   Living as a Christian requires that we allow Jesus' philosophy of life to become our own, without any attempt to modify it. The hard part about Jesus' philosophy is that it cuts across the grain of our natural human tendencies. For example, to put God first and love our neighbor as ourselves calls for a way of life that moves self from the center and rearranges our priorities.

As babies, we arrive in this world with the desire to immediately become the center of the universe. We want comfort, full stomachs, empty bladders and dry diapers, and we want them NOW! And if we don't get what we want immediately, we make the world aware of it by using our one and only weapon (for which there is no known defense): we wail to the top of our lungs! And since this initial philosophy of life works so well early on, it's hardly surprising to discover that most of us arrive at adulthood having made only slight modifications, and with our desires still firmly entrenched as the order of the day.

To be denied the things we want is a concept that most of us grudgingly accept only when it is forced upon us. And yet Jesus tells us that His way of life is to place other things ahead of ourselves, to deny ourselves, and to be willing to part with even our most prized possessions. To find life, He says, we must be willing to lose it. Are we willing? Perhaps Martha Snell Nicholson's little poem "Treasures" puts things in perspective for us.

> *One by one He took them from me, all the things I valued most,*
>   *Until I was empty-handed; every glittering toy was lost,*
> *And I walked earth's highway, grieving, in my rags and poverty,*
>   *Till I heard His voice inviting, "Lift your empty hands to Me!"*
> *So I turned my hands toward Heaven, and He filled them with a store*
> *Of His own transcendent riches, till they could contain no more.*
>   *And at last I comprehended, with my stupid mind and dull,*
>   *That God could not pour His riches into hands already full!*

A human life can contain only so much. Just as you cannot fill any container beyond its capacity, so our lives cannot be filled beyond

February

theirs. Thus, it comes down to dealing with the question of, "With what will I fill my life?" God has extended to each human being the choice (at least spiritually) of deciding what grows inside our hearts and souls. What grows within us is what we allow to be channeled into us. Paul gives us guidance in Philippians (4:8) when he exhorts us to fill our hearts and minds with that which is noble, just, pure, lovely, and commendable. That can be best accomplished by saturating our minds with the words of Jesus.

If our lives are already overflowing and there seems little room for Jesus, then the answer is to start removing things that waste our lives and take up space; make more room for the eternal things that Jesus offers. Look at your life today. What fills it? Where are you heading? Are you fulfilled spiritually? As long as you are alive you still have the right to make choices. Today, what will you choose?

Cheap Grace/Costly Grace

8 Dietrich Bonhoeffer, a Lutheran pastor who was executed by the Nazis in World War II, wrote a book entitled *The Cost of Discipleship*. He lived at a time in which he thought Christians were living in a manner that cheapened the grace of God. The following passage from that book seems all too true of many in the church of our own day.

> *Cheap grace is the preaching of forgiveness without requiring repentance, baptism without church discipline, Communion without confession, absolution without personal confession. Cheap grace is grace without discipleship, grace without the cross, grace without Jesus Christ, living and incarnate.*
>
> *Costly grace is the treasure hidden in the field; for the sake of it a man will gladly go and sell all that he has. Costly grace is the gospel which must be sought again and again, the gift which must be asked for, the door at which a man must knock.*
>
> *Such grace is costly because it calls us to follow, and it is grace because it calls us to follow Jesus Christ. It is costly because it costs a man his life, and it is grace because it gives a man the only true life. It is costly because it condemns sin, and*

grace because it justifies the sinner. Above all, it is costly because it cost God the life of his Son: "ye were bought at a price," and what has cost God much cannot be cheap for us. Above all, it is grace because God did not reckon His Son too dear a price to pay for our life, but delivered Him up for us. Costly grace is the Incarnation of God.

We make God's grace cheap when we take it for granted, when we squander it on self and neglect the responsibility to share it with others. We make it cheap when we refuse to give back to the church in service what the church has given to us in showing us the way to eternal life. We make God's sacrificial grace cheap when we find no value in worshiping Him, and instead, indulge ourselves in the pursuit of sinful pleasure rather than holy living. Wherever self is the center of one's existence, God's grace has been desecrated and the cross of Christ has been ridiculed.

God's grace is cheapened when we "bring out babies to the altar" for baptism but do not bring them up in church. It is devalued when we want to be married in a church but never worship in church; when we demand to have our name on the church roll but never darken its doors nor support its ministry. God's grace is made cheap when we are offended by the truth and choose to embrace the living of a lie. Grace is cheapened when we think we can be a Christian and not be a disciple and a servant.

Being a Christian is more than a name; it is a hunger, a yearning to know the God who lives and to be spent in serving Him. I will not add to the pain of Jesus' suffering by encouraging church members to indulge in cheap grace. We dare not take God's grace from a cross and use it as cheap wine. The full rich blood of our precious Lord is our grace, and we must be awed by its costliness. Jesus Christ, the Son of God, died for you and for me, and we must not live as if that doesn't matter. It matters very much to me. I pray it matters to you too.

The Search for Truth

9 I often quote E. Stanley Jones because I think he was one of the most deeply profound Christian thinkers I have ever read. Furthermore, his life revealed a peace and contentment I have

February

rarely beheld in others. In his book *Is the Kingdom of God Realism?* Jones makes the following statement: "There are two ways to raise questions — one is to raise them academically, discuss them, and thus search for a logical answer. The other is to raise those questions in one's own being and life and then give the answer out of life itself, by life itself (p. 45).

The person who is searching for the answer to the relevance of life will never find a satisfactory solution on the academic or intellectual level until and unless he or she is also willing to give consideration to the answers that arise from within the heart and soul. The answers to life inevitably will be derived from the Source of life. Science digs through archeological ruins, studies ancient bones and cultures, penetrates the world of microscopic life, searches the farthest dimensions of the universe, devotes itself to uncovering the mysteries of life—and always returns with only partial and incomplete answers that inevitably point to something beyond the capability of human wisdom and understanding.

E. Stanley Jones, referring to Jesus, says, "He was not a philosopher spinning theories about life, but One who was giving His answer to life out of life itself. You cannot tell where His words end and His deeds begin, or where His deeds end and His words begin, for His deeds were words and His words were deeds, and His deeds and His words coming together with what He was became the Word made flesh, a fact" (p. 16). A sarcastic student once asked Jones,

> "Have you ever caught God in a test tube?" He replied, "No, but have you ever caught love in a test tube? Is love thereby unreal? When science throws its net into the sea of reality, there are many things which slip through the meshes of its method when it draws its net to the shore of observation. And these things which slip through may be just as real as the things which were caught by this method." (*Is the Kingdom of God Realism?*, p. 14)

The person who sincerely seeks the truth will eventually find it in the life and teachings of Jesus or he or she will never find it at all. Jesus did not attempt to give answers to the questions of science, He

February

provided answers to the meaning of life. The scientist may think his hunger for knowledge is driven by the desire for scientific truth, but deep down inside it is being pushed by an invisible force which longs to reveal Himself as the creator of all truth.

There is nothing in this entire universe more relevant to life than that which Jesus has revealed about it. His words are the force that draws us back to the beginning, center, and destination of all life. Jesus makes us look inward to the soul and it is in the soul that we will come face to face with God. Science and technology are the creations of humanity, humanity is the creation of God. Why settle for half-truth when you can go all the way to the Source of all truth?

Hearing and Believing

10 Basically, we communicate with one another through the use of words. Words cause images to instantly travel through our minds and create pictures. For example, if I say, "The dog jumped over the fence," your mind creates an image of what you have long ago come to accept as being a dog. You see that animal leave the ground and rise over and clear a fence. You don't have to stop and think it out step by step; it simply takes place instantly as you read or hear the words. But hearing words and believing their truth is not the same thing as accepting those words and fashioning your life around them.

Jesus said, "Seek ye first the kingdom of God, and all these other things [food, clothing, etc.] will be added to you." We hear the words and basically we understand what they mean. We might even believe that there is truth in His words, but do we allow those words to radically transform our lives? Do we believe them enough to let them be applied to our lives? In other words, are we really seeking God's kingdom first for our lives, or are we only faintly interested in pursuing it? Truth is of little value to us unless we are willing to fully embrace it.

Sunday after Sunday, Christians throughout the world hear the truth preached. But how much of it are we willing to accept and incorporate into our lives? It was not by chance that the first commandment that God gave to Moses to give us was, "Thou shall

February

have no other gods before me!" In other words, God must be first and foremost in our lives above all other things. He must have our ultimate love and loyalty even above our family, our job, even our pursuit of leisure and pleasure.

"Seek ye first the kingdom of God" haunts us and pursues us like a relentless pack of hounds that will not leave us alone. We try to ignore it, run from it, block it from our consciousness, but it arises again and again and refuses to be banished. What we really want is a God who is willing to be there for us when we need Him, but remain in the shadows, removed from our sight until we call for Him to be present. We have yet to learn that God wants us to seek His kingdom first, not so we can be herded into line spiritually, but so we can begin to live in the joy, peace, and freedom in which we were created to dwell. We imagine that to seek first the kingdom means we must lose everything that is really important. But the truth of the matter is that what is ultimately and truly important will never be experienced apart from His kingdom. God asks us to seek His kingdom because He wants us to experience in majestic power the effect of His love upon our lives.

The spiritual life is not intended to be just the religious pursuit of ascetic monks secluded in some dark monastery. It is the discovery of who we were intended to be in the heart of God. We are and always will be restless and unfulfilled until we rest in God and we will never rest in God until we are willing to seek His presence above all other things. It does no good to hear the words of truth, or even believe them, if we are unwilling to let our lives be formed by them.

Abundant Living

11 What is abundant living? Does it mean that we make our way through this life by accumulating an abundance of things? As we look at ourselves and our friends and neighbors, the evidence seems to be that most, if not all of us, surely tend to do that. Isn't it amazing how much "stuff" we buy which at the time seems so important and indispensable, but before long ends up in a yard sale, being sold for a fraction of its original value?

February

Perhaps we think abundant living means being able to do more things and go and see more places. I had a great-aunt who often spoke with great pride that she had visited all 48 states—there were only 48 when she used to brag about her travels! Nothing wrong with travel and sight-seeing, but is that really abundant living?

Jesus said, "I have come to give you life and to give you life more abundantly." Yet somehow many of us have come to the conclusion that to become His disciple means we will have less in life, rather than more. That may be true, depending upon what you conclude is most important in life. We may rest assured that the purpose of Jesus' coming was not to ensure that we would all be wealthy and own a multitude of possessions. It may well be that many of us will have those things, and that indeed they may be within the will of God for us; but that was not His purpose in coming.

I believe that when He talks about the abundant life He is referring to the riches of knowing and living daily with our Father. Nothing we experience in this life is more important and valuable than inner peace, quiet joy, and a feeling of excitement about being alive with a consciousness of the presence of God with us. It is so sad to see so many "Christians" living un-abundant lives. Life has become a rat race and the next day is dreaded more than the current one they're experiencing. Not content to allow "the evil of today to be sufficient unto itself," they're already worrying about the evil of tomorrow (which may never come).

Try this prayer on for size—"Lord, help me to live this day with such a consciousness of your presence that all that I do and say will bring joy to your heart." One of the distortions of human understanding of life is that we can only find joy in doing what we want, rather than meeting the need in another's life. Could it be that at this very juncture, Jesus' words have meaning— "He who is willing to lose his life will find it, and he who seeks to save his life will lose it."

The abundance of life which Jesus promises to bring is the inner life— the place of your heart, soul, and conscience. The place no one sees but you and God. It is here where real living takes place. This is the shelter from the storm of life's outward demands. It is here that the divine and human will intersect and the mysteries of life will begin to

February

be revealed, one by one. In this arena of existence the presence of God becomes merged with our own presence and we finally begin to understand what life is meant to be. Abundant living begins within and from that starting point will manifest itself outwardly to the world.

Solitude with God

12 One element in a Christian's life which is essential to spiritual growth and maturity is solitude. I'm not simply talking about time spent alone—that can become a source of anguish that leads to loneliness. Lord knows there are too many people who live in loneliness. The solitude of which I speak is time set apart for the specific purpose of being alone with God. Our tendency as "modern" people is to fill our consciousness either with the presence of others, or with devices such as TVs, radios, or books that tell us what thoughts to put into our minds. Even if we go away on retreats we go with others and we generally let them dictate to us what we will be thinking about. Richard Foster writes, "Loneliness is inner emptiness. Solitude is inner fulfillment. Solitude is not first a place but a state of mind and heart" (*The Celebration of Discipline*, p. 84).

Jesus found it essential to separate Himself from those He loved for the purpose of communing with His Father. Time and again He went aside to pray, to meditate, and to be strengthened by God for the purpose to which He had been called. Tradition tells us that Jesus' ministry lasted approximately three years and that He was about thirty-three when He died. What about those first thirty years? All we know from those years are the brief stories surrounding His birth and the one incident at the Temple when He was twelve years old. For thirty years God was preparing Him for three years of ministry.

After the apostle Paul was dramatically converted, he found it necessary to go into the desert wilderness of Arabia for three years to prepare himself for the work to which God was calling him (Galatians 1:17-18). John the Baptist spent a large part of his life wandering in the wilderness. Moses encountered God in the burning bush in the desert—a place where, with the exception of the sheep he was tending, his time was spent in solitude. Likewise, other prophets from the Old

February

Testament found their relationship with God in the isolation of the wilderness.

If all of these giants of the faith found it essential to spend time alone with God, why do we think we will have a deep relationship with Him when we are never alone with Him? Solitude with God is not the constant chatter of our own voice talking out loud to Him or even silently communicating with him within the walls of our minds; it is a time in which we seek to become still and quiet and listen to what God is saying within us. We either have lost or never discovered the ability to hear the voice of God speaking inwardly to our souls. God's ability to communicate with us is not limited to audible sounds or even holy words printed on a page. He often speaks most profoundly to us when we hear His voice within our heart.

When was the last time you consciously and intentionally listened for the voice of God within? You can hear that voice speaking inwardly even if you are standing in the midst of a crowd; but you will develop that ability only as you have been able to discover it in solitude. Jesus said, "My sheep hear my voice. I know them and they follow Me" (John 10:27). Are you hearing the voice of Jesus? Are you spending time in solitude with God?

The Necessity of Accountability

13 Integrity, character, ethics, honesty, and morality used to be concepts that did not need to be defined or defended—especially by those who took their Christian faith seriously. But in today's society even Christians seem bewildered by these issues. We have so clothed ourselves in the preaching of grace that we have come to the conclusion that sin need not be taken seriously. Since we have been taught that we ought to forgive and that we should never judge, we have become reluctant to insist on moral living in the lives of others or our own. The notion that we are accountable, to God and one another, seems to have vanished.

In a national poll, a majority of respondents said that the character and morality of a political candidate would have no bearing on whether they voted for him or her or not. It seems to no longer matter whether one is honest or not since we are all human and therefore

February

fallible. It used to be expected that ministers would live their lives on a level that was beyond moral reproach, but now many are content to allow ministers to engage in the same immoral debauchery as the rest of society and say, "I don't want to hear about it. I make mistakes too, so I won't hold them accountable." Worst of all we have justified such thinking as being in keeping with what Christ expects of us.

The church not only has the right but the responsibility to insist that we be accountable to one another, not for the purpose of condemnation and expulsion, but for the hope that there might be remorse and repentance. To assume that God does not take sin seriously is to be unbelievably ignorant of the meaning of the cross. Yes, the cross is the revelation of God's love for sinful humanity, but it also stands erect on the horizon of human life to proclaim that God took so seriously the destructiveness of what sin does to us that He was willing to die for us in order to redeem us from its power. Our sin brought forth the Son of God's death. He did not brush it under a rug and say it doesn't matter; He said it matters so much that the only way it can be driven from our lives is by His suffering and dying to get rid of it.

Quoting Reverend Tim Keller: "The Christian gospel is that we are not saved by moral living, we are saved for it. We are saved by grace alone, but that grace will inevitably issue in a moral life. . . . You are not living as though you are loved! As his child! It is not because he will abandon you that you should be holy, but because at inestimable cost he has said he won't ever abandon you! How can you live in the very sin that He was ripped to pieces to deliver you from?" (*Leadership*, Winter 1996, p. 114).

We cannot pretend sin doesn't matter and think we are doing what God expects of us. Jesus exhorts us to "judge righteous judgments" (John 7:24). Righteous judgment is allowing one's life to be compared to the standard of God's law. If we make no judgments at all then we are saying there is no such thing as sin, and integrity is unnecessary. We are called to holy living, not living wholly as we choose. Where God's Spirit is present redemption takes place and where redemption takes place sin will not be glorified or embraced as the norm for Christian living.

February

Buried Treasure

14   Our lives have been woven together both by genetic fiber and by the events and experiences of life which have made us who we have become. Much of that weaving we had no control over. Yet, no matter who we have become there is within each of us a yearning, a hunger, a longing to be something other than what we are. It is as if there is some invisible magnetic pull that we can't identify which refuses to allow us to be content with life as we know it.

The Word of God says that when humanity was created we were made in the image of God. If God is the ultimate source of our life then it stands to reason that our life will bear the brush strokes of the One who created us. Each painting by Rembrandt, Michelangelo or Picasso bears the unique characteristics of its creator even though each painting is different. Likewise each of us is uniquely one of God's masterpieces. We are all alike, yet all different. We bear similarities, but we also reveal remarkable differences. Stamped indelibly on the canvas of our soul is the image of God. It is within us waiting to become outwardly revealed. It is that inner part which Jesus referred to as the abode of the kingdom of God.

Unfortunately, our own human nature has been so distorted by our propensity to sin that our consciousness of our spiritual nature has been buried by a mountain of guilt, shame, sin, and regret. The treasure that God has placed within us is struggling to come forth from beneath that heap of unwanted baggage. There is an inner hunger to be in perfect union with our Creator. We sin, but we find no peace and joy in our sinning. It may bring momentary physical pleasure or satisfaction, but it fades as quickly as the dew in the heat of the rising sun. How many years of our life will we waste, ignoring or denying the soft gentle call of the Master as He beckons us to come to Him and find the joy in living we were meant to have?

For decades we try life "our" way and we will always find it to be deficient. It seems unthinkable to us to yield to the call of the Spirit and try life God's way, because we are too afraid to surrender our will and our desires to anyone—including God. Besides, it takes a lot of effort to listen for and discover the voice of God speaking within.

February

We need to finally realize that we were created by a divine being to live and function in a certain way and as long as we try to go another way we will never be happy. The key to our happiness lies within our heart and soul and only as we are willing to begin looking there will we ever be headed in the right direction. God created us not just to be a physical being but also a spiritual one. Those two are not separate; they are one. When we put all the emphasis of living on one aspect of our being and ignore the other, then we are living against our own nature.

There is within you a hidden treasure. If you will seek it and yield to it you will discover the secret to living life in peace and tranquility. But only you can uncover the treasure, no one can discover it for you.

The God of Brokenness

15 The nature and character of God is dramatically revealed in the manner in which He deals with brokenness. At various times in each of our lives we have experienced the reality of brokenness. Sometimes it comes to us in the pain we feel at losing a loved one to death. Maybe it comes in the form of a marriage that could not survive "until death do us part." For others it is the shattered feeling that comes when we are betrayed by a trusted friend, or the anguish we feel when we have made a foolish mistake. For some it is the brokenness that comes when one's health is shattered by prolonged and serious illness.

Brokenness is a common human experience. Yet, how we deal with that condition will determine whether we rise from it stronger or weaker, sicker or healthier, wiser or more foolish. Everywhere Jesus went in life He encountered human brokenness. He did not condemn it; rather, He embraced it, absorbed it into Himself and returned it to the person from whom it came as wholeness. The sick He made well, the tormented He set free, the sorrowful He made joyful, the lost He made to be found, the sinful He redeemed, the dead He made alive!

Perhaps there is some brokenness in your life right now! If so, bring it to God and lay all the fragments at His feet. Confess that you have not the wisdom or power to make it whole again, but that you believe that He does. Surrender it, and believe that part of God's salvific plan for you is to make you whole in every way. At the heart of the word salvation is wholeness. To put "salve" on a wound is to put an ointment on it that brings soothing healing and wholeness.

Like all of you, I have known the experience of brokenness in body, spirit and soul. But I have also known how God cannot only restore me to wholeness but how He can take the very thing that was broken in my life and use it to help someone else deal with their own brokenness. There is no joy quite like the joy of seeing God use the painful things of your life as a means of helping and healing another human being. Brokenness yielded to God becomes contagious wholeness for those around you. Vance Havner once wrote:

> *God uses broken things*
> *Broken soil to produce a crop,*
> *Broken clouds to give rain,*
> *broken grain to give bread.*
> *Broken bread to give strength.*
> *It's the broken alabaster box that gives forth perfume.*
> *It's Peter weeping bitterly, who returns to greater power than ever.*

As children many of us learned the nursery rhyme about Humpty Dumpty. We dutifully recited the line, "All the king's horses and all the king's men couldn't put Humpty Dumpty together again!" Now I would finish that rhyme with—"But God could." I say that because I believe with all my heart that God can heal any brokenness —as long as we don't insist on telling Him how it must be healed. Sickness may be healed with death, which means eternal life. Broken marriages may be healed by restoration of self-esteem and life with or without another human being. Whatever the condition that lacks wholeness, God has the power to remake it. But God will remake nothing in our lives that we do not bring to Him in trust and surrender.

The Way of the Cross

16 During the season of Lent we shall dwell on the cross because the cross is at the very heart of Christianity. It is to the cross that our sins must be drawn; it is through the cross that

February

God's forgiveness and righteousness are imparted. Jesus said that whoever would claim Him as Lord must first deny him or herself, take up his or her cross daily, and follow Him. In light of such a strong admonition, it is essential that we fix our gaze on the cross and ponder how it should shape our lives.

When we think of the cross of Jesus, we think of the central cross, but just as there were crosses on either side of Jesus in death, so there are crosses that we too must take up and to which we must be crucified. The cross for the Christian to bear is the cross of self-denial—a concept that is repugnant to the modern mind! We flee from it with the zealousness of Jonah who sought the comfort of Tarshish rather than the cross of Nineveh. In Tarshish, Jonah could pursue his will; in Nineveh he had to be obedient to God's.

At the heart of human sin is the desire to elevate one's self above all other things; and that is the very point at which Jesus tells us the road to redemption must begin—by acknowledging that we are **not** the center of life—God is. As long as we insist on elevating our will above that of the Creator then we will live life on the plane of un-redemption—a place where life is fragmented and distorted.

The cross is about heaven and hell; places that in our misguided understanding of life we have assigned only to the afterlife. The truth of the matter is that we experience, in part, heaven and hell in this life. E. Stanley Jones, speaking about Jesus' coming to earth says, "He came, therefore, not [so much] to get men into heaven but to get heaven into men; not to get men out of hell but to get hell out of men" (*The Christ of the Mount*, p. 52).

In Jesus, heaven and hell met at the cross and heaven triumphed. The evidence of heaven's victory, however, was not manifested until Easter morning—in the resurrection. When we allow our will to be nailed to the cross of self-surrender, the immediate experience seems to be death, but the result is resurrected life. Paul plainly told us that until a seed is sown in death it cannot be raised into life (I Corinthians 15:35-36). In order for a person to discover life he or she must be willing to die to life. These are words that most of us don't want to deal with. We quickly read over them and hurriedly brush them out of our thoughts. And yet the answer to real life will only be found in the hidden truth that lies within the words of our Lord.

In the cross, Jesus denied Himself. He willingly lost His life in order that we might find ours. As you read this, you have a choice—you can spend time meditating on it and seeking God's will for your life, or you can quickly discard it and go on with the mundane things of life, never giving heed to the beckoning call of God's Spirit. One choice will be the path of life; the other will be the path that leads to death. God has not asked anything of us that He did not require of Himself. Now we must decide to follow Him or go our own way.

Lent

17 I cherish the season of Lent because it pulls me back to the centrality of life and faith. At the center of life is God and at the heart of God is the Cross. I marvel at the thought that God would have chosen a cross to be the place from which the greatest revelation of divine love would emanate. But there is no other place we will ever go with a searching heart, that will more clearly and profoundly reveal the depth and impact of holy love. We will never grasp the transforming power of the grace of God until we stand before an old rugged cross, clothed only with the rags of our life that we call sin. All the darkness that is within us is suddenly illumined by the pure light of God's holiness: holiness that reveals itself not in divine condemnation, but in unmerited mercy and grace.

We shield our face as if to deflect divine wrath, only to discover the warmth of sacrificial love gently dissolving away the darkness that too long has encompassed us. It is not our tears that cleanse us of sinfulness, but holy tears shed in Gethsemane and at Calvary for a fallen world that chose to live in darkness rather than light. The writer of Hebrews describes it even more poignantly than the Gospel writer when he paints the majestic portrait of Christ's suffering for our sake: "During the days of Jesus' life on earth, he offered up prayers and petitions with loud cries and tears to the one who could save him from death, and he was heard because of his reverent submission. Although he was a son, he learned obedience from what he suffered and, once made perfect, he became the source of eternal salvation for all who obey him" (Hebrews 5:7-9).

February

Yes, we stand in the presence of Holy Love and we feel the cleansing power of divine tears washing away the stains of our sin! We look down and no longer do we see sin-soiled bodies and guilt-riddled hearts, but flesh without spot or blemish and hearts without pain, shame, or sorrow. We are amazed, for there is no rational human reason for such transformation. It defies human logic, it mocks human understanding and it transcends human ability. Such indescribable joy overwhelms us and we experience the power of divine peace in the turmoil of human life.

Now our eyes move from ourselves and become transfixed on the brilliant light that has bathed our body in holiness, and we see it—finally, we see it! There, impaled on a cross, is the Lamb of God, and the purity of His being is now enshrouded in the dirty rags of our sin. His tears and blood have cleansed us and His body has become our own. "For He made Him who knew no sin to be sin for us, that we might become the righteousness of God in Him" (II Corinthians 5:21, NKJV). He suffers, He cries out, He dies!

Now I am broken in sorrow, for my freedom from sin's power cost God the life of His Son. I would wither away in the brokenness of unquenchable sorrow except for the sudden realization that the body that was broken on the Cross for me now stands before me in the glory of resurrection. It is more than I can grasp, it is too good to be true—but it is! That's the Gospel! God forgives all that we do and makes us whole again! I love Lent, for it draws me back to the center of life and faith; and once more I find life, not death, on a cross—amazing, amazing grace!

When a Cross Becomes a Cross

18 The cross is perhaps the most dominant religious symbol in the world. It appears atop church steeples, on altars, hanging on walls and banners, and around people's necks on chains. It is a symbol that really needs no explanation because the story has been told again and again.

Unfortunately, we have made crosses so attractive and glamorous that we have robbed the cross of its theological truth. The cross that the Lord of life died upon was not smooth and attractive, not

February

bedecked with diamonds and rubies, not covered in gold or polished brass. It was rough and heavy, filled with splinters and soaked with divine blood. It stood on a lonely hill, surrounded by an angry crowd so blinded with sin that they could take delight in watching a man slowly die an agonizing death. We Protestants have diminished the impact of the cross by insisting that our crosses be empty. At least the Catholics have crucifixes that show the suffering Son of Man who loved us all so much that He endured the humiliation of that horrible instrument of torture.

We overlook the fact that God **chose** to suffer. He willingly surrendered His body to the cross. Legions of angels stood ready to spare Jesus such agony but He would not come down and escape the pain. Why? Because it was important, no, essential that we human beings realize how great God's love is for us. It's easy to say, "I love you." It has far more impact when love reveals itself sacrificially.

Often I have heard people say they have crosses to bear. "My child is on drugs and I guess that's my cross to bear." "I have to take care of my elderly parent, there's no one else to do it; so it's my cross to bear." Understand: a cross is only a cross when one willingly accepts it in love. When one chooses to make a sacrifice out of love, not duty, then it can be properly called a cross. Imposed crosses are instruments of pain with no redemptive value. Crosses that are willingly embraced are opportunities for redemptive power to be imparted to us through the sacrifice of our precious Lord.

S. J. Reid writes, "Paul did not build a theology around the cross, until he had nailed his life to it; then his theology became a most precious possession" (*Do Not Sin Against the Cross*, p. 71). Once Paul understood in his soul the significance of Jesus' life and death, he could write with unwavering conviction: "I have been crucified with Christ and I no longer live, but Christ lives in me. The life I live in the body, I live by faith in the Son of God, who loved me and gave himself for me" (Galatians 2:20). Note the personal pronouns Paul used. He made the crucifixion of Jesus a personal event.

Jesus died for each of us individually, not just for the world in general. He died for you! Say it out loud, "Jesus died for me!" If I were the only sinner who ever lived, God loved me enough to endure

February

the cross. No one has captured that thought more beautifully than Charles Wesley, in his hymn *O Love Divine, What Hast Thou Done* (# 287 in the Methodist Hymnal). Take time to read it. The cross was for you! It was to show you how greatly God loves <u>you</u>. Revel in its glory and let its glory become your own.

The Cross and the Pain of God

19 When we think of the cross, we almost always think about the suffering of Jesus for our sins. We sometimes even meditate upon how horrible it must have been for Mary to watch her son dying on a Roman gibbet. Yet in our limited understanding of the union between Father and Son, we rarely consider the pain of God the Father in the suffering of His Son. In obedience to the Father's will, Jesus surrendered His own and endured the agony of the cross. Our interpretation of that theological truth leads us to **wrongly** assume that since the Father wanted the Son to embrace the cross that the Father's heart was not broken too.

I can imagine few things in life that would bring greater pain to the heart than having to helplessly stand by and watch one's child suffer. Perhaps the only pain that could surpass such an experience is to know you had the power to stop it and yet restrained yourself from helping. Who do you know that is so noble and virtuous that they would willingly allow their child to suffer and die in your place? The hard reality is that God did not allow His Son to suffer for righteous people, but for sinners who are totally unworthy of His love and grace!

If it is possible for the immortal God to weep, then heaven must have been flooded the day the events of "Calvary" took place. I have long felt that the theory that Jesus' death on the cross was required in order to appease God's anger and restrain God from destroying us was a perversion of the love of God. In essence, we are saying that Jesus' noble love wanted to save us, but the anger of God wanted to destroy us. If that is so then does not that mean that the Son loves us with a love far greater than the Father's? But how could that possibly be, since Jesus said that He and the Father were One, and He always wanted to only do the Father's will?

February

We do grave injustice to the Father's love for us when we imagine that He would rather have destroyed us than save us. Jesus didn't die in order to change the Father's mind, He died in order to reveal the Father's love! When Jesus suffered on the cross the heart of God suffered there too. There was no division of purpose, no conflict of wills, no battle between Father and Son for the souls of humanity. There was perfect oneness, perfect purpose, perfect love. The heart of the Father was shattered as He willingly sacrificed His only begotten Son out of love for the creation of His hands. "But God demonstrates his own love for us in this: While we were still sinners, Christ died for us" (Romans 5:8).

We need to ask forgiveness of the Father for so misrepresenting and ignoring the suffering brokenness of His heart. Perhaps this Lent, when we are remembering with gratitude the love Jesus has for us, we might also say a prayer of thanksgiving to the Father for loving us enough to not only give us His Son and watch Him suffer, but for suffering with Him for our sakes.

Sacrifice and the Cross

20 The cross is the supreme symbol of sacrifice. If sacrifice is understood to be the total surrender of one's self for another, then nothing will ever surpass what Jesus did on the cross. His entire ministry was about sacrifice and from the beginning "His face was set for Jerusalem." The Roman instrument of torture which we know as a cross was only the final step in Jesus' unwavering path toward total self-denial. He gave us everything and kept nothing for Himself.

No one has ever given more sacrificially than Jesus. He gave up the splendor of heaven and surrendered the majesty and glory of angelic beings praising Him day and night. He laid aside His claim to equality with God. He took upon Himself the robe of human flesh and then embraced the role of a servant rather than a king. He could have left us sinners His anger—instead He left us His love and forgiveness. His very mother He left to the care of a trusted disciple. The only clothes that He owned were given to the soldiers who crucified Him.

February

His body would be given to two Pharisees—Nicodemus and Joseph of Arimathea. His Spirit He entrusted into the hands of His heavenly Father.

The message of the cross is the message of sacrifice. It is God sacrificing Himself for the creatures He created. But the message of Jesus is that we too are called to sacrifice and self-denial. "If anyone will come after me," He proclaimed, "let him deny himself, take up a cross daily, and follow after me." "If you will find your life, you must first be willing to lose it." "If you would be first, you must be willing to be last." If you cannot discern the call for sacrifice in those words from the Master's lips, then you have no concept of what sacrifice is as it relates to your own life.

The cross is about suffering love—a love so great that nothing, absolutely nothing could prevent it from revealing itself. Sin is about self-elevation—making our will, not God's, the supreme motivating force in our lives. The cross is about self-demotion—not my will but yours be done, my Lord. Only those whose hearts are moved by the passion of God on a cross will ever find it within themselves to seek out their own cross.

The church is the body of Christ. Yet it struggles again and again because it is composed of human beings who hear the message of surrender, but continue to pursue the seductive illusion of being in control. We proclaim that all we have belongs to God, but cannot bring ourselves to return to Him one tenth of what we possess. We declare Him to the Lord of our lives, but refuse to serve Him when given opportunity to lead. Churches throughout our land are weak and feeble because we refuse to do with our lives what we so glibly proclaim with our lips. We have so hardened our spirits to the beckoning call of God's voice that we have forced our ministers into being servants who must constantly beg and plead with their members to faithfully support the very Body that gives them life.

Look once more at the cross. my friends, and as you gaze into the loving dying face of God's Son, as you behold the totally spent body and soul of the One who is dying for you, see if you can possibly find it in your heart to say, "Lord, please show me what I can do for you." And when He answers, go and obey.

February

The Cross—Divine/Human Intersection

21 Why is an instrument of human torture the dominant symbol of divine love? The cross, one of the most excruciatingly painful methods of punishment, adorns Christian churches throughout the world. How horrified we would be if we walked into a church and saw fastened to the wall an electric chair or a guillotine! Yet the Christian community elevates the cross to a place of central importance and prominence.

How ironic that sinful humanity thought it had to nail down the hands of God in outstretched position, when all along God came to the world with His arms stretched wide in love. Perhaps we are captivated by the cross's alluring magnetism because we are forced to see a God who allowed His hands to be nailed down in order to show without words the power of His love.

The cross became the cosmic crossroads of all human life. It was there that divine love and human sin intersected. Goodness confronted human rebellion and a cross was set up. That which is vertical—the divine, crossed that which is horizontal—humanity. Humanity apart from God can never rise above its level plane of existence. Only that which is divine can descend and then ascend. In order for humanity to be lifted up, God had to come down. In order for humanity to live, God had to die!

At the cross, Law and grace merged and sin was washed clean by divine righteousness and penalty was swallowed up in forgiveness. Law apart from grace will always result in death and grace that rejects Law robs God of His holiness. It was at the cross that darkness receded before the light and love overcame all there is in life that separates. Sin divides, love unites; hatred kills, love restores life. All the wars ever fought in human existence pale before the battle which took place on Calvary. For it was there that eternal goodness fought with finite evilness. Our evil encountered God's righteousness—and God won!

The cross stands erect because in order to see it one must look up. And when one looks up one must look at something beyond one's self. In dying on a cross God was suspended between the glory of

February

heaven and the hell we've made of earth. He found a way to bring heaven to earth and take hell out of humanity. The cross represents the worst in humanity and the most noble in God—suffering love.

The cross is a beacon, serving both to warn humanity of the potential destruction of unrepentant sin and at the same time a harbor light to guide one safely into the arms of God's love. How profoundly Jesus put it, "And I, when I be lifted up from the earth, will draw all people to me." Are you being drawn to the God on the cross? Have you yet experienced in your soul the healing power of such divine love? If not, then run to the cross my friend, and return to the source of all life. Discover there the only power that can calm the storms of your life and give you a peace that no one can take from you. Until you meet Jesus at the cross, you will never meet Him anywhere else.

Love, Suffering, and the Cross

For the message of the cross is foolishness to those who are perishing, but to us who are being saved it is the power of God. I Corinthians 1:18

22 The above words of Paul are still relevant for our generation. There are those today for whom the cross is an offense—a stumbling block. Like the Jews of Jesus' day, many of us are uncomfortable with the concept of a suffering Savior. Yet the words from the Master's own lips testify to us that it was not by the whim of sinful man, or by being overcome by the circumstances of life, that He marched steadily toward the cross. He said, "Now my heart is troubled, and what shall I say? 'Father, save me from this hour'? No, it was for this very reason I came to this hour" (John 12:27).

We cannot fully understand nor comprehend the meaning of human suffering, much less the meaning of divine suffering on the cross. There are a few human beings in this world who, through courage and nobility, willingly allow themselves to suffer for the sake of another. But, for the most part, they suffer for those whom they consider good and righteous. Jesus suffered for those whom He knew to be sinful and unrighteous.

February

Even before He was born, Jesus' destiny was the cross. Prior to the incarnation—centuries before the world beheld Him in human flesh—the Father and the Son were making plans for a place called Golgotha. Why do I believe that? Because the suffering servant passages of Isaiah, written six hundred years before Jesus was born, prophetically testify to the reality of His suffering death. Isaiah 53 makes no sense apart from its application to Jesus' death on the cross.

Look at the cross. What do you see? I know what you ought to see: incarnate love—pure love that has clothed itself in human flesh. Love that says, "I hold back nothing; I give you all that I have." That suffering seems even more senseless than the suffering mere mortals experience. Strange, is it not, that our salvation—not only from the despair of sinfulness, but the experience of human pain—was born out of God's willingness to suffer as a human being?

The plain truth is that Jesus' suffering did not eliminate human suffering. We know too well what pain is! But what His suffering did do, beyond the atoning act of suffering the penalty for our sin, was to show us that not only does God understand human suffering, He is willing to share in it. The writer of Hebrews reminds us, "For we do not have a high priest who is unable to sympathize with our weaknesses, but we have one who has been tempted in every way, just as we are—yet was without sin" (4:15).

There will always be those in every generation who will view the cross as foolishness. They will demean and ridicule those who embrace its relevancy and efficacy. Even among some "Christian" scholars and theologians there is condescension and self-righteous disdain toward those who view the cross with whole-hearted reverence. However, as Paul so keenly understood, there is a power in it that defies human comprehension—a power that is more than sufficient to provide not only salvation in the world to come, but hope in the heart of those who suffer in this world.

Reflections on a Crucifix

23 It was a cool day and I was attending an Evangelism meeting at the Avila Retreat Center located on Mason Road in Durham, NC. Avila is the Catholic retreat center that is

February

operated by several delightful nuns. After lunch, I went outside to sit in the warmth of the midday sun, and to meditate on my relationship with God. Rising up from the ground before me was a concrete crucifix about twelve feet tall. Fastened to the cross was the life-sized image of Jesus, who had succumbed to the evil of humankind.

Though the lifeless image was only sculpted from stone, it nonetheless made Christ's death on the cross more real and meaningful for me than just imagining it with my mind. The sun's rays penetrated through the gently swaying tree limbs that stretched over the crucifix, causing dancing shadows to bathe the lifeless form of Jesus with flickering hues of light and darkness—almost making Him appear to move. Lost in deep thought, I found myself wanting to run to the cross and wrap my arms around Christ's body. "Let me take your place, Jesus!" I cried inwardly. "You don't deserve to be there."

But once more in my life, I was reminded that it could not be so—even if I had been present at the actual crucifixion. Jesus is the Savior and I am just one of the saved. He could take my place, but I could never take His. It really was my sins that nailed Him there and not Roman spikes. In the recesses of my memory, I could hear Paul saying, "God made him who had no sin to be sin for us, so that in him we might become the righteousness of God" (II Corinthians 5:21). Tommy Lewis, a Baptist preacher, put it more simply, "Jesus became on the cross what I am, so that I might become in glory what He is." Some trade, huh? His righteousness for our sin, His love for our hatred, His acceptance for our rejection, His peace for our turmoil, His body for our soul.

In reflecting on Christ's death for us, I once wrote, "It is not the rationalization of my human mind as it beholds a crucified man that draws me to the throne of grace, but the heart and soul of my sinful self that is finally awed by the sacrificial redeeming love of God." For us individually, Christ's death at Calvary is meaningless—until we finally and truly realize that He literally died for the sins we have committed.

Salvation cannot occur until we recognize the reality of sin, feel deep sorrow within that we have committed it, and yearn for our unworthy soul to be in union once more with God. So much of our

February

life is spent devoid of peace and mired down in the experience of estrangement—and we don't seem to have a clue as to why. When will we let Jesus be our Lord? If we are to grow spiritually, it is absolutely essential that we make time for Christ in our life. When almost every waking moment of our lives is filled with things that let us avoid Jesus, then we may rest assured that what we put at the center of our lives will not only reveal, but perpetuate, the emptiness of our existence.

Just as every living plant that comes from the ground reaches upward for the sun in order to have life, so we too must reach upward for the Son in order to begin to live. As I looked up into the face of the "crucified" Lord that day, I saw flowing down the corridor of eternity a flood of grace rushing to embrace me. As my heart ran to meet it, I experienced once again the cleansing power of God's love and the renewing power of the Holy Spirit as He strengthened me once more to face the life that lay ahead.

Death on a Cross

24 Hours of suffering have been condensed into a few spoken words written on a page—as if one or two sentences of simple compassion would suffice to paint a portrait capable of spanning eternity. The nails that tore his flesh and ensured that he remained fastened on a cross were indifferent as to whose flesh they impaled. There is no mercy in rough, iron nails; and there was none in the hearts of those who drove them. In the long agonizing hours that followed, he had time to think thoughts driven by pain, and relive memories filled with regret. If only he could go back in time, perhaps he could figure out some way to avoid this horror. Alas, time for change was gone. At first, his torture brought forth thoughts of anger and hostility; but eventually his words would reveal transformation and acceptance.

Some who die are able to see their lives played back before their eyes in a matter of seconds. If this occurred for him, I wonder what he must have been thinking and reliving as minutes dragged on into hours? Perhaps he thought of pleasant childhood memories—of times that he ran through the streets of a small village and played "soldier and robbers" with his childhood friends. Maybe he remembered and

February

longed for the touch of his mother, just once more before he died, or hungered for one more fishing trip with his father along the Galilean shore. How wonderful it would be to hear just one voice speak a word of kindness to one who felt so despised! But alas, his fate was settled now, as surely as if it had been written in stone. He was suspended between earth and heaven, hung out to die, denied even the gentle caress of a loving hand.

He thought of the teachings of the rabbis in the synagogue as he grew up. Such harsh words—an eye for an eye and a tooth for a tooth! He knew there were certain things for which the penalty was death, but he could not have imagined that one day he would be the recipient of such a terrible sentence. Yet here he was, dying on Golgotha, sharing a lonely hill with two other men whose lifeblood was also flowing quickly down through the hourglass of time. Guilty and innocent were sharing a common lot: two men who had done evil and One who had done none. But that is the way of the world, is it not—to be blind to the difference between good and evil? In the confused morality of the time—of any time—always blending good and evil together, until any distinction becomes indiscernible.

The sky had been enveloped in darkness for almost three hours. An eerie silence filled the air that felt as heavy as a soaking-wet blanket. Strangely, the crowd had stopped mocking, the soldiers had stopped gambling, and everyone fixed their gaze on the dying men. It was too late now; all hope was gone. In a few moments, his eyes would look for the last time upon the land he loved and the people who hungered for his death. How his heart hungered to feel the caress of love one last time. Suddenly, a pain-filled voice spoke to him the last words he would hear on this earth: "Today, you shall be with me in paradise." As his head slumped, perhaps those last words trickled from his own lips, "Today, I shall be with Him in paradise." A thief closed his eyes at the gates of hell, and discovered the presence of paradise waiting instead! Grace is amazing, isn't it?

The Cross

25 There were thousands of crosses upon which men, women, and children were nailed when Rome ruled the earth. Prior to that time, under the Greek general, Alexander the Great

February

crucifixion was widely practiced and thousands died agonizing deaths while nailed to crosses. Yet only one became the focal point of the world, the chief symbol of a religious faith. In spite of what many think, its powerful attraction is not a testimony to the cruelty of human malevolence, but to the mystery and power of God to embrace and be embraced by the very worst in humanity in order to redeem it. Even the most avowed atheist or skeptic needs to come to grips with the mystery of why the cross of the Nazarene became so significant in the lives of untold millions.

Beautiful and important as Jesus' words are, it is the "power" found in the One who hung on a cross that seizes us and refuses to let us go. Perhaps it is because the life of the man who died at Golgotha portrays a nobility, a mercy, a grace that transcends the lives of all who have lived before or since. Out of the innocence of His pain and suffering, we see revealed the incomprehensible willingness of God to suffer, not only at the hands of His creation, but more importantly, for the sake of His creation. Jesus did not die on a cross so that He could understand what humanity feels when we hurt or suffer; rather, He died so humanity might understand what deep pain God feels for us when we suffer the sickness of sin. The cross is about God so identifying with humanity that humanity is finally able to grasp, even if but faintly, the meaning of grace. It is our nature to strike out when we are wronged: it is the nature of God in Christ to absorb the wrong and transform it through a willingness to suffer, even when He is the one who has been wronged.

As did the malicious crowd gathered at the foot of the cross, we mock the suffering of God—not so much with our words, but with our lives. We do not scream, "If you are the Christ, come down from the cross!" But we do grow comfortable with His pain, and worst of all become unmoved by its depth. Beyond the obvious reality of His suffering, there is divine mystery permeating the world through the cross. The mortality of human flesh is being wedded to the immortality of the human soul, and the crucible in which the two become one is in the suffering form of Him who is impaled on a cross. We must learn to look beyond the obvious dying of a crucified man: we must become aware of and moved by the suffering of the crucified heart of God.

February

We live with a holy restlessness until our hearts and minds find rest in the healing balm of God's grace. Grace reached its pinnacle when it revealed itself from a Roman cross. Sin has dominion over our soul until faith in God's suffering love finally drives home to our hearts the truth that we are loved. When that moment comes, the mystery of divine love's transforming power ceases to be an intellectual concept, and suddenly becomes a powerful heart-felt reality.

The idea of grace may have begun as a seed planted in the mind, but it becomes full-blown and gloriously reveals itself when it takes root in the soul. Are you looking for God? Do you desire to feel loved? You will find both those things at the Cross; for it is there that they reveal themselves as one.

The Glory of the Cross

26 What happened on a dark day in history two millennia ago on a hill called Golgotha refuses to be diluted or brushed aside by time or human indifference. We cannot encounter Jesus Christ unless we are willing to meet Him at the cross. Time and eternity flow through the cross. Salvation and eternal life come forth from it like a mighty rushing torrent. As long as we wander in the desert places of life, places untouched by the cross's power, we will remain unredeemed.

What's so significant about a man dying on a cross, you ask? It was God turning the world upside down, revealing that the Creator loved humanity so much that He was willing to allow the created order to crucify Him who had given them life. It becomes clear that the motivation behind the cross was God's love. If we are capable of heroic suffering and sacrifice for the sake of those we love, then it is because we have inherited that characteristic from God our Father.

We live in a world of suffering, often intense suffering. People die horrible deaths, and people do horrible things. We struggle to find meaning in that which seems beyond understanding. Then the cross rises up and human suffering is absorbed into the mystery of divine suffering. Is it not significant that out of God's greatest experience of

February

suffering was born the reality of human salvation? In order for a child to be born into this world, the mother must endure the suffering of childbirth. Could it be that far beyond the limits of human comprehendsion there lies the truth—that suffering **can be** redemptive? Just as the mother's pain in childbirth becomes the doorway to human life, so the Savior's pain on Calvary became the doorway to eternal life.

Still, we are left with the question, "Why the necessity of pain and suffering?" I do not know; I only know that it is so. With the reality of love there comes the inevitable possibility of pain. Love is defenseless. To the degree that it seeks to set up self-protective barriers, its power is diminished. You cannot love without the eventuality of pain for someone. There will be pain when we feel rejection, the pain of being left alone, the pain of yielding up that which we love to death. There will be the pain of watching one we love suffer, the pain of searing words that shatter our hearts. Only when we feel no love are we capable of feeling no pain (on the spiritual and emotional level).

And so, on the cross, God identified with humanity in a way unlike He'd ever done before. He risked all in the hope that some would grasp the depth of His love and be transformed by it. I honestly feel that it is impossible to experience salvation apart from appropriating God's grace and love at the cross. This is why I believe Jesus said, "No one comes unto the Father, except by me. And I, if I be lifted up [on a cross], will draw all people to me."

You cannot do better this Lent than to meditate on the cross. And if you look closely enough you will find that in the vastness of its mystery you can become immersed in the eternal love of God. Indeed, let us be willing to affirm with St. Paul, "God forbid that I should glory, save in the cross of our Lord Jesus Christ" (Galatians 6:14, KJV). Peace and grace to you through the suffering of our Lord Jesus.

The Revelations of Pain

Pain, like the razor-sharp scalpel in the surgeon's hand, has a way of cutting away the exterior that hides from the human eye the real person that lies beneath the skin.

February

Sometimes the pain is emotional, not physical, but still its presence has the same effect. The physical part of a human being is really a mask that reveals little about what lies underneath. All the feelings that so carefully hide in the interior of who we are rise swiftly to the surface when the great liberator, pain, sets them free. Out they pour like some volcanic eruption hurling their existence haphazardly upon any who happen to be standing nearby—anger, resentment, hatred, fear, unforgiveness, revenge, prejudice, self-centeredness, insecurity, and distrust. No longer restrained by the robe of painlessness, no longer held back by the security of physical contentment, they regurgitate from our bodies in all their undesirable ugliness.

Such was the case on a cool spring morning twenty centuries ago, when three men looking down from a hillside beheld a crowd of people gathered at their feet. Their half-naked bodies were tormented with pain as they hung suspended on crosses before those who had placed them there, and those who were powerless to prevent it. Two thieves and the Son of God. The scripture reveals that there were many in the crowd that day that laughed and mocked and ridiculed. Included in that number were **both** thieves whose pain-filled bodies revealed the darkness hidden deep within them (Mt. 27:44, Mark 15:32).

Likewise, the Man on the middle cross, tormented by no less pain than theirs, revealed the essence of what lay beneath His outer covering. The first words from His lips were to offer forgiveness to those whose hatred put Him there. Then His concern turned toward His mother, for whom He made provision even while nailed to a tree. Next, His thoughts were directed at a repentant thief who apparently had been changed by observing the nobleness of His suffering. Only then did He allow His own needs to reveal the depth of His humanity as He first cried out in despair, then in thirst, next in fulfillment, finally in the faithful resignation of His Spirit into His Father's loving hands.

The pain of Calvary revealed to the world the inner part of Jesus. And what was revealed on that gloomy hillside was the noblest heart that ever beat; the purest soul that ever was housed in human flesh. Pouring forth from the middle cross was a divine love so holy and

February

precious that it carried within it the power to transform a world—one person at the time. Out it flowed until the darkened heart of a crucified thief lit up with a light that revealed the way to Paradise. Down it flowed, until the hardened heart of a seasoned Roman centurion could recognize the Crucified Son of God. Into the heart of the stranger it went (the one that had been forced to carry His cross) changing his life so much that his sons, Rufus and Alexander, later became leaders in the early church. Up it went to the very streets of heaven, where angels watched and wept as it saturated the holy place of God's presence. No quickly passing summer shower, this torrent of love continues to flow around the world affecting one life after another with its life-changing power

Each year during Holy Week we proclaim once more the story of the Cross. Yes, we know resurrection will follow, but it is the cross and how it affects us that will reveal to us the heart and soul that lie beneath our own skin. In the reflection of Jesus' pain, what does your heart reveal?

The Choice

28 Strange, when you think of it—the most prominent focal points of the Christian faith are an instrument of execution and an empty grave. The cross and the tomb rise from the dust of history at the center of the world's greatest religion. No matter how moving and important were the words that Jesus taught, the power in His message always comes back to His death and resurrection. Paul, the greatest of the apostles, said, "For I resolved to know nothing while I was with you except Jesus Christ and him crucified" (I Corinthians 2:2). Clearly, Paul considered this to be at heart of the Christian message. Speaking again to the Corinthians, Paul proclaims, "For what I received I passed on to you as of first importance: that Christ died for our sins according to the Scriptures, that he was buried, that he was raised on the third day according to the Scriptures . . ." (I Corinthians 15:3-4).

For almost two thousand years human beings have meditated upon, rationalized, dissected, and explored the mystery of the cross,

February

and yet we have never fully plumbed its depths. It is shrouded in holy mystery and rewards those who ponder it with only momentary flashes of divine revelation. Just as the horizon enveloped in darkness reveals its presence with only momentary flashes of lightning, so the cross stands silent, speaking its message of redemption only to those who approach it in bursts of faith. The skeptic might forcefully argue that it is an unkind God that would require death on a cross in order to accomplish salvation, until that skeptic finally realizes that the death that was required was His own!

At a meeting of 2,000 delegates in Minneapolis in 1993, Delores Williams, a radical feminist theologian from Union Theological Seminary in New York told the group, "I don't think we need a theory of atonement at all...atonement has to do so much with death . . . I don't think we need folks hanging on crosses, and blood dripping, and weird stuff . . . we just need to listen to the god within." I would argue, "Then you don't understand divine love, for God is love, and it is the nature of love to suffer for that which is loved."

In our self-made worlds and in the fallacy of our finite wisdom, we prefer to create a world in which vengeance rules the day, where wrongs are addressed with acts of spite and where hostility is the response of choice. We prefer to slap the other cheek, not turn the other cheek; to live under the direction of the "spirit of this world", not the Spirit of Christ that longs to dwell in us. By our very acts we proclaim, "We will not be guided by your cross, Lord Jesus, we will choose our own way," and thus we add to the divisiveness of the world. In so doing, we cavalierly dismiss Good Friday and thumb our noses at Easter morning.

Each of us needs to pause and take stock of our lives. Are our choices and our responses guided by Christ, or by some unredeemed portion of our own sinful nature? Jesus said to each of us that we must take up a cross if we are going to follow Him. That, my friends, is a clarion call to self-crucifixion. Only we can crucify ourselves— no one else will. Only the person who is willing to nail one's self to the cross Jesus offers will ever know the power that comes through redeemed, resurrected life. The cross isn't easy; but resurrection apart from it is not possible. That's why Jesus chose it!

February

The Great Exchange

29   Many years ago, when I was only four or five years old, I recall standing on a street corner along with my older brother and sister, my best friend and his sister (all of us within four years of each other). Diagonally across the street was a white frame house of an elderly woman, who had only hours before passed away. We stood there not to gawk, nor out of some morbid curiosity, but because even at that age the mark of a childlike faith was already engraved upon our hearts. We sang to our departed neighbor at the top of our little lungs, a song that was my grandmother's favorite and was to become one of mine—*The Old Rugged Cross*. You know how it goes—*On a hill far away, stood an old rugged cross, the emblem of suffering and shame; And I love that old cross, where the dearest and best, for a world of lost sinners was slain.* Do you remember the chorus? *So I'll cherish the old rugged cross, till my trophies at last I lay down; I will cling to the old rugged cross, and exchange it someday for a crown.*

The song speaks of "clinging" and "exchanging". It reveals a truth that we need to ponder—there are many things in this life to which we can cling, but only one thing that will allow for an eternal exchange. The one thing in this life to which we can cling and exchange in the next life is the cross. When we reach the great divide and ask God for the crown of glory (eternal life), He will want to know if we have clung to the cross. It is not enough to cling to Jesus the carpenter, Jesus the healer, Jesus the teacher, or even Jesus the One who raises the dead. We must be in touch with the Jesus who died on a cross. It is at the cross where redemption takes place: not in the Temple, not at the marketplace, not the hills of Judea. It happened on Calvary.

But alas, Jesus also said to us, "If you will come after me, you must be willing to take up your cross daily and follow Me." "What are you saying, Lord, that we too have a cross? You mean that I must crucify myself in order to belong to you?" Jesus' response would be, "Yes, but not on a cross like mine. You must be willing to nail your heart to my cross. To live you must be willing to die and in dying to yourself you will finally begin to live."

March

Surely, A. W. Tozer must have thought so too, when he wrote:

> *In every Christian's heart there is a cross and a throne, and the Christian is on the throne till he puts himself on the cross; if he refuses the cross he remains on the throne. Perhaps this is at the bottom of the backsliding and worldliness among gospel believers today. We want to be saved but we insist that Christ do all the dying. No cross for us, no dethronement, no dying. We remain king within the little kingdom of Mansoul and wear our tinsel crown with all the pride of a Caesar; but we doom ourselves to shadows and weakness and spiritual sterility. (The Root of the Righteous, p. 66)*

On that great and wonderful day when we stand in God's presence in glory there will be a great exchange—a cross for a throne! But as long as we are on earth, it must be a throne for a cross.

The Heart of God

1 "But I, when I am lifted up from the earth, will draw all men to myself" (John 12:32). One might argue that these words of Jesus were in reference to His ascension into heaven had not the writer of John's Gospel included the words, "He said this to show the kind of death he was going to die" (John 12:33). Who can grasp the mystery of why Jesus said what He did, when He did, and how He did? Later on, just before His death, He left no room for misinterpretation (". . . the Passover is two days away—and the Son of Man will be handed over to be crucified" Matthew 26:2). Perhaps Jesus was trying to spare His followers the immediate shock of suddenly and unexpectedly seeing Him crucified on a cross. But the cross was inevitable; for Jesus there was no turning back.

So there it stands, its long shadow extending both forward and backward across the pages of history. It has become the crossroads of human life: the gate through which eternity is discovered. Not content to die for a few, God died for all humanity. No one was excluded, though many choose to exclude Him. It was the darkest day since God

March

said "Let there be light!" On that day in Genesis, physical light exploded into the darkness and the darkness receded, forever subservient to the light. But out of the darkness of Calvary, there came forth the true Light that shone its glory on human sin and burned away the darkness within us. Burnett H. Streeter wrote, "The Cross of Christ must be either the darkest spot of all in the mystery of existence or a searchlight by the aid of which we may penetrate the surrounding gloom" (*Words of Life*, p. 55).

Tens of thousands died on Roman crosses, but history focuses on just one. All other crosses were mere instruments of death: this one became the stairway to life. Christians have studied it, sung about it, and adorned their bodies and homes with its symbol. We pray about it, we fall prostrate before it; but it is not just the rough wood spattered with blood and splinters to which we are drawn, but to the Man who allowed Himself to be placed upon it. In a moment of time, God condensed the eternal magnitude of His love and placed it in one mortal body for the sake of humankind. The cross is the heart of God—bruised, battered, and bleeding before an indifferent world. Its cruelty left wounds on the hands and feet of Jesus; it also left scars on the suffering heart of God.

I never grow weary of the cross. I never get tired of teaching it or preaching about it. With Elizabeth Clephane I join my voice:

> *Upon the cross of Jesus mine eye at times can see, the very dying form of One who suffered there for me; and from my stricken heart with tears two wonders I confess; the wonders of redeeming love and my unworthiness. I take, O cross, thy shadow, for my abiding place; I ask no other sunshine than the sunshine of His face; content to let the world go by, to know no gain nor loss, my sinful self my only shame, my glory all the cross.* (*Beneath the Cross of Jesus*, p. 297, United Methodist Hymnal)

Many long for the eternal city, hoping for streets of gold and walls bedecked with jewels; but I, I would be forever content to sit before that old rugged cross and bathe my soul in the fountain of love that cascades from its center. If you have never knelt before the cross,

March

you have never drawn very near to the heart of God. God invites you to come!

The Great Intersection

2 It was a simple thing with only two parts: an evil thing, conceived in the human heart and fashioned with human hands.

Its intent was to create fear and to proclaim the power of men. Fashioned in hate, devoid of compassion, it became the thing upon which the blood of humanity would be freely spilled. It came to be called a "cross." This instrument of suffering, of torture and humiliation, God embraced with divine love. If God can transform a cross into the symbol of redeeming love, little wonder that He has the power to transform the evil in us into vessels of grace and peace.

No meaningless exercise, this contemplation of the cross, for hidden within its mystery is the answer to the deepest questions of life. It is not the super-intelligent that will unravel its secrets; not those who perceive themselves as righteous, not those who think to master its greatness with their tiny little minds, but only those who approach it with eyes cast down in humility, with a heart hungry to be fed, and a faith that will not let them look away. It is the person with childlike faith, with a willingness to see with the heart and not just the mind, that will soon find a river called Grace gushing from its center. Those whose soul's grasp exceeds the reach of their limited understanding will tap into the power that flows from it; for like an artesian well whose supply resides deep below the surface, the power in the Cross draws its energy from a Source hidden from human eyes.

How could two pieces of wood, one vertical and one horizontal, become the altar that would change the course of human history? On a Roman gibbet, the contrast between love and hate was as pronounced as the distinction between the vertical and horizontal beams that suspended God's Son between heaven and earth. That singular act in history contained within it more power than can be expended in the splitting of the atom. Seemingly isolated and insignificant, Christ's death on the cross exploded into history with a spiritual power as dramatic as the first nuclear explosion—sin was consumed in the unleashed power of divine redemption. Like ever-widening circles

March

caused by the proverbial rock thrown in a pond, God's love flowed out from the center of His heart revealed on a cross and the outward movement of its power has never been diminished.

How poignantly has Paul Scherer described the power contained in the cross. "The Cross is any place where a saving love goes out to undergird this life of ours and comes back with the hot stab of nails in its hands." The cross is the message of the healing heart of God absorbing into itself the wounded heart of humanity. It is grace defeating sin, life conquering death, holiness transforming sinfulness.

Here is a mystery! Good could destroy evil only through offering itself as the sacrifice! The cross will live as long as there is one person left who allows his or her heart to become the dwelling place of the Living Christ. The cross is the great spiritual intersection in history—the place where the goodness in God intersected with the evil in humanity and evil lost the battle. Where Christ dwells the cross will forever be present, for the cross is the place where one loses one's life in order that life might come forth in power. Even so, Lord Jesus, come forth in power in us!

It's Springtime Again!

3 It was a spring day—the kind of day when warm, gentle breezes lightly rustled the newly sprouting blades of emerald-hued grass. Trees had begun to bud and flowers bedecked the roadsides with beauty and a soft, delicate fragrance. It was that unique time of the year when every aspect of nature was proclaiming its message of life and hope and promise. In the midst of that inviting environment, I discovered myself standing alone, shaking in violent sobs in the quiet seclusion of the men's restroom at Duke Hospital. The year was 1966 and I had just heard the doctor tell my mother that my father had terminal cancer.

I vividly recall my conversation with God that day. I was confused, baffled, even angry. "God, you know how good my father is. He's a Lay Leader, Sunday School Superintendent; he sings in the choir and has held virtually every office in the church. Why, God, are you letting this happen?" My thoughts about him were put on hold as

March

I began to recall the story of Job and how he lost all he possessed, all his children died, and his wife came to him and said, "Curse God and die!" Job's response was "Though He slay me, yet will I trust Him." Slowly I began to repeat Job's words out loud and by the third time they had become my own. That day, at the age of twenty-three, God's grace and mercy became real to me—not fully developed, but real!

I say all of the above because it's now another time in life, almost springtime, and for the third time in two years I find myself in the hospital dealing with the effects of treatment for cancer—this time a horrible reaction to chemo or radiation therapy. The name the doctor's have assigned to my condition is Erythema Multiforme Major (sometimes known as Stevens-Johnson Syndrome). My entire body, from head to toe, is covered with bulls-eye skin lesions. I go from the extremes of high fever to bone shaking chills. I have learned that 50% of the people who get this syndrome will not survive it.

So, how is this affecting my faith? It isn't. "Why doesn't God heal me?" is a question I never ask. Not because I'm afraid of the answer, but because for me the answer is not something I need to know. The ways of God are beyond me. I bow before Him in utter humility and trust. I live in His grace and always His grace is sufficient. When I entrusted my life, my soul, my all to Him I meant it. He never promised my life would be lived free from suffering, but He did promise it would be filled and sustained with grace. Paul's words have become my own: "I reckon that the sufferings of this present time are not worthy to be compared with the glory that shall be revealed in us" (Romans 8:18, KJV).

Do I enjoy suffering? No, but I can rejoice in it, for it has brought glory to my Lord and that brings joy unspeakable to my heart. If all that I have been through is only the dawn of my suffering, then I have no fear or dread of the future because, "Even through He slay me, yet will I trust in Him." Blessed forever be the name of our precious Lord Jesus! And so, I go through life singing my song of love for Jesus. It is easy to love Him in the good times, but I have found it even easier to love Him in the difficult times, because it is in those times that I feel His love the greatest. It's springtime again—but then with Jesus, life is always springtime!

March

The Extravagance of Love

4 Most of us do not usually connect the word extravagant with the word love. We all know what love means, but perhaps we have settled on a middle-of-the-road kind of love that is content to live on a level plateau rather than risk sinking to the depths of rejection or rising to the peak of ecstasy. But such was not the case with Mary as she anointed Jesus with the costly perfume described in John 12. She possessed a vial of perfume that was extravagantly expensive (worth a year's wages for a common laborer).

In *Windows of the Soul*, Ken Gire, Jr. wrote beautifully and powerfully when he described Mary's act with the following description:

> *The aroma of extravagant love. So pure. So lovely. Flowing from the veined alabaster vase of Mary's broken heart—A heart broken against the hard reality of her Savior's imminent death. Mingled with tears, the perfume became—by some mysterious chemistry of Heaven—Not diluted, but more concentrated, potent enough behind the ears of each century for the scent to linger to this day.*
>
> *Doubtless, the fragrance, absorbed by His garment, as it flowed from His head accompanied Christ through the humiliation of His trials, the indignity of his mockings, the pain of his beatings, the inhumanity of His cross. Through the heavy smell of sweat and blood, a hint of that fragrance must have arisen from His garment—until, at shameful last, the garment was stripped and gambled away. And maybe, just maybe, it was that scent amid the stench of humanity rabbled around the cross, that gave the Savior strength to say: "Father, forgive them, for they know not what they do."*
>
> *And as Mary walked away from the cross, the same scent probably still lingered in the now-limp hair she used to dry her Savior's feet—a reminder of the love that spilled from His broken alabaster body. So pure. So lovely. So truly extravagant. It was a vase He never regretted breaking. Nor did she.*

March

There is a mystical power in love that lifts us above that which is simply rational or self-serving. It causes us to see such value in another person that our own value, though not diminished, finds its joy and fulfillment in union with that other person (spouse, child, or friend). Even so, there is no love greater than that which we experience when we finally realize we are loved by God. When pure love gives itself to that which is impure then love has reached the pinnacle of extravagance.

How many human relationships deteriorate and disintegrate because we never reach the level of extravagant love? Love that holds back nothing for itself but gives simply because it cannot do otherwise. Gire was right when he points out that in Christ God has poured upon us the sweet fragrance of the perfume of His love. Are we touched by its scent? Do we touch others with its aroma? Paul writes about the mystical quality of God's love when he says, "Thanks be to God, who . . . manifests through us the sweet aroma of the knowledge of Him in every place. For we are a fragrance of Christ to God among those who are being saved and among those who are perishing" (2 Corinthians 2:14-15).

The Cross Speaks Again

5 There was a moment in time in which the focus of the universe was fixed on a place on earth called Calvary. The eyes of heaven and the attention of the demonic forces of hell were riveted on the most critical event in human history. The salvation of every human being hung in the balance as Jesus surrendered His body to the sinful whims of humanity. Would He yield to the weakness of human flesh and flee? Would He change His mind and say we weren't worth the trouble? Would He relinquish His own will and drink the cup the Father gave Him to drink?

Today we know the choice He made and we need to come to grips more profoundly with the significance of the cross. Like a powerful magnet, it draws us into the cloud of its mystery. We think we understand it but the more we meditate upon it the more we become aware that we can never fully comprehend its power or its meaning. And yet we must try, for if we are to have eternal life, that life must flow into our souls through the fountain of the cross. Since that middle cross stood erect on Golgotha's hill, humanity has never been able to escape its grasp. We run, we deny, we seek to ignore it, but wherever we turn we see the Son of Man lifted up before us and we hear the resounding echo of His words as they enter our ears and descend to the bedrock of our souls: "And I, if I be lifted up will draw all people to me."

What gives the cross such power? Is it not because we cannot but be awed by a righteous and holy God who would be willing to reveal His love to us through suffering? In this world of human flesh, who shall escape without at some time experiencing the reality of suffering? On Calvary we see manifested God's willingness to share in and take upon Himself our suffering. "Surely he has borne our griefs and carried our sorrows; . . . But He was wounded for our transgressions, He was bruised for our iniquities; the chastisement of our peace was upon Him, and by His stripes we are healed" (Isaiah 53, KJV).

I never grow weary of the cross! I come to it again and again, and always I leave more whole than when I arrived. In the cross of Christ I behold the face of God, and in that face I see a God who loves me. In the mirror of the cross I see myself as I really am—unworthy, but not worthless; unlovable but not unloved; once lost but now found. I am awed at the greatness of God's love and now I know why Jesus died there. Nothing that He ever said, no matter how profound, no miracle that He ever wrought, no matter how magnificent, no other act of love that he ever performed can reveal to me how much He loves us in the way that I see it in the cross.

How I wish that I could have been there on that day. I hope that I would have had the courage to offer Him a cup of cold water and to share His suffering with my tears. If only I could have touched His feet and been able to look for a moment into those eyes of love and let Him know that I loved Him and that my heart broke because He was dying for me. If only . . . But I have that privilege just as you do, for Christ is with us even now. We can tell Him all those words we would have said, because the Christ of Calvary is the resurrected Lord of glory. Thank God for the cross and the Christ who loves us!

March 6

Crucified With Christ

I have been crucified with Christ; it is no longer I who live, but Christ lives in me; and the life which I now live in the flesh I live by faith in the Son of God, who loved me and gave Himself for me. (Galatians 2:20, KJV)

Go back and read again the beautiful words above! Are they your testimony along with St. Paul's? Have you come to the place in life that for you to live is to be so surrendered to the will of our Lord that He can live out His will through you? Paul did not mean that he had lost his individual identity and was now a mindless clone of God. What he was saying was that he genuinely sought to know and do God's will and freely set aside his own will for the sake of knowing Christ.

To be crucified with Christ means nothing less than to nail one's selfish will on the cross of Christ. This will never happen until you hunger to experience the reality of Christ's presence in your life. A wise commentator has written, "The only God a man will never outgrow, and therefore never lose, is the God he knows in a present tense experience, a God larger than the world" (*The Interpreter's Bible*, Vol. 10, p. 489). We can not successfully live a spiritual life on a childhood Sunday School faith. If our faith in and experience of Jesus has not come to the point of being a present experience and reality then we're not growing along the faith journey.

It is quite easy to say, "I am a Christian," it is something altogether different to say, "I am crucified with Christ." The writer of the Gospel of John describes the experience as "being born again"— that is, to be born through a spiritual birth brought about through the dynamic power of God. When we have reached the point that the driving force of our lives is to live life on the level of spirit rather than the simple satisfying of the flesh, we will have begun the journey toward spiritual maturity. To be crucified with Christ means that nothing should be more important to us that to do our Father's will. And what freedom there is when we live in the Father's will!

J. Rufus Moseley said, "In Him, there is so much Heaven on the way to Heaven that one wonders how Heaven itself can be much better than the going to Heaven. . . . In Jesus we lose nothing worth keeping and get everything worth having" (*Perfect Everything*, p. 20, 21). Paul did not rejoice in being crucified with Christ because it made him miserable, but because it brought him ultimate joy and peace. There is certain basic information we can learn about Christ without ever committing ourselves to Him. But we can never live in the bliss of His presence until we become willing to be obedient to Him.

It can all begin with a simple prayer like this: "Lord, I have lived life too long on my terms and it has brought me to the point that I feel despair. Help me to yield my will to yours and in so doing, begin to live life in your strength and power. Then I will be in union with the Creator and all that He has created. Even as You allowed your own will to be crucified on a cross, help me to be willing to allow mine to be crucified with you. Amen."

If Only You Had Known . . .

7 Palm Sunday was a sad day. What a day of contrasts—people cheered and Jesus wept. Who knows what expectations were in the people's hearts—what dreams or aspirations they had for Jesus as He slowly made His way through the city gates? Who knows the depth of disappointment that was in the heart of Jesus? He approached the city, straddling a small donkey while crowds screaming, "Hosanna!" surrounded Him. The scripture says, "And when He saw the city, He wept." Something seems terribly wrong with this picture! We call that day the Triumphant Entry, but aren't triumphant entries supposed to be happy times? Why then did the Lord of history reveal it to be a sad time?

The answer comes from the words that came immediately from His own lips. "If you, even you, had only known on this day what would bring you peace—but now it is hidden from your eyes" (Luke 19:42). God was in their presence and they were blind to His glory because their expectations of Him were in opposition to the plan of God for humanity. He was a gentle Man who, more than anyone who has ever lived, longed for peace in the hearts of humanity. Within Him was the peace for which creation longed, and it would not receive it. The winds and waves bowed before Him, not just because He spoke the words, "Peace, be still!", but because He **was** peace in the midst

March

of the storm and where the peace of God dwells, peace must come.

Jesus looked at the city and He saw no peace. Worse still, He saw no desire for peace—for peace is an inner thing. It's a calmness, an assurance that bubbles up from that place we call soul or spirit. The soul is that part of us that has the power to commune deeply with God and be transformed by God. No one changes on the outside until first he or she is transformed on the inside. As Jesus scanned the faces of the crowd, He must have been appalled at the shallowness of their souls for He found that He occupied no space in that part of them where they would understand His peace. They had no idea what "things made for peace". The hot, scalding tears that flowed down those tender cheeks revealed a compassion that was surpassed only by the heart that beat beneath them.

Down through the centuries come those haunting words—"If only . . . if only . . . if only!" Down to our own time, down to America, to our own city. . . With your mind's eye, look across the horizon of your city some warm spring morning and maybe you'll see the faint outline of the Man on the donkey; all alone, shoulders shaking with uncontrollable sobs, huge tears cascading down His cheeks, dropping from His chin onto His lap. Is Jesus weeping for your city? For the churches in your community that cannot accept Him for the Savior He is? Does it break His heart all over again to see us, we who call ourselves Christians, living lives that reveal no peace, no trust, no adoration? What about you, O reader, is there peace in your heart?

Palm Sunday is almost here and the Man of Peace rides once more in the direction of our lives. When He reaches the outskirts of your life and He draws near enough for you to behold His face, will you see tears, or will your heart and soul have embraced Him to the point of bringing a smile to His face? Instead of hearing Him say, "If only you had known . . ." wouldn't it be wonderful to hear Him say, "You know! You know!"

Day of Triumph?

In the Gospel of John, Jesus' triumphant entry into Jerusalem is preceded by the chapter recounting the raising of Lazarus

March

from the dead. No doubt the news of such a miraculous act had quickly spread and many were excited about the possibility that this revolutionary teacher might just be the Messiah/King they had longed for over the centuries. How ironic that the death and resurrection of one man would quickly lead to the death and resurrection of another.

The crowd wanted to make Him king but that was not their prerogative and certainly not within their power. Fred Craddock writes, "Jesus is King, but not because the crowd elevated him or made him so. He is King by virtue of who he is. Not even faith makes Christ King; faith only recognizes that he is" (*Preaching Through the Christian Year B*, p. 168). Such a statement is similar to the one that E. Stanley Jones makes concerning the Kingdom of God. He writes:

> *The New Testament never tells us that we are to build the Kingdom. We are told to "see," to "enter," to "receive" and to 'proclaim" the Kingdom, but never to build it. The difference? It is profound and far-reaching. For if we are to build the Kingdom, then it is something that we bring into life, something that we produce. But the Kingdom is already in existence; it is a fact, so it is something we "receive".* (*Is the Kingdom of God Realism?*, p. 63)

Jesus rode into Jerusalem on Palm Sunday as King, simply because He is. But where He wants to be King is in the hearts of those who will "receive" Him and His kingdom in faith. The kingdom that matters most to Him is the kingdom of our heart. There He will enter only by invitation and will remain only through accepting and continuing faith. We have no power to make Jesus King but we do possess the power to let Him be King within us.

All of us hope that we will go to heaven when we die. Jesus offers us heaven now! The heart that accepts Him as Lord and King is the heart that has been filled with heaven's glory. *Blessed assurance, Jesus is mine! O what a foretaste of glory divine!* There can be only one king in each heart. Something or someone will occupy that throne and we are given the choice of who or what it will be.

Jesus wept when He entered Jerusalem because the people proclaimed Him as king with their lips but would not allow Him to ride

March

into their hearts. Those doors and windows were closed tight and latched, and so His day of "triumph" was for Him a day of great sadness. Can you, with your mind's eye, see the cheering crowds again? Can you search the multitude of faces until at last you find your own? And as your eyes meet His, can you see into the soul of this "man of sorrows"—the anguish He feels of unrequited love? Well now's your chance to change His tears to laughter, to transform His sorrow into joy. Now proclaim Him King of your heart, mind and soul. By faith unite your life to His—and if you do, then Palm Sunday will at last truly become a day of triumph!

Six Hours

9 Six hours doesn't seem very long—the length of time between lunch and dinner—one fourth of a day. About the length of time it would take to drive 350 miles—six hours—360 minutes. A few thousand tick tocks of the clock and we're there. But then, how long would six hours seem if there were nails driven through your hands and feet and the entire weight of your body hung from the sensitive sore tissue of your hands that was pressed firmly against a wooden beam that had become saturated with your own blood? Six hours He was impaled on a cross, and the entire future of every soul hung in the balance.

Six days, the Bible tells us, it took God to create a world. Six hours is about right to redeem it, isn't it? How much can you accomplish in six hours, especially if half of them are experienced in darkness? It was a bright sunny morning, around 9 a.m. when the strong hands of a Roman soldier held His hands against the beam. Another one placed the iron spike in His hand, and with the hard, swift blows of a mallet, drove it through holy flesh into the tree that was helpless to stop it. Overhead, soft, white, billowy clouds gently floated by as the soldiers raised Him upright. The weight of his own body began to tear skin and muscle away from each other as a blue sky became the backdrop for His silhouette suspended on a cross. See, the world hasn't changed. Jesus is dying and the world goes on.

Moneychangers are already back at work in the Temple, extorting everyone that needs temple coins to put in the treasury.

Pharisees are returning to their candlelit rooms to once more pore over the law—split a few more theological hairs and make the world a more difficult place in which to live. Pilate is once more consumed with the affairs of Rome and the nasty business of suppressing the conquered masses of Judea. Herod, perhaps, is being entertained by another of his exotic dancers while he sips his wine and slips into another drunken stupor. Caiaphas is now putting on his high priestly robe in preparation for his yearly entry into the Holy of Holies. I wonder if that was where he was when the veil of the Temple was rent from top to bottom.

Nature could stomach no more. Almost as if to try to regurgitate humanity from itself, earth becomes shrouded in darkness as the sun refused for three hours to give earth its light. There would be no cosmic spotlight provided for humanity's darkest hour! The sweet voices of singing birds fell silent. Clouds thickened, twisted, and contorted as they turned as dark as freshly-mined coal. Lightning erupted in angry, frenzied flashes. The sky dumped tons of driving rain, as if to try to wash away the filthiness of humanity. The earth shook at its foundation and rocks tumbled to and fro. The wind blew, assisting trees and plants in bowing their heads in shame and sorrow. This was nature's reaction to humanity's dastardly deed!

Six hours! What can possibly be accomplished in six hours? In six hours, from the altar of a cross, Jesus gathered up the sins of the entire world, placed them in His own cup, and drank the last drop. His body became like the divine cosmic black hole, gathering up and condensing down every sin until it filled every crevice of His own soul. And when He had gathered them all, His work was done and He died. How do I know He got it all done in six hours? I know because the last thing He said before He left was, "It is finished."

Watch With Me

10 "Then he took Peter, James, and John with him. Distress and anguish came over him, and he said to them 'The sorrow in my heart is so great that it almost crushes me. Stay here and watch'" (Mark 14:33-34, TEV). Strange, isn't it, that God should express a need for human companionship? Is it possible that God so

March

understands the anguish and distress of human emotion that He cries out to human beings to just be consciously present with Him? Have you known a sorrow so great that it almost crushed you? So did Jesus! Have you been so afraid of the future that you shrank back in horror? So did Jesus! Have you known the heartbreak of wanting someone to just be there with you and they totally missed the deep need in your heart? So did Jesus!

God needed someone to stand with Him in a time of great distress, and humanity slept. God needed someone to step forward and say, "I'm here with you Lord," and we left Him all alone. Still, He loves us! Who can grasp love so divine? But all our opportunities are not lost, for there are still human beings who need us to stand with them, to sit in quietness and listen—to simply express that we are sensitive to and aware of their deep anguish. And each time we do, we are keeping watch with Jesus because He said when we did it to the least of these His brethren, we have done it unto Him.

Churches, like people, go through times of deep need—a time when the future seems so uncertain, a time when we need the strength of shared faith and the uplifting power of a common purpose. We need to come together in one accord and to make intercession to our Lord for the sake of His Body the church. We must rediscover the power of prayer! How unfortunate that so many of us use prayer like a spare tire. We only pull it out when there is a great crisis of need. Pray for your church. Ask God's direction for it and for your part in it. Do not be content to quietly sit by or sleep through those times when your conscious awareness is needed.

Jesus went to Gethsemane for two reasons. One was to seek comfort for the distress in His soul, and the other was to seek God's will and to submit Himself to it. The two became merged into one and the result was that both were accomplished. Yes, He passed through a time of suffering and distress, but the result was glory! Sincere prayer will always lead to victory. It may not be the victory that we had anticipated but it will be the glorious victory that God will bring to fruition; and that will be better than anything we could have imagined

The church's battles are fought in the arenas of prayer. Places called Gethsemane. The church is the spiritual body of our Lord and its battles must be fought in the spiritual realm. Our Lord has a plan for the future of His church but it will never come about and we will never even know what it is until we discover it in the sanctuary of prayer. There is no great secret to praying; it is a simple act of the will in which we make known to God the things that are in our heart and mind. Do you love your church enough to pray? Or will the cry of Jesus to come and watch with Him silently fall once more on the sleeping ears of His friends?

The Depths of Divine Love

11 Isn't it strange how we can live so much of our life without truly feeling a deep love for Christ? Sometimes it's because we were not introduced to Him until later in life; sometimes it's because we have grown complacent with His presence and fall into the trap of indifference that so often accompanies the love in marital relationships. Every once in a while someone will say or write something that shocks us back into the reality of how greatly Jesus loves us and it rekindles the deep feeling of love within us that we have for Him. Such was the case when my wife read to me some poignant words from a daily devotional this past week. They were written by Max Lucado in his book *And the Angels Were Silent*. Lucado said:

> *The Battle is won. You may have thought it was won on Golgotha. It wasn't. You may have thought the sign of victory is the empty tomb. It isn't. The final battle was won in Gethsemane. And the sign of conquest is Jesus at peace in the olive trees. For it was in the garden that He made his decision. He would rather go to hell for you than go to heaven without you.*

When at last we really begin to comprehend the eternal depth of God's love for us, when it finally settles down in our hearts and takes root in our souls that Jesus loved us enough to enter the gates of hell for us, then perhaps our hearts will be moved to embrace Him with tears of gratitude. But as long as Jesus is only a historical concept,

March

only the subject of a nice biblical story alongside other stories we have heard along life's way, then we will never be moved to feel any deep love for Him and certainly not inspired to commit our lives to Him in any meaningful service. I do not think that it overstates the case at all to say our love for Jesus can be measured by how willing we are to serve Him in response to the leading of His Spirit.

We need to somehow realize, difficult though it may be to comprehend, that the very Son of God agonized in Gethsemane, suffered humiliation and indignities before Pilate, was severely beaten in a courtyard and unmercifully suffered impalement on a Roman cross, not because He loved humanity, but because He loved each of us as individuals. When we allow ourselves to be lost in the anonymity of a mass of humanity, then we fail to see the uniqueness with which God values us. As long as we are content only to experience God's love as one of a mass of billions, then we will never feel any compulsion to serve Him as an individual.

The One who loves us like no other crashed the very gates of hell (I Peter 3:19) to battle Satan for the souls of humanity. No one is insignificant to God and He will not rest until every divine effort has been made to ransom the soul of every individual who ever lived. How can you not love a God who would not ascend to heaven until after He had plumbed hell's depths for you? If the knowledge that God loves you that much cannot move you to serve Him, then nothing on earth, heaven, or hell ever will!

Center Stage

12 It was amazing how many people found their lives centered on the life of one man that day—His family, the disciples, hundreds if not thousands of His followers, a king, the governor, Roman soldiers, two thieves, Pharisees, Sadducees, scribes, high priests, the seventy who made up the Sanhedrin. There must have also been those who had benefited from His healing who were present—blind, deaf, lame, lepers, and the formerly demon-possessed. Surely Lazarus, whom He raised from the dead, was there. And of course, there were the curious who always show up at a public execution, and the pilgrims who happened to be coming to the city for the Passover celebration. They all converged at the cross and watched a man die. Some gawked for a while and quickly moved on; they had more important business to take care of. Others felt grateful that they weren't the ones suffering at Rome's hands. Some were gleeful, others filled with sorrow; worst of all, most were indifferent.

Four men were required to be there; they weren't given a choice. Long hardened by their profession, they felt little pity for those dying, no compassion for the loved ones who grieved over the crucified. Mercy was a concept they could not grasp, for they were men who drove nails through human flesh, who lashed the backs of men until they bled; they broke the legs of the dying with heavy mallets and drove spears into sides to ensure that the dying were really dead and not pretending. So blasé were they about human suffering, their biggest concern seemed to be how to divide His garments. He called out in despair for a simple drink of water and they offered Him sour wine. They did nothing to still the mocking crowd, and looked with scorn upon the King whose crown was common thorns.

All that Jesus had owned was the clothes that He wore, and now they were fighting over who would get those. What would a Roman soldier want with a carpenter-preacher's garments? But among His scant belongings there was a seamless robe, perhaps woven by His mother. It was too good to be torn into four parts, as His other garments had been divided. So they gambled to see who would win it. One did! He became the proud owner of the coat that had warmed the Son of God. What must it have felt like, to feel draped over his shoulders the cloth that had graced the body of Him who knew no sin? What would you give to hold it in your hands for just a moment—the cloak that belonged to Jesus? How would you treat it? Would it bring tears to your eyes? Would you touch it gently to your face, press it firmly against your heart? Max Lucado writes,

> *Something about the crucifixion made every witness either step toward it or away from it. And today, two thousand years later the same is true. It's the watershed. It's the Continental Divide. It's Normandy. And you are either on one side or the other. A choice is demanded. . . . No fence sitting is permitted. That is one luxury that God in his awful mercy,*

March

doesn't permit. On which side are you? (No Wonder They Call Him the Savior, p. 73)

Do you realize that the entire world was at the cross that day? I was there. So were you. Now, what are you going to do about it?

Life's Ups and Downs

13 Life is always filled with ups and downs. One moment we may feel happy and contented, the next we find ourselves in the miry bog of discontent. At times we feel the love and support of family and friends; at other times we feel isolated, alone and perhaps misunderstood (certainly under-appreciated). It was no different for Jesus. He too had highs and lows, peaks and valleys. He knew what it meant to be the recipient of accolades from the crowds, and the next day to hear voices calling for His death.

Palm Sunday is considered by many to be a peak moment in Jesus' life. He was entering the city of Jerusalem to the welcoming cheers of the multitudes. Smiling faces greeted Him; eyes filled with love and affection were everywhere. Yet Jesus entered Jerusalem not with laughter in His voice, not with overwhelming joy in His heart, but with a flood of tears flowing down His cheeks. The English translation of the Greek word in Luke (19:41) is rendered "wept," but that does not fully convey the emotional anguish He was feeling. The word actually means, "shaking with violent and uncontrollable sobbing."

Why would the King of kings, who was finally being acknowledged as Lord and Messiah, find this an occasion for weeping? Perhaps because Jesus understood all too well the fickleness of human hearts. How often we praise Him with our lips, acknowledge Him with our voice, but deny Him access to the place of our being where He longs to reign—our heart. Had He not once said, "This people honor me with their lips but their hearts are far from Me"?

And yet Jesus continued on with life, maintaining that steady course that inevitably led him to the cross—the place that He always knew awaited Him. Every obstacle, detour, and setback in life He was able to overcome because His trust was always ultimately in the love of His Father who never failed Him. He looked to a Source beyond the

March

limitations of His human strength and was therefore always able to be re-energized and renewed. We can learn a lesson here! If we too would come to the place that we faced adversity not in the uncertainty of our own strength, but in the power of the God who loves us eternally, we would discover that there is nothing that can ultimately defeat us.

On that first Good Friday, as the Man of Sorrows hung suspended from the cross, the entire world (including His own followers) viewed His life as ending in failure. But what the world calls failure, God transforms into victory. The cross was humankind's symbol of the agony and uncertainty of life. It was an instrument of torture, an admission of defeat in terms of our ability to control life. It represented the worst in humanity, for it showed our disdain for the reality of God's presence in our lives. We had God with us and our reaction to His presence was to put Him to death.

But God cannot be defeated, even by our rejection. For His love is greater than our hate, His power is greater that our weakness, and His desire to embrace us with acceptance is greater than our ability to flee from His presence. Life will always present us with peaks and valleys, but in the power of God we shall always have victory.

Resurrection Living

14 Christians cannot meditate on the meaning of Easter without inevitably being drawn to thoughts of the Resurrection. But in order for there to have been a resurrection, there first had to be a death. Jesus understood that from the beginning; His followers did not, until after the event had occurred. It is the nature of the redeemed life to require death before "life" can be experienced. The spiritual experience of "new birth" was expressed in those terms by Jesus, because He knew that for humanity to be redeemed, it must first encounter the experience of death of the old nature. To be born again one has to die to self and thereby fulfill the condition for new birth. That's why Jesus said, "He who will save His life must first be willing to lose it."

Dwell for a moment on the latter half of that sentence—"must first be willing to lose it." The key word is "willing." Do you hunger enough for the redeemed life that you have reached the place that you

March

are willing to lose the old life in order to experience the new? Jesus said in the Sermon on the Mount, "Blessed are they who hunger and thirst for righteousness, for they shall be filled." The "righteousness" about which He spoke was the redeemed life. When we come to the point that we crave it, hunger for it and desire it above all things, then we will discover for ourselves what it means to be redeemed.

Jesus is the ultimate example of one who was willing to die to self. Not only did He surrender His own will to that of the Father, He poured out His entire life for the sake of humanity. He is the Redeemer because He was the One who was completely willing to die for the sake of others. In Revelation 5:9, the hosts of heaven proclaim Him Savior with these words (note what they say "qualifies" Him to be Savior): "Worthy are you to take the scroll and to open its seals, <u>for you were slain, and by your blood you ransomed people</u> for God from every tribe and language and people and nation . . ." He was worthy (to be the Savior) because through His willingness to die for us He became our Redeemer. Before His death on the cross, Jesus told His disciples, "No one takes my life from me, I have the power to lay it down and I have the power to take it up again."

When we become so in love with Christ that we are willing to die to self (that is, to put His will ahead of our own) then we will cease to be afraid of the actual experience of death, and will be forever set free from its power over us. You will find life when you become willing to lose life. It is paradoxical—a mystery of God that few experience because it defies human reason. I may have cancer, but cancer cannot hold me captive because my will is lost in Christ's will and therefore cancer has no ultimate power over me. Long ago I became willing to lose my life for Christ's sake and in so doing I have discovered true life—life that cannot be bound by the possibility or the reality of death. That's living in the experience of Easter now! That's living in the experience of resurrection—a foretaste of the glory which is yet to be!

People of the Resurrection

15 We have just passed through Lent and now are into the season of Eastertide—from the season of the cross to the season of the resurrection. The lessons we can learn from

March

these two events can be life-transforming. Life will always be filled with difficulties and with questions, but ultimately life will always rise above them. E. Stanley Jones writes, "If Calvary raises these questions, Easter morning answers them. The cross raised the questions, Easter morning raised the Man who gathered up the questions in himself. . . Life's last word is not a cross but an Easter morning" (*The Christ of Every Road*, p. 85-86).

All of life points toward a conclusion, but what awaits us at the conclusion is really the beginning. Along the way, we are shaped and molded by both good and bad, ease and pain, laughter and sorrow, sin and redemption. To conclude that this life is a "throw away" existence that was merely created to prepare us for the next one is crummy theology. God created life here to be good and it is in this life that the kingdom of heaven becomes established. We are not Buddhists longing for the mythical Nirvana where life dissolves into a neutral nothingness. We are not Hindus who believe that we suffer as a result of previous lives and are reborn again and again until we get it right. We are Christians and what our faith teaches us is that life is good (even when things go wrong) and that Jesus said He came to give us peace, abundant life, and joy NOW!

We are not Pollyannas who run around pretending that life doesn't have problems. We are people of faith who cling tenaciously to the truth that life has storms, but storms pass and people, by God's grace, can rise above them. The resurrection of Jesus affirms the existence of both the physical and spiritual. It proclaims that God is in both, that God created both and that we are not just one or the other, neither now or in the world to come. Some folks live as if this life is merely something to be endured until we can get to the next one. I think that is an affront to God who gave us this life and declared it to be good. To take the attitude that we merely hang on for the next life is to denigrate the beauty and sanctity of life now.

If your view of Easter is that God is only saying, "Just hang on for a few decades and I will end your misery here," you know nothing about the will of God for life. Get up in the morning and greet life with expectancy. Break out of your dull, mundane, life-robbing habits and start to discover the incredible adventure of your aliveness. We

March

live in a nation that has more wealth, more opportunity, more of life's goodness than any nation on earth and we behave as if we are children in a candy store who are forbidden to sample the infinite varieties of sweetness. This very day the Resurrected Christ wants to live life with you. He wants to show you the wonder of the world you inhabit and the innate goodness that flows through it.

In the Old Testament, God promised the Hebrews a land that flowed with milk and honey. When they got to the Promised Land, they didn't see anything but rocky ground with little water and a lot of hard work and they quickly turned away from God. In doing so, they missed the joy all around them. Life lived apart from communion with the Living God is always life lived in a spiritual vacuum. Life lived with Him will always be life lived on the highest plane of peace and joy. So quit living as if there was and is no resurrection! Because He lives, and desires to live in us, we ought to be rejoicing.

Grief, Hopelessness and Easter

16 It was a scene that would be forever etched in their memory—the lifeless body of Jesus, blood-spattered, beaten, dirty, drenched with sweat now grown cold. As gently as they could, Joseph of Arimathea and Nicodemus removed Him from the cross. His eyes stared blankly into space revealing the absence of that "spark" we know as life. Skin that just minutes earlier had the vital force of life-energy flowing through it now took on the characteristics of mere matter devoid of movement. His arms and legs hung limp, flopping involuntarily from side to side as they lowered Him to the ground. Unquenchable sorrow surrounded the Lord of Life as loved ones and friends wept uncontrollably and without shame. All of life's hopes had been attached to Him, and now He was DEAD.

No power on earth can rob us so completely of hope as does death. It seems so final! No matter how gravely ill a person is, no matter how slender the chance of survival, as long as there is life, hope can never be completely extinguished. But when the last breath leaves the body of the one we love, tears and sorrow erupt from the innermost part of our being, washing away the last vestige of hope that can no longer maintain its grip on our heart. As it leaves us, a huge deep void is created inside and nothing can immediately fill it. A dark emptiness is formed in which despair and hopelessness now embrace each other. The joy of living is sucked out of us. The desire to carry on the routines of life evaporates. Aimlessly, we wander from one meaningless event to another. The appetite vanishes and the craving for food is replaced with a stomach that feels full because of sorrow.

The morning after death has made its visit, having endured a fitful night of interrupted sleep, we awaken to daylight and our first and immediate thought is, "Oh no, it can't be, it wasn't a nightmare, it's true." Now comes the second wave of torrential tears. The shaking sobs, the coming to grips with that which we do not wish to know. This is the reality of grief; the soil that nurtures grief is hopelessness. In the fertile ground in which no hope resides, sorrow and despair grow as quickly as kudzu in the southern summer sun. Stretching its tentacles, hopelessness grips the heart and crushes it with paralyzing force. It intertwines itself around our mind and soul and squeezes and tightens until we feel that our very life is being taken from us.

Is there no answer to such human dilemma? Fortunately, there is. It's called Easter! Easter is the eternal proof that life does not end in a grave. It is the historical evidence that the lifeless body of Jesus lives again; and He said, "If I live, you will live also." It proclaims that the loved one to whom we said "Goodbye" will once again say to us, "Hello." Easter morn came and the darkness of death and hopelessness gave way to the glorious reality of eternal hope and eternal life! The stone that had been rolled in front of our heart where hopelessness dwells is rolled away and hope rushes in again. Weeping gives way to laughing, despair gives way to joy; death yields all its power to life. Grief reigns no more. That's the message of Easter! That's the reality of life!

Between Good Friday and Easter

17 In the hours between Good Friday and Easter, those who loved Jesus became intimately acquainted with the human experience of sorrow. Peace was an elusive luxury that hid itself well. How could there be peace when the One who held the

March

power to speak the words that bring peace had been silenced? As resilient as the human spirit may be, it is not capable of instant acceptance when death invades its perimeters. A mystical, invisible shield seems to be built into our humanity that allows only so much grief to be absorbed and dealt with at one time—otherwise, our hearts could not bear the pain. It is only in small increments that our hearts and minds absorb death's sting.

When one we love dies, our consciousness is flooded with a tidal wave of memories—a mixture of both good and bad. We sort through them seeking to glean anything that will postpone having to face the reality of death's power. Wonderful memories from the past bring smiles and warmth, but suddenly turn into tears and coldness. The tiny threads that composed the cords of love, cords that bound us to the loved one, have begun to be severed—one at a time. As each one snaps, the pain goes deeper and the consciousness of our loss grows greater. It begins to become clear now, that loving someone requires that we sink the deep roots of ourselves into the soil of their lives.

This thing called love that gives life its color and richness also brings with it the power to leave us feeling totally empty and without purpose when the one we love is snatched from us by death's grasp. Living life between Good Friday and Easter is a common human experience; it is a cup from which we all must drink. But do I hear you say, "Easter will not come for the ones to whom we have bid farewell"? You are wrong, my friend. For them Easter was never more real! It is we who must wait for their Easter experience to become our own. Jesus' death and resurrection was far more than the experience of just one solitary life; it was the prototype, the pattern, the mold for all human life. If ever the concept of hope had any place from which it could be born and blossom, it has to be in the resurrection of Jesus. All life emanates from a single Source, and in Christ, human reason is given the privilege of beholding that Source.

Reason tells us that eventually life runs into the insurmountable wall called death and it has no power to overcome it. But in the resurrection of Jesus we have seen that Life meets death head-on, passes through it and comes forth the victor. We view the world upside down; God sees it right side up. Death does not defeat life; life always

March

overcomes death. Death is darkness; life is light, and light always makes darkness recede until it becomes no more than a harmless shadow that only bears witness to the reality of that which it reflects. Death, you see, is but the shadow of life.

While it is true that we must sometimes dwell in that place in time between Good Friday and Easter, now its impact is greatly diminished by the reality that Easter is as certain to occur as the sun rising each new day. Jesus said, "I am the resurrection and the life, he that believeth in me, though he were dead, yet shall he live, and whosoever lives and believes in me shall never die." Easter removed for all time any doubt as to whether those words of Jesus are valid.

The resurrected Lord is not stuck in between Good Friday and Easter; He came forth alive and lives among us. With that knowledge to guide us, never let your soul be crushed by sorrow, for by faith, we already live on this side of Easter.

"It" Brought Easter

18 "It is finished! Father, into Thy hands I commit my spirit." These were the last eleven words Jesus spoke before He died. Before His life-giving body became lifeless, He proclaimed to the world that all He had come to do was now accomplished. It is finished! What is the "**it**" of which He spoke? Two small letters in English, yet large enough to encompass the world. All humanity can be squeezed into those two little letters—at least, all of humanity that desires to be.

The "it" was God's plan of salvation, which Jesus had faithfully and perfectly carried out. Nothing was left undone that needed doing. No human being's salvation was overlooked. Every sin had been embraced, every grief had been borne, every sorrow absorbed into His being, every ounce of love poured out, every desire of the Father faithfully and obediently carried out. The physical pain endured paled before the spiritual pain He experienced. And what was the spiritual pain? The pain of becoming intimately acquainted with the dark, destructive power of sin! "He who knew no sin was made to be sin, so that we might become the righteousness of God."

March

How fitting that His body, now emptied of life, was placed in a dark tomb and with the sealing of the entry, was cut off from light and sound. How graphically it portrays the reality of His body being immersed in the darkness of our sin. How poignantly it proclaims the truth of Scripture, "And this is the judgment, that the light has come into the world, and people loved darkness rather than light because their deeds were evil" (John 3:19. And so He embraced our darkness that we might bathe in His light! First, He had emptied Himself of the glory of heaven and now He emptied Himself of the life which He had incarnated in human flesh.

In the darkness of the tomb, the tiny glow of God's light began to expand and swell until it burst the shroud of darkness, threw off the power of gloom, overcame the strength of sin, and shattered forever the grasp of death. The most powerful government on earth at that time in history could not keep God in a tomb. The most devout religion in the world could not inter Him within the mountain of legalistic regulations that buried people in pseudo-righteousness. Satan's demonic power could not enslave Him in the veil of death, for death can never overcome life. Darkness can never shut out the light and the horrific power of sin cannot displace the mighty power of redeeming grace.

The resurrection was inevitable because God is the source of life and life cannot be sealed in a tomb. Easter is more about life than it is death. When the glory of Easter bursts forth on the horizon of life, then death quickly becomes an afterthought. It is the light of God-given life which will always banish the darkness of sin and death. It cannot be otherwise, for we find our being in the love of God and the love of God hungers to overcome the sin within us with the glorious power of new life in Christ. It's Easter, my friends. Rejoice in new life!

The Unsealing of a Tomb

19 How do you remove nails from human flesh without mashing or bruising the hands and feet of the One who has been impaled on a cross? No matter that there is no longer life in His body, this is the precious body of the One who was loved as no other man was ever loved. Surely Nicodemus and Joseph of

March

Arimathea must have tried to be as gentle as they could. Scalding tears flowed down their cheeks as they looked into those eyes that no longer sparkled with love and compassion, but were fixed in lifeless gaze through half-closed lids.

The eyes are the window to the soul and when life leaves the body and you gaze into the corridors of the empty shell which remains it is not difficult to see that more than breath has left the body: the soul no longer resides there. Mystery! Mystery! Mystery! Where has life gone? From whence did life come? Does not God's Word tell us? "And the Lord God formed man of the dust of the ground, and breathed into his nostrils the breath of life; and man became a living soul" (Gen. 2:7). If the soul came from the presence of God does it not seem reasonable that it returns to Him from whence it came?

For a few lonely hours the caretakers of our Lord's body tenderly handled it and carried it to its resting place—a dark hollow cavern carved from the hardened flesh of mother earth. Sorrow had swept through their own souls like wind blowing dry tumbleweed through a ghost town. Within them were only emptiness and the gloom of desolation. How difficult it must have been to look one last time at the incarnation of God's love and hear the awful sound of a "Thud!" as the stone was rolled in place. Sealed in a tomb! Separated from light and life! Gone forever!

Darkness now covered the earth as the sun receded below the western horizon. All that was heard was the muffled sound of shuffling feet, stirring up dust along the road leading to grief-filled homes. There is no pit so dark and deep as the heart and soul from which all hope has been drained. "We thought He was the Anointed One, the One who would save and redeem and live forever." Midnight comes and tear-soaked pillows cradle the heads of sleepless men and women whose minds will not stop racing and whose hearts will not stop breaking. Wonderful images of love and miracles that will no longer take place dance once more across the screen of their memories and their souls are disquieted within them.

The Sabbath, from sunset Friday until the setting of the sun on Saturday, is endured in sorrow and the anguish and sense of loss has

March

only intensified. No physical pain ever hurt more than the pain in the hearts of those who felt that Jesus was lost to them forever. Slowly the sun completes its predestined journey across the sky and sets for the last time on the sealed tomb that could not hold life within it.

It is now just before dawn on Sunday morning. Suddenly, there is an explosion of energy and life springs forth once more in beauty and power. Angelic hands roll back the stone to let the world look in upon an empty tomb. No longer does it cradle death; now its empty ledge proclaims life. It is Easter—the first Easter—and Christ is risen! Light and Life come again!

The Day After

20 Like the day after Christmas, the day after Easter is often the bridge that beckons us to return to the old life—the way things were before that special day intruded into the routine of our living. As Easter approached, we felt a crescendo of excitement as we anticipated once more the magnificence of what it meant. Finally, it arrived. All over the land, a handful of people rose from their beds before daylight in order to stand in a church parking lot or cemetery and be the first to proclaim with their presence, "He is risen!" Others chose to remain in their slumber and put off the celebration until a less intrusive hour.

When the hour came, into the church they poured and joined their voices in singing Charles Wesley's mighty hymn,

> *Christ the Lord is risen today, Alleluia!*
> *Earth and heaven in chorus say, Alleluia!*
> *Raise your joys and triumphs high, Alleluia!*
> *Sing ye heavens and earth reply, Alleluia!"*

Surrounded by Easter lilies, they listened to the familiar Gospel story and heard the preacher try once more to instill resurrection faith in the hearts of modern Christians who struggle with the issues of skepticism and the miraculous. For a few minutes they felt a strange rumbling down in their heart; perhaps all the way down into their soul. Something was being said that rang true, but somehow seemed almost

March

too good to be true. There was the quiet stirring of the Spirit as He blew His breath of gentle grace across the rough calloused surface of their hearts. With kindness He probed the openings that we offered and sought to nestle down within the brokenness and despair we so desperately seek to hide from the world.

For a few minutes, our spirits felt lifted as we caressed the fingertips of grace and sought to grasp more firmly the Hand of God and let Him pull us up higher onto the plateau of faith. Like the distressed father who came to Jesus pleading for the healing of his son, we silently whispered, "Lord, I believe, help thou my unbelief." There was a warm stirring, a lightness to our burdens: maybe this was the moment that we would take that giant step into the realm of true discipleship. God dying, God rising, God beckoning! We longed to say, "Yes, Lord, I hear you, I feel you, I believe in you, I yield to you, I will serve you. I am yours; you are mine. I surrender!"

But then came the day after Easter. We awakened to a day of post-resurrection—a day that looked very much like a thousand other days we had lived. Soon the weight of routine living pulled us back into the rut of our daily lives and the joyous chorus of "He lives" began to fade into the recesses of our minds more quickly than the fading distant notes of the hymns which we had sung just the day before. Easter, like Christmas ornaments—lights, tinsel, and bright wrapping paper—is gently packed away and put back on the shelf until next year. The shadow of the cross fades quicker than the dogwood blooms. The empty tomb is forgotten, and life returns to normal. But it doesn't have to be that way—unless we choose to let it be.

The Illogic of Faith

21 Having just experienced another Holy Week and the wonder of Maundy Thursday, Good Friday and Easter morning, my thoughts still linger, clinging longingly to the power and mystery of our faith. The Christian faith is so illogical, from the perspective of human reason. The Jews have always had difficulty with the concept of a God who suffers and dies for His people. The world continues to have problems with belief in another life and a thing called "resurrection." Strange, that God would choose

March

"foolish things to confound the wise." Paul said that he carefully avoided trying to preach about the cross with "eloquent wisdom" because to do so would "empty it of its power" (I Corinthians 1:17). Thus, the power of the cross lies not in understanding it with human wisdom but experiencing it in childlike faith. A. W. Tozer wrote:

> *The truth of the cross is revealed in its contradictions. The witness of the church is most effective when she declares rather than explains, for the gospel is addressed not to reason but to faith. What can be proved requires no faith to accept. Faith rests upon the character of God, not upon the demonstrations of laboratory or logic.*
> *(That Incredible Christian, p. 11)*

Every preacher of the gospel declares more than he or she knows. By that I mean it is not necessary that the preacher fully comprehend and understand with human logic the power and complete purpose of the gospel. Our job is to proclaim it with faithfulness, like the sower who sows seeds and allows them to fall in all sorts of soil. I do not understand electricity, but that does not keep me from using it.

How sad, that like the first disciples after the glory of Easter, we quickly retreat to the routines of our daily lives. Jesus had to search them out and remind them that if they loved Him they had to "Feed His sheep." Likewise, He discovers that we quickly allow the glow and glory of Easter to fade into the past as rapidly as darkness covers the earth at the descending of the sun. But must it be so? Can we ever peer into the empty tomb and be quite the same? The visible evidence of one who has encountered the truth of the risen Christ is the changed life! Sometimes the change comes quickly and sometimes it is quite slow. Sometimes it is dramatic and sometimes it takes hold of us in small subtle changes—but change we must. No one meets Jesus and remains the same—that is not possible.

As they reflected on their post-Easter encounter with Him, the two disciples that met Jesus on the road to Emmaus proclaimed, "Were not our hearts burning within us while he talked with us on the road and opened the Scriptures to us?" (Luke 24:32). Does your heart burn within you as a result of having encountered the living Christ? If it

March

does not, return to the cross and linger a little longer. Make your way back to the empty tomb and gaze deeper into the shadows until you see that all that remained were empty garments. If He has risen, that means He is alive! If He is alive, that means He is near. Don't stop looking until you find Him!

The State of Your Mind and Soul

22 Rufus Moseley writes, "We are born of whomever and whatever we choose to receive and to give ourselves to" (*Perfect Everything*, p. 36). Those are profoundly true words. If we give ourselves to God we become godly; if we give ourselves to evil or allow evil to have its way in us then we become evil. In this body of flesh we will always be in need of constant redemption of the soul. No one has ever given themselves to the will of God more than did Jesus. The result was that Jesus became the revelation of the presence of God in the world. We are not the Son of God and we do not have the ability to do perfectly the will of our Father; thus we cannot be the incarnation of God. But we can, through surrender to God's will, become instruments of our Lord that reveal to the world the character and nature of God living in us.

God is love. When we manifest love in our life we bear witness to the world that God loves them. When we show hatred, prejudice, or injustice to the world we bear witness to the power of Satan in our lives and God is denied glory. One of our frustrations in wanting truly to be Christian is that we long for the change in us to be immediate and complete. That rarely happens. For most of us the change is slow and gradual and occurs over a lifetime. No human being comes into this life fully grown. We begin as a one-celled embryo and slowly develop until we reach physical maturity. Even God did not enter our world fully grown but came as a babe in a manger, born from the womb of a woman.

There is a correlation between spiritual growth and physical growth. It takes time for both. The key is not to give up and throw in the towel before the power of God has the chance to remake us. Love planted in our heart and soul needs time to develop. It begins small and slowly develops into mature love—if nurtured and allowed to grow.

March

The miraculous power of love is that it has the capacity to absorb evil and transform it into good. But love planted can only be nurtured by the power of God, and the power of God will only nurture that love within us that we surrender to Him in obedience. No mother can feed the baby that refuses to open its mouth. God cannot redeem the soul of the person who will not open his or her heart.

The unredeemed soul will always exist in a spirit of discontentment because the body, mind and soul of humanity were designed by and for God. Again quoting Moseley:

> As Luther saw, if man, separated from God who is Love, had been able to hold that heavenly love in the separation, he would of himself have been a god. But when he was banished from Paradise man lost love except for himself and what seemed to promote his self-interest. Nevertheless in the separation he still had faith which is the power to receive and pass on love as a tube receives and passes on water. If he had not had this power he would have been hopeless. (p. 38)

You and I were created for God, to live in union and harmony with Him. Only when we are willing to accept that re-union through faith will our lives know the tranquil experience of dwelling in the presence and power of God. Like it or not, to a large degree, you choose what the state of your mind and soul experience.

The Dark Night of the Soul

23 When did it happen? When was that moment in time that our hearts became so encrusted with the routine living of life that we failed to be moved any longer by the mystery and power of the Word of God? We hear God's Word read and proclaimed and it no longer stirs the still waters of our soul. The words enter through our ears, dance merrily across our minds and cascade swiftly out of our consciousness. Our hearts are not "strangely warmed" like the heart of Wesley once was, and we make our way through each day with a noticeable absence of the conscious directing power of God's Spirit.

March

There is an emptiness to life that defies explanation. We try to analyze it but it eludes our comprehension. "What's missing?" we ask; but no answer springs forth. How is it that we can rise to greet a new day and feel no sense of purpose, no joy in being alive, no desire or inspiration to be about anything? We feel like a ship without a rudder, tossed and blown in whatever direction the strongest wind blows us. Life seems dull and headed nowhere.

Could it be that we are in one of those periods of time that John of the Cross, a sixteenth century monk, aptly named "the dark night of the soul?" A time in which, for no apparent reason, our journey toward God seems to have reached a dead end. Did not Jesus pass through such a time while nailed to the cross? Indeed, has any one ever experienced more completely a "dark night of the soul" than when He cried out to God in despair, "My God, My God, why have you forsaken Me?"

It is in such times as these that our faith abruptly descends and flows in the underground caverns of our heart and soul. No longer able to analyze it, or even comprehend faith's presence with our intellect, we are forced, like it or not, to make our way through the day simply trusting that God is with us in unseen ways. It is a frightening journey, much like the passage must have been from our mother's womb, down the darkness of the birth canal and finally into the light we had never known. For some the journey was swift; for others the labor is long. But in either case it was an essential part of our birth into aliveness.

Being born into the spiritual dimension of life is in some ways more traumatic than physical birth because in spiritual birth we bring with us the burden of a conscious mind that demands that each step along the way be explained and understood. It rarely is! Who can explain how the tiny seed, planted in the "dark night" of the soil, cut off for a while from the longed-for light, is able to be transformed from what appears to be a lifeless hardened object into a fruit-bearing vine or tree? Yet the process of darkness is essential to life and to growth.

If you are struggling now with faith, with no sense of direction, with a feeling of hopelessness, then take heart—you do not struggle alone! We all make similar journeys. But never doubt that the God who has given you life is making the journey with you. And though

March

His presence may not be seen nor felt, it is the power of His love and grace that will always see you through!

Dealing with Temptation

24 We all have to deal with temptations that come to us in life. How we learn to deal with them will ultimately determine whether we succumb to them or overcome them. To try to overcome the temptation simply through the strength of our own will may suffice for awhile, but will ultimately fail us. Will power is not enough. That's why the catch phrase for resisting illegal drugs ("Just Say No!") is not very effective in helping young people win the battle. The best way to resist that which is evil is to embrace and be embraced by that which is good.

The power of temptation lies within us, not without. Whether we resist it or are overcome by it will be determined by what dwells at the center of our heart and soul. When those moments of trial come, whose voice sounds most alluring—the voice of Satan or the voice of Jesus? We do not resist temptation in our own power but by the power of Him whom we allow to dwell in us. When Satan tempted Jesus, he was put to flight because the Word of God was anchored in the heart of our Lord. Each temptation was met with the words, "It is written . . ." Jesus listened to the voice of His Father and the sound He heard was more beautiful and more powerful than the alluring promises of Satan. The illusive sound of hell sought to draw Him downward, but the sweet music of heaven pulled his heart upward.

The Apostle imparted great wisdom when he gave to the Ephesians (and us) guidance in dealing with temptation.

> *Finally, be strong in the Lord and in his mighty power. Put on the full armor of God so that you can take your stand against the devil's schemes. For our struggle is not against flesh and blood, but against the rulers, against the authorities, against the powers of this dark world and against the spiritual forces of evil in the heavenly realms. Therefore put on the full armor of God, so that when the day of evil comes, you may be able to stand your ground, and after you have done everything,*

March

to stand. Stand firm then, with the belt of truth buckled around your waist, with the breastplate of righteousness in place, and with your feet fitted with the readiness that comes from the gospel of peace. In addition to all this, take up the shield of faith, with which you can extinguish all the flaming arrows of the evil one. Take the helmet of salvation and the sword of the Spirit, which is the word of God. And pray in the Spirit on all occasions with all kinds of prayers and requests.

Putting on the armor of God and standing faithfully is accomplished not in our own power but in the power of Him who shields us. When temptation comes, you are ready to do battle for you will be clothed in truth, righteousness, peace, faith, salvation and with your one offensive weapon—the Word of God.

The Lord's Prayer reminds us that we ask to be spared from the power of temptation, but when confronted with it, to be delivered from it by His power. In the strength of His words we find deliverance, but only if we are listening.

Living Life on the Level of Spirit

25 Do you love God for Himself, or what you think He will give you or do for you? If there was no promise of heaven, no assurance that anything exists beyond the grave, would you bother to pray, to read the Bible, to come to church? The mysteries of spiritual life are hidden within the realities of physical existence, but they will be revealed only to those who seek them with a searching heart.

Life is really about relationships and the discovery of how to be united in love, on the deepest spiritual level, with other human beings. Love, as God intended, is truly experienced at its greatest depth when it is realized at the place of spiritual union with another. The greater the spiritual union the closer we return to the true intent God had when He created humanity.

In seeking to give expression to the possibility of union with Himself, Jesus compared our relationship with Him to the relationship of marriage—He is the Bridegroom and we are the bride. At the heart

March

of the marriage union there must be love or there is not true union. The concept and reality of love is the divine expression of the nature of God, capable of being experienced on the level of our humanity. When we care for people simply for themselves and not for what they can give us, then we have begun to experience love.

God did not create the world and place us in it because He needed us to make it complete, nor because He needed our love. He created our world and us in order to give tangible expression to the reality of His love. In the first man and woman there existed the union of love between God and His creation. That union was broken when man's love for himself became greater than his love for God. Out of what began as divine union came forth human brokenness, which was the result of humanity's sinfulness. In spite of that, the love of God for humanity was so pure, so magnificent that it was willing to maintain its side of the union even when it broke down on the human side.

In order to be reunited with humanity, divine love was willing to sacrifice itself at the level of the cross. On the cross divine love willingly absorbed all the evil and division that humanity could hurl at it, and in absorbing our sin, thus created the possibility that we could be united once more with Him who gave us life. God loved us for ourselves, not for what we had become. Only in union with His divine love can we ever return to what we were created to be. This divine/human re-union is the new birth. It is what Jesus called "being born from above." He who created life out of chaos has redeemed our life out of the chaos that we created.

To the degree that we love ourselves more than we love God, we remain estranged from Him. We who were created for love must be willing to live in love which manifests itself in the realm of the spirit, or forever experience separation from that which is divine. When we hunger to love and serve God for Himself and not for what He can give us, then we will begin to live life on the spiritual level—the dimension of life for which we were created.

Love Will Set Us Free

26 Ask the average person to define sin and more than likely he or she will rattle off a long list of things we shouldn't do:

March

for example, murder, adultery, stealing, lying, coveting, etc. In reality these are but the outward evidence of our inward sin. Sin is that inward longing within us to turn away from the God who made us. It might reveal itself in many outward acts but the root cause is within our very being. As Paul Tillich puts it, "It is not the disobedience to a law which makes an act sinful but the fact that it is an expression of man's estrangement from God, from men, from himself" (*Systematic Theology*, Volume 2, pp. 46-47).

Time and again Jesus tried to get the Pharisees (and us) to see that sin is born in the heart. For example, He tells us that adultery can be committed within the heart without ever engaging in the outward act. Paul tells us that there is an inward war that goes on in each of us (Romans 7:7-25). Indeed, his words make it seem almost like our very being has been invaded by a spiritual force called sin, under whose power we become helpless. We want to do good, but don't. We desire to refrain from evil, but find ourselves engaging in it. In despair Paul cries out, "Wretched man that I am, who will rescue me from this body of death?" His answer? "Thanks be to God through Jesus Christ our Lord" (7:24-25, NRSV).

It is sin that not only separates us from God but also from other human beings and from ourselves. It is a spiritual disease that wreaks havoc with our minds and souls and makes us feel alienated. In this state of alienation we are incapable of experiencing peace and joy except for momentary flashes which only cause us to feel more miserable when they have gone. If we were to strike the end of our little finger with a hammer, even though it is a tiny part of our body, the whole body suffers. We feel pain, and our conscious thoughts immediately become centered on that finger. All of our attention is focused on it and all other reasoning and acts stop until the pain begins to subside. So it is with sin. Outwardly, it may be almost indiscernible but inwardly it corrupts our entire being. It is like some malignant spiritual tumor that drains us of energy and desire.

At the root of drug and alcohol abuse is the tyrant of sin. Its intent is to cause self-destruction and often, in the process, the destruction of others. Likewise with hatred and prejudice, the end result is not only the hidden desire that others be harmed but also a

March

hatred for one's self. The Bible says, "If you cannot love your brother whom you have seen, how can you love God whom you have not seen?" I would suggest that if you cannot love your brother and sister with whom you share this world, then you cannot truly love yourself.

The good news is that God has not left us in this dilemma to die. He has made a way for us to be set free from the destructive power of sin—through faith and trust in His Son. The penalty of sin is death, and Jesus has forever broken the power death has over us. Come to Him in humility and be set free by the power of His love.

The Heavenward Call

27 Do you feel the Spirit of God calling you heavenward? From the day we are born each of us starts a journey that inevitably leads us to the conclusion of our life on this earth. For most of us that journey is long; and as we make our way through life we discover firsthand how becoming what God would have us be is really an inward struggle to discern His will and then find the faith to be obedient to it. Unfortunately, we also discover that there is an inner voice beckoning us away from God, away from heaven and toward a path that leads us toward self-destruction. It does not reveal itself to us as self-destruction, but that is the end result.

In the choice between right and wrong, most of us know what the right is, so discovering God's will in that area of our life isn't that difficult. The difficult part comes in **choosing** right over wrong. If we follow our natural impulses we will invariably choose the wrong, simply because our minds and bodies have been corrupted by the hidden power of sin. We can deny this all we please, but it is nonetheless true. Can a person still be a Christian and yet sin? Of course! No one that I know of has ever entered a state of sinlessness in this life. Yet, the Christian who sins will always feel convicted within by the wrongness of his or her act. God's Spirit will not cease to deal with our disobedience and hopefully it will eventually pry us loose from sin's power over us.

A sure sign of the active power of God within us is the awareness of a hunger to do good, even if we have not yet attained the power to do it. How wonderful of God to relentlessly pursue us and not give up on us! He allows us to feel miserable inwardly in the midst of our sinfulness! There is written within the fabric of each human being the longing to be what God intended for us to be. We may suppress it, resist it, override it, and even eventually still the quiet beckoning of His voice, but it is still within each of us.

In talking about this state of becoming what God would have us be, Paul writes to the Philippians:

> *Not that I have already obtained this or have already reached the goal; but I press on to make it my own, because Christ Jesus has made me his own, but this one thing I do: forgetting what lies behind and straining forward to what lies ahead, I press on toward the goal to win the prize for which God has called me heavenward in Christ Jesus" (Philippians 3:12-14, NRSV).*

All of us have been and are being called "heavenward" by the Lord who loves us. We need to follow Paul's example and forget the things of the past, which we cannot undo, and reach for that which is yet in our future—in other words, the ideal for which Christ would have us strive. We become serious about our faith as a Christian when our sincere desire becomes a longing to be what Christ would have us be. Apart from His power we cannot become that. But with the assurance of His grace to guide us, neither can we fail. Pause now in your life and look within. Do you hear the voice of God calling, "Come this way, my child"? Then you are being called heavenward. Why wouldn't you want to go?

The Reality of Jesus

28 In the Gospel of John our Lord says, "You diligently study the Scriptures because you think that by them you possess eternal life. These are the Scriptures that testify about me, yet you refuse to come to me to have life" (John 5:39-40). These words are applicable not just to the Pharisees to whom He spoke, but to anyone who thinks that anything (even the Bible) will gain them eternal life apart from our Lord. The Bible is the revelation of God; the book itself is not to be worshipped.

March

Churches that are alive and growing are churches in which Jesus Christ is recognized as Lord and where individuals live in a daily relationship of love with Him who died to redeem them. It is not enough to simply say, "Jesus is Lord of my life." We must reveal that truth by allowing Him to direct our lives. He said, "If you love Me, you will keep My commandments. . . . Apart from Me, you can do nothing." At the heart of a Christian's life there should be more than religion, there should be "a relationship." Jesus is a real live being, He is far more than words on a page, even if the book is called "Holy." Jesus is the Word of God made flesh! He is all we ever need to know about who God is and how God relates to our world. It was not a Book that was crucified on a cross for us, but a Person.

Why, one might ask, should I love Jesus? Why should I give Him my utmost loyalty? The answer is really quite simple. Because it was He who not only gave you life, but redeemed it after you lost it in sin. We love our parents because they gave us life; they loved us and nurtured us into maturity. Jesus is greater than our parents and loves us far more than they, no matter how great their love for us may be. There is no greater transforming power in the world than the power of love. It can take the worst among us and transform him or her into the best. It can take a legalistic Pharisee named Paul, who was having Christians put to death for their faith, and make him into the greatest apostle the world has ever known.

Jesus' love has the power to take the darkness of our lives and make them become instruments of glorious light. He can take our greatest weakness and empower it to become one of our greatest strengths. He can take the heaviest burden we have to bear and set us free from its weight. "Oh, that's just pious nonsense!" you say. But it isn't! The happiest people I know in the world are the ones who walk daily with Him whom they call Lord. They have discovered and tapped into the Source of life and the author of happiness and holiness.

Jesus offers us more than eternal life; He offers us joyful life now! We human beings are slowly discovering that we cannot have joy and peace in life apart from Him who is the embodiment of those things. "My peace, I give you; not as the world gives, give I unto you," Jesus says. I fear that we have let a lifetime of hearing words about

March

Jesus dull our senses and hide from our perception the reality of His real presence. Let us begin to truly search the Scriptures for Him and allow the Holy Spirit to bring to our consciousness the reality of His Presence. Come, let's begin the glorious journey together!

When You Don't Feel Needed

29 Has there been a time in your life that you were so busy you felt like there wasn't enough of you to go around? Then count your blessings! How wonderful it is to feel needed! We all begin to look forward to retirement; then we settle into a routine of having little meaningful activity in our lives and we are disillusioned. One of the things that gives our life purpose is to feel needed. Unfortunately, many people—a lot of them senior citizens—begin to feel like their lives don't matter anymore. As a result they feel sad, lonely, and depressed.

It doesn't have to be that way! Every human being is important to God and should be important to us. No one is placed on this earth without a purpose. No matter who you are, your life touches and interacts with other human beings. You influence people in ways you cannot imagine. Perhaps you're homebound or bedridden and you feel that your life doesn't count for much. But how many people's lives can be made better by the courage they see in you, by the smile you can offer out of the midst of life's problems?

In *Book of Comfort* (p. 94), Alvin Rogness writes,

> *He never knew it, but I needed him. He was totally paralyzed with arthritis, lying in his bed like a board. Except for his alert, sparkling eyes and his warm smile, he didn't move, but he had an inner radiance. I never left him but any lingering self-pity was smashed to bits. He put me on my feet again to face life with cheer. He was no obsolete machine. He may never have known how important he was to me and to others, but God knew. It must have been such awareness that led John Milton, blind at 44, to say in his ode,* <u>On His Blindness</u> *"They also serve who only stand and wait."*

March

The measure of our importance is not how much we produce, but if we have added any value to another human being's life. Each of us can do that! Try walking down a hall at work, or in a hospital, or on the street, and when you meet a stranger give them a smile and say, "Hello, how are you?" Simple, isn't it? Yet in that brief moment you have let a complete stranger know that their aliveness is acknowledged; that another human being is taking note of their presence, and you have allowed them to see a tiny bit of your heart through your smile.

Brother Lawrence (a 16th century monk) wrote, "We should never grow weary of doing little things for the glory of God; who regards not the greatness of the act, but the love in which it is performed" (*The Practice of the Presence of God*). Few people do "great" things; everyone can do small but important things! If you are at a point in your life in which you don't feel needed, do something that will make someone else feel needed. Out of their need being met you will discover your own self-worth.

For years I watched my wife's mother endure the excruciating pain of severe rheumatoid arthritis. She didn't live a day without intense pain. But I never heard her complain that she had been treated unfairly. She always had a good word to say and a smile to offer. When I left her home I always felt the world was made richer because she was in it. Likewise, the world is made richer because you're in it too! You are important. You are needed!

Thankfulness in the Midst of Trouble

30 It's not difficult to feel thankful when good things happen to us. If we have a serious illness and pray for healing and it comes, we feel great joy in our heart—which almost always erupts in prayers of thanksgiving to God. Or, if we are abundantly blessed with the material things of life, there is often a secure feeling in our heart which leads us to thank the Lord for our blessings. But are we able to give thanks to God when we are in the midst of scarcity, or when things aren't going all that well?

It is interesting how similar the passages are in Paul's letters to the Ephesians and to the Thessalonians. To the Ephesians (5:18-20) he writes: ". . . be filled with the Spirit, speaking to one another in psalms, hymns, and spiritual songs, singing and making melody in your heart to the Lord, giving thanks always to God the Father in the name of Jesus Christ.". In his advice to the Thessalonians (5:16-18) he says, "Rejoice always; pray without ceasing; in everything give thanks; for this is the will of God in Christ Jesus for you."

Did Paul practice what he preached? Look at Acts 16:23-25. Paul and Silas were severely beaten by the Philippians and had been thrown into prison in chains. You would think that they would have been complaining to God about how unfair it was; after all, they were attempting to do His will and for their trouble He had allowed them to be beaten and imprisoned. Instead, the scripture says that at midnight, Paul and Silas were singing hymns and offered praise to God. In the midst of their praising God, the earth quaked, the walls shook, the doors of the cells flew open, and the chains around their arms and feet fell loose to the ground. In dramatic fashion, God sent us a message— there is freedom to be found in the mystery of praise and thanksgiving!

When we praise God in the midst of our problems, our problems may not suddenly disappear, but the imprisonment of our hearts and souls will dissolve. In the place of worry and anxiety God sends forth the freedom of peace. Frustration gives way to trust and the power of God becomes energized in our life. I know of what I speak. In the midst of the traumatic news of being told I had a large malignant mass in my abdomen, I turned to God in praise, thanking Him for His goodness and asked only that He be glorified in my illness. The result? There was never a moment when I was robbed of peace. Indeed, I was drawn closer in love to God than I had ever been in my life. Will I be cured of cancer? I don't know and it really isn't a priority in my life. What is most important is that I be given the joy of living my life with a conscious awareness of how great my Lord's love is for me. I have that awareness and it is joy beyond words.

Some will say that to praise God in the midst of trouble is escapism; it is a refusal to live with reality, and withdrawal into denial. I refute such claims, for I have found that to praise God in the midst of trouble is to enter the realm of the spirit where life is most real. Every day can be a day of Thanksgiving. Rather than spend that day

March

depressed about our troubles, let us pause and give thanks to God for His goodness, even if we find ourselves in the midst of some problem.

The True Kingdom

31 Jesus Christ came into the world to establish a spiritual kingdom, of that there can be little doubt. If that is true, then we will never be within that kingdom until we become conscious of and willing to discover the importance of our own spiritual nature. We may offer prayers with our lips and with thoughts which are derived in our minds, but unless we are willing to allow them to flow from the depth of our spiritual nature, they will largely be ineffective.

In John's Gospel (3:5), Jesus informs Nicodemus (a very religious man) that unless a person is born of water **and the spirit,** he or she cannot enter the kingdom of God. The reference to water is apparently to baptism, since two chapters earlier (1:33) John the Baptist makes a connection between the baptism of water, and the baptism of spirit which is brought about by Jesus Himself (". . . the One who sent me to baptize with water said to me, 'He on whom you see the Spirit descend and remain is the one who baptizes with the Holy Spirit'").

Baptism is a sacrament of the church because it was commanded by our Lord for those who would follow Him (Mt. 28:19). But baptism apart from the spiritual presence of God in one's life is really meaningless. Water baptism is but one step in a person's life in becoming what God would have us be. In baptism, God's grace is actively at work in the person's life, but it does not end with the ritual. Far more significant than having water poured or sprinkled on one's head, or being immersed in water, is the baptism that comes through the Spirit of God. As I understand the Bible, that baptism will come only to the heart that hungers to have God's presence live within. God does not invade and conquer the human heart, He comes in only by invitation and a sincere desire on the part of a person to make room for His presence.

If you carefully study the teachings of Jesus, you will find that He always placed the greatest emphasis on the inner person. Even in the Sermon on the Mount where moral and ethical instruction is given,

April

Jesus makes quite clear that it must begin in the heart and soul. The Beatitudes (Mt. 5:1-12) talk about inner realities (meekness, poor in spirit, merciful, hunger and thirst for righteousness, etc.). Even the outward act of adultery He proclaims to be a problem that emanates from the heart already corrupted by sinful lust. Any way you look at it, sin is a spiritual problem even though many of the outward manifestations of its presence may be seen in some observable physical act.

The Pharisees thought they could be right with God simply through the outward observance of laws or in refraining from doing something that was observable as a sin. But Jesus said, "Unless your righteousness exceeds that of the scribes and Pharisees you will never enter the kingdom of heaven" (Mt. 5:20). The Pharisees worked at trying to be holy, but it is only the Spirit of God that can create holiness within us. Self-derived holiness will inevitably lead to self-righteousness which is sin in itself. Only God's Spirit actively working within us (by invitation!) will ever draw us into the true kingdom. Our baptism of water is important, but without God's Spirit making us into a new creation, it will never usher us into the kingdom.

The Process of Becoming

1 Misty Mowery tells the story of a man who bought a home with a tree in the backyard. It was winter, and nothing marked this tree as different from any other tree. When spring came, the tree grew leaves and tiny pink buds. "How wonderful!" thought the man. "A flower tree! I will enjoy its beauty all summer". But before he had time to enjoy the flowers, the wind began to blow and soon all the petals were strewn in the yard. "What a mess", he thought. "This tree isn't any use after all".

The summer passed and one day the man noticed the tree was full of green fruit the size of large nuts. He picked a large one and took a bite. "Bleagh!" he cried, and threw it to the ground. "What a horrible taste! This tree is worthless. Its flowers are so fragile the wind blows them away, and its fruit is terrible and bitter. When winter comes, I'm cutting it down." But the tree took no notice of the man and continued to draw water from the ground and warmth from the sun and in late fall produced crisp red apples.

April

Some of us see Christians with their early blossoms of happiness and think they should be that way forever. Or we see bitterness in their lives, and we're sure they will never bear the fruit of joy. Could it be that we forget that some of the best fruit ripens late? People often dismiss the reality of Christianity because they look at the lives of those who claim Christ as Lord and see very imperfect creatures. What they fail to realize is that being a Christian is a journey toward perfection, not an immediate experience of it in this life.

We are not born with fully developed bodies. We start small and grow. Along the way our bodies encounter diseases and we're knocked down, but slowly our immune system takes hold and most often rids us of that which would take life from us. We do not come into this world with minds saturated with knowledge and wisdom, but only over a lifetime of living do we gain insight and understanding. Why then do we think that our spiritual development should be instantaneous? Our bodies grow and develop as we feed and nourish them. Our minds expand and become useful as we allow information to flow into them. Our spirits will blossom when we are willing to nourish them with the Spirit of God and feed them with the Word of life.

All of us are in the process of becoming. It's a lifetime process that best develops as we yield ourselves to the will and power of Him who has created us. If we live to be old, the body will eventually reach a point where it begins to decline and deteriorate. It will grow weaker and eventually give way to death, because it was not created to last forever. However, the spirit, allowed to be nurtured by God, will only grow stronger and more complete because that is the part that God intended to be eternal.

Therefore, rejoice, my brothers and sisters, for no matter what our weakness, no matter how far short we fall of perfection, we have the assurance that, if willing, we will eventually be transformed into that wondrous fruit that God intended for us to become.

Living in Christ

In his book *The Hidden Adventure*, Tim Hansel writes, "Contrary to what you may have heard, we are not called to live for Christ. We're called to live in Christ. . . . The Christian life

April

is not just one of imitation—but habitation." As long as our desire is to live for Christ, we ensure that we will be the ones who maintain control of our thoughts and our actions. But when we come to the place of yearning to live in Christ, we have surrendered our wills to His.

We cannot truly live godly lives until we are willing to let God live in us. The more of the Spirit of Christ that we allow in, the more the Spirit of Christ can flow out of us. J. Rufus Moseley reminds us: "We will be what we want to be when we receive from Him what He is and give what we receive and give only what we receive" (Perfect Everything, pp. 68-69). That part of us where we will not let Christ dwell is the part of us that we will not allow to be redeemed. When we harbor resentments, unforgiveness, unclean thoughts, hidden anger, selfishness, and unkind feelings, we have built protective barriers around those things within us which God longs to redeem but which we will not yield to Him. Thus, we try to build our relationship with God by constructing little dams within ourselves. When we do not allow God's Spirit to flow through us, we become stagnant and limit God's ability to use us for His glory.

We cannot give that which we do not have and we cannot keep that which we will not give away. The loving Spirit of God was not offered to us to be hoarded but to be given away. Do you long to live in union with Christ? Then you must be willing to let the Spirit of Christ dwell in and flow through you. When we allow Christ's Spirit to go out from us to another, it comes back to us in increased measure.

The Christian life is one that is lived in the realm of holy love. To dwell in that kingdom is to dwell in the midst of holy love and to be willing to give holy love. Holy love is love that is God-centered, God-directed, and God-empowered. It is not simply human goodwill, human kindness, and human concern. The purpose of holy love is not to injure or destroy, but to heal, build up, and lift others to the plane of resurrected glory. When we seek God only for ourselves, we search in vain. When we seek God for the purpose of giving ourselves to Him in obedient service then we discover the magnificence of His love.

Jesus tells us in John's Gospel, "I am the vine, you are the branches. He who abides in Me, and I in him, bears much fruit; for without Me you can do nothing." The purpose of abiding in Christ is

April

not self-gratification, but selfless service. Too many want the glory of Christ without the cross of Christ. We want the peace, joy, and happiness God promises, but we don't want to surrender the things within us which would allow those qualities to be ours.

When we come to the point of being willing to dwell in Christ we will have discovered the abiding place of love, peace, and joy. Until then we continue to be the architects of our own unhappiness.

Free From the Fear of Death

3 Someone once said that human beings are the only animals that have a consciousness of their own mortality. We may not dwell on it, but we each know that there is a day out in the future in which our life on this earth will be over. More so than any of us, Jesus was acutely aware of His death and the means whereby it would come. And yet, it did not frighten Him, nor did He seek to avoid it. Perhaps that is so because He was equally aware that what we call death is not the end of life but, in a real sense, the beginning.

If we find ourselves afraid of death, we need to ask why. Are we afraid because we are uncertain of what lies beyond? Do we feel fear because we have not made peace with God, other people, or perhaps ourselves? Have we fallen so much in love with this world that we would rather cling to it than embrace the beauty of eternity? To fear death is to deny faith the opportunity to bring peace to your soul. It is **not** the will of God that we should be afraid of death, for its power is not greater than God's.

When our fear of death ceases, our ability to live in peace and joy in this world increases. We are no longer bound, no longer held captive in this life by death's power. Instead, we are set free to enjoy each moment here for we know only that which is better awaits us. It all comes back to God. In His power is life and death and if we are His then life is always His gift to us. If the only power death really has is to usher us into that eternal life with God which He longs for us to have, then why should we be afraid?

You may say to yourself, "But I have sinned and God will condemn me and punish me eternally for my sin." But read again the

April

words of John 3:17. "God did not send His Son into the world to condemn the world, but that the world through Him might be saved!" Or read Romans 8:1-2, "There is therefore now no condemnation for those who are in Christ Jesus. For the law of the Spirit of life in Christ Jesus has set you free from the law of sin and of death." Read II Peter 3:9, "It is not God's will that any should perish, but that all should come to repentance." And if you say, "All that may be true, but my own heart condemns me for I know the terrible things I have done," then read I John 3:20, "For if our heart condemns us, God is greater than our heart, and knows all things."

Only God could break the power of death; not only its power to end life as we know it, but its power to hold us captive in fear of its coming. By experiencing death on the cross for us, and rising from the dead, Christ forever showed to the world that death's power is only an illusion—a mask that attempts to hide from us the reality of its impotence. Believe our Lord's words and you can be set free to live life here without a moment's fear of that point in time in which you make the great transition from this life to the life that God has longed for you to have. Jesus said, "I have come that you might have life, and have life more abundantly." Will you dare to believe Him? It's the truth! "Then you will know the truth and the truth will set you free. ... So if the Son sets you free, you will be free indeed" (John 8:32, 36).

Faith on a Tombstone

4 Faith cannot be put under a microscope and analyzed. It cannot be touched or seen except as it blossoms forth from the life of someone who has chosen to live it. We discern faith in the trusting acts of people who sometimes—in spite of overwhelming odds—rise above that which seeks to defeat them.

One of the greatest examples of faith I ever came upon I found in an old cemetery outside of the small town of Enfield, NC. It was at a little white wooden church called Whitaker's Chapel (a national historic site of one of the earliest churches in Methodism). On that particular warm spring day, I decided to stop and walk through the old cemetery that dated back to the Revolutionary War. As I made my way slowly through the grave sites, I came upon a plot that was filled

April

with some old markers. I stooped down and brushed away the dirt that had become encrusted over the engraved letters. A name appeared with this inscription—*Annie May Wheat, 1851 - 1852, The Lord gave and the Lord hath taken away; blessed be the name of the Lord.* I felt a stab of intense pain as I reflected on how it must have hurt those parents to have lost a child that was less than a year old.

I stood up to move on but noticed another little tombstone next to the one I had just read. Again I brushed away the built-up dirt and found these words: *Lawrence Gary Wheat (Son of L.C. and Annie H. Wheat), Dec. 1852 - March 1855, Suffer the little children to come unto me, and forbid them not; For of such is the kingdom of heaven.* How tragic! L.C. and Annie Wheat, had lost a second child that was only two years and three months old. I wondered what horrible disease or accident had taken their children from them and marveled at the evidence of faith revealed in the scripture verses they had chosen. They did not condemn God; rather, their statement of faith revealed that they believed their children were in the hands of a loving Creator.

Once more I rose to leave, but froze in my tracks as I noticed another small tombstone next to the first two. I began to think, "Surely they didn't lose another child!" With haste and anticipation I removed the remaining dirt from the little stone and my heart ached as I read the brief words which told the story—*Charles M. Wheat, age 11 years and 8 months.* (No dates were given so I don't know the year he died). What I did know was that this couple had lost a daughter and two sons while they were still children. How shattered they must have been! My eyes became fixed upon their final inscription on this little stone that would become a monument to their faith. The words read: *I've buried the last one under this fresh made sod. With a heart broken, yet trusting in God.*

A huge lump arose in my throat and warm tears flowed down my cheeks. What tremendous faith these parents must have had! All three of their children taken from them—hearts that were broken, and yet, still trusted in God. More than a century after Annie and L.C. had laid to rest their beloved children, their faith in God continued to be proclaimed to all who would pause and behold it. My faith got a boost that day. I learned a lot about God and myself. I also learned that faith can be measured in the words and lives of those who are willing to reveal it.

The Touch of Faith

5 Trust is such an elusive thing; one moment we feel we have it and the next it has slipped away from us and we feel the creeping walls of doubt and fear pressing in against us. We hunger for something firm to hold on to that will cause our uncertainty to evaporate.

Perhaps we are like the little girl who was touring the Carlsbad Caverns in New Mexico for the first time. Her father was walking just ahead of her, carrying her younger brother. That arrangement was fine as long as the path was broad and level. But the path grew narrow and a bit steep as they descended into the Cavern. She said, "Daddy, hold my hand!" Her father reassured her at once, "Honey, you're just fine. I'm right here with you."

This calmed her for a time but suddenly the trail was rougher and slick from water dripping from the formations. The little girl, relatively brave up to now, again spoke, "Daddy, hold my hand!" Once more, her father demurred, "I can't, I'm holding your brother. You're all right. Why don't you believe me?" The girl had an instant reply, "Because only my ears know you're ahead of me. My hand doesn't" (Source Unknown).

Faith is an easy concept to grasp but sometimes a difficult reality to hold on to. When all is well it's easy to make pronouncements of belief, but when life begins to squeeze us, our faith and trust in God dissipates when our requests aren't instantly granted in the way that we have asked them. We become very aware of the limitations of our humanity and we want to feel the hand of God firmly grasping our own.

God often comes to us through the words and touch of other human beings. To deny someone that encounter when they need to feel God's presence is a disservice. When you visit someone who is sick, don't be afraid to touch them, to hug them, to speak words of affection, for those acts can literally become acts of healing. It was not by chance that the early church offered with prayers for healing, the

April

laying on of hands. There's nothing magical about touching someone; it simply meets a deep hunger in the human soul to be touched when life is going wrong.

As children, when we are frightened or hurt, the one thing we long for more than anything else is to be touched and loved. Kissing the mashed finger of a child really does make it better because a child's soul soaks up the healing power of love in ways we seem to forget when we are adults. How unfortunate it is that as we grow into adults we often leave behind the most profound feelings of trust and faith, because somewhere along the way we conclude that it is childish to trust.

Isn't it interesting that when God designed our bodies, He made our arms long enough to surround another in embrace (which depicts the act of pulling one inside our hearts)? Jesus' death on a cross uniquely reveals that God stands before us not only sharing the pain of human life, but also stretching out both arms to welcome us into the love of His heart. Do you need to be touched? So does someone else. Never forget, when you touch someone else you are being touched as well.

The Empowering Renovation

6 While sitting in one of the workshops at Frazer Memorial UMC in Montgomery, Alabama, I was listening to the speaker talk about our role as Christians in terms of our living our faith in our church communities. I found myself writing the following words in my notebook: *Jesus did not die on a cross so that we could sit in a pew and feel grateful. He died on a cross so that we could be empowered to go into the world and serve Him.* I think that too often many people who join churches assume that what is expected of them is to simply come to church and absorb whatever is offered them in worship; rise from their pews and then go out thinking that their Christian responsibility to Jesus has been satisfied.

Everyone who sincerely desires to become a Christian is led to that decision by the alluring grace of God. We may not be aware of it, but it is God's Spirit gently leading and sometimes prodding us to

April

come to Him and commit our lives to where He leads. Whom God calls, God empowers. To be empowered means to be given the gift, talent or grace to serve God in some area of ministry. I truly believe every single Christian is given some talent, gift or ability that not only can be used for God's glory, but is expected by God to be used for His glory. Our challenge is to first discover what that gift is and then be willing to yield it in service to Him who died to empower us.

What makes Frazer Memorial a unique and powerful church is that they have tapped into the power of God in individual lives. Laity have been taught, and have embraced the idea, that God desires and expects them to serve one another with the gifts which He has provided them. The most beautiful thing about what I observed was not only the sincere desire to serve (that I saw on the faces and in the lives of the laity of Frazer) but the joy which they revealed in committing their lives to active and intentional ministry to their community.

One of the great tenets of the Protestant Reformation which we as United Methodists profess to believe, is the concept of the "priesthood of all believers." That means that we believe each person who comes to Christ is given the responsibility to minister to others. Unfortunately, what has occurred over the years is that we have wedded ourselves to the notion that ministry is what the paid ordained person does. That was never the teaching of the early church. If you have accepted Christ as your Lord, then you have accepted the idea that you are called to serve Him.

Most churches are sleeping giants that have not awakened to that notion. If you will take the time to look carefully at your church, you will begin to see evidence that God is moving you to deeper commitment and service. People need to discover joy in their faith and fulfillment in their service to our Lord. There needs to be a renewed hunger to learn about our Savior and to devote ourselves to deepening our relationship with Him. Churches are one commitment away from witnessing the birth pangs of a new creation. If you want to be part of the mighty moving of God, then go to church and behold the outpouring of God's Spirit. I promise you the renovation of one's soul will far outshine the renovation of a building.

April

Because We're Christians

7 Some time ago a pastor-friend of mine called to keep in touch and see how things were going. He is now serving a United Methodist church up in the mountains of western Pennsylvania. Greg was telling me about a family in their community whose house caught on fire. The community in which he lives consists of about a thousand people.

In response to the need of this family, his church took up an offering to try and help. They raised over $800. Later in the week, one of his church members asked Greg, "Preacher, why are we helping those folks? Why, they aren't even Christians!" Greg's response was simple and to the point: "We are!"

Sometimes we too fall into the trap that Greg's parishioner fell into—the trap of being only concerned with ourselves and those who think and act as we do. The famous words which were inscribed on John Wesley's tombstone reveal his attitude and what that of Methodism has always been, "The world is my parish!"

Many churches make the mistake of turning inward, which is the surest way to become a dying church. Jesus' command was "go into **all** the world, and make disciples." Just as turning inward is a certain step toward spiritual disaster, conversely, for the church to focus its attention outwardly is a dynamic sign of a growing, thriving church, alive with the Spirit of Christ.

The basic inclination for fallen humanity is to center life on ourselves and on those whom we love. That in and of itself is not bad, unless our concern excludes others outside the small little circle we have drawn. The reason that Methodism swept this nation by storm in its early years was because people seemed to genuinely care for the bodies and souls of strangers. Circuit-riding preachers followed the wagon tracks as far west as they went, and wherever a settlement was begun, the Methodist preacher was there to proclaim God's grace to those who would listen.

As powerful and significant as the preached Word was to early Methodists (and I think it was one of their greatest strengths), they were not content to save the soul and ignore the body. Schools and

April

orphanages were established. Clothing was distributed to the poor and help was provided for the unemployed and those unable to care for themselves. Loans were made to help those with financial needs and dispensaries were established to help those who were sick.

Our Methodist ancestors were on the cutting edge of social concern for those who suffered with deep need. It was a balanced mixture of passion to save souls and compassion for human need. The two are inextricably joined in a church that is faithfully following the teaching of our Lord. Take a look at your church and ask yourself how you think you are doing. Do you have a balanced ministry that involves much of the congregation? Why not begin to be a church filled with meaningful activity, not just for yourselves but for others? Then when someone asks you why you are doing what you're doing, why not just say, "Because I am a Christian."

Nothing Wasted

8 In the book *The Fire of Your Life*, Maggie Ross recounts the story of Emma, a survivor of the Holocaust, who regularly at four p.m. each day stood outside a Manhattan church and screamed insults at Jesus. Finally, the pastor, Bishop C. Kilmer Myers, went outside and said to Emma, "Why don't you go inside and tell him?" She disappeared into the church.

An hour went by, and the bishop, worried, decided to look in on her. He found Emma prostrate before the cross, absolutely still. Reaching down, he touched her shoulder. She looked up with tears in her eyes and said quietly, "After all, he was a Jew, too."

At the heart of the gospel is the message that God intimately identifies with our pain, our sickness, our sin, and our guilt. "God was in Christ reconciling the world unto himself. . . . For he hath made him to be sin for us, who knew no sin; that we might be made the righteousness of God in him" (II Corinthians 5:19, 21, KJV) "Surely he has borne our griefs and carried our sorrows: . . .He was wounded for our transgressions, he was bruised for our iniquities: the chastisement of our peace was upon him; and with his stripes we are healed" (Isaiah 53:4-5, KJV).

April

There are times in life when things go wrong. People we love get sick and die; friends or family members are struck down by some horrible tragedy. We lose our jobs, or we are betrayed by a spouse or loved one. A thousand calamities can befall us and in those moments when we feel most alone, most downcast, we need to do like Emma and prostrate ourselves before the cross. For it is there that God dramatically reminds us that He cares so much about our pain that He suffers with us.

Jesus was a Jew, and yes, Jews have known more than their share of suffering in this world; but Jesus suffered for every human being, not a select few. When finally we begin to realize that God suffers with and for us, perhaps our pain will not be quite as intense; we will not feel quite so alone, and we will finally have begun that first step toward being made whole again.

A wise person once said, "He who is born in the fire will not fade in the sun. If God therefore lets us be born in the fire of adversity and difficulty, depend upon it, He is only making sure we will not fade in the sun of smaller difficulties of human living." (Author Unknown). In his classic book *Christ and Human Suffering*, E. Stanley Jones says that there is nothing about our lives that God allows to be wasted, not even our pain. Jones writes: ". . . either He will heal us from the infirmity or else he will give us power to use the infirmity" (p. 90)."

The image of Jesus willingly dying on a cross for us should forever remind us that God has never allowed us to endure anything alone. He shares it with us. Bring your pain to the cross and there you will discover that in the heart of God, it has already been nailed.

Is Church Really Important?

9 Is there really any value in attending church? I once asked a group of children during a children's sermon to tell me what they liked most and least about church. One child, in obvious reference to the sermon, said he disliked the <u>long</u> commercial! Why do people come back Sunday after Sunday to hear someone talk to them again and again about a story they already know? Is it just possible that something is being imparted that is more significant than any

April

combination of words or noble thoughts which the preacher might convey?

In an article in an issue of *Glass Window*, a contributor recalls that several years ago, *The British Weekly* published this provocative letter:

> *Dear Sir:*
>
> *It seems ministers feel their sermons are very important and spend a great deal of time preparing them. I have been attending church quite regularly for 30 years and I have probably heard 3,000 of them. To my consternation, I discovered I cannot remember a single sermon. I wonder if a minister's time might be more profitably spent on something else?*

For weeks a storm of editorial responses ensued . . . finally ended by this letter:

> *Dear Sir:*
>
> *I have been married for 30 years. During that time I have eaten 32,850 meals—mostly my wife's cooking. Suddenly I have discovered I cannot remember the menu of a single meal. And yet . . . I have the distinct impression that without them, I would have starved to death long ago.*

The apostle Paul once wrote, ". . . it pleased God through the foolishness of preaching to save them that believe" (I Corinthians 1:21). Worship and preaching may seem foolish to some, but when a person has a spiritual encounter with the Living Christ, "church" becomes an immeasurable blessing. As long as one attempts to experience God only with the mind, the reality of the presence of God will seem very small. Only when God is encountered with the heart, soul, and mind will one begin to realize the value of worship.

When John Wesley had his heartwarming experience at Aldersgate, it was not due to the eloquent preaching of some distinguished minister, but through the words of a layman who was simply reading Martin Luther's Preface to his commentary on the Epistle to the Romans. Wesley states that he went "very unwillingly"

April

to the service that night (May 24, 1738), yet, it became a life-changing event for him. Why? Because he was searching for God with his heart and soul and was willing to put himself in a place where the simple message of God could transform his life.

Never underestimate the importance of your church. Through the years it will nurture you, by God's grace, in ways your mind cannot grasp, but without which your soul will be eternally poorer.

What Would Jesus Do?

10 Over the years, many lives have been greatly affected by the book, *In His Steps*, written by Charles Sheldon. It is the fictional story of a small community that was transformed by the visit of an unemployed stranger. Nobody in the community wanted to help the man and in a few short weeks he died. His death prompted the minister in the city to preach a sermon to the congregation imploring them to reconsider what it means to be a Christian. In order to do that, he suggested that they all agree to ask themselves the following question before making any major decision in their lives: "What would Jesus do?"

It seems to me that question is a good one for all of us to ask ourselves in attempting to make decisions. I once wrote an article to the editor of the local newspaper, lending my support to the proposed establishment of a house across the street from the church that I was serving. The purpose of the house was to help people with mental health problems. As a result of that letter I received both positive comments and negative ones. Many in our community (some of whom were members of my church) had reservations about using the house for the purpose stated. There were basically two major fears that were expressed. The first was that the neighborhood would be less safe if they brought in criminal elements of society (i.e., drug offenders, sex offenders, etc.). The Mental Health officials had assured us that would **not** be the case. The clients would be only those who have chronic mental health problems such as severe depression and other mental health issues that impair them from functioning in society. They would not be staying overnight.

April

The second objection was that such a facility in the community would cause property values to decline. However, studies done in other areas in which such homes had been established indicated that property values did not decline. In making my decision to support the home, I asked myself the question: "What would Jesus do?" For me, the answer was not difficult. I cannot possibly imagine Jesus doing anything other than welcoming such people into His presence. Indeed, the scriptures teach us that He was constantly condemned because He was perceived as spending too much time with those considered as outcasts by society—people such as prostitutes, tax collectors, lepers and "sinners."

Unfortunately, many people with mental health problems are often treated as outcasts. They are viewed with suspicion; sometimes with disdain. These people need our empathy, love, and support—not our rejection. I do not claim to have all the answers to such problems, but this much I believe with all my heart—God has called us to love one another and to intentionally reach out to those whose lives have been broken, no matter what the cause is for that brokenness.

When issues like these arise in your community, I hope that each of you will give prayerful thought to such matters and allow God's Spirit to guide you in coming to a decision. Jesus' haunting and comforting words that I hear are: "Come unto me all you who are heavy laden and burdened and I will give you rest."

Are We Truly the Church?

11 The word used in the Greek text of the New Testament for church is *ecclesia* (pronounced, eck clay see uh). It means "those who are called out" (called to live life different from the standards of a sinful world). And yet, those of us who make up the church are sinners ourselves. That which separates us from those outside the church is not self-attained righteousness, but that we believe in a Savior who will save sinners. We have faith!

Hans Küng, in his book *The Church,* says:

Faith in an ultimate and radical sense cannot be distinguished from love. It is a personal activity towards a personal recipient.

April

Faith is never, in the final analysis, a matter of adherence to objects, rules, or dogmas, but is the sacrifice and self-giving of one person to another.

In other words, what we have faith in is a Person, and that faith is revealed to those around us by our willingness to sacrifice our self-will for the benefit of others. In surrendering ourselves to Christ in faith, we surrender ourselves to others in service. To simply join a church with the thought in mind that membership ensures salvation, is a cruel deception. **Faith in Christ ensures salvation.** Devotion and service through the church is the outward manifestation of one's faith in Christ.

Where faith is genuine, the true church exists within the man-made church. Where true faith exists, the gifts (charisms–Gk.) of the Spirit are evident. It is a foolish notion that any leader in the church should think that the true church can function apart from the gifts of the Spirit which God willingly bestows upon those who are "the called out." Perhaps one of the major reasons that the institutional church is often ineffective is because we seek to do "religious work" rather than allow our faith to flow through the gifts of the Spirit which are the outward manifestations of God working through us.

Some of the gifts of the Spirit (listed in I Corinthians 12:7f) are: wisdom, knowledge, faith, healing, miracles, prophecy, spiritual discernment, tongues, and the interpretation of tongues. These are not the only spiritual gifts which God bestows; others are listed elsewhere in Scripture, such as: service and teaching (Romans 12:7), helping and administration (I Corinthians 12:28). All the gifts are given for the purpose of mutual benefit for the building up of the community of faith. They are not intended to be used for personal gain, or spiritual self-righteousness.

If we are the "called out," what are we called out from? What makes you different from the non-Christian? And please don't answer, "I go to Sunday School and Church." That's religion and *may be* evidence of faith. But in large measure your faith will be revealed more by what you do Monday through Saturday, than by what you do on Sunday morning. I'm looking for our church to be the ecclesia. Are you?

April

Membership or Discipleship?

12 In 1967 Daniel Walker wrote in his book *Enemy in the Pew*:

> *There is a natural tendency for us to equate membership in the church with discipleship to Jesus Christ. But they are not synonymous, and the one does not necessarily follow from the other. Membership nails down; discipleship pulls us loose. Membership draws us in; discipleship sends us out. Membership pays its dues and claims its rights; discipleship makes any sacrifice, asking nothing in return.* (p. 6)

Perhaps years ago he put his finger on what should be obvious but apparently isn't—membership in a church does not make us Christian disciples any more than owning a piano makes us a musician. I think that mainline churches have stopped growing because we have lost our zeal to make disciples and instead we have settled on adding names to a roll (or worse yet, refused to be concerned about the continuing dramatic decline in the numbers of people committing their lives to Christ). Unwittingly, we have done exactly what Dietrich Bonhoeffer wrote about when he talked about how the church had made God's grace cheap. He said in part that grace is made cheap when:

> *The sacraments, the forgiveness of sin, and the consolations of religion are thrown away at cut rate prices. Grace is represented as the Church's inexhaustible treasury, from which she showers blessings with generous hands, without asking questions or fixing limits. Grace without price; grace without cost!* (*The Cost of Discipleship*, p. 45)

The difference between a church member and a disciple is that one joins an institution by repeating required words, while the other unites him or herself with a Person through faithful obedience. To be a disciple requires us to move God to the center of our life and our own will to the periphery. It means we learn first hand how differently God views our world from the comfortable way we see it. Modern

April

society has grown comfortable with choosing that which makes our life the easiest and requires the least from us. As a result, not only have our bodies grown flabby and weak, our minds dull and uncreative, but most importantly, our souls have become spiritually anorexic.

We have fallen victim to the Siren call of the world that deludes us into believing that following Jesus demands too much and gives too little. The reality is that to truly follow Jesus—no matter what the cost—gives more to our lives than anything we can buy, trade, or possess. You cannot buy peace, joy, hope, love, happiness, and contentment. You cannot manufacture it, steal it, or create it. They are all gifts that come from God to the heart that surrenders in joyful obedience to the very One who created your life from the beginning.

Whether your church declines or joins the ranks of churches bursting at the seams with growth will be in direct proportion to your congregation's willingness to seek God in prayer and surrender to Him in the faithful obedience of discipleship. For the church that truly seeks discipleship, growth isn't an option, it is an inevitable result.

I Have Learned . . .

13 The past few days we have learned that cancer has returned to my body. According to the doctors, three one-inch tumors have grown on my left kidney. Soon, I will be having surgery to remove the kidney and hopefully the remaining vestiges of the original tumor. I face this surgery with the same faith and trust in God that I had prior to my first operation.

My heart is heavy, not for myself but for all of you who seem so genuinely concerned and distressed about this latest discovery. Because I am not distressed by the illness, I think some folks feel I am in denial or unaware of the seriousness of this illness. But I'm not! I did not come to this place of faith overnight. For all these years, through all my mistakes, problems, sins, and weaknesses, God has been quietly working behind the scenes of my life, strengthening me for such an occasion as this. Truly, cancer has no power to make me afraid. Yes, it can rob my body of health, even cause my physical life to end. It can bring pain, nausea, and discomfort, but it cannot shake my faith in the God who has loved me even before my conception.

I struggle to put into words the joy and peace I feel in God's presence. Like Paul, I have truly learned in whatever state I am in, therewith to be content. If Satan's battle plan is to shake my faith and shatter me with cancer, he's wasting his time. I'm convinced that it is Satan that causes sickness and brings on death. The writer of Hebrews (2:14) says that Jesus came to "destroy him who has the power of death, that is, the devil, . . ." It is the nature of God to redeem, make whole and give life; therefore, since I know I belong to God, why should I fear Satan, sickness, or death?

What you see when you observe me happily going on with my life is not a man who is delusional or afraid to face the facts of life. To the contrary, what you are observing is the miraculous power of the living God sheltering me from the impotent power of Satan to rob me of the joy of my Lord. I find joy in my salvation. All that cancer has succeeded in doing is to cause me to snuggle ever more securely into the arms of Him who loved me and gives me life.

Satan may be permitted to pummel my body with illness, inflict it with cancer, causing doctors to remove part of me one organ at a time; but I bear witness to this truth—when I am down to the last part of me that is able to survive and that part also becomes afflicted, like the stones that would not be silent, I shall rise up and bless the Name of my Lord. I will sing His praise and declare the greatness of His love. And when at last this body lies silent, my soul will join the chorus of those who have gone before me and will bow before our God and cry, "Worthy is the Lamb to receive honor, glory, and praise."

I live on the mountaintop because that is where God has led me. Never in my entire life have I ever been happier or more content. Therefore, do not sorrow for me, but rejoice with me and give glory and praise to my God and yours.

Faith is Trust

14 Eugene Peterson tells of seeing a family of birds teaching their young to fly. Three young swallows were perched on a dead branch that stretched out over the lake.

April

"One adult swallow got alongside the chicks and started shoving them out toward the end of the branch—pushing, pushing, pushing. The end one fell off. Somewhere between the branch and the water four feet below, the wings started working, and the fledgling was off on his own. Then the second one.

"The third was not to be bullied. At the last possible moment his grip on the branch loosened just enough so that he swung downward, then tightened again, bulldog tenacious. The parent was without sentiment. He pecked at the desperately clinging talons until it was more painful for the poor chick to hang on than risk the insecurities of flying. The grip was released, and the inexperienced wings began pumping. The mature swallow knew what the chick did not—that it would fly—that there was no danger in making it do what it was perfectly designed to do." (From *Run with the Horses*).

Faith is really trust—trust that the God who has given us life will be with us in life and that no matter what happens to us He will see us through it. Jesus reminds us, "Your heavenly Father knows what you need, even before you ask Him" (Matthew 6:8). To live in a relationship of faithfulness with God is to believe that God is aware of our need and will provide for that need.

For the most part, I have come to the point in life where I no longer feel it necessary to lay out in great detail what I desire God to do in my life. Rather, I simply say, "Lord, here is my life, you know my needs better than I do, do in me that which pleases you and brings you glory." I have learned to trust God to meet the needs of my life in ways that please Him.

Do I hope that my body is healed of cancer? Of course I do! But even if it isn't, it does not cause me to question God's love for me. It has taken a long time, but I have reached the place where I can truly trust God with the details of my life. My energy is no longer spent in trying to figure out God's will for me, but in surrendering myself to Him and allowing Him to reveal to me ways He can use me; ways that I would never have chosen or imagined. I am discovering in the most profound ways the absolute reality of the peace and joy that comes with letting God be in control. Faith is discovering that the heart, mind, and soul are shielded by the power of God from anything that

April

desires to do them harm. The storms may blow, troubles may come, but the grace of our Lord stands in the breaches of life. He is the bridge over troubled waters. He is the rock upon which we stand. He is the Light that lightens our path. He is that power which the forces of hell cannot shake. And wonder of wonder, He tells us that we belong to Him!

Today is Our "If Only" Time

15 25,566—that's how many days you will live (counting the extra day in leap years) if you live seventy years. Days quickly come and go and like grains of sand in an hourglass cascading down the slippery side of the narrow funnel, they descend into the irretrievable receptor of the past. Of the days and hours you have lived, how many can you remember? How many have you allowed to be swallowed up in the void of insignificance because you used those moments in time by unthinkingly passing through them in some meaningless routine?

How much of life we take for granted! Somehow, we have encapsulated ourselves in the thick veil of illusion which hides from our consciousness the inevitability of our mortality. We go through day after day consciously denying and refusing to consider the possibility of our own death. Instead of viewing each day as a blessed and treasured gift of God, we squander it by allowing the routine and often mundane activities of our "typical" days to steal from us the glory and beauty of simply being alive. As thorough-going American capitalists we are consumed with the pursuit of making a living while we totally lose sight of making a life.

Our children grow up before our eyes and those treasured moments and experiences which we might have been able to look back on in later years will never be remembered because we didn't take time to let them happen as we passed through life. Work was more important, or school, or a dozen other things which seemed more appealing at the moment. While it is impossible to remember what we never experienced, it is not uncommon to think back with remorse and regret about what might have been. If only I had known . . . If only I

April

had taken the time . . . If only I could go back . . . If only, if only, if only . . . Today is our "if only" time. What we can't do next week or next year, we can do today.

Perhaps God gives us no greater blessings on this earth than our families, our friends, and opportunities to live life with Him. Unfortunately, like the prodigal son, we squander our treasures and too often they are irretrievably lost. I am reminded of the words of the Psalmist: "This is the day that the Lord has made, let us rejoice and be glad in it." How often we lose the joy of today because of our fear of tomorrow; only to discover that when tomorrow comes the fear was only an illusion. Even when future fears become reality, we have allowed them to invade our present and deprive us of the joy we could have known had we not let them consume our thoughts.

What is there that you have always wanted to do, but never took the time to do? What kind and loving word that might have been shared with another has plummeted to the depths of your forgetfulness because you let slip the opportunity to express it to another? Words and deeds of priceless value became engulfed in the abyss of "never happened" because we wouldn't take the time. Stop right now! Don't let your mind catapult you to some awaiting task, but stop and treasure the moment of your aliveness! Look around you—what blessings fill your life! Pause now, and give thanks to God, not only for all that has been given to you, but all the promises He holds out before you. Make up your mind that each day that passes you will diligently seek to be grateful for it, and do at least one thing each day which will bless another. You might just be surprised at how radically different life will become.

Resting In God

16 The past few weeks several people have remarked about my faith and said they wished they had it. It is not that I have great faith, it is I have discovered the joy of resting in God. When my wife told a friend of hers what I had said, her friend said, "Then tell him to teach me how to rest in God." That isn't easy to teach because for me it has come through a lifetime process of hungering to know God more intimately. Psalm 37:7 says, "Rest in

April

the Lord, and wait patiently for him." To rest in God is to seek Him in quietness and relax in His presence.

When I was a child I took swimming lessons at the local pool. One of the first things they tried to teach us was to lie on our backs and float. We had to learn to trust the water to keep us up. At first it was difficult because my natural tendency was to kick with my feet and splash with my hands. All that succeeded in doing was to make me sink. When finally the instructor convinced me to relax and be still, I discovered that my face remained above the surface of the water. It is somewhat the same with resting in God. If we are afraid He will let us sink, we panic and life overwhelms us. But if we take God at His word and trust Him, relax in that trust, we discover that nothing in life can overcome us.

Throughout scripture, reference is made to the "rest" which God provides. Quite often the rest spoken of is describing that state of absolute peace found in eternal life; but in other places it is speaking of a condition of calmness, trust, peace, and joy in the present life. A passage in Isaiah (30:15) finds the prophet telling the people of Israel that God offered them rest but they refused it: "For thus says the Lord God, the Holy One of Israel; In returning and rest shall ye be saved; in quietness and in confidence shall be your strength; and you would not" (KJV).

I have discovered that resting in God calls for obedience. When we become willing to seek His will and honestly try to do it, the peace of His rest comes upon us. Resting in God is living in union with His Spirit. It is discovering that there is no greater state of existence than to dwell constantly and consciously in the loving presence of God. When we finally reach the point that trusting and believing in God's love for us is the most important thing in our lives, then we will know what it is to rest in God. Then we will find that loving this world and remaining in it becomes secondary, **not unimportant,** but secondary to the joy of allowing God to set the course and boundaries for our lives.

There's a song that goes, *Turn your eyes upon Jesus, look full in His wonderful face, and the things of earth will grow strangely dim, in the light of His glory and grace.* There is tremendous truth in that

April

verse. It is not escapism from reality, as some vainly imagine; it is to enter a spiritual plane of existence that makes life most real. I can say God loves me, and that's one thing; but it takes on a totally different meaning when I begin to live my life as if I believe it is true. That is resting in God and that is what brings peace to the heart, mind, and soul. In that state of existence pain, sickness, cancer, and death have no final power, for they too must bow their heads in submission to a God whose love for His creation demands that they yield to His power.

The Wonder of Love

17 The human capacity for love is a powerful and wonderful thing. Perhaps it is one of the greatest evidences of God's presence in human life. In his book, *When God Doesn't Make Sense (pp. 32-33),* Dr. James Dobson shared the following letter, written by a father to his daughter Bristol.

My Dear Bristol,
   Before you were born I prayed for you. In my heart I knew that you would be a little angel. And you were. When you were born on my birthday, April 7, it was evident that you were a special gift from the Lord. But how profound a gift you turned out to be! More than the beautiful bundle of gurgles and rosy cheeks—more than, the first-born of my flesh, a joy unspeakable—you showed me God's love more than anything else in all creation. Bristol, you taught me how to love.
   I certainly loved you when you were cuddly and cute, when you rolled over and sat up and jabbered your first words. I loved you when the searing pain of realization took hold that something was wrong that maybe you were not developing as quickly as your peers, and then when we understood it was more serious than that. I loved you when we went from hospital to clinic to doctor looking for a medical diagnosis that would bring some hope. And, of course, we always prayed for you—and prayed—and prayed. I loved you when one of the tests resulted in too much spinal fluid being drawn. from your body and you screamed. I loved you when you moaned and cried, when your mom and I and your sisters would drive for

April

hours late at night to help you fall asleep. I loved you with tears in my eyes when, confused, you would bite your fingers or your lip by accident, and when your eyes crossed and then went blind.

I most certainly loved you when you could no longer speak, but how profoundly I missed your voice! I loved you when your scoliosis started wrenching your body like a pretzel, when we put a tube in your stomach so you could eat because you were choking on your food, which. we fed you one spoonful at a time for up to two hours per meal. I managed to love you when your contorted limbs would not allow ease of changing your messy diapers—so many diapers— ten years of diapers. Bristol, I even loved you when you could not say the one thing in life that I longed to hear back—"Daddy, I love you." Bristol, I loved you when I was close to God and when He seemed far away, when I was full of faith and also when I was angry at Him.

And the reason I loved you, my Bristol, in spite of these difficulties, is that God put this love in my heart. This is the wondrous nature of God's love that He loves us even when we are blind, deaf or twisted—in body or spirit. God loves us even when we can't tell Him that we love Him back.

My dear Bristol, now you are free! I look forward to that day, according to God's promises, when we will be joined together with you with the Lord, completely whole and full of joy. I'm so happy that you have your crown first. We will follow you someday—in His time.

Before you were born I prayed for you. In my heart I knew that you would be a little angel. And so you were!

Love Daddy

The ability to love is a wonderful thing; so full of wonder that it must have had its origin in the heart of Him who is Wonderful, Counselor, the Mighty God!

A Living Well or a Swamp?

18 In his book *The Kingdom Within*, John Sanford describes a well from which his family drew water when he was a

April

child growing up on an old farm in New Hampshire. He said the water was "unusually cold, pure and a joy to drink." As the years passed by his family was eventually able to afford "indoor plumbing" and so the old well was covered over. Years later, he decided to uncover the well and once more taste the delicious water that he had enjoyed as a young boy. But much to his surprise the old well was bone dry. He was so disappointed and puzzled by the dried-up well that he decided to try and find out what had caused it. All the years his family had used it, even when other people's wells had run dry during terrible droughts, their well had always provided an ample supply of water.

He made an interesting discovery. An old well like theirs was fed by hundreds of tiny underground rivulets which allowed small but steady streams of water to seep into the well. As long as water was drawn from the well, the rivulets remained unclogged and the water supply was replenished. But when the water was no longer drawn out, the tiny rivulets closed up, sealing off the supply of water to the well. Sanford concluded their well had run dry not because of a shortage of water, but because the water had not been used.

From this beautiful illustration, Sanford drew a deeper and more significant conclusion—"The soul of man is like this well. What happened to the old well can also happen to our souls if the living water of God does not flow into us." Jesus promised us that if we believed in Him, the Holy Spirit would flow from our heart like rivers of living water (John 7:38). The only way to keep the Spirit of God alive and flowing through us is to continually draw on that source for life. If we choose to rely on our own strength, wisdom, and abilities as the primary center and source of our living, then we will quickly discover that the source of living water within us will evaporate and we will become as dry wells.

It is an immutable law of nature that what one does not use one will eventually lose. The source of inner strength for the Christian is the Spirit of the Living God. To refrain from drawing on that inner strength will ensure spiritual starvation and deprivation which leaves us to live life almost completely, if not totally, on the level of the physical while barely scratching the depths of the spiritual. Living waters are waters that flow and have life within them; waters that have

April

power and a continuing source of supply. Swamps are huge puddles of water that have no continuous flowing supply. Thus they become stagnant and undesirable.

If we are to have healthy, vital spiritual lives we must <u>constantly</u> draw from the source which provides us with spiritual health. To never look inward, to never intentionally seek to nurture the inner being is to ensure that we will become spiritual swamps or dried-up wells. There needs to be within each of us a conscious and intentional awareness of God and a desire to live with Him on the deepest level we can experience. Whether we become a well or a swamp will depend upon how seriously we seek God's presence.

Discovering our Aliveness

19 How unfortunate it is that we have either lost or never discovered the joy of our aliveness! From infancy, our lives are molded into the routine of daily existence until we finally become oblivious to the unique creatures we are. We are taught to eat, bathe, dress, talk (or be quiet!), sleep at the appropriate time, and to train ourselves to work. Like wind-up soldiers we are paraded through an education system that attempts to turn out human intellectual clones. Who is there that takes the time to help us discover our uniqueness?

In reality, our uniqueness will be discovered in the depths of our spiritual existence. How we relate to God will determine whether or not we discover the marvelous wonder of the created beings we are. Human bodies, while different, are nonetheless much the same. But the spirit, the soul that is at the center of our existence, is where we will discover who we really are. Once all the layers of disguise built up over the years are peeled away, we finally will discover the wonder of what God has created which is eternal.

Jesus said to Nicodemus, "You must be born again." In other words, you must surrender yourselves to the power of God and from the mutated creature you have become, allow Him to bring forth from you a new life, a new YOU. Yet in reality, it isn't a new you, it's the original you that God intended you to be all along. The Apostle Paul says, "If anyone is in Christ Jesus, he or she has become a new

April

creation." From the deadness of our selves apart from God, we grow into the aliveness of our true selves in God.

To be in Christ is to begin to view the world through His eyes. We discover beauty which we previously had been too blind to see. We discover value in each human life that we had always overlooked. We begin to have within us a sense of self-worth that for too long had been stolen from us. The Creator God not only gave us life, but He re-creates life in us when we turn to Him in faith. Before God can cause us to discover the joy of who we are in Him, He must first tear down the old creation we have built. It is not easy and it can sometimes be painful. Letting go of the false things we have built our lives upon is no small task. Following Jesus is always a **radical** transformation! That's why so few people ever fully embrace Him. We would rather cling to the false security of what we think we have than to let go and take hold of the true security that can only be found in Him.

When God made you, before you were created in your mother's womb, you were birthed in the heart and mind of God. You are uniquely and wonderfully made; loved and cherished and cared for by your Creator. Loved so much that God's Son willingly surrendered His life in order to bring you home where you have always belonged. If you are reading this you are alive! I exhort you this day to pause in prayer and discover the YOU that God intends for you to be. It will be a YOU that you will marvel at and will begin to love again. There is no stain on your life that God's love and grace cannot wash away. Then in the glory of your aliveness you will stand before Him without spot or blemish. That's living, my friends; that's living in God's presence.

Living in Two Worlds

20 The Christian is called upon to live in two worlds even while we live out our lives in this one. Paul writes to the Corinthians:

> *Though outwardly we are wasting away, yet inwardly we are being renewed day by day. For our light and momentary troubles are achieving for us an eternal glory that far*

April

outweighs them all. So we fix our eyes not on what is seen, but on what is unseen. For what is seen is temporary, but what is unseen is eternal. (II Corinthians 5:16-18)

The danger, of course, is always twofold. We can ignore the world that is to come and thus pay little heed to what is future and eternal. But we can also disparage this life so much that we miss the joy and beauty of our temporal existence. There are some who proclaim a message that makes living in this world seem like something that has to be endured just so we can arrive at the one for which we were created. It's almost as if they make living on earth a litmus test whose only purpose is to qualify us for eternal life. They have made heaven so important that life now is declared to be unimportant. I don't think that is the biblical approach to life. Jesus never despised this world, He loved it. God created it and declared it to be good. All around us are things that are beautiful and meaningful and should bring joy to our heart. Each day we live should be viewed as a sacred gift from God to be enjoyed and experienced to the fullest.

Having said that, I also am reminded that this life is temporary, even if we live to a very old age. Eventually we will face the reality of eternal life and therefore it is essential that we not neglect that truth and that we prepare for it. As we make our way through this world we spend the early years of our lives preparing ourselves for our life's work. We study and learn and experience as much of life as we can so that when we set off on our journey as adults we are well prepared and secure. To do otherwise is pure foolishness. Well, it's no different with eternal life. How foolish we would be to come face to face with that great event and be unprepared!

The only way to be prepared for eternal life is to study what God's Word has to say about it and to live in right relationship with the One Person who has the power to give it to us. If we are living the way God intends, we will find great peace and joy in living in this world, because by faith and trust we know that the world to come is equally as real and is God's promise to us. We do not have to despise this world in order to believe in the value of the next one. Neither do we need to be so consumed by this one that we ignore the reality that a great experience awaits us after death.

April

To believe that God loves us and desires to redeem us, to accept the fact that we belong to Him and live our lives as if that is so, ensures that we are able to experience peace and joy in this world even as we steadily make our way toward death. Long for heaven, but live in the glory that God has already bestowed upon you while you are on earth. It's true, we are pilgrims passing through this world, but we ought to enjoy every moment of life that God gives us now. Yes, it is possible to fix our gaze on heaven and not miss the wonder and joy of this world. Indeed, we live in two worlds, but our hearts long for that which is eternal.

The Treasures of Darkness

21 God's Word is instructive and uplifting. We can draw strength and guidance from the words our Lord spoke through His prophets and inspired writers of old. One such passage that comes to mind today is from Isaiah 45:3: "I will give you the treasures of darkness, riches stored in secret places, so that you may know that I am the Lord, the God of Israel, who calls you by name." I understand that text to mean that when times of trouble come to us, God will transform those experiences from a burden into a blessing; He takes trouble and makes it a treasure.

Much of what we learn in life comes through the experience of something negative (e.g., fire can burn; playing in the street can harm you, water can drown you, etc.). Unpleasant experiences can and will come to each of us. But God's message to us is that if we are willing, He will be with us in the problem and bring something good out of it. As much as we would prefer for everything to always be good and healthy and happy, in reality the bad experiences can make us see the value in life in ways that we might otherwise overlook.

Oswald Chambers says it this way:

> *There is nothing more wearying to the eye than perpetual sunshine, and the same is true spiritually. The valley of the shadow gives us time to reflect, and we learn to praise God for the valley because in it our soul was restored in its communion with God.* (Source Unknown)

Most of us fight and resist trouble when it comes. What would be more helpful would be to grab it by the neck and insist that it yield its treasure to us! God created the world out of nothing; surely He has no problem bringing good out of that which is bad. The key is to allow God to reveal the lesson and not demand that He resolve things according to <u>our</u> will.

In the passage from Isaiah quoted above, we are reminded that in trouble God reveals His nature and His power. We are also instructed that He makes known the close, intimate relationship He shares with us by reminding us He knows us by our name. We are not strangers to God; He has known us even prior to our birth (Jeremiah 1:5). Surely we must believe that a God that knowledgeable and concerned about us would not be oblivious to the deep need we experience in troubled times. To be drawn to God in times of need is to be made aware of the greatness of His love and the extremity of our weakness. When trouble comes, rest in God's promise; discover your soul being renewed and restored.

I am not suggesting that we engage in a game of mental gymnastics in which we stoically pretend that problems don't exist in our lives. What I am saying is that the Christian should demand that trouble yield up its treasure. Who would ever suspect that a slimy organism that dwells on the bottom of the sea, encased in a dark, ugly shell could possibly contain the beauty of an exquisite pearl? Someone has to force open the shell and demand that it give up its treasure; otherwise the treasure is never discovered. When a tiny grain of sand invades an oyster and begins to irritate it, the oyster encases that tiny grain with a slick coating that eventually becomes a pearl. The oyster has learned how to turn trouble into treasure. Have you?

Which Day Are You Living In?

22 When we are young, we almost always are looking forward to the future. Then, as we grow into the middle years of life, most of us become consumed with the present. As we enter the latter years of our lives we begin to spend a lot of time dwelling on the past. From the middle years onward many people

April

seem to find more happiness in reliving in their minds past experiences that were joyful or pleasant, rather than risk taking on the world and claiming new experiences of happiness.

Happiness is that elusive quality of life that darts in and out of our lives like a butterfly chaotically fluttering through the air. Have you ever tried to catch a butterfly? What some of us never seem to grasp is that happiness does not lie outside us, but within us. It saddens me when I visit folks and they never talk about anything but the past. Sad because if you are alive life is just as real now as when you were a teenager. One thing young people don't spend a lot of time doing is dwelling on the past. For them, there are new worlds to be discovered, new people to meet, new experiences to be encountered, new avenues of life yet unexplored. Where is it written that such an outlook must stop when one reaches or passes middle age?

At Frazer Memorial United Methodist Church in Montgomery, Alabama they formed an adult choir of people who were all over fifty-five. They call themselves the Speeder Choir. (They're all over the speed limit!) I've heard that choir sing and they sing with zest and joy. They sing like people who don't realize they're getting older. Could that be one of the secrets of remaining young—to not dwell on how many birthdays you have had but to live life to the fullest no matter how old you are? There is no more beautiful portrait of what God intended life to be than to find an elderly person who is vibrant, happy and joyful. "But", you say, "I have aches and pains, I don't see or hear as well as I used to." So what? God is still able to take what you offer Him and cause your life to become a blessing to someone else, and thus bring a blessing to you!

You have often heard me say, "Don't stop living before you die!" I suppose my saying that has been accepted as being somewhat valid in light of the gloomy outlook I have been receiving from the medical profession concerning my health. The experience of having cancer has taught me many things, not the least of which is that whether we are healthy or sick, feel good or bad, we have never been able to live but one day at a time. Since today is the only portion of time I can live in, why should I ruin it by worrying about tomorrow or wasting it with regrets about the past?

April

God has given you today! Read or do something that makes you laugh or smile. Forget about your own problems for a minute and allow someone else to tell you about theirs. You might find yours are small in comparison! Today is a precious gift; don't squander it. Do something that makes you feel alive. Vary your mundane routine. Go outside for a few minutes and look at what a beautiful world God has made and realize that it pales in comparison to what is yet to be. But until He gives you what is yet to be, soak up all the joy, beauty, peace, and happiness that today has to offer. Live in the present. Not even the youngest among us can live in more than one day at a time.

Spiritual Living

23 One of the most beautiful and powerful of all the Psalms is 139. It speaks of a person who is intimately acquainted with the transcendent power of God in his life. A power that was the creating force behind his very existence—"For you created my inmost being; you knit me together in my mother's womb" (v. 13). Furthermore, the Psalmist writes with a conviction that God is genuinely concerned about every aspect of his life, even the most minute—"You are familiar with all my ways. Before a word is on my tongue you know it completely, O LORD" (vs. 3-4).

He rests in the knowledge that God is always with him. No matter where life's circumstances take him, God is present; indeed, has preceded him there—"Where can I go from your spirit? Where can I flee from your presence? If I go up to the heavens, you are there; if I make my bed in the depths, you are there. If I rise on the wings of the dawn, if I settle on the far side of the sea, even there your hand will guide me, your right hand will hold me fast." (vs. 7-10). God never leaves us, even in our darkest, most rebellious moments. We discover that like Jonah we cannot hide, nor is there anywhere we can run from His love. For years we may neglect Him, turn our backs on His grace, drive the very thought of Him from our minds, and still—God is patiently, persistently searching after us, calling us to home again.

When at last we cease resisting and allow ourselves to become aware of His presence our lives begin to be transformed. It is not a transformation that comes against our wills, but one that now becomes

April

fully embraced by our own desire. Sometimes the shift is dramatic, sometimes it comes with subtle stillness. However it comes, we begin to feel a stirring within our hearts that draws us ever deeper into His grace. When that moment comes, we find ourselves feeling the words the Psalmist so beautifully expressed— "Search me, O God, and know my heart; test me and know my anxious thoughts. See if there is any offensive way in me, and lead me in the way everlasting" (vs. 23-24).

For the Christian who is growing spiritually there will come an increasing desire to surrender to the shaping touch of God. While there still will be sinful thoughts and acts that we commit, no longer do those acts satisfy us; instead, they disturb us. Our hearts become broken by our own words and deeds and we bring them to the throne of redemption and pour them out before the Lord. God in His grace takes the blemished brokenness of our lives, and like malleable clay in His hands, scoops it up and reshapes it into a thing of beauty. Now our hearts are being drawn to Him and our lives begin to settle into this inexplicable state of peace and contentment. When we have come to this point then we are truly living on the level of spirit.

In the realm of spiritual living, praise for God comes forth as naturally as breath fills our lungs. "I praise you, because I am fearfully and wonderfully made" (v. 14). This is a Psalm for one who is learning to live in the joy of God's presence. It is a Psalm that was written for you! Have you yet discovered its truth and power?

Love and Obedience

24 We come into this world demanding our own way. Even as infants we seek to set the rules concerning the few things that are within our power—when we will eat, when we will sleep, and when we will dirty our diapers. The world of a newborn is very much a self-centered world. Everyone else's desires and schedule must yield to the disturbing sound and arresting call of non-stop wailing. The sound meanders down the hall and permeates every cell of the adult body until we can no longer delay, but must respond.

Then the battle for supremacy and control begins. The parent begins to establish eating and sleeping schedules; potty training is finally implemented, and rules are taught and enforced. And all along

April

the way we resist, quietly (sometimes not so quietly) struggling to still be in control. Obedience becomes a repugnant word and discipline a concept that is repulsive. The teen-age years arrive and as our bodies grow closer to the size of our parents and our wills begin to reassert themselves, the tug of war for independence begins in earnest. We long to be free from parental control and to establish our own boundaries and priorities.

Finally we reach adulthood and think we have arrived. But alas, we discover that there are others (employer, government, spouse and children) that still exercise control over us. The bottom line is that we have spent a lifetime building up a resistance to obedience and discipline. Then along comes our religion and portrays a Jesus who says we must be obedient to His Word. And so the resistance continues. If, however, we have a mature understanding of obedience and have discovered that the guidance our parents, teachers, and others have offered us had value and purpose, then there is also the possibility we will be receptive to the teaching of our Lord.

There can be no spiritual growth apart from a willingness to obey our Lord. There is no need in asking to know God's will if we are unwilling to do it once He reveals it to us. Jesus said, "If you love me, you will keep my commandments." He did not say, "If you fear or begrudge me, you will keep my commandments," but "If you love me!" Obedience is born out of love, not the other way around. God is love and everything we experience about Him is derived from love. You will never sincerely love that which you fear. You will only truly be obedient to that which you love with all your heart.

Loving God releases the power of His Spirit into our lives. The more we love Him, the more of Himself He is able to share with us. As long as we see God as a mighty tyrant who simply wants to manipulate us, we will never surrender to Him. When finally we see Him as the source of life, wisdom, and knowledge, who desires to share Himself with us in love, then we will surrender and His Spirit can remake us into that which we were created to be. To seek God's will and to desire to do it is the key to discovering the purpose of our very being. Anything less than that will only lead us to dead-end paths that leave us miserable and unfulfilled. First comes love, then comes

April

knowledge, then obedience. That is the order that leads to spiritual growth, indeed to life itself.

Does Your Life Matter?

25 What is the one thing most people (especially church people) are seeking an answer to as they approach the latter years of their life? I'm confident that there would be many different answers to that question, but I believe that there really is one thing that people hunger to know as they reflect back on their life's journey—has my life mattered?

Very few people will have their lives recorded in history books. Of the billions who live, few will be kings or queens, presidents or members of Congress. There are only a few Jonas Salks, Mother Teresas, Billy Grahams, Alexander Graham Bells, Shakespeares, etc. In fact, other than knowing their names, I know next to nothing about my great-grandparents and their forbears. Yet without every single one of them, I would not exist. Therefore, to me, they are vitally important.

I think the problem with our reasoning is that we assume that in order to be remembered, to be considered important, we must accomplish extraordinarily great things. That's the way we have been taught to think! Being the top stone on the pyramid is the most important thing. And yet without every stone beneath the top one, it could not stand. Bill Gates is a billionaire, considered one of the wealthiest men in the world. But with all his insights and intelligence he is dependent, just as you and I are, upon the common worker to perform the tasks that make him rich.

The wonderful thing about God is that He doesn't measure our value by what we accomplish, by how much we possess, or by the soaring height of our I.Q. We are not important to God because of the office we may hold, by how many lives we have impacted, or even how talented and gifted we may be. God is not impressed by worldly fame and acclaim or even how many good things we have done. God, I believe, values us simply because we are the creation of His Hands. It was out of His mind our existence came to be. It brought joy to His heart for us to behold the aliveness He brought forth from each of us.

April

There are two Biblical stories that make me think that God values what the world overlooks. One is the story of the widow in the Temple who put in two pennies when others had perhaps given thousands (Luke 21:1-4). Jesus said she gave more than them all, because she rendered to God out of her poverty while they out of their abundance. She loved God so much that she was willing to withhold nothing from Him. It wasn't the monetary value of her gift that touched the heart of Jesus, it was the depth of her love for God.

Then there's the story of the tax collector who hid himself in the shadows of the temple and simply confessed that he was a sinner (Luke 18:9-14) No eloquent elaborate prayer, just seven simple words—"Lord have mercy on me, a sinner." Jesus loved him because He knew the man recognized the worthiness of God and the unworthiness in himself.

When you ask yourself if your living has mattered, why not try looking at it from God's perspective instead of the world's? Your life, every life, will find its true value in the heart of God. Any place else doesn't really matter at all.

The Mountain or Mountain Mover?

26 In Isaiah 36 and 37 we are told the story of how the king of Assyria, Sennacherib, threatened Jerusalem and King Hezekiah the king of Judah. The Assyrian king had easily overpowered every city and land that lay before him and now he stood on the outskirts of Jerusalem, ready to conquer the city and destroy the nation of Judah. Because of his military success, he was arrogant and taunted King Hezekiah. Worst still, he mocked God and tried to instill fear in the hearts of the people of Judah by telling them their God could not save them.

King Hezekiah was afraid, but nevertheless, he took the handwritten message from the Assyrians and carried it in the temple and spread it before the Lord. He prayed over it! Even out of his fear and sense of inadequacy he brought his troubles to the Lord and laid them before the altar. It was an act of faith and trust, even though the King may have been afraid. Logic dictated to Hezekiah that he didn't stand

April

a chance. No one had been able to stop the Assyrians. City after city had fallen. Judah was outnumbered and had no defense that was capable of stopping the mighty army from the north. The people were ready to flee in fear. Still Hezekiah prayed. He simply told God what the situation was and waited to see if God would save them.

Can we not learn a lesson here? There are moments in life in which we are overwhelmed by circumstances and events. There are times in which we see no human solution to our dilemma, no way out of our problems. From the human point of view things seem hopeless. We look at the obstacle and it appears to us as a mountain. Maybe the answer lies in looking at Him whose power is great enough to remove mountains! Take your spiritual eyes off the problem and place them on the One who is able to solve any problem. Perhaps it would help to write down on a piece of paper what the problem is and literally place it before the Lord, just as Hezekiah did. Tell God how you feel and while acknowledging your weakness, also recognize His power.

Prayer does change things! Perhaps not always like the scenario that we lay out, but God does respond to the cry of His children. If there is any great weakness in the church today, I think it is in the area of prayer. That's why I believe the way to renewal, for any church, is through a concerted, intentional ministry of prayer. No matter how much you are already praying, double your efforts and see what happens. Where possible, every church should have a prayer room—a room set aside for nothing but prayer. What a blessing it would be if it was used every day by people who would commit one hour a week or a month to come and pray for the needs of the church and the needs of individuals who would share their concerns with them. Would you be willing to be one of the "prayer servants?"

By the way, if you're wondering what happened to Judah and Hezekiah, God told Sennacherib that he would never enter the city of Jerusalem. The next day He sent <u>one</u> angel who slew 185,000 of the Assyrians and the king returned to Nineveh, where his own two sons murdered him. Even in the face of overwhelming odds, nothing is too great for the power of our God. What problem do you have that you have yet to share with your Lord? Bring it to Him and discover which is greater—your problem, or God?

April

Abide in Christ

27

Abide in me as I abide in you. . . . Those who abide in me and I in them bear much fruit, because apart from me you can do nothing. . . . As the Father has loved me so I have loved you; abide in my love. . . . I have said these things so that my joy may be in you, and that your joy may be complete.   John 15:4, 5, 9, 11

Who is there that would not like to live in the experience of inner joy? The words of Jesus in John 15 carry a poignant message. The God who made us knows what we need in order to experience joy. The joy that Jesus wants us to have is the same joy that is within Him. The only way we can experience His joy is if we abide in Him and He within us. There is a mystical merging of body and soul with the Source of all life which brings about inner peace and joy.

To abide in Christ is to **consciously choose** to live in His Presence. It is to invite Him into your heart and to hunger to live in His. Too often we live in Christ like the cold-natured person who goes to the pool for a swim and dreads the thought of the cold water. First, he sticks a toe in to test the water, then the foot and ankle; finally the calf. It takes the longest time to submerge the whole body in the water and as a result we prolong the intense discomfort of being partially in and partially out of the water. Only when we finally are fully settled in the water do we adjust to its temperature and begin to feel comfortable.

Too many Christians are miserable and unfulfilled because we have only submerged a small portion of ourselves into the loving presence of Jesus. You will never be happy in Jesus if you give only a small part of yourself to Him. Total surrender brings total joy; partial surrender brings only enough joy to make us miserable and incomeplete. I think the reason so many people will only give Jesus a tiny part of themselves is because they are afraid—afraid to let go of being in control of the direction of their lives. We are afraid that Jesus may take us somewhere we don't want to go, or ask us to do something we don't want to do. The terrible irony is that our choice to be in control inevitably will lead us to a life of unhappiness and emptiness. Years

April

and years will pass by and we will run from one temporary experience of happiness to the next. Like fireworks launched into the air there is an instantaneous moment of ecstasy and glory and then it quickly fades in the darkness and falls in ashes to the ground.

How wonderful it would be if we could recognize that Jesus has not come to make us miserable but to make us happy! He has not come to burden us with life, but to take life's burdens from us. He has not come to deprive us of joy but to bring us joy. When we abide in His love, we live in peace; not just outward peace but inner peace—that deep place within where no human being has the power to create calmness apart from the soothing presence of the Creator's Spirit.

Are you abiding in Christ or are you living outside Him? No one has to tell you; in your heart you know. Heaven begins on earth because heaven is where God is and God can be in you now!

The Power of Prayer

28 Samuel Ireneaus Prime, an American Presbyterian clergyman, wrote in his memoirs, *The Power of Prayer*, "Prayer is the chain that draws the soul to God and brings down promised mercies to us; or, like the hook which draws the boat to the shore, though the shore itself is immovable. Prayer is to the church what the breath of spring and the sun, the rain, the dew of summer, are to the earth. Without them, the church and the earth must remain in their wintry shrouds" (From *Companions for the Soul*, Nov. 27).

Prayer is that which connects us to God in a conscious way. When the mind is turned toward God, the spirit is naturally drawn to Him. When the spirit rests in God, the heart is transformed into a place of peace and contentment. We often fall victim to the misconception that because we have no conscious experience of God in an audible or physical way when we pray, that prayer must not be very effective. And so we often give up almost before we begin. But to what can I liken prayer? Perhaps it is like planting a seed in the ground. For the longest time the only awareness that we have that anything took place was the fading memory we have of our hand releasing it into the soil which soon covered it over. Days pass;

April

perhaps weeks, and we see no evidence that our effort accomplished anything. Then one day a small tiny green sprout protrudes through a miniscule crack in the earth's skin. It spreads its tiny limbs toward the light and a miracle is born.

Prayer requires not only trust but patience. We must learn that God does not operate on the hurried schedule by which we live our lives. There is "our time" and there's "God's time." We must adapt to His! Just because we live in a fast-paced, instant world of our creating, we cannot expect that God will fall in line with instant prayer response. Jesus had much to say about the importance of persistence in prayer (Luke 11:5-8; 18:1-8). God does not need to be reminded about what we need; we need to learn patience and faithfulness by coming to Him again and again with the concerns of our heart.

Jesus prayed often. Whenever important decisions were required, He spent long hours in prayer. If Jesus, God's Son, found prayer needful and helpful, how much more should we! (Read Matthew 14:13; Luke 5:16; and Luke 6:12, 13.) We can learn from these scriptures the importance of solitary prayer. Jesus most often prayed alone. There were no interruptions or distractions, for He found a secluded place where He could spend time immersed in the presence of His Father. Corporate prayer in church has an important place, but it can never supplant the necessity of prayer alone with God.

Those long hours spent in prayer are not wasted hours. Indeed, they are perhaps the most important hour we will spend in the day. Martin Luther was quoted as saying, "I have much to do today, therefore, I must spend much time in prayer." Our reaction usually is to say, "I have much to do today, I don't have time to pray."

Have you discovered the value of prayer? The wonderful thing is that it is never too late to begin! Spend time with God today. You'll be glad you did.

The Homeland of the Soul

29 No one can be in touch with God who is not in touch with his or her inner self. To be oblivious to the reality of one's soul or spirit ensures that communion with God is not

April

possible. The very desire to commune with God is given birth in the soul, which is the womb of our very consciousness of God's aliveness. How profoundly the Psalmist proclaims it: "As a deer longs for flowing streams, so my soul longs for you O God. My soul thirsts for God, for the living God" (Ps. 42:1). The soul is one of God's great mysteries of creation. Its form is hidden from the physical eye and resides in us like an inner garment. Like the quiet rhythmic beating of our heart that maintains our physical life, so the soul steadily beats behind the scenes to maintain the channels of contact with God, ensuring that the spirit remains alive.

Most of our lives we focus on the needs or the appetites of the body to the neglect of the soul. Indeed, when the soul that has been ignored cries out, we are bewildered as to where the voice came from. It sometimes affects us like the annoying cry of an inconsolable child in the middle of the night, and we long only for the peace of quietness and wish the soul would go back to sleep. But it will not be stilled, for it has been given life by God and will not go quietly into the darkness of life. In ways that sometimes we cannot comprehend it nonetheless harkens to us, "Awake, awake, thou that sleepest, and give heed to the God who has made you!"

"The fool says in his heart there is no God," but like stones that have been given life, the soul rises up and shouts, "You are wrong!" It is in the soul that happiness is discovered; and when at last we acknowledge that the soul is the place of inner peace, we can begin to live in an uninterrupted state of tranquility that previously was elusive. J. Rufus Moseley writes, "God is the homeland of the soul. We are no good away from home, except to return" (*Perfect Everything*, p. 138). Union with God can take place only as we seek to live in union with Jesus. He is the Door, the Gate, the Light, the Life. He is the One by whom and only through whom all can come to the Father. He is the Truth that sets our souls free to soar, and our hearts at liberty to sing.

Listen, O Christian: you were created for joy! Out of the infinite love of God's heart you were formed to bask in the glory of life. You were not created for despair, for sorrow, for unquenchable anguish. Jesus is peace, joy, love. In Him your soul will indeed find rest and when it finds rest it finds life. No wonder the underlying current of all

April

St. Paul proclaimed was to be "in Christ." He had discovered the union with Life, and nothing would draw him away. I too have discovered what Paul proclaimed and it has forever changed my life for Him. In Him we live and move and have our being. Apart from Him we dwell in darkness, in desolation, and in unhappiness.

Does your soul dwell in the Light? Are you in touch with your soul? Note how often the Psalmist addresses his own soul (e.g., "Why are you downcast, O my soul? Why so disturbed within me? Put your hope in God, for I will yet praise him, my Savior and my God." Psalm 42:11). Communion with the soul is essential. Within the soul is the answer to life's deepest needs!

Life – A Sacred Trust

30

We live with the knowledge that life is fragile and even at its longest is very brief. For some it ends all too soon and tragically. The world is still stunned by the senseless death of Princess Diana. Only thirty-six years old and mother of two young boys, her life was snuffed out by a drunken chauffeur and the relentless hounding photographers (infamously known as "paparazzi") who not only refused to allow her privacy but sought to enrich themselves no matter what the cost to her.

Even though we human beings are conscious of our mortality we tend to assume that our end is always in the distant future, no matter how old we become. But now and then some of us are afflicted with serious illnesses that remind us of how much we take life for granted and how quickly it could be over. What would you do differently if you knew your time on earth was short?

By the time you read this, I will have had a CT Scan and will have received the report from the doctor as to the status of the cancer in my body. We will know whether the chemotherapy was helpful, or not. If it did not help, then the prognosis will not be very encouraging. And so I have asked myself over the past few days, "What will you do if the news is not good?" I suppose no one can truly know until the moment comes, but I think I know. I will go on with my life pretty much as it is, trying to continue to faithfully serve our Lord and be

May

the best pastor I can be to the church where I am privileged to serve.

There are some lessons we cannot learn apart from the experiences of life. I am discovering the spiritual truth in the powerful words that Paul wrote to the Romans in 5:2-5:

> *We rejoice in the hope of the glory of God. Not only so, but we also rejoice in our sufferings, because we know that suffering produces perseverance; perseverance, character; and character, hope. And hope does not disappoint us, because God has poured out his love into our hearts by the Holy Spirit, whom he has given us.*

Regardless of what the doctor tells me this week, I will choose to continue my life as a minister of the Gospel of Jesus Christ. Whatever amount of time I have left on this earth, short or long, I intend to spend in service to Him who loved me and gave Himself for me. My world has not changed nor have my responsibilities been altered. My love for God is not dependent upon my longevity. His Word has been and continues to be the strength of my life and I trust His divine providence to do in me that which is pleasing to Him. I do not see my service to God as duty, but a sacred trust. That trust has not been increased nor diminished because I live with the reality of cancer. He has blessed me through the good times and He has faithfully abided with me through the tough times. I have no reason to think the future will be any different.

Living Life Faithfully

1 If asked to measure the greatness of someone's life, what would you use as a standard? What can a person accomplish in life that will have any lasting value when they are gone? How will your life be remembered by those you leave behind? More importantly, how will God evaluate the measure of your life?

How is it possible that a woman of such small statue, who by worldly standards had no physical beauty, who possessed almost nothing of material value, who lived the most austere life imaginable, who had no money, no home to call her own, and who spent her life in complete dedication to the sick and dying, could be so revered that her

May

death has saddened the world? Mother Teresa, a diminutive little nun in Calcutta, India, dies, and the entire world feels the loss. She was once asked how she could hope to make any difference in the slums of Calcutta when the sick were dying each day by the hundreds. Her reply was, "Unlike you, I do not add up how many are saved. I simply subtract from the number that are dying."

There are few Mother Teresas in this world. They are exceptional and rare and seem so far above us that we will always feel unworthy when we compare our lives to theirs. But people like Mother Teresa have discovered the true undercurrent of life—that the noblest way to live is the way of self-sacrifice. Jesus taught it: few of us embrace it. We live in an age in which almost everything around us demands that we put self first. Take, for example, advertisement and TV and movies. Even in the church, the message is often, "If I claim God as Lord, He is obligated to bless me." Bless, yes, but rarely ever in the sense of material reward. And yet the airwaves are filled with television evangelists who proclaim the "prosperity" gospel message. They claim that God is obligated to enrich the person who seeks to follow Him. I find that message not only repugnant but unbiblical.

Because our lives don't measure up to the standard of a Mother Teresa is no reason to fall into despair and refuse to live as nobly as we can. God will measure the value of our life, not against the standard of another's life but against the standard of how faithful we were with what we had and who we were. God doesn't need a million saints to go to Calcutta, He needs faithful servants to serve where you are. Love, kindness, and compassion are needed everywhere. We are each quite capable of expressing those feelings to others, if we are willing.

Living life faithfully is not determined by where you are, but who you are. It is not a way of life that God will squeeze out of you, but one that He gently requests of you. How beautifully the prophet Micah put it when he said, "And what does the LORD require of you? To act justly and to love mercy and to walk humbly with your God" (6:8). Only those who have accepted in their hearts how greatly they are loved by God will ever feel compelled to express thanks for that love through a life of self-sacrifice. When the depth of God's love is experienced in the soul, the physical life is drawn to Him in willing

May

service and devotion. We may not be a Mother Teresa, but we can strive to be what God calls us to be, wherever we are.

The World We Alone Can See

2 In secret the battles are fought. A place where no human eye can focus; where mortal discernment cannot intrude and where the utter truth of a human life lies veiled. Housed within layers of human flesh the soul becomes the battleground for the spiritual struggles we all encounter. We rise each day and leave the confines of our home to show our face to the world, always careful to disguise and protect the fragile inner tenderness that we zealously guard. To bare the soul would be to allow the world to see the most vulnerable part of our being and that is something most of us are unwilling to do. It is within this realm that we know the truth about ourselves. We see our weaknesses and our strengths; our sinfulness as well as our goodness. In undiluted truth our real self, good and bad, makes itself known.

Already we each live in two worlds: the world that is seen by those outside us and the world we alone can see. Regardless of whether one is Christian or atheist, religious or pagan, there is a consciousness of this "private world" that cannot escape our thoughts and will not let us dance merrily through life without paying it homage. Within this hidden consciousness our hopes and dreams run free; our fears and insecurities steadily march in the company of our successes and failures. Here the moral choices are made (or not made) and when we choose the wrong, our souls give birth to another child called conscience. And from this newborn infant of the soul there flows forth a stream of remorse within us that reveals itself as guilt. It fastens itself to our hearts and will not allow us to go on without it.

Within this sacred place the voices of heaven and hell state their case like the great scene in Eden in which the soul-battle revealed itself for the world to see. God established the boundaries and Satan sought to undo them. Temptingly he said, "Eat of this tree and you shall become like gods." With a single choice, paradise was lost and the soul went underground. No longer visible in purity and tenderness, it was destined to be covered by the outer garment that veils its presence from its human neighbors and reveals itself to God and self.

May

But God did not forsake us; He followed us into our newborn world and constantly beckons us to dwell in His presence. And when we humans could not grasp the depth and sincerity of His love, He said, "I'll place my Spirit in flesh like theirs and then they will see me as I am." So, Christ came and dwelt among us, housed in the tent of human flesh. Yet He chose to bare His soul and let all the world look in. And what we saw was tenderness, love, and self-sacrifice. We saw a Man whose soul was pure and whose greatest desire was to share life with us.

And now, into the murky shadows of our soul the voice of God gently comes. And His voice says, "You are the creation of my hands, my child; come home and dwell with me." And deep down inside of us, where no human eye can see, in the place where honesty must prevail, we will hear our voice answer— "I hear you Lord and I . . .!"

The Great Transformation

3   There are few things in life more shocking to us than to suddenly see ourselves as we are. In the seclusion of our own hearts we secretly try to convince ourselves that the person we are really isn't the person others often see. Then one day we come face to face with our real selves in those moments of weakness when we cannot maintain the pretense any longer, and the person we really are stands before us in unveiled truth.

Such was an occasion for the shivering man who stood near the glowing coals of the courtyard fire. The penetrating dampness of the early morning dew sent cold chills along the surface of his callused, leathery skin. He regarded himself as a strong man; one not given to fear of many things in life. Disguised by the pre-dawn darkness and counting on his unfamiliarity to the huddled crowd, he gathered enough courage to stand in the midst of those who would despise him—if only they knew who he really was. He had thought that he knew his own heart and that his heart was honest before the One He loved so deeply. But in a few brief moments he was to see the real self that he had long denied existed.

The flickering light of the charcoal fire danced aimlessly across his face as the woman at the gate asked the first question that began to

May

shatter his anonymity. "Aren't you one of the men who was with Him?" "I am not!" was his emphatic answer. Then others in the crowd asked, "Weren't you one of his followers?" Another adamant response of, "No, I am not!" quickly erupted from his lips. When the third challenge came, the old Peter rose to the surface and like a volcano spewing molten lava, his language turned to profuse cursing and swearing. Even before the echo of the cock's cry faded into the distance, Peter beheld his real self in the light of undeniable truth. His own words became the judge and jury of his soul. The self that is not immersed in Christ is a self that is left standing in the cold darkness of life, naked before the world.

As the last syllable of Peter's caustic denial reverberated through the courtyard, Jesus turned and looked deeply into his eyes, indeed, beyond his eyes all the way down to his soul. No words were necessary; no public condemnation required. Pouring from the soul of Peter was indescribable brokenness; a pain so intense that only the love of God could soften its crucifying power. Hot, salty tears flowed down the beaten fisherman's cheeks, matting his graying beard to the sides of his distraught face. "Oh, what have I done? How could I have done it?" echoed through his mind. And when the words became so heavy that they almost crushed his soul, they slowly gave way to the words of the Master who had comforted him in advance, "Simon, Simon, Satan has desired to have you and sift you like wheat. But I have prayed for you, and when you have turned again, give strength to your brothers."

In the course of time, the Spirit of God made whole the brokenness of that man. Only when Peter came face to face with the man he was apart from Christ did he ever become the man he was in Christ. So it must be for us. In the loving presence of Christ, we give up what we are and become what we were meant to be—if we are willing!

The Growing of Faith

4 Life has taught me that faith is a living journey. It is conceived within us by the power of God. It is not something that we can create by ourselves, any more than one person has the power to create the life of a child. To give birth to a child takes two

May

people even though only one of them becomes the living home in which the new creation begins as a tiny seed; over a period of nine months it is formed into the miracle that comes into the world.

Faith has life and everything that has life is created by God's power and is caused to grow by God's power. Our role in the process is to be willing to become the surrendered home of God's creating energy. Everything that has life begins small and if it develops into the mature creation it was intended to be, it goes through a process of growth that slowly, sometimes imperceptibly, brings it to that place of development where it functions as it was intended. In order to live in a conscious awareness of God's presence we are required to have faith. But that which God requires, He always provides.

The Hebrews were required to discover God's presence in the wilderness. But every step of their journey was guided by His Spirit and every need they had was provided by His presence. Water flowed from a rock, manna rained down from heaven, and doves descended in their midst to nourish their bodies. His presence was evident to them in the cloud by day and the fire by night in order to quench the spiritual hunger within them. No real need was left unsatisfied!

The need of our souls is faith and the only source for faith is God. It is no complex process, no catechism of correct understanding that we must achieve before we are given the gift of faith; it is simply child-like trust that asks that the One who loves us eternally give us this precious gift of faith. When a woman becomes pregnant, weeks, sometimes months pass before she is conscious of the new life within her. Yet life within her is just as real the first day of conception as it is the day she gives birth. So it is with faith. God plants it within us even if we are unable to feel it, or define it, or understand it. As we seek more of His presence, hunger to be guided by His Spirit, surrender more of ourselves to His leading, we become more aware of this mysterious creation that is taking hold of our life.

Faith is like a muscle; it must be exercised in order to grow strong. The only way it grows strong is to test it against something that causes resistance. And so, faith finds its strength, energy, and life as it is put to the test. The purpose of the test is not to destroy but to build up. When we are faced with life's challenges, God is at work

May

building up our faith that we might have greater understanding of His constant loving presence. To pass safely through the storm and look back reveals to us the presence of God that we often were unable to see in the midst of the storm. If you have asked God for faith, then settle it in your heart that He has given it to you. Now, simply allow Him to cause it to grow. It will bring glory to Him and peace and joy to you. What a wonderful God we have!

The Great Encounter

5 Along the dusty road of life Jesus encountered many people—Nicodemus, the woman of Samaria, the rich young ruler, Zacchaeus, the disciples, Mary, Martha, and Lazarus, and many more. There were thousands He met who are unknown to us, but they all shared one thing in common—to encounter Jesus of Nazareth demanded that you make a decision regarding Him. You can meet someone like me in life and you don't have to decide anything about me. But with Jesus, you come face to face with the Source of all life, including your own, and you do not have the freedom to simply ignore Him. There is something about His nature, His personality, His being, that will not allow you to ignore or simply dismiss Him.

Each of us has been given the right to live life as we choose, but we are not free from the consequences of our choices. Somewhere along your life's journey you have met the Christ. How has it affected you? Have you yet come to that point in your journey in which you are convinced that to live life His way is better than the way your natural sinful nature is inclined to take you? Or are you still following the alluring, seductive voice that calls you away from God rather than toward Him?

To follow Christ is to follow life. To turn away from Him is to walk toward eternal death. The tragic truth is that there are many who are walking away from Him and are oblivious to the terrible choice they have made. The Church calls us to follow Him. Many join its ranks but decline to walk in Jesus' footsteps. I think one reason is that they consider the cost too high. Jesus had many followers—until He began to talk to them about a cross. Then they walked with Him no more. In your conversation with Jesus, have you come to the place of

May

the cross? It won't appear to you as a wooden instrument of death with a vertical and horizontal cross beam; rather it will reveal itself at the point of the sacrifice of your own will.

The world met Jesus and it demanded His crucifixion. He hungered to give them life, but they only wanted His death. The reason they wanted His death was because they were unwilling to live in a world that was incarnated with the constant presence of God. To live in the presence of God makes us uncomfortable and will not allow us to find joy in our sinning—because He is holy and we are not. Like children who disobey their parents, we go against God's will and when we see the pain written across His face we are left with the reality of our sinfulness and the brokenness of God's heart. This we cannot bear and so we long to flee from His presence.

By God's grace, one day we come to the point that we stop running from His love and we surrender to it. But lo, instead of being consumed by it we are remade by it. All at once we discover that to follow in the footsteps of Christ, even if it does lead to a cross, is the most wonderful way to live life. Total surrender leads to total life. *Make me a captive, Lord, and then I shall be free. . . My will is not my own till thou hast made it thine; if it would reach a monarch's throne, it must its crown resign. It only stands unbent, amid the clashing strife, when on thy bosom it has leant, and found in thee its life.* (Make Me a Captive Lord by George Matheson) *Even so, come quickly Lord Jesus!* Amen.

The Presence of Tribulation

6 It was different this time. Unlike my previous surgical experience, there was a window of time during the days following the procedure that I did not experience the constant peace and presence of my Lord. Quite the contrary, for three days of pain, restlessness, and extreme nausea, I felt forsaken and spiritually alone. I prayed and prayed and was aware only of a growing despair, isolation, and desolation. In a period of 72 hours I only slept a total of five hours, and that fitfully.

It was one of those "dark nights of the soul" that the mystics often wrote about in which a conscious awareness of God's nearness is, for some inexplicable reason, removed from us. In those moments of literal torture it seemed as if my very faith was being ripped from my soul. Suddenly, I encountered the power of Satan as he began to taunt me by insisting: "There is no God, Christianity is a myth, you're living a pretense, you've called and your Jesus has not come to help you. When you die there is nothing else to experience; it all ends in the grave."

I discovered that in the daily devotional book that I had brought with me to the hospital, five of the seven daily writings that week dealt with trouble, tribulation, and a time of testing. The selection for October 9, the middle day of my ordeal, discussed the word *tribulation*, and described how it was derived from the Latin *tribulum* which was a threshing instrument used by Roman farmers to separate grain from the husks. Later a Latin Christian writer transformed the word into revealing a higher truth—that tribulations (sorrow, distress, and adversity) are a means for separating in us those things which are light, trivial, and poor from the solid and the true. It is a process that leads us to a new level of spiritual growth as we make our journey toward eternity.

Psalm 6:6 became my own living reality, "I am worn out from groaning; all night long I flood my bed with weeping and drench my couch with tears." Indeed, many of the Psalms are filled with the cry of a writer who is writhing in despair and desolation and cries out to God to come and rescue him. Often, it seemed no answer came. My situation was more perplexing with this surgery, because during the surgical experience the previous year there wasn't a moment that I was not aware of and comforted by the presence of my Lord. This time it seemed I cried out in vain. As I sought the healing consoling presence of my Lord, the words of the Welsh hymn writer and Methodist minister, William Williams, come to mind, *Guide me, O thou Great Jehovah, Pilgrim through this barren land; I am weak, but thou art mighty, Hold me in thy powerful hand.* Still the anguish continued unabated!

Ultimately, the old adage proved true—that which does not kill us makes us stronger. After three long days, a consciousness of God's presence returned as my body and soul began to recover; as if being ministered to by angels. How reminiscent of the story of Jesus' forty

May

days in the wilderness, when the battle was over, "Then the devil left him, and behold, angels came and ministered unto Him" (Mt. 4:11, NKJV). I bear witness to the goodness of God, who, even in the midst of our tribulation, will always renew us, while all the time drawing us nearer and deeper into the depths of His own heart and soul.

Time Alone With God

7 One grows in fellowship with Jesus not by accident or fate but by a deliberate and disciplined effort to know Him on a deeper and more personal level. If we have a close relationship with our family, it is because we have consciously chosen to set apart time with them, found ways to express love to them, and discovered a sense of fulfillment in sharing life with them. The same is true for one's spiritual relationship with Christ.

Finding time alone with God is absolutely essential for spiritual growth. Jesus must have thought so, for Matthew writes about Him: "After he had dismissed them, he went up on a mountainside by himself to pray. When evening came, he was there alone" (Mt. 14:23). Other examples can be found in Matthew 4:1-11; 14:13; 17:1; 26:36; Mark 1:35; Luke 5:16, 6:12,; John 6:15. Just as the human body needs refreshing and reinvigorating, so does the human spirit. As meaningful and necessary as corporate worship is, we all, nonetheless, need time alone with just God and ourselves.

There is an inexplicable strengthening that comes from disciplined times of solitude. In *Spirit of the Disciplines* (p. 160), Dallas Willard writes that one scientific experiment revealed that it took twenty times more the amount of amphetamine to kill a single mouse than it did when he was in a group of other mice. In fact, they also discovered that a mouse which had been given no amphetamine at all will die within ten minutes of being placed within a group of mice that were on the drug. The point is that we are more influenced by groups and masses of people than we realize. In moments of solitude life becomes more sharply focused and we are given insights that we will never gain if we are always immersed in the thinking of the masses—whether those masses are in the form of the actual physical presence of individuals, or radio, TV, or newspapers.

May

When we are alone, we are left with just God and our own thoughts. There are few times in our lives when our spirits will be in better position to hear the voice of God speaking to us inwardly. Often, we do not hear the inner voice of God because from waking to sleeping our lives are immersed in noise and distractions. Again quoting Willard, "Of all the disciplines of abstinence, solitude is generally the most fundamental in the beginning of the spiritual life, and it must be returned to again and again as that life develops" (p. 161).

The curse of living in the twenty-first century is that we have been convinced that we are so busy with so many things to do that we just don't have time for the spiritual disciplines such as setting aside time for solitude. Jesus asked the rather poignant question, "What does it matter if you gain the whole world and lose your soul?" What do we possess that is more important than our eternal soul? If we treated our new-born babies with the same neglect and indifference that we treat our fragile souls, we would be arrested for child neglect and abuse.

Even as you finish reading this devotion, do you feel the Spirit of God tugging at your heart and saying, "Come aside and learn of me"? If so, what are you waiting for?

The Storehouse Called Faith

8 Early in life we tend to settle into comfortable routines which seem to give stability to our lives—getting up at a certain time, eating at the same time during the day, doing the same sorts of things each day, going to bed at the same time. Though ordinary routine days can sometimes seem monotonous or boring, they also bring a certain sense of security and stability to us and after awhile we grow so accustomed to them that when there is a sudden change or challenge we begin to squirm with fear or dissatisfaction. Over time, we learn to become relatively self-sufficient and we develop a sense of independence that seems adequate to meet the dictates of life.

God's place in all this is pretty much nominal and on the periphery of what seems important because there doesn't appear to be any overwhelming need for His assistance or guidance. Then it

May

happens—that unexpected event that intrudes into our life and reveals its power to be greater than ours to control—some problem that we can't fix or overcome. So hastily we turn to this God we have been told about since childhood and petition Him to come to our rescue. Isn't that what God's purpose is, we surmise—to rescue us from trouble and to deliver us from the things we can't handle?

We live in an instant, fast-fix, disposable world and therefore assume that the necessary ingredient for communing with God—faith—can be instantly produced. But it doesn't work that way. Faith comes with spiritual maturity and just as our bodies do not mature instantly, neither does our faith. Faith is more than a feeling, it is more than analyzing situations through human logic, it is more than the sum total of our previous experiences. Faith is oftentimes the act of swimming upstream against what we have experienced to be true in the past. Real faith is more than simply intellectually accepting the doctrines set forth by the church. Faith is simply trusting that God truly is, that He loves us, and that He never forsakes us. It is belief that there is a Power greater than ourselves that is intimately and intensely interested in our well-being; that no matter what happens to us in life, regardless of what mountainous obstacle we must face, God's power and His love for us are greater than our problem.

The acquiring of faith cannot be put off until the crisis is imminent. You don't start boarding up your windows when the hurricane is upon you. Faith cannot and should not be viewed as that which we call up only when the troubles of life descend upon us. Contrary to what we think, faith begins to develop its roots when things are going right in life and we are still hungry to experience the love and presence of God in our lives. When we desire to commune with God in the good times of life, we are building up a reservoir of spiritual strength from which we can draw in the times of trouble. Then, in moments of tribulation we can pull back the veil from our souls and discover that God's precious Spirit is so entrenched in our lives that we feel shielded by His love and grace.

The growing of faith is a process, a lifetime journey. Is it a journey you have begun in earnest, or is it something that up to now you have only toyed with? God longs to fill the recesses of your soul

May

with the power of His Presence. It will be from the strength of that Presence that you will discover that faith flows freely.

The Origin of Faith

9 One of the most profound passages in the New Testament is found in Ephesians (2:8-9): "For by grace you have been saved through faith, and this is not your own doing; it is the gift of God—not the result of works, so that no one may boast." Paul expressly states that the thing that has the power to make us right with God is God's own grace (grace being love, mercy and compassion that are freely and willingly given to undeserving recipients). He who is righteous chooses to share Himself with all of us who are unrighteous. And so His grace is given to us, but it is given and can only be received through the channel of faith. Now comes the surprising part! The only way we can benefit from God's grace is through the means of faith, and God is the supplier of faith! Not only is grace His gift to us, but also the measure of faith which is necessary in order to receive the benefits of grace.

If you were hungry and I desired to alleviate your hunger with food, I could tell you to go to the supermarket to get food. But even though you might stand in the midst of massive amounts of food you would still need money in order to get the food. Grace is the spiritual food that nourishes us and faith is the means whereby we acquire it. God is the supplier of faith. Paul indicates in Romans 2:3 that God is the one who gives us "the measure of faith." Yet, like the master in the parable who gives his servants certain talents to use, what we do with the measure of faith given to us determines whether our faith shrinks or grows. God plants the seed of faith within us and we either nourish it and cause it to become healthy and vibrant or we let it die and become powerless.

How does one receive faith? "Faith comes by hearing, and hearing by the Word of God" (Romans 10:17). When we open up our minds and hearts to the Word of God, faith is ushered in and begins to dwell in us. It is as if each of us becomes spiritually impregnated by the presence of God's love. In Galatians we are told that faith is one of the fruits of the Spirit—that is, one of the evidences of the presence

May

of God dwelling in us. The more of God's Spirit we are <u>willing</u> to receive, the greater will become our faith. You will note that Jesus never said that we must have great faith: indeed, He said that all that is required is faith that is no greater than the smallest of seeds—a mustard seed (the smallest known seed in His day).

God is holy and requires us to be righteous in order to dwell with us. But God supplies the righteousness. We are made righteous by the redeeming power of His grace and His grace comes to us through faith which He gives to us out of His own heart of love. In other words, God requires nothing of us that He does not willingly supply! Faith becomes the supply line that connects us to God and God supplies the line! We cannot create faith but we can do things which will cause faith to grow. We cannot create butter beans or corn, but we can take the seeds that God has created and plant them, nurture them and do things to them that cause them to flourish. Such is the case with faith. God gives us the seed of faith; what we do with it will determine whether it becomes sufficient to establish and build a relationship with God or whether we let it die and go our own way. You have been given the seed of faith. What have you done with it?

Necessities for the Spiritual Life

10 I recently read a sermon in which a preacher made the following statement: "The [spiritual] life of a true Christian originates in salvation, develops in fellowship and issues in testimony" (<u>Keswick Week 1946</u>, *Three Aspects and Activities of Faith*, p. 208). That statement rings true to me. There is a process to the spiritual life that is not unlike the growing process we go through in our physical maturation. Physically, we begin in our mother's womb, develop our personality and character in the fellowship of family and friends, and bear witness to what we have become in living out our adult lives.

Salvation is where the spiritual life begins. It is the new birth brought forth by the power of God. His will, revealed through the power of His grace, shapes and molds us into the new creation we

May

become in Christ. "If anyone is in Christ, there is a new creation: everything old has passed away; see, everything has become new" (II Corinthians 5:17). Spiritual birth begins with God and is brought forth only as we willingly surrender to His re-creating power; thus, spiritual life, like physical life, is dependent upon another for its very beginning. In the act of receiving our salvation we begin to view life differently. The things which once seemed important no longer do, and the things that before seemed insignificant now become priorities. Outwardly, we might appear to be the same, but inwardly the process of "remaking" has begun.

For one's spiritual life to survive beyond its initial conception, Christian fellowship is essential—fellowship with God and fellowship with other Christians. Just as the burning coal soon dies out when removed from the company of other glowing embers, so the spiritual life will dim and cease to be if fellowship is ignored. The Christian life was not intended to be a solitary existence but an experience to be freely shared with others. Its source is grounded in God but shaped and molded by the experience and witness of those who are also seeking to grow in the Spirit. We are in no small measure shaped by the things and influences with which we surround ourselves. Live in the company of evil long enough and it will take its toll on your character. Commune daily in the presence of goodness and like waves beating upon the shoreline it will slowly but surely transform your nature. We become like that which we embrace!

The spiritual life that is healthy will by its very nature proclaim the goodness of God. Jesus spoke a great truth when He told the Pharisees that if the people did not proclaim His lordship the very stones on the earth would cry out! We cannot truly be "in Christ" and not bear witness to His glory. Just as children cannot restrain their feelings of joy and excitement when their eyes behold their gifts around the tree on Christmas morn, so the Christian born of and living in the Spirit cannot be silent when he or she has received the gift of God's redeeming love in Christ.

There is no greater blessing in life than to live in the presence of God's Spirit. In His presence we become immersed in love and grace and that becomes nourishment for our souls. That's spiritual life!

May

The God Who Speaks From Within

11 The modern world in which we live is not conducive to contemplation and introspection. It is a world that is filled with noise, busyness, motion, and distraction. The beauty of silence is lost to most of us because we have grown so comfortable with the radio, tape player, CD player, and television that we find little time to think our own thoughts. Are we afraid to be quiet with ourselves? Indeed, it has become quite difficult to find any place that is totally quiet. I truly believe that spiritual growth, intimacy with God, can come only as we discover who we are in His Presence and like Moses at the burning bush, we must come aside if we are to discover the holy.

> There is a place where thou canst touch the eyes
>   Of blinded men to instant, perfect sight;
> There is a place where thou canst say, "Arise"
>   To dying captives, bound in chains of night;
> There is a place where thou canst reach the store
>   Of hoarded gold and free it for the Lord;
> There is a place—upon some distant shore—
>   Where thou canst send the worker and the Word.
> Where is that secret place—dost thou ask, "Where?"
>   O soul, it is the secret place of prayer!
>   ~ *Alfred Lord Tennyson*

The soul is the primary fertile ground upon which we become aware of the Being who is greater than we are. St. Teresa of Avila describes the human soul as a beautiful castle that we must learn to enter and there we will find God awaiting us. She writes: "So, as far as I can understand, the door of entry to this castle is prayer and meditation" (*Companions of the Soul,* Nov. 29).

There is a restlessness within us that mystifies us. We never seem to be able to grasp its origin or purpose. We can't explain it and have trouble even identifying it; we only know it is within. Could it be that it is the suppressed voice of our soul crying out to be nourished? Like a newborn child who has not the ability to express its desires with words but only with the singular sound of wailing, our soul cries out to

May

us in the only way it can get our attention—an inner restlessness that longs to be noticed. A loving parent will run to a crying child and hold it close to his or her heart until the need in the child has been discovered and met. Will we do less for our own soul?

Spiritual awakening occurs when we behold that the Creator God whom we always think of as being "out there" is continually speaking to us from within. Like Samuel in the Old Testament we need to find a quiet place and say, "Speak [Lord], for your servant is listening" (I Samuel 3:10). God can be experienced and enjoyed in the midst of noise and confusion, but only when first He has been discovered in the discipline of quietness and serenity. The One who made the soul is the One who cries out to us from the center of that which He created.

Almost all communion with God will be inward. It will cause faith to manifest itself in outward acts, but it will emanate from the center of our souls. What have you discovered about your own soul? Do you even realize that you have one? Is God speaking from within and have you yet to recognize His voice? Come aside and listen!

Choosing a Dwelling Place

12 The Bible is the story of the relationship between God and humanity. The telling of that story reveals that human beings have always faced adversity, even those who sought to be faithful to their Creator. From Adam and Eve in the paradise of the Garden, to John on the desolate island of Patmos (Genesis to Revelation), each person's experience in seeking and being sought by God seems to be formed in the crucible of trials and tribulation. All the great heroes of the faith found the path to God and life to be filled with difficulties to be overcome, for that is the nature of life.

For the person who seeks to grow closer to God, adversity becomes a doorway to grace. While one always has the choice of "cursing the darkness", he or she can also choose the alternative of "lighting a candle." Light seems never to shine brighter than when it is ignited in the bleak darkness of struggle. The struggles of life cause us to emerge from the mundane day to day living and come face

May

to face with our own mortality and the crucial issues and relationships of life. Each person writes the story of his or her own life, and while we may not be able to control the direction of our destiny, we are always free to choose how we will face it—in fear or with courage, with resignation or with engagement, with hope or with despair.

My own battle with cancer has brought me more into the light of God's grace and love than good health ever did. I have faced this illness not in my own strength—which is only weakness—but in the strength of my Lord, which is all-powerful. I have discovered that at the center of the storm there truly is the "eye of peace." His presence is peace and I have basked in the glory of it. In those moments in which I thought the ferocious storms of life would rip me apart, I found an indescribable calmness that held life together.

While recuperating in the hospital from my surgery, that beautiful song by Ray Boltz (*The Anchor Holds*) kept reverberating through my mind.

> *The Anchor holds, though the ship is battered.*
> *The Anchor holds, though the sails are torn.*
> *I have fallen, fallen down on my knees as I faced the raging seas.*
> *But the Anchor holds; O, in spite of the storm.*

The storms of life do not have to destroy; they can build us up.

My search to know God and my struggles with the common experiences of humanity have brought me to the place of dwelling in God's love. It is a spiritual dwelling and not one of our own making. It has been constructed for us by the hands of a loving God and its doorway is always open to anyone who would come in out of the storm. But like all places of habitation that are built by another, whether one chooses to enter it or remain outside of it is an individual decision. When the biblical story began, two human beings faced life by having to make a decision—to dwell in the presence of God or seek to live outside it. They made the wrong choice, just as we often do. But in spite of their decision, God in His mercy offered another opportunity and another place to dwell with Him. What will be your choice?

May

Peace Like a River

13 In 1873, Horatio Spafford, a Christian lawyer from Chicago, placed his wife and four children on the luxury liner *Ville de Havre* sailing from New York to France. Spafford expected to join them in about three or four weeks after finishing up some business. The trip started out beautifully, but on the evening of November 21, 1873, as the ship proceeded peacefully across the Atlantic, the ship was suddenly struck by another vessel, the *Lochearn*, and sank thirty minutes later, with the loss of nearly all on board.

On being told that the ship was sinking, Mrs. Spafford knelt with her children and prayed that they might be saved or be made willing to die, if such was God's will. A few minutes later, in the confusion, three of the children were swept away by the waves while she stood clutching the youngest. Suddenly the youngest child was swept from her arms. Mrs. Spafford became unconscious and awoke later to find that she had been rescued by sailors form the *Lochearn*. But the four children were gone.

Back in the United States, Horatio Spafford was waiting for news of his family, and at last, ten days later (after the rescue ship had reached Cardiff), it came. "Saved alone" was his wife's brief message. That night Spafford walked the floor of his room in anguish, as anyone would have done. But that was not all. As he shared his loss with His Lord, a loss which could not be reversed in this life, he found, as many have, that peace which indeed passes all understanding. Toward morning he told a friend named Major Whittle, "I am glad to trust my Lord when it has cost me something."

As some have told the story, Spafford boarded a ship to sail to France to be with his wife. When the ship approached the approximate place that the *Ville de Havre* went down, the captain of the ship informed Spafford, who stood gazing at the dark rolling water. He was inspired to write this hymn:

> *When peace like a river, attendeth my way,*
> *When sorrows like sea billows roll;*
> *Whatever my lot, Thou has taught me to say,*
> *It is well, it is well with my soul.*

May

Though Satan should buffet, though trials should come,
   Let this blest assurance control,
That Christ has regarded my helpless estate
   And hath shed His own blood for my soul.

My sin—Oh, the bliss of this glorious thought,
   My sin—not in part but the whole,
Is nailed to the cross and I bear it no more,
   Praise the Lord, praise the Lord, O my soul!

And Lord haste the day when the faith shall be sight,
   The clouds be rolled back as a scroll,
The trump shall resound and the Lord shall descend,
   "Even so"—it is well with my soul.
           (Story from *Illustrations Unlimited*, pp. 243-44)

Indeed, "peace like a river" does flow in the fullness of God's grace to those who embrace it in faith.

Come Aside and Pray

14 There are moments in most of our lives in which prayer seems a futile and ineffective exercise. Yet there is some inner compulsion that tugs at us to pray, even when we remind ourselves how often we have done it and no answer seems to have come. Why do people speak words into the great void of silence that surrounds them; hoping, somehow expecting that there is some Power greater than themselves that will pick up the sound of their inner or outer voice and compassionately consider their heartfelt request? Do not quench the leading of God's Spirit when those times of tugging occur, for I am convinced that they are those precious moments, when in the weakness of our own strength, God is beckoning us from within to call once more on the Source of Life.

By His own example Jesus has taught us the essentialness of prayer. Time and again the Gospels paint a vivid portrait of the Son of Man who found it necessary to routinely go to some quiet place of withdrawal and consciously bare His soul to the One He called Father.

May

.Several examples of this are: Luke 5:16 - "But Jesus often withdrew to lonely places and prayed." Matthew 14:13 - "After he had dismissed them, he went up on a mountainside by himself to pray. When evening came, he was there alone." Luke 6:12-13 - "One of those days Jesus went out to a mountainside to pray, and spent the night praying to God. When morning came, he called his disciples to him and chose twelve of them, whom he also designated apostles."

Those passages tell us that He went to the wilderness and He went to the mountain *alone*, to share His innermost feelings with God. There is a time for corporate prayer—when Christians gather in the communion of fellowship—but there is also the necessity of individual quiet time spent in silent reflection with the Savior. The value of those moments cannot be measured! Praying, like believing, is an act of faith. It is looking into the face of all our own doubts and saying by our action that we still believe that God hears our cry. Those are not wasted moments when prayer is offered out of a heart that wonders if God hears anything it says; that is an act of great faith. Faith is always pleasing to our Father and will invariably bring about spiritual growth.

When our physical bodies are passing through those early years of growth, we cannot see ourselves growing. Our limbs do not stretch before our very eyes. But as the months and years march on, we can look back and measure our growth by what we were in the past. So it is with spiritual growth through prayer; only when those moments of faithful prayer are observed in hindsight do we see how far our Lord's Spirit has led us on our journey of growing nearer to Him.

Many churches provide their members with a "quiet wilderness"—a "set apart mountain" to which they may retreat and pray. They call it a Prayer Room. As you enter there and you sit quietly and alone in that special room, you will be filling the same space that some faithful prayer servant has previously occupied. An aura of the Spirit will develop in that room, because it will be the place where communion with God will have been experienced by many who came before you. If your church does not have such a room, I encourage you to try and establish one. It will add immensely to the ministry of your church and to the spiritual development of your congregation.

May

Spend Time With Yourself

15 Do you spend enough time with yourself? Seems like a dumb question when first you read it, doesn't it? But the reality for most of us is that we are so locked into routines and outside influences and other things, and the people who so often fill our day, that we come to its conclusion feeling like some helpless child swept downstream by a raging current. We lay our head down on the pillow at night and wonder where the day went and what we really accomplished?

There were times when Jesus must have felt much the same. When He realized the greatness of the demands, He would go aside to some quiet place and be alone with His own soul and with God. One such occasion was the time He fed the multitudes. Matthew records the event in the fourteenth chapter. Jesus had received word that His cousin, John the Baptist, had been beheaded by Herod. He needed time to grieve and comprehend His loss and so He withdrew to a deserted place by Himself. One could interpret Matthew 14:13-14 to mean that He got into a boat by Himself and rowed out away from the shore; there He could at least for a while insulate Himself from the demands of the crowds.

His time for quiet reflection was interrupted by the hunger (spiritual and physical) of the crowd; so He came back to shore and ministered to them. But note that immediately after He had fed them, He sent the disciples out on the boat and He went alone to a mountain, perhaps drawn there by the alluring exhortation of the Psalm:

> *I will lift up my eyes to the hills, from where will my help come? My help comes from the Lord who made heaven and earth. He will not let your foot be moved; . . . The Lord will keep you from all evil; he will keep your life.* (Psalm 121: 1-3; 7, NRSV)

Jesus knew that He must have time for Himself to commune alone in the presence of His Father.

I fear we do not spend enough time apart from the consuming, shaping forces of life. We let demands and events rob us of spiritual

May

sustenance. No one can have a strong spiritual life if time is not routinely set aside to ponder one's thoughts and to reflect upon them in the quiet presence of God. What is sadder than the person who feels no need for a spiritual life? To walk through life with nothing more than our own strength and wisdom to sustain us is to live a hollow existence. When the storms blow we are powerless to rise above them because none of us has such innate power. Jesus could cause a raging sea to become calm because He emptied Himself again and again so that the power of His Father could dwell in Him. He first calmed the inner storms of His own soul and then was able to calm the storm on the Sea of Galilee.

What storm of life is tossing you to and fro? Is it grief, loss, anger, loneliness? Do you feel rejected, used, forsaken, afraid? Are you battling some illness or holding feelings of resentment? Then come aside to a quiet place and discover with the Psalmist, "From where does my help come?" God hungers to lift you up, heal you and restore joy to your heart. David wrote in Psalm 23, "He restores my soul." Meditate on that verse and let the Spirit of God speak to your deepest need. Does your soul need to be restored?

The Value of Pain

16 We all are aware that we live in a world that is often filled with pain. If not our own pain, we witness the pain in other's lives as they deal with the tragedies of sickness, death, loss, and estrangement. Pain comes to us in two forms, physical and emotional. Sometimes it is difficult to discern which hurts the most. "Why," we will ask, "does God allow human pain? Of what possible use is it? Why could He not create a 'good' world that has no pain? How can He ever begin to comprehend what pain does to us?" Then came Jesus!

Pain is not useless, nor is it an experience that God knows nothing about. We often become so caught up in our own pain that we totally ignore the reality of the pain of God. Kazoh Kitamori writes:

God in pain is the God who resolves our human pain by his own. Jesus Christ is the Lord who heals our human wounds by

May

his own (I Peter 2:24). . . . Accordingly, the pain of God which resolves our own pain is 'love' rooted in pain. (Theology of the Pain of God, pp. 20-21)

Love never suffers more than when it beholds the suffering of the one who is loved. God in Christ beheld the world in its suffering and made it become His own. God on a cross endured more than physical pain; as the last remnants of His life were flowing out, from the cross, He beheld a world that mocked His love and it must have broken His heart. How deep and searing is the emotional pain of being rejected by the ones that you love! Kitamori is right, the magnificence of God's love is truly rooted in the pain He suffers for us.

In our ignorance of the nature of God, how often we overlook that the Father and Son were so intimately united in Spirit and will that what One endured, the other experienced also. The pain of Christ on a cross was also excruciating to the Father in Heaven, who willingly surrendered His Son to suffer pain and death for His creation. Pain that cuts from within the heart is no less real, no less difficult to endure, than pain that severs the flesh and robs the body and mind of the tranquility of peace.

But pain is not useless, for it alerts us to things that are wrong and it unmistakably reveals to our consciousness the value and depth of love. To be incapable of feeling pain is to be incapable of comprehending the depth, breadth, and height of love. Out of the depths of pain we come face to face with the worth and preciousness of human life. Furthermore, we can begin to comprehend the treasure of being loved by a God who shares not only our pain, but takes upon Himself the pain of the world.

Pain can be a treasure hidden in darkness. It can become a means of transformation, of reawakening, of redirecting the course of our life toward more noble goals. It shakes us out of the staleness of complacency and demands that we acknowledge the reality of being alive. When pain awakens us to the value of love, it has become a dear friend. That which causes us such great discomfort, in reality becomes that which will reveal earth and heaven's greatest blessings—if we will allow it.

May

What a Savior!

17 What do you want from Jesus? Or do you want anything at all? Some folks feel so self-sufficient that they imagine that they are totally independent. They have been blessed enough in life that they have never felt a need for anything or anyone; never felt any sense of inadequacy; always thought they knew the answers, and never struggled with the rightness or wrongness of issues. Such seems to be the case of the Samaritan woman at Jacob's well in Sychar. She came one day to draw water and there she met a stranger. She thought she had life under control and then she looked into His eyes and she discovered she had been living an illusion.

He asked for a drink of water, and startled her because He had broken the long- standing tradition of a Jewish man not speaking at all to a Samaritan woman—especially in public. When she questioned Him as to why He did, His response was, "If you knew the gift of God and who it is that asks you for a drink, you would have asked him and he would have given you living water" (John 4:10). A strange response to a simple question. But Jesus always goes to the heart of the matter. Even when we are unable to, He sees our deepest need and seeks to address it. In *God Came Near,* Max Lucado beautifully described Jesus' encounter with the woman of Sychar with these words: "Silently the Divine Surgeon reached into his kit and pulled out a needle of faith and a thread of hope. In the shade of Jacob's well he stitched her wounded soul back together. 'There will come a day . . .' He whispered" (p. 28).

Perhaps the greatest need in all our lives, and the one so many of us never realize, is the need to have our souls mended and our inner hurts healed. There are wounds that each of us carry within that can only be mended by the Great Physician, who not only can heal bodies but who can heal souls. Perhaps it was an emotional injury from childhood, or a lesion inflicted on your heart by one you love. Maybe it was a sense of betrayal that bruised you deeply and never healed within, but continues to ache each day you live. A thousand things can hurt within and rob us of contentment in life.

The God we serve is not powerless, but powerful. He knows more about us than we know about ourselves. Hearts and souls are His business and He knows just what they need in order to make them whole. The process of healing must have a beginning and most things aren't healed instantaneously. The healing balm must be applied over and over again and sometimes the healing process is painful. But God is faithful and He refuses to leave our lives in brokenness. Come He will, and when we encounter Him in the most unlikely places along life's road, He will see the need. If we are willing to receive it, He will offer the healing.

Once in the heat of the day, on a dusty road outside a small village a woman met a stranger. Unable to give expression to the deep need in herself, she chanced to encounter the Source of all life, and lo, He looked into her soul and saw the place she needed wholeness and not only did He heal her wounded heart, He gave her the gift of life that is eternal—the gift that heals the soul. What a Savior! What a Savior!

Love Birthed in Brokenness

18 Brokenness of spirit prepares the heart and soul for the replenishment that comes through God's grace. Perhaps that was what Jesus had in mind when He spoke those beautiful words: "Blessed are the poor in spirit, for theirs is the kingdom of heaven." Was it mere coincidence that this was the first beatitude? The human heart was not made for sin but for holiness. When we sin, a spiritual emptiness begins to permeate our soul and we become aware that something in our life is missing—the peaceful contentment of a right relationship with God.

Do we love God and therefore He forgives us, or does He forgive us and thus cause us to love Him? Does our love for Him precede His forgiveness of us, or does He forgive us even before we love Him?

A perfect portrait of such a theological riddle occurs in Luke, chapter 7. An uninvited guest appears at a banquet given by a very "religious" man known as Simon the Pharisee. The dinner is being given in honor of Jesus. The meal is prepared, the guests are reclining around the table and are engaged in light conversation. Quietly, out of the shadows, a woman appears. Shoulders slumped, head cast down, her face solemn and forlorn, tears streaming down her cheeks, she

May

makes no noise except the quiet rhythmic sobs she tries to muffle deep down in her throat. She does not speak, but simply kneels at Jesus' feet. Scalding tears drip from her eyes and chin and splash gently on Jesus' feet. No one speaks; everyone stares in stunned silence. Simon waits to see if Jesus will rebuke her; for he and probably others recognize the woman as a "sinner." In their eyes she is unfit to be in Simon's house and if Jesus really is a prophet, He should recognize her unrighteousness and demand she get away from Him.

But He doesn't rebuke her. He watches with tender compassion as she lets down the long tresses of her hair (in that day, an act of utmost humiliation for a woman to do in public) and begins to wipe His feet dry with the softness of her hair. Lovingly, tenderly, she caresses His feet and begins to gently touch her lips to them. A communication is going on between them which transcends words. Love, grace, guilt, sin, forgiveness are being intermingled as their two spirits unite; and when the scene is played out, two people emerge pure—the One who was pure from the beginning, and the one who has been made so by a divine love and grace so powerful it transforms human sin into divine righteousness.

When Jesus finally does speak, He pronounces that she is forgiven and comments on the greatness of her love for Him. **Before the woman was told that she was forgiven, she loved Jesus deeply.** She loved Him because in His presence, even with the knowledge of her own sin, she felt accepted. When one feels accepted, especially when the acceptance is offered by One who is greater than one's self, then one will experience the emotion of deep love.

Despite our sinfulness, God loves us. It is that love which draws us to Him; and when we are drawn there and feel accepted by Him our hearts will melt with remorse and regret. Out of our brokenness He brings wholeness; and once you have been made whole by God's love, you will never be the same.

God's Hidden Image

19 Life has a way of wearing us down as we grow older. Not just physically, but down in our spirit—our soul. As the years roll by we see too much suffering, too much sickness,

May

pain, and grief. We find ourselves asking the unanswerable question, "Why?" If God really exists why does He allow this? Why doesn't He do something? We fling our questions toward the heavens and they fade into the thin air of a dark empty silence. But my mind is drawn back to the biblical account of creation in Genesis where we are told that **we** are created in God's image.

Perhaps God is saying to us, I have placed a part of myself in each of you, I will do something about the world's suffering through you. We can't eliminate all the anguish there is in this world but we can touch some lives with God's compassion. It's wonderful to pray for someone in need, it is also wonderful to seek to meet that need. Unfortunately, many of us, as we grow older, turn more and more inward and self-consumed. We harden our hearts toward those around us who cry out (often silently) for someone to care about their need. We settle into our daily routine of busy work, of simply existing through the day. Often our time is consumed with sleeping, watching TV, or just letting the hours of our day slip away. It's as if we are simply hanging on, waiting for our end to come. That's not living!

Every human life is important and every human being has something to contribute to living. The emptiness we feel within can begin to recede when we decide we will use our life for something good and positive. When life treats us badly, rather than withdraw into some isolated corner, how much better we will be if we stop engaging in self-pity and use even our own pain for the benefit of someone else who might also be hurting. God often changes the world through us if we are willing to let Him.

The church was called into being, as I understand it, for two basic purposes: to worship and glorify God, and to serve one another in the power of His presence. The church was not called into being so that we can use it like a spiritual gas station, where we drop in, fill up, and go our own way. The church is a place where we should come to give ourselves to God and then allow His Spirit in us to give Himself to others. How was it that Paul put it? "I have been crucified with Christ and I no longer live, but Christ lives in me. The life I live in the body, I live by faith in the Son of God, who loved me and gave himself for me" (Galatians 2:20).

May

Where the Spirit of God is present in the church, it will reproduce itself. God's Spirit is never static, stale, or selfish; it always flows outward from the lives of those who have surrendered themselves to its leading. The Source of all life comes to us in prayer. If you never pray or rarely pray, you will always be spiritually anemic, devoid of power, and a not particularly happy person.

Life doesn't have to be meaningless or unhappy. There really is an answer, and the answer is a Person. His name is Jesus! Those who have truly found Him are those who not only live in peace, but those who are doing something about making the world better. Has the image of God in you risen, or have you buried it deep within?

Self-love or Self-loathing

20 It has been my experience as a minister that the vast majority of people don't feel very good about themselves. It is not always too much self-love that causes people to be unhappy and unfulfilled, but sometimes too much self-loathing. Look at the stories in the gospels of Jesus' encounter with individuals. The lives that were transformed and the overwhelming majority of His ministry was spent with people who seemed to have little self-worth. The religious establishment referred to them as "sinners" and convinced them that in God's sight they were of little value. Jesus was condemned for spending too much time with tax collectors, harlots, and sinners; people like Zacchaeus, Levi, Mary Magdalene, the woman of Samaria, and others.

Each of those lives that He encountered He restored to a sense of self-worth. Self-worth because He revealed to them that God loved them even if they did have faults (real or imagined). Our value as human beings is not so much determined by being reminded who we are but by Whose we are. Christ changed people by loving them, not pointing out their faults. Most of us are all too aware of our faults and don't need a lot of help in discovering what they are. What we often need help in believing is that we are people of great worth, because God has declared us to be so through the sacrificial death of His Son.

May

Jesus taught us that we are to love ourselves. He tells us this in His commandment, "Thou shall love thy neighbor as thyself." The truth in those words points out that the reason we may not love our neighbor is because we don't love ourselves. Maybe one reason—perhaps the primary reason—that prisons don't rehabilitate many people is because in that environment they are constantly told that they have no value. The small percentage of those who come out of prison and stay out are those who in spite of their imprisonment have discovered within themselves something of great worth.

Our true value is determined not so much by what we do or don't do, but by the fact that we were created by a loving God, for the joy we bring to His heart. God created and then pronounced that His creation was good. True, we all play a part in making His creation less than what He wants it to be, but He overcomes our weakness, our sinful propensities, by redeeming and transforming us from the inside out. It is in our heart and soul that God does His greatest work. When the light of His glory shines on our inward parts, then our consciousness of the value of our being begins to become profound.

We matter to God, we are loved by God, simply because we are. We cannot make sense of divine love because in our sinful confusion it all seems so illogical. There is nothing logical about lavishing love on a returning prodigal son, or paying all laborers the same whether they worked one hour or ten, or forgiving people who are putting you to death, or calling the most intense persecutor of the church to be the greatest of all the apostles.

We will discover our worth, and thus be freed from the prison of our self-condemnation, when we discover the depth of God's love for us. You are valuable—simply because God declares you to be!

Spiritual Pigmies or Giants?

21 How often we cling to the trivial, the mundane, the comfort of the familiar, the security of the "already experienced", rather than take the risk of an adventure into an unknown experience where God awaits to reveal new insights to us about ourselves our world, and His glory. We have been well-

May

disciplined to only put trust in that which we readily comprehend and that which has proven itself to us to be predictable—thus controllable. Isn't that really what we want in life, the assurance that we can always be the one who is control? Isn't that what is behind the arguments we have with our spouse, our children, our friends? And if that is true about our relationship with other human beings, could it not be true about the kind of relationship we try to establish with God?

The dilemma we are faced with, however, is that God requires a relationship with us built on our willingness to surrender, not maintain control. "That's not fair!" you say. But wasn't Jesus (the very Son of God) committed to living His life totally surrendered to the will of His Father, and thus to our needs? Even if we go back to the biblical account of the fall in Genesis, the underlying factor which ultimately caused humanity to be estranged from God was the need, the desire to be in control. God forbade, humanity rebelled. Little wonder the first of the Ten Commandments—which Moses recorded on the tablet—pronounced that there is only one God (and it isn't us!).

The older we become, the less inclined we are to risk much. Over the course of our lives we have discovered the things that cause us the least distress, the least expenditure of energy (physical and spiritual) and like water, we always seek the course of least resistance. Somewhere along the way we settle into the contentment of just getting through another day of life without really exploring the hidden treasures buried in the adventure of each new day. What will you do today that you haven't done a hundred times before in days gone by? Will you risk trying something totally new, something that might yield a windfall harvest, but yet brings with it a certain amount of uncertainty?

Strength and growth, both physical and spiritual, are brought about by testing ourselves against that which provides resistance. In order for muscles to develop they must be exercised against some force or object that causes them to be stretched and challenged. So it is in our spiritual development. The great men and women of the faith, who often stood out as giants among the rest of us, were those who devoted themselves to a disciplined life of seeking God. The "spiritual disciplines" are those activities we freely choose to engage

May

in which cause our spirits to be challenged, tested and stretched. To discipline one's self to the study of God's Word, a regular prayer time, a time for meditation, journaling, and fasting, develops the depth of one's relationship with God and creates within us a healthy spirit.

If we always settle only for that which we already know, already have experienced, already know the outcome to be, then we will forever be spiritual pigmies. Like Moses at the burning bush, God calls us to come aside and learn something new about Himself. We will never exhaust the treasure house of God's Spirit and grace!

The Wonder of Grace

22 I have become increasingly aware that we are often blind to the many ways God's grace comes to us. Rarely does it appear in mystical spiritual moments of ecstasy; more often it comes in quiet deeds of love and devotion through the selfless acts of those who love us and are unwittingly used by God to touch us, comfort us, yes, even to heal us. Their touch, smile, prayers, and deeds of kindness are like little tributaries of God's love that come to us from the very heart of heaven and pass through these human channels that become for us immeasurable rivers of divine grace.

In our modern world of skepticism and despair many lash out that God's love is not to be found, that His grace is nothing more than the empty words of religious zealots, that it does not have the power to touch the human spirit. But they are like a blind man who stands in the midst of indescribable beauty, surrounded by soaring snow-capped mountains, and pristine lakes lined with cathedral forests; he is totally oblivious to what is there because he has not the ability to see. Only the prevenient grace of God (that grace which precedes us) will open the blinded spiritual eyes of those who will not or cannot see.

Many live out their lives in spiritual darkness. The life in which there is only darkness is the life that has yet to be permeated by God's grace. It is like the primordial chaos described in chapter one of Genesis: before the Spirit of God swept across it, the earth had no light because God's spirit had not yet produced in it the joy of life. But God's grace, like the first tiny rays of dawn, explodes into the darkness and chaos of human life and the darkness must recede before its

May

power. "In him appeared life; and this life was the light of mankind. The light still shines in darkness, and the darkness has never put it out" (John 1:4,5, *The New Testament in Modern English*, J. B. Phillips translation).

God's grace is not hidden from those who seek it; it will not be denied by those who refuse to behold it. Sometimes it trickles down like a soft gentle rain; at other times it gushes forth like a mighty rushing torrent, always for the purpose of bringing divine presence into human existence; always lifting up, building up, restoring, refreshing and renewing. Sometimes it comes as judgment to reprove us and free us from the burden of sin and guilt. Oftentimes it bathes us in soothing waves of mercy that heal our brokenness and calm the turmoil in our lives. Sometimes it beckons and leads, and other times it gently prods from behind; directing us toward that eternal place we one day will call home. It pursues us relentlessly and will not cease until we either have utterly rejected it or embraced it in fullness in the depths of our soul.

Sometimes grace reveals itself only in hindsight—when one has passed the point of struggle and looks back from the vantage point of peaceful serenity—that place which mystically has been built on the foundation of uplifting grace. Grace is the expression of God's love made manifest in the breaking down of spiritual barriers that blind us to the reality of His presence. Grace is God's precious love gift to you in the midst of all that life brings. All you have to do is stretch out your hands, open your heart and let it come to rest in the dwelling place of your soul. Will you do that? All that you need to do is lift up your empty hands to God and with a simple prayer say, "Lord, fill me with your grace!"

What Are You Following?

23 One of the interesting things about reading the gospels is that we discover that they center on a Person, not a doctrine. Each time Jesus met someone and proclaimed the imperative to follow, He said, "Follow Me"—"Me" being the person of Jesus Christ. To follow someone, especially Jesus, involves risk. It becomes a detour in the way we were heading, the way we were

May

living. Rest assured that no matter how nobly you may be living, no matter how morally upright you may be, no matter how honest and ethical you might consider yourself, to follow Jesus will require that a new path be blazed in your life. The reason—because Jesus is not just honesty, morality, and ethics, He is the embodiment of all that is good; all that is God.

When the apostles went out to proclaim the message of the Christian faith (check it out in the Book of Acts), the message was really a Person. Doctrines have their place, but a doctrine is not alive, it is a concept, even if it is just and right. It was not a concept that was nailed to a cross for our sins, it was a Person. Furthermore, it is not a dead person that we proclaim as Lord, but He who **was** dead and is alive forevermore!

When Moses went to Egypt and convinced the Hebrew slaves to follow him to the desert, he did so because He persuaded them that the Living God awaited them there. Following God involves risk precisely because we are asked to leave behind the old life with which most of us have grown quite comfortable. We've spent years coming to the conclusions we have (some of which are wrong) and a lifetime in growing comfortable with the things we embrace which we think make us feel secure (but never can). We are like the disciples who cling to the security of the boat beneath their feet and look astonished when Jesus, standing outside the boat, says, "Come to me on the water!"

The way God leads doesn't always make us feel comfortable. In fact, there are times in which it makes us feel very uncomfortable. Once in the wilderness, we begin to think like the Israelites and say to ourselves, "I felt much more secure when I was a slave in Egypt." The old life calls us to come back and settle back into our bondage. But be aware that if we return to the old life we can never inherit the Promised Land. No doubt there were many times the disciples felt inclined to return to the old life because the new life came with demands. But Jesus' words to them were these: "Everyone who has left houses or brothers or sisters or father or mother or children or fields, for my name's sake, will receive a hundred fold, and will inherit eternal life" (Matthew 19:29). I always remember that verse because 1929 was the year the stock market crashed. How ironic that in using

May

those same numbers, we can remember that Jesus gives us a promise that will never fail or falter!

The reward of following Jesus will always far exceed the cost. Perhaps like me, you have discovered that the most precious things we attain in life, more often than not, have come through great trial or struggle. For Jesus, the cost was immense and ended with a cross! Yet His willingness to give up all for us ended ultimately with His being proclaimed King of Kings and Lord of Lords! If He is indeed that, what better person could you be following?

What's Missing?

24 How can a person miss that which he or she has no memory of ever having? Nonetheless, I have come to believe that God has written upon the fabric of the human soul an innate longing for Himself. There is an emptiness within us that presents itself to our consciousness from time to time, and causes us to be aware that there is an inner void that cries out to be filled. One is not often conscious of their stomach—until it becomes empty, and if not soon filled begins to stir and growl and remind us that it longs to be filled.

We may not possess any conscious memory of experiencing the presence of God in our lives in any meaningful way, but His Spirit will spend **our** lifetime seeking to draw us to the reality of His dwelling place. Heart, soul—what are these mystical inner sanctums of our being which defy our ability to ignore or suppress them? They push themselves into our consciousness and gently remind us that they are an integral part of that which makes us a being made in the image of God. We gleefully indulge the appetites of our flesh while we constantly suppress the hunger pangs of our spirit.

How superficially we live, extravagantly wasting the resources of our lives as frivolously and carelessly as the Prodigal Son. But will we, like him, ever come to an awareness of the poverty of our souls? Will we ever come to the point that we recognize that we are unfulfilled and hollow inside because something very valuable is missing? What the Prodigal realized was missing was the love and presence of his father in his life. When we seek to live life without

God at its center, we are building our lives on sand and it doesn't take much of a storm to send us cascading down the slope of despair.

Are you as close to God as you would like to be? "O God, you are my God, earnestly I seek you; my soul thirsts for you, my body longs for you, in a dry and weary land where there is no water." So pines the heart of the Psalmist (Psalm 63:1). Does that describe your desire to dwell in the presence of the One who created you? One of our most frequently used excuses for putting God off is that we don't have time. But time is the one thing we are given. Each person on this planet will have the same twenty-four hour day; and to a very large degree, we will determine what we do with it. What are you going to do with today? Is half of it already wasted on activity that will have no lasting value, or have you spent it in such a way that it has a positive impact on your relationship with God now, indeed even into eternity?

We live in a nation that provides us with great freedom, even the freedom to carelessly fritter away the days of our lives on things that will forever leave us spiritually impoverished. Only YOU can change the direction of your life from emptiness to fulfillment, from meaninglessness to purpose, from despair to peace. You are in charge: don't look for someone to blame or make decisions for you. Decide today whether you are content with the state of your soul or whether you long to experience the peace and fulfillment that God dwelling in you can bring. It's your soul. Is something missing?

What Are You Living For?

25 Is pondering the meaning and purpose of human life simply the domain for the professional philosopher or would we all do well to consider our unique existence? Have you ever sat down with yourself and wondered who you are and why you are here? Does your life have any significant purpose or do you simply slip through each day not knowing where you are going? There has to be a greater purpose to living than putting in eight hours in a factory or office, mowing grass, painting walls, eating, piddling in the yard, attending meetings, accumulating material items, or wasting meaningless hours before a TV screen.

May

Have we demeaned our very existence by ignoring the wonder of it? The Psalmist said to God:

When I look at your heavens, the work of your fingers, the moon and the stars that you have established; what are human beings that you are mindful of them, mortals that you care for them? Yet you have made them a little lower than God, and crowned them with glory and honor. (Psalm 8:3-5, NRSV)

Here, I think, is the key! We come to understand our uniqueness, our worth, our purpose, as we discover our value in God's sight. We uncover the mystery and wonder of our aliveness as we look beyond our self to the glory of God revealed in the majesty of creation. Take a simple flower, for example. Rather than casting an admiring glance at one, why not sit down with one? Examine its texture, its color, its tenderness and fragileness. Smell its fragrance and be awed by its exquisite beauty. Jesus said, "Consider the lilies of the field, how they grow: they neither toil nor spin; and yet I say to you that even Solomon in all his glory was not arrayed like one of these" (Matthew 6:28-29).

As you reflect back on your life, what is the legacy you will leave behind? Will you be remembered as a grouch, a recluse, a selfish person, one that was mean-spirited or intensely prejudiced, self-consumed and devoid of compassion? Will your neighbors miss you or hardly notice that you're gone? Or will hearts feel deep sorrow at your parting, regret that your days were not longer? Will the world in which you live feel a void, a loss that can never be filled? And will people, when sorrow has faded with time, reflect back upon your life with a smile and give thanks to God that their lives were touched by the uniqueness of yours?

I don't know about you, but I don't want to have passed across the horizon of this world without doing my best to have made it better. I do not wish to add to the evil of the world but to its goodness. Compliments and accolades I have no hunger for; but I would desire that I will have added something good or positive to the measure of each life I will have encountered. How about you? Are you satisfied with being remembered as things are now, or is God (even through

May

these simple words) awakening your heart to the grains of sand left in the hourglass of your life? Awake from your slumber, dear friend, and begin to discover the value in you to touch the lives of others with your own. Pour out the remaining days of your life in the beauty of goodness, in the tranquility of service to God, and in the joy of bringing smiles to the lives of all those whom you will encounter. God has a purpose for your life and you may rest assured it is a purpose that will bring Him glory, you peace, and your neighbor joy.

Soul Glory

26 I read a story recently about Michelangelo pushing a huge rock down a street. A man sitting on his porch observed him struggling with the rock and asked him why he was going to all that trouble for an old stone. Michelangelo's response was: "Because there is an angel in that rock and it wants to come out." (*Disciplines for the Inner Life*, p. 316). The story caused me to ponder the thought that within each of us there is something of significant value which is hidden and wants to be acknowledged.

The soul is not simply a part of us that was created for the purpose of being kept in storage until we reach eternity. If it was, then God would simply have waited until we got to heaven before we received it. Body and soul are not separate entities but are woven together to form the person we are. Unfortunately, most of us tend to focus all our attention on the part that is visible and forget the invisible segment which is no less significant than our bodies. Our souls long to be nurtured, cared for, loved, and developed by the grace and Spirit of God.

The soul is the inner part of ourselves that lives on beyond the body. It is the part that survives the grave and dwells somewhere in eternity. It is our "inner ear" whereby God communicates with the inner us. Spiritually we are guided and directed as our souls respond affirmatively to what they hear God saying. Most often, prayer is the physical means whereby we energize the inner voice which is spiritual. The less you pray, the less God's Spirit communicates. Jesus asked the rhetorical question, "What good will it be for a man if he gains the whole world, yet forfeits his soul? Or what can a man give in exchange

May

for his soul?" (Matthew 16:26). The implication of His question is that the soul is more valuable than the wealth of the world, and once it is eternally lost it cannot be regained. If our soul is that valuable, we would do well to ensure that it is recognized and nurtured. None of us would intentionally starve our bodies; why then do we constantly malnourish our soul?

When the mind is troubled, the soul that has been well-kept will bring to it the balm of calmness, for the soul can refresh the mind and usher it into the soothing presence of the Almighty. In Matthew 12:18 (KJV), God acknowledges Jesus with the words, "Here is my servant, whom I have chosen, my beloved, in whom my <u>soul</u> is well pleased." God has a soul and when we communicate with Him it is soul to soul. When we come before Him in prayer our souls touch His and we are cleansed, renewed, empowered.

In Genesis, when God created man, it says God breathed into him and he became a living soul. Perhaps a part of God, the soul, was implanted in each of us and it is that which is eternal. The Psalmist writes, "What is man that you are mindful of him, the son of man that you care for him? You made him a little lower than the heavenly beings and crowned him with glory and honor." (Psalm 8:4-5). We are endowed with glory and honor and it is manifested whenever we allow the soul to have its rightful place in our consciousness. Let your soul shine, for it will reveal the glory of God!

Paper Doll Days

27 If you were the parent of a small child and the time you spend with him or her was the same as the time you spend in communion with God, what would become of the child? Can a child be nurtured in any meaningful way if we acknowledge that child's existence for only a few minutes or a couple of hours a week? Yet in our relationship with God, it is not God that will be diminished or undernourished by our unwillingness to spend time with Him, but us! *In Man's Quest for God* by Abraham Joshua Heschel, we find these profound words of truth: "Prayer is 'our' humble 'answer' to the inconceivable surprise of living. It is all we can offer in return for the mystery by which we live" *(Disciplines for the Inner Life,* p. 66).

May

We have lost the childhood ability to be awed by the mystery of our aliveness. When we were children each new day was an adventure to be anticipated. There were hidden worlds to be explored, treasures of knowledge to be discovered, new friendships to be established. Then we grew up and narrowly set the parameters of our lives, greatly limiting what came in and went out of our tiny little world. How infinitely sad and how egotistical we are to think in our short span of years (no matter how many that may be) that we have tasted and exhausted all the experiences of life that God holds out as possibilities!

How sad and tragic it is that so many of us go through life with so little desire to grow closer to the One who created us. Years ago we established our daily routines for getting through the day and we have become so ensconced in our limited, tiny worlds that we have little desire to escape from their bondage. Like the homeless person who grows content with eating scraps found along the way and retiring each night to a house constructed from a cardboard box, we settle for a mere pittance of what God desires that we should experience. The hardest prison from which to escape is the one we have created for ourselves. That's because we alone hold the key to unlock the door and we have become so accustomed to our spiritual apathy that we can't muster the courage to be embraced by anything greater than ourselves.

And so we plod through "paper doll" days, each one as predictable, identical and meaningless as the one which preceded it. We make appointments for things we perceive to be important (doctors, auto maintenance, business meetings, dinner engagements, etc.) but think it ludicrous to make appointments to meet our Lord. It never occurs to us that when we have no time for God in our day, we are saying with our life that God is a low-priority, unimportant Being who means very little to us (until a crisis arises). How hurt we would feel if the **only** time our children contacted us was when they were in the midst of a problem.

I challenge you to re-think your life. Begin today to proclaim to the world that your life is "under new management" and the manager's name is Jesus. Make time for God in your life and discover the joy of being alive. Life doesn't have to be boring and mundane. Why not

May

resolve that you will have no more "paper doll" days? Now each one will be an exciting new adventure, hand in hand with God.

Faith is a Journey

28 Faith is not a destination; it is a journey. Just as we cannot suddenly by an act of the will make ourselves adults when we are children, neither can we will ourselves to have immediate and unshakable faith. Faith is a process of becoming. We can no more cause faith to grow than we can make the seed planted in the ground suddenly become the plant or tree we impatiently want to see arrive. Faith is a gift from God that we allow to grow in us. We can do things that give faith more opportunity to increase itself in us; things that in essence nurture and nourish this tiny seed of grace implanted in our heart, mind, and soul. Yes, faith is a gift of grace! God asks us to have faith; then, for those who are willing, He instills within us that precious gift which grows until it becomes outwardly obvious.

Faith is that mystical element of our being which builds a bridge across the chasm of despair and allows us to cross over without being mired in a pit from which we cannot extricate ourselves. When we feel attacked from every side, it is that shield of God which deflects those things or people who otherwise would do us spiritual harm. Faith becomes the light in our darkest moments that lightens our path into the presence of God. It is that burst of spiritual energy which heals our inner wounds and soothes the hurts that otherwise would leave us bitter.

Faith is that inner strength that is provided to help us through the valley of sorrow. Even though our hearts may be aching and our sense of loss intense, faith will not allow us to succumb to the temptation to quit living, but to keep on going even when we cannot clearly see the road ahead. Faith is God intervening in our lives, even when we cannot see or hear Him, to guide us in ways that our minds cannot begin to comprehend. It is like the air we breathe, essential but unseen; and like the very air we breathe that sustains us, it always is there even if we do not know from whence it comes.

May

Perhaps it was implanted in us when we were baptized as infants; or maybe it came to us when someone who loves us first read to us a Bible story. Yet again, it might not have taken root until we were older. Somehow it seems the longer we have lived without it the more difficult it is to allow it to establish itself within us. As children we are so open and trusting; as adults we become far too skeptical and wary. That's why Jesus said that to enter the kingdom of God we must be willing to be like children. Faith is more than feeling something—in fact, it does its most powerful work in us when we cannot feel it moving within. Faith is when you keep going even though you cannot see what is over the next hill of life. It is trusting that God (like the highway crews we put such trust in) has gone before you and smoothed the road, filled in the holes, built the bridges and created a highway whose destination leads to Himself.

When at last we reach the presence of God, we have arrived at that destination which faith has been carrying us toward for most, if not all, of our lives. What an adventure it has been, to discover little by little that God indeed can be trusted with our lives and with our souls. As we look back, we finally realize that faith is truly a journey.

Time for God

29 Finding time for God is essential to spiritual growth. If we are honest with ourselves, most of us will have to admit that more often than we not treat God as if He were a distant cousin—we recognize Him as family but aren't too moved to seek Him out and spend time with Him. We give God the leftovers of our life when there is nothing else to do, or if there is a special need that is beyond our power to fix. Daily we go merrily on our way, attempting to get through the day without consciously making time for God, and then have the audacity to wonder why we are so often unhappy and unfulfilled.

Oswald Chambers, in his book *Christian Discipline, Vol. 2* writes:

> *"Enter into thy closet." Did you ever say anything like this to yourself, "It is so difficult to select a place"? What about the time when you were in love, was it impossible to select a*

May

place to meet in? No, it was far from impossible; and beware of self-indulgence. Think how long our Lord has waited for you; you have seen Him in your visions, now pray to Him; get a place, not a mood, but a definite material place and resort to it constantly, and pray to God as His Spirit in you will help you" (From, *Disciplines for the Inner Life*, p. 218*)*.

God asks us to love Him above all things; yet we seem to love all things above Him. J. B. Phillips translates a passage of scripture from Paul's letter to the Romans (12:2) this way, "Don't let the world around you squeeze you into its own mold, but let God re-make you so that your whole attitude of mind is changed." The nature of modern living is that the world does try very hard to squeeze us into its mold. In the process God is squeezed out because we convince ourselves there is no time available to get serious with Him.

God comes to us each day in many ways and if we do not take the time to acknowledge Him, we will eventually reach the point that His presence is unrecognizable. What if, when Moses encountered the burning bush in the desert, he had simply said, "I have a full day's work today just looking after these sheep. I don't have time to go aside and find out what that bush is all about." He would have missed his opportunity with God. How many opportunities do we miss everyday because we simply won't take the time?

Spiritual discipline won't just happen. It will occur only when an individual decides it is a valuable part of his or her life that merits attention. If you get up on a cold winter morning and the house is freezing cold because the heating unit has broken, will you just sit there and assume that eventually the heat will start up on its own, or will you call the repairman to come and get it going? How is it possible that we have become so content with spiritual emptiness?

Don't wait until tomorrow. Right now, right this moment, even as you read these words, pause and say to God, "Lord show me how to make room for you in my world. Lead me aside and teach me how to live in the joy and peace that you have always longed for me to know. There is nothing in life more important than living in a consciousness of your presence Lord. Show me the way!"

May

Paradoxical Living

30

Much of what Jesus taught us about living is paradoxical—that which is seemingly contradictory but nonetheless true. For example, in the area of giving He taught: "Give and it shall be given to you; good measure, pressed down, and shaken together, and running over, will they pour into your lap" (Luke 6:38). Most of us do not find giving to be an easy thing. We acquire things in life and we tend to hold on to them rather tenaciously. Grudgingly, we let go of them.

Let's forget about material things for a minute and simply address ourselves to that which is intangible—for example, love. How freely do you express love to others? Can love truly be love if it is given only to those from whom you expect it to be returned? I once wrote, "You cannot give that which you do not have and you cannot keep that which you will not give away." It was true when I wrote it, and it is no less true now. There are some things in life that can only increase as we are willing to let go of them. If we love little, we will be little loved.

Some of us suffer from "hidden manna" disease. Remember how God told the Israelites when they were in the wilderness that He would feed them with manna from heaven; but they were forbidden to hoard it? They were to collect only enough for one day—the point being that they were to take God at His word, trust Him, and not worry about storing up enough for the next day or week. Those who disobeyed and hid some away discovered the next day that it had decayed and was filled with maggots. Ugh!

Love is really like manna from heaven. It is a precious gift which God imparts to us for the purpose of giving it away. If we try to hoard it for only ourselves or a small chosen few, it soon becomes stale and shrivels away. But if we will freely and generously give it away not only will we discover that it flows from us in unending supply, but it soon returns to us in an abundance that is almost miraculous—good measure, pressed down, shaken together, and running over.

God has set certain principles in motion in this world and we, like strong-willed children, are determined that we will defy them,

May

prove them to be untrue. In the process we rob ourselves of joy that we otherwise would have experienced. In any relationship, whether it is marital, parental, filial, or whatever, where love is rationed out it will come back to us in tiny measures (if it comes back at all). If you want to be greatly loved, then give love greatly. To restrain love is to strangle love. To give love is to trust God to increase its measure just as one kernel of corn, released in faith to the soil, can bring forth a stalk that will yield a hundredfold.

But alas, we refuse to embrace the paradox of God's Word and insist on hoarding the hidden manna. In so doing, we ensure that we will always live in scarcity rather than in abundance. Paradoxical living is faith living, and faith will surrender its treasure only to those who freely give.

Obedience and the Spirit

31 While attending Annual Conference in Fayetteville, NC, I was privileged to hear Dr. Eddie Fox, one of the guest preachers, make the following statement: "The great sin of the United Methodist Church today is not omission or commission but no mission." He went on to say that it was essential that the church open itself up to the power of the Holy Spirit. He said, "No Holy Spirit, no church." The average person in the pew, so it seems, is quite content to live out the routines of his or her life, secure in the fallible and limited power of self. The church has not been called into being to become an institution, it was called into being to be the living, breathing, witnessing body of Jesus Christ in the world.

Where the church is truly the church the evidence of God's wondrous grace will make itself undeniably known. We sometimes get so lost in meetings, committees, boards and agencies that we lose sight of our mission, which is, as I understand it, to offer Christ to the world and to live before the world in such a manner as to clearly reveal the presence of Christ in our lives. If such a concept does not turn you on to get busy, then maybe you need to ponder how much of God's Spirit you have allowed into your life. If we were Christians in Jerusalem in the months following Jesus' crucifixion and resurrection, and put forth no more effort to share that good news with the world than we seem to do today, then the church would never have survived the first century.

We have tried to substitute the concept of church membership for the active reality of genuine discipleship. Jesus did not call you to become a member of an organization; He called you to become a follower of the Way—His Way. In his renowned book, *The Cost of Discipleship*, Dietrich Bonhoeffer said, "Christianity without the living Christ is inevitably Christianity without discipleship, and Christianity without discipleship is always Christianity without Christ" (p. 63). In talking about Jesus calling the disciples, Bonhoeffer said, "The response of the disciples is an act of obedience, not a confession of faith in Jesus" (p. 61). Words are easily spoken but apart from genuine discipleship they are useless.

To follow Christ should be the goal of everyone who claims to accept Him as Lord. J. Rufus Moseley writes:

> *Willing to do His will, and then doing it in so far as you know it to be His will, is the Way to an increasing knowledge of Him. We do not know by study alone, we know by obedience. Obedience is the organ of knowledge and the condition of revelation. . . . There is no need of His revealing His will until we are ready to do His will. (Perfect Everything*, p. 30)

Coming to know Jesus in an intimate way then, is paradoxical, like so much of what Jesus taught. We know Him through obedience; we do not come to obedience only after we have fully known Him.

The more obedient we become to Christ, the more fully His Spirit comes to rest in us. The more fully His Spirit rests in us, the less difficult it becomes to serve Him. The less difficult it becomes to serve Him, the easier and greater becomes our love for Him. The greater our love for Him, the easier it is to love self and others.

The Healing Balm of Grace

1 G. Campbell Morgan was one of 150 young men who sought entrance to the Wesleyan ministry in 1888. He passed the doctrinal examinations, but then faced the trial sermon. In a

June

cavernous auditorium that could seat more than 1,000 sat three ministers and seventy-five others who came to listen. When Morgan stepped into the pulpit, the vast room and the searching, critical eyes caught him up short. Two weeks later Morgan's name appeared among the 105 rejected for the ministry that year.

Jill Morgan, his daughter-in-law, wrote of him in her book, *A Man of the Word*: "He wired to his father the one word, 'Rejected,' and sat down to write in his diary: 'Very dark everything seems. Still, He knoweth best.' Quickly came the reply: 'Rejected on earth. Accepted in heaven. Dad.'" G. Campbell Morgan went on to become one of the greatest preachers of the twentieth century. His sermons are treasures of expository excellence.

No matter how dark the day seems, life will inevitably turn again toward the good. Many people find themselves in moments of deep despair, moments when it doesn't seem possible that life can ever be good again. Yet if we will but hang on, circumstances will turn once more to a time in which it will seem wonderful to be alive. Following my divorce, I discovered the anguish and despair that comes with a broken relationship. Depression set in and the will to keep living became a heavy burden to be borne. The joy of life evaporated, pain cut deep into my soul, and I could not imagine that I would ever laugh again.

But God's grace cuts across the bonds of human despair. When the soul becomes mired down in the bog of hopelessness, when even laughter has receded into nothing more than a faint and fading memory, when everything around us seems shrouded in darkness and the light of living seems but a shadow, if we will recline spiritually in the presence of God, He will restore us to wholeness and shatter the chaos of our darkness with the glorious light of His grace and love. Paul writes in Ephesians 1:19, "How tremendous is the power available to us who believe in God" (Phillips translation).

How well and how soon we escape the dungeon of our dark despair depends upon where we place our focus. If we choose to dwell on our circumstances, if we rehash and relive our mistakes over and over again, if we heap upon ourselves guilt upon guilt, then we will be constantly crushed by the weight of our self-imposed burden. But if we look to God in faith, if we place our hope not in our own strength but in His ability to restore our brokenness with the joy of living, sooner than later our feet will once more tread the path of peace and happiness.

God created life to be good, not unbearable. He is in the restoration business of healing wounded hearts and souls. Place your burden upon Him, and discover the healing balm of His grace once more!

The Best of the Past

2 Sometimes I sit and ponder how different the church today looks from the one described in the Bible. The portrait that emerges from the pages of God's Word is a picture of everyday people, not overly educated, certainly not in possession of much of the world's wealth, not very religious (in the sense of being like their Pharisaic leaders wanted them to be), meeting in houses, yet absolutely filled with amazing power. There's nothing in the New Testament about elaborate liturgies, highly formal and strictly structured services of worship, or preachers who tried to impress their congregations with their academic accomplishments or great theological insights.

The thing about the early church which jumps off the biblical page was that they were in love with a Person, not an institution. Jesus was not a historical concept to them, not just because they weren't centuries removed from when He lived, but because they daily experienced His aliveness within the innermost part of their being. What was most important to them was daily communion with the God who had become Emmanuel (God with us); not the polity of a denomination, or the latest fad in technological evangelism. They didn't increase their numbers for the sake of quarterly reports to the home office, but through the unbridled power of the Holy Spirit and for the glory and praise of God. The living Spirit of the holy God had settled into the commonplace corners of their daily lives and breathed into them the joy of being alive.

Though I am sure there were times when the sermons of Peter and Paul might have been boring and less than inspiring, they didn't just walk out the door at noon and go home and forget that what they

June

said mattered. I don't think that the people in Peter and Paul's day were really any different than those in our day—human nature and need remains pretty much the same regardless of which century we happen to live in. The difference seems to be that they were unsophisticated enough to open their hearts to the power of the Holy Spirit and discover that He could come in and transform their lives from the inside out.

Most denominations have a wonderful heritage and wonderful churches. We grow comfortable with our way of worshiping and the building in which we worship. But my friends, no one was ever saved by a denomination, no structure or liturgy died on a cross for the souls of humankind. I am not suggesting that we throw out the familiar trappings of our churches, I am imploring us to look at them as only a means of pointing us to what is really important. What matters, and matters eternally, is whether Jesus Christ has been allowed to become Lord of your life. Churches don't give you eternal life. Only God's precious Son, dying on a cross, has the power to give you what down in your soul you long for, and maybe don't even recognize as your craving.

We can't return to the first century, nor should we. But a living, vital faith in Christ is timeless. There are some things about the past that we ought to bring with us into the future and a Holy Spirit-energized, grace of God-empowered faith is one of them. Too much "religion" and not enough of God's Spirit will never transform us into what we were created to be.

The Battle with Fear

3 We live in a world that is filled with fear. Even people we know and assume to be strong often hide or try to mask the fact that deep down inside they are afraid. We often fear things which have not yet happened (and may never happen). We are afraid of failure, of not being loved, of becoming sick, of dying. We are afraid that we might not be liked or appreciated, that we might become unable to care for ourselves when we are old, and have to be placed in a nursing home. Some live in apprehension that they won't have enough money to retire on; or their children won't care about them

June

when they're old. The list could go on and on. But God is not the author of fear. He is the One who abolishes it.

Fear is a thief—it robs us of peace; it steals from us happiness and it causes us to be riddled with jealousy which in turn makes us unlovable. It sneaks its way into our hearts and sows its seeds of destruction in our relationships with people and more importantly, in our relationship with God. Fear gives birth to doubt, doubt begets suspicion, suspicion brings forth anxiety, and anxiety, like cancer, eats away at the joy of living. When fear controls us it usurps the place of God in our lives. If our trust is in God, and if God is faithful to His Word (as He always is), then we having nothing to fear. But if we embrace fear we have surrendered ourselves to a power that is less than God and that is approaching idolatry.

The Word of God says, "There is no fear in love. But perfect love drives out fear, because fear has to do with punishment. The one who fears is not made perfect in love" (I John 4:18). Think about how many times Jesus said to people, "Do not be afraid!" In the Gospel of Mark we read about Jairus' daughter dying. When word reached the synagogue leader that his daughter was dead (prior to Jesus arriving), Jesus' words to him were, "Don't be afraid; just believe" (Mk. 5:36b). Belief and trust in God is the key that banishes fear.

Perhaps nothing causes many people greater fear than dying. But in Hebrews 2:14-15 we are told that Jesus came in the flesh "so that by his death he might destroy him who holds the power of death— that is, the devil—and free those who all their lives were held in slavery by their fear of death." When fear controls us, we become its slave. It summons and we obey, it threatens and we shrink in alarm. It has the power to totally consume us, causing us to find no joy in being alive. What a great victory that is for Satan! But Jesus said, "I have come that you might have joy and peace." His death on the cross was for more than just the redemption of our sins; it was to set us free from everything in life that spiritually binds and enslaves us. The person whom the Son sets free is free indeed!

Today, I exhort you to take your fear to God. Tell Him how it binds your life, robs you of peace, causes you sleepless nights and anxious days; and ask Him to set you free. If God is your heavenly

June

Father, and surely He is, then what can ultimately harm you? Learn to say with the Psalmist, "The Lord is my light and my salvation, whom shall I fear? The Lord is the stronghold of my life—of whom shall I be afraid?" (Psalm 27:1). Indeed, what is there to fear?

The Temporary and the Permanent

4 I gaze out my study window and see two bulldozers scooping up great mounds of dirt as they prepare the surface for our church's extended parking lot. I smile as I reflect on how busy man always is, rearranging what God created millions of years ago. But, we have His blessing, for He told Adam in the garden to till the soil and to work the land. I suppose years from now someone else will be on a bulldozer on this land, rearranging what our generation has built, just as the old white wooden church that once stood on this site gave way fifty years ago to the dream of that generation. That's how it should be!

It all reminds me how temporary things in this life really are. Change is built into the fabric of life and if we do not change then we surely will be left behind. And yet, the irony is that as we grow older we become more and more resistant to change and long to hang on to the things and ways with which we have grown comfortable. How refreshing it is to see an elderly person who has so retained the zest for life, that he or she is open to new things and new adventures. It is always a joy to be around folks like that because their delight in life becomes contagious.

God's Word reminds us that "if the earthly tent we live in is destroyed, we have a building from God, an eternal house in heaven, not built by human hands. " (II Corinthians 5:1) Perhaps Paul calls the human body a tent because it was designed to be temporary. Tents are made to be taken down and moved from place to place. But the home God has prepared for our soul is a building, made by God Himself; and it is permanent and eternal. If that is so, why do we live as though the flesh which covers our bones is here forever?

We need to spend more time preparing for the eternal future and less time dwelling in the past, or just idly watching the days of the present slip by. We say that we believe in a spiritual dimension to life, but we spend so little time living as if we do. In preparing for a life in ministry, I spent 10 years in college and seminary—time well spent in preparing me to minister to the physical and spiritual needs of my people. But I find so few who seem at all interested in discovering the vibrant spirit within. Earth's alluring pursuits claim their time and desires while the soul within languishes with starvation and cries to be fed. "Not me!" you say. But ask yourself, "How often do I read God's Word?" Once a week, once a month, only when I'm in church? "How often do I pray?" Once a day, once a month, almost never? "How often do I worship God? How much of what He has blessed me with am I willing to return to His work and service? How many people on this earth have ever heard the name of Jesus come from my lips?" How you answer those questions should give you some idea of how far down the road to spiritual awareness you have traveled.

Life changes, the world changes, people change, but the one constant thing in all the universe is God's love for you and His desire to be in communion with you. Are you willing to open up your heart and soul and allow the bulldozer of His Spirit to remake you? It will only happen when you desire it, when you request it. Will you?

The Eyes of the Soul

5 Has God become real to you yet? Strange question, you may be thinking, to be asking someone who's probably a church member. But I wonder how many people who attend church make their way through life never quite certain that this being we call God really exists. "I've never seen Him, or heard Him, or touched Him," you might say, "therefore how can I possibly know that He exists? And if He really exists why should He care about me? Who am I, that God should care?" Sort of like the Psalmist, aren't we, when he wrote, "What are human beings that you are mindful of them, mortals that you care for them?" (Psalm 8:4, NRSV).

We sometimes ponder: "Why does God seem to hide Himself? If He would only come out into the open where we can see and hear Him then we would have no trouble in believing in and serving Him."

June

When that happened to the Hebrews in the wilderness, they were so frightened by the mighty presence of God that they asked Moses to tell God not to speak to them again; to let Moses convey God's messages to them. Nonetheless, I think God does reveal Himself to us in many ways; we just aren't "tuned" in to listen. There are hundreds of radio stations sending signals into the air all around us, but we will only discern them when we tune our radio to their frequency.

In the book, *The Disinherited Mind*, Erich Heller relates the following story about Karl Vallentin, one of Munich's greatest clowns. ". . . the curtain goes up and reveals darkness; and in this darkness is a solitary circle of light thrown by a street light. Vallentin, with his long-drawn and deeply worried face, walks round and round this circle of light desperately looking for something. 'What have you lost?' a policeman asks who has entered the scene. 'The key to my house.' Upon which the policeman joins him in his search; they find nothing; and after a while he inquires: 'Are you sure you lost it here?' 'No,' says Vallentin, and pointing to a dark corner of the stage: 'Over there.' 'Then why on earth are you looking for it here?' 'There is no light over there,' says Vallentin" (from *Opening Blind Eyes*, by John Claypool p. 95). So it is in our search for God: if we only look for him in the places we feel secure, we may never find Him.

My experience has been that God has always revealed Himself to me in the times of my greatest insecurity, my biggest doubts, and my greatest failures. Still, most of the awareness that I have of His nearness in those moments came upon reflection when viewed in hindsight. Often it is in the darkest moments of life that we discover the light of God's presence. When the eye of our soul first catches a glimpse of the tiny light of His presence and then focuses on that light, the consciousness of God's reality grows in magnitude and clarity.

God comes to us more often in quietness rather than noise. Elijah discovered Him in the still small voice, not the whirlwind, lightning, and thunder. On a dark, cold, and quiet night the Babe of Bethlehem slipped into our world and except for a very few, His presence went unobserved. God is present with you; He isn't hiding, but you will see Him only when you seek Him in faith with the eyes of your soul.

June

The Boomerang Principle

6 The words of Jesus are not complicated or difficult to understand. Whatever the reason may be that we do not live up to them, it is not because we do not understand them. More than likely it is because we do not ponder them in our heart and choose to apply them to our lives. Take for example the simple statement (simple but profoundly true), 'Whatsoever you sow, that shall you also reap." We can grasp that for we know enough about planting gardens or flowers to know that the seed you sow will produce its own kind. Yet Jesus has said that the same axiom applies to the spiritual aspect of our being. If we are grumpy and mean-spirited, just like a boomerang that is what will come back to us. If we are selfish and stingy, then we will not receive the multitude of blessings that others would confer upon us. If we are self-centered and egocentric then the world will ensure that we live in our self-imposed isolation.

We become like that to which we give ourselves. We cannot reveal the spirit of Christ to anyone until we give ourselves to His spirit. In reality, the human life becomes a reflection of that to which we have given ourselves. Human beings do not have within them the power to remake themselves. A "self-made" man" is a contradiction, for no one can make themselves (at least not in any spiritual sense). To give our lives to anything that is less than Christ will ensure that we will reflect everything but Christ.

The Apostle Paul was acutely aware of the weakness of human flesh. Read Romans 7:14-25 and see how Paul struggled with the frailty of his own human nature (". . . the good I would do, I do not do, and the evil which I don't want to do, I find myself doing. . . "). He realized that he did not have the power to change himself, but discovered that Jesus could change Him "What a wretched man I am! Who will rescue me from this body of death? Thanks be to God—through Jesus Christ our Lord!" (Romans 7:24-25).

At the heart of Paul's gospel is the proclamation of living "in Christ." Again and again he uses that phrase in describing his own life. He sowed the weakness of his flesh into the life-changing soil of the spirit of Jesus and it changed his life forever. He began to reveal Christ because he sowed his life in Christ. We will give our lives to

June

something—that is a foregone conclusion. And what we give ourselves to will be made manifestly evident to all those around us. If we give ourselves to anything that is less than God then we will begin down a path that inevitably leads us to where love isn't.   J. Rufus Moseley writes:

> *The only possible way for God to be God (Love) and remain God (Love) is for Him to Love us and love the universe into loving. The only possible way to respond to His love is to love. (Perfect Everything,* pp., 69)

Realizing then that the simple words of Jesus are profoundly true, what are you sowing? Are you sowing kindness, love, mercy, and peace; or anger, hate, strife, and turmoil? People who give love will inevitably be loved. How loved are you?

The Assurance of Salvation

Many people, I am discovering, have a difficult time in trusting in the efficacy of their faith. Most of their lives they have done their best to faithfully serve the Lord and yet still, in the back of their minds is the nagging question, "Have I been faithful enough?" Invariably, their minds will bring to the surface of their consciousness one incident after another in which they failed to do the best they could. They will allow past mistakes and failures to unmercifully torment them into believing that they are outside the power of God's redeeming grace. How sad that must make our Lord who understands human frailty so well!

At the very heart and core of the gospel is the unchanging message that God loves us in spite of ourselves. Yes, He asks us to love Him and to try our best to faithfully serve Him, and yet, God has room in His love for our failures. The human being that loves us the most on this earth does not stop loving us when we say or do some unkind thing in a moment of weakness. Why should we think that God's love is less noble?

John Wesley, founder of the Methodist Church, had faithfully served God from the time he was a child, and yet he found himself tormented with the fear that God would not save him. It was only in a

June

moment of spiritual awakening at Aldersgate that he finally settled it in his heart that God forgave him when he failed and loved him in spite of his failures. He was thirty-five years old when that realization finally took place and by that time he had already traveled to America and had been preaching for years. Listen again to his uplifting words as he went very unwillingly to a church service at Aldersgate: "About a quarter before nine, while he [a reader reading from Luther's preface to the Book of Romans] was describing the change which God works in the heart through faith in Christ, I felt my heart strangely warmed. I felt I did trust in Christ, Christ alone for salvation; and an assurance was given me that He had taken away my sins, even mine, and saved me from the law of sin and death."

God does not want us to doubt our salvation because our salvation is not based upon our goodness but upon the faithfulness of God to love us even if we are sinners. All He asks is that we accept through faith what He so freely and graciously gives—life eternal. But even if we continue to have residual feelings of doubt, God will not withhold His love from us, for God's faithfulness is not dependent upon our strength. Does that mean that we are therefore free to live as sinfully as we choose? Of course not! God expects us to live in faithful obedience to His Word. But He also understands that no human being's faith is perfect. One moment it seems strong, the next it appears weak. One moment it convinces us of the assurance of God's love, the next it fails to persuade us that there is anything in us that is even good.

I guess the point I'm trying to make is that your faith and God's faithfulness are not dependent upon how you "feel." Long before Wesley received his "assurance," God's love and acceptance of him had never wavered. It was only in the mind of Wesley that his salvation seemed uncertain. It was never that way in the mind and heart of God.

Grace and Assurance

8 We admire and are sometimes in awe of the great Christian leaders of the past such as Augustine, Luther, Wesley, and others. But if you read their biographies you will discover that they

June

experienced many of the same doubts and fears that most of us encounter in life. We do ourselves, and them, a disservice when we fail to recognize their "normal" humanity. Take for example Wesley's great transforming experience at Aldersgate (referred to in yesterday's meditation). For years he had struggled to find inner peace regarding the assurance of his own salvation, and finally it came. But then he went off the deep end and began to preach that unless a person had that inner assurance then he or she was not saved.

As the years passed by, Wesley began to realize that what he was requiring of people was not only discouraging them, more importantly it was biblically wrong. In the latter years of his life he wrote to a friend (Melville Horne) and said,

> When fifty years ago my brother Charles and I, in the simplicity of our hearts, told the good people of England that unless they knew their sins were forgiven, they were under the wrath and curse of God, I marvel, Melville they did not stone us! The Methodists, I hope, know better now; we preach assurance as we always did, as a common privilege of the children of God; but we do not enforce it under the pain of damnation, denounced on all who enjoy it not. (Sermons, I, 82, f.n.)

There is a tremendous difference between requiring someone to feel assured of their salvation and saying it is a privilege that someone can have if they want it. It is essential that we not cause people to believe that they can only be saved by God's grace if they "feel" saved. Wesley wrote (Letters, V, 358-59) ". . . I have not for many years thought a consciousness of pardon to be essential to justifying faith." You may do something that hurts me and I tell you I forgive you. Then you may go off somewhere and say, "He couldn't possibly forgive me for that; he must still hold it against me." What you think or even feel about my forgiveness does not determine whether I actually forgive you or not. My ability to forgive is not dependent upon whether you think I have, or not. Neither is God's forgiveness of us determined by our knowing it without any doubt.

Grace is called grace because it stands on its own and is undeserved. If we deserved it, earned it, or had a right to it, then it

June

wouldn't be grace. God forgives because it is the nature of God to forgive. Forgiveness is a gift offered in advance of our asking for it. Grace precedes repentance, though repentance is necessary in order to receive grace into our hearts. Grocery stores are filled with life-sustaining food. But the food that is there is only helpful to us when we willingly partake of it.

God does not lie. He has proclaimed, "This is the will of my Father, that **all** who see the Son and believe in Him may have eternal life; and I will raise them up on the last day" (John 6:37). Accept that you are saved, simply because God promises that you are if you believe in His Son! Don't trust in your own goodness to save you—it can't. But the goodness of God can. That's His promise. That's the truth!

A More Beautiful Melody

9 The presence of temptation in human life is a common dilemma. When we fall victim to its power we are made painfully aware of the weakness of the human mind and spirit. In the Middle Ages, devout Christian men and women tried to resist temptation by isolating themselves from the world in monasteries, thinking that if they weren't exposed to the sins of the world they would be able to remain sinless themselves. They soon discovered that sin was an inner problem of the heart, mind, and spirit, and that solitude and asceticism did not have the power to banish sinful thoughts and desires.

We can learn a valuable lesson about resisting temptation from Greek mythology. When Ulysses was sailing the seas on one of his wandering journeys, he had to pass by the island of the Sirens somewhere near the coast of Italy. These beautiful enchantresses purportedly had the power to sing such beautiful songs that no man could resist their alluring melodies and turned their ships toward the island where their boats were smashed on the rocky shoals—they died in the ecstasy of delight. Ulysses, aware of the danger of their enchanting melodies, ordered his men to plug their ears with wax and tie him to the mast of the ship, thus allowing him to hear the beautiful

June

music without sailing into destruction. He flirted with temptation and survived only by extraordinary restraints on himself and his men.

Later, when the Argonauts were in pursuit of the Golden Fleece, they too had to pass by the island of Sirens. But Jason, their leader, knew a better way to resist the bewitching melody that flowed across the waves. He ordered Orpheus, a musician of rare talent, to play his lyre and sing a song more beautiful than the Sirens. His song was so sweet and majestic it far surpassed that of the Sirens and the ship sailed safely by. (Adapted from *Milestone Papers*, by Daniel Steele, p. 145-46).

We cannot resist the wiles of the Tempter through will power and sheer determination. Satan does not come to us revealed as he really is; he always comes in alluring disguise, beautiful and appealing, tempting and enchanting. We best resist his power not through the force of our will but by listening to a more beautiful melody—the melody of our Lord. When our minds, hearts and souls are fixed on Jesus, when we invite Him into the center of our lives, then we can resist the wiles of evil because the music of life which our Lord sings to our souls will always surpass in beauty and power the destructive melody of the fallen one.

Daniel Steele said it well:

> *Melody had surpassed melody. Here is set forth the secret of the Christian's triumph. Joy must conquer joy. The joy of the Holy Ghost in the heart must surpass all the pleasure of the senses. When all heaven is warbling in the believer's ear, the whispers of the tempter grate upon the purified sensibilities as saw filing rasps the nerves. . . .The Orphean lyre is a better safeguard than the Ulyssean wax. Lashing one's self to the mast may be heroic, but is it is not the highest style of heroism. Jason acted a braver and wiser part than Ulysses. To be sure, it is better to incapacitate one's self from sin than to be cast into hell "having two hands and two feet." But it is still better to present the whole body a living sacrifice, and with all our faculties unimpaired and free, to love the Lord with all the strength.* (pp.146, 47)

June

Called to Follow

10   As a child, it never struck me as unusual that people such as the tax collector Matthew would suddenly drop all that they were doing and take off after Jesus when He simply said, "Follow Me." But since I have become an adult, I have realized that their willingness to leave all behind and suddenly change the course of life seems out of character with what I have come to learn about human nature. Assuming that the biblical narrative is true, I am left with the conclusion that there must have been something so powerfully compelling about Jesus' nature that He drew forth from men extraordinary behavior. It could not have been that they understood a great deal about Jesus, for it appears this was a first encounter. Therefore, it must have been Jesus' ability to convey an overwhelming sense of love that drew men, women, and children to Him.

One naturally assumes that to make the commitment to follow someone with your life, you need to fully understand him or her. But as Frederick Buechner points out, "You do not come first to understand a person fully and then to love him, but love comes first, and then it is out of the love that understanding is born" (*The Magnificent Defeat*, pp. 98-99). Matthew must have felt intensely loved by Jesus and that love was made all the more real because Matthew knew that he not only was not generally loved by people—indeed, he was despised. Jesus saw in Matthew not so much what he was, but what he could become.

Divine love is the power that draws faith out of us. A person can believe in, follow, and commit to someone who loves him or her unconditionally. Again quoting Buechner, "Faith is the word that describes the direction our feet start moving when we find that we are loved. Faith is stepping out into the unknown with nothing to guide us but a hand just beyond our grasp" (p. 99). The biblical story of Jesus is the story of how God has decided to overcome the hell of human sin with the heaven of divine love. Love is the magnet that draws us into the holy presence of God whereby our entire being becomes changed by the transforming power of holiness and righteousness. We follow because some inner part of our being causes us to know that we **must** follow, even if we don't know exactly where we are going.

June

God beckons and we follow. It is a strange process that seems enshrouded in mystery because we discover that following by faith "will take us not where we want to go necessarily but where we are wanted, until, by a kind of alchemy, where we are wanted becomes where we want to go" (*The Magnificent Defeat*, p. 99). Read the biographies of the great leaders of the Christian faith and you will discover that without exception they all came to the point of yielding their entire lives to the directing Spirit of God. Self became lost in service. Pride was consumed by humility. Sin and rage were replaced with holiness and peace. And love became the bond that bound life together in meaning and purpose.

The world in which we live is not devoid of the voice of God. It is all around us, but we dismiss it. We dismiss it because we either do not yet perceive how deeply we are loved, or we do not feel worthy of such love and so we run from it. But by God's grace, one day it will overtake us and then we can do nothing less than to follow because our unworthiness will be washed away in the light of unfathomable love.

Sing Me a Song

11 The Psalmist, finding himself unwillingly carried into exile in Babylon, pours out his heart to God. His captors had demanded that he sing songs of merriment while they feasted and laughed. He writes in Psalm 137:

> *By the waters of Babylon, there we sat down and wept, when we remembered Zion. On the willows there we hung up our lyres, for there our captors required of us songs, and our tormentors, mirth, saying, "Sing us one of the songs of Zion."*

Then he asks the rhetorical question, "How can we sing the Lord's song in a strange land?" There seem to be times in every Christian's life when it is difficult to sing the Lord's song; times when our lives seem exiled to a foreign land—not literally, but mentally, spiritually, and emotionally.

Trials and tribulations come to us all and Christians, like all other human beings, are not exempt. A marital conflict, a wayward

June

child, the loss of a job, the betrayal by a friend, the suffering of a loved one, the unwelcome news that we have some serious illness—all these are captors who seek to drag our spirits into exile in the foreign land of despair and depression. And we, like the Psalmist, ask ourselves, "How can I sing the Lord's song in a foreign land?" In other words, how can there be any peace, any joy, any hope in my heart when these burdens of life have overwhelmed me?

One thing I have learned in my own experience is that peace can come to us in the midst of whatever trouble we are facing. We do not always have the ability to change the things that are troubling us, but we do have the ability to trust the One who can change them. In order to discover that trust, however, we must first be willing to seek the One who is worthy of trust.

Maxie Dunnam writes about Maggie Savoy (a very talented society editor of The Los Angeles Times). Maggie had undergone surgery for abdominal cancer and recovered. The disease was in remission for five and a half years and then returned. Here are some of Maggie's thoughts on the subject of her own mortality and battle with death:

> *Dying is more beautiful the second time around. No easier. But there is joy to be wrung from the second time.... Like the fact of cancer, I learned another fact. I may not have the choice over what kills me, but I do have a choice over what I kill. I have the power to shape, make, spend, use every single hour still on the books. And I have the power to shape, make, and build love. These are the only things I really own, the only ME there is.* (*Living the Psalms*, pp. 96-97).

I would add to Maggie's testimony that we have the power to discover the joy of our Lord's presence in the desolation of our exiles. We can sing a joyful song within our hearts and souls even in the midst of life's captivities, because no matter where we find ourselves captive, God has not been left behind in our homeland. Indeed, our homeland is always where God is, and God is always where we are. When trouble besets us and mocks us, taunts us with the words, "Let me hear you sing us a song," we can respond, "All right, I will sing

June

you a song about the God who never deserts me, who promises to meet my every need, and who is even now preparing my home to receive me. It's a joyful song and one that you cannot take from me." Peace!

Tears in a Bottle

12 If you have ever read many of the Psalms you discovered that a great number of them deal with the writer crying out to God for help in time of trouble. I suppose that is why so many people find them comforting and uplifting. Such is the case in Psalm 56 in which the Psalmist proclaims that God is aware of his sorrow and distress. He writes: "Thou hast kept count of my tossings; put thou my tears in thy bottle! Are they not in thy book?" (56:8, KJV) Putting tears in a bottle is a strange concept to most of us, but to the Psalmist it was a normal part of the culture in which he lived. When great trouble or death struck a family member, the tears of the family would be gathered in a bottle and in the case of death, were often buried with the deceased. The intent was to show that they all shared in the suffering.

Tears are a part of human life. Indeed, we begin life with tears when we come forth from our mother's womb. They give expression to the deep emotional and sometimes physical needs within. They are a part of the way God designed us to function. Through the tears that we shed, the pain of our emotions finds release and our spirit cleanses itself of anguish that can be set free in no other way. Tears also reveal the depth of the bond we feel with the suffering of another. Their pain in some strange mystical way, becomes a part of our own emotional well-being.

Maxie Dunnam recounts the story of a young woman in his church who had recently lost a great-aunt who was almost like a mother to her. She had cried a great deal and her six year old daughter, Katy, was concerned about her mother. She painted her a picture and gave it to her saying, "I want you to feel better." That night, when she was putting Katy to bed, she thanked her and told her the picture had made her feel better, but added, "Katy, I want you to know that Mommy may cry a lot more, because I loved Ola so much."

"But Mommy," Katy said, "I'm afraid you'll turn into a tear."

June

"Well," she said, "If I turned into a tear, would you wipe me up?"

"No," said Katy, "I'd put you into my eye." (From, *Living the Psalms: A Confidence For All Seasons*, pp. 74-75).

The Psalmist asked God to put his tears in a bottle because it was a way of affirming that God shared his suffering. It is somehow comforting to us when we are in pain to know that God is not oblivious to our distress. One way that we can be sure that is true is revealed by the suffering love of God for us on a cross. Isaiah said, "Surely, he has borne our griefs and carried our sorrows," (53:4, KJV). Part of Christ's atoning sacrifice was not only to absorb into His own being our sins, but also to take upon Himself our sorrows.

No matter how isolated we may feel, we are never alone. The God of grace and compassion is always standing in the shadows of our lives weeping with us when we weep and suffering with us when we suffer. The long hours of the night, when we fitfully toss and turn on our beds, are observed by the One who keeps watch with us. Take comfort in knowing that no matter what you must face in life, you will always be able to meet it in the added strength of the Shepherd who keeps watch over you.

Building or Body

13 *It happened one day that St. Thomas [Aquinas], who was a Franciscan monk, was sitting in the Vatican with Pope Innocent IV, when masses of gold and silver were being carried into the Papal treasury.* "You see," said the Pope with a touch of self-satisfaction, "the age of the Church is past when she could say, 'Silver and gold have I none.'" "Yes, Holy Father," replied the Angelic Doctor, "and the day is also past when she could say to the paralytic—'Take up thy bed and walk!'" (*Companions for the Soul*, April 4).

There is always great danger to the church when it accumulates wealth for its own benefit. If we are not careful, over a period of time and in almost imperceptible ways, the church turns inward upon itself and loses sight of its mission and its ministry. From time to time,

June

churches become the benefactors of large amounts of money that are willed to them by some loving parishioner. As a result, the congergation faces the challenge of how best to use the money. Far too often they choose to spend it all on themselves and are quite hesitant to channel it into missions and outreach. They give little thought to the fact that buildings disintegrate into rubble as time marches on, but ministry, carried on in the precious name of Christ, has eternal implications. Large monetary gifts bring with them the potential to be a blessing or a curse. What they become will be determined by whether we look inward or outward.

Church buildings may be desirable and even necessary, but if all we use our building for is to bless ourselves in comfort and neglect the call of God to minister to others, then we will have surely lost sight of why we were called into being. At the heart of our faith is the message of salvation and that message was given in order that it might be shared. Does it concern us that there are people living in the shadow of our churches who hear or know nothing about our Lord?

For the committed pastor and layperson, nothing is more important than being a channel whereby the kingdom of God can be made known among His people. The reality is that we don't build anything that is spiritual; we receive what God builds and we are nothing more than unworthy vessels who have the joyous privilege of passing it on to others. We cannot build the "kingdom," we can only pass on what we receive.

If we truly live our lives as if we believe there is a heaven and a hell, we will not be content to sit passively by while the world around us marches on in blissful ignorance. The power of the first-century church was not found in its material wealth—it had none! Its power and attraction was revealed in hearts surrendered to the power of the Holy Spirit and in its desire to share the message of salvation with the world—no matter what the cost.

In Acts, chapter three, Peter and John were on the way to the temple to pray when they met the man lame from birth. He asked them for alms. Peter's response was, "Silver or gold I do not have, but what I have I give you. In the name of Jesus Christ of Nazareth, walk." What do we give to those around us whose need is no less?

June

The Value of Small Things

14 We live in a nation and in a time in which little value is given to small things. A person's worth (according to conventional wisdom) is determined by the size of the bank account, the number of square feet in their house, what kind of automobile they drive, whether they belong to the "biggest" church, or how popular they are in the community. The "little" people are often brushed aside as pawns to be used for nominal tasks that are beneath the elite.

With Jesus it was not so. Strange how differently He viewed things. He gave value to that which was declared to be insignificant—the widow's tiny mite, the unclean leper, the cup of cold water given in His name, the smallest infant in His midst, the one lamb missing from a flock of a hundred, the adulterous woman thrown at his feet, the vineyard laborer who only worked an hour, the young boy with two loaves and five fishes, the tiny mustard seed, the tax collector who hid in the shadows of the temple, too ashamed to lift his eyes to heaven. He saw more beauty in the lilies on a hillside than He did in all of Solomon's glory—and on and on it could go. Jesus never measured the value of a person's life with the standards that the world sets forth.

From the world's perspective, most of us will be viewed as insignificant. Our names will not be recorded in any history book, monuments will not be erected in our honor; indeed, a hundred years from now only a very few of our future relatives will even recall our names. But God will never forget, and we will never be looked upon by Him as valueless. Every tiny kind deed we do for His glory and honor is proclaimed in the streets of heaven. Every time we boldly bear witness to His Name, the angels in heaven rejoice. Each time we choose good over evil His heart is filled with joy.

Brother Lawrence, in *The Practice of the Presence of God,* said, "We ought not to be weary of doing little things for the love of GOD, who regards not the greatness of the work, but the love with which it is performed" (*Fourth Conversation*, p. 8). So I say to you, my brothers and sisters in Christ, you are eternally significant to God. Every kind deed you do in His name shall not lose its reward. Every time your

June

heart is humbled with the sorrow of your own sin, God's Spirit takes note and draws nearer to you. Whenever you feel alone and think no one cares about your needs, God's heart reaches out to you.

Your value as a human being is not determined by the world but by the Word. If your body has become feeble and your mind has become forgetful you are still important not only to God, but to all those who love you. Even amidst the limitations of failing human strength, continue to practice small acts of kindness and offer tiny gifts of grace, for by the time your act reaches the corridors of heaven it will be viewed not as some meaningless, unnoticeable deed, but as a marvelous thing in the sight of God. What the world called great, Jesus declared to be small. What the world said is unimportant Jesus said makes up the kingdom of heaven. So rejoice in what you perceive to be your "insignificance" because that just makes you important in God's sight.

Adversity–Rock or Stepping Stone?

15 Assuming that you have good health, for what would you trade it away? Would you take $100,000 for it, or a million? "What an absurd question," you say! In fact most of us would spend almost all that we have to regain good health if we were seriously ill. Many people do indeed spend their life savings, or go into debt for years in order to try and regain health that has been lost. But Jesus asks a question that's a little different. He confronts us with, "What will you give in exchange for your soul?" Does it ever occur to us that spiritual health is just as important as physical health? Indeed, it is more important. But how much time and money do we spend ensuring that we are healthy spiritually?

One of the strange paradoxes of life is that it is often when we lose what we consider to be valuable that we finally discover what is really most valuable. Maude Royden once said, "When you have nothing left but God, then for the first time you become aware that God is enough" (*The Secret of Suffering*, by Rolf L. Veenstra, p. 42). The relationship with a loved one seems to become intensely more valuable when we realize that we have lost them to death. Why are we human beings so hardheaded and self-consumed that we cannot grasp the value of people while we still have them in our lives?

June

I want to suggest to you that one of the most valuable things that we can have in our lives is adversity. Adversity forces us to comprehend what is significantly important. The irony is that most of us seek to avoid adversity at all costs, and when it does come to us, rather than let it become our teacher, we seek to escape its grasp with all deliberate speed. Jesus' life was filled with adversity and yet He always found a way to use each incident as a stepping stone to rise higher in glory. The ultimate adversity wasn't the cruel impalement on the Roman cross, but His obedience in embracing in His very soul the weight and despicableness of our horrendous sin. And yet that very act ensured that He has a name that is above all names, "that at the name of Jesus every knee should bow, in heaven and on earth and under the earth, and every tongue confess that Jesus Christ is Lord, to the glory of God the Father" (Philippians 2:10-11).

There is no greater teacher in life than adversity. Yet how we face it will determine whether it destroys us or makes us stronger. It is like the undertow along the shoreline; if we are caught up in it we can either fight against it and spend all our energy and be pulled down by it, or we can simply relax, allow the current to take us for a brief journey and emerge from its unrelenting power, strong and whole.

One of the very reasons that the Jews rejected Jesus as Messiah was because they could not embrace a Messiah that was willing to suffer. Yet Jesus has taught us that since suffering seems to come to everyone it needs to be faced with courage and determination. E. Stanley Jones writes of Jesus: "He withdraws from life only to advance further into life, he surrenders life only to get a better hold on it; he lets life do its worst and then through it shows the very best that God or man can show" (*Christ and Human Suffering*, p. 82). Are you using adversity as a stepping stone to spiritual wholeness, or are you fighting it with all your might and being crushed by its weight? You do have a choice!

The Bondage of Sin

16 In his book *Christ and Human Suffering* (p. 21), E. Stanley Jones says: "Evil is of two kinds—one which arises from within from the choices of our wills; that evil we call sin.

June

The other evil comes from without, from our environment of society and of the natural universe; that evil we call suffering." Jones wrote this in an attempt to explain why Christians suffer just as non-Christians do. It becomes quite obvious that when we sin we often bring suffering into our lives and the lives of others. Not only physical suffering that can result from violent and hostile acts, but inner suffering of the heart and soul that comes when we betray, disappoint, or deceive someone who loves us.

There is always a consequence to sin. Assuming we take our Christian faith seriously, even if our sin is kept secret there will be inner suffering with feelings of guilt, shame, and self-deprecation; often mingled with tears of sorrow and remorse. And if we don't feel those things as a result of our sin, then we suffer by having our soul and conscience eaten away from the inside out. Sin that is allowed to go unchallenged, though it may not be outwardly apparent to others, destroys the inner fabric of our being as surely as a colony of termites slowly and imperceptibly eats away the foundation of a house. The only way a person with cancer can be healed is to have the cancer destroyed or removed. The only way a termite-infested house can be saved from destruction is by the extermination (removal) of the termites. The only way a person engaged in sin can have their soul healed is by the removal of sin through confession, repentance, and the acceptance of God's forgiving grace.

The field of medical science has already shown that there often is a correlation between certain illnesses and the feelings of guilt that come from sinning. Sometimes the result is migraine headaches, depression, or weight loss (which can lead to other medical problems). Human beings are one entity—body, mind, and soul. What affects one part affects all. We cannot neatly compartmentalize and isolate these areas from one another. If we love our children and one of them is hurting, we hurt with them. Why then do we think we can separate the spiritual aspect of our being from our physical bodies?

Sometimes the body can be healed of illness only when the soul is ministered to first. The person addicted to drugs will never be healed of the detrimental physical effects of drugs until the mind and will are dealt with, which cause them to keep injecting its evil power into their

June

bodies. One must always go to the source of the illness in order to set in motion the healing process. If the source of our problem is sin, then we must go to its origin which is the heart, mind, and soul. This is an area in which the Spirit has great power to bring healing. Jesus said, "You shall know the truth, and the truth shall set you free. And that person whom the Son has set free is free indeed."

As long as we refuse to turn to the source of life for the gift of inner wholeness and freedom we shall always be captive to the evil of our own creation. That which humanity creates apart from the will and purpose of God, will almost always be evil and can bring self-destruction. There is, however, a way to be set free—that's why we call Him Savior.

The Poor in Spirit

17 The Sermon on the Mount (Matthew 5-7) begins with the Beatitudes—powerful words spoken by Jesus to reveal the essence of the joy one can discover in the kingdom of heaven. Strange, however, that Jesus begins this powerful sermon with the words, "Blessed are the poor in spirit for theirs is the kingdom of heaven" (Matthew 5:3). Immediately, He comes at life from the exact opposite point of view that the world takes. The world declares that there is nothing "blessed" about poverty, be it material or spiritual. What Jesus is declaring is that it is those who are poor in spirit who can claim the kingdom of heaven as their own.

But what does it mean to be "poor in spirit?" It certainly doesn't mean that a person is "blessed" if he or she has a weak or impoverished spiritual life. Perhaps William Barclay comes closest to its meaning when he paraphrases the verse with these words: "O the bliss of the man who has realized his own utter helplessness, and who has put his whole trust in God, for thus alone he can render to God that perfect obedience which will make him a citizen of the kingdom of heaven" (*The Daily Study Bible Series*, Matthew, Vol. I, p. 92).

Happy then, to the highest degree, are they who finally discover that without God at the center of their life they are of all people most poor. For in that discovery they will see where true riches come from and will reach out and be granted spiritual enrichment. Spiritual enrichment comes when one begins living in the kingdom of God.

June

When we describe a person who is an egotist, we often say "He is full of himself." In other words, at the core of his being and motivation is self. Outwardly, that person may appear to be happy and in control, but inwardly there will be a restlessness and emptiness that will ultimately lead to a dead end. But the person who has discovered the true poverty of self without God will instinctively reach out to God and hunger to be filled with His Spirit. When that happens, that person has truly reached the highest state of joy and happiness that is possible for a human being to experience. It was the Psalmist who wrote, "...a broken and contrite heart, O God, you will not despise" (Ps. 51:17).

There is a vast difference between self-hatred (which is unhealthy) and a sense of worthlessness apart from God's life-giving presence. The Prodigal discovered self-worth when he realized that without his father's love he was empty and lost. God created no one to be worthless, indeed, we are of ultimate value. We were created to love ourselves, but we will only love ourselves when God is the center of ourselves. When we try to love ourselves apart from God's presence in us, it becomes idolatry and ultimately leads to self-dissatisfaction, self-hatred, and self-destruction.

When we choose to live life apart from the One who created us, we have chosen a path that will inevitably lead to a life of unfulfilled hunger and emptiness. We can only be full when we have been filled by Him who is the very essence of life itself. Jesus said, "I have come to give you life and life more abundantly. . . . I am the way, the truth and the Life, no one comes to the Father except through Me." (John 14:6). One therefore has the kingdom of heaven when one has Jesus, and when one has Jesus that person is possessed by God! When one is possessed by God he or she has discovered the greatest of all joys.

O the Joy of Mourning

18 "Blessed are they that mourn, for they shall be comforted" (Matthew 5:4). Each statement of blessedness in the Beatitudes is followed with a promise. Each promise brings blessedness because each promise is built on faith. Therefore, it speaks not only of the present but the future. The word "blessed" which begins each Beatitude means more than just "happy." The Greek word was used to denote the highest state of joy known by the gods. A better translation than "blessed" would be: "happy to the highest degree" or "the absolute bliss of." How interesting indeed that Jesus would approach life from the opposite point of view of the world. The world would never declare that there was anything blissful about being "poor in spirit," much less "mourning."

The word "mourn" in the Greek text is the word that was used for mourning for the dead, sorrow which issues in tears, sorrow which pierces the heart. How then can Jesus say, "Happy to the greatest degree are those who mourn?" The answer comes in the latter half of the Beatitude—for they will be comforted! There is no joy quite so intense as the joy of having sorrow undone. We mourn or grieve over that which we think we have lost, but when that which we thought was lost is returned, joy breaks out in uncontrollable emotion. The cornerstone of the Christian faith is belief in the resurrection. If Jesus' words are true, that through Him we have everlasting life, then for the Christian every loved one we have who has given their life to Him will one day stand before us in perfect wholeness.

When my daughter Angela was about nine years old we took her to the beach along with the rest of our church youth group. Several of us adults were at the cottage, three blocks from the water, when two of the older teenagers came running up screaming and crying that Angela and two others had been pulled under by the undertow and had drowned. I rushed toward the oceanfront, devastated and broken by the news that my precious child was dead. As I climbed to the top of a sand dune and saw the line of people stretched along the shoreline, I fell on my face in uncontrollable tears. Suddenly, one of the teenagers saw me and came running to tell me that Angela was alive—they had saved all three! In the flicker of an eyelash, my sorrow was turned into unbridled joy! Happy to the highest degree are those who mourn now, for one day their sorrow will be turned into joy when they once more behold the one they thought they had lost.

Jesus could see beyond the horizon of life and He knew that death, which brings us such pain and brokenness, is not the final word. The day will finally come when Death will bow its head in Jesus'

June

presence and ours, and it will proclaim that Jesus is Lord and God; He is indeed the Resurrection and the Life. Then the heart that has mourned will be comforted and then we shall discover in the fullest sense the happiness of those who have mourned.

Our Precious Savior does not mislead or taunt us. He has shared with us the truth of life. We who are Christian and mourn are not like those who have no hope. Soon, my mother will join my father in heaven and my heart will be heavy and broken, but I know in my soul that the day will come when "weeping may tarry for a night, but joy will come with the morning." Happy to the highest degree are those who mourn, for our Lord promises us we will be comforted!

On Going Home

19 They huddled together in quietness. No words unnecessarily interrupted the angelic smile which filled their faces. They were all there in eager anticipation of the arrival of one who had too long been separated from them. There was Elmer and Bill, Georgia and Lila, Hayes and Earl, Kate, Harley, and Dianne; Deanes and Lois, Melza and Aunt Mary and Ella Grace and a throng of others who had arrived much earlier. There also was her mother and father, hands joined, hearts in one expectant accord. Then it happened—at about 8 p.m. It must have begun with the soft voice of one angel in an almost quiet whisper, "Hallelujah." One by one they all joined in, accompanied by the throngs of angels until the streets of heaven were resounding in a chorus of Hallelujahs that could never be matched by anything on earth.

The One who had said, "I will come again and receive you unto Myself" was now approaching the celestial kingdom and in His hand, secure for eternity, was the hand of my mother Norma. In the twinkling of an eye the furrowed brow was made smooth, the eyes that had grown dim were gloriously bright, the tiny body that had known too much pain was young and vibrant—free at last! What a grand reunion took place! Hugs and kisses, hearts erupting in laughter and joy. Finally, Norma had come home.

Meanwhile, back on earth, in a room that was gray and somber; one filled with tears and heartache, a family huddled together in silence and struggled with the knowledge that life here is short, sometimes painful, and always difficult to leave behind. Like separate needles we stood in mama's presence and felt that the common thread that ran through each of us and bound us together had been broken, and suddenly the loss seemed overwhelming. The Christian cannot escape the reality of human grief, but neither can the Christian be crushed by it. For we do not grieve as those who have no hope. Our hope is in the Lord who made us, sustains us and loves us.

Each tear shed holds within its tiny little world a precious memory—the memories that now become the thread that continues to bind us together—one with Mama, one with each other, and one with the God we all love. Each tear becomes a drop of heavenly balm that slowly soothes the broken heart. Strange how one tiny little woman had within her such tremendous power. And yet, didn't Jesus always remind us of the value of small things—the little cup of water given in his Name, the tiny mustard seed of faith, the value of the widow's mite? Why then should we be surprised at the intense value Mama's life had for each of us?

And so, we must go on with life. It is not easy but it is required. There is a void that will never be filled until God fills it by His wondrous grace which one day will usher us too into the presence of the larger family that has gone before us. What a wonderful thing it is to be a Christian and to know without doubt that not only is our mother in the real world of heaven, but that God will not leave us to sorrow alone. For here is the reality—"Surely He has borne our griefs and carried our sorrows . . ." (Isaiah. 53:4, KJV). In the midst of sorrow, He is here again and once more I am awed by the power of His Peace! Blessed be the Name of our God!

Inheritance Through Humility

20 The third Beatitude says, "Blessed are the meek, for they shall inherit the earth." Unfortunately, in our society the word "meek" has become equated with weakness. A person who is meek is considered to be a patsy, a doormat, someone who can be run over. But the Greek word we translate meek (*praeis*) does not mean weak, but one who is humble and exercises self-control.

June

Numbers 12:3(KJV) says: "Now the man Moses was very meek, above all the men which were upon the face of the earth." Our image of Moses certainly is not that of a man who was a doormat. Quite the contrary, he is portrayed in the Bible as a man of great strength and leadership. Jesus described Himself with the words, "I am meek and lowly of heart" (Matthew 11:29, KJV).

Meekness properly carries the connotation of humility. To be humble actually is indicative of people who are secure within themselves. They recognize their own strengths but are also aware of their areas of weakness. Those who are humble do not boast about themselves, are not "pushy," and do not seek to lord it over others. Those who discover humility in their relationship with God are the ones who draw on God's strength and not their own. To be humble or meek is to willingly choose to not promote one's self, to not demand special attention or favor, to pattern one's life after the role of a servant, not one who demands to be served.

Mother Teresa was the epitome of meekness, but she was not weak. From all the accounts of her life, she was viewed as a woman of immense strength and courage. As a nun she took vows of poverty and chastity and did not really possess anything of a material nature, but truly she inherited the earth, for the world loved her. When Jesus speaks of inheriting the earth He was not alluding to ownership of land or property (a thought many television evangelists would do well to ponder). The Psalmist wisely proclaimed, "The earth is the Lord's and the fullness thereof . . ." Truly, in this life we are only stewards of what belongs to God. We have oversight of it for a few brief years, and then it is passed on to someone else.

The promise of the beatitude is that the meek person will **inherit** the earth. That which one has by inheritance is not something one has purchased or worked for. It is a gift that one receives as a result of someone bequeathing it. Once again Jesus confounds the wisdom of the world, for in essence He is saying that those who make no outrageous claims for themselves, will be the ones who receive that which they never could have owned on their own. Boasting is an attempt to force people to admire you. Humility is the living of one's life in simplicity and strength; thus declaring that one's self-worth and value are not determined by what others think or say, but by what one feels confident of in him or her self, as a result of recognizing that greatness belongs to God, not to human beings.

Each beatitude contains a promise. The promise of this one is to receive what only God has the power to give—the earth. The truth is that in a real sense we already possess it—for no one can rightfully claim ownership of the beauty and magnificence of the forests, oceans, mountains, and sunsets that bring exhilaration to the heart of all who are awed with their beauty. They belong to us as an inherited gift from our Lord!

The Joy of Being Thirsty

21 The fourth Beatitude given to us by our Lord proclaims: "Blessed are they who hunger and thirst for righteousness, for they shall be filled." When one is truly hungry or thirsty, that need or desire dominates everything else. The straggler in the desert who has been days without water is consumed with one desire—to find an oasis where the desire for water can be quenched. Jesus says when we desire righteousness like that, then we will be filled.

William Barclay describes this Beatitude as "the bliss of the starving soul." He says it is the most demanding of the Beatitudes because it is for those who desire righteousness as a matter of life and death. But note that Jesus does **not** say, "Blessed are they who are righteous," he says, "Blessed are those who desire righteousness with an all-consuming hunger or thirst." And just what is this thing called righteousness for which we should hunger and thirst?

Entire books have been written on the use of the word "righteousness" in the Bible. In Paul's epistle to the Romans, he uses the word "righteousness" 38 times. A good exercise to do would be to take a highlighter and mark each verse in Romans where the word "righteousness" appears. Righteousness, as simply as I know how to put it, is that standard of rightness or holiness one must have in order to be in a proper relationship with God. Since no human being is righteous by his or her own merit, we can only be "righteous" in God's sight as a result of that inner rightness or holiness which He gives to us as a gift. That gift comes through the atoning love and sacrifice of

June

Jesus. Therefore, it follows that when one hungers and thirsts for righteousness, one is hungering and thirsting for Jesus.

In the Book of Jeremiah, God says through the prophet, "And you will seek me and find me when you seek me with all your heart." (29:13, NRSV). Jesus said the greatest of all commandments was this: "You shall love the Lord your God, with all of your heart, mind, soul and strength." Rather obviously, this is not a casual interest in God, but an all-consuming desire that is the dominant desire in our life. How beautifully did the Psalmist express this marvelous truth: "As the deer longs for flowing streams, so my soul longs for you O God. My soul thirsts for God, for the living God" (Psalm 42:1-2, NRSV). "O God you are my God; I seek you, my soul thirsts for you; my flesh faints for you as in a dry and weary land where there is no water" (Psalm 63:1, NRSV).

The truth is that we can have as much of God in our lives as we desire. The problem is we desire so little. I would paraphrase the Beatitude this way, "Happy to the greatest degree is that person who desires to be in right relationship with God with a desire that exceeds all other desires, for the good news is that person will have that desire granted and his or her heart will overflow with inexpressible joy." Let this verse from a beautiful Christian song become your prayer: "Living God, consuming fire; burn the sin from my life. Make your will my desire. Take my life in your hands. Purify me with your love, 'til I shine far brighter than purest gold in your eyes." If you can pray that with sincere conviction, then joy awaits you, for you shall be filled with the glory of God.

The Joy of Showing Mercy

22 The fifth Beatitude is really at the heart of the gospel: "Blessed are the merciful, for they shall be shown mercy." Someone has wisely said that when we stand before God, no one will be asking for justice; rather we will be asking for mercy. In the Old Testament "mercy" occurs more than 150 times. Ninety percent of those references are God's actions toward humanity. Yet we have a very limited understanding of mercy if we only think of it in terms of withholding punishment or anger. It means much more than

June

just the remission of a penalty: it carries with it the clear connotation of active kindness.

The prophet Micah recognized the importance of mercy not only in terms of being in right relationship with God but also in how we relate to our fellow human beings. He wrote: "What does the Lord require of you? To act justly and to love mercy, and to walk humbly with your God" (6:8). He was not talking about loving mercy so much as a gift for one's self, but as a way of reaching out to others with our own acts of outgoing love.

Jesus entered the world at a time in which, for the most part, mercy was not a way of life. The Romans were well known for their cruelty and harshness in dealing with human beings and had little compassion for those who were weak or poor. Even the Jews themselves were very selective, and primarily excluded non-Jews from their list of who should receive the abundance of God's mercy. They had a saying: "There is joy before God when those who provoke Him perish from the world." Jesus said, however, "There is great joy in heaven over one sinner who repents." So miserly in their extension of mercy were the Jews that they had a law that forbade even the helping of a Gentile woman during the crisis of childbirth.

Charles Allen, quoting from *High Wind at Noon* by Allan K. Chalmers, tells the story of Peer Holm, a world famous engineer, who fell into poverty and returned to the little village where he was born to eke out a living as a farmer. His neighbor owned a fierce dog. Peer had warned his neighbor about the dog, but he sneered at him and ignored him. One day the dog attacked Peer's little daughter and killed her. The community was outraged and ostracized the neighbor whose dog had killed the little girl. When planting time came no one would sell the man grain and no one would speak to the man or help him. But not Peer Holm. Early one morning, he quietly took a half bushel of barley and sowed it in his neighbor's field. When the seed came up it was obvious who had sown the seed, for half of Peer Holm's own field was bare. As Allen said, "Mercy requires that we sow good seed in our enemy's field, even though it means that part of our own will be left bare" (*God's Psychiatry*, p. 146-47).

The Beatitude about mercy reveals that the one who shows mercy is happy to the highest degree, because that person is the one

June

who is assured of receiving God's mercy. To live in God's kingdom means that we have the assurance of receiving mercy at God's hand; but it also means that we have discovered the joy in being willing to give mercy as well as receive it.

The Joy of a Pure Heart

23 The sixth Beatitude is perhaps the most "spiritual" of them all. "Blessed are the pure in heart for they will see God" (Matthew 5:8). When the Bible speaks of the heart in relationship to God it gets to the very essence of our communion with Him. Jesus was not the first to speak of the necessity of having a pure heart. Centuries before, the Psalmist had said: "Who shall ascend the hill of the Lord? Who may stand in his holy place? Those who have clean hands and a pure heart; who do not lift up their souls to what is false, and do not swear deceitfully" (Psalm 24:3-4, NRSV; also see Psalm 73:1).

Purity of heart would appear to be an unattainable goal. Who is there whose heart is without spot or blemish; who is capable of such integrity and absolute virtue that he or she could declare their heart to be pure? If we think of a pure heart as being one that is totally without sin, then who can stand in the presence of God? Fortunately, I think the Bible gives us a direction out of this dilemma.

In the Book of Acts, Luke tells us about the dissension that was going on in the early Christian church over whether one could become a Christian without first being circumcised. In other words, without the outward (Jewish) act of circumcision one is unclean and unacceptable before God. Peter's response to the Council makes clear the answer. "And God, who knows the human heart, testified to them [the Gentiles] by giving them the Holy Spirit, just as He did to us; and in cleansing their hearts by faith He has made no distinction between them and us" (15:8, NRSV). Thus, our hearts are made pure by faith in the cleansing power of Christ's atonement through the work of the Holy Spirit. Peter had discovered this truth earlier when God gave him instruction in a vision about eating "unclean" food. "What God has made clean, you must not call profane" (Acts 10:15; 11:9, NRSV).

It is God who makes the heart pure through our faith, not our failed attempts to live flawless lives before His presence.

In the Gospel of John (15:3, 4, NRSV) Jesus says, "You have already been cleansed by the word that I spoke to you. Abide in me as I abide in you." When we hear the good news that Jesus brought to the world, invite Him into our hearts through faith, and desire to love and serve Him, then our hearts are made pure, not by our own righteousness, but by the love and grace He extends to us through His presence in our lives.

The pureness of heart of which Jesus spoke, and which is required by God, is a pureness that comes to us as a gift accepted in faith. The heart that is made pure by God is the heart that is allowed to behold His glory. Pureness is derived out of righteousness, and there is only One who is righteous. Only those who sincerely and earnestly seek to know God will discover Him. Only those who hunger for pureness of heart will ever bask in the joy that comes from dwelling in the presence of the Living God. Oh, the joy, the indescribable blessed joy, of standing in the presence of God, who accepts us as creatures of utter purity, because we stand clothed in the righteous pureness of the goodness of Christ Jesus. What a Savior!

The Joy of Peacemakers

24 The seventh Beatitude proclaims, "Blessed are the peacemakers for they will be called children of God" (Mathew 5:9, NRSV). From the beginning of time, God has been trying to establish a relationship of peace with His creation. Too often we think of peace only in terms of the absence of hostility, war, or strife. Yet from God's perspective it is not simply the absence of something negative, it is the presence of something positive. Peace brings calmness, happiness, contentment, acceptance, and unity with other things.

In the New Testament, the word "peace" occurs 88 times and is found in all 27 books. From Jesus to angels to the apostle Paul, the word flows from their lips with earnest longing. To offer someone peace was to extend a gracious gift. Peace becomes peace only when

June

it is both given and received. Note the beatitude does not say "peace-lovers" but "peacemakers." This indicates that peace can come about through positive action, not simply withholding ill-will. Making peace can involve anything that eliminates misery and suffering.

Inner peace involves three relationships: peace with God; peace with other human beings; and peace with one's self. If any one of the three is in conflict, then there is an absence of peace. When there is a lack of acceptance in any one of the relationships it carries over to the other two. At its core, peace is a spiritual issue. Unfortunately, where there is strife in the spirit there will be an impact on the physical. Basically, over the years we have unwittingly tried to divide the human body into separate compartments—body (physical) and soul (spiritual). When you go to a doctor, he or she will treat the body, for that is the area of their training. But sometimes, what has caused problems in the body has originated within the soul and unless the root cause is identified the problem will not be resolved.

It seems clear that in the mind of Jesus, one's peace was a powerful force that could be extended or withheld. He tells us in Matthew, "Whatever town or village you enter, find out who in it is worthy, and stay there until you leave. As you enter the house, greet it. If the house is worthy, let your peace come upon it; but if it is not worthy, let your peace return to you" (10:11-14, NRSV). Since Jesus, in this Beatitude, says that peacemakers are children of God, He is implying that to do the work of making peace is to do the work of the God who claims us as His own. In John's Gospel, Jesus said, "Peace I leave with you, my peace I give to you. I do not give as the world gives" (John 14:27, NRSV). True peace is a gift from God that is greater than any gift the world can bestow.

At the heart and center of inner peace is the reality of acceptance and trust. To say to someone that you accept him or her in spite of human frailties and mistakes and to love that person into self-acceptance, is to give that person the gift of peace. It is the work of God to change chaos into calmness, brokenness into wholeness, rejection into acceptance, and turmoil into peace. The promise of God is—Happy to the highest degree is the person who creates an environment where peace can be born, for that person lives as a child of God.

June

Finding Joy in Persecution

25 The eighth and final Beatitude is considered by some to actually be two since it contains two "blesseds." But since both deal with the subject of persecution most people consider it to be one Beatitude. Jesus said, "Blessed are those who are persecuted for righteousness' sake, for theirs is the kingdom of heaven. Blessed are you, when people revile you, and utter all kinds of evil against you falsely on my account. Rejoice and be glad, for your reward is great in heaven, for in the same way they persecuted the prophets who were before you" (Matthew 5:10-12, NRSV).

In the preceding seven Beatitudes, Jesus has been describing what it is like for the person who desires to live in the kingdom of God. If one chooses to embrace those principles then the promise is that you will eventually be persecuted. To live according to the Beatitudes is to live according to righteousness and that means people will criticize you, even lie about you because those who delight in unrighteousness have little compassion for those who seek to live righteously. Note that Jesus says the persecution He is talking about is "for righteousness' sake" and for "His sake." When you are willing to endure persecution for those reasons, then Jesus says, "Happy to the highest degree you will be, for you will have discovered the kingdom of God."

There has been and always will be a cost to following Jesus. Those who are looking for the benefits of faith without a willingness to accept the responsibilities and demands of the faith will inevitably be disappointed. Charles Allen writes, "No person ever really lives until he has found something worth dying for. You can never really possess the Kingdom of God until the cause of God becomes more important than your own life" (*God's Psychiatry*, p. 158).

William Barclay asks a profound question and then offers the answer:

There remains only one question to ask—why is this persecution so inevitable? It is inevitable because the Church, when it really is the Church, is bound to be the conscience of the nation and the conscience of society. Where there is good the church must praise; where there is evil the Church must condemn—and inevitably men will try to silence the trouble-

June

some voice of conscience. It is not the duty of the individual Christian to habitually find fault, to criticize, to condemn, but it may well be that his every action is a silent condemnation of the unchristian lives of others, and he will not escape their hatred. (The Gospel of Matthew, Vol. 1, p. 118)

The difficulty for the Christian will always be to **not** respond to criticism or persecution in an unchristian manner. Forgiveness, turning the other cheek, and loving one's enemies are essential ingredients for the person who genuinely seeks to live in God's kingdom of blessedness. If we respond to the evil of persecution in like manner, we will surely lose the joy of our life in the kingdom. Yes, it is a difficult path to tread, but never forget that we walk along a path that has already been worn by Him who carried a cross to Calvary. From that cross came the words to His persecutors, "Father, forgive them, for they know not what they do."

Making Friends with Grief

26 Grief is a reality that we all have to face. It is as much a part of life as living. We are told that there are three things that cause us to feel grief: 1) contemplation of the loss itself; 2) contemplation of a future without the lost object; 3) contemplation about the unexpected experience of grief itself, i.e., feelings about grieving (*All Our Losses, All Our Griefs*, by Kenneth R. Mitchell and Herbert Anderson, p. 61). Too often we lump feelings of grief into a single category, thus implying that all grieving is primarily the same. But in reality it is not. The dying person is letting go of the persons and things that are loved in order to prepare for death. The grieving person is letting go of what is being lost in order to begin living again. In a real sense, both are grieving, yet in different ways.

Grieving is all about loss and loss is a part of life that we begin to experience early on. The early stages of a baby's life are normally spent being almost constantly cuddled, held, fed, and nurtured. Within months of its birth it has to adjust, as it grows, to less and less attention as it slowly makes its way toward independence. Our first teeth begin to come out and be replaced. We go to a daycare center, kindergarten or elementary school and have to adjust to the loss of the intimate and

June

familiar relationship of being constantly at home under the protection of loving parents. And so, perhaps unwittingly, we begin to experience and adjust to small losses as we discover through experience that life is temporal and eventually will be left behind.

The depth of love that a person feels for the thing or person lost does not necessarily determine how well or poorly one handles grief. Losing that which one loves deeply may cause deep pain, but the ability to adjust to that loss will be greatly influenced by the **ultimate** value we put on something; and whether we deeply believe that God not only helps us through our sorrow, but will in the life to come restore to us that which we have given up in this life. Here, I primarily refer to relationships because I do not believe any material object in this world has an ultimate value. Many people have chosen suicide over the loss of job, wealth, or possessions (e.g., during the Great Depression) and by their very act indicated they had placed ultimate value on that which is not ultimate.

One needs to ask the question, "Why did God create us with the ability to feel grief and loss?" Real grief brings real pain, even if that pain is emotional. But emotional pain can become so intense that it literally creates a feeling of physical pain; it certainly brings on physical discomfort and sometimes illness. The human body was created with the ability to heal itself in many ways. For example, if you cut your finger, normally it will eventually heal over; if you break a bone it will mend itself. Likewise the human mind and emotions are capable of healing themselves of the pain of grief. That process, however, will be greatly enhanced if we somehow learn to let God share our sorrow.

Grief and pain have purposes in our lives that we will never fully understand. But I do not believe God allows them for our detriment. Somehow they must serve a purpose in causing us to grow in grace and knowledge of the value of love and the depth of love that He feels for us. To make friends with grief, therefore, is not a bad thing!

Grief over Material Things

27 Continuing the theme on grief—it is informative to realize that, according to Kenneth R. Mitchell and Herbert Anderson, there are six major types of loss which can bring

June

on grief: material loss, relationship loss, intrapsychic loss, functional loss, role loss, and systemic loss (*All Our Losses, All Our Griefs*, p. 36). All human beings are affected at some time in their lives by one or more of these. Understanding them will help us deal with the emotion of grief that we all feel. Drawing on Mitchell and Anderson's insights, we will examine these six major losses.

We live in a world that by its very nature is material. As a result, we form attachments to material things: from houses and cars to less expensive (but no less treasured) articles such as heirlooms, favorite photos, and special gifts. If those things are lost, stolen or destroyed we grieve; often quite deeply. Somehow we've allowed ourselves to become merged in some immeasurable way with an object. Thus, to lose what "was ours" brings about a deep sense of loss, as if we had lost part of ourselves. The grief that we feel when we lose a beloved pet is deep because we realize at the deepest level of our emotions that it cannot be replaced. That's why in Jesus' parable about the lost coin, the woman rejoiced so greatly when the coin was finally found. It was as if part of herself had been recovered.

Grief takes place in the very center of our being, the place from which our emotions are derived. When one grieves deeply all of the rest of life seems to be put on hold. Nothing brings happiness; laughter is a forced imposition, nights are often sleepless, the appetite vanishes, energy level plummets, and our minds become consumed with despair over what has been lost. It may take weeks, months, or sometimes years, before a person adjusts to the loss. How long it takes to adjust will depend upon how deeply intertwined one's life was with the thing that is gone.

Often when treasured objects are lost, a person will try to replace it with something of close or equal value. When a child's bicycle gets stolen we comfort them with the assurance, "Don't cry. We'll get you another one." Some people do this when pets die, even though we may have said, "I'll never get another one." If we do quickly replace them, we in essence treat pets like objects, even thought they are living creatures.

When one is in the midst of loss there is a necessary preoccupation with self because it is a psychological attempt to survive. We constantly think about the lost person or object and tears flow freely; we relive memories and we ache for that which can no longer be. The person who suffers great loss and then seems to show no grief, but goes on as if nothing has happened, is in denial. Grief denied is grief delayed and grief delayed is grief prolonged. It will inevitably come out again somewhere and often in an unexpected traumatic fashion.

Whether dealing with children or adults we must allow time and freedom of expression as they come to grips with loss. To belittle or ridicule them when grief is genuine is to only add to their sense of loss and bewilderment. While grief is a common experience, each person deals with it and adjusts to it in his or her own unique way.

Grief When Relationships End

28 The most intense kind of grief for most people involves relationship loss. Such loss can span the gamut from casual friends all the way to immediate family members. It often occurs early in life as children experience the grief associated with moving away from friends; or the deep loss encountered in divorced parents, or the death of family members. As children, part of our stability and self-understanding comes from close relationships. When those relationships are broken then the security of our world is shaken. Our lives become very much like a structure supported by four posts, one of which has now been removed.

Even when relationships are sometimes filled with strife there is usually grief when those relationships end. Divorced people often say they "miss the strife." If strife has become a large part of one's world, then the absence of that strife leaves a void. In an unhappy marriage there is a sense of security and comfort that is developed even in a dysfunctional relationship. Some have said that divorce is worse than death because in death there is irrevocable closure while in divorce, especially if children are involved, the contact with the divorced spouse usually continues—often with arguments over visitation and custody. In divorce, there is no funeral or memorial service, no gathering of friends and family for a formal rite of passage.

In the case of the death of a loved one, the depth of love may or may not determine the intensity of the grief. There is no "norm" or

June

"standard" for how people grieve. Yet, I believe, in large measure it will be determined by the perceived importance the deceased had on the life of the one left behind. Even in situations where contact with the person who died had been limited over the years, the loss can nonetheless be felt with great emotion and stress—if that person occupied a special place in the life of the one sorrowing.

To experience the death of a loved one will inevitably bring on a period of reminiscing. Memories will be explored and relived over and over again. It is not uncommon for loved ones to be "romanticized", giving them virtues that exceed those which they actually had. An internal dialogue with one's self may take place as the good and not-so-good qualities of the deceased are revisited. Sometimes, grieving people actually find it helpful to talk out loud to the deceased person, either at the gravesite or at some place that was special in their relationship. Others find they feel angry at the person over some unresolved issue. All these feelings have to be worked through and in most people they usually are, though not according to an orchestrated time schedule.

Where then, we must ask, is God in all of this? God has created the human heart and mind with the capacity to experience what we call grief. Somehow in that mysterious process of healing, God enables us to keep that which is healthy and healing, and work through that which is destructive and damaging. His word tells us "Surely, he hath borne our griefs and carried our sorrows" (Isaiah 53:4, KJV). I do not believe they are meaningless words; rather I take them to be God's promise that in **all** our sorrows, He willingly shares them with us. If God Himself takes our sorrow (just as He does our sins) how then can we not eventually be made whole?

Grieving Over Lost Hopes and Dreams

29 The third loss in our series on grieving, is called "intrapsychic loss." That's an unfamiliar word for most of us but simply means "the experience of losing an emotionally important image of oneself, losing the possibilities of 'what might have been,' abandonment of plans for a particular future, the dying of a dream" *(All Our Losses, All Our Grief*s, p. 40). At one

June

time or another almost everyone will grieve over the loss of something that "might have been." Perhaps it was a hoped-for relationship with a person that never materialized, a job that one never acquired, a promotion that never came, or the realization that most of your life is behind you and you never attained the goals in life that you had imagined. For some, the experience won't be traumatic; indeed it passes almost without notice. For others, however, the grief can be deep and prolonged.

When my son was about six years old, he earnestly wanted to grow up and be a "garbage" man. He thought it was wonderful that they got to ride on the back of those big trucks and push that lever that made garbage go away! It wasn't too many months before he changed his mind and his grief over the unfulfilled dream passed with hardly a notice (he finally became a mechanical engineer).

Many people experience the grief of intrapsychic loss when they create an idea in their mind as to how something will be and then discover that the person or thing isn't really that way at all. This can sometimes occur in the early months of a marriage when it's discovered that "prince charming" has an un-princely side, or that the "girl of his dreams" is not everything he thought she would be. Grief sets in and the person must work through the loss of an "ideal" that was never real from the beginning. Or sometimes grief occurs when we have worked on a job or project for months or years and once it is completed, even if quite successfully, there is a big let-down that follows. For most people, there is a need for new goals that cause us to have to stretch ourselves in order to meet them. When there are no goals, or we are physically or mentally unable to make new ones, we grieve.

We can also experience intrapyschic loss when we feel that we have lost our faith or courage. We look inside and discover that the inner resources we thought were there have deserted us and we grieve and often feel depressed, worthless, or lost. All of these experiences of loss are a result of an inner hope or aspiration that somehow didn't occur and as a result we give up on the dream as lost. So how do we deal with these feelings?

I believe, as Christians, we must start by taking our feelings to God in prayer. Absolute honesty with God is the beginning of healing.

June

A realistic look at life shows us that not only does everyone have unfulfilled hopes and dreams but that even those lost dreams can become steppingstones to growth. There is nothing that happens (or doesn't happen) to us in life that God is not able to use for our good, if we will let Him. The gospel message from Jesus has always been about surrender of self to God. He must have had dreams and hopes, but He was given a cross. From that cross Jesus found His greatest desire—His love for God and humanity—fulfilled in the most unlikely of ways. The grief over inner loss, surrendered to Christ, can be healed!

Grieving When We Lose Ourselves

30 The loss of the body's ability to function in "normal" ways will inevitably bring grief to the person who suffers the loss. It may be that the person and his/her friends do not recognize the reaction as grief, but that is really what is behind the emotions being experienced. When a person loses a limb to amputation, there is pain that is physical which must be endured, but often there is lasting grief that will inevitably accompany the loss. Part of one's self has been lost and the grief is not dissimilar to that of the grief we feel when a person we are close to dies.

When a woman loses a breast as a result of cancer, it will often be accompanied by an acute sense of loss that displays itself with all the characteristics of grief—denial, anger, bargaining, depression and eventually acceptance (there is no specific order in which these feelings may occur). The same is true for men when they become sexually dysfunctional because of prostate surgery or an injury. There can be no more intimate association than that which we feel with the parts of our own body; and when one of those parts is taken from us or becomes dysfunctional, especially if it is one that shapes the image of ourselves, then we experience grief. Normally, one does not grieve when an appendix or some non-vital organ is removed (though the trauma of surgery may create an emotional struggle).

Grief is also experienced as we make the journey into our twilight years when our energy is less, our muscles grow weaker, our eyesight and hearing dim and we begin to realize that the process of

July

aging is beginning to make itself known to us in undeniable ways. When we lose the ability to be mobile, or significant loss of sight or hearing, we are in essence losing an important part of who we are—our autonomy. We are discovering that the physical vitality which once gave us a sense of being in control is now lost, and therefore we grieve. If we live long enough we will eventually have to stop driving; not be able to go to all the places we once went, and become more and more dependent on others, even for our basic needs. In times like those it is helpful to remember that God is not only with us but is intimately aware of the process and the feelings we are experiencing. By faith, we believe that living to an old age is not a journey into obscurity but preparation to receive the greatest of all God's promises—eternal life.

Grief is a process, and while each person experiences and deals with it differently, there are no shortcuts through it. Just as God gives the human body the ability to heal itself of many things such as injuries and certain illnesses (flu, colds, and viruses), He also gives us the ability to heal the emotional trauma we experience through the process of grieving. One needs to remember that it was God who designed the human body with the ability to cry. Tear ducts are more than a means of cleansing the eyes of foreign objects: they also allow the heart and soul to be cleansed of inner pain. Recent studies have shown that emotions that precipitate tears also cleanse the body of certain impurities that nothing else will.

Normal grieving is a way of dealing with loss. In a sense it is a God-given gift because grieving allows us to be healed. The promise of God, regarding the loss of function or even a part of our physical body, is that He will be with us and that in the life to come we will be made perfectly whole with strength which time will no longer take from us. Once again my heart rejoices at the goodness, love, and mercy of our Lord!

Grieving When We Lose Our Role

1 The experience of grief dramatically reveals how complex the human mind and emotions are. From the time we are born our perception of our world and ourselves is being formed by every

July

experience we have. As we form relationships and adjust to various roles in life we attain a degree of comfort and confidence within that role. Obviously, we start out as a son or daughter: if we have siblings our role as brother or sister is formed; and then we begin to understand ourselves in our role as friend or companion. By adulthood, most people have learned to adjust and adapt to "fitting in" to the role that we are assigned or pursue. What has that to do with grief, you might ask? Because as life progresses and we let go of roles in which we have found fulfillment or security, we grieve over their loss.

The high school graduate who leaves for college must come to grips with a diminished role as a family member no longer living in the security of the daily household. Off to new worlds and people and experiences, they encounter excitement and anxiety but also feel a sense of loss in leaving home. We call it "homesickness" and yet it is really the intense experience of grief over something that gave our lives meaning and purpose that is now left behind. Over time, we have found psychological security in our role and for the most part have been totally unaware that it has been forming.

When a person starts a new career, even if the previous one wasn't overly happy and fulfilling, there is a sense of grief and loss at letting go of what heretofore had been a secure place in one's life. Likewise, when one marries, the role changes dramatically, not just from the status of being single, but in the new role as spouse, adjusting to the new family of in-laws, the friendships that come with the spouse, and the new environment of being less autonomous. The "down" feelings that people experience are often the process of grief being played out as we adjust to the lost or diminished role we formerly enjoyed but has now been dramatically changed or lost altogether.

Perhaps one of the greatest role losses we will experience is the one that comes with retirement. Our entire adult lives we have worked and become comfortable with who we are as defined by our occupation. Most of us are not fully aware of how much our work has influenced who we perceive ourselves to be. When that work is no longer part of our lives we can suffer a tremendous sense of loss. We go through a period of disorientation, feeling that somehow our lives

July

no longer have meaning or value; that we are less than we were because we no longer have a place to contribute.

It is essential that we come to realize that our worth in God's sight, or anyone else's if they think for a moment, is not determined by what we do for a living. Our worth comes from within and ending a career does not require that we stop contributing to the good of the world. Grief over role loss can best be dealt with by discovering, perhaps for the first time, that we have value simply because we are a creation which God has made and whom God loves with an everlasting love. Role loss does not have to be self-worth loss. We can begin the exciting adventure of finding new ways to use the value that God has placed within us.

Grief When the Circle is Broken

2 The final major loss which we shall look at that often results in grief is "systemic loss." Most of us are not aware of it but we have found a sense of security and comfort in the various "systems" of our lives in which we have settled. We would never call it a system and probably wouldn't realize, until it is pointed out, that we are part of something that helps us define ourselves. Mitchell and Anderson define the systems we move in as "some interactional system in which patterns of behavior develop over time" (*All Our Losses, All Our Griefs*, p. 44).

These systems develop at home as we find our place within the family structure. Later, they develop at school as we begin to mesh with classmates and structured environments, and eventually in the work place as we settle into the work that is assigned for us to do. The longer we do these things the more comfortable we become and the more dependent we become (usually subconsciously) on the meaning and purpose they bring to our lives. But things change. Eventually we leave home and are off on our own; we graduate from school and go off to college or work. Many people change jobs and start over with new responsibilities and new people with whom to work. As a result, we experience loss, some anxiety, and grief.

We need to also keep in mind there is systemic loss for the family or group the person leaves. When a child goes off to school or

July

moves out of the home, a very important part of the family's sense of identity and cohesion is missing, so parents and siblings experience loss and confusion, just as the person leaving does in his or her new environment. My youngest sister was eight when I got married and moved out of the home. I was the last of her siblings to leave and as a result she went through a period of intense grief as a part of what had been important in her life was no longer present in the home.

But God has made the human body and mind resilient. Most people adapt after a reasonable time and the sense of loss begins to wane as new friendships and opportunities bring with them their own sense of security and well-being. Families adjust to the "missing" member as it becomes clear that though the person's daily presence is no longer there, there is still communication, and the person comes back for visits and contact. Human beings were not created to live alone, God made that clear in Genesis. 2:18, and so there is this innate quality in us that causes us to seek out new relationships in which to share our lives.

And so we come to the conclusion of this series on grief with the understanding that grief is as natural a part of living as breathing, loving, and laughing. Just as there is a mystery to why God made the human body capable of physical pain, there is a mystery as to why grief is also a prominent part of human experience. Yet I refuse to believe that God allows us to pass through this sometimes traumatic experience without some edifying purpose that can be gained by it. I do not believe that God wastes anything in our lives; not our pain, not our loss, not our grief. What I have learned from my own experience is that if we will surrender even our grief to Him in prayer, not only will He heal our brokenness and loss, He will find some way to bring something good out of it.

What Comes First?

3 Sometimes we read a passage of scripture from the Bible and read right past a simple but profound statement. Perhaps such is the case with a verse found in II Corinthians 8:5. Paul is addressing the issue of "giving" and is using the example of the churches in Macedonia who were persecuted and in poverty and yet

July

were extremely generous in the giving for the ministry of the church. Paul writes: "they gave themselves first to the Lord . . ." (then they gave their money). That has always been the key ingredient to financial stewardship in the church. To try and do otherwise is like a piece of fruit trying to create itself without benefit of the tree.

The person who consecrates his or her life to Christ will find that the areas of the stewardship of life are not burdens to be borne but opportunities to serve our Lord. When our commitment to Christ is half-hearted and partial, our lives will reveal it in service and giving. It irritates us to have to acknowledge that whatever we place ahead of our Lord is that to which we give honor and worship. We do err when we try to gradually work our way piecemeal into full commitment to Christ. We are like the rich young ruler who stopped to count the cost of discipleship and regrettably concluded that he was only willing to give part of himself in discipleship.

First, foremost and fully, we must give ourselves to God and then the requests He makes upon our lives will not be burdens but joyous opportunities to express our love and our loyalty. In II Samuel 24, we are told the story of how David had sinned in the Lord's sight and the nation of Israel was being punished. In repentance David was going to build an altar and offer a sacrifice unto God on the threshing floor of the Jebusite, Araunah. Araunah offered to give the site as well as the animals for sacrifice to David, but David's response was, "No, I insist on paying you for it. I will not sacrifice to the LORD my God burnt offerings that cost me nothing" (24:24). How much of what we offer God costs us little or nothing?

In this life we hoard and store up, we accumulate and collect, we save and lock up, we buy and possess and at the end of the day, when life reaches its conclusion, we are dispossessed of it all. It seems that for most of us it takes the entirety of our lives before we discover what is really eternally important. In all my years in ministry, I have not once stood by the bedside of a dying person and heard them grieve over the wealth and possessions they are about to leave behind. Most often, if there is sorrow it is over the people they are leaving behind.

It is not necessary to wait until the beginning of a new year to take inventory of our lives. What's first in your life today? Is it God?

July

Possessions? Family? Work? We need to ask ourselves what should be first? Then we need to decide to make it so, not so much by the profession of unfulfilled words and promises, but with the commitment of our lives to God in service. Paul had some excellent advice for the Corinthians and for us: "First they gave their own selves to the Lord . . . ." Have you?

One Nation Under God

4 How easy it is to forget one's beginnings! There are those today who try to deny the spiritual foundation of this nation and do so with the same measure of accuracy as those who would seek to deny the reality of the Holocaust. The fifty-six courageous men who signed the Declaration of Independence affixed their names beneath the last line that read, "With **a firm reliance on the protection of Divine Providence**, we mutually pledge to each other our lives, our fortunes and our sacred honor." It was not upon human intellect they relied, not upon human talent and vision, not upon human goodness and power, but upon Divine Providence—the all-knowing, all-powerful leading of the Hand of God.

It cost these men dearly to give us our nation. Someone wrote:

> *Of the fifty-six, few were long to survive. Five were captured by the British and tortured before they died. Twelve had their homes, from Rhode Island to Charleston, sacked, looted, occupied by the enemy, or burned. Two lost their sons in the army. One had two sons captured. Nine of the fifty-six died in the war, from its hardships or from its bullets. (The Rebirth of America. p. 15)*

They risked all they had; put their lives, fortunes and sacred honor on the line to give us a nation of liberty and freedom. We need to once again hear the immortal words of these great men ringing in our ears.

John Quincy Adams wrote: "Posterity—you will never know how much it has cost my generation to preserve your freedom. I hope you will make good use of it." Thomas Payne wrote in 1776, "What we obtain too cheaply, we esteem too lightly; it is dearness only that gives everything its value. Heaven knows how to put a price upon its

July

goods, and it would be strange indeed if so celestial an article as freedom should not be highly rated." Thomas Jefferson once asked, "Can the liberties of a nation be secure when we have removed the conviction that these liberties are the gift of God?"

George Washington in his inaugural address to Congress clearly declared God's role in the birth of this nation when he said, "No people can be bound to acknowledge and adore the invisible hand which conducts the affairs of men more than the people of the United States. Every step by which they have advanced to the character of an independent nation seems to have been distinguished by some token of providential agency. . . We ought to be no less persuaded that the propitious smiles of heaven cannot be expected on a nation that disregards the eternal rules of order and right, which heaven itself has ordained."

Let us pay great heed to the wise and enlightened words of the great founders of our nation, those who walked with the hand of God in one hand and the hand of a nation in the other. Abraham Lincoln put it concisely. "It is the duty of nations, as well as of men, to own their dependence upon the overruling power of God and to recognize the sublime truth announced in the Holy Scriptures and proven by all history, that those nations only are blessed whose God is the Lord."

In our present crisis following 9-11, there are those who decry the joining of a nation's heart and sorrow with our services of worship. I think the history of our nation and the words of those who gave this nation birth prove them wrong!

Strength in our Weakness

5 There are moments in each of our lives when we become painfully aware of our weaknesses and inadequacies. Our day-to-day living has revealed to us that there are some things we have not the skill, ability, or even the willpower to accomplish. And yet there are things in life that demand that we deal with them. In times like that we find ourselves being drawn to a power beyond us.

A simple story regarding one of Poland's greatest concert pianists, Ignace Paderewski, reveals a profound truth. A mother wanted to encourage her young son to play the piano, so she bought

July

tickets to Paderewski's concert. The night of the performance she went to the huge concert hall and found their seats. Soon the mother got lost in a conversation with a friend and the boy slipped away. He wasn't missed until the time for the concert began and suddenly, as the spotlights centered on the Steinway at center stage, there sat the little boy on the piano bench innocently picking out "Twinkle, twinkle, little star." The mother gasped but before she could get to her son, the great pianist sat down on the bench beside him and whispered, "Don't quit—keep playing." With his left hand Paderewski began filling in the bass part to the simple song. Then he reached around the child and began to add a running obbligato. Together the master pianist and the young child, with beauty and harmony, mesmerized the audience.

There are times in our lives when we feel like we can't go on. Life's demands have become too difficult and the strength within us seems all too inadequate. If we are willing, that is the time when the Master can surround us with His arms of strength, take the simple melody that we can offer, and transform it into a chorus of unsurpassed beauty and grace. We have been created by a Hand that made us, by necessity, to depend on something or someone beyond ourselves. The person who feels so self-sufficient, so much in control, so all-powerful that they think they need no one, is living a delusion.

We are not "islands unto ourselves" placed on this earth to live at enmity with or apart from God's creation We are put here for the purpose of living in harmony with God and His created order. The person who chooses to live in isolation is estranged from the very world God created us to be immersed in. We have been given eyes to see, ears to hear and mouths to speak in order to be in communion with one another. And the sad thing is there are people who, because of health and age, are left in isolation as shut-ins or in nursing homes to live out their days in loneliness.

As Christians we are called of God to share our lives with His children. We who have strength and vitality, who have the ability to come and go when we choose, have the opportunity to lessen the loneliness and the despair of others, simply with the priceless gift of our presence. We can become the arms of the Master who reaches around that lonely frightened one, and plays the harmony to their melody. We can be the voice of the Master that says to this precious child of Christ, "Don't quit—keep playing." Just as God in Christ strengthens you, will you be willing to become His strength to another?

Faith Beyond the Turning Points

6 There are turning points in time; pivotal moments in which upon looking back, one can readily discern when things shifted.

Such a moment is recorded in Scripture following Peter's confession of faith in Jesus at Caesarea Philippi. It was a momentous event, culminating after years of teaching His disciples. "You are the Christ, the Son of the Living God," Peter had proclaimed (Matthew 16:16). What follows is startling. **"From that time on** Jesus began to explain to his disciples that he must go to Jerusalem and suffer many things at the hands of the elders, chief priests and teachers of the law, and that he must be killed and on the third day be raised to life" (Matthew 16:21).

It defies human reason to assume that Jesus' pronouncement spontaneously erupted from Him, as if this was the first time He had given any thought to it. Long ago, He had settled it in His heart and from the beginning of His ministry He had known that a cross waited at the end. But He could not set that series of events into motion until first someone in the inner circle finally recognized who He was. Once that historic moment took place, and Peter finally saw clearly who this simple carpenter really was, Jesus' life took a dramatic turn—"He set His face to go to Jerusalem!"

Figuratively, the ground shifted beneath the disciples' feet and slowly they began to realize that this man whom they loved and whom they had followed for almost three years was on a path that would bring heartache and sorrow. They could not possibly understand that the outcome of that sorrow would be "a peace that no man can take from you." Beyond the cross was the resurrection—a historic event that would forever change humanity's perception of death. But between Peter's confession of faith and the resurrection there was a period of darkness and confusion that would become the crucible for the creation of faith.

July

All of us reach turning points in our lives. We may not realize it at the moment, but we will later on when we look back from a clearer vantage point. I have become convinced that there is nothing that happens to us in life that God is not willing and able to redeem into something that can be positive and good. Not even suffering and death are outside the domain of His power. Surely Paul discovered this when he wrote, "We know that all things work together for good for those that love God, who are the called according to his purpose" (Romans 8:28, NRSV). Nothing is beyond God's power—not powers, nor tribulation, not suffering, not death!

Perhaps you are at a turning point in your life right now, or you look back and you suddenly are aware of one that happened a while back. Maybe you lost a job, went through some terrible illness, lost a loved one, felt betrayed by someone you trusted. It could be many things and somehow that event made you feel vulnerable, helpless, afraid, and unsure of your future. The message of the Bible is that God is able to take anything that happens to us, even if it leads to prolonged suffering, and transform it into something that is beneficial—if we will let Him. We will cease to fear the future and we will no longer be apprehensive about the present when we finally discover that God is aware of our turning points and His grace precedes our steps.

Are You Donating to Life?

7 The Living God never created a single life that did not have within it the potential to be valuable. God does not measure as we measure; the value of a human life is not determined by longevity, by wealth, or by popularity. It is determined, in part, by the contribution one makes to the lives of others without the desire to be rewarded. To **not** be recognized for one's noble accomplishments in no way lessens the value of what was achieved. Peter Marshall, one of America's greatest preachers, said, "The measure of a life, after all, is not its duration, but its donation" (*Mr. Jones, Meet the Master*, p. 16).

Without question, the most selfless life that was ever lived was that of Jesus. In three scant years of ministry, He lived a life that literally transformed the world for all time. He built no great bridges,

July

skyscrapers, or monuments. He left no oil paintings of Himself on board room walls. He made no medical discoveries, such as vaccines. He owned no property, had no bank account; and as far as we know had only one change of clothing. He never ran for office and He never lied to His followers. He never took advantage of a single human being; and never spoke an unkind word about anyone (except those religious leaders who were misleading God's people). He had no college degrees but was the wisest of all men. He received no earthly honors, but has the Name that is above all names. He sought no fame, but is revered throughout the world, not just in the century in which He lived, but for all time.

We claim to be His followers, but how reluctant we are to pattern our lives after His! If we seek to emulate His life in order to be adored by others, it will never happen. Jesus never sought glory for Himself, only for His Father. The glory that is sought for self is no glory at all; it's only an illusion. It's sort of like the old cliché, "Humility is the one thing when you think you have it, you lost it." What is there within us that makes us want to be praised? Why do we find it so difficult to do good simply for the sake of doing good? The term "do-gooder" is a negative concept because it describes someone who seeks to do good for the wrong reasons.

Who is there among us who cannot look back over his or her life and find things for which to feel regret? No one, if we are honest! But no matter what we have done in the past, it is no excuse for how we live in the present or in the future. When I was a boy I was a Boy Scout (it seems like a hundred years ago now) and one of the things I remember being taught was to try and consciously do at least one good deed each day. That's good advice, regardless of one's age.

I am aware that good deeds do not save us—yes, we are "saved by grace alone through faith." But I am also aware that where faith is genuinely present, good deeds will flow as naturally as the water in a mountain stream must flow down the side of a mountain. In reality, good deeds become outward evidence of inward faith. Kindness is one of the fruits of the Spirit (Gal. 5:22). Where kindness is absent, God's Spirit is not present. The Apostle Paul's parting advice to the Galatians was, "Let us not become weary in doing good, for at the proper time we will reap a harvest if we do not give up. Therefore, as

July

we have opportunity, let us do good to all people, especially to those who belong to the family of believers" (Gal. 6:9-10). Seems applicable today, does it not?

What Do You Bring To Church?

8 When you go to church, what do you expect? If we could have our wish, what would church be like? Should not church be a place where we experience the presence of the Living God? A place where we are so caught up in the awe and majesty of His presence that we are spiritually enriched? Should church not be a place where we feel the pressures of life being relieved and the hurriedness of life slowed down? Should not church be a place where we feel safe, free from attack, loved and accepted in spite of our shortcomings?

Churches become reflections of the people who make them up. If they bring strife to the setting then the environment is permeated with discord. If they bring peace then peace will be as dominant as each heart allows it to be. If we come seeking forgiveness others will be the recipients of forgiveness. If we come with anger and hatred in our heart, the tranquility of the service will be shattered by our inner demons. If we come with self-centeredness and concern only for ourselves, many will leave empty feeling no one cared about them.

We live under an illusion if we think church will be any different from what we make it. God is pleased to dwell mightily in the places where people make room for Him. When we come with cluttered minds and selfish hearts, where is there for Him to dwell? When we come expecting nothing, we usually leave with that which we expected. When our minds are closed to the revealing of God's truth through the hymns that we sing, the prayers that we pray and the Word that is proclaimed, then we leave no better than when we came. In fact, we leave perhaps worse, for once more our expectations have led to disappointment and disappointments lead to despair.

I guess what I am saying is that in large measure, church will become what we bring to it and what we sincerely desire for it to become. Too many churches wither and die because those who make it up refuse to follow the guidance of our Lord and insist on making the church after their own image rather than His. There should be no "mean spiritedness" in church and yet, like household bacteria, it thrives in the damp darkness of our souls. When tongues wag and people constantly find fault with each other, condemn and never commend, then God's presence gets squeezed out. Most of the malicious gossip that gets spread is untrue to begin with and people get hurt and lives are ruined because someone has told a half-truth or an outright lie. I am constantly amazed at how quickly some people are to believe the worst about someone without any evidence whatsoever, except the statements of those who have nothing better to do than criticize and tear down. Finger pointing and self-righteous judgment will always ensure that a church will grow—grow stagnant!

And so, I ask, what do you bring to church when you come? Do you bring praise for God, forgiveness for your neighbor? Do you bring a hunger to experience God? A desire to be used in service by Him? Do you come to serve or be served? Do you come to lift up or tear down? Do you criticize more than you praise? Do you find fault more than you seek virtue? Do you long for His kingdom to grow, or are you content to see it stay right where it is? If what the church becomes is what you bring to it when you come, what kind of church will your church be?

A Friend Inside

9 We live in a time in which honor and integrity seem no longer to be important to many in society. The political scene of the past few years has vividly revealed how little value is placed on the importance of truth, honor, and integrity. No doubt, there has never been a time in which those virtues were practiced to perfection, but it seems to me that we as a nation, and as individuals, are on a slippery slope when we either accept dishonesty as a way of life, or equally as bad, are indifferent to it. The very fabric of human relationships, if they are to have any lasting value or merit, must be constructed on the foundations of honesty, integrity and virtue. To build on anything less is to build one's house on sand.

Yet somehow, we have reached an era in which the person who stands for honesty, who seeks to steer a course of moral uprightness, is viewed as either odd or a nuisance. Often they are ridiculed and

July

ostracized. Society demands conformity; when one, by honest virtue, appears to rise above society's norms, he or she is attacked with a vengeance. When we give in to the pressure to conform to that which is less than virtuous, our character is whittled away little by little. One day we will wake up and be shocked at the person we have become.

Sometimes it is difficult to do what is right when popular opinion is running the other way. We live in a time in which too many decisions seem to be made based on polls. I don't know if it is still practiced today, but there was a time at West Point, at the Sunday worship service held in the chapel, that the cadets repeated the "Cadet's Prayer." In part it says,

> *"Strengthen and increase our admiration for honest dealing and clean thinking, and suffer not our hatred of hypocrisy and pretense ever to diminish. Encourage us in our endeavor to live above the common level of life. Make us to choose the harder right instead of the easier wrong, and never to be content with a half truth when the whole can be won. Endow us with courage that is born of loyalty to all that is noble and worthy, that scorns to compromise with vice and injustice and knows no fear when truth and right are in jeopardy. Guard us against flippancy and irreverence in the sacred things of life."*

Every day we face choices that can build up or tear down our integrity one small segment at the time. We can give in to our prejudices or we can take the higher ground and stand for a greater principle. We can twist the truth and color it to suit our needs or we can have enough integrity to let it stand on its own. We can sacrifice praise for virtue's sake or we can run with the herd and seek self-glorification. To choose the right can be lonely and difficult. But it is the way of righteousness that God sets before us.

Few have faced harder choices than did Abraham Lincoln in the midst of the Civil War. He was opposed by the people in the South and disparaged by the people in the North. He had tough decisions to make, choices that ultimately led to his assassination. He once wrote, "I desire so to conduct the affairs of this administration that if at the end, when I come to lay down the reins of power, I have lost every

July

other friend on earth, I shall at least have one friend left, and that friend shall be down inside of me." The Christian who is filled with God's Spirit will always desire to listen to that voice within one's self, which we trust is God speaking to us. When life is over, and all has been said and done, what will matter is whether God is pleased with our choices and whether deep down inside us that is confirmed by a feeling of peace down in our souls—a friend inside!

Head and Heart

10 There are many simple but profound verses in the Bible which quickly get to the center of essential things. One such verse (which seems rather self-evident) is "And without faith it is impossible to please God, because anyone who comes to him must believe that he exists and that he rewards those who earnestly seek him" (Hebrews 11:6). Almost always, God reveals Himself only to the person who seeks Him through the doorway of faith. Faith is more than knowledge or intellectual acceptance; it is that moving of the Spirit that rises up from within the heart.

We live in the Information Age: a time in which great emphasis has been placed on tapping into and acquiring more and more knowledge. Knowledge is power. Knowledge is king! Yet knowledge divorced from the restraining guidance of the heart will inevitably lead to disaster. The person who seeks to find God only with their mind will always be disappointed. Facts about God, even biblical historic facts, do not prove God's existence; they only point us in the direction where He is to be found so that He might be encountered by faith. Faith is not born in the head; it is conceived in the heart. A woman in childbearing years may have within her very body an egg that has the potential to produce a child: she may have all the medical and anatomical knowledge necessary to give birth to a child, but until that child is conceived within the womb of her body, it will never come into reality.

A person may have knowledge about the acts of God in one's head; he or she may indeed possess more information than the average person, but unless God is approached with the heart the experience will be like two ships silently and unwittingly passing each other in the dark. Faith is about trust (reasonable trust, but nonetheless, trust).

July

When one flies in an airplane, just possessing knowledge of how airplanes work isn't sufficient to get you on board. First, you must place trust in the people who built the plane, those who maintain the plane, the pilot who flies the plane and the air traffic controller who guides the plane. Getting on board is the act of faith that brings to life the experience of flying. Deciding to "risk" following Jesus is the act that brings about the experience of His presence.

The person who has built his or her life on intellect alone will always struggle with the issues of faith because they are willing to trust only that which the mind can perceive and grasp. Everything must pass the test of analytical scrutiny and must neatly fit into the pigeonhole of human rationality. If it doesn't, it gets rejected. God cannot be conveniently squeezed into our intellectual capacity; He is too great a Being. When one falls in love it is not the result of knowledge, but a feeling within the heart. In a real sense when we have true faith in God, we fall in love with the One who has given us life. Love sometimes isn't very logical, but there is nothing that exists which is more real.

Faith cannot be dissected and analyzed but it can be observed. It is observed in the acts of those who trust the God whom their eyes have not seen. Faith reveals itself in each simple decision we make to live life with the assumption that there is a God. It is the ultimate risk, but it brings with it the ultimate reward—a relationship of love and trust with the God of the universe. Head knowledge is important, but in matters of faith, heart trust is essential.

People of the Way

11 The name that was given to the earliest followers of Christ was not "Christians" but the people of "the Way" (Acts 9:2; 19:9, 23; 22:4; 24:14, 22). The name described people who lived their lives a certain "way." There was something about how they lived that was so different from those around them, that their very way of life bespoke who they were. Christianity is more than simply embracing a certain set of theological principles. It is more than just trying to live a moral and ethical life. It is more than studying and trying to live by all the things Jesus has taught.

July

What appears to be unique about the people of "the Way" was that the Holy Spirit of God dwelt in and empowered them to live a distinctively different way of life. Obviously, Jesus understood the need in His followers to be strengthened to live the Christian life after He had departed this earth. In his book *Your God is Too Small*, J. B. Phillips writes:

> *He [Jesus] knew very well, for example, that the followers of His own day would very quickly collapse when the support and inspiration of His own personality were removed by death. He therefore promised them a new Spirit who should provide them with all the courage, moral reinforcement, love, patience, endurance and other qualities which they would need.* (p. 118)

Any person, regardless of the century in which that person lives, who strives to be a Christian without the Spirit of God as their empowerment, will always struggle because a godly life apart from the Spirit of God is not possible. Modern people find it difficult to embrace the idea that there is really a power outside themselves which can dwell within them and shape their lives for good. We are far too much a product of a way of life that has taught us the supreme importance of self-reliance, working your way to the top, and the innate power within the human mind and psyche. We have been programmed to dismiss the supernatural and worship only at the altar of that which is "natural." We approach the door to God's presence and it remains forever closed to us because we think we can open it with the power of our mind and will. In reality, it is only opened by the trusting step of faith.

Why must we be like we are? We are like the person who stands in a great hall with a thousand doors, one of which is marked "The Way to God." But before we open that door we insist on trying all the others first. Like St. Augustine, our prayer becomes, "Save me Lord, but not yet!" The purpose of Christ's coming was not just to reveal the true nature of God, but to transform the corrupted nature of humanity. Redemption does not mean simply accepting us as the sinful beings that we are, but transforming us into the changed people that we can become. We constantly live life against itself. We crave

July

peace and joy, but we are forever seeking it in the places where it can never be found.

Peace and joy are qualities of God's nature and those qualities cannot become our own until we willingly become His own. To Americans, surrender is a repugnant word; but in the real world of the Spirit, that is the only way true life can be found. When we are willing to give up all that we have become, then and only then is He able to help us become all that we can be. Then we will be the people of the Way.

The Voice in Silence

12 Prayer is not a word that causes us to stumble with ignorance when it is used, for we all know perfectly well what it means. We may not be intimately acquainted with the multi-dimensional aspects of it, such as intercession, petition, adoration, praise, and thanksgiving, but we all have a general idea of what praying means—it is conversing with God. Here's a simple thought—what kind of a relationship would you have with your spouse, your children, your parents, or your friends, if you talked to them no more than you talk to God? Better still, what kind of children would our children become if we spoke to them no more than we speak to God?

Ever since there has been more than one creature in existence, the need for communication has been essential. Oddly enough, communication can consist of far more than the meaningless exchange of empty words; it can occur through the simple impact of a person's presence. Many husbands and wives find great closeness in simply abiding in each other's presence without the necessity of verbal communication. Sometimes the most meaningful communication takes place in the profundity of silence. Part of our problem with each other is that we live too much in the world of noise—it drowns out, it distracts, it consumes.

I suspect that very few of us have experienced the powerful impact of sitting quietly in God's presence without bombarding Him with questions, requests, or our opinion on everything and everyone else. Our prayers are almost always a monologue because we never

July

give God any time to respond. Oswald Chambers has written many great books filled with deep wisdom. In one of those books, he makes the following statement, "We have to pray with our eyes on God, not on the difficulties" (From *God's Workmanship*). Is that how you pray when you have troubles? Is your focus on God, His power, His goodness, His grace, His love, His care for you? Or is all your attention so concentrated on your problems that you become oblivious to the God who has the power to help you through your time of trouble?

The Bible tells us that Jesus **often** spent time **alone** with His Heavenly Father in prayer. It does not describe all that was said (or not said) but I suspect a great deal of that time of communion was spent not only in audible silence but in mental silence—that is, Jesus wasn't just talking to God silently with words in His mind, He was quietly listening to the inner voice of God's Spirit as it began to give direction to His life. Here's a suggestion: Go aside to some quiet place where you won't be distracted or interrupted, sit down and get comfortable. Briefly greet our Lord with a few opening words and then just try to rid your mind of any and all thoughts. It won't be easy; thoughts like persistent children will tug at you for attention, but gently brush them aside and tell them you will deal with them later. For now, just sit quietly in God's presence without attempting to direct the thought process.

It is possible that you may doze off—that's okay. But it is also possible that God might finally be able to break through the mass of barriers that we have unwittingly erected that keeps Him from being able to communicate with us. It might just be that in that rare moment of "letting go of controlling the conversation," God might just speak to you in the most profound of ways. Are you willing to chance it?

Honest Questions

13 When you read the Psalms you will discover that the writers often asked questions—questions that erupted from the deepest part of their soul: questions that transcended human knowledge and cried out to God for any semblance of an answer. Such is the case in Psalm 8 when the author asks, "What are human beings that you are mindful of them, mortals that you care for

July

them?" (NRSV) If the Psalmist asked, why then shouldn't each of us feel at ease in asking God our questions? Listen in as I explore the thoughts and questions hidden deep inside my own heart.

Lord, I look at us humans and I see flesh and blood, bone, tissue, and cells that brim with life and energy. We have the gift of consciousness, of being aware of our aliveness, and those things that exist around us. We know the acuteness and shock of pain, the enticement and exhilaration of pleasure, the continuum that exists between the extremes of joy and sorrow, health and a sense of well-being, sickness and the inevitability of death. We also experience the contentment of inner peace and the perplexity of fear and despair. We have the unfathomable gift of seeing beauty in things, places, and people, as well as the ability to give and experience kindness. We are a mixture of vice and virtue, goodness and evil, wisdom and ignorance, mercy and vengeance. We know right and good, yet, we often choose wrong and evil. We are capable of adoring You and defying You, loving and betraying You, worshipping and denying You.

You have given us the ability to grow and change, think and re-think, advance and retreat. We have been entrusted with the power to create and the ability to destroy. We are capable of dreaming and imagining; of giving birth to new creations through thoughts and ideas. We have the capacity to remember the past and the unique ability to envision the future. We are born, we live, we die. Like the glancing, darting flash of the sun's rays on a spinning mirror, we are here and are suddenly gone. In the context of creation, we are but a drop in the ocean of time, a fleeting life viewed for a moment and then gone.

What is there about us that will be remembered, O Lord; or will we be lost in time, as are the millions who have preceded us? Is there anything about us that will be preserved and exist eternally, or will we rise and set on life's horizon as quickly as one sunrise and sunset in the brief span of a single day? Why do you allow so much evil to exist, not just in human beings but also in the acts of nature? We could ask you a thousand questions God, but it seems that you are often slow to give us answers.

Nonetheless, Lord, when my tiny little mind has thought as deeply as it is capable of thinking, when the outer boundaries of my

July

understanding have been stretched to the uttermost of their limits, when once again I have come face to face with all that I am and all that I am not, I am left with only trust in You. I don't understand my existence, O God, and I don't comprehend the greatness of Your Being, but I thank You for allowing me the privilege of questioning that which I cannot contain, and trusting in that which I do not behold. If we can be but one tiny cog on the wheel of Your will, O God, use us for Your glory and for the benefit of those you have created!

Power in His Presence

14 Those who scoff at Christianity with its call for an ethical and moral standard that seems unattainable have failed to grasp the fact that such a standard is attainable when empowered by the indwelling Spirit of the resurrected Christ. People will always fail and will inevitably become frustrated if they try to live a life of holiness and righteousness based on their own power. We fall into the same traps and mistakes that all humans experiences when we focus our attention on ourselves rather than on our Lord.

Oswald Chambers observes:

> *If all Jesus came to do was to tell me I must have an unsullied career, when my past has been blasted by sin and wickedness on my own part, then He but tantalizes me. If He is simply a teacher, He only increases our capacity for misery, for He sets up standards that stagger us. But the teaching of Jesus Christ is not an ideal, it is the statement of the life we will live when we are readjusted to God by the Atonement. . . . Unless I am born from above the only result of the teachings of Jesus is to produce despair. Our Lord's teaching has no power in it unless I possess His nature.* (The Oswald Chambers Daily Devotional Bible, p. 895)

When we seek to be Christian without the empowering Spirit of the living Christ dwelling in us we will not only fail again and again, but we will eventually be driven to frustration and despair. Trying to be Christian without Christ is like trying to be human without a body. It's like trying to breathe without air; trying to swim without water.

July

When those outside the church look at those of us inside the church and see that we are no different from the world, they have no desire to waste their time. We will never be different from the world until we exchange our love of the world for a deeper love for Jesus.

The Atonement, rightly understood, is not just Jesus dying on a cross for our sins, but literally exchanging His nature for ours. That's why the story didn't end with a cross and a resurrection, but continued on to Pentecost where the empowering Spirit was poured out upon human flesh. Apart from God's Spirit, the best we can hope for is nominal and flawed goodness. With God's Spirit, we can be transformed into a "new creation." Physically speaking, we may not look much different on the outside, but inside there will be a total renovation.

It is sad, but true, that many church members live their entire lives trying to be what they think God wants them to be without ever realizing that apart from His power they are doomed to failure. Empowerment comes with surrender. It is recognizing and confessing to God that by ourselves we cannot succeed. Paul wrote in Romans. "The good that I would do, I do not, and the evil that I would not do. I find myself doing." Then he gives the answer, "O wretched man that I am! Who will deliver me from this body of death! I thank God through Jesus Christ our Lord!" (Romans 7:19, 24-25, KJV). Living for Christ means not only living with Christ, but most importantly of all, having Christ live in us. Does Christ dwell within you, or do you insist that He reside on the outside?

The Tree of Life

15 How often we overlook the things that are around us which enrich life immeasurably! Have you ever thought about the beauty, mystery and power of a tree? Are you aware of their significance in the Bible? They appear in the first chapter of Genesis and in the last chapter of Revelation (and many books and chapters in between). Life began in a garden; a garden whose décor was the handiwork of God—masterfully painted in the brilliant colors created by God and unmatched by earth's greatest artists. "And the LORD God made all kinds of trees grow out of the

July

ground—trees that were pleasing to the eye and good for food. In the middle of the garden were the tree of life and the tree of the knowledge of good and evil" (Genesis 2:9).

Without trees, life on this planet would soon cease to be. It is the green trees and plants that take the carbon dioxide we breathe out and transforms it into life sustaining oxygen. From these marvelous creations we build our homes, construct our furniture and create things of beauty that enrich our lives beyond measure. The ark of the covenant was handcrafted from wood; the Psalmist declared the righteous to be like "a tree planted by streams of water which yields its fruit in its season" (Psalm 1:3). The writer of Proverbs describes wisdom as ". . . a tree of life to those who embrace her; those who lay hold of her will be blessed" (Proverbs 3:18).

One of the most significant trees in the Bible was the one on which our Lord was crucified. How like us humans, to take the Creator and kill Him by means of His own creation. Interestingly enough, Paul never calls the instrument of execution of Jesus a "tree" (*xulon* in the Greek) but always refers to it as the cross (*stauros*) perhaps to differentiate between the cross as the creation of human hands while the tree is the handiwork of God. But Peter, and he alone, refers to the cross as "the tree." Preaching in Acts, he reminded the Jewish leaders that they took Jesus ". . . whom you had killed by hanging him on a tree" (Acts 5:30). In I Peter 2:24 he says of Jesus, "He himself bore our sins in his body on the tree, so that we might die to sins and live for righteousness; by his wounds you have been healed."

Just as water in baptism has no efficacious power of itself to cleanse from sin, neither did the tree on which Jesus died have any power within itself to redeem us from our sins. The power was within the One who was dying. If trees had feelings, how broken it must have felt that it had been singled out to share in the execution of the Lord of life. Like Simon of Cyrene, who was forced to carry the cross, the tree was forced to participate in the evil of humankind. God has placed within the power of humanity great control and effect over creation. Rather than be one with the created order, we seem far more interested in destroying it.

July

The biblical story of history ends with the establishment of a celestial city. Flowing in the center of the city is a river of the water of life. And on either side of the river is the tree of life. Whatever that tree may be, surely it has its spiritual roots in a tree called the cross, a tree that forever will be stained with the blood of God's Son. That's the real tree of life!

I Thirst . . . I Thirst . . . I Thirst!

16 Bishop Francis Stafford, former Roman Catholic bishop of Memphis recounts the story of an experience he had at a retreat with Mother Teresa several years ago. The two were walking along together in an enclosed cloister in the monastery. They walked in silence until they came to a statue of the crucified Christ. They stood for a long time in front of the statue and the bishop overheard Mother Teresa whispering, "I thirst . . . I thirst . . . I thirst." The bishop said that in that moment he discovered the saintly nun's secret. It was her desire—her burning thirst for more of Christ.

The secret to peace and serenity in the Christian's life will not be found in events, in retreats, in books or even in sermons. It will be discovered in one thing only and that is in the person of Jesus Christ. We can read and meditate, search and inquire, but until we are willing to dwell in the presence of the Christ who lives, we will not have peace in our life. Does your soul thirst for Christ? Have you come to the place of the Psalmist who could declare, "I lift my hands to you in prayer. I thirst for you as parched land thirsts for rain" (Psalm 144:6, NLT).

The unfortunate truth is that most of us do not thirst for God. Most days we probably don't even think about Him and if we do, it's probably just long enough to fire off an "instant" prayer (in keeping with our instant everything world). Modern civilization has so filled its world with "things" that we have no room for God in our day. We have become so comfortable in our overflowing routine days that we have unwittingly squeezed God out of our desires and out of our consciousness. When we observe a crucifix, be it one made from gold or a life-sized one chiseled from stone, do our minds marvel at the craftsmanship of the artist or the suffering of the One he or she has tried to portray?

We will have become serious about our faith when we begin to make time in our day for Jesus. As you read this, what time of the day is it—morning, noon, or evening? Think back, have you gone aside to seek the Lord's presence? Is your heart whispering, "I thirst . . . I thirst . . . I thirst"? Or are you saying to yourself, "I just didn't have time"?

One day, long ago, Jesus encountered a woman who had come to draw water from a well—a Samaritan woman. He made a simple statement to her that changed her life and He makes that same statement to each of us. "If you knew the gift of God and who it is that asks you for a drink, you would have asked him and he would have given you living water" (John 4:10). That day she put aside all of the things that made demands on her life and she made time for Jesus and her life was forever changed.

Where does Jesus fit into your daily life? If He's not in your life daily then He really isn't much in your life at all. He's not a part-time God or an on-call errand boy. He makes it quite clear that He does not want part of our heart; He longs to possess it all. That which He completely possesses He gives back, "good measure, pressed down and running over." He stands before you right now. Perhaps even now He hears you saying, "For you Jesus, I thirst . . . I thirst . . . I thirst!"

The Jesus Who Disappoints

17 There were many times in their brief relationship that Jesus was a disappointment to His friends and followers. He will inevitably disappoint every person who follows Him— if you try to impose on Him what you think He ought to do and be! The Pharisees were disappointed because they thought He was weak on upholding the Law. The Sadducees were disappointed because He spoke of a resurrection. The disciples were disillusioned because He kept talking about going to Jerusalem to die. Peter was dismayed because he wouldn't let him defend Him with a sword. Judas was appalled because He wouldn't use His miraculous power against the

July

tyranny of Rome. Many Jews were disappointed because He told them they should love their enemies (which included the Samaritans). His own siblings distrusted Him because He claimed He was the Son of God. The list could go on and on. Everyone who encounters Jesus brings to Him his or her own expectation of who He ought to be and what He ought to do.

Unlike today's politicians who often make decisions based on polls, Jesus never decided anything simply because it was the popular thing to do. The only opinion that mattered to Him was that of His Father. He refused to be shaped by the might of Rome, the intransigent Jewish religious leaders, Greek culture or the adulation of the masses. He was in the world and the world was made by Him, but the world could not make Him in the likeness of its own image. No one before or since has walked a path through life with such utter nobility and purity of heart. All the wealth the world had to offer, all the ego-stroking comments that people uttered, all the pain and sickness of the world could not force Him into a pattern of life or behavior that would deter Him from the singular mission He had in life.

It is for good reason that those who become Jesus' disciples are called followers. He leads, we follow! He will not alter his path for us or for anyone. He alone knows the way to eternal life and He will not allow us to sidetrack Him or delude ourselves into thinking there is any other way. He longs for us to come to Him with our needs and our requests; but He will answer those petitions only in a way that reflects His will, not ours. Every prayer we offer with a heart sincerely content to discover and accept His will shall be honored. It was not insignificant that when asked to teach us to pray, He included "Thy will be done on earth as it is in heaven." Can you possibly imagine heaven to be a place where God's will is done less than perfectly?

Our Lord cannot be manipulated, neither will He force us to do His will. The sad part is that there is within each of us a desire to be in control, to dictate to God how life ought to be. As long as that part of our nature seeks to dominate, Christ will always disappoint us because He will not yield to the baseness of our sinful nature. Our desires too often are shaped by sinfulness, His are born in holiness. Our vision does not extend beyond the present, His extends into eternity.

July

Has Jesus disappointed you? If so, then your will was not in alignment with His. Grace allows us to seek our own way. Mercy reaches us when we go astray. Love pursues us until His will becomes our own. Then, we are never disappointed in Jesus.

The Simple Truth

18 Sometimes we human beings fail to comprehend deep spiritual things because we overlook the obvious. For example, we might argue, "How can I understand a God whom I cannot see, who never speaks audible words to me, who is so mysterious and quiet that I cannot grasp who or what He is like?" He does not speak to us from the clouds in the sky. He does not appear before our eyes so that we can discern His nature and character. How then can we know this Being whom we call God?

The truth is, everything we need to know about God has been revealed in Jesus Christ! God did come down from the lofty heights of heaven and assume a form and a voice to which human beings could relate. Jesus said, "The Father and I are one. The person who has seen Me, has seen the Father." Over the centuries scholars, theologians and philosophers have debated the nature and characteristics of God and have succeeded in totally burying Him beneath an avalanche of human rationale. There is nothing wrong at all with honest inquiry about God, but we must be careful to let God reveal Himself and not attempt to create the God we want with our own human limitations.

Perhaps at the heart of our inquiry about God lies the most significant question we all have. Is it possible that God loves me? After all, I am a sinner; there is much about me that is unlovable. There is a clear and unmistakable answer to that question in the Bible. Look how Jesus related to "sinners" in His day—He loved them! He nurtured them. He lifted up the downtrodden and they soaked up His love like sponges. He prayed for forgiveness for the very ones that demanded His death and He carried a thief with Him to Paradise on the day that He died. The cross is eternally God's answer to how much He loves us. There is a profound little verse that I have hanging on my study wall, "I asked Jesus, 'How much do you love me?' He answered, 'This much.' And He stretched out His arms and died."

July

What could God possibly do to show you He loves you, beyond dying for you? Jesus said, "Greater love has no one than this, that he lay down his life for his friends" (John 15:13). Jesus took all the laws that accumulated over the centuries, laws that were supposed to govern human behavior, and He reduced them to two. He made it so simple that we shouldn't get confused. "Thou shall love the Lord thy God with all thy heart, mind, soul and strength. And thou shall love thy neighbor as thyself" (KJV). If you are looking for guidelines for living then spend time meditating on those simple but profound words.

God has chosen to relate to us on the level of the spirit, not the flesh. When we begin to seek Him with our spirit, we will begin to become aware of His nearness. It will be a difficult task because we live in a time and with a generation of people who demand instant gratification and empirical provable data. God will not be rushed in His revelation, but like a steady, slow, flowing stream that carves great canyons through mountain ranges, God's Spirit shapes and molds the person that is willing to be shaped by His love. The simple truth is that God has shown us what He is like in Jesus. The question then becomes, are we willing to accept what Jesus has revealed about God, or are we going to insist on making a God that suits us?

The Simple Invitation

19 Every day that we rise from our beds, let us remember the words of the Psalmist: "This is the day that the Lord has made, let us rejoice and be glad in it" (Psalm 118:24). Self-sufficient creatures that we imagine ourselves to be, how little thought we give to the fact that each day is a gift of grace. We think that it is a given that we have many more to live, and yet the reality is that it could all be over with our next breath. Then what? James 4:13-15 describes humanity's cavalier attitude toward life with these words:

> Now listen, you who say, "Today or tomorrow we will go to this or that city, spend a year there, carry on business and make money." Why, you do not even know what will happen tomorrow. What is your life? You are a mist that appears for a little while and then vanishes. Instead, you ought to say, "If it is the Lord's will, we will live and do this or that."

July

Life is fragile and delicate. From its very beginning it hurtles toward its inevitable conclusion. The moment we draw our first breath and the loving eyes of our parents behold us for the first time, we have begun the journey toward life's end. For some the end is not far down the road; for others it becomes a long journey of passing through the cycles of youth, adulthood, and old age. Our bodies begin in weakness, they discover the joy of strength and health, and then they become reacquainted with weakness. Along the way, we drink from life's mixture of good and bad. We grow, we learn, we experience, we laugh, we love, we know anger, we struggle with disappointments, and bend under the weight of sorrow. Each event (even those that seem unimportant) shapes and molds us into what we become.

In the process of living, we are exposed to the reality and presence of God. But some will have become so focused on self or on the material world that they will be totally oblivious to His presence. In the vainness of their own little world, they will imagine that the Creator could not possibly exist. Like Adam in the garden, they will choose to give up their walk with God in the cool breeze of the evening and they will hide themselves from His presence. What a terrible loss, to trek through this life without the joy of a conscious knowledge of God's loving presence.

In every nook and cranny, we look for that mysterious element of life that will bring happiness to our heart and peace to our soul, never realizing that those are gifts that come only from the hand of the One we seek to avoid. In our busy days we can find no time to give Him entry, no space to allow Him to occupy. Loving God that He is, He patiently waits in the shadows, ever longing for that moment when with outstretched hand we reach up for the comfort and consoling touch of the Source of grace and life.

Today, this very day, the One who granted you life waits to share life with you. It happens only by invitation: **your** invitation to invite Him into the sanctuary of your soul. And when you do you finally will have discovered not only the One who loved you into being, but the one Person that can bring peace to your troubled soul. It's not complicated; it's as simple as saying, "Come, Lord Jesus, live in and with me today!"

July

The Peace of God's Presence

20 From time to time, it is important to spend time alone in the solitude of nature. Separate yourself from that which is created by human hands and discover the simple purity of that which was fashioned by divine hands. Observe the delicate but precise construction of a blade of grass or a dark green leaf. Smell the deep aroma of a magnolia blossom or a gardenia bloom. Feel its softness, marvel at its texture; observe its serenity. How wise of our Lord to remind us to observe the lilies of the field, how they neither toiled nor labored, yet how magnificently they are arrayed. "Solomon," He said, "in all of his glory was not clothed like one of these" (Matthew 6:29, NRSV).

Some warm day, stretch out a blanket on your lawn, lie down and look up at the soft, powder blue sky and the white fluffy clouds that dance across the horizon before you. Quietly, gently they move, changing shape before your eyes with their hypnotic rhythm, and calm peaceful presence. Listen to the wind as it rustles the leaves in the top of one tree while leaving another beside it undisturbed. Tiny fingers on skinny limbs faintly clapping their hands in glory to their Creator. Feel the gentle breeze caress the miraculous tiny nerve endings that cover your face; little receptors—free gifts of grace that grant you the privilege of experiencing the soft, loving breath of God. Breathe deeply the freshness of the air, filled with the nectar of nature, and become aware of the gratitude down in your soul as it seeks to burst through the barriers of your crowded mind and over-burdened heart.

Sit by a pool and catch the glittering sunlight as it bounces off tiny ripples of water. Glistening like diamonds, it dazzles the eyes and gives a miniature foretaste of the glory of God. Cast a tiny pebble a few feet from shore and observe the perfect concentric circles that radiate from the center of its splash. Note how at one all of nature is with itself. Birds sing their soothing songs to one another. Bees and flowers work together in perfect union, each giving something to the other. Butterflies zig and zag with erratic bounces from flower to flower; and hummingbirds dart from tree to tree, almost quicker than the eye can see.

July

Stand on a sand dune and be awed by the might and majesty of breaking waves rolling themselves flat on the shoreline as seagulls cry aloud to one another. As steady as the ticking of a clock the waves beat against the shore, then retreat back into the dark vastness of the sea, as if teasing us to come and join them. Dark, bluish-gray water suddenly becomes white bubbly foam as it laps at your feet. Do you feel one with your world yet?

All these things God has placed before you and they are free! He charges you not one penny for this exquisite beauty that no artist's brush can match and no sculptor's chisel reproduce. In the quietness, beauty, and solitude of nature, commune with God and marvel at how "peace like a river" gently flows over you. We are not pantheists who claim God is in nature, but we can be Christians who proclaim that God's handprint is clearly found there. In the busyness of your day, will you make time to seek God's peace, His presence? Or will you let the human-made clutter of your life blind and deafen you to His glory all around you?

Let's Hear it For Tears!

21 The Psalmist writes, "I praise you because I am fearfully and wonderfully made" (Ps. 139:14). This body in which we reside is indeed marvelously intricate and complex. Not only does it function to allow us to exist, it houses within it the spirit, the emotions, and the soul. Emotions are those feelings we have which cause us to feel joy or sadness, laughter or inner pain, happiness or despair, peace or turbulence. They are the fountain from which flow love or hate, anger or calmness. As far as I know, human beings are the only creatures on this earth that have been given the capacity to feel emotions.

All these things are interconnected with the body of flesh and bone. There are moments in which we feel great sorrow, and if the sorrow is deep enough it might evoke tears. Yet those same tear ducts can also emit tiny droplets of emotion when we feel great joy or great love. How beautifully has Max Lucado described tears:

July

> *Those tiny drops of humanity. Those round wet balls of fluid that tumble from our eyes, creep down our cheeks, and splash on the floor of our hearts. . . . They are miniature messengers, on call twenty-four hours a day to substitute for crippled words. They drip, drop, and pour from the corner of our souls, carrying with them the deepest emotions we possess.*
> *(No Wonder They Call Him the Savior, p. 106)*

Is there any other creature on earth that has the ability to give expression to its feeling through the shedding of tears? When animals are physically hurt they may whimper, growl, or yelp, but they don't cry tears. Tears are a precious gift from God that allows our inner pain to make its way upward from our heart and soul and find an outlet for its expression. I wonder how we could bear the deep pain of loss, if it were not for the release of that sorrow in tears. When our feelings are hurt with untrue or unkind words, some of the sharpness of that hurt is dulled and diluted by the pain that comes out in those tiny little droplets of balm. Each one brings with it a tiny piece of pain encapsulated in fluid to cleanse us and to usher it outside of our heart.

Little boys are often taught, "Men don't cry." Who, I wonder, was the author of that piece of misguided advice? To constantly suppress tears is to imprison within one's self a world of pain. Pain that is granted no outlet will take its toll on the heart and stifle the soul. It is God who in His wisdom gave us the ability to cry. He knew that the human body is also a soul and the soul sometimes must be granted an avenue of expression. Sometimes the need is for only a few tears and sometimes they erupt like flash floods, sweeping away the hidden debris that has clogged up the inner paths of our lives.

Three times we are told in the New Testament that tears were found on the cheeks of our Lord. The Gospels record that He wept over Jerusalem and another time at the tomb of His friend Lazarus. According to Hebrews 4:7, He also wept in Gethsemane. If the incarnate God could weep from the pains of life, why should we feel shame at allowing so precious a gift to become our own? The next time you feel a tear on your cheek or behold them on another's face, stop and remember they are there to help bring wholeness. What a wonderful Lord we have, who made a way to take away the pain from our soul!

July

Yesterday, Tomorrow and Today

22

A wise man has written:

*The God separated a spirit from Himself and fashioned it into beauty. He showered upon her all the blessings of gracefulness and kindness. He gave her the cup of happiness and said, 'Drink not from this cup **unless** you forget the past and the future, for happiness is naught but the moment. (The Treasured Writings of Kahlil Gibran, p. 3)*

When our thoughts become weighted down with anxiety over past mistakes, or we become consumed by fears for the future, we totally lose any possibility of knowing happiness in the present. It was our Lord who exhorted us, "Take no thought for tomorrow . . ." He was not suggesting that we not plan for the future; He was clearly saying that we should not worry about the future. Why? Because the future is in God's hand, and God will provide for our needs.

Is it not sad that the older we get the more bogged down our minds become with either dwelling on regrets from the past or worrying about what will become of us in the future? The result is we totally let go the happiness of the moment. It is impossible to return to the past, nor can we skip ahead to the future. The only life you can live is the one you live in the present moment. Thank God we cannot see the future, for if we could we would look ahead and discover that moment in our future in which something bad happened to us, such as some sickness or the loss of someone we love, and we would become consumed with that event. We would agonize, worry, and fret and not allow anything in our present life to bring joy to our heart. Unfortunately, even though we can't see the future, we still try to conjure up what "might" happen and we let what "might" take place rob us of today's joy.

When we aren't consumed with our future, we sometimes seek to journey back into our past and dredge up terrible mistakes we have made. We carefully take them from the worn and tattered files of our memory, weave them together until they make a fine braided whip, and then commence to beat ourselves unmercifully. When at last we

July

think we have created enough pain, drawn enough spiritual blood, we put down the whip and settle into our self-imposed misery. Here's the sad shocking news: When we won't let God be the God of our past and future, we don't let God be the God of our present. Life lived in the present without an awareness of God's deep love for us is life that is inevitably filled with strife and worry.

Hear the Word of God, "Though your sins are like scarlet, they shall be as white as snow; though they are red as crimson, they shall be like wool" (Isaiah 1:18). "As far as the east is from the west, so far has he removed our transgressions from us" (Psalm 103:12). "For I will forgive their wickedness and will remember their sins no more" (Jeremiah 31:34). God is the great eraser of past failures. **Any failure** taken to God in repentant prayer, God erases. He depends upon us not to keep dragging it up from our memory.

As for the future, we cannot see beyond our next breath, much less next week, month, or year. We must be content to place our hand in the Hand of the One who can see beyond time's horizon and trust that His word is true, "I will be with you always, even unto the end of the age." Whether you are rich or poor, all anyone has is the present moment. Therefore find joy in today; yesterday's gone and tomorrow isn't here.

Life is Made For Sharing

23 It is an unsettling thing to be left alone. Human beings are not designed for isolation and separation from human contact. In the beginning, right after God created Adam, He proclaimed an astounding truth regarding human companionship, "It is **not** good that man should be alone." So God created a woman to be man's companion. Prior to Eve, Adam had the matchless beauty of a paradise, but there must have been an emptiness within him that God knew could only be filled by sharing his life with other creatures who were like himself. Perhaps one of our greatest failures as human beings is to disregard the immense importance of our most precious relationships. Not just spouses, important as they are, but children, mother and father, brother and sister, and cherished friends.

July

The sun rises and quickly we begin to fill our day with routine activities. We assign supreme importance to the trivial and make trivial that which is supremely important. We let our occupation become more important than the time we spend with those whose very lives are interwoven into our own. We become so intent on making a living that we lose sight of how to make a life. For years we bow down to the gods of this world and unwittingly become slaves to every event that demands power over us. So consumed are we with our distorted values that we become totally blind to that which should be at the center of our lives—God, family and friends!

Each day becomes a replica of the day before; we have become so entrenched in the ordinary that we miss the extraordinary. Years pass and the time we long ago intended to spend with those we love has now eluded us and one day we discover ourselves sitting in our homes alone, staring aimlessly out a window at an empty world that seems forever to have lost its beauty. They are gone and those mystical moments of joy that once we might have known have now slipped quietly into the irretrievable past. Some people put off into the never-arriving future the most important things life has to offer and forever miss the beauty of the outstretched arms of the present moment.

As Jesus prepared to depart from the disciples, He sensed their grief and the innate need within them for the power and joy of His presence. And so He gave to them words pregnant with soon to be grasped truth, words filled with promise and hope and comfort: "I will not leave you as orphans; I will come to you" (John 14:18). He was not speaking of His second coming but of His sending to us the living Spirit of Himself in the form of Holy Spirit. Therefore, the truth is that we are not alone; by faith we forever have within us the comforting Spirit of our Lord. Can that replace the spouse or child or friend that we have lost? No, but it can begin to heal us until we can once more discover that there are people on this earth with whom we can continue to share our lives. It can sustain us until we reach that moment in time when that which has gone from us will finally be restored.

Even in pockets of loneliness, the Christian lives in genuine hope. For while we cannot recapture in temporal time that which is no longer part of our lives, we can live expectantly for eternal time in

July

which God makes all things new again. Life is made for sharing. Go out and share yours!

Poverty of the Soul

24 This week I was reading once more from a magnificent little devotional book by Thomas R. Kelly entitled, *A Testament of Devotion*. One of many penetrating statements that he wrote grabbed my attention and I pass its truth on to you:

> The deepest need of men is not food and clothing and shelter, important as they are. It is God. We have mistaken the nature of poverty, and thought it was economic poverty. No, it is poverty of soul, deprivation of God's recreating, loving peace. (p. 123)

The world is filled with poverty but the greatest place of deprivation is the soul. If we could but look inwardly at that vast mystical chamber, we would discover that it weeps in loneliness and is bloated from malnutrition.

The common experience of human life reveals to us that only a very few ever experience the audible presence of God. For the vast majority of us, if we have any conscious awareness of His presence, it will be as we commune with Him on the level of spirit. Most people will not take the time to look there, for we have become too much a society that demands experiences based solely on the five senses—sight, sound, touch, smell, and taste. Anything beyond that, we conclude to be unreal. As a result, we miss the most real thing of all—communion with the Creator on the level of creating love. In a world crammed with the demand for frantic activity and structure, we have no time and room for meditation, quietness, and inward searching. Yet it is there that God will be discovered in greater fullness; it is there that the peace, serenity, and joy of life that we hunger for will be revealed.

Some will give this process a brief fling, but will quickly reject it because it will not yield to the demand for instant results. In our "instant everything" world we will only relegate a tiny block of time for that which is eternal because for most of us eternity is perceived as always future. Blind, spiritual illiterates that we are, we have not

July

fathomed that the eternal is birthed in the present. We are like the expectant parent who desperately wants a child but ignores the necessity of nine months of formation that have to take place before birth can become a reality.

We have never grasped the spiritual truth discovered by Elijah in the doorway of a mountain cave (I Kings 19:11ff.): that God is not found in the power of a violent wind, nor in the bone-shaking tremble of an earthquake, nor in the consuming heat of the dancing fire, but He is found in the soft quietness of "a still small voice". God will be found only by those who will come aside to see why the burning bush is not consumed; those who will dare to encamp in the wilderness away from the rush of life, those who will commit time in their busy day and make an appointment with the God who is Eternal.

There is no veil that hides God from us—except the veil that we create with our stubborn self-will. Is your soul shriveled and starving? Does it hunger for living water and the bread of life? Then find a quiet peaceful place, be still, close your eyes, turn your empty palms up, confess to Him who surely hears you that you hunger to commune with Him on the deepest level of reality—the spiritual. Patiently wait, faithfully pursue, joyously encounter the God who lives, who loves, who comforts. Come aside and meet the One who has waited from the beginning of time to greet you!

The Clothing of Prayer

25 There is, I believe, within each of us who claim Christ as our Savior, a spiritual yearning to be in communion with Him. Yet we are quite willing to go days, maybe even weeks or months without seeking a conscious awareness of His presence. When we do that, we become spiritually weak and devoid of inner tranquility; there is no sense of oneness with the One who called us into being. Our souls will seem troubled, our lives too often feel empty, and we will stumble through too many days without any sense of joy. At the heart of such a dilemma, we will discover, is the absence of a prayer life.

It is amazing that we can be content to live our lives without a desire to give God a major part in it. Sometimes we seem to be like

July

arrows that have been launched into the air, flying straight and fast without any consciousness of the power that put them in motion. But the conclusion of their flight is inevitable, for without the power of the bent bow that set them in motion, they will soon begin a downward descent that will bring them to an abrupt halt. Prayer is the doorway that leads us to Him who empowers us to soar. Here is a spiritual paradox—in order to stay in motion we must learn to be still in prayer.

Oswald Chambers wisely wrote, "Unless in the first waking moment of the day you learn to fling the door wide back and let God in, you will work on a wrong level all day; but swing the door wide open and pray to your Father in secret, and every public thing will be stamped with the presence of God" (*My Utmost For His Highest*, p. 173). None of us would think about rising from our beds and going out into the world physically unclothed, but how often we greet the world spiritually naked because we have not put on the garment of our Lord before we left our home. We of the "older" generation often decry the lack of discipline in young people today, yet how undisciplined we are when it comes to the mastery of our spirit. Like a spoiled, self-willed child, we let our fallen spirit run roughshod through life, indulging its excesses and flinging its tantrums.

The weakest of all excuses for not praying is to say, "I don't have time." No one has more than twenty-four hours in any day, and for most of us, how we spend those twenty-four hours is our own choice. Praying is an act of the will. It is making a conscious choice to seek God and to yield body, mind, and spirit to the scrutiny of His loving presence. "Search me, O God, and know my heart; test me and know my anxious thoughts. See if there is any offensive way in me, and lead me in the way everlasting" (Psalm 139: 23-24). To build a spiritual house is no less demanding that to build a physical one, and it only happens one brick at the time. To imagine that one or two days of five-minute prayers is going to make us into spiritual giants is as foolish as thinking that one or two bricks will create a mansion.

The human body begins with one cell that divides into two, then two into four, and so on. It is a process of growth that takes place in the womb of the one who gives us life. To become spiritually mature is a process that is born in prayer and God's presence is the womb in which we are formed into a vibrant living spirit. When we live outside of the womb of His presence we stop growing. I exhort you to learn the mystery and the power of prayer to shape and form you into that lovely magnificent creation God yearns to see you become. In Christ, we truly become a new creation!

A Consciousness of God

26 Most of us, when we pray, spend the vast majority of our time making requests of God for some perceived need in our life or in the life of someone else. There's nothing wrong with prayers of petition, but they are only one part of what praying is about. Oswald Chambers says, "We look upon prayer as a means of getting things for ourselves; the Bible idea of prayer is that we may get to know God Himself" *(My Utmost For His Highest,* p. 176). Imagine trying to have a conversation with a person that never lets you speak. Try hard as you may, you are never allowed to get a word in edgewise. How frustrating that is! And yet when we pray (converse) with God, if we are only conscious of Him for the length of time we have His attention in asking something of Him and then go on to something else, how can we expect to learn anything about Him?

How often Jesus told us His will was to do the will of the Father. He could not possibly know the will of His Father if all He ever did was simply ask for something. The beginning of His ministry included forty days and nights in the wilderness. It was then that He yielded to the leading of the Spirit to discern the Father's will. There must have been many hours spent on a rocky ledge, on a hillside or on a moonlit night in which Jesus simply sat quietly in the presence of His Father, seeking to find direction for His life. Those who know God most intimately are those who discover Him in quietness.

Find yourself a quiet spot where you won't be interrupted (preferably in nature rather than the confines of a small room). Come to God in humility and simply say, "Lord, I have not come to ask for anything except the joy of your presence; reveal to me yourself as you desire to make yourself known to me." Then sit in quietness. Don't try to think anything, don't allow yourself to slip into a mental conversation with God, just simply "be" in His presence. Close your

July

eyes and smell the freshness of the air; marvel at the sounds of nature that you have missed because you have allowed man-made noise to drown it out in the routine of your daily life. Sit quietly and just be conscious of your own aliveness. Surrender your mind to God's direction and let Him fill it with thoughts, ideas and concepts that you might never have chosen.

I seriously doubt that you will see any visions (though some do) or hear any audible voice speak (though some have). Most likely you will simply begin to develop a conscious awareness of a "nearness" that you cannot see or touch but that you sense deep within yourself is there. Don't be in a hurry! Be patient with God. God is certainly patient with us! If you try this and the first time you do, nothing happens, don't give up. Your faithfulness in seeking God will soon be rewarded. Everyday that you live you routinely feed your body. Learn how to daily and routinely provide nourishment for your soul.

The most memorable moments you spend in prayer will not be those moments in which you ask for things, even if your prayer requests are answered, but those moments in which you seek to know God and discover how wonderful and glorious is His presence. It will be that moment when that precious peace comes over you and your heart overflows in joy as you finally discover the power that comes in knowing you are truly loved by your Creator.

Spiritual Thirst

27 The journey had been long and difficult, the noonday sun was scorching, and the traveler was weary from the long walk. He came to a well outside of a city and sat down beside it. The well was deep and He had no means of drawing water. Before long, a woman approached with a bucket and a long rope and He asked her for a drink of water. Rather than immediately comply with His request she began to interrogate Him about why He, a stranger and a member of another race, would even speak to her. His response was unsettling. "If you knew who I was and if you knew anything about the love and grace of God, you would be asking me for a drink."

July

Startled by His response, she asked the obvious: "How can you give me a drink of water when you don't have anything to draw water up from the well—which is very deep?" What He said next was even more disturbing. "Everyone who drinks this water will be thirsty again, but whoever drinks the water I give him will never thirst. Indeed, the water I give him will become in him a spring of water welling up to eternal life" (John 4:13-14). Where do you go to quench your thirst when your soul is parched and your spirit is dry as dust? Do you drink deeply from the salty wisdom of the world, or have you found that eternal fountain that bubbles with cool clear water in endless supply?

When all in life is going well we build an illusive wall of self-contentment around the cravings within and we convince ourselves that we have all we need. We seek to ignore that mystical stirring within that says all is not well at the center of our being. We stifle the weeping of our infant soul and turn deaf ears to the rhythmic sobs that pulsate upward into our conscious mind. "Be quiet my soul, for I have no time to listen to your needs! The cares of this world are all that I can handle and their needs must come first." Little do we know that the place where we will find peace has been ignored or rejected as we vainly search in places where it can never be found. We are like the woman at the well who wanted that which eternally satisfies, but like her, we are forever looking in the wrong places to discover it.

What is this "spring of water gushing up to eternal life" of which Jesus spoke? He reveals it more clearly in John 7:37-41,

> *"If anyone is thirsty, let him come to me and drink. Whoever believes in me, as the Scripture has said, streams of living water will flow from within him." By this he meant the Spirit, who those who believed in him were later to receive. Up to that time the Spirit had not been given, since Jesus had not yet been glorified.*

The living water that springs up from within us is the Holy Spirit. It is the presence of that Spirit which brings to us eternal life and satisfies the cravings of our famished souls.

July

The only one who can give that Spirit, that living water, is Jesus. He gives it only to those who seek it and who ask for it. God's Spirit will invade no one's heart apart from a personal invitation. The starting place is to acknowledge that something deep down inside is crying to be cared for. The soul that will stretch its arms out in openness to the grace of God's Spirit is the soul that will never thirst again and which will discover the eternal peace that is derived from the constant presence of the One who loves eternally.

Waiting For God

28 I once met an elderly woman in the mountains of Virginia who said she had never been to a city, never seen the ocean, and in fact had never traveled more than 20 miles from her home. She had no electricity and her "running water" was water that she obtained by walking several hundred yards down to the creek every morning and filling her bucket. Her life was quite simple, to say the least—no television, no radio, no modern appliances. She seemed quite happy and content. Yet her perception of the world was no broader than that which she had allowed herself to experience. I don't know if she looked at pictures in magazines or not, but if she didn't she would have been completely unaware of the vast and diverse beauty in this world which God has given us. While there is much that can be said for the simple life, there was much that had been forever missed.

I use the above illustration to suggest that many of us are like this elderly lady when it comes to our spiritual lives. We've never ventured very far in seeking to discover a vast beautiful spiritual world that lies beyond the immediate horizon. We aren't even sure it really exists because we have chosen to devote ourselves to our immediate needs and surroundings. It has been my experience that God has not cloaked the spiritual world in complex, unattainable mystery, but extends it to us through the simple act of inquiring obedience. We occasionally think about heaven and life eternal, but we don't let ourselves dwell on it, perhaps out of some misguided fear that we will make it come sooner than we want.

July

Listen to the exhortation of Holy Scripture, found on the very lips of our Lord Jesus, "God is spirit, and his worshipers must worship in spirit and in truth" (John 4:24). Do you worship God in spirit and in truth? Have you ever even pondered what that means for your life? If you wear glasses, have you ever propped them up on top of your head and forgotten where you put them? You look everywhere for them but can't find them because they're out of your line of vision. We have a spirit within us that's ours and yet we seem oblivious to its presence because we never look for it in the right place. To worship God one must begin by looking inward.

Find a quiet spot—I often emphasize quietness because I think we will rarely ever be conscious of God's presence in the midst of noise (until we have first discovered Him in quietness). God longs to be the center of our lives, not one among many things that battle for our attention. By going aside into quietness, we are physically acknowledging our desire to be in communion with only Him. We must discover the mystery and benefit of "waiting" for the Lord. Listen to the Psalmist, "For God alone my soul waits in silence, for my hope is from him" (Psalm 62:5, NRSV). "My soul waits for the Lord more than those who watch for the morning, more than those who watch for the morning" (Psalm 130:6, NRSV). "Lead me in your truth and teach me, for you are the God of my salvation; for you I wait all day long" (Psalm 25:5, NRSV).

Isaiah writes, ". . . those who wait for the Lord shall renew their strength, they shall mount up with wings like eagles, they shall run and not be weary, they shall walk and not faint" (40:31, NRSV). The beginning of spiritual worship starts by waiting for God. Are you waiting? Meditate on this and see if God won't begin to become more real to you.

Coming Home

29 I wonder how many days had passed since last the eyes of the prodigal's father had beheld him—a detail of the story that we have not been given. Day after day, week after week he must have gone to the window and looked wistfully down the dusty road until its two edges merged into a single point in the distance. I

July

imagine he would watch sometimes for hours, always with the same result; the absence of the familiar and yearned-for form of the one he loved so deeply. Their parting had been sudden, strained and unexpected. Feelings were hurt and issues had been left unresolved. Now, inner wounds, wounds which could not heal in solitude of estrangement, were constant reminders of the price of love.

Strange, how one can be alienated from a part of one's self. Aptly named are our children—offspring—for how often do they spring off! Separated by more than just miles, we find ourselves separated by dreams, desires, and hopes—ours being one thing, theirs another. The parent soon learns, painful though it may be, that children grow up and have minds of their own. The child is beginning the adventure of life with new discoveries to be encountered. The parent, having grown weary with discoveries, longs simply for the comfort of the child's presence.

In time children will learn the same lesson, but probably not until they have grown old themselves and have discovered what only living can reveal—relationships are what matter most in life. Meanwhile, in our story, the young man forgets all that is home and lives each day for the moment. Satisfying the desires of his own heart, for the time being the loss within himself remains hidden from his eyes. But one day the partying grows old, the excitement of new places seems dull, the money is gone and "friends" have gone off in search of new highs. There are few experiences more revealing than to become conscious of the reality of one's self.

It's unbelievably clear now. Everything that really mattered about living is found in the sharing of one's self with those who loved him the most. The Bible puts it this way: "He came to himself." And so the journey toward "home" begins. There are many miles to cover and much time to think. Fears rise up; will he be accepted or rejected—will he be cursed or welcomed? For the first time in his life he becomes aware of the pain he has inflicted on his father—even though it was not his intention to hurt him. He has time now to meditate on the hurt and disappointment he has caused and he resolves not to ask to be restored to his place in the family but only to work as a slave: even in that role, at least he will be back home.

July

But home is not a geographical spot; it is not a building or a special room. Home is not just being where the heart is, home is being in the heart of the one who loves you. From that place, the son was to discover that he had never been allowed to leave. For when he reached home, the eyes of his father, that often viewed the empty road through tears, now beheld the one who was always loved, and stretched out unhesitant arms of welcome. In a single moment in time, two hearts that had been separated by a long journey called life were melded into one. That's the way it is with God. That's the way it should be with each of us. Are you in the process of coming home, or are you still dwelling in the "distant land?"

When Tears Bring Rainbows

30 In the exuberance of youth there is no place for pain; there is only room for excitement, new discoveries and self-fulfillment. We seem to come into this world with a propensity to weave our way through life dodging any and every obstacle that will hinder our experience of constant pleasure and happiness. Laughing is good, tears are bad; exhilaration is wonderful, pain is horrible; health is magnificent, sickness is despicable; tranquility is marvelous, problems are repugnant. And yet, for whatever His reasons, God has allowed human life to be quite filled with all the things we seek to avoid. Perhaps it is because it is the hard things of life that are the greatest teachers.

Many people grew up when life was tough and hard work was the norm. Material possessions weren't plentiful and the very scarcity of things gave them their value. Life soon teaches us that what comes easy or without effort is usually devalued: conversely, that for which we labor or struggle increases in value. In view of the fact that life comes with hardships, maybe we would do well to ponder the great significance and value of the difficult things in life. When we look at the life of Jesus, we are struck with the difficulties that He had to face. There were many crosses to endure before He faced "the Cross." And yet He despised not the crosses, but used each one to prepare Him for the greater task that lay ahead.

George Matheson, the great hymn writer, once wrote:

July

My God, I have never thanked Thee for my thorns. I have thanked Thee a thousand times for my roses, but not once for my thorns. I have been looking forward to a world where I shall get compensation for my cross: but I have never thought of my cross as itself a present glory. Teach me the glory of my cross: teach me the value of my thorn. Shew me that I have climbed to Thee by the path of pain. Shew me that my tears have made my rainbow. (From *Come Before Winter,* pages 489-91, by Charles Swindoll)

Life that has value will be a life that has known its measure of heartache. The wonder and majesty of God is that even the things in life that we would prefer to avoid, He uses to make us grow. We can grow sweeter by them, or we can grow bitter. To make our way through life seeking to avoid at all cost the things which can cause pain will create a life that is shallow and hollow. It is the difficult things in life which chisel out within us what comes to be called character. How was it that Paul put it? ". . . we also rejoice in our sufferings, because we know that suffering produces perseverance; perseverance, character; and character, hope. And hope does not disappoint us, because God has poured out his love into our hearts by the Holy Spirit, whom he has given us (Romans 4:3-5). A diamond in the rough has no beauty; it is only when the cutter, with loving care, chisels away the excess that it sparkles and glows.

Today, rather than complain and act bitter about what life has brought your way, why not pause and thank God that even in the midst of your struggles He is with you and will ultimately turn it into something good in your life. The very things that have the power to bring us pain also have the power to bring us the clearest vision of the valuable things in life.

The Hidden Place

31 There is a secret place hidden within each human being. Some call it heart, others call it soul. It is the place where treasured things are housed—a place no human eye can see; no unwanted visitor can behold. It is the place where treasured memories of those we love are gently cataloged and stored. We plant

July

them there in the deep, rich soil of love. Time and nurture cause them to sink their roots deep and inextricably into the fabric of our being.

I don't know how or when, but at some point these treasures become so much a part of ourselves that when they are gone from us, a wave of pain is set in motion that reverberates within our inner being, constantly reminding us of their priceless value. This "hidden place" is a hallowed cave chiseled out within us and those we love lay claim to that sacred spot that no one else can possess. There is no limitation to how many can be kept in this hidden place, except the limitation of our ability to love. Those who love little will have few treasures, those who love much will know first-hand the meaning of "good measure, pressed down, shaken together and running over" (Luke 6:38).

In the center of this storehouse resides our greatest treasure. We have been given the freedom to determine what that will be. No parent, no teacher, no tyrant or captor can control what we choose to place in its center. However, what we choose to put there will affect everything else in the living out of our lives. This spot—over which we have absolute determination—God desires to occupy. Still, He has given us the option of allowing Him in or blocking His entrance. Gently He stands at the door and knocks. It is a quiet, soft rapping that makes itself known but does not frighten or alarm us. Often He will hear, "Go away, I don't want you here now!" Then He retreats for awhile, but soon returns with divine persistence.

When at last we let God occupy that center place, the other treasures that are stored there near Him are affected by the glow of His presence. Spouses are loved more faithfully, children are cherished more deeply, siblings are valued more greatly, and friends are nurtured more lovingly. "How can this be?" one might ask. It's because when God is given the throne room of our heart, then love dwells on the throne. Where love resides life becomes transformed; it is changed from the inside out. It was the gentle Carpenter who said, "Where your treasure is, there will your heart be also." Just as easily He could have said, "Where your heart is, there will your treasure be also." In reality they both mean the same thing.

When someone you love is gone, either through the separation of distance or death, and you feel that strange pain at the loss of their

August

presence, you now know that they are one of your treasures and neither space nor time, neither life nor death, has the power to remove them from their hallowed spot within you. What one treasures one never loses, even when life or death seeks to create a great divide, for they are forever bound within you by the mystical power of love. Only when your love dies will they be removed from you; until then they will be forever a hidden treasure.

The Eternal Treasure

1 Perhaps one of the greatest tragedies of human life is our propensity to overlook that which is most precious. How much of life we waste in our constant pursuit of that which we do not have while we squander away the treasures that we innately possess. A reasonable person would agree that the thing which is of ultimate value is that which is eternal (assuming that there are things that are eternal—that which passes beyond mortality and extends into a world hidden from physical sight). The things that matter most are the things that one cannot possess with money nor claim with selfish desire. Yet, how much of our lives we spend in pursuit of that which is less than ultimate!

The history of humankind is filled with the wreckage of wasted lives, wasted days, and wasted years of those who were content to live life at its lowest level. Few there have been who would sacrifice the pursuit of finite things for the sake of discovering infinite things. Though Jesus only left us with a limited number of words and instructions, we somehow have the uncanny tendency to misinterpret and completely overlook the significance of the truth He imparted. He walked among the lowly ones in life and offered them a portrait of themselves as seen through the eyes of God. The greatest sinner He ever encountered was given the opportunity to see the saint he or she could become.

Material wealth is one of the greatest barriers to a consciousness of the soul. It brings with it the power to acquire more things that but distract and temporarily entertain. It blinds us to the sacred things of life and hides from us our eternal value to God. Until we truly learn how deeply God loves us, we will never be able to love ourselves with

August

a healthy love. An unhealthy love of self is one built on the satisfying of physical desires to the exclusion of nourishing the soul. Every material thing on this earth that we possess, we lose at death. Everything we have pursued and gained that is spiritual is immortal and we keep that forever. In light of that truth, hear again the words of Jesus, "He who would find his or her life, must be willing to lose it."

Unquestionably, the central teaching of Jesus concerned the kingdom of God. He declared that kingdom to be a spiritual realm. (John 18:36) Why then do we insist on placing such importance on one made of finite matter? We may boast of our Bible knowledge, we may bask in self-endowed praise, we may exult about how many times we have read The Holy Book, but unless we have truly heard the voice of Jesus in the Word we have not discovered the truth; all we have done is to read burdensome words. Unless you think Jesus was mistaken or deranged, you must take seriously His words when He said to Pilate, ". . . for this reason I was born, and for this I came into the world, to testify to the truth. Everyone on the side of truth listens to me" (John 18:37).

Each of us in our own way is in pursuit of a treasure. Many will lay claim to fool's gold, to an illusion, to a temporary fix, and at the end of life will find it nothing more than dust in their hands. Others will secure away in their hearts that which is truly a treasure and when life has run its course they will discover that they have laid hold to that which is eternally without price, and no one will be able to take it away from them.

The Locked Gate

2 When our stomachs are empty, we stop what we are doing and find something to fill them. When our minds crave nourishment, we fill them with books, activities, or some form of intellectual stimulation that satisfies their craving. But when our souls erupt with hunger pangs, we stifle or ignore them. Many of us have no concept of the value of solitude in God's presence. We have so fashioned worship into a routine that we have inoculated ourselves from its potential power. It has become like some spiritual vaccine we give ourselves just enough of that we ensure it will prevent us from being

August

infected with its real and life-changing power. Routinely we get out of bed each morning and almost mindlessly make our way through the day, like water seeking to follow the path of least resistance. That seems to carry over to church on Sunday morning. We arrive with no great expectation that worship this Sunday will be any different or better than most of the other Sundays of our lives. When the service is over we leave pretty much as we came.

Why is that so? Because most of us do not come truly seeking God, we come seeking the conformity of a safe and familiar past experience. That which is new is perceived as unsettling. That which is different becomes frightening and undesirable. The God with whom we feel safe, and of whom we are willing to be tolerant is the God that will not surprise us, challenge us, or be different from what we expect Him to be. Whether we acknowledge it or not, we really don't want God to reveal anything more of Himself than that with which we long ago grew comfortable. Oh, the arrogance of the human mind; to think that the God of the universe can or should be no larger than the limits of our past experience, nor greater than that genie bottle to which we have confined Him!

One reason so many of us live such empty and unhappy lives is because we are willing to seek God only for His blessings and not for Himself. When was the last time you approached God in prayer simply to give Him praise and thanksgiving rather than to bombard Him with requests? When was the last time you entered the sanctuary doors of a church sincerely hungering in your heart to experience the presence of the One who gave you life? Does not your soul even now beg to be fed? Does it not send message after message to your heart to hear its cry? What daily routine today will distract you from its plea and override its petition until once more you ignore it and banish it to the soundproof cell of neglect?

If we will not discipline ourselves to seek God in the morning we will not likely encounter Him in the afternoon or evening. Cursed is the modern civilization that will not believe in or seek after that which their minds did not conceive or control. Why are so many people more comfortable believing that we evolved from nothing, simply by chance, rather than believing that a Being who loved life so

August

much decided to extend it and give it to humans? God is as much alive as you who read these words, and His heart aches to share life with you. Unfortunately, our desire to share life apart from Him is stronger than His will to force Himself upon us. We have erected a wall with a gate between God and ourselves and we hold the key that unlocks the gate.

A Sheep's Song

3 Several year ago, in a sermon, I used a paraphrase of the Twenty-third Psalm that I had written. Following the service, several people asked me for a copy. Below is a copy of the interpretation I had given to the psalm:

Jesus is the Guardian and Protector of my life and my soul. I discover in the boundaries of His will that nothing I need goes lacking. He leads me to quiet places where I can find comfort and spiritual rest; places where my soul can feast bountifully on the spiritual food that no one else can give me.

In the balm of His presence and grace my tired wounded soul finds rest and healing. When I follow Him my life is embraced by that which is good, noble, and uplifting; therefore, I am able to bring honor to His precious name.

In those moments in life in which sickness and death draw near like ominous, foreboding clouds that cast dark shadows over me, His Presence shields me from their power to destroy and lifts me up from the dungeon of fear into the light of peaceful contentment.

His words of discipline give direction to my life, and challenge my desire to live selfishly; in so doing, they set my feet upon the path of freedom. When I am surrounded by those who misunderstand me, who condemn and criticize me, who inflict painful injury upon my soul and spirit, the tenderness of His love anoints me and my wounds are soothed and made whole by the power of His unmerited grace. My starving soul is nourished by the banquet feast He sets before Me, and I always rise from the table of life with a full soul and satisfied spirit.

All the days of my life He has revealed Himself to me as goodness and as loving mercy; therefore, I have no reason to

313

August

doubt that the constancy of His love will be my hope and joy as long as I live. And when that moment shall come that life as I have known it on earth no longer exists, I am absolutely convinced that I will live forever in my eternal home in the glory of His Presence.

As a way of deepening your own understanding and experiencing first hand the comforting power of God's Word, why don't you take a Psalm or favorite passage and prayerfully try to put it into your own words. God's Word is not static; it is dynamic and alive, filled with life-giving and life-changing power. You might just be amazed at how beautifully God will be able to speak to your heart when you quietly and intentionally meditate upon His goodness.

Living For Life

4 Impoverished is the soul that never contemplates the glory and mystery of life. What greater waste, what more horrific tragedy than to live on this earth and never marvel at the wonder of being alive? To suddenly "be" and not ponder one's aliveness, not search for a meaning to one's existence and one's destiny is to be little more than a robot. Life must have a beginning; every living thing we encounter proclaims that truth. And if it has a beginning, what or Who caused that beginning to be? In order for human life to be perpetuated, two human beings must give up part of themselves in order to form another. In God's will for human life, conception is born out of love and out of a mutual desire of two people to share their most intimate selves with each other. The result is a new life.

In order for God to create a living world, surely He gave away part of Himself, part of His aliveness in order to create life. It was a conception born in love with a desire to give to the created the most intimate part of Himself. According to Genesis, in the beginning He walked with us in the cool of the evening and He declared that all life was good. But created life that seeks to find itself apart from that which created it is destined for loneliness and loss. Where creation is born in love it will always find its self-worth in relationship to the love that created it. Does not God's Word show us this when He wrote:

August

> *He was in the world, and though the world was made through him, the world did not recognize him. He came to that which was his own, but his own did not receive him. Yet to all who received him, to those who believed in his name, he gave the right to become children of God—children born not of natural descent, nor of human decision or a husband's will, but born of God.* (John 1:10-13)

When God created life and gave away part of Himself, mystically, He lost none of Himself in the same sense that when a man and a woman create a child by giving to each other part of themselves, they consciously lose nothing but gain a child. Life must be given away in order to create life. And if that is so in the physical realm of existence, I believe that it is even more true in the spiritual realm. God so loved the world that He gave [away] His Son so that they might have life eternal. Jesus said if we would have life we must be willing to give it away. When our norm for living becomes living for self we accelerate the process of our own death. To live only for self is to live for death; to live for others is to live for life.

Why would anyone imagine that life concludes in a grave? Scientists tell us that matter cannot be destroyed: it simply changes form. Is it too difficult then to believe that neither can the "essence" of life be destroyed? It too merely changes form—from that which is temporary to that which is permanent. Lorenzo de' Medici wrote, "Those are dead even for this life who hope for no other." Thomas Wilson said, "No man must go to heaven who hath not sent his heart thither before." Heaven is the goal for which our souls hunger, for heaven is the place where life's Source began. Blessed is the one who discovers the joy of living now, for that person has captured a vision of what life is to be eternally.

Does Jesus Care?

5 God often speaks to us through the voice of others. There is a book I commend to you entitled, *God Calling*. It is written by two women who chose to remain anonymous and gave themselves the name Two Listeners. These two women were poor and lonely, one to the point of despair with life, when Jesus spoke to them in their

August

helplessness. Day after day He spoke to their hearts and together they recorded His words. It's amazing how on a certain day, when I open the book, there is the voice of my Lord saying what my soul needs to hear. Call it coincidence if you choose, but it's like a message has been sent to meet the need of the day.

Recently, one such message in the book was this:

> *That voiceless cry, that comes from anguished hearts, is heard above all the music of Heaven. It is not the arguments of theologians that solve the problems of a questioning heart, but the cry of that heart to Me, and the certainty that I have heard."* (p. 215)

Have there been moments in your life that you felt overwhelmed with life and felt the joy of your life taken away? You desperately search for answers and no human voice holds the key to unlock the door. You cry out in the darkness for God to intercede and the heavens remain silent. You sit in motionless quietness waiting for some angelic or divine voice to shatter the deafening silence, but the only sound you hear is the pounding of your heart and the routine noises of indifferent lives around you.

Does Jesus care when life seems desolate and without any sign of hope on the horizon? Does He notice when our hearts are heavy, when our efforts have run the gamut of human wisdom? Does it matter to Him when the nights are long and the pain is deep; when it seems that sorrow could not possibly grow heavier? Could He possibly imagine how alone a human being can feel, even in the midst of a crowd? He must! For on a crowded hill one day He cried, "My God, My God, why have you forsaken Me?" His divinity became fully acquainted with human despair and He became oblivious to the presence of the One who called Him "My beloved Son."

There was a brief pause and evidence was given that His consciousness of God's presence returned. "Father, into Thy hands I commend my Spirit." Would He have committed His spirit to that which He did not feel was present? He discovered that our Father really never leaves us, we simply lose sight of His presence. That moment when we are ready to turn once more and behold Him, He is there because He never really left.

August

It is a comforting thought to know, even before times of desolation come, that God has not left us. Our pain sometimes draws a dark veil across our spiritual eyes and we are temporarily blinded to the fact that He is present. The hymn writer Frank E. Graeff said it best in his moving hymn, *Does Jesus Care*:

> *Does Jesus care when my heart is pained too deeply for mirth or song, as the burdens press, and the cares distress, and the way grows weary and long? Oh yes, He cares, I know He cares, His heart is touched with my grief; when the days are weary, the long night dreary, I know my Savior cares.*

Yes, Jesus cares!

Love – Evidence of God's Presence

6 Love—poets, philosophers, theologians, young lovers, old couples, and average people have sought to plumb its depths and claim its riches, but always rise from the deed with scant understanding and partial treasure. Where was its origin? What is its source? It cannot be cupped in the hands nor dissected with the scalpel. It cannot be seen with the eye nor heard with the ear. No artist has ever imprisoned it on canvas and no composer has confined it to music. It may be the greatest of all human mysteries for it challenges the average mind and eludes the wisdom of the wisest seer.

What indeed is this thing we have named "love" and pretend to know so well? Love is that mystical essence that flows in and out of every human heart that will allow it entrance. It becomes most powerful and visible when it gives itself away, when it offers the other cheek to the hand that strikes it, and when it keeps no record of the times it is wronged. Like hoarded "manna" it sours when hidden away in the selfish corners of our lives and evaporates like a heavy morning mist when mercilessly exposed to the heat of selfish desire. It cannot be purchased and it cannot be sold; it is priceless, but can be acquired without payment. Its birthing place is the heart, and its creator is God.

Love has the unique ability to see beyond human fault and imagine the possibility of what someone might become. It grieves at the sight of sin, but will not withhold its balm of healing from the repentant heart. It is the wind upon which forgiveness soars and it is

August

the power that brings forth life out of brokenness. Faith and hope ride on its crest and when their journey is complete, love spirals upward in glory bright and bows its head in humble sight of Him who is Eternal light. It is divine power in gentle form. It is that element that most reveals the likeness of Him in whose image we were made.

When applied to wood, linseed oil brings out its beauty. Likewise, love when rubbed into daily living brings forth the best in humanity. Rock-hard hearts have wilted in its presence and animosity dissolved into banished vapor. Calmly and softly it silently moves through the cells of our being until it cleanses the hidden stains and heals the heart of endless pain. Like wind, it hides in mystery's shroud, yet moves our lives in echoes loud, until our souls in words proclaim the glory of its precious name. It makes the ugly disappear and takes away the useless fear that life was meant to only be living without eternity.

We ponder its meaning and discover once more that love exceeds our mental power. It exists in a realm that is beyond human reason. It dances through our lives, sweeps through our hearts, kisses our souls, and we—we can only marvel at its power and be awed by its beauty. In the end, we must state the inevitable—that love is a gift wrapped in grace and offered without price. It embraces both those who are good and those who are bad. It is never diminished; it is never overcome. It is the one thing that is left standing when all else has passed away. Love is unsearchable because the truth we will ultimately discover is that love is the irrefutable evidence of the presence of God.

The Place to Live

Yesterday, today, and tomorrow—three realities, separate, but inextricably connected; each uniquely distinct, demanding the attention of each of us. They fight their battles in the valley of our heart, each wanting to rise above the other and claim our thoughts as their throne. "I am most important," cries one, "for I have shown you what was." "Nay," says the other, "I am, for I reveal to you what is." "You both are wrong," says the third, "for I unveil what is yet to be." And most of us choose the first or third, dissatisfied with the second; for we imagine it to be not enough to satisfy our inner longing. Our

August

yesterday, today, and tomorrow have not yet learned to live in harmony, and as long as we are content to let them joust for supremacy in our hearts, our hearts will be troubled and devoid of peace.

Yesterday contains the past; the things we have done right and the things we have done wrong (as well as the things over which we had no control). A short visit there is all very well, unless we dwell too long with pride in our good deeds or too long with sorrow for our mistakes. Yesterday can give us little, for what we learned in its kingdom we experienced then and brought with us into today. Reflection may sharpen the picture of the past, but the experiences of yesterday are gone. If you must journey to the land of yesterday, make your visit brief, for life was not created to be lived in the past, it was created for and can only be experienced in the present.

Tomorrow flirts with the mind and teases us about what might be, but cannot guarantee that it will be. We can go to that distant land only in our imagination, not with our literal being. Tomorrow is like the distant wave forming on the surface of the sea; as it makes its way toward us, its form changes and when it breaks on the shoreline of our lives it no longer looks the same. Hopes and dreams are the only way we can look into tomorrow; and while they may stimulate us to keep going, they can only be fully realized when we do today what will lead us to, and prepare us for, our hopes and dreams. Tomorrow is forever the carrot on the stick; always beyond our reach and no matter how fast we run, we can never catch up to it.

And so we are left with today; discontent with it though we may be, it is the only place we can live. It is the one thing that is real, the one thing that can be shaped and formed and experienced. As the minutes tick by we can waste them with tears of unquenchable regret (brought with us from yesterday); we can fritter them away with unrealistic daydreams about what is yet to be; or we can savor each one, clinging to it like Jacob did to the angel, demanding that it yield up to us, **in this present moment,** the best that it has to give. The tragedy for many of us as we grow old is that we live too much in the past, glance too fearfully into the future, and miss far too much of the glory of the present. The Psalmist said it so simply; "This is the day the Lord has made, let us rejoice and be glad in it."

August

Yesterday and tomorrow can be experienced only faintly—in memory and in imagination. They are places of escape, places that really don't exist. How much of your today do you squander in your visits there? God cannot reach you in the past, nor can you encounter Him today by dwelling on the future; for whenever you encounter Him, it is always today!

In Search of Life

8 Words are a form of communication. They become a symbol for something that creates a mental image. The word "house" for example, creates in your mind a picture of a structure with doors, windows, a roof and any other characteristic that is indicative of a house from your experience. Words have the power to cut and create pain. I'm sure you can think of a time when someone said something to or about you that caused you to hurt deep within. Or perhaps you can reflect back to a time when your words carved deep chasms of pain into the heart of someone you knew. Words can also heal and uplift, like when someone praises you or tells you how deeply they love you.

But there is a great deal of difference between mere human words (important though they may be) and the words of Jesus. The words of our Lord were much more than letters from an alphabet—consonants and vowels that were formed to create mental pictures. They were more than just the conveyance of information or even of ethical and moral guidance. Contained within His words is spiritual power. Remember, He said, "The words I have spoken to you are spirit and they are life" (John 6:63). He said that in response to the disciples' bewilderment at His proclamation:

> *I tell you the truth, unless you eat the flesh of the Son of Man and drink his blood, you have no life in you. Whoever eats my flesh and drinks my blood has eternal life, and I will raise him up at the last day.* (John 6:53-54)

The skeptics among us will dismiss His claims as barbaric and ludicrous. Some will attribute His comments to the delusional ranting of some early Christian scribe who added these mystical words to

August

clothe Jesus in mystery. Others will simply brush aside His claim as irrelevant to their life, and will look no further than the printed ink on a page. And alas, they will banish from their presence the very words that have the power to enrich their lives here and ensure the majesty and glory of life that is yet to be. Because the spiritual life is discovered only by faith and discipline, they will postpone the search or never begin it at all. Content to live out their lives in the tiny confines of a miniscule physical world that extends no farther than their ability to see or control, they will miss the eternal vastness of that which is forever.

But thank God there are some, few though they may be, who have caught a tiny glimpse of His glory; who have been stirred deep down in their souls and who hunger and aspire to become something more than the sum of their past experiences. They have danced in the majesty of the spirit and have trembled in the shadow of His glory. Like children drawn by the mystery of the unknown, they refuse to believe that it is beyond their attainment. They persistently search, they wade through discouragements, they climb over disappointments, they do battle with the fears of darkness, and press on toward that tiny but steady light that glows in the hallways of the spirit within them. One day, praise God, they shall rest in the arms of grace, bask in the magnificence of divine love, and hear from Him who is Spirit and Life: "Well done, my good and faithful servant!"

All Things Work Together for Good

9   I sometimes think we overlook the immense value that comes with the struggles of life. Our human nature often leads us to want to avoid difficulties and take the path of ease. But I have come to see that there are lessons to be learned in hard times that would otherwise never be mastered. Moreover, there are relationships that are often formed in the crucible of heartache and adversity that become the very bedrock of one's life.

Kahlil Gibran, one of my favorite writers, wrote the following verse about sorrow and friendship:

> *The sorrowful spirit finds rest when united with a similar one. They join affectionately, as a stranger cheered when he*

August

sees another stranger in a strange land. Hearts that are united through the medium of sorrow will not be separated by the glory of happiness. (*The Treasured Writings of Kahlil Gibran,* p. 886)

How strong become the bonds of affection between those who have faced and shared similar adversity. Veterans of war who endured the same shelling, the same threat to their very lives and survive, will share forever a camaraderie that others will never experience. Parents who have children with terminal illnesses, such as brain tumors, join support groups of parents who have suffered similar pain and discover a bond that they will hold on to for life.

I can think of moments in my own life in which I felt that living had reached its lowest depth; everything seemed wrapped in gloom and I felt as if I would never see the light of joy again. In those moments, someone seemed to always emerge who had known similar pain and extended to me the gift of grace. I felt the pain in their life melded mysteriously with my own and somehow my pain began to lessen. I think back over the struggle of my seminary years; the demands of a student pastorate, the 180 miles of daily commuting four days each week for three years, and of the blessed friendship with a fellow minister that was born out of that adversity as we shared similar challenges while driving to school together. Years later we continue to share a bond that nothing has been able to shake. When pain creeps into his life, I discover that it also invades mine, and my heart reaches out to him in empathetic love, just as his does to me.

Gibran was trying to show us that friendship does not fade in the glory of happiness, because it has been nurtured by tears and bonded together by the cement of inner pain. The struggles that we shared became the very soil into which the roots of our hearts sank and became forever intertwined. At the time, we could not see the beauty of what was being formed, but it revealed itself quite clearly later on. How biblical, that out of the chaos of struggle, new life came forth in strength, in loyalty, and in lasting friendship.

Perhaps you are struggling now with some deep pain that seeks to overwhelm you. If so, look for the one around you who knows a similar struggle and discover that pain that is shared is pain that is lessened. Who knows, maybe out of the pit of despair God will draw you wondrously into the heart of a new friend who will become one of the greatest gifts God will ever grant you! I know of what I speak!

A Living Soul

10   There is only one person you are with during your every waking (and sleeping) moment—yourself. How well do you know YOU? Is there a part of you that you choose to hide away in the shadows of life, even from yourself? Is there a part of you that is cradled in nobleness, bedecked with honor, and is the fountain of your virtue; and yet you have long ago decided to remain unacquainted? I wonder sometimes how well we really know ourselves. Are we afraid to confront that part within that lies hidden in the privacy of our inner being? Are we too frightened of what we will discover to bring it into the light of God's scrutinizing gaze? We deceive ourselves if we think that by ignoring the cries of our soul we will thus shield it from God's awareness of its plight.

Did not God create the soul? With the knowledge of His ageless wisdom did not He house the essence of who we are in the sacred temple of our inner being? What the world sees when it looks at us is only that which we allow to be seen. No one can see your soul until you yourself first have come face to face with its reality. We display the soul when finally we have learned to live at peace with who we are. Until then we keep it locked away in the cellar of hidden inner secrets.

The soul is the "living" room where God communicates the clearest. His voice speaks here without the necessity of words, and quietly we hear His thoughts. They are more than "Dos" or "Don'ts" that we hear, they are the inner guidance that gently chastises, or the still small voice that builds up and reveals our inner worth. It was not merely for temporal flesh He died, but for that immortal part within us which transcends the limitations of bone, blood, and skin. That which creates does so by giving part of itself, and God is the absolute source of all creating life. In order for us to have this thing called life, God implanted part of Himself into every living being. Gently, He who is Life housed life within the created and breathed upon us and we became a living soul made in the image of God.

August

The human soul that seeks to exist apart from the life-sustaining power of God is a dying soul, for the branch cannot long survive when disconnected from the Vine. According to John's Gospel (20:22), just prior to His leaving the disciples, Jesus "breathed" on them and said, "Receive the Holy Spirit." In receiving the spiritual life-sustaining power of the Holy Spirit, the disciples became connected to the Vine and thus to spiritual life. Later, the Holy Spirit was given to the remaining disciples to transform and empower them to become living souls in God's presence.

You will not discover the certainty and reality of God until you have sought to meet Him in your soul. If you know nothing about your own soul, how can you ever expect to encounter the God who gave it life? Rhetorically, Jesus once asked, "What good will it be for a man if he gains the whole world, yet forfeits his soul? Or what can a man give in exchange for his soul?" (Matthew 16:26). Clearly, your soul is the most valuable thing you possess and the only thing that you possess that will live on beyond this life. Perhaps our soul is somehow connected to the "priceless pearl" hidden in the field, and maybe the field is our inner self. Have you looked inside for God lately? Maybe that's where we need to begin!

Dependence

11 We consider ourselves to be free and independent. Once we attain the stage of life called maturity, we conclude that we are now in control. Still, we are but composites of those who have taught us and the experiences in life which have shaped us. Elements of truth were set before us, and along the way we chose some over others and built our lives upon them. Just as we give little or no thought to the skeleton within us that holds our body erect, so we have grown oblivious to the very things we have absorbed over time which make us stand as we do on issues of ethics, morality, integrity, religion, and politics. We are woven together with strands of love and hate, joy and sorrow, peace and turmoil, goodness and evil, fear and trust, truth and falsehood, pride and humility, virtue and vice; we are the sum total of the things which have shaped us over time.

August

V̲ainly we imagine that nothing can restrain us, for **we** are the lords of life! We have mastered the earth and all that dwells upon it. We have conquered the seas; climbed the highest mountains; and challenged the limitations of space. We imagine and invent; we tear down and we build up; we create and we destroy. We sit upon our self-made thrones and think nothing has power over us; nothing can restrain us! And then ... something as tiny, soft, and gentle as a snowflake falls from the sky in infinite numbers. They join hands together and we awake from our slumber and discover that we are held captive in our homes by pristine purity and beauty. Suddenly, the routines of our lives come to a screeching halt and we are forced to stop and become conscious of our world.

As I sit and gaze out the window onto my snow-covered deck, I see a tiny sparrow huddled in a frozen corner. I find myself moved with compassion for a creature considered by most of us to be insignificant. It shivers and vibrates its wings trying to shake the freezing moisture from its tiny body. Vainly it seeks food, but a thick white blanket has buried it deep, and out of reach. There stirs within my heart a crescendo of emotion and I rise from my chair and begin to break a slice of bread into tiny morsels and throw them on the outside wooden threshold of the dining room door. First, the sparrow flies away in fear, but soon returns—revealing that hunger can overcome even the great barrier of distrust. It cocks its head, glancing first at the door from which I came, then at the bread lying in the corner. In an act of desperate trust, it lights on the door sill and begins to devour that which its tiny body needs to survive.

In a single moment, on a cold, snowy day, two of God's creations once more found union—brief though it was; the existence between a human being and a tiny bird merged into a place where long ago it began in trust and harmony. I seem to remember Jesus once saying, "Not a single sparrow falls to the ground without your Father's awareness." And did He not also say, "Consider the ravens: They do not sow or reap, they have no storeroom or barn; yet God feeds them. And how much more valuable you are than birds!" (Luke 12:24).

I was reminded again this week that both sparrows and human beings are dependent upon the same Creator. Perhaps God sometimes

August

sends snow storms to cause us to stop and look around; to meditate upon our insignificance and helplessness, and to discover just how dependent we are. Strange, how in just an hour He can transform the ugliness of our world into a glorious world of love and beauty.

Another Day

12   The day stretches itself before us like a snow-covered road through the woods, upon which no one has traveled: soft, pure, inviting—waiting to record the tracks of anyone who ventures forth. We can stand where we are, drink in its beauty, marvel at its allurement, or we can venture out and begin a journey. In the process some of the beauty is lost, part of the mystery is removed and the plodding steps mar the landscape. A day is given in order that it might be lived, explored, enjoyed, and yes, sometimes even endured. Sad—the plight of one who fears to dive into the day and challenge the unknown. Sadder still, the one who has lost the childhood excitement of unhesitatingly viewing the day as an adventure waiting to be discovered.

This morning when you awoke just like the billions of other human beings on this earth, you began the same day. Your eyes beheld the same rising sun, breathed the same atmosphere, experienced the same aliveness called "life" and dwelt on the same earth made by the same God. And yet, on this day, while some will find joy, some will do good, and some will make life richer, others will curse the light, dread the day, and wallow in impotent resignation. To a very large degree, the day will be what we choose to make it. Some things we can't control, and those we will simply have to deal with as they come. But other things we have the power to shape and influence for good or for evil. Every day will come with opportunities and challenges.

If it is morning when you read this, what do you plan to do with today? How much will you uselessly fritter away; how much will be selfishly hoarded for yourself? What part of this day will you grant for the benefit of another? If it is evening, what have you done with today? "Oh", you say, "I have other days to live and on those days I will expand my circle beyond myself!" But, do you have other days?

August

Might it not be possible that this is your last day on this earth; and if it were, and you knew it, how would you live it? My guess is that if you **knew** it was your last you would certainly not live it as you have, or as you otherwise intended. Most likely, you would find someone you love and share a close moment. You might call a friend and share a final few moments of friendship. Upon contemplation, you might even think of someone you have hurt and try to mend broken fences. Quite possibly, you would write down a few words to your family that too long you have ignored. Maybe you would set aside time to pray—that before never got squeezed in.

How often we take for granted life, health, happiness, family, friends, church, God! Some will find time for God today; most will relegate Him to another day. Some will spend the day living, others will unwittingly spend it dying. Some will make beautiful tracks in the snow, revealing that life was meant to be lived, not just observed. Others will stand still in the same place, no visible sign given that they were ever there. The wonderfully marvelous thing is that God has given each of us this day and for the most part we have the choice of what we will do with it. What will you do, or what have you done with today? Has another life been blessed by yours, ignored by yours, or made worse by yours? You have/had a choice! What will you do?

Amazing Grace

13 The congregation was singing that old familiar hymn once more, "Amazing Grace." It was at the funeral of a dear friend of mine, a retired United Methodist minister, Jack Smith. I must have sung that hymn hundreds of times and know most of the words by heart. But after singing it again, as I sat back down in the pew the words to the second verse began to dance again through my thoughts. *'Twas grace that taught my heart to fear, and grace my fears relieved, how precious did that grace appear, the hour I first believed.* Grace—what is this wondrous thing of which we sing?

I listened as an elderly minister recounted his 50 years of knowing and loving Jack. He told about Jack's faith and his call to ministry, his love for the poor and his lifetime commitment to serve

August

them. Years ago, Jack encountered this thing we call "grace" and it snatched his life out of the pit of self-will and placed his heart, now fearless, on the path that otherwise he would not have trod. I was reminded of a verse of scripture from I Peter 2:7: "To you then, who believe, He is precious" (NRSV). Peter, of course, was talking about Jesus and His love for us, and His willingness to sacrifice His very life for our sake.

"How precious did that grace appear the hour I first believed." "To you who believe, He is precious." Behold, grace and Jesus are synonymous! Until one encounters the reality of God in Christ, not only is grace not viewed as precious, it is incomprehensible. Until we embrace in faith the unmerited love of God revealed in Christ, we cannot know what grace is, at least not deep down in our heart and soul. Grace cannot be fully grasped with the mind; it can only be understood as it is absorbed into the depths of our soul. When a person is bathed in grace that person no longer sees God through the same eyes. Grace becomes the salve which removes the thick covering from blinded eyes. Until that moment, we are like the blind man in the Bible who could only see "men as trees walking." There is no focus, no clear vision, no understanding of what it means to be loved and redeemed until Christ resides within.

Grace does not look past our sin, grace runs to meet it. It embraces it, absorbs it and carries it to a cross and there allows its body to be impaled; all the while bearing the weight and ugliness of all that separates us from God. In the dying body of Jesus, our sin is immersed and the dark stains on our soul suddenly disappear. I step back and I gaze inward at my soul and I am awed that I find no spot or blemish. Amazingly, I appear to be clean, indeed made holy. Amazing grace! Amazing grace! Amazing grace . . . that saved a wretch like me! You are precious, O Jesus, because what you do no human being could even have imagined. Your grace is amazing because it does the unthinkable—it accepts us as we are and transforms us into what we can become.

I remember Jack, and when I think of him I will always recall the preciousness of Jack's life, because in that life I beheld the working and moving of grace—the wondrous power of grace to come

August

into one who believed and take a simple human life and turn it into something wonderfully good. Grace is amazing, to those who believe. Have you been touched by grace? Have you yet believed?

The Darkness of Silence

14 Who is there who has not at times prayed for guidance and waited in quietness, only to receive the answer of silence? So, we prayed more diligently, more emphatically, more sincerely, more passionately (if that were possible), and still there was no voice, no sign, no revelation of the Spirit. Our despair increases, our faith seems to diminish, and our sense of helplessness becomes overwhelming. Max Lucado writes the following in his little book, *The Gift For All People*,

> *It wasn't right that people spit into the eyes that had wept for them. It wasn't right that soldiers ripped chunks of flesh out of the back of their God. It wasn't right that spikes pierced the hands that formed the earth. And it wasn't right that the Son of God was forced to hear the silence of God. It wasn't right, but it happened. For while Jesus was on the cross, God sat on his hands. He turned his back. He ignored the screams of the innocent.*

Perhaps Lucado overstates the case when he says God turned his back and ignored the screams of the innocent. I don't believe God did that to Jesus, nor do I believe He does it to us. But surely God did not respond in any recognizable way to Jesus, and often He doesn't with us. It is in such moments that our faith is put to the greatest test. Yet ironically, it is in such moments that our faith grows the strongest. The muscle that is not challenged, exerted, and stretched is the muscle that atrophies and becomes useless. It is the metal that is immersed in fire that eventually becomes the strongest when tempered.

Those who take their faith seriously can undoubtedly attest to "dark nights of the soul"—those times when one feels isolated from God, for no apparent reason. They are those times in which we seek with all of our hearts to experience God's presence in a conscious way, and yet find ourselves still feeling alone. But God has no more

August

deserted us than has the oxygen in our atmosphere. Our senses are oblivious to its presence, but nonetheless it sustains our very life. There are long periods of time in the winter in which days pass without any visible evidence of the sun in the sky, other than a dark, gloomy, cloudy day—just slightly brighter than the night time. Yet eventually the sun reveals itself to us again, and warms us with its glory.

Those of us who are parents know the inner pain that we experience when we pass through those stages of our children's lives and must teach them the necessity of both dependence on us and independence from us. For their good we sometimes step back and allow them to learn lessons through hardship and struggle. We cannot teach them math by always finding the answers for them. We cannot teach them self-discipline by never requiring anything of them. If those times are hard for us in dealing with our children, is it too much to believe that God's heart aches for and with us when He must allow us to learn lessons the hard way?

If you are in one of those dark times, somehow find the strength to believe that even in silence God loves you far more than you can imagine. He has not deserted you nor forsaken you, for He promised He never would. Bleak though things may seem now, they will pass, and the sun of His love will warm you again! Trust Him, and wait upon the Lord.

Death—Only a Servant

15 Death—a small word; two vowels and three consonants—yet a word that has the power to strike fear in faithful and faithless alike. As surely as sunrise comes, we all know the day will come for each of us when this ominous reality we call death will intersect the path of our life. There will be no escaping or avoiding it for as the Bible says, "It is appointed for mortals to die once, and after that the judgment" (Hebrews 9:27, NRSV). And so we make our way through life, giving as little thought as possible to what we know is inevitable. Because death is shrouded in mystery, because it takes from us that which we love, be it our own life or the life of someone else, we do not look kindly upon its presence. It seems to have the

August

final say to our existence and when it approaches, there is never a moment in our life that we feel more powerless or less in control.

We gaze down at the lifeless body of one who only a few minutes before was as "alive" as we are and we are awed by death's power to interrupt living. Like time and tide it cannot be stopped or held back and so we treat it as if it were the greatest of enemies. But is it? If God's Word is true, should not death be seen as simply a passageway from life to life? Rather than view death as a heavy, thick door through which we must walk but cannot see beyond, shouldn't we view it as the gate of a chain-link fence that can be looked through to what awaits on the other side? Sometimes we fear most that which we cannot see nor understand; but death can be seen beyond through the words and promises of Jesus.

He said, "I am the resurrection and the life. He who believes in me will live, even though he dies; and whoever lives and believes in me will never die" (John 11:25-26). The essence of the power of life rests in God and is extended from Him to us. He is life's Creator; He is the One who causes life to be. To believe in Him, He says, is to ensure that we never die. But how can that be? One must ask, "What is death? Is it really the cessation of all life, or just life in the form that we presently experience it?" Just suppose that all death is is a bridge to greater life—a passageway from a lesser life to a greater one. Let's imagine for a moment that God can be trusted and His word is true—that there is an existence in which pain, sickness, and sorrow no longer exist. Imagine, if you will, life without interruption (death).

It's hard to believe, you say, in any life beyond this one. Why? Why is it harder to believe in eternal life than it is to accept that you are alive now? If God could create this life, with all the good that's in it, why do we imagine that He has not the power to create something better? Our Lord has said, "As the Father has life in himself, so he has granted the Son to have life in himself" (John 5:26). Life resides in God and there is no way to get to eternal life except through the channel of death. Therefore, I view death not as an enemy but as a gentle friend that takes me by the hand and ushers me into the presence of Him who loved me and walked the dark valley before me. I love this life, but I love eternal life more. Death does not make me

August

afraid; it gives me hope for that which is better. When it comes for me, I shall make it be my welcomed guest—nothing more than a servant of Him who is Life.

The Pursuit of God

16 Is life defined by the beating of a heart, the inhaling of air into lungs, the rapid transit of blood flowing through our veins and arteries, the tiny electrical signals sent from brain to tissue? Were we created for no other purpose than to successfully span the years from cradle to grave by surviving illnesses, working hard enough to gain food and shelter, forming a few close friendships, perhaps give life to one or two offspring, retiring, and then exit time to no longer exist? Some of us engage in a lifetime pursuit of seeking to discover the reality of God and how He relates to our living. Others show minimal or no interest in learning about (much less experiencing) the mystical invisible Being revealed in the Bible. If God is real, why does He hide? If God is Creator why does He not speak so we can hear Him? Why does He leave us to struggle with the mysteries of life, to say nothing of suffering through the tragedies of life?

Some will quickly give up their pursuit in frustration; some will stoically try to endure to the end; some will mock those who seek to live life on a level called "faith", and others will catch a glimpse of the eternal and tenaciously cling to an inexplicable mystery. Those who demand that God reveal to them all the secrets of His wisdom, who dismiss Him from their thoughts when He does not instantly respond to their demands, and who refuse to accept belief in a Being that will not reveal Himself according to their dictates, are doomed to die dissatisfied. Their inner being will be as hollow and empty as the stomach that has known no food for days; the mind that has never been filled with experiences and information—because no risk was ever taken to learn.

In our puffed-up wisdom, we imagine that our tiny little brains can grasp the greatness and glory of a God who could create a universe. In ignorance, we seek to define God by the limitations of our life's experiences. What might unwittingly be behind our desire to

August

place God in the mental box of our creating? That which we fully comprehend, that which we condense down to manageable levels, we feel we can control. There is something within us that wants to control God; not be controlled by Him. There seems to be in most, if not all, of us this need to be in charge. But alas, when we find ourselves being allowed to be in control, we discover quite quickly the immense limitations of our abilities and our wisdom.

The older I become the more certain I am of how *little* I know. Perhaps life was created to be a struggle for truth, because it is in the crucible of struggle that wisdom is acquired and the myriad of life's mysteries are slowly revealed. God painted for us a portrait of Himself, not on the canvas of a distant sky, but in the flesh of an only begotten Son. Do you desire to discover the mystery of divine life? Then you must find it in the words and life of a man called Jesus— One who did **not** say, "I have the truth," but said, "I am the Truth." Does that offend you, that truth could be embodied in one single Person? Well, for most of His earthly life Jesus' presence was a constant offense to someone. If you are interested in discovering truth, the purpose of life, and the glory of the Creator, you will find it when you finally encounter Jesus.

The Absence of Joy

17 Is there any difference between happiness and joy, or are they two words that simply mean the same thing? I believe they are different. Joy takes happiness to a higher level, for joy is experienced on the level of the spirit not just the plateau of human pleasure. Just as there is a huge difference between smiling and laughing, so there is between happiness and joy. Happiness may touch the mind but joy will touch the heart and soul—the inner being where deep mysteries unfold.

Jesus, preparing His disciples for His death and resurrection, warned them of a deep sorrow that they were going to experience when they watched Him die, but He said, "Now is your time of grief, but I will see you again and you will rejoice, and no one will take away your joy" (John 16:22). He also had said earlier, "I have told you this so that my joy may be in you and that your joy may be

August

complete" (John 15:11). Joy is exhilaration within the soul. It is the place where Life is reunited with life. We experience joy when we begin to behold the reality of truths that are derived from that which is eternal. In other words, when we finally begin to see, believe, and experience the truth revealed by God, we find ourselves ushered into an arena of life that supersedes the level of the commonplace.

Joy can be experienced even in the midst of trouble (e.g., Christian martyrs singing as they are dying; Paul rejoicing while beaten and imprisoned in chains in Philippi; Peter and John—after having been beaten—rejoicing that they had been counted worthy to suffer for Christ). Joy and peace are intertwined for they grow from the same root. That root is the consciousness of God's love and grace. A person can be aware that he or she is dying with a terminal illness and still live on a level of peace and joy that is astonishing, if one is able to believe that he or she is securely in the hands of the God who loves them.

Paul Tillich discovered one of the keys to understanding the mystery of joy when he wrote:

> *Joy is possible only when we are driven towards things and persons because of what they are and not because of what we can get from them. . . . Every human relation is joyless in which the other person is not sought because of what he is in himself, but because of the pleasure he can give us and the pain from which he can protect us.* (The New Being, pp. 145-46)

I understand that to mean that when we seek God simply for Himself, and not for what we think He can give us or do for us, we will have plunged ourselves into the great mystery of joy. When we seek people and love people just because they are, instead of for any pleasure we think they can give us, we will find joy in that relationship.

One of the tragedies of human existence, however, is that many will spend most of their lives pursuing people and things for what they think they can get from them. As long as we are content to do that, our lives will always be a witness to the absence of joy. How quickly we banish to the "junkyard" of life statements that we imagine are no more than clichés. Statements like, "It is more blessed to give, than to

August

receive." In our narrow little worlds, we conclude that the author of that statement got it backwards. We never risk trying to see if it's true or not. The result is an absence of joy in our lives.

Is There Any Word From the Lord?

18 King Zedekiah asked the prophet Jeremiah, "Is there any word from the Lord?" That is a question that many will probably ask from time to time. The skeptic or the agnostic may ponder the question sarcastically. "Show me evidence that a God exists, much less communicates with human beings, and then I will believe." Some who struggle with issues of faith may ask the question despairingly, hoping that somehow there will be some divine response. My reply to all who would ask the question would be, "Yes, there is word from the Lord and He speaks to us primarily through His written word and through the moving of His Spirit within those who believe." That will not satisfy many, but the time will never come when God will allow human beings to dictate to Him when and how He chooses to reveal Himself.

Christian theology proclaims that "the Word became flesh and dwelt among us, and we beheld His glory, the glory of the only begotten Son of God." In other words, God reveals Himself to us in the life and teaching of Jesus. Many will not accept that; but what is it they must have? Do they need a 500 foot heavenly being walking the earth beside them? Must His word be viewed as legitimate only if it comes as a loud, booming voice descending from a cloudless sky? Will their belief in God only be confirmed if His self-revelation comes with flashing lights and multitudes of angels surrounding Him, with trumpets blowing and fireworks exploding? If this is what they require, most likely they will go to their grave entrenched in unbelief.

Perhaps we can learn how to discover God by considering a tiny seed. A farmer holds a seed in the palm of his hand; he looks at it, examines it, and can discern within it no life—no power or evidence of aliveness. But then, in **faith** he plants the seed, he waters it, fertilizes it, and tills around it. All of this **before** he sees any evidence that the seed has any life. Then suddenly, tiny shoots begin to appear and what seemed impossible and unbelievable now becomes commonplace and

August

acceptable. How unbelievable—we place more faith in a seed than in the God who made it! What if the farmer had said to the seed, "I will not believe there is life in you until you first reveal your glory to me: only then will I plant you in the ground in faith." If that were the case, the farmer never would see the glory in the seed, simply because he could not bring himself to initiate an act of faith.

Faith, you see, includes trusting in something we have not seen, believing in something that we have not created, and accepting something that we do not control. It is a willingness to allow God to reveal Himself to us when and how He chooses; not as we choose. Some have said that in order to believe you must exercise "blind faith." But the faith I'm talking about isn't blind faith. We have the visible evidence of millions who have gone before us and built their lives upon the reality of Jesus' aliveness. All we need to do is follow where they have led. Is there any word from the Lord? Yes, history and the very world around us are filled with it. It proclaims itself to us every day. We just aren't willing to listen.

Law or Grace

19 God gave us the Law (Ten Commandments). Primarily, they are couched in negative language—"You shall not." There are a couple that are positive—you shall love and honor your parents and you shall keep the Sabbath holy. With knowledge of the law comes the awareness of our overwhelming inability to keep it. When we don't keep it, we feel guilty (unless we have managed to successfully suppress our conscience). After repeatedly trying and failing to keep the law, many people give up in despair and turn away from God because they have decided that if they cannot keep His law perfectly, He is unwilling to have a relationship with them.

Thus, we come to comprehend God in terms of law, not grace. We begin to believe that His love for us is dependent upon our unwavering obedience to His law. When we fail, we lose all sense of self-esteem and we throw up our hands in spiritual despair. We arrive at this point of despair precisely because we have misunderstood God

August

and the purpose of His law. Max Lucado writes: "To limit God's revelation to a cold list of do's and don'ts is as tragic as looking at a Colorado road map and saying that you'd seen the Rockies" (*God Came Near*, p. 27).

Why is it that we can never seem to grasp that God loves us simply because we are, not because of what we do (or don't do)? No sane parent would withhold love from his or her child because the child isn't perfect, or because the child is sometimes disobedient, or even because the child sometimes shows little love for the parent. If human parents are capable of loving their children "in spite of" the things they do wrong, does it make any sense for us to say God is less capable? The Apostle Paul puts it this way, "But God demonstrates his own love for us in this: While we were still sinners, Christ died for us" (Romans 5:8).

It is right that our hearts should feel broken when we become conscious of the horror of our sin. But it is not right that we should refuse to acknowledge that in our brokenness God draws nearer to us, not farther away. Again, what parent, when he or she sees one's child in pain or despair, does not do everything in his or her power to meet the child's need? Do we accuse God of doing less? Are we so blinded by the power of the Law that we cannot behold and experience the reality of grace?

Grace is love that is given that is undeserved. Love that is deserved (earned) will never come to us as grace. The Word of God says that "grace and truth came by Jesus Christ." In other words Jesus is the embodiment of God's loving grace. So what can we learn by observing Jesus' life? With whom did Jesus spend most of His time? With those whom the "righteous" declared were unworthy. And since they were deemed unworthy, the "righteous" thought God had no desire to pour His love upon them. Do you feel unworthy? Then know without doubt that God loves you. Do you feel like a failure? Then know that God stands ready to lift you out of your despair. If you are hurting, then discover that like a loving parent, God yearns to bring you healing. Discover and accept this truth—that it is grace that loves and heals; something the Law could never do.

August

Estrangement

20

Estrangement is a word that we do not frequently use. Unfortunately, it is all too much a part of everyday life. One dictionary defines the word this way: "to make (someone previously friendly or affectionate) indifferent or hostile; alienate, as affections." To be estranged is to no longer dwell in an environment of love and acceptance. It is to live with a sense of separateness, a feeling of tension, an awareness of division. It happens with husbands and wives, it happens with our children and our friends, it happens among church members and it is surely an experience we all have felt in our relationship with God. It is this latter relationship that I want to address.

Our feeling of estrangement from God becomes most apparent when a consciousness of the division within ourselves becomes most intense. We feel a sense of bewilderment, an isolation from God, an inability to communicate with Him; but we are unable to discern the cause.

God does not withdraw Himself from us; we separate ourselves from Him. Sin is at the heart of estrangement. It is the great divisive force which gives birth to all division in relationships, whether that relationship is with human beings or with God. It is tragic that most people never recognize or acknowledge the source of their division. There is a war that goes on within each of us that begins early in our childhood. As children we begin to discover that there is within each of us a desire, and an ability, to do both good and evil. Too often we choose the side of evil. That choice will reveal itself as the outward evidence of the presence of the sin that is within us. Sin is not the outward act, sin is the inner desire that causes us to choose to do wrong. The outward act simply becomes the manifestation or evidence of the inner problem.

Sin creates estrangement and estrangement will lead to guilt. Guilt that is left unresolved can turn into self-hatred and inevitably that will drive us away from that to which we long to be united. There can be no outer peace (loving acceptance between ourselves and another) until we have first discovered how to acquire inner peace. Inner peace becomes possible when we quit denying the presence of sin and self-

August

centeredness. and start acknowledging and confessing that we cannot redeem ourselves. At that point, grace meets sin, conquers it and banishes estrangement. God's unmerited love (grace) does in us what we cannot possibly do for ourselves. It accepts us in spite of ourselves—not because of ourselves. In God's acceptance of us, sinners though we are, we discover that it is alright to accept ourselves.

We are reborn in the womb of grace and it is in the crucible of God's acceptance and our self-acceptance that we not only find redemption—we can become instruments of reconciliation. Out of redemption flows the source and power to bring about acceptance of others and their acceptance of us. No one sets out to create estrangement from that which he or she loves, but it will inevitably happen if we fail to recognize the power of sin, and the fact that each of us is vulnerable to it. Estrangement is removed through grace. Grace is God's healing acceptance of us sinners.

It's A Small World

21 We live in a world that is getting smaller. Not because of technology which allows us to instantly communicate with those on the other side of the globe; nor because we can board an airplane and travel thousands of miles in mere hours. Our world grows smaller when we become so content with the little part of it in which we move daily that we fail to remember that the world consists of more than our immediate surroundings. We become so caught up in the routines of our day and the immediate acquaintances with whom we live, that we lose sight of the fact that there are other people on this planet who God made and who are as loved by Him as much as He loves us.

Our world grows smaller when we fail to remember that every human being is a creation of the hand of God. It is not enough to simply say "If He wants to love them, that's His business; as for me, I will greatly limit those for whom I will show concern." Neighborhood children who often fail to live up to the standards of acceptable behavior that we hold are rejected by some as undesirable. How easily and quickly we can relegate human beings to the scrap heap of life; giving little thought to the fact that the precious blood of Christ was

August

poured out for their redemption too. They meander into our midst desperately searching for a loving expression, a kind word, some semblance of acceptance, and see only stern looks that offer them the stale, dry bread of rejection.

The world becomes smaller when we grow content with the distortion of life that convinces us that the only race of humanity with ultimate value is the one to which we belong. How easy it is for the human heart to hate total strangers when we fail to realize that a person's value has nothing at all to do with the color of their skin. People are not just a reflection of the environment, the neighborhood in which they grow up, or the predominate culture in which they move; they often become what they are because they have dwelled too long in a society that rejects them before they are even given a chance to reveal their worth.

We make the world smaller when we limit our love and concern only to those who are our own family or the ones to which we feel closest. In so doing we live in a world within the world. We need to become more like the person described in Edwin Markham's poem *Outwitted*:

> *He drew a circle that shut me out—*
> *Heretic, rebel, a thing to flout.*
> *But Love and I had the wit to win:*
> *We drew a circle that took him in!*

Our world is smaller because the older we become the more we desire to shrink it rather than expand it. We draw in the reins, board up the windows of life, and become content to live out our days only in the tiny areas of life with which we have become comfortable. Scientists tell us the universe is constantly expanding. God keeps pushing the boundaries of life farther and farther outward. Maybe we ought to follow our Creator's example and risk making our world a little larger.

On Being Remembered

22 There is within most of us a desire to be remembered. How often have you heard someone asked, "How would you like to be remembered? When you are gone, what do you

August

think people will say about you?" What is there about your life that is so distinctive that it will stand out as the thing for which you will be recalled? The world has been inhabited by billions of people over the centuries, but very few are still remembered. We're born, we live the length of our days, and then we die. For a few years, maybe even a few generations, we continue to exist in the memories of our families. Perhaps long after we are gone some enterprising relative will trace a family tree and our name, the dates of our birth and death, our marriages, and our offspring will appear on a crowded list beside the names of other relatives long-forgotten.

Even those who were famous enough to be recorded in history really become little more than legend or myth. For example, we know a few facts about George Washington. From paintings we have a general idea of what he looked like. We have documents that he wrote and articles that were written about him, but we really don't know him at all. No one who lived when he did is still around to hold in their memory accurate glimpses into his personality and the deep things in him which made him who he was. Even the stories about him that have been passed down are questioned by some revisionist historians.

The Biblical stories of the Jewish people clearly reveal a desire to be remembered. The covenant God made with Abraham was so intertwined with him that to remember the covenant was to remember Abraham. In the Old Testament passages, God Himself constantly reminds the people that they must remember Him and not forget. We tend to remember that which we consider valuable and important, so conversely, we assume that if we are not remembered we are not important. The thief, dying on a cross with Jesus, made one request. "Lord, remember me when you come into your kingdom."

The truth is that no matter how great our accomplishments, no matter how well-known and respected we are among our families or peers, the essence of who we really are **cannot** live on in the minds and memories of future generations; for they too will pass away and every succeeding generation's knowledge of us will become more and more diluted and removed from who we were. There is only one Being whose memory of us really matters and that is God. It matters because He alone determines the eternal dwelling place of our souls.

August

If our souls are the immortal essence of who and what we are, and if only God can control the ultimate destination of our being, then it is essential that He remember us. And in this life, it is equally essential that we remember Him in faithfulness since our eternal future is dependent upon His grace and mercy.

The real question then becomes, "How will God remember you?" When all is said and done, that's the only remembrance that really matters. Perhaps what is most important about what God remembers about us won't be what we said, or what we did; it won't matter where we traveled to or what we owned. Maybe what will really matter is what we believed in our heart concerning His Son. When you are gone, how will God remember you?

Life through the Eyes of a Child

23 Are you able to remember the time when you were a child? Most of us can recall memories that are both good and bad. But think for a moment only about the good memories. Do you recall that you hated to go to bed at night because you didn't want to give up on the day? And you looked forward to tomorrow because it held out an abundance of exciting things to do— new things that had never been experienced before. When you finally did drift off to sleep it was a sleep that was unsurpassed in peacefulness and without interruption until morning (and you didn't have to get up and go to the bathroom)!

As a child the concept of worry was as foreign to you as the stranger who lived on the other side of the world. There is no one so carefree as a child. Everything seemed bigger, clearer, and more beautiful. The biases and prejudices of life had not taken hold and as a child you were oblivious to the distinctiveness of other races. You were unaware that some people were considered to be ugly while others were deemed beautiful. You had no consciousness that money was so valuable that it needed to be hoarded, or that life could possibly ever end.

You felt safe with your parents and took for granted that any need you would ever have would be met by the power of their love. Love did not need to be explained because love was self-evident.

August

Springtime appeared more glorious and the fragrance of the air after a summer shower had a sweetness of its own that naturally caused you to pause and take deep breaths. The stars seemed brighter and the "lightning bugs" awed you with their flickering little tail lights. Can you recall your first view of the ocean and how awesome that much water seemed? How frightening it was the first time your parents held you by the hands as you beheld the onrushing waves crashing against your legs! Do you still have faint memories of the first time you realized that boys and girls are really different and there was this strange attraction inside you as you were drawn to one in particular?

Perhaps you can recall a hundred other childhood experiences that made it exciting to just be alive. And then one day adulthood set in, and suddenly life became demanding, mundane, repetitive, unfulfilling. The dreaded word "responsibility" arose and the weight of answering to and looking out for others settled on your shoulders with a resounding "thud." The routine of daily work and the disappointments and frustrations of life piled up and squeezed out the wonder of joy from your heart. Old age which heretofore was unthought of now became a looming reality. Where did the excitement of living go?

My answer—it has gone nowhere; it has simply been buried under a ton of things that hides its possibilities. We cannot ever return to the newness and innocence of childhood, but we can recapture the wondrous excitement of our aliveness. The same wondrous world God gave us in childhood is still all around us. We just need to take the time to rediscover and be awed by its presence.

The Fall of a Nation

24 The downfall of mighty nations, history records, rarely comes through sudden and catastrophic events. It usually comes through a slow and gradual deterioration of the moral fiber and strength of its inner structure. Like hidden termites eating away at the inner structure of a house, it is the small, seemingly insignificant things that slowly take their toll. A nation is the sum total of its people. Thus, nations fall when the people grow comfortable with the gradual chipping away of their integrity, honor, and liberty.

August

On June 19, 2000, the Supreme Court ruled that public prayer at a high school football game is unconstitutional. There will be little outcry from the majority of the public because we have grown comfortable and complacent with the continual erosion of freedom and liberty in this country. One right, one privilege, one freedom is taken away at the time. Slowly, but surely, the spiritual health of our nation grows anemic while we sit back and watch one more effort to make this nation become a secular, immoral society that places its trust not in God, but in its own corrupted strength.

This country was founded on religious principles. The Supreme Court, in my judgment, has totally corrupted the intent of the part of the First Amendment which deals with religion. "Congress shall make no law respecting an establishment of religion, **or prohibiting the free exercise thereof** . . ." Clearly the Court has made a ruling that prohibits the free exercise of religion. If that was the intent of the founders of this country, why did they establish that each house of Congress would have its own chaplain and begin each session with prayer? Why does the phrase "In God We Trust" appear opposite the President of the Senate and is inscribed in the marble backdrops of the Speaker of the House? Why are those words included on our money? Above the head of the Chief Justice of the Supreme Court are the Ten Commandments. Engraved on the metal cap atop the Washington Monument are the words "Praise be to God." The Library of Congress has engraved on its walls numerous quotations from Scripture. The monuments and buildings of Washington are replete with religious symbols and references to God.

We would do well to heed the words of Abraham Lincoln (April 30, 1863) as he proclaimed a National Day of Fasting, Humiliation, and Prayer:

> *We have been the recipients of the choicest bounties of heaven. We have been preserved, these many years, in peace and prosperity. We have grown in numbers, wealth and power, as no other nation has ever grown. But we have forgotten God. We have forgotten the gracious hand which preserved us in peace and multiplied and enriched and strengthened us; and we*

August

have vainly imagined, in the deceitfulness of our hearts, that all these blessings were produced by some superior wisdom and virtue of our own. Intoxicated with unbroken success, we have become too self-sufficient to feel the necessity of redeeming and preserving grace, too proud to pray to the God that made us! It behooves us, then to humble ourselves before the offended Power, to confess our national sins, and to pray for clemency and forgiveness.

One would think the above words might have been written today; they are so descriptive of how many in our nation behave. We would do well to carefully study the history of other nations who fell. Who knows, our turn may be just ahead.

Inner Healing

In his book *Lion and Lamb* Brennan Manning recounts the following story.

Several yeas ago, Edward Farrell, a priest from Detroit, went on a two-week summer vacation to Ireland to visit relatives. His one living uncle was about to celebrate his eightieth birthday. On the great day, Ed and his uncle got up early. It was before dawn. They took a walk along the shores of Lake Killarney and stopped to watch the sunrise. They stood side-by-side for a full twenty minutes and then resumed walking. Ed glanced at his uncle and saw that his face had broken into a broad smile. Ed said, "Uncle Seamus, you look very happy." "I am." Ed asked, "How come?" And his uncle replied, "The Father of Jesus is very fond of me. (pp. 21-22)

Has it yet dawned upon you that the Father of Jesus is very fond of YOU? Indeed, more than that, He loves you with an eternal unwavering love. If that thought does not stir something within you, then you have not yet come to realize how deeply you are loved. I state the above because it has been my experience that there are so

August

many people in this world who find it difficult to love themselves. Because of mistakes they have made, bad decisions, and some terrible sin in their lives in the past, they view themselves with disdain and suffer terribly from almost no self-esteem.

We who are parents say we love all of our children the same, and I suppose that is probably true, as much as it is humanly possible. But love is not always revealed in the same measure. It is the child (even if they have grown to become an adult) who is hurting that draws forth from us the greatest evidence of our love. In most people there is this innate tendency, when we see something or someone wounded, to pour out all the love of which we are capable. If that is true for us, how much more true it is of God. When He looks at us with all our faults, with all our guilt, with all of our inner pain, it is His nature to pour more and more of His love into our life and upon the source of our pain.

Love heals. It is the only thing that can heal the pains that are within. If it is possible for God to love us as we are does not that mean it is not only possible but desirable that we should love ourselves? When a great artist paints a canvas, there are characteristics of his unique abilities and talents that are evidenced in his or her work. When God created us in His image the evidence of God's nature was written into our very being. We can love, because the One who made us and put part of Himself into us is Love. Just as God designed our physical bodies so that we are able to heal ourselves from outer wounds (e.g., a cut finger), so He has, through His creative grace, placed within us the ability to love ourselves so that we can be healed from our past mistakes. In reality our healing is a result of the presence and power of God within, not something that we have imagined or created on our own. Yet in giving us our freedom God also allowed us the choice of blocking or not receiving that inner healing that He longs for us to receive. It's like someone has given us a beautifully wrapped Christmas gift and we put it under the tree and never open it.

And so, if today you are having a difficult time forgiving and loving yourself, just remember: if God loves and forgives you, shouldn't you follow His example?

August

Giving In or Going On

26 Have you ever had a day in which things seemed so bad, life seemed so hopeless, and loneliness felt so overwhelming that you didn't feel any joy inside? One you loved so deeply seemed oblivious to your pain and carelessly rejected your overture of love. You had tried at some noble task and failed miserably. The "Oh me's" arrive like a thundering herd of buffalo and run right over you. Suddenly you feel your worth as a person is somehow dependent upon the broken relationship you shared with another. That person rejected you, not so much as a conscious choice, but by the careless words they hurled at you or perhaps by the indifference they showed to your pain.

There is a special place in each of us that is vulnerable to such experiences. At such times we come to realize just how interwoven our lives are with the lives of others. As children growing up, we don't question our dependence upon others, we accept it as a given. But as we grow into adolescence and then adulthood we begin to put our hunger for independence upon the throne of life. If we can just be on our own, do our own thing, establish our own world—a world we create—then we will be happy! Alas, we soon find out that the world we create is inextricably connected to the worlds that others create and we awake one day to discover that the independence we think we have achieved is only an illusion. We eventually will see that, in reality, our world is built upon the lives of others who, one way or another, seek to meet their own inner needs.

Every human being will suffer loss, and loss will make us acutely aware of our interconnectedness with others. The loss may come in the form of death, divorce, unemployment, sickness, harsh words, lost romance or a thousand other possibilities. When it comes we are left with two basic choices—give up and let it dictate to us how we will live out the moment, or muster up the inner strength God has given us and rise above it.

It is in moments of loss that we begin to profoundly discover who we really are and the strength that is hidden within us. Life is filled with successes and failures, good times and bad, gain and loss.

August

Ironically, we grow the greatest inwardly when we have faced and overcome the loss. Ralph W. Sockman once wrote:

> There are parts of a ship which taken by themselves would sink. The engine would sink. The propeller would sink. But when the parts of a ship are built together, they float. So with the events of my life. Some have been tragic. Some have been happy. But when they are built together, they form a craft that floats and is going someplace. And I am comforted.
> (*Dawnings*, p. 202)

There is much that happens in our life over which we have little or no control. But we don't have to let the individual moments of life dictate how we will live our entire lives. We are never alone; God is always with us. Rise up therefore and face life, live it, rejoice in it, weep with it, overcome it! Lest you forget, life is eternal and the One who created it is the One on whom you are most dependent—and He never fails you!

Life – Death – Life

27 Written into the fiber of our nature as a living being is the desire to survive—it is sometimes called "the survival instinct." Not only is this true of human beings, it appears to be true of all forms of life. Human beings, unless they suffer from depression or some form of mental illness, seek to avoid and escape from those things which might do us physical harm or possibly cause death. The evolutionist would attribute this to the necessity of the survival of the species. Though some may consider it simple-minded, I attribute it to the hand of the Creator who chose to give us life and prolong it. Life is a precious gift and we cling to it with a tenacious grip, refusing to let it go.

In order to be able to face the reality of death, we must come to understand and value life. In order to comprehend and appreciate the significance of life we must grasp the terrible reality of sin. If ultimate life is spiritual, then sin is the disease which seeks to destroy ultimate life. Like some microscopic spiritual termite, sin quietly, sometimes almost unobtrusively, eats away at us from within. If our physical houses were infested with termites, we would call an exterminator to

August

remove them and then seek to repair the damage. Crude though the analogy may be, Jesus is the one who comes and rids us of the spiritual infestation within us (sin) and also repairs, by grace and love, the damage which we have done to ourselves.

To see no purpose or possibility to life beyond the grave is to totally miss the biblical understanding of the value of life. God, who is Life, chose to expand life by creating. He is not a God subject to whimsical moods, He is a God with an eternal plan. That eternal plan we have come to know as "salvation."

Every human being has value, regardless of the place on this earth upon which he or she dwells, regardless of the color of one's skin. To devalue any human being, born or in the womb, is to devalue life. It is to miss the eternal purpose for which God created. I believe that God creates because creating is a part of the nature of God—a part of Himself, by the way, which clearly has been incorporated into the nature and essence of living things. Why do people write music? Why do they paint pictures on canvas? Why do they build beautiful edifices and magnificent structures? Why do we have this innate love for the beauty we see in plants, flowers, trees and shrubbery? I think we express all these things because the ability to create and the love for creation has been woven into the fabric of our being by the one who imparted to us His own nature.

Out of the billions of humans who have inhabited this planet, only a few will achieve lasting fame. But every life matters because every life, in its own way, either contributes to or takes away from the sanctity of life. Though most would not recognize it, the desire to pursue knowledge is in reality a desire to pursue the Source of knowledge. Truth is not created by human beings; it is uncovered. If something is discovered that means it already existed but was temporarily hidden. Knowledge is not the "one" way we are led to God, but it complements the ultimate way, which is through faith.

When at last we come to understand why God created life, then we will come to understand why death cannot be the final answer to life. God placed within human beings a soul which ensures that the essence of who we are will not end in a grave. That, I find to be fascinatingly wonderful!

August

Faith and Love

28 Faith is a small word, yet contained within its meaning is the bridge between God and humanity. God has chosen to build a relationship with His creation, primarily based on the concept of trusting faith. Rarely is God experienced with the perception of the physical senses of our bodies, but through the hidden senses we know as heart, mind, and soul. The word faith almost defies being defined. Yet, we must try, or the word becomes useless.

The renown Catholic theologian Hans Kung, in his book *The Church*, says:

> *Faith in an ultimate and radical sense cannot properly be distinguished from love. It is a personal activity directed towards a personal recipient. Faith is never, in the final analysis, a matter of adherence to objects, rules, or dogmas, but is the sacrifice and self-giving of one person to another.* (p. 55)

Faith, in the biblical sense, is expressed in a vital relationship between God and human beings. In proclaiming the kingdom of God, Jesus depicted it (especially in the parables) in terms of a relationship—not just of awareness, but of commitment and obedience. One can say with words that one has faith, but the evidence of faith is not so much proclamation as it is in obedient living. Obedient to what, you ask? Obedience in following the teaching and guidance of the Living Christ who reveals Himself to us through the inner working of the Holy Spirit.

The evidence of our faith comes through the way we choose to live our life. For example, a couple takes holy vows that bind them in a marriage covenant. The proof of their acceptance of those vows is revealed in their faithfulness in keeping them. That is why when a person breaks the vow of fidelity, they are described as being "unfaithful." When we break our vows of fidelity to God, then we, at least in that moment, have been "unfaithful." Faithfulness to God expresses itself through the relationship of love. That which one truly loves, one honors with fidelity. The great commandment in Judaism, which Jesus acknowledged and proclaimed is, "You shall love the

August

Lord your God, with all your heart, mind, soul, and strength." In other words, with your entire being. So, from the beginning of your relationship with God, you build a relationship based on the foundation of love; a relationship that is not based on fear, because one will never truly love the person of whom they live in fear.

In this life, love and faith either flourish together or die together; they really become inseparable. That which we love or have faith in we do not treat casually, but rather with deep commitment. God has declared that He loves us. That means He treats us with kindness, with goodwill and with faithfulness. Even when we are unfaithful, He still remains faithful. When one feels genuine sorrow for one's sins (the first stage of repentance) and experiences first hand the unmerited grace of God in forgiveness, how is it possible not to love the One who has never been unfaithful? That's when love becomes transformed into biblical faith. Paul profoundly said there were three great qualities in life—faith, hope, and love; and the greatest of these is love. Perhaps he said that because by the time we reach eternity, love will have absorbed the other two into itself. When we stand eternally before God, there will be no need for hope (it will have been fulfilled); and no need for faith (for God is now seen and experienced in fullness). But there will still be a need for love.

Oak or Morning Glory?

29 From where did we come? I am not talking about the biological explanation that delineates our conception as an embryo in our mother's womb. Nor am I referring to the widely accepted scientific explanation that we are no more than the product of evolution that began with the "Big Bang" and over time evolved from a one-cell organism in the ocean. There is a complexity to our body, to the functioning of our mind, to the expression of our emotions, which demands that I reject the notion that life was **not** created by an intelligent Creator with a purpose. There is nothing more foolish than the person who considers him or herself to be wiser than the Being that created life. Did not Paul forewarn us when he wrote, "I will destroy the wisdom of the wise; the intelligence of the intelligent I will frustrate. . . . For the foolishness of God is wiser than

August

man's wisdom, and the weakness of God is stronger than man's strength" (I Corinthians 1:19, 25).

I stubbornly refuse to accept the notion that human life is the result of mere chance. We were brought into being for a reason. Why do human parents have children? True, some are conceived unintentionally, but many are planned, desired, and longed for. Only a radical evolutionist would say, "We have children to simply carry on the species." No, I believe the person who longs for a child does so because there is deep within that person a desire to express the nature implanted in us by our Creator to create—create a living being for the purpose of loving. There is a oneness, a mystical connectedness that exists between a parent and child, that transcends human understanding. To love the child one creates is in essence to love a very part of oneself.

In the heart, if not the understanding of the person of faith, there is this creative desire to give birth to that which is immortal. It is not simply a desire to continue the species as much as it is a desire to play a role in the eternal order. God's Word tells us that we have been created in His image. To me that means, in part, that we have within the fabric of our very nature a need to create. Humanity has always created—houses, buildings, monuments, art, music, drama, floral arrangements, and a myriad of other things; but the ultimate creation is to create life. In reality, however, we do not create life; physiologically, we simply pass it on. Still, we play a role in creating through the child that is conceived—a being with an eternal soul and destiny.

So, you have created a child! What now will you pass on to that child spiritually that will assist him or her in a journey toward eternity? What an awesome task! Maybe we should ponder the words of Edward Leigh Pell:

> *I would rather plant a single acorn that will make an oak of a century and a forest of a thousand years than sow a thousand morning glories that give joy for a day and are gone tomorrow. For the same reason, I would rather plant one living truth in the heart of a child that will multiply through the ages than scatter a thousand brilliant conceits before a great audience*

August

that will flash like sparks for an instant and like sparks disappear forever. (*Dawnings*, p. 153)

The question then becomes, "What 'living truth' have you implanted in the heart of your child (or anyone's child)?" Is it the seed of a morning glory or an oak? Will it fade with the setting sun, or will its impact reach eternity? What power, what opportunity God has entrusted to us!

Kindness

30 Did you know that "kindness" is one of the fruits of God's Spirit? In Galatians 6:22, Paul lists nine fruits of the Spirit among which is the word "goodness." When you look up the work in a Greek lexicon you will find that the word used in Galatians is *chrestotes* which is translated by the words "gentleness, kindness, or goodness." Some places in the Bible the translators used the word "kindness" other places they translated the very same word "goodness." In my mind, the word kindness indicates one's attitude and behavior toward others, while goodness might describe the inner state of one's being.

All the fruits of the Spirit, that is, the characteristics that are given birth or produced in the Christian's life by the power of God's Spirit, are characteristics which are descriptive of who and what God is. God is the source of and the epitome of kindness. When the fruit of our life reveals kindness, then we have in essence allowed the Spirit of God to dwell within us—at least to the extent that His kindness is part of us.

Like forgiveness, kindness does not necessarily have to be initiated by waiting for a "feeling," but by the deliberate act of one's will. On a given day, in a certain circumstance, you may not "feel" like being kind to someone, but because you innately know it is the thing God would have you do, you act kindly anyway. Do I hear someone say: "That's hypocritical!"? No, it's not. It is never hypocritical to choose to do good rather than evil.

We live in an age in which life is lived at such a rapid pace that we think we don't have time for kindness. If that is true then we have

August

made an ongoing tragedy out of life. There is a profound little verse that someone once wrote that bespeaks a great truth:

> *I have wept in the night*
> *For the shortness of sight*
> *That to somebody's need made me blind;*
> *But I never have yet*
> *Felt a tinge of regret*
> *For being a little too kind.*
> Anonymous

We can observe in the world of politics how especially ugly and ungracious people can be. Half-truths and outright lies are spewed forth to distort the record and character of one's opponent; and it seems each year it gets worse.

Is the church any different? How difficult is it, and how far back do you have to think in order to recall hearing a church member saying some unkind or ungracious comment about another church member? I submit to you that whenever we say unkind things we are uttering those words, not from the Spirit of our Father, but from the spirit of the Enemy. Who is there among us who can stand up and say, "Of that, I am never guilty"? And if we are guilty, wouldn't our church, wouldn't our world, indeed wouldn't we be much better off if we uttered words of kindness rather than words that create pain? If kindness is a fruit of the Spirit, does your life reveal an abundant harvest, or a devastating crop failure?

The Walk of Faith

31 It is not difficult to walk by faith when things in life are going well. But when troubles come and we are driven to the place of dependency and helplessness, we discover that "trusting God" becomes more difficult to do. How do you simply trust that which you cannot see and listen to that which you cannot hear? In his devotional book *Grace for the Moment*, Max Lucado records the following words that were scratched on the wall of a Nazi concentration camp by one of the victims of the holocaust:

August

*I believe in the sun, even though it doesn't shine.
I believe in love, even when it isn't shown.
I believe in God, even when he doesn't speak.*

I also recall reading a book entitled *Night*, by Elie Wiesel, a survivor of the holocaust. In despair he had watched his family exterminated one by one by Nazi soldiers. His entire family had been devout Jews and they looked to God in despair. Wiesel wrote, "I prayed to the God in whom I no longer believed." Contrary to what his words seem to say, Wiesel undoubtedly believed in God or else he would not have been praying to Him. I doubt any of us have ever, or will ever, experience anything as terrible and traumatic as did those who were herded through the gates of concentration camps. But we all will encounter moments in life in which our faith is put to the test.

Faith is more than believing God exists: faith is trusting your very being to God. It is a willingness to say, "No matter what happens, I trust that God will be with me and that ultimately His will shall be done." Faith is looking death in the face and saying, "Even if you win this temporary victory, I will rise above you." Believing in God only as long as He gives you what you ask is not faith. When faced with illness, faith is not demanding of God that you be made well; it is trusting God so much, that even if you die He will give you life. One does not acquire such faith on the spur of the moment: it comes through years of prayer and searching. People who are wise do not attempt to board up their windows in the midst of the hurricane, but long before it arrives!

Believe it or not, it is the "little" tests along life's way that begin to build up faith—not tear it down. Anyone who knows anything about body-building knows you only increase muscle mass as you exercise it under the stress of challenging it with resistance. The muscle that is never "stretched" is the muscle that will soon atrophy. If a person desires to lift 300 pounds, they don't do so by beginning with 300 pounds, they start out with a lighter weight and work their way up by small increments over time. When "small" troubles come use them to draw nearer to God in faith and let each one become a building block to withstand the greater troubles that may come later.

September

Faith is a journey; it is not a destination. The destination is God and when we stand before Him in eternal life, faith will no longer be necessary, for then we shall see Him as He is. In the meantime, like an infant learning to walk, we must take small steps. When we fall down, we must get up and try again, until one day we will have mastered the art of walking by faith. The child who quits the first few times he or she falls is the child who will never learn to walk. Success is a matter of getting up one time more than you fall down!

The Cross of Servanthood

1 One of the more difficult, and sometimes frustrating, aspects of ministry is encountered during that period of time in which we seek to nominate people to hold offices of leadership in the church. Among many, there seems to be a built in resistance to want to lead. Some will accept jobs only if it is something they like, never considering that just maybe God is calling them to do something that is difficult. The easy things almost anyone can do; the hard things are where God challenges us to be faithful.

When we read the words Jesus spoke, we cuddle up to the ones that make us feel loved and comfortable and flee from or ignore the ones that challenge us in our self-constructed contentment. There is a cost to discipleship: Jesus made that unequivocally clear. One such saying is, "No one who puts his hand to the plow and looks back, is worthy of the kingdom of God." We do not escape the demands of such a saying by simply refusing to put our hand to the plow! I can imagine Jesus also saying, "Anyone I call to the plow who refuses to consider it and take it up, is unworthy of the kingdom of God."

The strength of a church is not so much found in the talents of exceptional leaders, but in the power of God in the lives of humble servants who are willing to offer what they have, even if they think their talents are small. It is in our weakness, not in our imagined strength, that God's strength is made perfect. The true church is the living body of Christ, dwelling in the lives of ordinary people who are willing to be used by Him to do extraordinary things. Every person God calls to a task, God will empower to do it!

September

Edward Everett Hale once wrote:

> *I am only one, but still I am one.*
> *I cannot do everything, but still I can do something;*
> *And because I cannot do everything*
> *I will not refuse to do something that I can do.*
> *(Words of Life, p. 199)*

As we grow older our skin loses its elasticity, but it is not necessary that our soul and our heart lose theirs. The Bible is filled with stories of how greatly God's power was revealed in those who had achieved many years of life. Abraham was 75 years old when he gathered up his family and belongings and obediently followed God's call. Moses was 80 when he encountered God in the burning bush of the wilderness and submitted himself to be used by God as a deliverer. God does not scour the earth looking for great leaders, He searches for servants who are willing to be greatly used. Read Paul's words in I Corinthians 1:26-31. Do they not speak to all of us?

Each year your church asks many of its members to step forward and put their shoulder under the yoke of Christ as He beckons them to serve. If asked, will you refuse even **before** you ask God if it is His will for you? We are the body of Christ! The question becomes, "Are we a living body or a dying one?" "God is not the God of the dead, but of the living." In the name of Jesus Christ, I exhort you to step forward and be willing to be used in service for His glory!

A Living Expression of Grace!

2 Have you made someone's life better? Have you given them the gift of yourself when it meant that you had to deny yourself? Have you absorbed the harsh words, the unkind comments and allowed the wounded love within you to break the cycle of anger? Have you embodied for another the reality of forgiveness as you returned their scorn with deeds of loving kindness? Have you smiled through the day and closed your eyes in sleep at night, head cradled on a pillow made damp from tears? Have you learned the price of loving that makes itself known in love rejected? Have you learned yet that loving someone really can bring pain, intended or not? Yet, to not

September

love is to condemn oneself to a life of indescribable loneliness and to deny oneself the hope of the Divine hand that gave you life.

Have you lived life so much for yourself that you have become oblivious to the pain in another, or has your heart with gentle longing reached into the heart of another and secretly borne the burden not bearable with mere human understanding? Has God revealed to you the cost of compassion, the price of caring, the weight of another's burden? Have you ever sought to look below the surface of the negative qualities in a person who angers you, to see that even in them there is much to value and love? Have you tried to help others be better than they are? Have you stepped down that they might step up? Or have you shunned the quiet call of humility and aggressively embraced the alluring call of pride? Have you sought to make yourself bigger by seeking to make someone smaller?

It is a noble thing to walk in the shadows and allow someone else to walk in the light. On such occasions, I believe, the great richness of God's presence abides quietly and more fully with the one in the shadows. It is a noble thing to love without demanding, to give without wanting to receive, to sacrifice without complaining, to honor without regretting, to bring light into darkness, to cleanse another's mistakes with hidden inner tears that build up instead of tear down. I once discovered a poem entitled *Love*, written by Roy Croft, that speaks nobly of a person who embodies the wonderful qualities listed above. One of the verses says the following:

> *I love you for the part of me that you bring out;*
> *I love you for putting your hand into my heaped-up heart*
> *And passing over all the foolish, weak things*
> *That you can't help dimly see there,*
> *And for drawing out into the light*
> *All the beautiful belongings that no one else had looked*
> *quite far enough to find.*

I have experienced the wonder of that kind of love in the most beautiful person I know. Her name is Gaye and as of today (August 28, 2000) she has blessed my life for seventeen years as my wife! Truly, a living expression of God's wondrous grace! I pray that each of you who read this have, or will have, a similar gift of love given to you by the hand of a loving God.

The Bedrock of Life

3 If one were to condense the biblical message from God to humanity into a single concept it would rest firmly on the foundation stone of forgiveness. The biblical story begins with "the fall." The result of the fall of Adam and Eve was that the relationship that they had shared with God was changed forever. Prior to the fall (the entrance of sin into the human heart), the divine/human relationship was based on unblemished trust. In the fall, trust was broken and God became the party that was wronged. When wrong is committed against a person (divine or human), the one who has been wronged can allow the relationship to be healed and resumed or die.

The Bible tells the basic story of human sin and weakness and God's desire and plan to redeem it. The word "forgiveness" is one that we all know well, but have you allowed the full meaning of the word to sink into your soul? To forgive does not mean that the wrong committed can be undone; it does not mean that it can be simply forgotten and swept under the rug of life. What it does mean is that in spite of being wounded, the one wronged chooses to treat the person who has wronged him or her with grace, love, and acceptance. That is clearly the message revealed in the life and teaching of Jesus. His very first words from the cross were, "Father, forgive them, for they know not what they do."

In my opinion, there is no story in the entire Bible that better illustrates the message Jesus came to share than the parable of the Prodigal Son. Told on a level that anyone should be able to grasp, the story vividly reveals the lost, hopeless plight of humanity, and how in spite of being mistreated, the father welcomes the child back to the home he chose to leave. Long before the prodigal ever thought about returning home, the grace of the father flowed down that long wayward road like a mighty rushing stream, and surrounded him in love. Before it ever entered the heart of the prodigal to feel remorse or repentance, the vigilant father stood faithfully at the window of life, longing for the return of the one who had wronged him. He longed for

September

him to return, not in order to condemn, punish, or remind him of what he had done, but in order that the son might be made whole by the father's love.

Jesus was severely condemned by the Pharisees because He chose to spend His time with the common sinners, outcasts, the lower strata of society, the sick, the mentally tormented, the ones who clung to life by a thread of hope. To them He came and His life became the soothing balm that bound up their wounds and made them whole again. And for that He was harshly condemned.

Two thoughts I would leave with you: 1) We **all** are sinners who stand in need of God's forgiveness—a gift which He joyfully holds out to us. 2) If we have been healed and blessed by forgiveness, our act of gratitude should reveal itself in that we will also be willing to forgive when we feel we have been treated unfairly. When God created the first human being, divine forgiveness became a prerequisite for life. When he created the second one, human forgiveness became essential in order for two or more people to live in harmony.

Hide, Whine, or Serve

4 Have you ever found yourself having to do a task in the church that you didn't feel qualified to do? Have you approached it with a sense of uneasiness and reservation because you didn't think you had what it took to do the job? Did God make a mistake in allowing you to be the one chosen? Well, take heart! Most of us have been there. Now the good news from scripture! The Word says, "But God chose the foolish things of the world to shame the wise; God chose the weak things of the world to shame the strong. He chose the lowly things of this world and the despised things—and the things that are not—to nullify the things that are . . ." (I Corinthians 1:28). If that doesn't make you feel better, try this one, "But he said to me [Paul], 'My grace is sufficient for you, for my power is made perfect in weakness.' Therefore I will boast all the more gladly about my weaknesses, so that Christ's power may rest on me. That is why, for Christ's sake, I delight in weaknesses, in insults, in hardships, in persecutions, in difficulties. For when I am weak, then I am strong" (II Corinthians 12:9-10).

September

If that still doesn't light your fire, here's another word from our Lord. "I can do all things through Christ who strengthens me" (Philippians 4:13, NKJV). What we Christians tend to forget is that when God calls us to a task, His Spirit becomes the empowerment to accomplish the task. It pleases God for us to recognize our weakness because then when we accomplish something good, He receives the glory and we get the satisfaction of having been mightily used to honor Him. I believe that God is able to do far more through the person with limited talent that is yielded to Him, than He can through a greatly talented person who seeks to do something in his or her own power.

If you will read the biblical stories of those whom God chose to be strong leaders, you will discover that He chose them from the weakest. Take for example Moses. When God called him to go to Egypt, Moses had been hiding out in the Midian desert for forty years tending sheep. When God spoke to him from the burning bush, Moses gave one lame excuse after another as to why he couldn't do what God asked him to do. "I'm nobody Lord, why send me?" Then, "If I go nobody will pay any attention to me, and besides I don't even know your name." God still said "Go." But Moses continued to argue, "But what if they don't believe me or listen to me?" His objections go on: "But I'm not eloquent enough, I don't have a way with words." Finally, as God dismissed all of Moses' arguments, Moses got down to the bottom line: "O my Lord, just send someone else" (Read Ex. 3-4).

Eventually, when Moses gave in, God was able to do great works through this weak whiner that would change forever the history of the world. As a result of Moses' obedient surrender, the Jewish nation and religion emerged out of slavery. From the Jewish religion came the Messiah and from the Messiah came the Christian faith. No one whom God calls to faith, is left powerless. Your faith must not be in yourself: it will flourish only as it is placed in God. Do not seek to glory in your strength, but rather, glory in your weakness. When anything of significance is accomplished through your weakness, then you know first-hand that God was in it. There is no greater satisfaction than knowing that you have been obedient to God and that God has honored you by using your life for His own good purpose. So, let us quit whining and start daring. Let us stop hiding behind

September

excuses and start serving, not in our own strength, but in the strength of Him who is not weak.

The Special Place of Peace

5 *Not that I speak from want, for I have learned to be content in whatever circumstances I am. I know how to get along with humble means, and I also know how to live in prosperity; in any and every circumstance I have learned the secret of being filled and going hungry, both of having abundance and suffering need. I can do all things through Him who strengthens me.* (Philippians 4:11-13, NASV)

Paul, writing to his Christian friends at Philippi, was attempting to console them regarding his present suffering. He wrote this letter from prison (probably in Rome). Rather than complain about his predicament, instead of lashing out at God for letting him suffer in spite of faithfully serving Him, Paul chose to live in peace with his condition and continue to give glory to God. It seems that it is basic human nature to complain when things don't go our way. Think back on your life, perhaps even your recent past, when things went wrong. Did you complain or try to resolve the problem? And if the problem wasn't resolvable, did you simply trust God to deliver you in spite of it? If you complained, did that make the problem go away?

Please note, from Paul's own words, such acceptance of life did not come instantly; he says, "I have learned." The experiences of life taught him the futility of living in turmoil and anguish. There are things in life that happen to us or to those we love, which we simply cannot control or change by our will or effort. In times like that we can either struggle and drive ourselves to despair, or we can do our best to trust that God will see us through. There can be peace in the midst of life's storms. Storms frighten us and make us aware of our finitude. But peace in the midst of the struggle makes us marvel at the power of God to sustain.

It was Jesus who said, "Peace I leave with you; my peace I give you. I do not give to you as the world gives. Do not let your hearts be

September

troubled and do not be afraid" (John 14:27). The difference between Paul and us is that he accepted the words of Jesus as truth and found sanctuary in their power. We doubt their power and thus remain in the turmoil of our condition. It really all comes down to faith and how we view human life. If we think this life is all there is, or if we cling to it as if it is **ultimately** important, then we rob ourselves of heavenly peace which can be experienced right now. I have known perfect peace when it comes to living with cancer, because I believe with all my being that God loves me and has prepared a better place for me. Since May 9, 1996, when I was told there was a huge mass growing in my body, I have lived without the burden of fear. Is that because I have great faith? Absolutely not! It's because we have a great God, and I chose to place my trust in Him.

Perhaps you are in the "learning stage" of life and have not yet come to that special place of peace. If so, don't give up! When life knocks you down, lean all the more on Him who promises you eternal life. Jesus said, "I have come that you might have life, and life more abundantly." He has not come to make us miserable, but to bring us hope and peace even when life treats us miserably. He has not come to make our burdens heavy but to lighten them through the power of the cross. He has not come to leave us desolate in despair, but to walk the dark valley with us until we come into the glorious light. Today, simply pray, "Lord I trust you, give me peace." You might just be surprised!

Guidelines for Living

6 When does it happen—that moment in time in which we begin to take life for granted? That dark moment in our lives in which we lose the wonder of being alive? When did we stop being awed by the creative power of God and begin to feel indifferent to the majesty of the created universe? At what point did the melodious lullaby of chirping birds greeting the dawning of a new day cease to be a song of delight and become an annoying disturbance? When did you stop gasping in reverence at the priceless panorama painted on the horizon at twilight's coming, or the spectacular glory of a rainbow's arch splashed on the canvas of a blue-gray sky? How oblivious we have become to the glory that is all around us!

September

How do you live your days? Are you simply waiting on death's coming, or are you living your life with all the zest of which you are capable? Have you resigned yourself to the fact that most of your life is behind you and there are no new, exciting days left in your future, or do you still find exhilarating joy in just being alive? Does the innocent expression written on the newborn's face no longer amaze you, or do you still marvel at the miracle of new life? Has love lost its excitement and now seems mundane, or do you still find it amazing that the special person in your life can love you so deeply? Have you forgotten how to love? More importantly, have you lost sight of the Source of love which is God?

As each day of your life passes like grains of sand in an hourglass and you reflect back on the day, how did you live it? What were your goals? Did you have any, other than making it through the day? Did you show someone kindness or were you content only with the satisfaction of your own most basic human needs? If someone used your yesterday of living to measure the value of your life, what would they conclude about you?

The circumstances of life often shape and give direction to the day we live, but we still determine **how** we live it. With each decision, with each act, with each word we utter, we have the power to choose. God trusts us with today and makes us the steward of our own vineyard. When the Master returns at eventide and asks for an accounting of the day, will we shrink in sorrow and regret or will we, with joy, offer the report of a faithful servant?

Perhaps the simple but profound words of Richard Baxter can guide us in the living out of our days. Maybe each of us should use them for a simple guideline for living. He wrote:

> *Spend your time in nothing which you know must be repented of; In nothing on which you might not pray for the blessing of God;*
> *In nothing which you could not review with a quiet conscience on your dying bed;*
> *In nothing which you might not safely and properly be found doing if death should surprise your act.*

September

God has entrusted you with today. Are you living it well, or do you need to pause and make some adjustments? Hold it as treasure in your hands and heart, for this day will come not again!

On Being a Christian

One reason so many us struggle in our attempt to live the Christian life is because we seek to make ourselves become something that inwardly we do not have the power to be. One cannot be Christian through will power but through will surrender; and that the modern independent-minded American resists with a passion. Since the beginning, with Adam and Eve, human beings have sought to supplant God's will with their own. We want to be like God, but we want to do it apart from His direction. This will never be!

The Christian life is one that is lived in the realm of holy love. To dwell in that kingdom is to not only dwell in the midst of holy love, but to be willing to give holy love. Holy love is love that is God-centered, God-directed, and God-empowered. It is not simply human goodwill, human kindness, and human concern. The nature of holy love is not to injure or destroy, but to heal, build up, and lift others to the plane of resurrected glory. When we seek God only for ourselves, only to satisfy our selfish desires and whims, we search for Him in vain. When we seek God for the purpose of giving ourselves to Him in obedient service, then we discover the magnificence of holy love.

One cannot enter into the holy presence of God clinging tenaciously to the things which we put ahead of Him or seek to hide from Him. That which we withhold from God becomes the obstacle that blocks the healing power of God and prevents Him from making us whole. That which we surrender to God becomes the bridge which spans the chasm that separates us from His love and power. To live the Christian life is more than going to church and claiming to be good. It is living a life that discovers resurrection in the self-crucified corpse of surrendered self-will. I believe the church today fails so miserably at drawing people to Christ because we imagine we can do it with pious words apart from spiritual power. We cannot give that which we do not have and we cannot keep that which we will not give.

September

The loving Spirit of God was not offered to us to be hoarded like hidden manna, but rather to be given away. Do you long to live in union with Christ? Then you must be willing to let the Spirit of Christ dwell in and flow through you. Be warned, there is a danger here for both the orthodox and the liberal who seek to claim the name of Christ. In *Perfect Everything*, J. Rufus Moseley wrote:

> The special temptation of the custodians of orthodoxy is to say "Lord, Lord," as a substitute for doing His will. The special temptation of the liberal is to seek to bear the fruit of the heavenly Vine without being in the Vine. (p. 140)

The pages of history are littered with the ruins of human lives who thought that they could go through life claiming Christ's name without having Christ live in them. In some ways their lives may have reflected Christ's glory, but His glory never dwelt in them. It is not in reflected glory that we are transformed but in glory that penetrates to the deepest recesses of our souls. In a word, we cannot be Christian without Christ living in us and that will never happen until we surrender ourselves to Him.

A Simple Truth

8 Think back to yesterday. Do you recall meeting God along the way? Is there some conscious moment that you can point to that His presence seemed real to you, or at least you acknowledged it by having a conversation with Him (prayer)? Or must you answer honestly, "You know, I don't recall conversing with God yesterday." It is an unfortunate truth, but most of us usually discover that what we put off to later doesn't get done. I ran across a little poem written by Ralph S. Cushman that just might help explain our dilemma.

> *I met God in the morning*
> *When my day was at its best,*
> *And His presence came like sunrise,*
> *Like a glory in my breast.*

September

All day long the Presence lingered,
All day long He stayed with Me,
And we sailed in perfect calmness
O'er a very troubled sea.

So I think I know the secret,
Learned from many a troubled way:
You must seek Him in the morning
If you want Him through the day.

Most of us live very busy lives. And if we have somehow convinced ourselves that our schedule for the day is so full that there is no time to speak to God, what should that tell us? Martin Luther once said, "I have much to do today; therefore, I must spend much time in prayer." If it is your habit to only pray to God at the close of the day, does not that suggest that you have sought to live the day in the strength of your own power? No wonder we are tired by the time we lie down for the night! I have discovered a strange thing. Even though I am only 57 years old, my strength and energy are far less than they used to be (please don't remind me that it's going to get worse)! Oddly enough, the demands on my life have increased even as my strength seems to be decreasing.

I wonder why it was that Jesus, even while still in his early thirties, found it necessary to spend much time alone with His Father? Could it possibly be that He realized that human strength needs to be supplemented with God's strength? Is it possible that there might just be an inextricable connection between spiritual strength and physical strength? The Hebrew mind never understood body and soul to be separate entities. They considered them to be one inseparable being. Therefore, while we might feed the physical body with food and thus gain physical strength, if we starve the soul of spiritual nourishment, it will take its toll on the body. Body and soul may be one, but they need uniquely different forms of nourishment.

It is so very sad that many will discover the truth of how much they need God in their lives only as their physical bodies are dying. For years, their starving souls pleaded for the life and strength He alone could offer—only to be neglected. What a great loss!

September

Godly Discipline

9 Like many other words, the word "discipline" can have more than one meaning. It can mean for example, punishment for misbehavior. It can refer to a set of rules or guidelines that govern a church (such as the *United Methodist Book of Discipline*). It can refer to the studies collectively embraced in a course of study. Finally, it can describe systematic training or subjugation to authority or subject, such as exercise, meditation, and behavior.

The Apostle Paul in writing to Timothy exhorts him to ". . . discipline yourself for the purpose of godliness; for bodily discipline is only of little profit, but godliness is profitable for all things, since it holds promise for the present life and also for the life to come" (I Timothy 4:7-8, NASV). Paul wrote these words in the context of warning Timothy to be prepared for the Second Coming of our Lord, which would bring history to an end. Since none of us knows exactly when that might occur, we should always be prepared through vigilance and self-discipline.

We live in an age in which the word "discipline" seems to have fallen into disfavor. Regardless of whether one is young or old there seems to be little motivation to bring the body, mind, or spirit under the discipline it requires to rise above the average. The summer Olympics have just concluded and many of us marveled at the skills of athletes (runners, swimmers, divers, and others) who prepared themselves through years of grueling discipline, subjecting their bodies and minds to the toil that was necessary to draw out of them the excellence that allowed them to compete with "the world's best." There are not many people who are willing to spend hours each day for years, pushing their bodies to the limit in order to run a race that will be over in mere seconds or minutes. But those who do not train extensively are incapable of competing at that level.

What is it to discipline one's self for the purpose of godliness? First, it requires that one be willing to take seriously the spiritual dimension of life. This is done through regimented exercise of the spirit and mind, just as those who want to build up their body would undertake a deliberate concentrated regiment of physical exercise in a

September

gym. If you were to drive by the health clubs around town, you would see that the parking lot is usually packed with cars almost any time of the day or evening. Inside are people committing themselves to the building up of their bodies through disciplined and strenuous exercise. But I wonder how much time they dedicate to their soul? Are we so naïve as to think our bodies will outlast our souls, and therefore they are more important?

To discipline one's self to godliness is to consciously choose and commit one's self to make important those things that build up our spiritual relationship with God—prayer, meditation, fasting, reading of the Bible, faithfulness in worship, and commitment to service, to name just a few. Spiritual discipline is anything that is God-oriented for the purpose of building up and nourishing the soul. It is discipline because it is not easy, and it requires extraordinary effort. The real question comes down to, "Do you want to be closer to God?" If you don't, your spirit will show it! If you do, then you will be viewed by others as someone who has tapped into a Source they have never known. Here's the good news—you're never too old for this kind of exercise!

Two Groups in One

10 The congregation in every church is composed of at least two parts—there is the group that forms the Body of Christ, and there is the group that allowed their name to be added to the list of a religious institution (otherwise called "the membership roll"). All who joined took the same vows. For some the vows had meaning that attached themselves to their soul—others merely uttered words because it was the expected thing to do. In a cynical age in which one's word is not expected to have much value, vows to God are no more significant than any other broken promise.

Much of the difference between the two groups can be traced to the fact that one made a commitment to a Person, the other to an institution. The group that offered sincere vows of fidelity to Jesus is the group that is empowered to be the Church—the Body of Christ. That is so because He becomes the power within their lives that pulls them back again and again to the way that leads to life. The group that

September

simply joined an institution soon discovers that they have no power within to keep them faithful.

Jesus once said, "Apart from me you can do nothing" (John 15:5). Those who do not wish to dwell in Christ show no evidence in their life that they have any desire to serve, they feel no compulsion to give, they reveal no desire to love and praise and be instruments of grace. They look for excuses to **not** serve and never ask the question of Jesus, "What would you have me do?" They are the ones who give little to the church, even if they have an abundance from which to give. What concerns them most is their own need, not the needs of others.

The person who is in Christ feels compelled to serve—not out of fear or coercion, but out of love. No one can truly belong to God and not desire to serve Him. One cannot have the Spirit of Christ within and not desire to be an instrument of His love and grace in the lives of others. Do Christians do it perfectly? Of course not—they are mere imperfect vessels, not Christ Himself. However, it apparently pleases our Lord to use imperfect vessels. In the course of a lifetime, if they are willing, He will slowly transform them into people growing toward perfection. When they fail, Christians feel great sorrow; but even that God can use and transform into something good. He can take the sorrow of their heart and the tears in their soul and use them to soften the hardened parts of their lives in order to shape and mold them into a new creation.

Many people become disillusioned with the church and church people and "drop out." They choose instead to fill their Sundays with extended slumber, and pore over the pages of all the bad news the world can print in newspapers, rather than scouring the pages of the Book of Good News that offers them life. They would rather listen to the Sunday morning talk show hosts interview politicians than listen to a preacher speak words for God. They joined an institution and now they have dropped out, lain down, tuned out, and live their lives in the impotence of human weakness. But those who joined themselves to Christ get up, go out, sing praise, offer grace, and live for something besides themselves. In every church there are two groups—to which do you belong?

September 11

It's What's at the Center

(This article was written a few days after the horrific events of 9/11, 2001. Our nation was in turmoil and we struggled to find our equilibrium. Much needed to be said. Therefore it's a little longer than the other meditations in this book

On July 14, 1994, I began an article for the church newsletter with the following sentence:

> *Everything has a center, a primary source around which everything else moves. In our solar system, the sun is our center. The planets move in elliptical orbits around this center of our part of the universe. The energy, size, and power of the sun affect and control life as we know it.*

That thought came back to me as I read an article on the internet about why the World Trade Centers collapsed. The project engineer, Hyman Brown, said, "Each tower was built around a central core that kept the building up, supporting each tower's so-called dead weight. But when the steel melted, like dominoes it fell." In other words, when the building lost its center, the entire complex collapsed, pan-caking straight down, one floor upon another.

If our sun were suddenly to disappear, all life on our planet would end and the solar system of which we are a part would fall into chaos. Human beings have a center as well as all other things. At the center of humanity is the soul. How well we do depends upon what's at the center of our soul. Jesus said, "Where a man's treasure is, there will his heart be also." In other words, that which we treasure most of all becomes the center which controls us. The terrorists who thought they could shake this nation to its foundation and perhaps bring it crumbling down like the twin towers, will discover that all they did was make this nation once more get in touch with its soul.

When the towers fell, an ominous cloud of dust and debris rapidly mushroomed out in every direction, wrapping those in its path in a veil of darkness. But more rapidly than the dust clouds, there spread across this nation a sense of unity that followed hard on the

September

shockwaves that reverberated from east to west. Suddenly millions of individual citizens began to realize that we are one people. People who heretofore had buried their sense of patriotism suddenly found it exploding to the surface. Rather than the "core" of this nation melting down it became tempered as steel passing through the fire. A great nation has now been forced to become reacquainted with what made it great. What makes our country great is not the vast wealth that makes us materialistically the richest on earth; it is not the technology that is both a blessing and a curse; it is not the acquisition of knowledge accumulated in vast libraries; nor is it our industrial complex that leads the world. What makes this nation great is what is essentially at the heart of this country—a basic goodness and a desire to share with the world the blessings that have been ours.

And from whence does that goodness come? It comes from a faith, though sometimes dormant, in the One who is Goodness. Those who do not know or believe that this nation was built on the core of faith are ignorant of our history. You cannot melt down faith! Tyrants have tried to do that for centuries and all they do is cause the core to grow stronger. In England, centuries ago, when Hugh Latimer, bishop of Worcester and his friend Ridley were about to be burned at the stake by Queen Mary, Latimer looked at his frightened companion and said, "Be of good comfort Master Ridley and play the man, I trust that we shall this day light a fire in all England, that shall never be put out."

Several years ago, the University of Houston did a ten-year study of the early documents of this nation's history. They looked at over 15,000 documents and discovered that 94% of them were based on the Bible; 34% were direct Bible quotations; and 60% were from men who based their ideas directly upon the Bible (*Decisive Issues Facing Christians Today*, John Stott, p. 19).

When the Pilgrims landed at Plymouth Rock in 1620, William Bradford, who was elected Governor, set the tone for our nation in the Mayflower Compact when he wrote:

> ... *having undertaken,* ***for the Glory of God and the advancement of the Christian Faith*** *and the honor of our King and country, a voyage to plant the first colony in the northern*

parts of Virginia, do by these presents solemnly and mutually in the presence of God and of one another, covenant and combine ourselves together into a civil body politic.

We may be a nation that has its share of doubters, but we are still a nation that believes in and trusts God. Hate-filled tyrants seem to never learn that murdering Americans in mass simply reawakens faith that makes them stronger. Over the years we may lose sight of what's at our center; we may, like the prodigal, journey a long way from home and live too long in riotous living, but eventually we will come home and when we do, when once more God is at our center, no one can make this nation fall, except to fall on our knees, not before terrorists, but before Him who gives and sustains our very lives.

Fear or Faith

12 It is amazing that a handful of men filled with hatred have the power to throw the entire world into the bottomless pit of fear. Four airplanes guided by religious fanatics caused the normal lives of millions of people to suddenly be changed forever. Among those affected have been Christians who suddenly find the legs of their faith as wobbly as the newborn colt standing up for the first time. But it should not be so, certainly not for those who claim Christ as the Lord of their lives. Fear is not of God, it is a tool of Satan. Let us heed the powerful words of the Psalmist: "The LORD is my light and my salvation—whom shall I fear? The LORD is the stronghold of my life—of whom shall I be afraid?" (Psalm 27:1).

The greatest weapon of the terrorist is not bombs or planes used as missiles; it is the scourge of fear. Over 3,000 people died on September 11 as a result of the tragedy created by crashing planes, but ten thousand times that many have been driven into the darkness of doubt and fear. Who holds you securely in his hands—a terrorist who has the power to end your life, or God who has the power to redeem and resurrect it? The only thing a terrorist can do is be the catalyst that ushers you into life with Christ forever. Should we ignore the reality of the threat of violence? Of course not—but we dare not live our lives in fear of what might be!

September

In 1789 the sky of Hartford, Connecticut darkened ominously, and some of the representatives, glancing out the windows, feared that the end of time was at hand. Many urged that the House of Representatives adjourn immediately and that representatives be allowed to go home. But the Speaker of the House, Colonel Davenport, rose to his feet and boldly proclaimed, "The Day of Judgment is either approaching or it is not. If it is not, there is no cause for adjournment. If it is, I choose to be found doing my duty. Therefore, I wish that candles be brought."

It seems clear to me that how one faces the things in life that have power to threaten or harm us is in proportion to how secure one feels with the promises of the Living God. It is easy to "appear" to be a Christian when life is sailing along smoothly and nothing seems out of kilter. But the true measure of the depth of one's faith is revealed to each of us when we bump up against the adversities of life. Are we people of less faith than the terrorists who, misguided though they may be, fly planes into buildings, believing that the God they worship will provide for them eternally? The answer to fear is not to retreat into the cave of insecurity, but to march courageously into the arms of our Heavenly Father who promises us eternal life. Jesus trusted His Father—but there was still a cross to be borne! Trust does not ensure that we are immune from physical harm. It does, however, ensure that come what may, God has possession of our life.

Through the prophet Isaiah, God asks a question and then gives the answer: "Can a woman forget her nursing child, or show no compassion for the child of her womb? Even these may forget, yet I will not forget you. See, I have inscribed you on the palm of my hands." (Isaiah 49:15-16, NRSV) If you are inscribed on the palm of God's hand no terrorist can defeat you. Nor can anything else!

Life Yet To Be

13 Even among those who consider themselves to be Christians there are some who struggle to believe that there is a life beyond this one. It is not that they do not want to believe, they just cannot bring themselves to affirm with their life that which they have not experienced. And yet, if one would pause for a

September

moment and consider the miracle of life as we now know it, perhaps believing in life beyond this one would not be so difficult.

Ask yourself this question, "Why and how can there be life as we know it now?" Can you look at the miracle of your life, the wonder of your "aliveness" and not marvel that life exists at all? Have we become so unimpressed with how a microscopic cell can be transformed into a complex organism such as a human being? We begin as a being with a few cells; some cells become a heart, others form into lungs, others into a brain. The brain has millions of tiny electrical connections that send out impulses that give us the ability to think, to reason, to perceive. Consider the eye with its unique capability to transform bursts of light into images that allow us to see our world. Ponder for a moment the marvel of the ear that can take vibrations in the air and change them into tiny electrical signals that go to the brain and allow us to distinguish between a thousand different sounds. The marvel of life is overwhelming!

If all of the above is so, why is it difficult to believe that the same Being who created life would limit it to a few finite years and then allow us to be gone forever? Why is it that human beings are conscious of this unquenchable hope down deep inside that imagines a world greater than this one—that lasts for eternity? Why is it any more unreasonable to imagine a life that is yet to be than to be aware that we live in life now? At the heart of the Christian faith is resurrection. Jesus' entrance into this world and His message while here was to tell us, and convince us, that there is a kingdom of God that exists beyond that which we yet know. For Him to experience death and rise above it back to life should be clear evidence to us that life is more than we realize.

When questioned by Pilate, Jesus responded with the words, "My kingdom is not of this world." The obvious implication is that it is a kingdom beyond this world. When Paul wrote to the Corinthians about the resurrection he said, ". . . if Christ has not been raised, your faith is futile; you are still in your sins. Then those also who have fallen asleep [died] in Christ are lost. If only for this life we have hope in Christ, we are to be pitied more than all men" (I Cor. 15:17-19). But then he goes on to say, "But Christ has indeed been raised from the

September

dead . . ." (v. 20). It seems to me that there is something intrinsic about existence, which by its very nature proclaims that life is not temporary, but eternal. One of the things that is different between human beings and animals is our ability to dream, envision, create, imagine, and most importantly, believe in something greater and beyond ourselves.

I cannot prove to you that life exists beyond the life we now experience. I can only tell you that life seems literally to demand such a belief. If I can believe in a Creator who gave me this life, I do not find it difficult to believe His promise that He has created a life beyond this one. What's the point of saying you believe in God, if you don't believe what He says?

Learning to Listen

14 Have you ever prayed for guidance from God concerning some important issue in your life and you felt like you were left hanging with no discernible answer? I suppose all of us have at some time or another. However, the problem may be that we are expecting God to answer us in a manner that is not in keeping with the way He desires to answer. The following story, told by Max Lucado (*Grace for the Moment*, p. 336), illustrates the point:

> Once there was a man who dared God to speak: *Burn the bush like you did for Moses, God. And I will follow. Collapse the walls like you did for Joshua, God, and I will fight. Still the waves like you did on Galilee, God, and I will listen.*
> And so the man sat by a bush, near a wall, close to the sea and waited for God to speak.
> And God heard the man, so God answered. He sent fire, not for a bush, but for a church. He brought down a wall, not of brick, but of sin. He stilled a storm, not of the sea, but of a soul.
> And God waited for the man to respond. And he waited . . . and waited.
> But because the man was looking at bushes, not hearts;

September

bricks and not lives, seas and not souls, he decided that God had done nothing.

Finally he looked to God and asked, *Have you lost your power?*

And God looked at him and said, *Have you lost your hearing?*

When we think about it, it is somewhat presumptuous on our part to expect God to meet our demands with a certain kind of response. We do not relate to God on a level of "equality." He is Creator, we are the created; He is the Parent, we are the child. Maybe in some homes the child tells the parent what to do, but in God's home He is sovereign. None of this is to say that God does not desire to respond to our needs—quite the contrary: He desires to respond far more than we desire for Him to. But God knows best when and how we need to receive His guidance.

Time and again in the Gospels, when Jesus is teaching the people, He says, "Let anyone who has ears to hear, hear." The implication of His teaching is that much of what He has to say will be clearly heard and understood when we listen with spiritual hearing and with hungering hearts. God does not hide. We need to develop the ability to see and hear Him in the many ways and times in our lives that He chooses to reveal Himself.

Many of the answers to our questions are found in the Bible. It may not answer a question like, "Should I take this job or that one?" but it will answer questions as to how we are to live; how we are to treat our neighbor; and how we are to live in peace with ourselves. God did not speak to Moses out of the burning bush until Moses had made the commitment to come aside and see what was going on. Then, and only then, was Moses able to hear what God desired to say to him. Perhaps we have reached a moment in our life when we need to "come aside" and discover what God wishes to say to us.

Emotions

15 If you ever watched the old TV series "Star Trek", you will recall that there was a character played by Leonard Nimoy named Spock (half human and half Vulcan). There were two

September

dominant characteristics about Spock which defined who he was—his ability to think with absolute logic and the complete lack of any emotion. Sometimes, we might wish that God had made us without the ability to experience emotion. If so, we would never feel hurt when the words of people plunge searing swords into our souls; we would never feel despair when things didn't go our way; we would never feel sorrow when those closest to us suffered or died. We would never feel anger when we are wronged; we would never feel regret when we had done something unkind. But then we would never feel happiness when something good took place; we would never know joy when some wonderful incident stirred us to the depths of our soul with emotion that surpasses happiness and plunges to a deeper depth where joy resides.

God has His reasons for giving us the ability to experience emotions. We may never fully understand what those reasons are, but we can deduce from life's experiences why emotions can't just be positive. The only way the emotions we enjoy could have meaning is that there had to be the possibility of their counterpart. That which could never be lost could never be perceived as valuable. Love would be mere sentimentality if there was not also the potential to not only **not** love, but also to feel hate. Calmness would be meaningless without the present possibility of anger and despair. Every good emotion must have its negative counterpart or there could be no standard of measurement to determine the value of what is good.

Without valleys there can be no mountains. There can be no continuation of living things unless there is the reality of rain. Friendship is a meaningless term unless we are able to understand what life is like without it. It is in the dark moments of living, when our hearts are crushed and our spirits feel deflated, that we begin to perceive the value of love and friendship. To be able to experience love means we also have the potential to be wounded when love is withheld or lost. When that happens, the wounds of the heart cannot be healed by words, nor by the passing of time, but only through the balm of God's love that often comes to us through those who love us. Strength cannot be fully comprehended until one has known weakness. Laughter seems absurd unless one has known the tears of sorrow.

September

Laughter and tears erupt from the very same origin—the deep spring of the soul. Foolish people that we are, we live life so much on the level of the physical that we ignore the spirit within; and in time some imagine that it doesn't exist at all. We indulge in things we think bring us pleasure, never realizing that pleasure has value and lasting purpose only as long as it is born in that which is noble, honorable, and virtuous. Pleasure apart from honor is fleeting and inevitably gives birth to sin. Sin apart from godly sorrow is destined to eternal loss and destruction.

We may never understand our emotions; we may never discover how to master them; but let us never imagine that we possess them by chance. They are God's gift to help us grow into the best we can become.

God in Today

16 How did you greet the day when you arose this morning? Did you dread getting out of bed? Was there some task that awaited you which you have put off as long as you can? Did you greet it with the same indifference as many other mornings of your life? Perhaps you felt fear as you dealt with the uncertainty of some medical test or doctor's appointment. Maybe you have lived life so long without any excitement or anything out of the ordinary that it's just one more day of life to get through. If this is how you view life you are squandering it. It all comes down to attitude. Most days are as good or bad as we make them. Perhaps we should see the day from a different perspective, poetically like Oswald W. S. McCall saw it when he wrote the following prayer:

> *O God, I saw Thee push the black bolts back today and set ajar the Gates of Dawn, and the Spirit of Morning coming through at once was everywhere. The golden torrent of her hair she shook wide and free and lightly tiptoed up the sky, while all her trailing skirts spread glory. She blew a whisper through the woodland and it broke in song; she glanced along the streams and they mirrored heaven; she ran across the lawns, through gardens enamel-petalled and aroma-drunk. They stood unutterably still and rich as if their soul had come.*

September

Glorious God, I saw Thy Morning, and it seemed like resurrection to a life once dead in trespasses and sins. (Words of Life, p. 211)

There is no guarantee that today will be filled with joy and ecstasy. There is, however, the assurance that it will be filled with the presence of God. Think of all the days in the past that you dreaded so much. They have all passed and sooner than later, another day brought the return of peace and goodness. So this day, whether filled with good things or bad, will reach its conclusion with the coming of sunset, and as we pass through the dark hours of the night, God will bring forth a new day with the potential to be far different and better than the hardships of a previous day. Difficult though it may sometimes be, we must try to recognize that there is more good than bad in any day. Are you sick? The promise is that one day you will be well—in this life or the next. Are you troubled? Remember, you serve the God who calms storms, even those of the heart. Are you afraid? Jesus said, "Fear not, for I am with you." What is there that you must face that is more powerful than the love and grace of God that encounters it with you?

The reason that most of us who call ourselves Christian experience such anxiety and depression is because we have focused on the wrong thing. We cannot always control the negative things that happen in our lives, but we **can** always go to the One who can transform every negative into a positive. When problems arise, let your thoughts center on Christ, not the problem. Bring the problem into His presence in prayer and plop it down in God's lap. There has never been a problem so great He could not solve it. Remember, it is in our weakness that His strength is made perfect, not in our imagined strength. Therefore, discover joy in today!

Guilt

17 I have long believed that there is a correlation between the physical and spiritual laws that govern life. When God created our world, He set in motion certain principles such as those in physics and biology that allow life to function in a meaningful

September

and somewhat predictable way. Theologians, in discussing the creation story of Genesis, quite often use the word "chaos" to describe the nature of things prior to God's bringing order to existence. For life to have meaning and purpose, certain principles had to be established. We may not fully understand those principles—we may even complain about them, but they are an essential part of life.

For example, the human body has the ability to feel physical pain. If we step on a nail or cut our foot on a broken bottle, a signal is sent to our brain alerting us to the injury with such extreme discomfort that we are compelled to take action to minimize the damage done to our body. If we ignore the injury, infection could set in which has the potential to end our life. One might ponder why God did not find a "less painful" way to alert us to injury, but the fact remains that it is a principle that was established **for our own good**. Similarly, I believe that "a sense of guilt" is to the soul what pain is to the body.

It is not by chance that we have the ability to experience guilt when something is going deeply wrong in our spiritual life. Unresolved guilt that is ignored, like physical pain that is ignored, can cause the soul or spirit to continue a pattern that leads to self-destruction. I believe God created us with the ability to experience guilt, not for the purpose of making us miserable and unhappy, but for the purpose of causing us to make corrections in our behavior which bring the restoration of wholeness and interrupt a journey toward spiritual death. The counselor or psychiatrist that seeks to banish guilt from a patient without acknowledging and respecting the spiritual function that it serves, provides only a partial and inadequate solution to the spiritual damage which has led to the warning signal provided by God.

When we feel guilt we are experiencing the principle which God has initiated that seeks to warn us about harm to our soul. The underlying purpose of "healthy" feelings of guilt is not to make us feel that we are a bad person, but to cause us to seek inner healing. To simply seek to suppress the feeling, rather than to resolve and remove the cause, is to compound the problem. There is built within the human psyche the ability to inwardly know when something we do is wrong. The stronger our consciousness of right and wrong, the stronger will be our feeling of guilt and shame when we do what we

September

inwardly know to be against God's will. It is possible to continually deny and reject our feelings: in so doing, we can eventually still their voice. In other words, we can sear our conscience to the point that it no longer serves as a warning signal to our souls. When that occurs we have done irreparable damage to our spirituality. It's like removing the battery in a smoke detector—you render it useless and defeat its purpose.

All this to say, the next time your conscience causes you to feel guilty, begin to take steps to remove the cause of the guilt in order to restore peace to your soul. Then thank God for so gracious a gift.

Hope

18 In the beautiful passage of scripture found in I Corinthians 13, the apostle Paul eloquently describes the supremacy of love. In arriving at that conclusion, however, he first points out that in terms of the value of human living there are three things in this life that are essential—faith, hope, and love. None of them have to do with the possession of anything material, but have to do with the inner reality of the spirit. The qualities described are intangible. None of the three can be placed in a test tube or observed through a microscope in order to define and understand them. Love is revealed through outward acts of kindness and sacrifice. Faith makes itself known in the way a person lives life based on certain principles and behavior. Hope is revealed in the dogged determination to not let go of something that in the present moment is beyond one's attainment. It is the last of the three to which I draw your attention.

Hope is an inner desire that longs for something beyond the present. It looks across the limited horizon of "now" and hungers for something that exists in the future. For the Christian, the greatest of all hopes is the desire for eternal life. If one does not have such a longing desire, then life is diminished of meaning and purpose. The great barrier to the realization of our hope is the wall we call "death." It blocks our view of that which, by faith, we believe awaits us. Its dark thick veil will not allow us to observe what lies beyond this present world and behold what awaits us on the other side. And so the Christian's vision of life eternal is blocked, and we search frantically

September

for some vantage point that allows us to see beyond the dark fog. There appears in the blackness a tiny growing flicker that, like Moses' burning bush, draws us to it.

Had not the prophet spoken of such light? "The people walking in darkness have seen a great light; on those living in the land of the shadow of death a light has dawned" (Isaiah 9:2). In the Gospel of Luke, Zechariah prophesying through the power of the Holy Spirit said, "Because of God's tender mercy, the morning light from heaven is about to break upon us to give light to those who sit in darkness and in the shadow of death, and to guide us to the path of peace" (1:78-79). Behold, the light we see which gives us hope that clears the hurdle of death is Christ! He is the light of the world; He is the hope of glory! Paul says it in Colossians (1:27)—"Christ in you is the hope of glory!" If we cannot fix our gaze on what lies beyond the Great Divide then we must fix our spiritual gaze on Him who has traversed that division and brought heaven down to earth. Thus, our hope is no longer centered on distant life eternal, but on Him who has within Himself life that is eternal.

Human beings cannot long survive without hope. Prisoners of war who survive are those who cling to a hope within themselves that chains and torture cannot subdue—they hope, and their hope keeps alive within them the spark of life that cannot be denied. In this world we are held prisoner by the shackles of our own sin. The weight of our guilt and shame grows heavier and seeks to pull us beneath the surface of the joy of living. Suddenly we fix our gaze on the One whose hands are nailed to a cross and hear His words of hope, "I love you this much—for you I have died!" When the light of that truth comes crashing into our hearts and souls, there is no darkness in this world that can put out the light. Our hope is in Christ. Our hope for eternal life is assured. Praise God!

God's Thoughts

19 God speaks to us from Isaiah (55:8, 9): "For my thoughts are not your thoughts nor are your ways my ways, says the Lord. For as the heavens are higher than the earth, so are my ways higher than your ways and my thoughts than your thoughts."

September

We cannot be blamed for being unable to think thoughts as pure as the divine mind of God, for we are but imperfect human beings. Nevertheless, God does call us to try to elevate our thinking from the sinful, mundane perspective of human complacency and seek a higher level. The scriptures also tell us: "For as he thinks in his heart, so *is* he" (Proverbs 23:7, NKJV). If the thoughts of our heart are fixed on earthly things then our experience of the heavenly never gets elevated above the level of earthly existence.

Max Lucado illustrates for us the difference between how we think about things and how differently God sees them. He writes:

> We're thinking, *Preserve the body*; he's thinking, *Save the soul*. We dream of a pay raise. He dreams of raising the dead. We avoid pain and seek peace. God uses pain and brings peace. "I'm going to live before I die," we resolve. "Die, so you can live," he instructs. We love what rusts. He loves what endures. We rejoice at our successes. He rejoices at our confessions. We show our children the Nike star with the million dollar smile and say, "Be like Mike." God points to the crucified carpenter with bloody lips and a torn side and says, "Be like Christ." (*Grace For the Moment*, p. 370)

The human dilemma is that we tend to dwell on things which are temporary and thus less than ultimate. God takes the long view of life; we take the short view. God does not ask us to become profoundly brilliant in our understanding of life: He simply asks us to look to Him and His wisdom and place less reliance on our own. In the Book of Job, we learn in the early chapters that Job thought he could reason with God and plead his case from a position of equality. He wanted to go toe to toe with the Creator of all life. He soon found out that human wisdom is but a drop in the ocean compared to the wisdom of God. When he finally recognized the futility of arguing with God, Job writes in the last chapter of his book, "I have uttered what I did not understand, things too wonderful for me, which I did not know" (42:3).

God asks us to trust Him. When we board an airplane, we do not make our way to the front and proceed to tell the pilot how to fly

September

the plane. Neither should we attempt to tell God how to run the universe. What we do need to do is trust that God loves us and like any loving parent desires only our best good—even when the circumstances of life are going wrong. I began this message quoting from one of the latter chapters of Isaiah. Let me conclude by quoting words from the first chapter: "'Come now, and let us reason together,' says the LORD, 'Though your sins are like scarlet, they shall be as white as snow; though they are red like crimson, they shall be as wool'" (1:18). God doesn't expect us to have His wisdom, He only asks us to trust His!

The Weight of Regret

20 Quickly in life, we become acquainted with regret—that inner sadness that mysteriously thrusts itself upon the pristine landscape of our memory with such impact that it causes us to pause in the busyness of life and ponder some event that, given the chance, we would gladly undo. At what age did we first meet this uninvited guest and discover that there was something hidden within us over which we have little power? Children regret long before they are taught the depth of its meaning. Regret is a feeling that comes to us not from without, but from the depths of that mystical chamber within—the place where soul and spirit make their home in our inner being; the place where we have no power to physically see, and no ability to banish regrets by simply saying we do.

Regret is that silent voice that speaks first to the inner consciousness and, when experienced in its greatest power, causes tears to erupt like hidden geysers from unseen wells that flow deep beneath the surface of the face we manifest to the world. Regret is the begetter of the phrase, "If only . . ." It is the creator of the hunger to turn back time; the master of the desire to "undo." Regret makes us see, with hindsight, the true reality of a thing no longer hidden by unknown consequences. Suddenly revealed in all its painful truth, we no longer wonder or doubt the power of the thing we have done.

Regret can cause us to make changes in life which will make our life, and perhaps the lives of others, better. Where positive change can be wrought it serves a useful purpose—indeed a noble one. But regret

September

can also be a jailer that imprisons the soul and weighs down one's life with crushing fury. When regret only represses, when it only tears down with no desire to rebuild, it becomes a tool in the arsenal of the demonic. God did not give us life today for the purpose of being bogged down in the mistakes of the past. One or two aspirin for a headache can be a good thing: a whole bottle can be destructive.

We would all do well to heed the words of the wise man Kahlil Gibran who penned these enlightening words:

> Be not like him who sits by his fireside and watches the fire go out, then blows vainly upon the dead ashes. Do not give up hope or yield to despair because of that which is past, for to bewail the irretrievable is the worst of human frailties. (The Treasured Writings of Kahlil Gibran, p. 877)

We do not have the power to change the past or to retreat into its dark shadows. The only healthy thing we can do with the mistakes of the past is to confess them with repentance to the God who is timeless—the One who can transform one thing into another—the One who said, "Behold, I make all things new."

No one will pass through this life without an abundance of regrets. But regrets that become baggage are things that rob us of the joy of living. They weigh us down and inhibit the journey of peace and joy we were created to experience. We each must face the regrets that belong to us, but we bring God no pleasure, and ourselves no good, when we tote them alone through life, without releasing them into the cleansing hands of God's forgiving grace. What regrets do you carry today that weigh you down? Take them to God, confess them, and leave them there as you walk away. Letting go of regrets results in new-found freedom.

How Important Are You?

21 One of the big differences between the scientist and the theologian, as they look at life, is that the scientist's question centers on "How?" while the theologian's centers on "Why?" So consumed with the search for how life came to be, the scientist is

September

prone to spend little if any time considering why life came to be. I am not a scientist: rather, I am a theologian, at least in the sense that I am far more concerned about the purpose of life than I am the "how" of its origin. Have you ever meditated on the purpose of your life? We spend much of our life going through the motions; jumping through the hoops set before us by parents, teachers, and employers. Do you see yourself as a meaningless particle in a sea of humanity, or have you been able to grasp that your life has unique significance in the eyes of God?

I believe that life is far more than the mathematical possibility of being formed by chance, resulting from the ordinary sexual union of two human beings. Every being brought forth into life is uniquely valuable to God and was created for a purpose. We turn on our TV or pick up a magazine and for the most part it is only the "well-known" that get the attention. For example, the wife of the President is being given $8 million dollars in advance to write a book about her eight years in the White House. Why do people find her life (or any celebrity's life) more valuable or interesting than someone else's? Why do some cower down in awe or humility in the presence of any human being—whether it be a President, king, movie star, or bishop? Your life is just as important to God as theirs is!

Is it not significant that Jesus, while on this earth, chose to make his abode with the poor, downtrodden, and seemingly insignificant people of His day? Shepherds were the first invited to His birth and shepherds were some of the most despised and ostracized people of their day. Jesus did not frequent the palaces of kings and emperors, nor did He socialize with the high priest and the religious hierarchy. He would never have found His name on the society page of the *Jerusalem Herald* and the only reason He seems to have spent time with the wealthy was to remind them that they were obliged to share it with the poor. He did not shun "sinners," He embraced them. He had this strange compassion for tax collectors, smelly fishermen, and small-town prostitutes. Among those whom He seemed to think were the greatest in His day were the widow with only a few pennies, lepers with rotting flesh, children for whom His own disciples had no time, a devout Roman Centurion, and a thief dying on a cross. After His

September

resurrection, He sought out a feared and despised religious zealot trying to exterminate His church and chose him to be the greatest apostle!

Who am I, you ask, among such as these? I'll tell you who you are—you are a precious child of God! So valuable, that Jesus would have endured Calvary just for you. So precious, that the gates of hell were stormed in order to keep you out. So important, that no one can take your place. So great a treasure, that Jesus picked out a choice lot in heaven and has built a mansion for you there. Why were you created? In order that God might glorify Himself in you. You are the temple of His presence. You are a treasure for which He searches your whole life. Lift up your head! Begin to live like the child of the King that you are!

Loneliness

22 Human beings were not created to be alone. If we were, then the ability to speak would be meaningless. Speaking is communicating and communicating is done with other living things. Early on in Genesis (2:18), God said, "It is not good for the man to be alone. I will make a helper suitable for him." Most of us have a need and a desire to spend time by ourselves. We can use that time to deal with our inner thoughts and feelings, to get away from the busy rush of life and to calm our often stressed-out spirit. But inevitably we desire to return to the consoling presence of other human beings—be they spouse, family, or friends. To live in too much solitude robs us of the joy of aliveness because we are confined to the limitations of our tiny inner world.

You will note that when you remove the "l" from the word "alone" you are left with "a one." When a person is alone they are "a one." One is the number which symbolizes that which stands apart and by itself. In prison, some criminals are put into solitary confinement as punishment. In prisoner of war camps, captives were often isolated from their compatriots as a form of torture. To constantly live alone deprives the spirit of needed fellowship, and one's mental abilities often begin to diminish. There are people in our church and community who live in loneliness, not by choice, but because they are either physically unable to be in the presence of

September

others or they are forgotten and neglected. This should not be so, in a loving church!

Loneliness robs us of the joy of living. It attacks self-esteem, it strikes at one's sense of worth in community and it denies us the peace of feeling loved. It often brings on despair even as it steals from us hope for a future. While there are some people who prefer to be left alone; most people do not. To live in self-imposed isolation is to distort the plan of God for humanity. There will be no islands in heaven—there should be none here! Many of our elderly give up on life because they are forced into isolation. Either they are consigned to small, isolated apartments, or to the last place most of us want to be—a nursing home. We who still have strength and the vitality of life need to examine how we contribute to the loneliness of those around us because we are too busy to brighten their days with our presence. One of the greatest gifts anyone can give another is the gift of him or her self—our time.

Let us also be reminded that one does not have to be old to feel alone. There are those who feel lonely even in the midst of a crowd. One can feel isolated, even when surrounded by people! Children can feel alone when playmates ignore them or make them feel unimportant. Many children know the pain that comes with always being chosen last when teams are picked. They know the torment of being made fun of or ridiculed because of their appearance or simply for who they are. Slowly but surely, they retreat into the solitude of their inner aloneness.

We in the church have a responsibility to try to minister to the pain of someone's loneliness. You know someone right now who is alone, who feels forgotten, who feels unloved. Are you going to sit there and try to push them from your consciousness, or are you going to get up and share your life with them?

To Be or Not to Be–the Church

23 The television pictures tell the story—a woman clothed in Hindu garb, only partially revealed beneath the massive pile of concrete rubble that crushed the life from her body. Thousands more, adults and children, made lifeless by the sudden

September

devastation of an earthquake in India. The camera's eye captures the scene for the entire world to see. We yawn, then change the channel—after all, they are only Hindus in India and we are safe in America! Another scene—a dark-skinned child with a distended belly, limbs so frail they look like skin was painted on his bones, eyes distant and protruding, flies crawling around a tiny mouth that had known too little food. Hundreds, dying before our eyes as we gulp down our evening meal. Too bad, we think, but after all that's over in Africa. It has been that way for centuries; it will go on being that way.

It was Jesus who said, "There are none so blind as those who will not see." People gravitate to groups that are reflections of themselves. We do not want our consensus-formed worlds to be challenged by that which is different, or that makes us feel uncomfortable. Many years ago, I served a church in which a member wanted me to deny a little boy the opportunity to serve as an acolyte because he wore dirty tennis shoes to church. (It happened to be the only pair of shoes he possessed). Some are apprehensive about neighborhood children becoming involved with "our" children because they know too many curse words and their home environment is so dysfunctional they fear that it might have a bad influence on our children. Here's a radical thought—maybe "our" children could influence them!

If Jesus came to live among us for a month or two and we allowed Him to be in charge of our church, I wonder what changes He would make? Would we find His changes offensive? Would He walk through the streets surrounding our church and say, "Don't waste your time with these folks: they're dirty, they're poor, their culture is different from yours—just write them off and forget them." Have we secretly adopted the Marine Corps ad as the mission statement for our church—"We're looking for a few good men [people]!"

Which child, which human being did God create who is unworthy of His love? Which person has God declared to be outside the circle of Calvary's redemptive power? God did not make the church an institution—we did! Institutions choose and exclude. God declared the church to be the living body of Christ. The church is not a building; it is not a group defined by a membership roll; it is not a homogeneous group that is limited only to those who see everything the same. The church is a group of people who offer the world Christ. They become His hands, feet, and voice. They open their hearts to the least, the last, and the lost. They show by their deeds that there is room in God's heart for all who will come and receive Him. The church is the dispenser of grace, it is the healer of brokenness, it is the reservoir of God's forgiveness, it is the place where people feel safe, and where God's presence powerfully dwells. Are we the church, or are we simply an institution? We have a choice to make—to be or not to be the church.

The Pain of Rejection

24 There are some people who, from the time they were small, have been made to feel that they don't matter. Perhaps it was a parent who constantly criticized, a teacher who found fault with everything they did, or playmates who chose him or her to be the one to be constantly teased and ridiculed. It's sad that some children grow up wounded and carry inner pain that never seems to heal. They are robbed of self-confidence, deprived of self-worth, and feel compelled to shrink into the shadows of life where they feel safe. To venture into the "spotlight" of life is for them unthinkable, for they dare not risk more pain. Having once been burned in the flame of rejection, there is no desire to take such risk again!

Rejection is an experience almost everyone will encounter at some point in life—it is common to humanity. But rejection that is repeatedly experienced in childhood will take a lifetime toll. When one loses all sense of value as a human being, then one is scarred for life. I suppose there are some who unwittingly add to a person's struggle with self-esteem. They don't intend to be cruel, to make the person feel badly. In fact, if you were to ask them if they knew how much their words had hurt, they would probably be honestly surprised to learn they had added to another's pain. Yet words spoken without sensitivity and without forethought can often become flaming arrows that tear open an already bruised and aching heart.

Do you know someone who is hurting? Do you try to be sensitive to the feelings of those around you, or do you run roughshod over them and silently say, "Toughen up—it's a dog-eat-dog world!"

September

Perhaps you have never been hurt deeply enough by someone to feel utter despair. If not, then you will probably have little sympathy for someone who has. But if you have known deep pain in your own heart, you will quickly sense the pain in someone else's. Henri Nouwen wrote a little book entitled *The Wounded Healer*. One of his conclusions was: the person who has been wounded is the one who has the most power to heal another.

The person who goes through life feeling rejected is the person who has allowed others to determine his or her value. The truth is, however, that a person's innate value is **not** determined by human beings, but by Almighty God. The prodigal son did not understand his value as a person until he came back home to the father. His return did not undo the wrongs that he had done, nor did it wipe from his memory the consciousness of his own sin, but it did make him rediscover his value in the light of the father's forgiving love. I say "rediscover" because his value, in the father's eyes, had never diminished.

If you happen to be one of those people who, because of the way life has treated you, feels that you are of little value, I would leave you with this thought: He (Jesus) who was despised and rejected of men, thinks you are so valuable that He faced the fury of hell on a cross so that He might prepare a mansion in heaven for you! You might not think you are valuable, but God surely does!

Home

25 There is a distinct difference between the words "house" and "home." One denotes a building or structure, the other elicits images of a safe, comfortable, and appealing environment. Home is the place where we feel secure, loved, and valued. When we speak of places and attach to them the word "home," we give them special meaning. For example: hometown, home church, homeroom, homegrown, homestretch, homemade, homemaker, homebound, homecoming, and the list could go on and on. Home is the place we desire to retreat to when we have had a long hard day; the place where we can unwind and feel free to be ourselves—warts and all.

September

Home is where one returns to after a long trip, or perhaps years of being away. Home, in its best and most noble form, is the place we can go to and feel loved. At Christmas and special times during the year, if our parents are still living, we "go home" to spend time with them, often to reminisce and reflect on favorite times long since gone by. In moments like those, we shut out the world, leave behind our problems, and re-establish the bonds we have known over the span of many years.

There is a biblical story about home. It is the story of a young man who was not happy at home; he felt inhibited, confined, and smothered. The thing he wanted most was to be given his inheritance and to be allowed to break free from the shackles of his father's house; to spread his wings and fly to new places and new friends. You know the story of the Prodigal (Luke 15) and how after years of living life in the far country as he pleased, he awoke one day and discovered that he was miserable. Alone, deserted, penniless, and in despair, he discovered that the most valuable part of his life was not in the foreign land of delights for which he had longed, but was in the old familiar surroundings of the place he had called home. It was a lesson that could not be taught by word of mouth, but could be discovered for one's self, only through the process of living.

Many of us who are older have learned that lesson, but alas, we cannot go back, for home is no longer there. Beloved parents have died; the place we were born or grew up has been torn down and now exists only in the fondness of our memories. What would one give to have the opportunity to go back for a single day and once more sit on the lap of our parent? How comforting it would be to feel again those arms that were like no others, tenderly holding us to their breast. Or perhaps we would love to return to a time in which we could hold our own children and feel the trust and safety they felt with us. While no one can go back in time, one does not need to jettison the loving memories of home.

I believe that home is not just in the past, it is still in the future. It is a place that God has prepared for us—a place that we call heaven. Many of our parents and loved ones have already gone there. The older we become the more we are aware of a deep longing growing

September

within us to be there. This heaven-home is a place where love is, because it is the place where God is. The wearier this body becomes, the greater grows our longing to go home. One day I will go there—a place that I have never seen, and yet, the place where the longing of my heart and soul has always been!

The Burden of the Day

26 Has your heart ever borne the burden of the day? I'm not talking about some task at work, some housekeeping job at home, or something that demands physical exertion. I'm talking about the burden that you know inwardly; down inside you where heaviness drapes over the heart and soul like a soaking wet blanket. There can be an inner weight that pulls down the spirit and stifles the breath of the soul. Sometimes, you can't even identify what it is that's troubling you, you just know that there is no inner peace—no lightness to life. It may last for a few minutes, hours, or days. When it happens, you force yourself to go through the routine requirements of the day: all day long your body is doing its thing while inside you, you are somewhere else. A melancholy sadness settles in and there's no place you can go to escape it because it is inside you, and we discover we can't get away from what's inside us.

For lack of a better term, it feels like "spiritual oppression." Is it possible that this is tangible evidence that the world is composed of more than the physical matter that makes up our universe? Is there a spiritual dimension to life that defies the scrutiny of the eyes and can be seen only through the eyes of the spirit? St. Augustine in his *Confessions* speaks of a truth we can discern only as God becomes the "sweet light of my hidden eyes." Was the Apostle Paul merely a superstitious fanatic when he warned us about spiritual warfare in Ephesians 6:12? "For our fight is not against any physical enemy: it is against organizations and powers that are spiritual. We are up against the unseen power that controls this dark world, and spiritual agents from the very headquarters of evil." (J. B. Phillips Translation). Could this be why Jesus felt compelled to spend so much time in prayer with His Father?

September

Sometimes the things that burden us seem to come not from those we might label enemies, but those who we think of as friends. There is within each of us the "shadow self" that is suppressed most of the time, but is quite capable of rising to the surface and becoming an instrument, not in the hand of God but in the hand of the Enemy. Paul describes it with these words, "For what I do is not the good I want to do; no, the evil I do not want to do—this I keep on doing" (Romans 7:19). I have learned over the years that when God's people begin to get serious about serving God, the Evil One rises up and begins to seek to divide us from within. Satan is enraged by the praying Christian and will intensify his attacks when we begin to call on the name of the Lord.

Now for the good news! No burden borne for God's sake is ever borne alone! Our bodies and souls may become the battleground, but "greater is He that is in you, than he that is in the world!" My friends, I exhort you to lean on God's power. Let us fall on our knees, and through prayer, drink deeply from that well whose source is the river of Life. Let us draw strength and grace from Him who is more powerful than the Enemy; and let us no longer bear the burden of the day in our own strength but in the strength of Him who never slumbers nor sleeps. Remember, we can't rise up until we have first knelt down. The burden of the day is not made lighter by simply trying to lay it down, but by sharing it with Him who is able to bear it.

The Wonder of It All

27 Is it possible to live in a world created by God and never feel God's nearness? Is it possible to gaze upon creation and never long to know the Creator? Is it possible to know the blessings of life and never know the One who blesses? The child born into this world enters it with an insatiable curiosity. It grasps for things before its eyes that its hand is unable to reach. It looks from side to side, finding its gaze riveted on anything that shines or moves. When able to crawl, it scurries from object to object, room to room in order to explore that which it has never before seen or grasped. The child fears nothing—until something injures it or startles it. What I

September

have described is the innocent inquiry of a child for physical objects. But a child also has a spiritual curiosity that hungers to be satisfied.

As a child grows, it allows its mind to be filled with any story that is offered. It has no trouble accepting Santa Claus, the boogie man, the Easter bunny, gold at the end of the rainbow, or the tooth fairy. Cinderella, the Wizard of Oz, Snow White and the Seven Dwarfs, and Pooh Bear are just as real to him or her as the world in which the child lives. Then one day we change. We quit seeking, we quit expecting to discover anything new or different, we stop searching for and believing in a God we cannot see. We stop having the innocent faith of a child, a faith without which, Jesus says, we can never enter the kingdom of God. Is Jesus calling for us to embrace myths, fairy tales, stories that have no basis in fact? No, He is calling for us to pursue truth—truth that exceeds the boundaries of our limited understanding.

Somewhere in life we encounter a great winter wasteland. Everything seems to be buried in a "white" sameness; nothing seems alive or real. It feels frozen in time and appears lifeless. Laughter becomes infrequent, excitement is less intense and less often experienced. Living becomes routine and mundane, and one day seems like a replica of the one that just passed. Must we attribute it to growing old? Have we lived so long we have explored and experienced all that God could create? Have we fallen so much in love with the created that we have entirely missed seeing or desiring the Creator? The created becomes familiar and will often disappoint us. The Creator is new and fresh every day and is inexhaustible!

When we can discern the Creator's handiwork in the birds' morning song, it will no longer sound mundane. When we can imagine the genius it took to put color in nature and fragrance in a flower, life will no longer seem ordinary. When we can encounter the eternal soul that's deep within us, we will never again doubt the reality of a God whose love could not be confined to temporal time, but required Him to express it eternally. What we are lacking, my friends, is a consciousness of God—amazingly enough—in the very world that He brought into being. I exhort you to rediscover your childhood curiosity and seek again to explore the inexhaustible treasures of both the world that you can see with your eyes and the one that you will only discover with the vision of your soul. Life doesn't have to be dreary. It can once again become as exciting as it was when you crawled and stretched out your hand in childhood wonder.

The Simplicity of Faith

28 It's amazing how so many Christians struggle with the concept of faith. They all know the word: many feel despair that they do not have more, some take it for granted, others live their lives out of each day's measure. I believe faith is like the daily manna God provided the Israelites. It cannot be stored up and hoarded, it cannot be produced out of sheer effort; it can be used and experienced only in the present moment as we look to God to meet our needs.

In his intriguing little book, *The Pursuit of God* (p. 91), A. W. Tozer makes the following observation:

> *Faith is the least self-regarding of the virtues. It is by its very nature scarcely conscious of its own existence. Like the eye which sees everything in front of it and never sees itself, faith is occupied with the Object upon which it rests and pays no attention to itself at all. While we are looking at God we do not see ourselves—blessed riddance. The man who has struggled to purify himself and has had nothing but repeated failures will experience real relief when he stops tinkering with his soul and looks away to the perfect One.*

Many Christians seek to build up their faith, struggle to have more faith, hunger to be given more faith. Thus, they place their attention and importance on the wrong thing. What we should long for is more of God's presence, a greater understanding of His will and a deeper hunger to do it. We get the cart before the horse! More faith does not draw us nearer to God—seeking more of God creates greater faith. Unfortunately, many of us seek to use God like an ATM machine. We run low on something in life and we think we can drive by, insert our "prayer card," punch in our request and expect instant results. Along the way, we haven't bothered to consider if what we

September

want is what God wants for us. I think it was Steve Brown in his book *Approaching God*, that said, "Prayer is not getting what we want from God, but wanting what God wants for us."

Unfortunately, we try to do with God what many parents do with their children—role reversal—allowing the children to assume the role of parents and dictating to the adults the way things must be. God is the parent, we are the child! God will not play the role-reversal game. The evidence of deep faith is revealed when a person is willing to let God's will be done rather than demanding that their own be done. One of the greatest affirmations of the Judeo-Christian faith is: There is one true God and He alone shall be worshiped and served.

Like most profound things in life, faith is really quite simple. It manifests itself when you exercise it. If you come to a ditch four feet wide and say, "I have faith that I can jump it!" That's not faith. Faith is revealed by getting a running start and actually doing it. You can say, "I have faith in God", but that is only a statement. Real faith is revealed when you start living your life in a way that reflects your faith in God. The magnificent thing is, the more you try to live for God the more power He gives you to live for Him. Why not try it and see? But then that would require faith, wouldn't it?

Dealing with Discouragement

29 Who among us, from time to time, has not had to deal with the reality of discouragement? Things don't always go our way. Some people seem to find fault with everything we do. No matter how hard we try, something always goes wrong. Exciting dreams fizzle out and amount to nothing. Life seems stuck in a rut and appears to be going nowhere. Is that the way it's been for you recently? Guess what? It's that way for other people too. Let's look at a few biblical characters.

Elijah was one of God's mightiest prophets in the Old Testament. Yet, he fled from Jezebel and begged God to let him die. "I have had enough, LORD," he said. "Take my life; I am no better than my ancestors" (I Kings 19:4). Jonah is commanded to preach to the Ninevites—and they repented. We find Jonah saying unto God, "O Lord, please take my life from me, for it is better for me to die than

September

to live" (Jonah 4:3). As you read through the Bible you will discover that most of the great leaders of God's people encountered times of great discouragement, even to the point of wanting to die. But they hung on! As a result, God was able to continue to use them and their life found great purpose.

Discouragement is one of the greatest tools in the hands of Satan. He can take the most devoted saint and, in an instant, bring him or her to their knees. Discouragement attacks not only the mind, but also the soul. It gnaws away at self-worth and blinds one to the goodness and blessings of life. Ironically, it seems to come most powerfully right after one has experienced a great success or blessing. One reason we get so bogged down when discouragement comes is that it inevitably causes us to focus on ourselves. "Woe is me," we cry to ourselves and we start down a slippery slope that ends in despair. Discouragement occurs when we take our eyes and thoughts off of God and put them on something else.

For the Christian, the way out of discouragement is to focus one's thoughts on God and not one's self. Turning to God's Word and intentionally engaging in prayer will eventually lead one back into the sunlight. It is not an easy task but it is an essential one. Our natural tendency is to want to struggle with the discouragement and wrestle it like Jacob wrestled with the angel. Instead, we need to lay it at the feet of God and ask Him to help us deal with it. Some may disagree, but I believe that discouragement is a spiritual problem and can only be satisfactorily resolved in a spiritual way. No one understands us better than the One who created us. Therefore we need to go to the source of our creation in order to resolve the problems that affect us internally.

In his classic book *The Screwtape Letters*, C. S. Lewis portrays his chief character, Screwtape (an experienced devil), giving advice to his nephew, Wormwood (an apprentice demon), on how to tempt a Christian into sinning. Discouragement is one of the tools of his trade but can sometimes backfire. Screwtape warns Wormwood: "Our cause is never more in danger than when a human, no longer desiring, but still intending to do our Enemy's [God's] will, looks round upon a universe from which every trace of Him seems to have vanished,

September

and asks why he has been forsaken, and still obeys" (p. 39). Seeking God in obedience will inevitably defeat discouragement.

Hope for Disquieted Souls

30 The Book of Psalms is an open diary of the inner cries of the psalmist's soul. They are the revelation of a heart that often was weighed down with despair and deep longing. The Psalms speak to most of us because they are spirit communing with spirit. In many of the Psalms, the writer is engaged in a conversation with his own soul. For example, Psalm 42 is a powerful illustration of one man's effort to address the inner battle deep down inside himself. "Why are you downcast, O my soul? Why so disturbed within me? Put your hope in God, for I will yet praise him, my Savior and my God" (42: 5-6).

There are times in life in which we feel a lack of inner peace; a disturbing restlessness forces its way into our consciousness and refuses to be dismissed. We are unhappy and cannot discern why we are so uneasy—even to the point of tears and despair. The disquieted, cast-down soul is the voice of our inner being crying out for a calming peace that seems far too elusive. To address one's own soul is to finally seek to communicate with not only the internal, but the eternal part of one's being. It is to ascend to the level at which human beings most powerfully commune with God. When one addresses one's soul with such honest searching and inquiry, one is walking on holy ground, for it is here that God's Spirit moves in the most powerful ways.

In the verses quoted above the Psalmist identifies the reality of his own being (the disquieted, cast down soul) and also discerns the answer to his need (hope in God). The Apostle Paul did the same thing in Romans (7:14-25) when he acknowledges both his inner conflict and the solution to that conflict—Jesus Christ. Ted Turner (CNN billionaire mogul) was quoted as saying that "Christianity is for losers." Mr. Turner needs to have a conversation with his soul, for quite the contrary is true: Christianity is for those who would not lose their soul but who would come to be at peace with the part of themselves that lives eternally.

October

When everything in life seems to be going wrong, when one feels an inner distress that nothing has the power to remove, when one finds little joy in living and faint desire to keep going, the way out of the maze of despair is "hope in God." In Colossians, Paul speaks of "the mystery that has been kept hidden for ages and generations" (1:26) and how God has revealed the answer to the deep needs of the human condition. And what is the answer? It is "Christ in you, the hope of glory" (1:27). Whenever we put our ultimate hope in ourselves, we shall always be disappointed. When we place our ultimate hope in Christ, we shall always be lifted up out of the mire of despair into the glorious light of His presence.

Are you in one of those times of feeling lost and alone; devoid of peace, and beaten down by life? Then turn your thoughts, your heart and your soul to Jesus Christ. Cry out with the Psalmist. Put your hope not in yourself but in your God. And behold how from your inner being, God will bring forth living waters springing up unto eternal life. Do not be cast down and disquieted O my soul, hope in God and praise Him in the peace of quiet joy!

Forgiveness

1 Have you ever thought about the significance of the word *forgiveness*? The word in Greek (*aphiemi*) means, among other things, to lay aside, to leave behind, to let go of. Forgiveness is required when someone has done something that is wrong. Nothing that is said or done can "undo" the wrong that is done; it is in the irretrievable past. The question then becomes, are we going to insist on letting the past continue its division into the present and into the future? Forgiveness does not mean one forgets what has been done; we do not have the power to will ourselves to forget. Forgiveness means that a person refuses to allow the wrong someone has done to continue poisoning and destroying the possibility of reconciliation.

No human being lives a life without sin and without mistakes. Do we desire for God to apply to us the same standard that we insist on imposing on others? Did not Jesus powerfully remind us of that each time we pray the Lord's Prayer? "Forgive me the trespasses I

October

commit in the same way that I forgive those who trespass against me." While we cannot forget the wrong done to us, we can refuse to let that wrong continue to make us bitter. Forgiveness is **not** a feeling; it is an act of the will. One may still feel a deep hurt at what has been done to him or her, but that does not mean that a person cannot choose to do good to the person who has done the wrong. Indeed, that is what forgiveness is all about. Jesus reminds us of this truth in the Sermon on the Mount when He enjoins us to love our enemies (Matthew 5:43-48).

"Easy for Jesus to say," you mutter! Really? I remind you of the scene on the cross where He said to those who were crucifying Him, "Father, forgive them for they know not what they do." What about Stephen, the first Christian martyr, who was being stoned to death? What words did he have for those who were ending his life? "Lord, do not hold this sin against them."

Husbands, wives, parents, children, siblings, friends; all make mistakes. When they do, we have a choice—we can either continue to remind them of their mistake at every opportunity, we can throw it in their face and emotionally bruise them all over again, or we can pray that God will give us the grace to become part of their healing, which becomes the very essence of our own healing. Unforgiveness perpetuates division; it never expedites healing! To forgive someone is not saying the wrong was insignificant, it is saying our desire to live in harmony is greater than our desire to live divided.

Now for the really bad news (you may not want to hear). When a Christian refuses to forgive the wrong that has been done to him or her, that person has rejected their own redemption. We who claim to follow Christ are entrusted with the message of reconciliation (II Corinthians 5:16-21), no matter who you are. It is not optional; it comes with one's Christian confession. Forgiveness is the bridge to restoration. Resentment and retaliation are weapons that bring about destruction. Jesus put it as succinctly as it can be put, "But if you refuse to forgive others, your Father will not forgive your sins." (Matthew 6:15, New Living Translation). One day we will face God and we will bring with us our mistakes. He will treat us as we have treated others. What will that be?

October

Soul Purging

2 Any Christian who has lived very long soon discovers that to follow Christ does not ensure that life is all joy and ease. There are those in every age who teach that to follow Jesus ensures divine protection, including healing, financial success, and peace and harmony among friends and family. Nothing could be farther from the truth! Such teaching is neither biblical nor true to life. Were any of those things true of the first disciples who followed Christ? Jesus was a realist and He never hid the cost of what it might cost us to follow Him. He said:

Do you think I came to bring peace on earth? No, I tell you, but division. From now on there will be five in one family divided against each other, three against two and two against three. They will be divided, father against son and son against father, mother against daughter and daughter against mother, mother-in-law against daughter-in-law and daughter-in-law against mother-in-law. (Luke 12:51-53)

Jesus was not divinely protected from His enemies, nor was He ever financially successful, nor was there very much harmony among his friends and family.

Almost five centuries ago, in Spain, there was a devout Christian man who came to be known as John of the Cross. He went through an experience that he called, "the dark night of the soul." Many people throughout the centuries have come to know a similar experience in their own spiritual pursuit. Because of John of the Cross' deep faith, he went through a horrible time of suffering. He was kidnapped, beaten, and crippled for life, and yet he refused to be swayed from his spiritual pursuit of God. He awoke spiritually one day to discover that it is in the dark nights of loneliness and solitude that God often spoke the most profoundly. His advice to those who came after him:

Turn your soul, I say, to walk toward God when all seems blackest and there is no light of His presence to be seen anywhere. Though this seems harsh at first, you will soon

October

understand how this journey through dryness and darkness is God's chosen way of purging your soul. (The Soul at Rest, p. 165)

The "darkness of life" comes to us in many forms. Sometimes it is in spiritual tiredness, sometimes in loneliness, sometimes in despair, often in sorrow. Perhaps dozens of ways could be listed. How we dread the darkness and seek to run from it as quickly as possible! But what profound lessons of living we learn in those moments that seem too deep for words; too dark for any light to penetrate. My friend, God created a world out of darkness (Gen. 1:2). Do you imagine for a moment that the darkness of your little world is too great for God to break through? Rather than scream and kick against the darkness why not settle down in quietness and trust and wait to hear what word God will speak?

There is no problem in life for which God does not have an answer! The secret is to let God give us His answer, not insist that He accept ours. No sunlight, no gloriously blue sky ever seemed more exhilarating than the one that follows the most terrible and darkest of storms. God never leaves us in darkness. He abides with us in it and He has never failed to send back the light. Are you in darkness now? Do not curse it; wait quietly for God to dismiss it! It just might be that there is something in our soul that needs purging: something that can only be banished in the darkness. When God's Spirit has made it pure, then we will once more walk in the light!

Fear and Love

3 Fear is an emotion that we have all experienced. Usually, we are afraid of the things that we believe have the power to harm us or someone we love. That can include many things (e.g., an intruder breaking into our home, sickness, falling, being left alone, starvation). We fear the things we feel powerless to control or understand. For many, the word "cancer" strikes terror in the heart. They hear the word and suddenly jump to the conclusion that they have been given a sentence of death. In reality the majority of people survive most types of cancer. But even if we don't, for the Christian,

October

there is no necessity for being imprisoned by an event (any event) which is in the future.

One need be terrified of death only if one doubts that life goes on beyond this one. If you believe this world is all that exists, you will either cling too tenaciously to life and fear too many things can bring it to an end, or you will become so weary with life that leaving it seems insignificant. On the other hand, if you believe that there is an eternal life and yours is securely in the hands of a loving, grace-filled God, then there is no need to be afraid. The key to overcoming fear is to place your trust in that which is greater than the thing you fear. Does cancer frighten you? What is greater than cancer? God! If cancer consumes your body, does it have the power to touch your soul? And into whose power is your soul entrusted? Cancer cannot touch your soul!

Fear may begin in the mind, but it takes up residence in the heart. Fear is possessive and reclusive; it desires no companions. Where fear is allowed to remain, it will destroy whatever it touches. Fear eats away at faith until it leaves behind a lifeless skeleton. It blocks both the giving and receiving of love, for even love is seen as an intrusive competitor. There is an answer to this problem in scripture. The verse is found in I John 4:18, (NKJV) "There is no fear in love, for perfect love casts out fear!" Who is perfect love? Only God! The heart that is filled with God's love cannot fear. The heart that is only partially filled with God's love cannot escape fear.

Saint Augustine, in writing his classic book, *The Confessions*, made a brilliant observation about his own condition. Prayerfully he said to God, "Narrow is the mansion of my soul; enlarge thou it, that Thou mayest enter in." (Book 1, Ch. 5, p. 20) He recognized both his need of God and the barrier that kept him from experiencing Him. God cannot infill any soul that will only partially open the door. Are we capable of enlarging the "room" of our soul? No, but God is! God cannot dwell in clutter and He will share His glory with no one.

It is essential that we realize what faith is and what it is not. Faith is not a willingness to follow God only if He will bless us, but a willingness to follow Him whether we are blessed or not. Faith does not grow if we are only willing to accept healing; it grows when we

October

are willing to accept not being healed. And what if we are not healed? Then we have the blessed assurance, by the Holy Spirit, that we are made perfectly whole in the presence of Him who was willing not to be spared in order to bring eternal healing to us.

Birth, Death, Birth

4 We are formed in the isolated darkness of our mother's womb. I do not know at what point in the nine-month process that the child begins to develop a consciousness of its environment. The temperature is the comfortable body temperature of its mother. Its oxygen supply is provided through its mother, as well as the food and nutrients needed not only to sustain life, but create life. Whatever sounds it hears are filtered through the layers of bone, muscle, tissues, and skin that separate it from the outside world There is no light and there is very little freedom of movement. Though it can move its tiny limbs and twist its body in different positions, it is confined to the limited watery world in which it rests. This is the world of a child in the making—a world which offers protection, comfort, and everything it needs in order to survive and grow. It is a world with which the baby grows comfortable, and in which, if able to choose, would be content to remain.

Strange characteristic about life—it cannot remain the same. While it is true that there is a routine to life, a sameness in many respects, it is not the same. Doctors even tell us the human body is constantly renewing itself to the point that every seven years we are basically a new person (I have a little trouble with that one when I look in the mirror, for the face I see looking back doesn't look very new to me!). As we grow into maturity we establish thought processes and routines with which we grow comfortable. We soon learn how to find and secure the things we need to sustain life. Now our world is filled with approximately half darkness and half light. The dark part we generally sleep through, the light part we primarily are active in.

One of the things that is different from the first world we encountered (the womb) is that we have the freedom of movement and we have association with other beings that we can engage through communication. Our senses become fine-tuned, and our world is now

October

comprised of taste, smell, sound, sight, and feeling. Interaction and learning from others teaches us about the reality of good and evil, love and hate, joy and sorrow—thus our world is greatly broadened. Most of us love our world and grow quite satisfied with it; so much so that we would struggle and fight to remain in it. But remember, the one thing that is always true of life is—change. And so the day comes that the body in which we dwell is no longer able to sustain what we call life, and we are confronted with that which we know as death.

The child in the womb, on the day it is to "be born," if it had an intellectual consciousness of the process that was taking place, would probably consider it death. The world as it knew it was coming to an end. Everything that it valued, in terms of its surroundings, was being violently pushed aside by contracting muscles, forcing it into a world about which it knew nothing. Perhaps part of the pain of childbirth is the resistance of the child to leave the world it knows inside the womb. Likewise, maybe part of the pain of dying is a reluctance to leave the world we know outside the womb. Just as I wouldn't want to live forever in my mother's womb, neither do I want to live forever in this world's womb. Death is birth—birth to a new world where there is no more darkness. Knowing that, I think I shall resist dying less as that day comes. If dying means we are being re-born, the first experience taught me that it will be gain.

Inner Sanctuary

5 Wouldn't it be nice if God would speak to us audibly with a majestic voice that drowns out the noise of our world? Imagine walking down a sidewalk somewhere and stopping dead in your tracks as you hear the voice of God giving precise and undeniable direction. Or wouldn't it be wonderful if He'd just plop down an angel in front of us with a special message just for us? Unfortunately (or, fortunately) that's not how God chooses to communicate with us. It would seem that for the most part, God reveals Himself only to those who faithfully and persistently seek Him in the unexpected places. He whispers to the soul amidst the soft gentle breezes, and rides with power and might upon the lightning and thunder! Nonsense, you argue, those are just acts of nature that have nothing to do with God's presence. But is it?

October

For most of the years of my ministry, I have been captivated by the passage of scripture that says, "Let us make humankind in our image . . . So God created humankind in His image, in the image of God He created them; male and female He created them." (Genesis 1:26-27, NRSV). Whatever else that passage may mean, I'm convinced it does not mean that He created us physically to look like Himself. God created a being that not only shared the reality of being "alive" but had down within that aliveness a living soul, a spirit that transcends the physical world. There is a sanctuary within each of us where the holy can make itself known. It cannot be located with surgery or a microscope, for it is birthed in the womb of faith. Faith is intangible; it cannot be held, it cannot be seen with the eye, except as it clothes itself with the flesh of love and grace revealed in deeds of obedience and kindness.

Thomas R. Kelly once wrote,

> *Deep within us all there is an amazing inner sanctuary of the soul, a holy place, a Divine Center, a speaking Voice, to which we may continuously return. Eternity is at our hearts, pressing upon our time-torn lives. Warming us with intimations of an astounding destiny, calling us home unto Itself. Yielding to these persuasions, gladly committing ourselves in body and soul, utterly and completely, to the Light Within, is the beginning of true life.* (A Testament of Devotion, p. 29)

God is clothed in mystery and no human mind can confine Him to the boundaries of mortal understanding. For those who are too lazy or indifferent to seek God in the quiet tranquility of prayerful meditation, it is extremely unlikely that they will ever encounter Him in the noise of daily living.

Perhaps part of the curse of living so fully in the physical world is that we are so enthralled with what is tangible that we feel no need to seek and experience the intangible. Everything that is tangible will pass away, just as our bodies will one day return to dust. But the things that are eternal cannot be measured or discerned, apart from yielding to the hungering spirit within us. God is even now speaking to you out of your inner being. Can you not hear His voice within

October

yourself, saying, "Come aside and learn of me"? God can be discovered, but only as you are willing to look within. Our role is to come aside and listen. God's role is to honor us in the place of our chosen quietness, with the glory of Himself. He waits to meet you there!

God's Gift of Yourself

6 Do you like yourself? When you are alone with just yourself, do you like the person you are? I know that there is always room for improvement in each of us, but are you satisfied with the basic person you have become? Peel away the layers, the image the world sees, and get down to the core of who and what you are. Do you see kindness inside, or compassion, or the desire to be loving? If you had to live in a house for ten years with a person exactly like yourself, how would that make you feel? There is within each of us the potential for both good and evil. Even the most saintly person has within him or her the capability of doing something that is harmful. But God has placed within each of us the hidden capacity for more goodness than we can imagine.

Do you like the part of yourself that desires to do good? Then why not work to develop that part? It's sort of like Rev. John Ed Mathison (the pastor of Frazer Memorial United Methodist Church in Birmingham, Alabama) says about churches: *we should spend our time working on the church's strengths and not its weaknesses.* At first that seems wrong; but think about it: the more time we spend on increasing our positive traits, the less time our negative ones will have to lead us the wrong way.

In his book, *The Light Within You,* John Claypool writes:

> *In my judgment, there is no issue of any greater practical significance than this issue of self-image. How do you view the gift of God that is yourself? All depends on your response. To accept yourself positively and live creatively on the basis of what God has made you is the way to joy, but to deny and reject God's gift of yourself is the way to ruin.* (p. 41)

October

Loving parents would not despise their own child, no matter what the child has done or not done. I think that sometimes the parent values the child more than the child values himself. God is like that with us. We've heard it stated in many different ways, but it is nonetheless true: God did not die for "good" people, God in Christ died for sinners. If God can look at us and see a person of such deep worth that He was willing to surrender His life for our sake, why should we despise ourselves? If we as human parents are willing and able to accept the faults in our children and love them in spite of their faults, why do we find it difficult to believe that God does the same for us?

We are the creation of God. No, God does not make us do evil, He does not create in us a desire to sin; but God did give us life. Life, even our life, has value because God does not create anything that has no value. You are God's gift to yourself. And yet each of us is in a constant state of becoming. We are not what we were yesterday, and we are not what we will be tomorrow. No matter what we are or how far we have come, God loves us in spite of ourselves. I think Claypool was right, we will find joy in living when we find peace within ourselves, with ourselves. How about you? Do you like the basic person you are? If not, then just remember that God hasn't given up on you. So why should you?

Quiet Time

7 Have you discovered the reality of God's presence yet? I'm not talking about learning information about God, I mean have you ever felt God's presence? Knowledge of God is not limited to the intellect: He can be felt with the heart and soul. I think that one of the major reasons that many people do not experience God is the absence of quiet time alone with Him. The Psalmist writes: "Be still and know that I am God!' (Ps. 46:10). Isaiah the prophet wrote: "In returning and in rest you shall be saved; in quietness and in trust shall be your strength." (Isaiah 30:15, NRSV) **There is no substitute for quiet time seeking God!**

Because we live in a rush-about world, a world in which we have become acclimated to the "instant-everything" we think God can

October

be squeezed in whenever we have a free moment. We have microwaves to speed up our cooking, fast food restaurants when we don't have time to cook or eat a leisurely meal in a nice restaurant, instant grits, rice, coffee, and a thousand other "instants". We are provided with ATM machines to do our banking, we have remote controls to change TV stations with the push of a button, and countless other means and devices to make our world go faster.

God will not be speeded-up, nor will He allow Himself to be assigned only to a "free moment." He created time: He is not subject to it! He does not see us by appointment at our convenience, nor is He content to deal with us on the periphery of our lives. Listen again to His words to us from the Psalm, "Be still, and know that I am God!" Are you still? Have you slowed down enough to wait upon His presence? We must learn the discipline of slowing down; even slowing down our wandering thoughts so that they may be still in His presence. Have you ever noticed how, when you are sick or in the hospital, you suddenly have time that you could never find before? We think we are indispensable and we have deceived ourselves into thinking that the world will skip a beat unless we are "doing our thing." But the truth is it hardly notices when we are absent or no longer alive.

Oftentimes, when a basketball or football team is not doing well, the coach will spend practice time going back over "the basics". That means refocusing on the fundamentals of the game. The fundamentals are the foundation blocks upon which everything else depends. God is the foundation of our life. If we aren't securely built upon that foundation then life is lived in chaos. I don't know whether it is ignorance, indifference, self-absorption, or just plain stubbornness that makes us so neglectful of God, but regardless, it always ends with the same conclusion—unhappy, unfulfilled, and frantic lives. If ever there was a time in human history in which human beings are constantly in motion, it is now. Our spirit will not find nurture or growth in busyness and haste.

Spiritual strength is found in quiet rest. As our bodies are resting our soul is also being renewed—if we seek God in those moments. Moses discovered God in the burning bush; but only when He took time to come aside to see. We will discover God when we

October

come aside from the demands of living in a hurry-up world and seek Him in the quiet places of life. When was the last time you fellowshipped with God? When was the last time you came apart for quiet time? Does that tell you anything?

Unbendable Truth

8 People commit their lives to something, whether they realize it or not. Some people devote their lives to their work, others to their possessions, some to their family, still others to the pursuit of some elusive dream. Contrary to the opinion of some, I do not think all truth is relative. There are many religions and there is some truth in all of them, but not all that is in them is truth. Jesus said, "I am the way, the truth, and the life." He did not say, "I know something about what is true: I have discovered part of the truth". He made the outrageous statement—"I AM the truth!" Now we are left with a choice—either we can believe what He said, or we can refuse to believe it. If He is not the TRUTH then we are better off disbelieving Him. On the other hand, if it turns out He is Truth and we refuse to believe it—how great is our loss!

If a person takes the time to read the words of Jesus carefully (and there really aren't all that many of them), he or she will be astonished; for as the multitudes who heard Him speak said, "No other man ever spoke like this!" There is a power, an authority, a ring of "divine knowing" that flows from Jesus' words. He never wasted words; His sayings and stories were always brief and to the point—and a powerful point it usually was! Jesus did not play games with people: He did not argue philosophy, He simply laid the truth out there and you either liked it or you didn't; accepted it or rejected it. He said in the Gospel of John, "I have come that they may have life, and that they may have it more abundantly" (10:10, NRSV). Why would He say that? Weren't people already in possession of life? Ask yourself the question, "Apart from Jesus, is my life abundant?"

It seems that Jesus' words and the world's values are almost always in conflict. The sad reality is that we live more by the world's values than we do by His words. Is your heart at peace, or do many things keep it anxious? Jesus said, "Peace I leave with you, My peace

October

I give to you; not as the world gives do I give to you. Let not your heart be troubled, neither let it be afraid" (John 14:27). He prayed to the Father, in the 17th chapter of John, that we who believe in Him would have His joy fulfilled in themselves (17:13). He went on to ask the Father to "sanctify [make pure and holy] them by Your truth. Your word is truth." He asked the Father to make us one with Him and one with the Father and He asked that we be allowed to be with Him where He is and to behold His glory. These are not the words, the requests of a delusional self-absorbed philosopher. These words have a unique truthful sound to them.

"So what's the point?" you say. The point is: what have you built, or are you going to build, your life upon—the words of Jesus or the world's opinions? Remember, Jesus wants no part-time disciples. He has no desire for partial commitment, nor "sunshine followers." Grace that is amazing cannot be diluted. It either cleanses all of your soul or cleanses not at all. Our Lord said, "No one, having put his hand to the plow, and looking back, is fit for the kingdom of God" (Luke 9:62). Jesus does not give guidelines, suggestions, or possibilities for following Him. He demands all of you—heart, mind, and soul. We can't walk part of the way with Him to the cross—we must go all the way. Tough words, but He said them, not me! Tomorrow's meditation will offer a partial list of some of Jesus' "non-negotiable" truths.

Non-negotiable Truths

9 Yesterday I concluded the devotion by saying that I would follow-up with a partial list of some of the "non-negotiable" truths that Jesus taught. By non-negotiable I mean they aren't open for compromise. A person either accepts them in their entirety as truth or simply rejects the truth. Jesus made these proclamations and I invite you to embrace them by faith, as complete truth:

- Anyone who loves his father or mother more than me is not worthy of me; anyone who loves his son or daughter more than me is not worthy of me; and anyone who does not take his cross and follow me is not worthy of me (Matthew 10:37-38).

October

- No one can serve two masters . . . You cannot serve both God and Money (Matthew 6:24).
- If you do not forgive others, neither will your Father forgive your trespasses (Matthew. 6: 15).
- Whoever wants to save his life will lose it, but whoever loses his life for me will find it. (Matthew 16:25).
- Everyone who has left houses or brothers or sisters or father or mother or children or fields for my sake will receive a hundred times as much and will inherit eternal life (Matthew 19:29).
- Heaven and earth will pass away, but my words will never pass away (Matthew 24:35).
- I tell you the truth, no one can see the kingdom of God unless he is born again (John 3:3).
- I tell you the truth, whoever hears my word and believes him who sent me has eternal life and will not be condemned; he has crossed over from death to life (John 5:24).
- I tell you the truth . . . before Abraham was born, I am! (John 8:58).
- I am the resurrection and the life. He who believes in me will live, even though he dies; and whoever lives and believes in me will never die (John 11:25-26).
- A new command I give you: Love one another. As I have loved you, so you must love one another (John 13:34).
- I am the way and the truth and the life. No one comes to the Father except through me (John 14:6).

Listed above are only a small handful of the sayings of Jesus which are eternally true. Can I prove them to be true? No, I can only accept them as true by faith. If they aren't true, then Jesus really isn't who He says He is and He isn't worth following. But if they are true, you cannot detract from or diminish their truth by saying you don't believe them. If they are indeed true and we reject or ignore them, then we have thrown away our eternal future. Truth is truth! Either Jesus is the Son of God, the Savior of the world, or He is not. Whether we admit it or not, every human being on this earth will decide by the

October

way they live their life whether they affirm or reject these truths. Perhaps we should heed Jesus' words: "There is a judge for the one who rejects me and does not accept my words; that very word which I spoke will condemn him at the last day." (John 12:48).

Two Worlds

10 There are two worlds in which we live—the natural world around us with created beings and objects, and the world inside our minds. The natural world we have little control over; the inner world of our thoughts we can control to a large degree. No one is allowed to enter into our thoughts and read our minds (contrary to what the psychics claim). Sometimes our thoughts perceive and interpret the events of the natural world correctly; sometimes they do not. Each day we live we dwell in the midst of other human beings, none of whom have access to the secret world of our inner thoughts unless we choose to let them. But God does! He sees the good and noble thoughts but He is also aware of the dark and evil ones. It is in this inner world of existence that the great battles of our soul are fought.

No theologian (that I ever read) has ever been able to draw clear lines of distinction between the mind (consciousness) and the soul. In the inner world of our minds, our thoughts and feelings co-mingle until they seem as if they are one. We may go to bed one night feeling happy and fine and awake the next morning with some inexplicable feeling of doom. We can go from ecstasy to depression, often with little consciousness of how we arrived there. Modern thinkers have attempted to separate the human being into neat little pigeonholes such as, philosophy, psychology, and theology, as if we were capable of being so neatly compartmentalized. The reality is that unless one is mentally ill or incapacitated, there is an on-going battle being fought inside every human being. It is the battle between good and evil, truth and falsehood, the holy and the unholy, righteousness and sin, law and grace.

The Apostle Paul identifies this battle in the seventh chapter of Romans (7:13-25) when he describes it as the battle between the spiritual and the carnal. He further identifies the struggle in Ephesians

October

6:12 when he writes, "For our struggle is not against flesh and blood, but against the rulers, against the authorities, against the powers of this dark world and against the spiritual forces of evil in the heavenly realms." Paul is talking about spiritual warfare that goes on within each human being regardless of whether they consider themselves a "religious" person or not. One of the great weaknesses of many in the modern church is that they consider such thinking as archaic and outdated, and thus unwittingly surrender to spiritual oppression because it refuses to fight a spiritual battle it no longer believes exists.

We vainly imagine that an "enlightened" mind cannot accept the understanding of a first century man. The ancient sin of pride rises up within us, looks down its snooty nose at Paul, and sweeps his pronouncements into the dustbin of outdated thinking. In so doing we condemn ourselves to live in the darkness of self-deception and we stumble through life never grasping the significance of the war going on within us. It is in the inner being that God strives to reach us. It is there that we, like Jacob, wrestle with the angel; there, like Job, we try to make sense of our suffering; there, like Nicodemus, we hunger to discover the mystery of "being born again." My advice? We would all do well to spend a little more time with Paul and a lot less time with the wisdom of the world.

At the Heart of It All

11 There stands Jesus—the God-man: Divine being clothed in human flesh. He looks like us, but He is not like us. Blood flows through His veins like ours, refreshing the body with the power of life. Yet, life does not come _to_ Him, life comes _from_ Him—for He is life! We live in the post-Enlightenment era—the information age—in which we place such great value on knowledge; and yet, the mountain of our ignorance soars beyond sight. The more knowledge we think we possess, the less we think we need God. Well did the prophetic words of the Apostle Paul describe our generation: "always learning but never able to acknowledge the truth" (II Timothy 3:7). One would think that knowledge would naturally lead us to understand the mystery of God. The problem is that knowledge about God divorced from faith is inevitably distorted and perverted through the sinful pride of our humanity.

October

If it were possible to peel away the layers of Jesus' heart and arrive at the very center, I think we would discover love whose roots are grounded in forgiveness. The two are inextricably woven together; for in a world filled with sin, it is impossible to have one without the other—Jesus could not forgive apart from love, and love would not be love without forgiveness. The only thing that can possibly bridge the chasm between holiness and the sinful nature of humanity is forgiveness. Shortly after God created Adam, He created woman in order that the two of them might share companionship, fellowship with God, and perpetuate the human race. But where two humans exist there will always be the necessity of forgiveness; for inevitably, there will be conflict, difference of opinion, hurt feelings, and innumerable other divisive issues that can only be bridged and overcome by forgiveness.

What is forgiveness? It is the willingness of one person to accept the other person in spite of the wrong they have done. It is a conscious choice to place more value on the relationship rather than allowing the relationship to be severed. Can forgiveness heal every broken relationship? No, but unforgiveness will certainly ensure its death. Unforgiveness is the final blow that builds a wall so high nothing can penetrate it or climb over it—not even love. Forgiveness creates life, it renews, it resurrects, it heals, it embodies the true meaning of grace. If we are unwilling to forgive then let us not sing of *Amazing Grace* lest we sing with a forked tongue. How can we sing of God's grace when we stubbornly withhold our own? How can we claim to live in a relationship of grace with God when we choose to live in a divided relationship with other human beings?

Read the gospel stories of Jesus a thousand times, study them until the day you die, and still, you will always find that at their heart is forgiveness. The cross is the symbol of forgiveness; it denotes the intersection of two opposite poles. It is divine love coming down (vertically) and intersecting sinful humanity (horizontally). It is the crossroads of time in which holiness met sinfulness and through the sacrifice of itself built the bridge that leads to restoration. How can we accept such grace from God and withhold it from our brothers and sisters? How can we claim union with God and delight in divisiveness

October

with others? If we do, we delude ourselves; and in so doing dismantle the very bridge that allowed us to be in relationship to God.

The Gift of Comfort

12 Have you ever been comforted by another person in a time of trouble or crisis? Have there been times in which your heart felt desolate and afraid, and out of the blue, someone showed up unexpectedly and by their words or presence calmed the storm raging within you? Was it coincidence? Or is it possible that God's sovereign power works in ways that supersede our ability to discern His presence? There are spiritual gifts, and those gifts vary from person to person. There is the gift of compassion—although everyone is capable of feeling and expressing compassion, it seems that God gives a special gift to certain people. They always seem to know just what to say, or not to say, and by their very presence touch lives in ways others cannot.

Sometimes people learn compassion from the things they suffer. While I do not believe that God causes suffering, I do believe that God transforms our suffering into opportunities to help others. Look how many lives have been touched and helped through the suffering of Joni Erickson-Tada. She became a quadriplegic as a result of a diving accident. Rather than become bitter and wallow in self-pity, she chose to use her life for the glory of God and the benefit of others. Clutching a paint brush between her teeth, she paints beautiful pictures, signing each one with the letters PTL (Praise the Lord!). God wastes nothing about our lives—not even our pain or sickness.

There is a passage of scripture that is relevant to what I am saying: "[God] comforts us in all our troubles, so that we can comfort those in any trouble with the comfort we ourselves have received from God" (II Corinthians 1:4). If we are willing, our own experience of suffering will often open the doorway into the life of someone who is suffering a similar affliction. Those who are experiencing all the anguish that comes with cancer will take more seriously the words of someone who has also suffered from the disease. Support groups are effective precisely because it is the shared bond of experience that creates a legitimacy to the comfort that people seek to offer. The person experiencing the trauma of divorce can be greatly helped and comforted by the reassurance of those who have passed through that dark night themselves.

It is with good reason that Jesus referred to the Holy Spirit as the Comforter. To comfort in a godly way means more than to speak words of sympathy, to feel pity for someone, or to simply do a kind deed for one who is suffering. It means to be bonded to that person with the mystical bond of God's grace. When we embrace those who are suffering, when we cry with them, and hurt with them, we are comforting in the way that God comforts. To comfort in the biblical sense means to strengthen and fortify. In some strange way, suffering that is shared is suffering that is somehow lessened. Isaiah said of Jesus, "Surely he has borne our griefs and carried our sorrows . . ." God suffered for and with the world. Those who follow Christ are called to share in the sufferings of others by becoming for them a source of comfort. If you aren't suffering now, then comfort someone who is. If you are suffering, then let God comfort you through someone else.

A Closer Look at Love

13 Love, when it is purest, will pass through the land called humiliation without so much as a thought for itself. Love has been written about, sung about, and shouted about—perhaps because it is the most noble of all expressions. When it comes forth in purity, it stops the mind in its tracks. It descends into our innermost being and touches us with emotion that, before its arrival, we never knew we could feel. Love is at its best when it gives up itself for another. Recently, during one of my morning devotions, I read of an example of love that was simple yet powerfully moving. It was written by Karen Barber who described a touching moment in her life that she shared with her mother, who had suffered a stroke. She wrote:

> *Perhaps it wasn't so, but I couldn't help thinking people were staring as I wheeled my mother into the crowded fast-food restaurant after church that Sunday. It was Mom's first outing since she had been released from the rehabilitation hospital following a serious stroke. She was slumped in her wheelchair, her hands quivered, and a black patch covered her*

October

drooping eye. To cover my embarrassment, I busied myself settling Mom at the table while Dad ordered.

In the wheelchair bag I found a nice purple-checked bib with lace edging that Aunt Josie had made. As I tied it on Mom, I sighed. Even the lace couldn't disguise the fact that the bib was as big as a bath towel, big enough to cover Mom's torso and fold down into her lap to catch the large amounts of food she spilled.

Dad came over with a tray of food, sat down and quietly said the blessing. Then he rummaged through the wheelchair bag and got out a second bib. This one was a faded, ratty-looking terry cloth affair, with just a hint of blue left from the constant washing at the rehab hospital. Dad draped the bib over his suit, vest and tie, tied it around his neck, and then took a bite of his hamburger.

My tense shoulders relaxed at once. In a busy fast-food restaurant full of onlookers, my father had just shown me that the best cure for self-consciousness is a self-forgetful act of love. (2001 Daily Guideposts, p. 202-3)

Sometimes I wonder if I really know how to love. Perhaps we never know what love truly is until we willingly do something for another that costs us something of ourselves. Surely, the small things we do for others that really cost us nothing shouldn't be filed under the heading "Love." Maybe love begins to blossom when we refuse to strike back, refuse to curse when cursed, and refuse to keep lists of wrongs. Perchance love is born when we actually, by the act of our will, choose to suffer humiliation rather than to humiliate another; or don't allow them to suffer humiliation alone. Seems to me that is a lesson we can learn at the foot of the cross—the place where a half-naked man, horribly beaten, completely deserted, and unjustly crucified said to each of us, "I love you this much!"

At the Center

14 There is a center inside each of us from which everything about us that is observed outwardly ascends. By the time we are grown the center has formed; what we have become is

October

now directed and influenced by what the center has become. In every human being there is a mixture of good and bad. It is here, at the center, that the war is fought for the soul; for it is from within that both sin and the desire for salvation engage in battle. Jesus called this center the "heart." He said, "Don't you see that nothing that enters a man from the outside can make him 'unclean'? For it doesn't go into his heart but into his stomach, and then out of his body." (In saying this, Jesus declared all foods clean—spiritually speaking). He went on: "What comes out of a man is what makes him 'unclean.' For from within, out of men's hearts, come evil thoughts, sexual immorality, theft, murder, adultery, greed, malice, deceit, lewdness, envy, slander, arrogance and folly. All these evils come from inside and make a man 'unclean'" (Mark 7:18-23). "Heart" was not, of course, a reference to the muscle in our chest that pumps blood, but that inner place from which emanates the force that causes us to do the things we do—both good and evil.

It is not the mind that is the sole cause of our going astray—Jesus just told us that it is from the heart that evil thoughts come. Yet, if we put garbage into our mind, if we poison it with thoughts which of themselves contain evil, they will work their way down into this center and begin to transform us into what we "center" on. The apostle Paul said to the Christians at Rome, "Do not conform any longer to the pattern of this world, but be transformed by the renewing of your mind" (Romans 12:2). He exhorts the Christians in Philippi to fill their minds with virtuous thoughts (Philippians 4:8). We cannot plant briars in the soil and expect fruit trees to come forth.

Doctors say that cancer begins with one cell—one cell that has gone terribly wrong and begins to reproduce itself in rapid succession. Eventually it begins to overpower the good cells around it, and if left unchecked, will continue to grow until it consumes all the life out of the body in which it dwells. My doctor told me that the massive tumor that he removed from my body was consuming 75% of the nutrients that went into my body. Similarly, sin left unbridled in the human spirit will consume the person and drain all spiritual life out of him or her. Like most cancers, it grows quietly and unnoticed beneath the surface, until finally it becomes in such total control that it reveals itself. An evil deed erupts, uncontrollable anger bursts forth; harsh,

October

cutting words fly like razor-sharp swords through the air, making slashing wounds in the heart and soul of another. Now we see sin in all of its dark ugliness, and we are horrified that it emanated from within us.

Sin is a monster. It not only consumes the one out of whom it comes, it wreaks havoc on the lives it touches. How can we battle such a powerful enemy? Through faith in Christ! Sin crucified God's Son; but grace absorbed sin and destroyed it within itself. The kingdom Jesus came to establish was lordship over the human heart. He alone has the power to defeat the enemy within each of us. He alone can find His way to our center and cleanse that which seems uncleansable. How does your "center" look? Who is its master? It will have a master—either it will be Jesus or it will be the opposite of all that Jesus is. We each make our own choice!

The Hiding Place

15 There is a world where no one can go but us. It is the world of our inner self. We go there many times during a day and no one ever knows we slipped away, because to them we are still physically present. Sometimes we go there to make decisions, to talk to God, or to get in touch with ourselves. But even there it is often difficult to be totally honest, not because we wish to be intentionally deceitful, but because, the truth be known, it is not always easy to accurately know our own feelings and motivations. There are times we retreat to our secret hiding place because we are hurt and we go there to deal with the pain. Inner emotional pain can be just as devastating to one's life as physical pain, for it attacks us at the core of who we are. It has the power to acutely debilitate us just as having one's arm or leg severed from one's body limits us.

Emotional health and stability are as important to one's being as the very skeletal network of bones that support our muscles, organs and skin. Imagine trying to function physically in life with no bones! When one's emotions have been severely damaged, when one has been literally beaten down through abusive words and cruel acts of unkindness, then one is literally fighting for one's life, even though the wounds may not show on the outside. As a child growing up I

October

occasionally was the recipient of punishment from my father in the form of a few lashes from his belt. This was administered when he thought my behavior was inappropriate enough to merit it. For a few brief moments the sting of the belt caused pain, but soon passed. The emotional pain lingered a little longer. And yet the inner pain caused by angry words, words that sometimes made me question my self-worth, left scars that took years to heal, and to some degree still haven't completely healed. I have no doubt my father loved me, and he was not an unkind man: quite the contrary, in most respects he was loving and gentle. But those moments of weakness in him had a devastating impact on my tender inner being that no one was allowed to see.

When children are hurt or frightened they look for a place of safety to which they can retreat; a place where they feel secure and protected from whatever it is that either hurt them or has the potential to hurt them. But just as we look for a physical place in which to hide, so we learn early on that we can find an inner hiding place where we can go and hurt until the pain goes away—or at least diminishes. Here, in our inner sanctuary, we discover that we are free to lash out at the one who hurt us without feeling their retaliation. Here we can unleash words and thoughts that we would never utter in their physical presence. Here we can let the inner child cry without fear of being told to "Dry it up!"

God gave us our inner world. It is a place where not only we can go, but where (wonder of wonders) He can come along. Here we don't need to speak to an imaginary friend for we can converse with the One who created our inner being. We need not be afraid, we need not restrain our feelings, for He will always understand us. It is in being honest with God about our feelings that healing is allowed to ultimately come. It is also the place where we learn how to forgive. Perhaps in the security of our hiding place, the place where forgiveness is allowed to be born, the road to healing can begin.

In Search of the Holy

16 The Christian faith has been shaped and honed over the centuries in an attempt to make the church more like the world rather than to make the world more like the church.

October

There was a time that the words of Christ and the apostles who spread the Christian message after His death and ascension were what shaped the church.   A. W. Tozer once said, "The curse of the modern Christian leadership is the pattern of looking around and taking our spiritual bearing from what we see, rather than what the Lord has said" (*A. W. Tozer: An Anthology*, p. 120). Time was, the preacher would study God's Word and proclaim what it said as the means of shaping the church. Now preachers try to figure out what modern folks want to hear and scour the Bible in an attempt to find some pleasing passage that will send them out the church door feeling good.

There is nothing wrong with people leaving the church feeling good as long as the preacher and the congregation have yielded themselves to hearing and proclaiming what it is that the Holy Spirit has to say to the people. When one studies the heroes and heroines of the faith, you won't find extraordinary people content to do ordinary things, but ordinary people inspired by the Spirit to do extraordinary things. The reason they were able to do it is because they surrendered themselves to the leading of a Power that was greater than themselves. The Hebrew people looked at Goliath and saw an unconquerable giant; David looked at Goliath and saw a target he just couldn't miss! Peter, Paul, and the early apostles gazed out at a pagan world firmly in the grasp of a tyrannical government centered in Rome and saw a harvest of souls just waiting to enter a spiritual kingdom.

God has placed within the human heart a hunger for Himself. Unfortunately, we have become so worldly that we mistake that hunger for everything but God. Too many modern Christians have lost the desire (if they ever had it) for the holy. The medium of television with its multi-million dollar religious productions has made worship more about entertainment than about worshiping God. Worship services have modeled themselves after rock concerts. Preachers prance around on stages yelling and screaming cheered on by audiences that find their behavior delightfully entertaining. Others have healing ministries in which desperate and distraught people come to them hoping for a miracle and have to endure shouting and the literal slapping of hands on their heads or forceful arms pushing them to the floor. Can you imagine Jesus screaming at his listeners, or slapping them on the forehead as He yelled to the top of His voice,

October

"Be healed!" Do modern healers think all people are deaf, or that God is so far away one has to shout?

Surely there is a place and a purpose in worship where honest Spirit-led emotion is appropriate and desired. But for goodness sake, let it be emotion that is Holy Spirit-inspired and not humanly manipulated. We need to look to God for direction in worship and in Christian living and not use worldly models as prototypes. It was not in the loud fury of earthquake or whirlwind that Elijah communed with God, but in the holiness of the still small voice. There are times when God may shout; but more often than not, He speaks with a soft, gentle holy whisper.

A Different Perspective

17 Strange how one's understanding of something is radically shaped by the perspective from which one is viewing it.

From an airplane gliding at a thousand feet, an elephant seems rather small and insignificant. However, if you happen to be on the ground directly in its path as it charges toward you in a violent rage, you will experience an urgency and a fear that no one could make you fully comprehend by describing it to you with words. Everything in life has something to teach us. Some things we are willing to accept, other things we have no time or use for. One thing almost everyone desires to avoid is anything that can cause the slightest pain. Yet oftentimes we learn lessons through pain that we can learn no other way.

It is human nature to become blasé and unappreciative of the familiar, to view it with the eyes of disinterest and to lose the urgency to explore it. Perhaps that is why so many couples who are married no longer find excitement and value in a relationship that began at an altar with the anticipation of experiencing the intimate joy of another's aliveness. Part of the allurement in relationships is in the discovery of who the person is. Some discover that once that "aliveness" has been experienced, it no longer holds the magnetic fascination it once held. How unnecessarily tragic! One can no more fully comprehend the intricacies of a human life than one can grasp the beauty and depth of the sparkling starlight on a cool autumn night. We can focus on the negative in others and thus distort our perception of who they really

October

are; we can also only concentrate on the qualities in them that we find appealing and thus create an image of them in our mind that is always partial, making them appear to be more than who they really are.

Kahlil Gibran profoundly observed: "When you part from your friend, you grieve not: For that which you love most in him may be clearer in his absence, as the mountain to the climber is clearer from the plain" (*The Prophet*, p. 50). Perspective makes the difference! A person may lose sight of the value of another's life simply by allowing familiarity to dull one's senses. The answer to the dilemma is not in finding that which is new and unexplored in another, but in seeking a new perspective of the person that once drew us with fascination. Sometimes that perspective is created from the peak of pain, sometimes from the pain of being knocked down with illness. Sometimes it comes when the circumstances of life force separation; but come it will, if one is willing to simply observe.

Crippling familiarity has the power to affect anything—marital relationships, family relationships, business relationships, friendships, and yes, even our relationship with God. When we demand that life be experienced only on the level of the familiar then we have built a wall that separates us from the excitement of new discoveries. Children are excited and carefree because they have not yet built walls that shut out or limit the horizons of their world. They don't think they have explored everything or even fully know a person, so they get up each day with unbridled anticipation and excitement. Has life grown mundane for you? Has your relationship with someone you love become dull? Then try viewing them from a different perspective.

In Search of a Savior

18 No one will ever come to know God by simply using the mind alone. That would be like an alien trying to understand a human being by only studying the hand. One of the geniuses of John Wesley and other leaders in the early days of Methodism was the ability to join together the heart, spirit, and mind in the search to know and proclaim God. The Bible tells us that "God is spirit, and his worshipers must worship in spirit and in truth" (John 4:24). Truth may be comprehended with the mind,

October

but it is experienced in the spirit and sealed in the heart. Jesus did not come into this world just to tell us a few things that are true, but to reveal to us from where truth comes. The scriptures tell us that people were constantly "astonished" at His teaching because He spoke not as the scribes and Pharisees, but as one with authority.

Would you trust an automobile mechanic to fix your television? Would you go to an airplane pilot to fix your sore tooth? No, you would put your trust in the person whom you felt was qualified to understand and fix the problem. We are all in need of a Savior. To whom do you go? E. Stanley Jones writes, "The philosophers may enlighten me, the moralists may instruct me, the prophets may inspire me, but my need is deeper. I need a Savior. For I am deeply hurt—sin hurt" (*The Christ of Every Road*, p. 80). Human beings face many problems in life and encounter many issues—none more important, none more bewildering than the sickness of sin. How tragic that so many have not yet realized that at the heart of the human dilemma is the issue of sin. There is only one Person who can solve the problem of sin—His name is Jesus!

Truth does not originate from a concept; it comes from a single source—the Source is the One who holds the power of life. Truth is what He declares it to be because He is its Creator. Every truth we discover or uncover is a truth that already existed before humanity discovered it. Sir Isaac Newton may have pondered the reality of gravity and proposed in words the concept of gravity, but God created the reality of it. Columbus may have discovered America, but the continent existed before man ever set foot on it. There is an answer to every question, but there is only one source for that answer. Only one man that I have ever heard of claimed to "be" life, truth, love, and resurrection. Jesus did not tell us about life, He revealed that life was in Him. He did not teach us about truth, He claimed to be its source. He did not try to explain the reality of love, He manifested what love is. He did not inform us that there could be a resurrection, He said, "I am the Resurrection!"

Have you encountered Jesus yet? Dr. Jones wrote: "There was something about the Man that made the best of men feel that they were in deepest need. And yet the worst of men felt drawn to Him"

October

(p. 62). Imagine, the unholy being drawn to the holy; and rather than being consumed by it, the unholy becomes transformed by that which is eternally holy. Jesus' hands were for healing and when those hands were nailed to a cross, they became the means whereby the human soul was made whole. That's my Savior! Is He yours?

Spiritual Hunger

19 When the time between meals has stretched beyond its normal length we begin to feel the pangs of hunger. Sometimes it begins with gentle rumblings in our stomach—perhaps we call them growls because they sound strangely like the sounds a dog makes when you try to take its food away! An emptiness begins to rise from our stomach up through our esophagus to the back of our throat and we begin to become acutely conscious of a nagging desire to satisfy that feeling with food. The hungrier we become the more our minds dwell on the subject of food until we can hardly think of anything else. Finally, we give in, locate some food and fill our stomachs. In a matter of minutes the hunger has gone.

Have you ever realized that you also have moments of spiritual hunger? It has nothing to do with the emptiness of your stomach, but the emptiness in your soul. Your heart feels as if there is a void within it, and there is a longing deep down inside for something which you do not have. How else can you account for those unique moments when your thoughts return again and again to the significance of your life and you wonder if there is an eternity? You ponder, "If there is an eternity, where will I spend it?" A spiritual "rumbling" begins to occur and you are conscious of a deep need within. What do you do? Stifle the desire, or turn aside as did Moses, to inquire about the nature of the burning bush that was not consumed?

No one will ever be able to stand in the presence of God and truthfully say, "God never beckoned me to come and know Him." He beckons in a hundred different ways—we just choose to ignore the call. There are such things as spiritual disciplines that can enhance one's spiritual life. But alas, the very word *discipline* drives many away before they even begin. To discipline one's self is never easy, but why

October

do we always want what is easy? Most of us avoid physical exercise as if it were the plague, and then wonder why our bodies don't look firm and trim like those who *discipline* themselves to improve how they look and feel. This is no less true regarding a strong spiritual body. To ignore our spiritual need is to ensure that we will remain spiritual infants that are always anemic.

If you are interested in growing toward spiritual maturity, and are looking for a good book to get you started, you can't do better than Richard Foster's book, *The Celebration of Discipline*. Another excellent book is by Dallas Willard entitled *The Spirit of Disciplines*. One of the significant things that will happen to you when you become serious about your spiritual life is that you will become conscious of the holy. The holy doesn't turn you on? Then heed the words of Elisabeth Elliot (*Discipline—the Glad Surrender*), "Holiness has never been the driving force of the majority. It is however, mandatory for anyone who wants to enter the kingdom." Better still, ponder the words of St. Paul, "This is the will of God, that you should be holy: you must abstain from fornication; each one of you must learn to gain mastery over his body, to hallow and honor it… For God called us to holiness, not impurity" (I Thessalonians 4:3-4, 7). When the hunger pangs of the spirit come again, don't ignore them. Get up and seek to meet their need!

Spiritual Laziness

20 There is for clergy and laity alike the ever-present temptation to grow complacent about serving and worshiping God. It is easy to fall into the trap of doing nothing, or no more than "busy work" at the expense of the truth and power of the gospel. Some Christians are content to do as little for God as they can get by with. For them no task is too small to be perceived as a heavy burden. Not only is it disappointing, but also discouraging, when people join churches but refuse to "join forces" with those who are busy about our Father's business. Recently, I ran across the following prayer written by A. W. Tozer, on the occasion of his ordination as a minister. He entitled it *The Prayer of a Minor Prophet.* Every preacher should pray it, but perhaps the laity should as well.

October

> *Lord Jesus, I come to thee for spiritual preparation. Lay Thy hand upon me. Anoint me with the oil of the New Testament prophet. Forbid that I should become a religious scribe and thus lose my prophetic calling. Save me from the curse that lies dark across the face of the modern clergy, the curse of compromise, of imitation, of professionalism. Save me from the error of judging a church by its size, its popularity or the amount of its yearly offering. Help me to remember that I am a prophet; not a promoter, not a religious manager—but a prophet. Let me never become a slave to crowds. Heal my soul from carnal ambitions and deliver me from the itch of publicity. Save me from bondage to things. Let me not waste my days puttering around the house. Lay Thy terror upon me, O God, and drive me to the place of prayer where I may wrestle with principalities and powers and the rulers of the darkness of this world. Deliver me from overeating and late sleeping. Teach me self-discipline that I may be a good soldier of Jesus Christ.* (A. W. Tozer, an Anthology, p. XXI)

Little wonder that Jesus said, "small is the gate and narrow the road that leads to life, and only a few find it" (Matt. 7:14). Historians, looking back in time, assign names to certain eras (e.g., the Ice Age, the Iron Age, the Dark Ages, and the Middle Ages). Perhaps they will look back centuries from now and call our era the "Convenience Age." If it's convenient we consider doing it; if not, forget it! We live in a period of history in which we have more free time than any other generation, and very little of that time will we use for God. Americans are more "overweight" than any other nation in the world. Perhaps that applies as much to spirit as it does to body. We overindulge and under-exert (physically and spiritually)! Spiritual laziness will accomplish just about as much for our spirits as physical laziness does for our bodies. In the physical realm of existence, laziness brings on weakness, sickness, and early death. The old adage of "use it or lose it" comes to mind. Is that less true for spiritual health?

We may never be as committed to God's service as John Wesley when he said, "Leisure and I have taken leave of each other", but we ought to at least try to do more than we do. After all, it's our own spiritual health that's at stake.

October

Hope for the Broken-hearted

21

What breaks your heart? Perhaps life itself. You're lonely or you're unhappy and see no glimmer of hope. Someone has hurt you, deceived you, betrayed you. You want to forgive and get on with life but just haven't found the spiritual energy or desire to get past it. Maybe you sit and stare out the window, reminiscing about a happier time and you wonder how you got to where you are. The innocency of childhood seems a lifetime ago and there is a sad forlornness that permeates you as you wish that just for a day you could go back and bask in the glow of a carefree time in which life seemed so exciting and inviting. But the experience of life has taught you that there is no going back, no wiping clean the slate of your memory and beginning again. Your "gunnysack" of regrets and mistakes has overflowed and you bend beneath the weight of remorse.

Well, I have some good news for you in the midst of all that despair. It involves Jesus Christ and why He said that He came into the world. Listen as He preaches His first sermon in the synagogue in Nazareth and declares why He has appeared on the stage of history: "The Spirit of the Lord is upon me, because He has anointed me to preach the gospel to the poor; **He has sent me to heal the brokenhearted**, to preach deliverance to the captives and recovering of sight to the blind, **to set at liberty them that are bruised**, to preach the acceptable year of the Lord." (Luke 4:18-19, KJV) He said, "Today this scripture is fulfilled in your hearing." Can you dare believe that the verse above was meant for you? Yes, you can dare, because it was! Hear that verse again, as if it were being uttered for the first time, "**Today** this scripture is fulfilled in your hearing."

Let me tell you who the brokenhearted were in Jesus' day—it was a man born blind, a leper with no hope, a mother who had lost her daughter to death, a father who had lost his son, a harlot who found forgiveness, a tax-collector who was despised by his neighbors, Simon Peter who denied Him and went out and wept bitterly. It was Mary Magdalene, whose life was consumed by the demonic; it was His mother who watched Him die on a cross. It was ten disciples who fled and left Him alone to die; it was the ones to whom He said, "Whoever

October

will come unto me, I will in no wise cast out." Whatever has broken you, whatever is broken within you, Jesus Christ has the power and the will to make you whole!

Like children who bring their broken toys to their father to fix, let us bring our inner brokenness to our Lord and ask Him to heal and make us whole! Let us confess that we are not able to fix ourselves, not able to restore wholeness to our aching heart and our troubled soul. He who fashioned the heart and breathed life into the soul is capable and willing to fix it when it's shattered! Haven't you lived long enough in the prison of your thoughts and feelings? Go back and read the above passage again. Doesn't it say something about setting the captives free? Could it be that He had spiritual and emotional imprisonment in mind? Do you think that when Jesus ascended into heaven all that He came to do ended? No, my friend, that was just the beginning! He says to us, "I stand at the door [of your heart] and knock; if you will open the door I will come in. He whom the Son sets free is free indeed!"

The Prayer of Silence

22 Let's be honest! Really now, how much time do you set aside each day for God? Two minutes? Five? Maybe fifteen or thirty? None? No time for God? How much time do you set aside each day to read the paper? Thirty minutes? How much time each day do you devote to feeding your stomach? An hour or more? Now we come down to the nitty-gritty: how much time do you spend watching meaningless trivia on TV each day? Three hours? Six? Finding time for God and one's soul is really about setting priorities, isn't it? With whom do you expect to spend eternity? Do you imagine that God will be there? But why would you want to spend eternity with Someone who is unimportant to you now?

If you wait until you feel some powerful and dramatic inner urge, some undeniable moving of the Spirit within before you decide to seek God's presence, then the chances are slim to none that you will ever find Him. God isn't lost, we are! We first find God in the Scriptures; then we find Him in prayer! Henri Nouwen wrote:

October

> *Contemplative reading of the holy scriptures and silent time in the presence of God belong closely together. The word of God draws us into silence; silence makes us attentive to God's word." (Reaching Out: The Three Movements of the Spiritual Life, p. 136)*

I can remember when I was a child sitting in church, hearing the choir begin the worship service with powerful words that challenged the imagination of my juvenile mind: *The Lord is in His holy temple, let all the earth keep silence, before Him!* Have you learned the majesty of being silent in God's presence?

The church (the community of faith) that does not nourish itself with prayer is a community that will spiritually starve itself to death. Again quoting from Nouwen's book:

> *Sometimes it seems as if the Christian community is "so busy" with its projects and plans that there is neither the time nor the mood to pray. But when prayer is no longer its primary concern, and when its many activities are no longer seen and experienced as part of prayer itself, the community quickly degenerates into a club with a common cause but no common vocation.* (p. 148)

God has not called us to become a club; He has called us to be a holy people! Holy people have time for the One who is holy! Holy people engage in a holy vocation.

Have you ever discovered the hidden treasure of trying to be in prayer with God without bombarding Him with words? "How can you pray without words?" you ask. First, you find a quiet secluded place, a place away from noise and distractions. You begin with words; you invite God to be present, and you tell Him you just want to rest quietly in His presence. Then as best you can, try to clear your mind of conscious thoughts and simply allow yourself to "be" in the presence of the One who is Holy. "Ah," you say, "I'll just drop off in sleep!" So what? Is God not present when you sleep? Can God not commune with your spirit without directions from your mind? Will you dare to give it a try? Or is the little demon in the television far too tempting? Let us not forget that only as Elijah withdrew from the sound of the

October

whirlwind could he ever hear God in the gentle quietness of the still small voice.

Daily Inward Renewal

23 Do you ever feel like your life is overwhelmed with trouble and that things couldn't get much worse? Then ask yourself, "What is my mind focused on?" Is it focused on God or on your problems? Have you ever wondered how all those Christians in the early centuries could die with such courage and peace upon their faces? What did they have that we don't? The Apostle Paul, in writing to the Corinthians, revealed a tranquility of spirit that we all would do well to discover. He said:

> *Therefore, we do not lose heart. Though outwardly we are wasting away, yet inwardly we are being renewed day by day. For our light and momentary troubles are achieving for us an eternal glory that far outweighs them all. So we fix our eyes not on what is seen, but on what is unseen. For what is seen is temporary, but what is unseen is eternal.* (II Corinthians 4:16-18)

The peace that is within one's heart can be measured in proportion to the focus of one's soul on that which is eternal. Outwardly, everything may seem to be wasting away, but if our heart belongs to our Savior, inwardly we are being made stronger daily. The Christians in Paul's day, who faced the threat of extinction by a Roman tyrant, were able to face it with unwavering courage because they had allowed their bodies to be filled with the Spirit of the Living God. You cannot kill the spirit, you cannot kill the soul, and you cannot destroy that which is eternal. Upon what are the eyes of your heart and soul fixed?

Perhaps your body is afflicted with some terrible illness, perhaps someone has even dared to inform you that your condition is terminal. Guess what? Everybody who has been or ever will be born is terminal; it's just a matter of time. Perhaps that is your concern—the amount of time that is left. Well, nobody knows how long that is regardless of how informed or intelligent they think they are. And

October

even if they do and your time is short, let me remind you that eternity is long. So maybe that is your concern—"Where will I spend eternity?" That choice is left up to each one of us. Paul and the early Christians could live in peace no matter what happened to them because in their hearts they had fixed their gaze on the One who assured them of where they would spend eternity.

Think Paul had it easy compared to you? Listen to his words:

We are hard pressed on every side, but not crushed; perplexed, but not in despair; persecuted but not abandoned; struck down, but not destroyed. We always carry around in our body the death of Jesus, so that the life of Jesus may also be revealed in our body. For we who are alive are always being given over to death for Jesus' sake, so that his life may be revealed in our mortal body. So then, death is at work in us, but life is at work in you. . . . we also believe and therefore speak, because we know that the one who raised the Lord Jesus from the dead will also raise us with Jesus and present us with you in his presence." (II Corinthians 4:8-14)

I would say Paul and those like him had fixed their eyes on the eternal. Upon what have you fixed your eyes?

Silk Flowers

24 Like it or not, believe it or not, there is a spiritual dimension to life that is as real as the body in which you dwell. The church began with the incarnation of the Spirit in the man Jesus and grew to be the "true" church where that same Spirit still indwells those who through faith proclaim Jesus as Lord. Our roots as a people are in spiritual life, not physical accomplishment or materialistic acquisition. If we are truly a people of faith, we cannot build on the past unless we build on the aliveness of the Spirit that is the same yesterday, today and tomorrow. Bishop Richard B. Wilkie reminds us that:

Elton Trueblood used to say that we are a "cut flower" culture, drawing on the spiritual resources of earlier roots. . . .

October

Trueblood observes that we "cannot reasonably expect to erect a constantly expanding structure of social activism upon a constantly diminishing foundation of faith." (And Are We Yet Alive, p. 34)

The empowering force that shapes, grows, and enlivens the church is not the genius of innovative programs (important though they may be); not gimmicks for church growth nor charismatic leadership, but the moving of the Holy Spirit in the lives of those who are willing to **take the risk** to be surrendered to the moving of that Spirit. Even from the limited vantage point of over two centuries ago, as infant Methodism was beginning to explode in phenomenal growth, John Wesley prophetically warned, "I am not afraid that the people called Methodist would ever cease to exist either in Europe or America. But I am afraid, lest they should only exist as a dead sect, having the form of religion without the power." Individuals as well as denominations can, from all outward observance, appear to be religious but have no comprehension or experience of the Spirit of the Living God.

Human beings, being what we are, have institutionalized the church and in the process have become content to leave the Spirit out. Technology has allowed us to take the form and beauty of the natural flower and duplicate it with one that is made of silk. Both are beautiful but only one has life! The United Methodist Church is probably one of, if not the most organized institutions in the world. We would do well not to laugh at Bishop Wilkie's quip but take it seriously when he said, "God so loved the world that He didn't send a committee" (p. 33). The bishop puts his finger on the pulse of our denomination and asks the profound question, "When did we become primarily concerned with giving bread and begin to neglect the giving of the bread of life?" (p. 42)

Rather than ask yourself: "What's the status of my portfolio? How secure is my job? How well am I fixed for retirement? What's the condition of my health?" I challenge you to ask yourself, "How well is it with my soul?" Zero in on what's eternal and take a reading on your spiritual health and future. Until his Aldersgate experience, John Wesley was simply a religious man. When his heart suddenly

October

got warmed by the moving of the Spirit, then he became power in the hands of the Living God. Until God's Spirit blows the fresh winds of His breath across the fertile, receptive ground of our soul, we will be little more than religious silk flowers.

Refocusing Life

25 One of the interesting things in life is the way two or more people in the exact same situation can see things from entirely different perspectives. You recall the old query, "Is the glass half full or half empty?" Some people go to bed at night looking with excitement toward the dawning of a new day. Others go to bed either dreading the coming of a new day or with no expectation that it will be much different than the one before it. The older I become the more convinced I am that how we approach the beginning of the day will in large measure shape how the day unfolds. We have more control over the day than we think. The truth is, we **choose** to make decisions, no matter how small or insignificant they may seem, which set the tone for most of our day. What are your thoughts focused on as you contemplate tomorrow? Upon what or whom is your gaze fixed?

Somewhere, I once read a story about Alexander the Great, who with his army had just captured a small village. The citizens of the village were brought before Alexander, at which time their future was to be determined. There appeared before him a young man, his bride and his bride's mother. As they stood before Alexander, the young man was asked, "What would you give for your life?" upon which he replied, "I would give all my gold and silver, Sir." Then Alexander asked, "What would you give for the life of your wife?" to which he replied, "I would give my life, Sir." Alexander said, "Let them go free." As they left, the mother asked her daughter, "Did you see the golden coat Alexander had on?" "No," replied the daughter, "I could only see the one who said, "I would die for her."

In any given day there will always be some things which are more important than others. Unfortunately, we focus far too often on the things that are unimportant. For example, today many things have happened, or will happen, in your life. How much time did you spend

October

thinking about that which is most important to you? Did you set aside some time for your spouse or children? Did you bother to speak a kind word to someone who was hurting? Did you shore up the undergirding of an old friendship? Did you find time to share a few minutes with God as you began your day? Of all the things you have done today, how many have any eternal significance? How many would impress God or how many would God have approved? What did you do today that someone will be likely to remember next year, next month, next week, or even tomorrow?

Perhaps life hasn't treated you with kindness lately. Maybe you lost your job, your portfolio has taken a beating, your marriage has come crashing down, you've lost a loved one, or your children have rebelled and seem out of control. Maybe you've been told you have a terrible disease. Now, what are you focusing on—the problem or the solution? Is it not strange how deeply we often grieve over something that we, at one time, didn't have? It seems to me that when life gets out of kilter we have to come back to that which we know and trust. When our attention becomes focused on that, the way out of the maze of life begins to become apparent. When all is said and done, perhaps all of us ought to focus on the One who said, "I will give my life for him or her." The interesting thing is—He actually did. "Who did?" you ask. Jesus did!

Wanted: Happiness

26 It seems to me, as I wander in and out of the day to day life of ordinary people, that most of them don't seem very happy. First we turn life into a rat race and exhaust ourselves with non-stop activities; then, we reach retirement and make ourselves miserable because we have so little to do that is meaningful. Most people don't seem very happy with their jobs, yet lack the courage and determination to take the risk to change it. We'd rather be miserable and seemingly secure with the familiar than take a chance on changing our routine to something that is new and untried. As far as material possessions go, Americans are the richest people on earth. But on the happiness scale, we probably rank near the bottom. Is there a message here?

October

Perhaps at the heart of our failure to be happy is the inability to capture the joy in the present moment. We somehow have succumbed to the notion that we were happy years ago (living in the past) or that the things that will make us feel happy are in the future. There is an old Sanskrit poem that points to our dilemma.

> *Look to this day! For it is life, the very life of life. In its brief course lie all the verities and realities of your existence. For yesterday is already a dream and tomorrow is only a vision; but today, well lived, makes yesterday a dream of happiness, and every tomorrow a vision of hope.*

As you read these words, you are alive in the present. Perhaps you are unhappy, lonely, or depressed. Going to your home or to your room and secluding yourself from the world is guaranteed **not** to make you feel happy. Ah, you say, I don't feel like being around people! Well okay, settle down comfortably in your misery and have a good pity party! Repeat after me three times, each successive time with increasing volume, "Woe is me! Woe is me! Woe is me!" Are you feeling better yet? Are you breaking out into happiness? Felt any sudden surge of exploding ecstasy?

Well, since you're going to be miserably unhappy anyway, why not just get up and go out and see if you can do something that makes somebody else's day a little brighter. Why not try just forgetting yourself for an hour, even five minutes, and see if just maybe you can make someone else feel good. Here's a difficult one—the next person you meet, conjure up your most innocent smile and say "Hello, how are you?" Most people will smile back; and if for only two seconds, you have at least acknowledged their aliveness (to say nothing of your own) and have offered them the gift of a smile that brought a tiny ray of sunshine to their day.

Most people are miserable because we become too consumed with ourselves. The smaller we make the boundaries of our world, the more unhappy and less fulfilled we will become. Can't get out? Pick up the telephone! Don't have a telephone? Then write someone a "love note." I wonder what our world would be like, if for just five minutes, everyone in it forgot about their own misery and tried to

October

alleviate someone else's? I have this faint memory that a long time ago Someone said, "The person who is willing to lose his or her life would be the one who would finally find it." But then what did He know? He was only God!

The Night of Lightless Dark

Helen Keller, who became blind when she was a child, had the ability to see light where the sighted often never see it. She once wrote:

I have walked with people whose eyes are full of light but who see nothing in sea or sky, nothing in city streets, nothing in books. It were far better to sail forever in the night of blindness with sense, and feeling and mind, than to be content with the mere act of seeing. The only lightless dark is the night of darkness in ignorance and insensitivity." To be blind is unfortunate but to have the ability to see and to grow indifferent to the evidence of God in this world is tragic. (Unknown Source)

In the Gospel stories, the miracles of Jesus often included the restoring of sight to those who were physically blind. The crowds no doubt were amazed and fascinated to witness the restoration of sight to someone who had previously been unable to see. But for every physical miracle there is a spiritual one that far exceeds the importance and wonder of physical healing. The Gospel of John almost always brushes aside the physical miracle and dwells on the spiritual. For example, read the ninth chapter of John's Gospel. If you are spiritually interested, you will take the time to look it up, read it and ponder the meaning of the last three verses (39-41).

To attend church week after week and have no sense of the holy is to dwell in spiritual blindness. If you never feel God in the music, never have any consciousness of His presence, never hear His voice resonating in the reading of Scripture, never get a glimpse of His glory in the sermon, then you abide in the darkness of spiritual blindness. Dare you think that God's ability to reveal Himself is dependent upon the skill or eloquence of the preacher, the talent of the choir and

October

organist, or the beauty and aesthetics of the sanctuary? My goodness, in the Old Testament God spoke through the mouth of an ass! (Numbers 22:21-35). Jesus said that if God so chose He could make the very stones of the ground cry out and give Him glory! This same Jesus said, "There are none so blind as those who will not see." He did not say "cannot see" but "will not see."

The starting point in overcoming spiritual sightlessness begins with one's becoming aware of one's spiritual blindness. Nothing so moves the heart of God as the melody of sincere confession and the contriteness of a heart broken with awareness that something within is amiss. The thing that causes great rejoicing by the angels in heaven is not when someone who was physically blind is made to see, but when one who is spiritually blind suddenly beholds the glory of God's forgiving grace, embraces it in repentance, and feels the shackles of spiritual blindness fall away. Now that's a miracle! That's worth shouting about! The darkest night in anyone's life is the darkness of not knowing God.

Eugene Peterson's translation of the Bible (*The Message*) makes perfectly clear the predicament we're in. He wrote:

> *This is the crisis we're in: God-light streamed into the world, but men and women everywhere ran for the darkness. They went for the darkness because they were not really interested in pleasing God. Everyone who makes a practice of doing evil, addicted to denial and illusion, hates God-light and won't come near it, fearing a painful exposure. But anyone working and living in truth and reality welcomes God-light so the work can be seen for the God-work it is."* (John 3:19-21)

The Hidden Part

28 There is within each of us a part of ourselves which we keep hidden; hidden not only from the world, but often from those to whom we are closest. It is the place where we house our deepest fears and most vulnerable feelings. We neatly arrange them right next to our insecurities, our feelings of inadequacy, our self-doubts and our sense of unworthiness. I don't know exactly

October

when those things started to occupy this inner sanctuary—probably when we were quite small. Perhaps the impetus for this hidden chamber was a harsh or unkind word that was spoken when we were no bigger than a toddler. Maybe it came later when we not only were able to clearly understand words, but also to interpret tones and attitudes. Maybe it began one night when as a child we awoke in a dark room and felt the first tinge of fear.

Over the years, we have enlarged the room until it has become quite big, quite comfortable and quite secure. Time has allowed us to build a protective barrier around it that has become almost impenetrable. When we are hurt or disappointed we find somewhere we can be alone and we go there in our mind and spirit and nurse the pain we feel within. Strange, it somehow seems to help to allow the inner feelings to rise to our consciousness and be dealt with in the total isolation and security of our solitude. It's almost as if we have an inner friend that we feel safe enough with to allow the light of truth to be shone on our deepest feelings. But is it really helping?

Now comes a question we dare not avoid: Have we allowed God to enter our hidden part? Or do we feel so vulnerable that we seek to hide that part even from Him? If the chamber within you is bulging at the seams, that's a good indication you have never let God in. When God is allowed in, when we allow Him to see and touch us at the place we feel most frightened, then healing is inevitable and the "stuff" we've relegated to the hidden chamber begins to slowly disappear. Hard as it is for us to believe, God accepts us as we are and loves us in spite of ourselves. Most parents learn this in time as they discover the depth and power of their own love toward their children. We may not always approve of things our children do (or don't do), but their behavior has not the power to diminish our love. If that is so for us, how much more so is it true of God!

How often we have read that God is love (read I John 4: 7-12). Love accepts, love heals, love endures for the sake of the one that is loved. Where love is allowed to come in, fear, shame, guilt and insecurity must go out. "There is no fear in love. But perfect love drives out fear, because fear has to do with punishment. The one who fears is not made perfect in love." (I John 4:18) "Ah," you say, "but

October

how can I let God into my heart when my heart is filled with self-condemnation?" Because the Word of God says, "If our heart condemns us, God is greater than our heart, and knows all things." (I John 3:20)

The hidden chamber is the place within us we call "heart." From its dark chasm is derived self-hatred and self-condemnation. Here we mercilessly abuse ourselves. But listen: God is greater than our heart. He sees, He understands, He forgives and He heals. It's time to let God come in and clean out the hidden part.

I Know a Man . . .

29 The year was 1968. The room was small and dimly lit; just enough space for a bed, a small table, and a couple of chairs. It was clean, though it was filled with the medicinal aroma that is common to hospital rooms. I paused before entering because I heard the unexpected sound of a young man singing. I do not remember his name; it has long since faded into the file of my memory labeled "Not Necessary to Recall." What I do remember is that the young man stood at the foot of the bed upon which my father lay dying with cancer. Dad had heard the song a year or so earlier, and while he, like most folks in their fifties, had long since decided that it's the 'old favorite" hymns that appealed to him most, he was drawn to the power and conviction found in the words written by a young gospel song writer named Bill Gaither. The verses resonated with a message that was being lived out within his soul.

He had requested, I was told later, that the young man come to see him and sing for him once more those words that had taken on new meaning in his life. Though he never discussed with our family that he was dying with cancer, we knew that he knew; others less close to him told us that he had shared his moments of sorrow with them because he did not wish to "burden" us with the anguish he felt at leaving us all behind. You see, for my father, family was his most cherished treasure. He said in his will that his grandchildren had been "my rainbow after the storms of life." Dad was a big strong man, strong physically, but also in spirit and heart. Now it was being drained out of him one day at the time.

October

And so you can imagine how moving it was to stand just outside his hospital room and hear the words sung that soothed his mind and soul:

Shackled by a heavy burden, 'neath a load of guilt and shame,
then the hand of Jesus touched me,
and now I am no longer the same.
Since I met this blessed Savior,
since he cleansed and made me whole,
I will never cease to praise him; I'll shout it while eternity rolls.
He touched me, O He touched me, and O the joy that floods
my soul! Something happened, and now I know,
He touched me and made me whole.

The Bible tells us many stories of people that Jesus touched and made whole. Except for a very few, most of them remain nameless and most of them were healed physically. What is not so obvious to us are the multitudes of people that Jesus has touched and made whole spiritually.

There was a peace that pervaded my father the last months that he lived that allowed us to accept his death in the assurance of faith. His encounter with Jesus was not a last minute thing. He had served Him all his life. Yet it was in those last months that he discovered that what he had believed all of his life really was true. In our own day and in our own life the hand of Jesus still touches us. One day, like my father, we too "will never cease to praise Him. We'll shout it while eternity rolls." Because, you see, I know a man that Jesus made whole.

A Simple Man

30 When you think about Jesus' life what thoughts come to mind? Tall man in a robe, beard, long hair, sandals—bet His feet got cold in the winter! A man who seemed unconcerned about material things—He only had the clothes He wore, as far as we know. I imagine they weren't designer name brands. He seemed to enjoy people, but also found it necessary to separate Himself from them from time to time. His main desire seemed to be that He wanted

October

to please His Father and do His will. Apparently, He liked festive occasions, especially where food was served— I know that because He attended a lot of suppers and banquets and started out at a wedding. He must have really had a great time since His religious foes accused Him of being a glutton and a winebibber. I don't think they meant it as a compliment.

Jesus appeared to have a lot of patience with people, except for pseudo-religious people who were mighty confident about their own righteousness. Strange, He always had a lot of time for sinful folks, especially those considered to be the worst offenders. It's difficult to understand why He never seemed to take time to remind them of their faults. Jesus was obviously very familiar with the Old Testament (He quoted it a lot), but never sought to use it to club people into submission. When asked to summarize it He chose to point out something about loving God with all of the heart, mind, soul and strength and loving one's neighbor as one's self. (Now that's a condensed version!)

Apparently He was pretty devout about some things—attending church (actually it was called synagogue in His day), praying and deeds of kindness (He did a lot of that). Sick folks were important to Him, as well as those who were made to feel like outcasts. He didn't have a lot of words to say, certainly no long sermons at one sitting— okay, except for the one where He kept them so long He had to figure out a way to feed them. Maybe that's why most of us preachers are content to let folks go about lunchtime.

He wasn't satisfied with enjoying the pleasure of a small family but insisted on enlarging it to include anyone who also wanted to do the will of His Father. He stayed calm most of the time; except for that incident with the whip in the Temple. I wouldn't say He lost His temper—I think He was in perfect control, but I believe the folks He was angry at probably jettisoned the notion that He was a wimp! He strikes me as one who was serious but never unpleasant to be around. He placed a high premium on truth and had a way of sort of making you get in touch with your inner self. He never played games with folks but always was upfront with them about the cost of following Him. Seems like He demanded a lot, but then He did promise us

October

heaven and eternity as a reward, to say nothing of inner peace and joy here on earth.

Jesus never traveled very far, probably no more than a hundred miles or so from home. Never used big words, though He sometimes spoke in riddles. I suppose you could say He accomplished a lot in 30 plus years—became the Savior of the world, the King of Kings and Lord of lords; He claims the Name above all names and showed us what God is like. Simple fellow, but He sure made a big difference in the world.

Are You Listening?

31 Somewhere along life's way, many Christians came to the conclusion that prayer was basically convincing God to grant what you asked. That is no more reasonable than thinking that the role of a parent is to always give your children everything they request. "Okay," you say, "God doesn't have to give us everything we ask; only the major things like always being healthy." But what if God, who can see beyond the limits of our horizons, is able to discern a good reason for a person not to be healed? Does that make Him unfair or unkind? Only if you measure the degree of His kindness in human terms, and only if you think the most important part of life is physical life.

Our preconceived notions of who God is and how He should behave determine how we relate to Him. In addition, the faith and trust we place in Him also shape our relationship. As I have often said, my prayer to God in all the aspects of my life is that God should be honored and glorified in the way I live. Like all human beings, I often fail to live up to my prayer request. But this morning as I was praying, this thought came to me: *If there is any true honor to be found in this life, it is in obedience to and trust in God, no matter what comes.* Do we trust only when God does what we want, or do we dare trust when He leads us where we might not have chosen to go?

We cry out to God to speak to us, and when we do not hear what we expect, in the way we anticipate, we presume to think He has not answered. That is "fuzzy" thinking. Dare we imagine that God might speak to us in new ways outside the ordinary? Dare we think that He

November

might even speak to us in ways that aren't necessarily like those encountered by our biblical heroes? Just because the biblical canon has been set (nothing else can be added to the Bible), we make a mistake if we think God can only speak to or relate to us in a manner that has to fit one of the biblical examples. As far as I know, there was only one "burning bush" and only one incident of a still small voice being discerned after an earthquake and a whirlwind.

I don't think the problem is that God doesn't speak any more—it's that we aren't listening. Almost all our prayers are one-sided, We do all the talking and expect God to do all the listening. Have you ever been around someone who totally dominates a conversation? They seem to be talking twice as fast as a normal person and they run from one subject to the next, almost without taking a breath. Perhaps it was one such occasion that the old adage was formed, "I couldn't get a word in edge-wise." When finally you leave their presence you feel like you've just run a marathon. Wonder if God feels that way about the conversations we have with Him?

Do you remember the story of the boy Samuel in the Old Testament? Eli, the prophet, was asleep in his room and the young child Samuel was lying down in the temple. Three times the voice of God called out to him "Samuel! Samuel!" Samuel didn't know what to do, so he asked Eli. And what did Eli tell him to say to God? "Speak Lord, for your servant is listening." Maybe like Samuel, we ought to come to the place of prayer and say, "Speak Lord, for now your servant is listening." But maybe we don't because we are afraid He might actually say something to us.

Are You Wasting Your Life?

1 The feeling of hopelessness is not limited to a specific age or gender. I hear it expressed by elderly nursing home residents and also young people who are active, with most of their life ahead of them. The feeling is not imagined, certainly not desired, but is as real as the air we breathe. It is not a twenty-first century phenomenon but seems to span the course of human history. Job and Jonah both pleaded with God to let them die. The Psalmists cried out again and again from the depths of despair. Take Psalm 13 for

November

example: "How long, O Lord? Will you forget me for ever? How long will you hide your face from me? How long must I bear pain in my soul, and have sorrow in my heart all day long?" (Psalm 13:1-2, NRSV).

Hopelessness is not necessarily a result of one's being ravaged with illness (though that can certainly cause hopelessness in some people). Neither is it always brought on by a reversal in fortune or events which occur in ways that we do not intend. Hopelessness seems to overcome those who cannot look beyond the pain or despair of the moment. One can be unaware, for example, of the fact that cancer may be growing in their body. The person is happy and content with life until suddenly he or she is informed of this unwanted secret companion. But what really changes? Only one's attitude and what one chooses to center their thoughts on. No matter how old or healthy we are, none of us know what any day will bring, or how long we will live. In our lack of knowing we make ourselves content.

So is ignorance bliss? I don't think so. Ignorance can lead to disaster. Those who rise from the depths of hopelessness are those who have learned how to center their thoughts on something other than themselves. Each of us is quite capable of diving head-first into the inviting pool of "Oh me." But each of us is also capable of choosing to dwell in the land of "I'm alive today, I will live it to the fullest for the sake of God and others." Though the alphabetical letter is not contained within the word, hopeless begins and ends with the word "I." Hope begins with the word "Jesus." Yes, hope is born out of faith—faith in One who never allowed hopelessness to become a part of who He was, because His thoughts were always centered on His Father and not Himself.

The apostle Paul did not say, "Christ is the hope of glory." He said "Christ in you, the hope of glory." When Christ is allowed to live in us, hopelessness will give way to hope. When things go wrong, even if I lose everything, I still have Christ. If I live ten more years or die today, I still have Christ. If I am in a nursing home or living in a mansion, I still have Christ. What greater thing could I desire? Paul said that there are three great things in this life—faith, hope, and love. In reality, all three of those things are wrapped up in Jesus.

November

I know, as surely as I write these words, that Jesus desires that none of us live in hopelessness. We have this day and what becomes of it will in large measure depend upon what we choose to do with it. We can wallow in the mire of self-pity, or we can defiantly rise up and say, "Today I choose to live in the joy of my Lord!" We can waste life or live life usefully. It's up to us!

The Prayer of Relinquishment

2 In his book *Prayer—Finding the Heart's True Home*, Richard Foster begins the fifth chapter with the following quotation from Andrew Murray:

> *The Spirit teaches me to yield my will entirely to the will of the Father. He opens my ear to wait in great gentleness and teachableness of soul for what the Father has day by day to speak and to teach. He discovers to me how union with God's will is union with God Himself; how entire surrender to God's will is the Father's claim, the Son's example, and the true blessedness of the soul.* (p. 47)

Many Christians say that they seek spiritual unity with the Father, but if they are honest with themselves, they would acknowledge that they have not come to the point of being willing to yield their will entirely to the Father. As Murray profoundly points out, in order to have union with God we must surrender to His will. God never bends His will to ours. He may let us do our own thing and He might patiently pursue us as long as we have life, but He does not set aside His own will for ours, undoubtedly because His will for us is always the best.

I write this article the day before my third surgery for cancer. I have no reason to assume that the surgery will be anything other than routine. On the other hand, I have no guarantee of life, just as none of you do. So how am I feeling? I feel the calm, peaceful presence of Jesus so profoundly close that I can truly say I have no fear or anxiety. I suppose I have learned at this stage in my life the secret that so many Christians before me learned—when you entrust your life to God there is nothing that can rob you of peace. How did Isaiah put it? "Thou

November

wilt keep him in perfect peace, whose mind is stayed on thee: because he trusteth in thee" (26:3, KJV).

Creating a meaningful prayer life is a journey of learning. One begins with the simple childlike trust of children's prayers; then through the positive and negative experiences of life, we move down a continuum of trial and error until we arrive at the pinnacle of all prayer—relinquishment or surrender. To be able to pray "Thy will be done," and mean it with the total sincerity of one's heart, is to arrive at a place that God has created that is indescribable. God's peace is far more than the absence of fear, anxiety, or conflict; it is the presence of something that fills that void. It cannot be purchased or bartered; it cannot be passed on or stolen. It comes when one's spirit dominates the body, not by force or coercion, but through glad surrender of the physical. "God is Spirit," Jesus said, "and they that worship Him must worship Him in spirit and in truth."

The prayer of relinquishment is literally diving into the future, trusting and believing with all of one's being that God will be there to catch you. If the surgery goes well and I am home when you read this, that will be wonderful. But if by chance it should not, please know that I landed safely and securely in the precious hands of my Lord. The place of perfect *true blessedness of the soul*!

The Faithful Prayer

3 It's not difficult to become discouraged with prayer. When we pray we engage in an act of faith that the words we utter or that the thoughts we launch heavenward will be received, considered and acted upon by the Divine Creator. It's like planting a tiny seed in the ground—when you have done all you know to do you must walk away from it and trust that in the course of time God will bring forth from your act of faithfulness a plant that will grow and flourish. Most prayers do not receive immediate results. Some will require years to reveal an answer. If we are impatient, we may very well give up before the answer comes.

God is not boxed in, as we are, by the limits of time and space. His timetable differs from ours and we cannot force ours upon Him, no matter how noble and sincere we may think our request is. Years ago I

November

came to the conclusion that faith is a process, a journey through life: it is not an instantaneous acquisition of spiritual maturity. Faith is a gift from God that grows and develops as we consistently use it. Only a fool would enter a gym, lift weights for one session and expect that his or her body would suddenly become fully developed. There are consistent correlations between the physical and spiritual aspects of our lives. The more one exercises faith, the greater and stronger faith becomes.

Max Lucado writes:

The God of surprises strikes again. . . . God does that for the faithful. Just when the womb gets too old for babies, Sarai gets pregnant. Just when the failure is too great for grace, David is pardoned. . . . The lesson? Three words. Don't give up. . . . Is the road long? Don't stop. Is the night black? Don't quit. God is watching. For all you know right at this moment . . . the check is in the mail. The apology may be in the making. The job contract may be on the desk. Don't quit. For if you do, you may miss the answer to your prayers. (*Grace For the Moment*, p. 20)

We wrongly assume that God hasn't heard, or God doesn't care, or praying makes no difference, when the answer doesn't come as soon or in the way that we desire. God is never rushed! You will never hear God say, "Oops!" He never makes a mistake and He never has to back up and punt! What pleases God immensely and draws us ever closer to Him is the sinner/saint who, in spite of all odds, does not give up praying but continues faithfully on no matter how bleak the future may seem.

In the Book of Revelation, in his letter to the seven churches, Jesus offers Christians a promise of reward for their faithfulness. He uses the words "He that overcomes . . ." (which is another way of saying "The person who remains faithful") will receive the blessing of God. Come to God with your requests, but not with a timetable. Come to God with the desires of your heart, but not with a blueprint about how He must act. Come to God with faith and with trust, and you will discover the faithfulness of God.

November

4

Reminders of Grace

The first time He spoke the words, they must have seemed strange to those who quietly listened and observed as Jesus held up an unleavened piece of bread and said, "This is my body, given for you." What has a loaf of bread to do with Jesus' body? How does bread become the nourishing basic element of a meal? First, seed must be sown in the ground. In so doing, seed appears to be dead and buried. But eventually a sprout rises to the surface and it becomes a stalk that brings forth tiny little tassels of grain. The grain is stripped from the stalk and it is crushed and ground and beaten. Then it goes through the ordeal of fire and comes forth as a life-sustaining nourishing element of life.

Jesus, was stripped, beaten, and horribly mistreated. Isaiah said of Him, "But he was pierced for our transgressions, he was crushed for our iniquities; the punishment that brought us peace was upon him, and by his wounds we are healed" (Isaiah 53:5). If you've never read the 53rd chapter of Isaiah, you need to stop and read it. It is a portrait of the Suffering Servant who was to become our Lord. Jesus was not burned alive but His body endured the searing heat of pain and sorrow. The embodiment of innocence was suffering for the guilty and it was in every respect a trial by fire—fire in the sense that each step of the way He was forced to decide whether to continue or escape. At each juncture He chose to continue on until His body had endured the agony and consequence of human sin.

After the supper, He took a cup and said, "Drink it, all of you; for this is my blood of the new covenant, which is poured out for you and for many for the forgiveness of sins." How is wine in any way related to Jesus' blood? The grapes are harvested from the vine they are thrown into a vat and then squeezed and crushed until they yield the fluid contained within them. In the Garden of Gethsemane, Jesus wallowed on the ground among the olive trees, His mind and soul so tormented by the coming storm that His body literally sweated drops of blood. The very life force of the Son of God was being squeezed out of Him by the weight of human sin.

Who can fathom the mysterious depth of meaning found in the atonement? Was it to pay the penalty for sin? Was it to assuage the

November

anger of a furious God? Was it a substitutionary death—one person taking the place of another? This much I can grasp: the innocent Son of God loved you and me enough to not run from the cross but embrace it, because He loved us more than life. This the Bible teaches me, "God made him who had no sin to be sin for us, so that in him we might become the righteousness of God" II Corinthians 5:21.

When next you hold out your empty hands— signifying that you bring nothing of merit into the presence of God—and there are placed in your hands the consecrated elements of bread and wine, let the very essence of how they came to be remind you of all that Jesus was willing to endure in order for you to know peace and have eternal life. Bread and wine—common elements of everyday life—reminders of God's unfailing love for the creatures He made, who loved sin more than they loved Him. I see it now—bread and wine represent Grace. Perhaps that's why we call the meal blessing, "Grace".

Union with God

5 Rufus Moseley said, "God is the homeland of the soul. We are no good away from home, except to return" (*Perfect Everything*, p. 132). The soul was created by God; that is, it originated in His heart, and will find its rest and peace only as it journeys home to God. God never desired or intended for humanity to exist apart from union with Himself. But sin entered in, and the union of the divine with humanity was severed. Jesus Christ, as a human being, entered our world to restore that union. He is thus the bridge, the bond, and the means whereby fellowship with God is reunited. The hunger that you feel within that rises and falls in intensity, that seeks to draw you into spiritual union with the Godhead, is the vestige of the handiwork of the Divine hand seeking to reunite the creation with the Creator.

That which draws us back into union with God is the experience and acceptance of holy love. Holy love comes to us through the power of the Holy Spirit actively pursuing us through life. Whether we re-establish union with God or not depends upon our response to that love which is made known in the life, death, and resurrection of Jesus.

November

While Jesus was on earth His being was filled with holy love but was confined by the limitations of His human body. That is why He said to the disciples, "But I tell you the truth: It is for your good that I am going away [die and ascend to my Father]. Unless I go away, the Counselor will not come to you; but if I go, I will send him to you" (John 16:7).

The purpose of the Holy Spirit is to make known the reality of the love of Jesus. The Holy Spirit does not point to Himself, but to the work of Christ. When one is conscious of and accepts the loving work of Christ, and acknowledges that love by repentance of sin and acceptance of divine grace, one has finally reached the place of union with God (See John 16:12-15.) As a result of that union the two dominant feelings that one experiences are the feeling of being deeply loved and an inner peace that defies description. Birthed out of the feeling of being loved is the ability to love others. For love reproduces itself and finds life only as it goes out from the one who loves to others who are starving to receive love.

Moseley points out, "We become like whatever we receive and pass on. So, to abide and increase in union with Him, we must receive freely and give freely, give His love and give only His love. For if we give anything other than love, we go out in the thing we give out . . ." (p. 140). Whether we are aware of it or not, we each give out to the world what is within us. It might be love, resentment, or hate. It might be peace and joy or it might be hostility and conflict. It might be a willingness to give sacrificially or be a desire only to take—even that which is not our right to take. What we individually give to or take from the world helps shape and mold the world in which we live.

If our purpose in being created is to be in union with God, then the world will either be made better or worse by whether we accept that union or reject it. Are you in union with Christ? If not, then surrender and let the Holy Spirit make you one with Him.

The Starting Point

 The life of Jesus has been studied, dissected, scrutinized, analyzed, criticized and theologized. There has never been a

November

human being about whom more has been written. Yet if every shelf in the world was filled with books about Jesus it would not be enough to make Him Savior. You can learn every fact about Jesus that human beings are capable of knowing, but that will never make Him your Savior. The portrait of the Man is formed in the brain, but the Savior is born in the heart. There was something about Jesus that was unique, making Him different from any human being who has ever lived. Perhaps we get a glimmer of that truth in the words of E. Stanley Jones, "There was something about the Man that made the best of men feel that they were in deepest need. And yet the worst of men felt drawn to him" (*The Christ of Every Road*, p. 62).

The modern educated person takes pride in believing he or she is in search of truth. We believe truth is present, and yet is hidden. We think that all one needs to do is search and truth will reveal itself to us. Scientists, engineers, medical researchers, and a thousand other professionals pour over the various facets of our world, all in search of truth; and they find bits and pieces of it. But they will never find the origin and totality of it until they look for truth, not in a world of matter and minerals, but in a Person. Jesus did not come to earth in search of truth; He came to earth to proclaim and reveal truth. No, He didn't teach mathematical truth, or scientific truth, or medical truth; He taught ultimate truth. He taught human beings about the value of life, about the Source of life, and how to discover eternal life.

Jesus had no need to search the starlit sky with a Hubble telescope, looking for the origin of life. He knew Who was behind the origin of life because He was there when it all began. Human beings seek to work backward to God; Jesus is God working forward to humanity. In the Incarnation Jesus revealed the essence of God to humanity. At the heart of that essence is divine love. Do you want to know why the world was created? John tells us—because "God so loved . . ." The world was created out of love; incredibly, humanity could not comprehend it. And so God sent Love to the world in order to reveal our origin—and the world, through sin, crucified it.

But wonder of wonders, God's creative love proved to be greater than humanity's sin (sin which is lack of love) and it overcame it on a cross. The deepest need in all of humanity is the need for a Savior—

November

Someone to save us from ourselves. Salvation does not come through scientific discovery of truth, but through broken humanity embracing love poured out from a cross. It comes not when the mind encases truth in intellectual boxes, but when the soul embraces truth at the center of our being. Eternal truth is discovered through the channel of faith because faith is the only pathway to the soul. God is a Spirit, and spirit can only be discovered by spirit. If you are looking for truth that is eternal, you will find it at only one place—and the starting point is the Cross.

The Undivided Life

7 There is a battle going on inside each of us—sometimes consciously and sometimes not. This struggle within the human mind and spirit is a malady that has been brought on by an inner division. From a theological point of view, one could argue that the division can be traced back to the entrance of sin. Humanity was created for union—oneness—not division. A. W. Tozer writes:

> *One of the greatest hindrances to internal peace which the Christian encounters is the common habit of dividing our lives into two areas—the sacred and secular. As these areas are conceived to exist apart from each other and to be morally and spiritually incompatible, and as we are compelled by the necessities of living to be always crossing back and forth from the one to the other, our inner lives tend to break up so that we live a divided life instead of a unified life."* (The Pursuit of God, p. 117)

When we divide life into these two separate areas, the sacred part will almost always receive the least attention. The sacred is the time set aside for worship, studying God's word, praying, perhaps a daily time of devotion and meditation, and engaging in service. The secular is basically everything else.

Living a divided life was never God's intention, nor should it be our desire. Every moment of life should be sacred in the sense that we desire to live in the center of God's will. The perfect example of such Living was the life of Jesus. There was never a moment that He was

November

outside the will of His Father. As a result there was never a time in which He felt division in His soul (with the possible exception of His mystical encounter with sin while on the cross). All of life is sacred to God. He makes no division between sacred and what we have set aside and called secular. For example, we should not feel that we need to put God on the shelf when we go to work (though that is clearly society's desire). No one has the right or power to control your heart or your mind. Every business decision or transaction can and should be immersed in the will of the Father. Shady dealing, cutting of corners, intentional deceit, and climbing the corporate ladder on the backs of others is not the Father's will, but the will of all that is secular.

Perhaps Paul stated it most succinctly when he said, "So, whether you eat or drink, or **whatever** you do, do **all** for the glory of God" (I Cor. 10:31). In any given day, how much do we do for the glory of God? How many days do we live with scarcely a thought given to God? Again quoting Tozer: "It is not what a man does that determines whether his work is sacred or secular, it is why he does it. The motive is everything. Let a man sanctify the Lord God in his heart and he can thereafter do no common act" (p. 127).

How different our day would be if when we got up in the morning, regardless of what we had to do, we committed the day to God and sought to do all for His glory. If each unpleasant task that lay before us was surrendered to God and our effort to complete it was done "as if unto the Lord," suddenly there would be far more sacred than secular to our life. Peace cannot be found in the secular, for by its very intent the secular is that which is set apart from God (at least by the world's view). Inner peace is a spiritual reality, and as long as one is striving to be in the will of God, peace will flow as calmly and serenely as a gentle stream. That, my friends, is the result of an undivided life.

Intentional Stillness

8 Few books have been written with greater spiritual insight and power than A W. Tozer's book *The Pursuit of God*. Every Christian who has a sincere desire to grow in the Spirit should seek it out without delay. We run to and fro seeking answers to the

November

problems and mysteries of life, immersing ourselves in an ocean of words and ideas, and come back empty again and again. For many the reading of the Bible is a journey into a dry and barren desert. How profound and accurate are Tozer's words: "... it is not mere words that nourish the soul, but God Himself, and unless and until the hearers find God in personal experience they are not the better for having heard the truth" (p. 10). What one receives, even from the Word of God, is directly related to the attitude and desire with which one approaches the Word.

Jesus once said, "There are none so blind as those who will not see." We are surrounded by profound truth about God and we are totally oblivious to it. Again quoting Tozer: "The modern scientist has lost God amid the wonders of His world; we Christians are in real danger of losing God amid the wonders of His Word" (p. 13). Like Elijah hiding in a cave, we look for God in all the wrong places; as a result, we often fail to discover Him in the "still small voice." God is not a sunset, a beautiful blooming flower, a mighty roaring ocean, or the beauty of an infant's face—all those are but His handiwork, the creation of a Divine Being. God is a Person, and we must not lose sight of that. We may stand before a magnificent Michelangelo sculpture, or be awed by a da Vinci painting; we may be moved by the masterpieces of Shakespeare, but let us not lose sight of the fact that they are but the creation of the artist. The talent and gift dwelled in the person, not in the creation.

God is Spirit, and those who would know and worship Him must seek and worship Him in spirit and in truth. Since we seem to have such difficulty in discerning the nature of God as Spirit, He made it easy for us. He took upon Himself human flesh and came to us in the person of Jesus. Jesus said, "The Father and I are one, whoever has seen me has seen the Father." If we come to know Jesus as Lord, it will not be because our mind has simply revealed Him to us, it will be because our spirit hungers to know Him. When our spirit hungers for God, "As the deer pants for streams of water . . ." (Ps. 42:1), then will our soul and mind find God.

The modern churchgoer will not find the Living God as long as that person is content to place God on the periphery of life. God is not

November

discovered or experienced on the outer edges, but at the center of our desire. The pace of life for the modern man and woman is breakneck speed. The pace of God remains constant, steady, and never in a rush. How many there are who will miss God because they go rushing by at supersonic speed. We would do well to heed the words of the Psalmist of old (Ps. 46:10), "**Be still**, and know that I am God." It is in **intentional** stillness that God is to be found, not in the cluttered life that is being stretched in a thousand different directions. One thing that too many of us share in common is the absence of a quiet time set apart with God. Do you have such a time, or is there no place in your day to commune with the One who gave you life?

The Throne Room of the Heart

9   We live in a world that was brought into existence by the creating God, and the vast majority of human beings never experience His presence. A person who is physically blind cannot see the physical beauty of the world—not because it does not exist, but because they do not have the physical ability to see that which is all around them. Likewise, human beings who have not learned to see with their spiritual eyes are surrounded with the glory of God's presence but are totally oblivious to His nearness. There is one thing above all others that causes spiritual blindness and it is the love affair we have with self.

It was for good reason that the first commandment God gave to Moses on the mountain was, "You shall have no other gods before me." It has never been the pseudo-gods fashioned from rocks and metal that were the greatest detriment to spiritual oneness with God; it has always been the inner god we fashion in our hearts that seeks to elevate the "self" above the recognition and worship of our Creator. When the center of our will becomes "Me" rather than "Thee" then spiritual life becomes non-existent. Jesus' prayer was the prototype for putting self in its proper place—"Not mine but thy will be done." He reminded us that if we are to have life (spiritual life) then we must be willing to die to life (self-centered life).

Faith is the road that leads to God. As A.W. Tozer so poignantly reminds us:

November

> *Faith is redirecting our sight, a getting out of the focus of our own vision and getting God into focus. Sin has twisted our vison inward and made it self-regarding. Unbelief has put self where God should be, and is periously close to the sin of Lucifer who said, "I will set my throne above the throne of God." Faith looks out instead of in and the whole of life falls in line.* (The Pursuit of God, p.113)

It is self-evident that the physical body, in order to be renewed and restored, requires rest. The same is true for the spiritual body, but that truth never seems to occur to most people. The soul is renewed and enlivened when it rests in God, a state of existence which most people seem to avoid at all costs. The result—a sick and anemic spiritual life that is gasping for every breath. The person who will not intentionally set aside time with God will never be conscious of God's presence. A day is made up of 1,440 minutes. Approximately 480 minutes (8 hours) we devote to resting and renewing the physical body (sleep). How many do you give to renewing the soul? We feed the body and starve the soul. We satisfy the appetites of the flesh and ignore the pleading of the inner spirit. We trade the eternal for the temporal and wonder why we are unhappy and miserable.

The God of life cannot dwell in us as long as the god of self sits on the throne. Once more quoting Tozer:

> *Men have now by nature no peace within their hearts, for God is crowned there no longer, but there in the moral dusk, stubborn and aggressive usurpers fight among themselves for first place on the throne.* (The Pursuit of God, p. 30)

Heaven will not take the throne room of our heart by force, but only when we freely and gladly surrender it.

The Gate of Forgiveness

10 Why do we find forgiveness so difficult to extend? Could it be because we have not yet learned how to receive it, or worse still, think that we have never been in need of it? Jesus said to Simon the Pharisee, "He who is forgiven little, loves little." A "sinful" woman had just washed Jesus' feet with her tears

November

and dried them with her hair. Jesus tenderly told her that her sins were forgiven. Compassion for a "sinner" was unthinkable to Simon. Jesus, searching Simon's heart, could discover very little love within it. Therefore his statement: "He who is forgiven little, loves little." Where forgiveness is withheld, love shrivels and dies!

At the heart of human sin is the dominance of human pride. The person who withholds forgiveness would rather be cloaked in one's sense of "I'm right" than to be at peace with another through forgiveness. **Forgiveness is that gift which the person who feels wronged gives to another in order to restore union.** God in Christ Jesus extends to us forgiveness in order that we might once more have union with Him. The same principle holds true on the human level. We can choose to be in union with one another or to live apart from one another. When a wrong has separated two human beings, regardless of the relationship (brother/sister, husband/wife, parent/child, friend/friend, etc.), forgiveness is the **only** bridge over which they may cross in order to be once more in harmony with one another. There is no other way!

People who are unforgiving have entombed themselves in a world in which they vainly imagine that no one has ever been wronged as deeply as they have. Rather than allow the wound to heal through application of the salve of forgiveness, they pick at it through constant resentment and incessant reminders of how wrongly they have been treated. The goal of the unforgiving person is to seek to heal their own pain through the infliction of pain on another. Alas, the end result will always be the same—their pain will never be healed, even after the other person who has been banished from their life has long since been healed. It seems to be an axiom of life that those who cannot bring themselves to grant forgiveness never discover how to receive it. The sad part of that story is that **all** human beings will at some point need healing in their life—healing which can come to them only as they accept their forgiveness.

While hanging on the cross, Jesus made seven statements. Two were prayers to His Father, one was provision for His mother, one was for the spiritual needs of a thief, one was to acknowledge the human need of His body, one was to announce the completion of His work,

November

and one was His gift of forgiveness to the world. In ten simple words He unleashed on the world a torrential shower of grace which has never stopped falling—"Father, forgive them, for they know not what they do!" If we never allow that cleansing shower to wash away the stain and pain of our sin, we will forever find it difficult to give to those in need of our forgiveness the gift of healing which we could offer. By withholding forgiveness we perpetuate estrangement and we add immensely to the pain of the world. Foolish sinners that we are, when we refuse to grant forgiveness, we slam shut the gate that separates us from our own.

The Road Less Taken

11   I read the following verse and its profound thought haunted me and refused to leave my mind. "Do not follow where the path may lead. Go, instead, where there is no path and leave a trail" (Anonymous). I was reminded of the poem by Robert Frost, *The Road Not Taken*, in which he describes two diverging roads in a yellow wood. He is faced with having to make a decision regarding which one he would follow. The poem concludes with this thought: "Two roads diverged in a yellow wood, and I—I took the one less traveled by, and that has made all the difference." As we make our way through life, most of us will almost always take the path that looks most trodden, because the well-worn path is the least threatening and appears to be the one that seems easiest. God bless those rare courageous individuals who dare to chart a new path; to brave the challenges of the unknown and make a trail that others can follow.

Jesus was such a man. When He etched His footprints in the dust of this earth, He walked a path that no one had walked before Him. He dared to challenge the established norms; He ruffled the feathers of the complacent, the self-centered, the hard-hearted, the self-sufficient, and the self-satisfied. Even He talked of two roads— the broad and the narrow one. "Many will take the broad road," He said, "and it will lead to destruction. But few will choose the narrow one [the one less traveled] and it leads to life eternal." We would do well to ponder the profound truth conveyed in His words. But here's the good news—Jesus will not ask you to go one step down a road that He has not trod before you. The path may not seem well-worn (and it

November

won't be) but it is a path whose strength is grace and whose destination is eternal truth because it is the path that leads to life.

Let this unsettling thought reverberate through your mind: maybe Jesus is challenging you to do something that isn't easy—indeed, maybe it's something that is difficult. We are inclined to only "sign-up" for those things with which we feel comfortable, which make only small demands, while leaving the difficult tasks for others. The way of the cross doesn't seem easy to me, but Jesus said if we were to come after Him we had to find our own cross, pick it up, and follow Him. And then He had the audacity to suggest that we needed to do that daily! But crosses are such uncomfortable things! They are heavy and rough and in the end we get nailed to them. One thing is for certain—you won't have to wait in line to get one!

If you know Christ today, it's because along life's way someone had picked up a cross and carried it down an infrequently traveled path. They did not despise it but learned to love it; for while eternal life may be the destination, along the way of the cross, eternity comes to walk with us. Christians do not travel the way of the cross alone; God's Spirit walks before them and with them. If you are looking for Jesus, don't look for Him on the well-worn path. Rather, look for Him along the road that has only one set of footprints and a strange plow mark in the ground, as if something was being dragged. Crosses don't leave footprints, they leave plow marks. Until Jesus left the trail, the path had never been trodden.

The Place Called Faith

12 Ask the rhetorical question of churchgoers, "Do you have faith in God?" and most will say, "Yes" or "I hope so" or perhaps, "I think I do." If you were to be asked that question how would you respond? Before you answer, perhaps it would be wise to ponder what it means to have faith. Does faith in God simply mean that you believe He exists? Jesus said that even the demons believed in Him, but they are not saved. There is a difference between having faith and believing. Believing acknowledges something while faith is committed to it. You might believe that I could walk across a tightrope a hundred feet in the air pushing a wheelbarrow in front of

November

me; but you probably wouldn't have enough faith in me to be willing to get in the wheelbarrow.

In his book *The Church*, Hans Küng writes:

> *Faith in an ultimate and radical sense cannot be distinguished from love. It is a personal activity towards a personal recipient. Faith is never, in the final analysis, a matter of adherence to objects, rules, or dogmas, but is the sacrifice and self-giving of one person to another."*

If indeed faith **is** love, sacrifice, and self-giving to another person, then how would you now answer the question, "Do you have faith in God?" Faith includes believing, but goes far beyond it. You can believe there was a Jesus, you may even believe that He was and is the Son of God, yet it is possible to believe and not have faith.

Using Küng's statement as the standard implies that if we have faith in Jesus, we will love Him and be committed to serving Him to the point of self-giving and self-sacrifice. What part of yourself have you given or sacrificed for Jesus lately? Was it not Jesus who said that if anyone would come after Him (be His follower) that person had to deny self, take up a cross and then follow? What have you denied yourself for the sake of Christ? Going back to the beginning of Küng's premise: if faith cannot be distinguished from love, and an objective by-stander sought to determine the depth of your faith by the love you show for Christ, how much would be measurable? One can believe in something without loving it—including belief in God—but one cannot truly have faith in God without loving Him.

I think that it is also true that you cannot really love that which you fear. If you go through life trying to be a faithful church member because you fear that if you don't God will cast you into hell, then you will never truly love God. We cannot fully grasp or exhaust the meaning of the cross, but I believe part of the reason that Jesus hung there for us was to show us that God would rather die for us than to let us live life in fear of eternal punishment. In dying on a cross of His own free will, Jesus showed us the depth of God's love. "Greater love has no man than this, that he lay down his life for his friends." God calls us friends! Imagine that—YOU are a friend of God.

November

It seems to me that it shouldn't be too hard to love a God who is willing to die for us. Herein is the love of God revealed, in that while we were still sinners (people who were still constantly sinning) Christ died for the ungodly (those who rebelled against Him). Has your love for God reached the place called faith?

The Pseudo Power of Fear

13 Fear is a powerful emotion that more often than not affects us in a negative way. Some people are afraid of dying; others are afraid of living. Some are afraid of the dark; many are afraid of the light (and what it will reveal). I once read that every human being is born with four inherent fears—the fear of falling, the fear of loud noises, the fear of failure, and the fear of being deserted or left alone. Fear can be debilitating and crippling if it is allowed to be in control. There is a distinct difference in having a "healthy respect" for something that can harm us (e.g., storms, lightning, poisonous snakes, violence) and being paralyzed by the existence of those things in the world in which we live.

Has it ever occurred to you that Jesus never showed fear of anything? Not life or death, not emperor or tyrant, not failure or Satan. He wasn't afraid that He would be misunderstood, rejected, betrayed, or mistreated. He never lived a moment of His life in fear; not when the burden of the cross was laid upon Him, nor later when He was nailed to it. When we fear something our focus is placed upon the thing that we fear rather than that which has power over it. Someone has wisely said, "**Fear is having faith in the thing we don't want to happen.**" Fear is often directed at something that has not yet happened to us (and may never happen). Unfortunately, our fear often perpetuates and keeps alive the very thing of which we are afraid.

Sometimes fear is caused by our inability to understand. Racism is perpetuated because people of different races do not know and understand one another and make no effort to try. Many people are afraid of the future, basically because it is hidden in the unknown. There have been rare instances of people committing suicide because they were afraid they had a terminal illness—only to have the autopsy reveal that there was no such disease within them. The word "cancer"

November

can cause some people to shrivel up and die, long before the disease itself has brought them to that point. Life lived in fear is life lived in misery.

I hope it has not escaped your attention how often angels appeared to people in the Bible and the first words they spoke were, "Fear not!" You should also remember how many times Jesus spoke those same words to people whom He met in different situations. When He was with the disciples in a boat on the stormy sea of Galilee, He said, "Why are you afraid, do you have no faith?" When Jesus bade Peter to walk to Him on the waves he was doing just fine until he saw the waves and he was afraid—then he sank. Fear smothers faith; conversely, faith drives out fear. The writer of I John 4:18 says, "There is no fear in love. But perfect love drives out fear, because fear has to do with punishment. The one who fears is not made perfect in love."

When we place our faith in Christ, like banished demons our fears flee from us. When our attention is focused on God and not on that which we think has the potential to do us harm, fear retreats into the shadows. The Psalmist had it right: "The Lord is my light and my salvation, whom shall I fear? The Lord is the strength of my life; of whom shall I be afraid." What is it that you can fear that is greater than God's love for you? NOTHING! So . . . ?

Has the Church Become a Club?

14 The title and thoughts for this devotion were prompted by a passage in Henri Nouwen's book, *Reaching Out*. I quote the following passage from his thought provoking chapter: *Community and Prayer*. He begins by saying:

> *Prayer is the language of the Christian community. In prayer the nature of the community becomes visible because in prayer we direct ourselves to the one who forms the community. We do not pray to each other, but together, we pray to God, who calls us and makes us into a new people. Prayer is not one of the many things the community does. Rather, it is its very being. . . . Sometimes it seems as if the Christian community is "so busy" with its projects and plans*

November

that there is neither the time nor the mood to pray. But when prayer is no longer its primary concern, and when its many activities are no longer seen and experienced as part of prayer itself, the community quickly degenerates into a club with a community cause but no common vocation. (p. 156)

In essence, what Nouwen is saying is that prayer is the life-blood of the Christian church. There is no program, activity, or ministry in the church that will have any lasting value apart from prayer. If it has not been birthed in the will of God—a will that must be sought and discovered on our knees—then it will amount to nothing. Jesus said, "Apart from me, you can do nothing." How on earth (or heaven) can we have a part in Jesus if we do not come to Him through the means of prayer? Are you so in tune with the will of God that you never have to ask what it is? Are you so confident that you are directed by the leading of His Spirit that you never have to struggle with it in prayer? If you are, then spiritually you must be light years ahead of the rest of us.

Show me a church that is dying and I will show you a church that is seeking to function apart from the leading of God's Spirit—a leading that can only be discerned through the discipline of prayer. Where feasibly possible, every church should have a Prayer Room. I'm not just talking about the sanctuary, but a special room, set aside for the singular purpose of prayer: a place where a person can go and feel safe, comfortable, and alone with God; a place where spiritual energy can be focused and the very power of God can be unleashed upon and into human lives. We greatly underestimate the power that can emanate from such a place. Power that has not only the ability to change individual lives but also the life of the congregation as a whole.

Like Moses who argued with God when God was trying to convince him to do something new and different, we can make an avalanche of excuses for not using that sacred room (e.g., I can pray at home, I don't have time, I can't pray for 15 minutes, and so forth) but the truth is, we just choose not to take the time. We refuse to recognize and proclaim the discipline of intentional prayer as a necessary part of our spiritual life. Life built on prayer is just one of the many important things that sets the Church apart from the civic

November

club ... good and noble though civic clubs may be. The Church was not created to be a club, but the living Body of Christ—guided by, empowered by, and held together through the power of prayer. Are we a church or a club? Each of us must answer for ourselves.

The Secret

15 There are a few in every church who are able to see beyond the bricks, the mortar, the steeple and the structure. They look beyond the polity, the doctrine and the raucous theological debates that sometimes occur. They do not linger in the shadows waiting to be asked to serve, but take the initiative to seek that special quiet place that Mary discovered at the precious feet of Jesus. Jesus named that place for all time—He told Martha it was called the "good part that shall not be taken from her." Have you ever discovered the contentment of simply sitting in the presence of Jesus? Quiet time, uninterrupted time, time that is experienced without the necessity of words! Is there time in your day for just you and Jesus? If so, is it a regular appointment or are you a "walk-in" worshiper?

Ralph S. Cushman wrote a beautiful little poem that we would all do well to ponder. It's entitled *The Secret:*

> *I met God in the morning*
> *When my day was at its best,*
> *And His presence came like sunshine,*
> *Like a glory in my breast.*
>
> *All day long the Presence lingered,*
> *All day long He stayed with me,*
> *And we sailed in perfect calmness*
> *O'er a very troubled sea.*
>
> *Other ships were blown and battered,*
> *Other ships were sore distressed,*
> *But the winds that seemed to drive them*
> *Brought to us a peace and rest.*
>
> *Then I thought of other mornings,*
> *With a keen remorse of mind,*

November

When I too had loosed the moorings,
  With the Presence left behind.

So I think I know the secret,
  Learned from many a troubled way:
  You must seek Him in the morning
  If you want Him through the day!

How many more days of our lives will fade into the distant land of the past before we discover "the Secret"? How long will we bear the burden of unnecessary anguish because we would not seek the One who longs to share our load? Listen to Him: "Come to me, all you who are weary and burdened, and I will give you rest. Take my yoke upon you and learn from me, for I am gentle and humble in heart, and you will find rest for your souls. For my yoke is easy and my burden is light." (Mt. 11:28-30) If you don't meet Jesus in the morning, it's won't be because He was absent!

Where Are Your Roots?

16 Brennan Manning, in his book *Lion and Lamb,* says, "I can think of no other time in history where the name of Jesus has been so frequently mentioned and the content of His life and teaching so thoroughly ignored" (p. 70). Many claim the name of Jesus but show no desire to follow His teachings. Do not try to argue that you cannot understand the things Jesus said, for no one ever spoke more clearly or in simpler terms. Let's be honest; it is not that we do not understand, it is that we do not choose to follow.

We live in a time in which we are inundated with the "marketing" of Jesus. Turn on your TV and you hear preachers screaming at the congregation the "prosperity gospel" message. "Send me your money and God will bless you." "If you don't sow the seeds of faith with your contribution to my ministry, then God can't bring riches into your life." Whatever happened to Jesus' admonition to the disciples as He was sending them out, "Freely you received, freely give"? How many people did Jesus charge a fee in order to heal them? Where did we ever get the notion that God withholds His grace until we have paid enough to receive it?

November

Do we receive God's grace because we love Him, or do we love Him because He has given us His grace? Go find a quiet place and ponder that question for a while because it is not a trivial question! When our children come into the world, do we immediately love them, provide for them, protect them and cherish them, or do we wait until they have gotten old enough to love us and appreciate us and give something to us? Do we withhold our love until they have earned it through moral and upright living, or is it possible that we still love them even when they fail in life or disappoint us? If we do, does that make our love greater than God's, or have we simply never come to the realization that God's love for us is not dependent upon our righteousness?

Too much religion housed under the banner of Christianity has been distorted and perverted. We need to return to the simple basics that our Lord has taught us and it begins where He began: "Seek first the kingdom of God and all these other things will be added to you." If the seeking of God's kingdom is anything but primary in our life, then God is made secondary! Spiritual growth and strength are found most abundantly in the tranquility of quietness, not in the hubbub of frantic modem living. Toyohiko Kagawa said, "In times of quietness our hearts should be like trees, lifting their branches to the sky to draw down strength which they will need to face the storms that will surely come."

Have you put down your roots in the philosophy of the world, or have you heeded the admonition of Paul: "Do not conform any longer to the pattern of this world, but be transformed by the renewing of your mind. Then you will be able to test and approve what God's will is—his good, pleasing and perfect will" (Romans 12:2). Sounds to me like Paul is saying quit letting the world set the agenda for your life and discover that true living is found in seeking and doing the will of God. Strange thing about God's will—He doesn't force it on you!

The Spirit-filled Church

In the man Jesus, the fullness of God was pleased to dwell! (Read Colossians 1:15-20.) By that, I think Paul meant that everything that makes God who and what He is

November

was present in the person we know as Jesus. This was affirmed by the fourth century Nicene Council when they wrote the Nicene Creed (p. 880 in the *United Methodist Hymnal*). In part, the creed says regarding Jesus, that He is "God from God, Light from Light, true God from true God, begotten not made, of one Being with the Father; through him all things were made." Why is that important? Because the nature of our humanity is such that we cannot truly relate to a concept, but only to a person. If we wonder how God would react to a certain thing or situation, we need only observe the acts and behavior of Jesus. How does God feel about sinners? Look at Jesus! How does God feel about those who are sick or hurting? Look at Jesus! Does God desire to destroy or make whole? Look at Jesus!

Now to another kind of question: How are we to relate to God? What are we to think about and do about His will? If Jesus is to be the model for how we should strive to live our lives, then we have to acknowledge His words, "I have not come to be ministered unto, but to minister. . . . My will is to do the will of my Father who sent me." If Jesus submits His will to the will of the Father, what does that say about what we should do? Are you interested in knowing God's will for your life or are you so caught up in living according to your own desires that you never seek to know what God would have you do and be?

How much "spiritual power" can you observe in your church? Tozer once said, "The dead church holds to the shell of truth without surrendering to it, while the church that wills to do God's will is immediately blessed with a visitation of spiritual power" *(A.W. Tozer, An Anthology,* p. 184). While it is true that any church can benefit by the leadership of a spirit-filled, will-of-God-surrendered pastor, does anyone think that the God who could makes stones cry out is unable to grow a church apart from a single leader? A pastor is just one individual. The church is made up of many people. When the people desire God's will, and seek above all else to know and do it, then the will of God cannot be kept from being done in them.

If you want a spirit-filled pastor, then become a spirit-filled congregation. The more people within a church who surrender their will to the will of the Father, the more powerful and useful the church

November

becomes. This is never easy, nor without cost. Old prejudices must be allowed to die, and truth, grace, and love must be allowed to flow. I cannot conceive of the notion that God would not desire a church to grow. The very command of our Lord as He ascended was, "Go into all the world and make disciples . . ." (Matthew 28:19). Dying as a church is not an option for the Spirit-filled congregation. Giving glory to Jesus and growing in the Spirit is not only a necessity; it is inevitable for the church that seeks to know and do God's will. Which leads me to the final question: Does your church hunger to know and do God's will? Ultimately, what happens to it will reveal the answer.

Which Life Will You Live?

18 There are really two ways to live your life—with God, or without Him. God will always give you the choice. It is rather obvious that since we are not God, thereby not possessing the ability to foresee events and know all things, that our choices will always be imperfect and flawed. By virtue of our very humanity, our decisions will be shortsighted and without question we will make many mistakes. Furthermore, if we insist on making all the decisions, our wills inevitably will conflict with God's will. It is self-deluding rhetoric to tell ourselves we want to do God's will when we refuse to yield to it. How can we be guided by God's will if we are going to insist on telling Him how things must be done?

The time came for my next pastoral appointment. For months I prayed about it and though I did not attempt to tell God where He should send me, it was quite clear to Him (and me) that for many reasons I wanted to go in a certain direction. Eventually, I learned that I would be sent in the opposite direction. I was stunned and disappointed; not because of the church or the wonderful people there, but because my heart was set on a different direction. Suddenly it became profoundly clear to me that while I had been asking for God's will to be done, in reality I desired for mine to be done. While struggling with that inner conflict, I ran across this beautiful little poem that I had read years earlier, but had forgotten. Once more, it spoke words to my heart that I needed to hear.

November

I said: "Let me walk in the field"; God said, "Nay, walk in the town"; I said: "There are no flowers there"; He said: "No flowers, but a crown."

I said, "But the sky is black, there is nothing but noise and din";

But He wept as He sent me back, "There is more," He said, "There is sin."

I said: "But the air is thick, and fogs are veiling the sun"; He answered: "Yet souls are sick, and souls in the dark undone."

I said: "I shall miss the light, and friends will miss me, they say"; He answered: "Choose tonight, if I am to miss you or they."

I pleaded for time to be given: He said: "Is it hard to decide? It will not seem hard in Heaven to have followed the steps of your Guide."

I cast one look at the fields, then set my face to the town; He said: "My child, do you yield? Will you leave the flowers for the crown?"

Then into His hand went mine, and into my heart came He; And I walk in a light Divine, the path I had feared to see.

—George MacDonald— (*Streams in the Desert*, p. 348)

I wonder sometimes why God doesn't give up on us. We so often pull in the direction that He's not leading. Yielding to God's will is not always easy, but I am convinced that it is always right. Throughout life we will be given a choice— our way or God's way. By His grace, let us choose His way.

Are You Contented?

19 Years ago, when milk used to be delivered to a person's home, a milkman put a note on each of his customers' bottles: "This milk is not from contented cows. Our cows are striving to be better and better every day." Well might Christians adopt such a goal for ourselves spiritually. If an athlete becomes content with his current attainment, he will never exceed it. So it is with the Christian life. In terms of your faith, are you content with who you

November

became ten, twenty, or forty years ago? Has your faith never graduated from the elementary Sunday school class you attended while growing up? It seems to me that anything that is alive is either growing or dying.

Before you jump the gun and say, "Well, I'm 80 years old, so I guess I'm dying", I encourage you to stop and think. While it may be true that the body is growing weaker and the mind less reliable, one's spirit does not have to be governed by the body and mind. I know people in their nineties who spend their days in wheel chairs but their spirit is as young and fresh as the dawning of a new day. On the other hand, I know some folks who have just reached mid-life who act like the best of life is behind them. Those of advanced years who are young in spirit are those who are not "content" to live life solely in the past. Young people are energetic and enthusiastic about life in part because they don't waste the present by dwelling on the past. Each new day brings with it new opportunities and new experiences.

The apostle Paul left us with some wonderful advice and we would be wise to heed it: ". . . one thing I do, forgetting what lies behind and straining forward to what lies ahead, I press on toward the goal for the prize of the upward call of God in Christ Jesus" (Philippians 3:13-14). Notice that the statement has two parts— forgetting what has already past and straining (energetically reaching) for what lies ahead. Life lies ahead! Are your eyes fixed on life or on death? Jesus reminded the Sadducees that God is the God of the living, not the dead! (Matthew 22:32). Do you think God's plan for you ends in a grave? No, the prize of the upward call of God in Christ Jesus soars past the grave into eternal life. The upward call shouts to me, "Get up and stop being content with things as they are. Strive for things as they have the potential to become."

When you were a teenager, I'll bet you didn't spend a lot of time worrying about how many years of life you had left, or about dying. You got up each day and went about living. If you awake tomorrow that means you are alive; so get up and embrace the day and all that God will bring to you in the day. Get out into the beauty of His world and LIVE! Go to see someone, call someone, write someone a note, do a good deed, sing a song, write a poem, smile at someone,

November

touch someone, or show love to someone. You're alive, so start living and quit making friends with death. When you become content with life you have stopped "straining forward for the upward call" and you have begun to look backward to the past. God doesn't dwell in the past any more than life does. Life is now and life is future. Go for it! Don't stop living before you die!

A Single Act of Kindness

20 What have you done with your life? As you look back are you satisfied with how you have lived it? Have you added to or diminished the integrity of life? Have you brought people more joy or more sorrow? Have you shown kindness, or indifference, to those who are hurting? Have you made peace in the midst of turmoil or have you brought turmoil where there was peace? We cannot change anything that we have done or failed to do in the past. What we can do is begin where we are and go forward, doing our best to make someone's life happier. We cannot always alleviate pain but with our genuine concern we can share someone's suffering. We can restrain ourselves from engaging in gossip, character assassination, and the spreading of malicious, unsubstantiated rumors.

It's not so much that we don't know the difference between adding to life or detracting from it; it's a matter of disciplining ourselves to choose the high road rather than the low one. Just as a journey of a thousand miles begins with a single step, so the journey toward doing good rather than evil begins with a single act of kindness. To fail to do kindness hardens us as the years roll on, and we begin to become that which we despise in others. Would you rather have a heart that aches because you are too tender or a heart that aches because you have no compassion?

I hope it has not escaped your awareness that God chose to save the world through the submission of Himself to human suffering. In the midst of trouble, we often cry out, "Where is God when I hurt so badly?" My answer: "Hurting and dying on a cross for you and with you!" How often have we heard the age-old question: "Why do the good suffer?" The answer is that almost everyone suffers at some point—both good and bad. Human suffering has more to do with just

November

living than it does with whether one is good or bad. Still, to the degree that I can cause pain or happiness, I choose the latter.

When your life is over, what would you like to have written as your epitaph? The words of Ralph S. Cushman's, *The Parson's Prayer* would satisfy me:

> *I do not ask that crowds may throng the temple,*
>   *That standing room be priced:*
> *I only ask that as I voice the message, they may see Christ!*
>
> *I do not ask for churchly pomp or pageant,*
>   *Or music such as wealth alone can buy:*
> *I only ask that as I voice the message, He may be nigh!*
>
> *I do not ask that men may sound my praises,*
>   *Or headlines spread my name abroad:*
> *I only pray that as I voice the message, hearts may find God!*
>
> *I do not ask for earthly place or laurel,*
>   *Or of this world's distinction any part:*
> *I only ask when I have voiced the message, my Savior's heart!*

Discovering the Plan

21 Do you sometimes feel that God has forgotten you, or is at least disinterested in what is going on in your life? Do you see the dawning of each new day as simply the routine occurrence of another "random" series of events that will unfold before you without plan or purpose? Then listen to God speak to you from the words of the prophet Jeremiah:

> "For I know the plans I have for you," declares the LORD, "plans to prosper you and not to harm you, plans to give you hope and a future. Then you will call upon me and come and pray to me, and I will listen to you. You will seek me and find me when you seek me with all your heart." (Jer. 29:11-13)

Imagine! God has a plan for your life! But there's a catch. The plan will be fulfilled only if you yield to it. An architect can draw

November

detailed and masterful blueprints of a magnificent building, but they remain only lines on a page until someone takes the plans, follows them, and constructs the building. If you note the brief words above from Jeremiah, the first verse is inextricably connected to the latter one. God has a plan for your life—but you will only know what it is if you seek to know God. Even then, He will most likely reveal it to you only a little at the time. If God were to reveal to each of us at the very beginning of our life every aspect of where our lives would lead us, we'd probably give up before we start. So He gives us one day at the time and stands ready to guide us.

Regardless of the circumstances that life brings to us, God can take those circumstances and transform them into something good. Paul said it this way: "We know that all things work together for good, to those who love the Lord and are called according to His purpose" (Romans 8:28). Do you see the connection between "God's plan" and "good things" being brought out of the circumstances of our lives? We need to start reading God's Word as if it was written for us—because it was. The promises contained in the Bible apply to any generation that will embrace them. Was not Paul speaking for you and me when he wrote to the Philippians: "And my God will meet all your needs according to his glorious riches in Christ Jesus"? (4:19). Can we not say with Paul, "I can do all things through Christ who strengthens me"? So often, we profess belief in God's power but then live our lives as if He has none.

Is it not sad that too many of us get up too many days of our lives and march through the day without any consciousness of purpose, either of our own or of God's, and allow the day to dictate to us what we will do, what we will think, and what we will be? When you get up tomorrow, why not begin the day by asking God to reveal to you His plan for your life for that day? Ask for guidance; ask for the intervention of His Holy Spirit in the activities of your day. Ask for opportunities to serve Him and the wisdom to see them when they arise. Throughout the day pause and invite God to direct your path, your thoughts, your words, your deeds. Begin to believe that no matter who you are, where you are, or how old you are, God has a plan for your life. Whatever that plan is, it will be far better and greater than anything we could think up.

November

22

Profoundly Simple

It seems to me that the profound things in life are the simple things, not the complex ones. I once had in my library a set of books on Paul's letter to the Ephesians, written by a well-known author. As you probably know, Ephesians is only six chapters long and contains some of Paul's most profound thoughts. The author who wrote the commentary on Ephesians required seven books (that take up about ten inches of space on my shelf) to contain his thoughts on Paul's short epistle. I have never read the commentaries and probably never will because that's more than I want to know about anything! God gave Moses Ten Commandments. The Jewish rabbis kept adding to them until they had made them into 613 laws. It seems that human beings are never content to keep things simple; we always try to make them more complicated.

There is an old Quaker saying, written by Stephen Grellet, that most of us have heard. My father-in-law had framed it and hung it on his den wall. It's simple and to the point and it goes like this:

> *I expect to pass through this world but once. Any good thing, therefore, that I can do or any kindness I can show to any fellow human being let me do it now. Let me not defer nor neglect it, for I shall not pass this way again.*

That is profound. Even a child can grasp its meaning. But of what value is something that is profound if we do not heed it? Each day God sets before us countless opportunities. Often we ignore, neglect, or decide to put them off to another day. Alas, the chance is often lost forever!

Have you ever felt a deep inner compulsion to visit someone or write a note of appreciation? Maybe the person was sick or going through a hard time and you just dismissed the urge within and told yourself you would do it later—and later never came! The moment was lost, never to be regained. No matter who we are, no matter how young or old, none of us can go back and relive a single day. As the day unfolds itself before us, we must choose in that very moment to live it to its fullest and take every opportunity we can to create

November

something good out of it. Are we not wise enough to realize that we may never pass this way again? We live in an age that is too busy. No one ever heard someone on his deathbed say, "I wish I'd spent more time at the office!"

It seems to me that Jesus accomplished a great deal in His brief life. And yet there is not one single incident recorded in Scripture that tells us He was ever in a hurry. Even when word came to Him about Lazarus' imminent death, He did not hurry back to Bethany. "In the fullness of time," and "My hour has not yet come," were phrases that Jesus lived by. When one looks at the life of our Lord, it is not difficult to see that everywhere He went He did good! He touched people with His compassion and kindness and forever changed their lives. We are not Jesus, but we can follow His example. To do good to others as often as we can and in every place that we can is not a complex philosophy of life. Quite the contrary, it is profoundly simple.

The only question that remains is, "Will we begin to rethink the way we live or go on in the same rut we've been living in?" Today, God will give you the opportunity to show kindness and love to someone. What will you do with it?

The Joy Drought

23 All of us have probably heard the cliché: "When life hands you a lemon, make lemonade." I wonder, however, how many of us have ever thought a little deeper about that. A lemon is sour to the taste and in order to make lemonade palatable, you must add sugar. In order to transform that which is sour into that which is delightful to the taste, the sourness must be offset with sweetness. Have you ever allowed a small child to suck on a lemon, not knowing what he was about to taste until it was in his mouth? Immediately a shocked look flashes across the face and the innocent countenance becomes drawn up in wrinkled lines of bitterness. It is rather self-evident that you cannot make that which is sour or bitter taste sweet by adding more of that which is sour.

The lesson for the Christian should be obvious—when someone does something to you that leaves a bitter taste in your mouth, do not seek to remove the taste by creating more bitterness and discord by

November

responding in like manner, but deflect the bitterness and transform it into sweetness by adding sugar (i.e., respond to evil with good). Perhaps one of the greatest problems in human relationships is that we would rather respond with revenge when we are wronged than seek to heal and restore the relationship by absorbing the wrong and granting forgiveness. When we respond to being wronged by attacking the attacker, we perpetuate the brokenness and further deepen the wound.

There is a hymn we sometimes sing in our worship services that goes like this:

> *There's a sweet, sweet Spirit in this place,*
> *and I know that it's the Spirit of the Lord;*
> *there are sweet expressions on each face,*
> *and I know they feel the presence of the Lord"*
> (*United Methodist Hymnal*, p. 334).

The quickest way for visitors and strangers to feel the sweet presence of God in a sanctuary filled with people is to see it and sense it in the lives of those who worship there. If you were the sole measure of the presence of God in your service of worship, what kind of message would you be sending? Would the person sitting on the pew beside or behind you observe any evidence in you that God is a God of love, joy, and grace? Or would they glean from your countenance that God is a grump who simply tolerates your presence?

Once, while walking through the underground tunnel from the parking deck over to Duke Medical Center, I decided to try an experiment. Each time I met someone, I would smile and say, "How are you?" In the 120-yard walk through the tunnel, I met seven or eight people and spoke to each one. Only two responded back to me. Nonetheless, would you rather meet someone who smiles at you and asks, "How are you", or someone with a sour, grumpy look?

Each of us has a responsibility to make the world in which we live and move be a brighter, more joyful environment. One of the great purposes of Jesus' words is to sow joy into the believer's life. He said in John 11:15, "These things have I spoken to you, that my joy might remain in you, and that your joy might be full." How much of the joy of our Lord is there within you? How much of it do you share with a

November

world that is in a joy drought? Today, why not share a little of Jesus' joy with someone else?

Thanksgiving

24 Thanksgiving did not become a national holiday until 1863, when President Abraham Lincoln proclaimed the last Thursday in November to be a time of national thanksgiving. Strange that in the very midst of the Civil War Lincoln would desire to set aside a time for counting one's blessings. We tend to be thankful only when some monumental event occurs and causes us to give birth to expressions of gratitude.

The apostle Paul once wrote:

> *I am not saying this because I am in need, for I have learned to be content whatever the circumstances. I know what it is to be in need, and I know what it is to have plenty. I have learned the secret of being content in any and every situation, whether well fed or hungry, whether living in plenty or in want. I can do everything through him who gives me strength.*
>
> (Philippians 4:11-13)

We are familiar with being grateful in the midst of abundance, though even there we too often fall short of thanksgiving. To be grateful in the midst of scarcity is foreign to most of us.

There was a German pastor named Martin Rinkart, who in 1636 amidst the turmoil and tragedy of the Thirty Years War, had the demanding task of burying five thousand of his parishioners in one year. That averages out to about fourteen funerals a day. He lived in a time of intense human suffering, war, death, and economic deprivation. Yet, even as the world seemed to be crumbling around him, he sat one day at his window and wrote this table grace for his children:

> *Now thank we all our God,*
> *with hearts and hands and voices*
> *who wondrous things has done,*
> *in whom this world rejoices;*

November

> *and from our mothers' arms,*
> *has blessed us on our way*
> *with countless gifts of love*
> *and still is ours today.*
> (United Methodist Hymnal, p. 102)

Here was a man who had discovered that thanksgiving is not dependent upon outward circumstances, but upon the willingness of a person to open him or her self up to the moving of God's grace, even when surrounded with tragedy. No, it isn't easy to be thankful when on the surface there seems to be little for which to give thanks, but it can be done, and we are always the richer for doing it.

Life will always be a mixture of good and bad, happiness and sorrow, pain and joy, tears and laughter. Life becomes "out of whack" when we allow the bad things we encounter to blind us to all the good that comes to us as well. We need to rethink and refocus; not as one who denies the reality of evil and tragedy and trouble, but as Christians who in the midst of adversity believe and trust in a God who is greater than our troubles. We would do well to quit complaining so much and start doing more praising and thanksgiving!

Life is good! Therefore, let us resolve to make ourselves more aware of its goodness. Even if we are presently suffering from some unexpected adversity, let us look beyond it to the good that still permeates our lives. Let us learn with Paul to be content in whatever condition we find ourselves.

What Does God Have to Say About It?

25 Does God have anything to say to us about the poor and hungry? Let's look at Deuteronomy 15:11 for starters: "Since there will never cease to be some in need on the earth, I therefore command you, 'Open your hand to the poor and needy neighbor in your land'" (NRSV). This isn't a suggestion God is making, it is a command! The word "poor" (according to Strong's Exhaustive Concordance) appears 204 times in the Bible. If there is one thing in the Old Testament that seemed to infuriate God, causing Him to speak warning after warning to the people through the prophets, it was their neglect, abuse of, and general indifference to the poor in their midst.

When the laws governing the behavior of the Jews as a nation were being formed, central to their instructions was to care about the poor and the strangers in their midst. If they loaned money to the poor, they were to charge them no interest (Exodus 22:25). If they grew crops in their fields they were to leave enough behind for the poor to glean (Leviticus 19:9-10). Great effort was put forth to protect and defend the stranger in their midst, the widows, and the orphans.

When Jesus appeared on the scene, His compassion for the poor was a significant part of his ministry. He fed the hungry multitudes and He associated frequently with those who were thought of as outcasts. We may ignore the poor beggars on the street but Jesus would never have turned His back on them. Later on, when the disciples began to preach, they undoubtedly remembered what Jesus had taught them, for even when they had no money for themselves, they gave what they had. Peter and John, encountering the lame man outside the Temple, said to him, "Silver or gold I do not have, but what I have I give you. In the name of Jesus Christ of Nazareth, walk" (Acts 3:6).

It is easy to decry the plight of the poor, and it is easy to justify doing nothing because some of them will try to take advantage, but one thing I'm sure of: God will never ask you, "How many people did you allow to swindle you out of a few dollars?" I am equally as sure one question He _will_ undoubtedly ask is, "How many poor people I sent your way did you offer to help?" I know we aren't obligated to help someone we know is trying to con us, but God will never condemn you for sincerely seeking to help someone in need, even if they did take advantage of you. Our role is to do our part and answer for our conduct. God will hold them accountable for theirs.

Whenever we seek to help the poor, we embark on a mission of compassion and grace. Freely we have received, freely let us give in Jesus' name. The poor are all around us and we can either ignore them or seek to put bread in their hands and food in their stomachs. Jesus said: "And if anyone gives even a cup of cold water to one of these little ones because he is my disciple I tell you the truth, he will

November

certainly not lose his reward" (Matthew 10:42). What greater reward than to see someone who was desperate and hungry appear content because their stomach is no longer empty! "Lord, when did we see you hungry and feed you? . . . I tell you the truth, whatever you did for one of the least of these brothers of mine, you did for me" (Matthew 25:37, 40).

What Kind of Church Are We?

26 The church is called "the body of Christ." So what have we made of Christ's body? What do we contribute to its health, its life, its strength? We have taken what is supposed to be a vibrant, living, Spirit-filled, self-sacrificing, outward-reaching, disciple-making creation and we have institutionalized it, ritualized it, politicized it, and turned it inward to serve ourselves. In so doing, we have created an organization that only faintly resembles the New Testament church. If I understand at all our Lord's will for the church, it means that it was created to spread the word that Jesus Christ is Lord. It has been entrusted with the precious holy gospel—the good news that Jesus is Savior—and its primary purpose is to bear witness to that truth.

Where Jesus is proclaimed and acknowledged as Lord, the church will be a servant—not a master. The church was not created in order to rule over others or to be served, but to become a servant to God and His people. We assume we properly serve God when we more or less regularly make our way to a weekly service of worship. Sitting in a sanctuary for an hour each week does not fulfill our vow to be a disciple of Jesus Christ. Membership without service is not discipleship. Jesus' last words to His followers in Matthew was "Go into all the world and make disciples"; not "Withdraw into your sanctuaries and get comfortable." We insulate ourselves **from** the suffering that is all around us, and then convince ourselves that we have no responsibility to alleviate it. Our concern should be not **just** for those who are hungry and destitute, but also those who are hurting, and lonely, and broken, and lost.

We must never forget that the primary purpose of clergy and laity alike is to bear witness to the glory of Jesus. John Wesley's

November

admonition to his preachers was:

> *You may be elegant, you may be winsome, you may be a good financier, yea, you may be in great demand, but if you do not win souls, you are a failure. You are not called to do this or that, but to win souls.*

Perhaps the greatest failure of the modern church is that it has lost its passion for souls. We have become so enchanted with living the good life in this world that we have blinded ourselves to the reality of the world that is to come. Jesus pulls us back to reality when He confronts us with, "Of what value will it be to you if you gain the whole world, and lose your soul?" Are we so blind and naïve as to think that Jesus died on a cross so we could have a more affluent and financially secure existence in this world?

No, Jesus didn't die on a cross just so we could get to heaven (though that certainly was part of it). He died so that we could have life and have it more abundantly—life here and now, as well as life later. By abundance He did not mean an accumulation of material things on earth but the calm, peaceful inner assurance of the Spirit's presence. There is no greater blessing in living than to be at peace with God and with one's own soul. And so let us resolve to do our part to make the church become what the church was intended to be. It's Christ's body and we either help it to be healthy or we diminish its power and purpose.

The Melody of Life

27 Henry Wadsworth Longfellow once said, "Music is the universal language of mankind." There is a mystery and a rhythmic flow to music, whether vocal or instrumental, that has the capacity to reach past the eardrums and mental consciousness of an individual and to meander its way into the heart and soul. It touches not just the mind but also the emotions. It has the ability not only to fill an empty space within us, but also to draw feelings out of us in a way that nothing else has the power to do. Whose spirit has not been stirred by the musical masterpieces performed by skilled

November

orchestras or the world's great singers? One would think that even an atheist would have a difficult time sitting through Handel's Messiah without sensing the touch of God's hand arranging the notes in all their stirring and harmonic beauty.

The beauty in music is magnified and perfected when the melody is blended with the harmony of other notes. Yet when the other parts of a song are played without the melody, they often sound discordant or out of tune. It is the melody that carries the song, gives it a foundation, and draws the beauty and meaning out of the other notes. At times, it sounds as if the harmony has overpowered the melody and one has to listen intently to clearly hear the guiding sound—just ask any untrained choir members who are trying to pick out their part in the midst of the alto, bass, tenor and soprano notes.

In its own way, all of life is a song—a song with many notes and many parts. God's will is the melody that gives life its beauty and meaning. When we seek to live apart from His melody, life will seem discordant, out of kilter, and devoid of meaning and purpose. The universe is governed by an established set of laws and principles. When those laws are broken or interfered with, chaos can follow. For example, there is an axiom in physics that says, "Two objects cannot occupy the same space at the same time." As long as objects in space follow an orbit that does not cause them to collide, there is harmony. Likewise, the laws of God's will are written into the fabric of our being. As long as we are in harmony with the melody of His will our lives function in spiritual order. When we violate those laws, the melody of God's will becomes hidden and we live in uncertainty and inner turmoil.

The Genesis creation narrative describes how God created the universe out of a chaotic, formless void. He brought order and stability to that which was without order. When human beings introduced sin into the world, they brought chaos back into the order of life which God had established. Instead of the peace and tranquility that God intended, sin brought pride, shame, guilt, envy, and murder. No longer was God the underlying melody of human life; that part had been buried under an avalanche of human will, and spiritual chaos became the norm.

November

When we finally reach the place that we are willing to allow God's will to be re-established in our lives, then stability and order return. Suddenly, the melody of life can be heard again and even though the world in which we live may still be chaotic, the spirit within us will be at peace. "How can I find the melody again?" you ask. By embracing the One called Jesus!

The Ancient Beauty Within

28 It was revealed to us in the beginning, but somehow we manage to overlook the elusive truth hidden deep in the creating words of God. He said it in Genesis 1:26 (New Living Translation): "Then God said, "Let us make human beings in our image, to be like us. They will reign over the fish in the sea, the birds in the sky, the livestock, all the wild animals on the earth, and the small animals that scurry along the ground." To be made in the image of God has been studied, debated, and argued about for centuries. There is no one definitive answer that allows us to condense its meaning into a single sentence. But here's a thought: Could it be that God, in creating us, put a part of Himself in each of us that only becomes revealed when we search for Him? Jeremiah gave us a hint: "You will seek me and find me when you seek me with all your heart" (Jeremiah 19:13).

God is creating, life-giving energy. We exist and breathe because God wills it. That force of energy we call "life" comes from Him, and many of us believe that when we die that essence of life returns to Him. Listen carefully to what Paul tells us in Acts 17:26-28:

> *From one man he made every nation of men, that they should inhabit the whole earth; and he determined the times set for them and the exact places where they should live. God did this so that men would seek him and perhaps reach out for him and find him,* ***though he is not far from each one of us. "For in him we live and move and have our being."*** *As some of your own poets have said, "We are his offspring."*

One of the great classics of Christian literature is *The Confessions of St. Augustine*. Augustine, whose life spanned parts of

487

November

the fourth and fifth centuries, was a somewhat rebellious young man and was for a while consumed with satisfying the many lusts of the flesh. But one day he was converted and went on to become one of the great saints of the church. In his pursuit of the presence of God, he finally discovered that it had been with him all the time. Listen to his beautiful and revealing, almost poetic words:

> *How late I came to love you, O beauty so ancient and so fresh, how late I came to love you! You were within me while I had gone outside to seek you. Unlovely myself, I rushed towards all those lovely things you had made. And always you were with me, and I was not with you. All these beauties kept me far from you—although they would not have existed at all unless they had their being in you. You called, you cried, you shattered my deafness. You sparkled, you blazed, you drove away my blindness. You shed your fragrance, and I drew in my breath, and I pant for you. I tasted and now I hunger and thirst. You touched me, and now I burn with longing for your peace. (The Lord of the Journey, p. 73)*

In the Gospels, Jesus talks about the kingdom of heaven being within us. He talks about the "treasure hidden in the field, for which a man would go and sell all that he has in order to possess it." Is not the kingdom the presence of God and could it not be that the treasure hidden in the field is referring to the field of our heart? If you are truly serious about discovering God, no matter where the journey takes you, it must ultimately bring you back to your own heart and soul. That is where the "beauty so ancient and fresh" is pleased to dwell.

Love Discovered in Pain

29 In his masterful little book *Lion and Lamb*, Brennan Manning writes:

> *An old Hasidic rabbi, Levi Yitzhak of Berdichev in the Ukraine, used to say that he discovered the meaning of love from a drunken peasant. Entering a tavern in the Polish countryside, he saw two peasants at a table, both gloriously in*

November

their cups. Each was protesting how much he loved the other, when Ivan said to Peter "Peter, tell me what hurts me?" Bleary-eyed, Peter looked at Ivan: "How do I know what hurts you?" Ivan's answer was swift: "If you don't know what hurts me, how can you say you love me?" (p. 126)

We live in a world in which we are so consumed by our own lives that too often we fail, or refuse, to take note of the pain in the lives of those around us, even those closest to us. As a result, life is lived out in pockets of isolation although we are surrounded by crowds of people. There is truth in Ivan's response—how can we love someone if we have no comprehension of the pain within his or her life? And all of us experience inner pain.

Jesus had many qualities that made Him unique and special. But perhaps Brennan Manning is quite insightful when he points us to that quality in Jesus which makes Him so appealing to humanity—His deep compassion. Jesus came into our world as God/Man, not to stand above us in order to judge and condemn us, but to experience the depth of our pain within the tenderness of His own body and soul. Thus, Manning describes Jesus' compassion with the words "relentless tenderness."

There is a deep longing in each of us, whether acknowledged or not, to be accepted and loved. Nowhere will that love and acceptance ever be experienced more fully than with Jesus Christ. What drew people to Him then and now was not the awesomeness of His wisdom (profound though it is) but the compassion that flowed from Him like soothing medicine rubbed on a painful wound. The woman caught in adultery, the despised tax collector, the abused prostitute, the leper, the beggar—all encountered Someone who knew what caused them pain, and that became the crossroads of their life where they finally experienced love and healing.

Most of us are keenly aware of our failures, our sinfulness, and our separation from the ideal of perfection. Inwardly we brutalize and torture ourselves with condemnation and self-hatred, so much so that we isolate ourselves from both the love and pain of others. We cannot be the healing balm in another's life until we first become willing to be

November

healed. Perhaps one of the most difficult concepts for us to grasp is the reality that God can love us in spite of our sin. We react like Adam in the garden paradise after his fall; rather than run to the light of God's healing presence—where we finally can be made whole—we seek to hide ourselves from Him, fearing that He will condemn us. We forget the words of scripture, that Jesus "did not come to condemn the world but to save it" (John 3:17).

Where do you hurt? Self-condemnation? Estrangement from a loved one? Loneliness? Sickness? Sorrow? The "relentless tenderness" of Jesus yearns to touch you at the point of your pain and make you whole. Will you come and be made whole? And if you do, will you now become God's instrument of grace for someone else who is suffering? Often we will become whole ourselves when in a moment of self-denial we put aside our own pain in order to share someone else's.

A Name above All Names

30 What's in a name? When babies are born, parents often struggle to find just the right name to give to this tiny little creature that enters our world undefined by character and personality. Many things influence the choice we make—gender, family names, special people in our lives whom we wish to honor by giving our child their name (my middle name, "Byron" was the first name of the doctor who delivered me). Some draw from historic figures like John Wesley, Lincoln, or Washington, or sports heroes, but more often than not, we simply choose names that sound good together.

Our name becomes our identity. It is how we are recognized and addressed. My guess is that none of us was given a name because our parents foresaw what we would become and what we would do with our lives. But when Jesus was born, it was not left up to Mary and Joseph to choose a name for Him; the name He was given by the angel would define who and what He would become. The angel said to Mary, "You shall call Him Jesus, for He shall save His people from their sins." In Hebrew thought, names were chosen for children "for

November

its meaning in God—to acknowledge his gift, or to express hope or destiny in him" *(Interpreter's Bible Commentary,* Vol. 7, p. 253).

The name "Jesus" literally means, "The Lord is salvation." The emphasis is placed on the act of God to save. The angel makes this quite clear when he says, "He shall save His people from their sins." In the context of that statement, it is clear that the purpose of Jesus' life was that of Savior. From conception to resurrection, it was declared that Jesus' unique relationship to the world would be bound up in the concept of salvation history.

Salvation is centered in forgiveness. We can forgive people when they wrong us, but only God has the power or right to forgive sin, for sin is not committed against humanity, but against the Creator's righteousness. The Bible tells us that without the shedding of blood there can be no forgiveness. When our forgiveness was dependent upon God's willingness to shed His own blood, He did not withhold Himself. Little wonder that Paul could say so boldly,

> *Therefore God exalted him to the highest place and gave him the name that is above every name, that at the name of Jesus every knee should bow, in heaven and on earth and under the earth, and every tongue confess that Jesus Christ is Lord, to the glory of God the Father.* (Phil. 2: 10-11)

Goodness, nobility, and virtue are bound up in the name of Jesus. And He is called "Wonderful, Counselor, the Mighty God, the Everlasting Father, the Prince of Peace." We know Him as Emmanuel—God with us—as Savior, Redeemer, the Good Shepherd, the Son of God, the Lamb of God, the Root of Jesse, the Rose of Sharon, the Lily of the Valley, the Bright and Morning Star, the Great I Am, and by a dozen other names, but no name sounds so sweet and soothing to the soul, as the precious name of Jesus. "Jesus, Jesus, Jesus, sweetest name I know!"

How touched and moved I am by the wonderful name of Jesus—five letters and only two syllables, but what comfort and peace they bring to our soul. And that is so, because in ways that our minds cannot understand, but somehow our souls are able to grasp, in Jesus we have been saved from our sins. Hallelujah!

December

The Mystery of Love

1   I once wrote to my wife, attempting to describe to her what I believed about love. It hardly rivaled St. Paul's letter to the Corinthians, but it was my meager attempt to make what I felt come alive in words. Having experienced the deep pain of divorce I found in Gaye's love the healing power of God. Here, in part, is what I wrote:

That which infuses life where life has gone out is called love. Love always seeks to give itself totally and completely to another, for it can only sustain itself, replace itself, multiply itself as it seeks to give itself away. Love is that which, when it is hurt, heals itself by risking being hurt again. Love is able to feel and absorb the pain of another in such a way that the pain is taken within itself and released through the sharing of cleansing tears. Love knows anger only when the one who is loved is hurt or mistreated. Sometimes it is required to sit quietly and listen, to sort out words and feelings, and see beyond their surface meaning, all the while gazing into the depths of one's soul.

Love is never ashamed of itself, but sees itself in pure light because it is created by a pure God. Love dwells in hope, overcomes sorrow, creates joy, and rises above all things. Love looks deeply into the eyes of the one loved and pours out the essence of its own life. It is the mystical entrusting of one's very soul into the care and keeping of another. Love is forgiveness that is always offered before it is asked. It looks beyond the loved one's faults and sees what the person has the potential to become. Therefore, it joyfully and wholeheartedly accepts the person as he or she is. Love refuses to dwell on the past, lives today to the fullest, and looks forward to tomorrow with hope. Love exists only for the joy of giving itself to another, for without an object upon which to bestow itself, love fades as quickly as the rose plucked from the bush. Thus, love discovers its own life within the heart and soul of another.

Love is always costly because it gives itself beyond its own pain—therein, it manifests that it is priceless. Love is pure

December

because it seeks joy for another beyond its own joy—therein, it makes known its matchlessness. Love is beautiful because it makes everything it touches more beautiful—therein, it reveals its power to redeem. Love is eternal because God is its Author and has declared it so—therein, it reveals its timelessness.

When life as we have known it ceases to be, when mountains, and oceans, and worlds have passed into the receding history of time, one thing will rise up from the ruins in greater power than ever, into the promise of timeless eternity—love.

Deep inside of us, God has planted the tiny seed of love. Whether it grows, remains the same, or dies, depends upon what we do with it. What made people respond so deeply to Jesus was that He loved them even when their response to that love was to impale Him on a cross. But who would have thought a crucified Man could transform the world by His willingness to love them unto death? By dying to self, He gave us life. And so I have concluded that love is born out of the willingness to let self die. The mysterious miracle which then takes place is that love gives birth to the person we were intended to be. How great is our God! How marvelous is this experience of love!

Spiritual Enlightenment

2 Since the Enlightenment, Western civilization has embraced an approach to life that is almost totally based on rationalization that uses the Aristotelian division of the five senses. What cannot be seen, touched, heard, smelled, or tasted is often considered to be invalid or unacceptable. As a result, we modern Christians have been programmed to give little credence or importance to the depth and reality of the spiritual world. This is reflected by the absence of any meaningful and disciplined devotional/spiritual life among most of us.

Somewhere inside us, there is a hunger for deep things of the spirit, but because we are so consumed by the physical world, we are unwilling to look in the spiritual realm for them. The spiritual realm that I refer to is not some dimly lit room where people have gathered for a séance, nor the ghostly horrors so popularly displayed on the movie and TV screens. The spiritual realm of which I speak is that realm within one's self, wherein God is able to touch us at the deepest

December

level of our being. Psychiatrists might call it the subconscious; Paul would describe it as "the inner man." (Ephesians 3:16) Others would call it our spirit or our soul. Jesus said, "God is spirit, and his worshipers must worship in spirit and in truth" (John 4:24). One of the results of the Incarnation (Christ coming in human flesh) was that it drew attention to the spiritual world. Jesus told the Pharisees, "Before Abraham was, I am." He also said that He had come down from heaven and that His kingdom was not of this world (John 8:23).

The important lasting qualities of life that we all want, and which are always so elusive, are spiritual qualities. That's why as long as we seek to find them on the level of the physical, we will never discover them. Peace, joy, and love are attributes of God which we can have, but only if we are willing to receive them from the hand of God. One of the mysteries of the gifts of God's Spirit is that we cannot have the gift without the Giver. Therein is where humanity continues to go astray. We want the attributes of God without having to bow down before God.

It all began in a Garden called Eden, where a man and a woman thought they could become like God, and thus have no further need for God. We are like a person who wants to enjoy the delight of some scrumptious meal without eating it. Likewise, you cannot be soothed and comforted by a warm bath until you are immersed in it. Nor can you comprehend the beauty and grandeur of a mountain range until you stand in the midst of it. Only when we come aside in quietness and honest inward reflection are we ever going to discover why we were created, and for Whom. Our happiness will not be found in another person or thing. It is found within ourselves as we discover and become awed by that which God has done, is doing, and will do in us.

Apart from the spirit we cannot begin to comprehend God with the mind. That is not to say that we don't need to use our minds or that we should reject rational thought. But there is no way the limitations of human understanding will ever be able to grasp the magnificence of God. Even our spiritual natures cannot take in all that He is; but they will surely put us more in touch with that which God is than all our rationalizations ever will. It is time we quit being afraid of the spiritual and start seeking to embrace it. We need to look at scripture differently

December

and begin to see the deep spiritual fabric upon which it was written. To many of you this will sound like mystical nonsense. To others I say, "They who have ears to hear, let them hear what the Spirit says to the church."

The Hunger for Righteousness

3 When was the last time you "hungered and thirsted for righteousness"? You will recall, I trust, that one of Jesus' Beatitudes was "Blessed are they who hunger and thirst for righteousness, for they shall be filled." That passage, of course, comes from the Sermon on the Mount, found in the fifth chapter of Matthew. This particular beatitude goes to the heart and core of the Christian faith. The Greek word *makarios*, which is translated as "blessed," means happiness and joy to the highest degree, a joy above which there is no higher joy. Note that Jesus does not say that this joy is given only to the person who has attained righteousness, but to the one who hungers and thirsts for it. To hunger and thirst means to have a deep and strong desire for something that has not yet been fully attained. And yet the promise is that for the persons who hunger and thirst for righteousness, the day shall come when they shall be perfectly filled or satisfied.

I believe that the righteousness for which we are to hunger is Jesus Himself. He is our righteousness—that Being which takes our unrighteousness and transforms it into His righteousness. We live in a world of unfulfilled and unhappy people. Nothing seems to satisfy or bring to us any lasting sense of fulfillment. This is so because we too often choose the lesser things in life rather than reaching for the ultimate—God in Christ. Unfortunately, our hunger and thirsting is not for righteousness but for the satisfying of appetites that have little or nothing to do with Christ. Jesus Christ is moved to the periphery of our concerns. When He who is the center of life—the hub around which our lives ought to revolve—is placed at the outer edge of our living, our lives never run smoothly but are like a wheel whose center is way off-center. The ride is always bumpy.

If you carefully examine the life of the apostle Paul, you will discover that he found peace within himself by being "in Christ." Yet most of us choose the world over Christ, partly because we are afraid

December

of what we might be asked to give up in order to attain oneness with Him. J. Rufus Moseley, in his book *Perfect Everything,* writes, "In Jesus we lose nothing worth keeping and get everything worth having" (p. 21). Joy will not come by simply knowing the teachings of Christ apart from being in union with the Teacher. That which separates Jesus Christ from all other teachers is that He offers us the opportunity to be in spiritual union with a living Being we have come to know as God.

The more of Christ we seek, the more of Christ we shall have. The human body and spirit were not created for the purpose of sin, but for righteousness. Righteousness exists only in union with God. For fallen humanity, righteousness is not living in a state of sinlessness, but living in a state of redemption and forgiveness that has been offered as a free gift by Christ. As long as we seek oneness with Christ based on the premise of our own goodness, we will never be in union with Him. But when we allow the hunger within us to be satisfied by accepting from God that which we cannot earn or gain for ourselves, the beatitude becomes fulfilled in us and our hunger and thirst are satisfied. Then we begin to live in a relationship of unsurpassed peace and joy.

We all live busy, demanding lives, but the happiest person among us is the one who has been made rich by attaining the righteousness of God that is offered in union with Jesus. As you read these words, do you feel an inner hunger and thirst for righteousness tugging at your insides? Then do not quench the Spirit, but allow your body and soul to be fed by the righteousness of God that is found only in Christ Jesus.

God Suffers With Us

4 Who is there who has not wrestled with the reality and mystery of suffering? To experience the presence of suffering will inevitably lead to the question, "Why?" More often than not, we will leave the question with an unsatisfactory or incomplete answer. E. Stanley Jones wrote in his book *Christ and Human Suffering*:

> *A pure love suffers when it comes into contact with sin in the loved one, and the purer the love the more poignant the*

pain. When the pure and holy love of God comes into contact with sin in us, his loved ones, then at the junction of that sin and that love a cross is set up. . . . For love cannot be love and remain apart and aloof. If it be love, it will insinuate itself into the sins and sorrows of others and make them its own. . . . If, therefore, in the midst of our pain and suffering we cry out in protest that God has made a world in which sin and suffering are possible, let us remember that if it costs us a great deal to live in a world like this, it costs God more to make one like this. To make one like this meant that he had to live in it as Love. That meant his own cross. (pp. 152-53)

We often forget that God suffers too. Isaiah, in describing the Suffering Servant, said, "He is a man of sorrows and acquainted with grief." God does not remove Himself from our pain; He joins Himself to it. One of mysteries of the atonement is that Christ somehow mystically took upon Himself that which we suffer in this life. That does not mean that we are necessarily freed from pain and sorrow, but it does mean we do not carry the burden alone. God shares it with us! Paul Claudel submits that: "Jesus did not come to explain suffering nor to take it away: he came to fill it with his presence" (*The Lord of the Journey*, p. 351).

As we reflect on the pain and suffering of Christ, never let us lose sight of the suffering that took place in the heart of the Father. What parent can look indifferently upon the suffering of his or her child? The Father and the Son are one. The heart of the Father must have been broken as He restrained Himself from saving His Son. Only His deep love for humanity allowed God to permit such divine sacrifice. To have intervened in the Son's suffering would have removed the means of human redemption. Jesus said, "Greater love hath no man than this, that he lay down his life for his friend." Perhaps we might also ponder this thought: Greater love hath no one than this, that he allow his only son to lay down his life for the sake of others.

Once more quoting E. Stanley Jones:

. . . what fell on Jesus, fell on God, what he bore, God bore; his cross was God's cross. Then this outward cross that was lifted up in history is a sign of that inward cross that lies upon

December

the heart of God. When Jesus says, "He that hath seen me hath seen the Father," he means, among other things, that "he that hath seen me on the cross hath seen the Father on the cross." The cross, then, is God's heartbreak. (p. 151)

Christmas is approaching and we will rejoice in the birth of our Savior. It might be beneficial today to remember the suffering that awaited God and His child. Grace and peace through Christ our Lord.

When Peace is Elusive

5 There are certain places you can go that allow you to feel the presence of God in special ways. Some find it at the ocean, in the mountains, in the woods, or out on a lake or river. One such place for my wife and me is the peaceful feeling we experience at our retirement home near Kerr Lake, just outside of Henderson, NC.

Most of the time, the only sounds that interrupt the quietness there are the sounds of birds singing, crickets chirping, frogs croaking, or the gentle wind rustling through the trees. There are no other houses within a quarter of a mile. So beautiful are the surroundings that I built a bench in the backyard facing the sloping wooded area. Just to the left of the bench we planted a small flowerbed of coleus and impatiens. In the midst of the flowers, there sits a small life-like raccoon and rabbit overlooking a goldfish pond that mesmerizes you with the peaceful sound of a waterfall. Rising up from the flowers is a sign I carved which states in Hebrew: *Makone Leshalom Liphne Yahweh.* The English translation beneath the Hebrew reads, "A place of peace in God's presence." Many times I have sat there immersed in the peaceful presence of God's nearness.

But no matter how peaceful the surroundings, no matter how soothing one's experience of God's presence has been in the past, when the heart is torn and troubled there is no peace. One such time occurred for me in 1992 when I learned that my youngest teen-age daughter would be moving to Alabama and I no longer would see her every other week. I was reminded anew that peace is not a place; peace is an inner experience. I sat on the bench in our yard and prayed, but my troubled heart felt no peace. I knew God was there, just as He is

December

everywhere we go, but the pain I felt inwardly denied me the joy of feeling His nearness. I became aware of a second lesson: that when one cannot "feel" the presence of God, that is when we must go on depending upon the depth of our faith to reassure us that God is still with us.

I recounted in my mind the words of Jesus to the disciples: "Peace I leave with you; my peace I give you. I do not give to you as the world gives. Do not let your hearts be troubled and do not be afraid" (John 14:27). I believed those words with all my heart but the pain within me would not allow them to renew in me the peace that I longed to feel. Love for my daughter and the coming loss of her presence evoked too much inner emotion to brush the pain aside and abide in the peace that I knew God wanted me to experience.

Perhaps it only revealed the shallowness of my faith in a moment of crisis, but in all honesty, I have to confess that peace eluded me. From that experience, I learned a third lesson: that human beings cannot escape their humanity and faith is not an experience that is lived in perfection. When peace is not present, nonetheless, faith is just beneath the surface, waiting like a germinating seed to break through the hard layer of life's crushing disappointments. Oftentimes it is the tears of our heartache that moisten the soil of life's hardships and thus play a part in bringing forth the blossoming flower of life's hope. We need not add to our lack of peace the guilt of not "feeling" peaceful, for God understands our humanity. The greatness of His love and grace accepts us even in our weakness. The Apostle Paul was right: "In our weakness His strength is made perfect."

As for me, I still felt a great sense of loss. That inner restlessness was not quieted for a long time, but eventually the peace of God began to permeate the innermost part of my being, and I knew through faith that ultimately everything would be all right.

Is Your Savior Your Lord?

6 There seems to be a growing movement among many Christians toward a renewed interest and understanding of what it means to be a Christian. Simply joining a church and doing nothing more than just attending worship services now and then is

December

revealing itself to be inadequate in the nurture of one's spiritual relationship with God. There is a growing hunger to discover the purpose of life as it relates to communion with God. Discipleship is becoming a prominent word again. There is church membership and then there is discipleship—the two are not synonymous.

Maxie Dunnam, in his book *Congregational Evangelism,* says, "We can't claim Jesus as Savior without a willingness to surrender to him as Lord" *(*p. 28). Think about that for a moment. Have you surrendered to Jesus and allowed Him to be the Lord of your life? We want a Savior, but do we want a Lord? Have we in America become so wedded to the desire to be number one, to always be the victor, that we see "surrender"—in our spiritual relationship with God—as totally unacceptable? Is not this the very core of what sin is about—that we must be in control—that we must be the ones who sit on the throne of life? I know of no one who has a deep spiritual relationship with God who has not willingly yielded his or her will to God's. That was the essence of Jesus' life in human flesh. He said, "My will is to do the will of Him who sent me."

God is not merely a convenience—someone we should call on only when all else fails. If that is the way you treat Him, then without ever knowing the details of your life, I can know, with almost absolute certainty, that there is an emptiness and a nagging sense of unhappiness in your life. Many people reject discipleship because they correctly see that it brings with it radical demands. They are unwilling to ask Jesus what He would have them do, because they know the answer will cut across the grain of their own wills. "You can be my Savior, Jesus, but I will not allow You to be my Lord. For if You are Lord, then that leaves me with the role of servant; and I refuse to be subservient."

Too often, we fail to realize that spiritual growth and health are very similar to physical growth and health, in the sense that we have to do certain things in order for them to happen. Happiness and peace are inner experiences that are dependent upon spiritual disciplines. Just as we can starve our bodies by not providing them with the proper nutrients, so we can starve our souls if we withhold spiritual nourishment.

December

Each of us needs a personal encounter with the Lord of life. There can be no substitute for such an event. E. Stanley Jones spoke of his own encounter with Jesus with these words, "The center of my being was changed from self to the Savior. I didn't try by an act of will to give up my sins—they were gone. I looked into his face and was forever spoiled for anything that was unlike him" *(A Song of Ascents,* p. 28). There is the key—the change must not start on the outside, not by giving up our pet sins one by one, but by allowing the change to take place on the inside, at the center of all that makes us what we are. Jones goes on to say, "I don't have to persuade him to forgive me; he has forgiven me. It is a matter of my turning and my acceptance. He accepts me if and when I accept his acceptance. I do not have to overcome his reluctance. I have to lay hold on his highest willingness" (p. 22). It was the great church father St. Augustine who said it most profoundly, "We are made for God, and we are restless till we rest in him." Are you restless? I know in whom you can find rest—His name is Jesus!

Voluntary Poverty

7 Oswald Chambers once wrote:

> As we draw on the grace of God He increases voluntary poverty all along the line. Always give the best you have got every time; never think about who you are giving it to, let other people take it or leave it as they choose. Pour out the best you have, and always be poor. Never reserve anything; never be diplomatic and careful about the treasure God gives.
>
> "Give to him who asks you." Why do we always make this mean money? Our Lord makes no mention of money. The blood of most of us seems to run in gold. The reason we make it mean money is because that is where our heart is. Peter said, "Silver and gold I do not have, but what I do have I give you." God grant we may understand that the spring of giving is not impulse nor inclination, but the inspiration of the Holy Spirit, I give because Jesus tells me to. (*The Oswald Chambers Daily Devotional Bible*, p. 583)

December

The happiest people I have ever known are those who are generous givers. There are few possessions in their lives that they cling to as too precious to allow someone to have. As a result their souls are not bound to that which is material but are attached to that which is eternal. And yet, they seem to lack for nothing. They discover that Jesus' words fulfill themselves in their lives: "Give, and it will be given to you. A good measure, pressed down, shaken together and running over, will be poured into your lap. For with the measure you use, it will be measured to you" (Luke 6:38). Note how Jesus emphasized the greatness of that which will be received by the three descriptive phrases, "pressed down, shaken together, running over."

All the material things we possess do not seem nearly so important when we are faced with the reality of our death. One thing I have discovered in having cancer is that what one possesses becomes more and more insignificant, and how one relates to those we love becomes priceless. The value of living becomes fine tuned, sharply focused, and we discover the real treasures of life are to be found in relationships, not in possessions. The most significant relationship of all is the one that we have with the Lord Jesus Christ. When we come to know Him as He is, we discover that He voluntarily assumed poverty for our sakes. He left the glory and splendor of heaven and became the suffering servant who had nowhere to lay His head.

For what purpose did the Lord of life become poor? For the purpose of claiming us as His own. Take the time to read Paul's description of Jesus' "voluntary poverty" in Philippians (2:5-11). The greatest gift was the priceless gift of His righteousness which He willingly surrendered in return for our sins. What an exchange—righteousness for sinfulness! How is it possible to not love Someone who gave all that He has and is for our sake? And if we truly love such a Person how can we not willingly serve Him? And how does He ask that we serve Him? By loving one another and by freely giving even as we have been blessed by His giving. Here is the great paradox—when we become willing to be poor, that is when we will become rich. Are your treasures hidden away in a bank, or are they stored in the treasury of heaven?

December

The Mind Controlled by the Spirit

8 There is a spiritual dimension to our humanity that not only determines our eternal destiny, but also our happiness and peace in the present. Unless one is mentally ill, every human being wants to be happy—yet happiness is often an elusive reality. We live in a world of unhappy people. Many of us could ease the tension in our life and experience the reality of peace if we would simply get in touch with our inner selves (our spirit), and bring that spiritual part of our being into right relationship with God.

The chaos, violence, hatred, greed, and enmity that exist in the world are spiritual problems—not physical ones. God created humanity and from the very beginning, strife and animosity began. Adam and Eve sinned and immediately Adam blamed not only his wife, but also God. "The woman YOU gave me enticed me to sin," Adam reminded God. Then they had two children; and Cain killed Abel out of jealousy and envy. It is not difficult (at least for me) to see that the basic problem of humanity is a spiritual one.

When our spirit is in right relationship to God, there is no animosity toward God, neighbor, or self. But in every human heart there is a spiritual battle going on. Paul identified it when he wrote the seventh chapter of Romans: "I know that nothing good lives in me, that is, in my sinful nature. For I have the desire to do what is good, but I cannot carry it out. For what I do is not the good I want to do; no, the evil I do not want to do—this I keep on doing. Now if I do what I do not want to do, it is no longer I who do it, but it is sin living in me that does it" (7:18-20).

There we have it—sin. Sin is a spiritual problem and is at the heart of human misery. It eats away at our insides with an unquenchable appetite that is as deadly as the most malignant tumor. We have no power to undo it, remove it, or banish it on our own. So how do we get rid of this human/spiritual problem? Once more Paul writes, "What a wretched man I am! Who will rescue me from this body of death? Thanks be to God—through Jesus Christ our Lord!" (7:24-25).

We refuse to get in touch with our soul. It is on the level of the soul (or spirit) that we shall discover inner peace, and from inner

December

peace, outer peace will flow. Paul (and other Christians) could face their executioners with inner peace, because their spirit rested in God. They had allowed their inner selves to be perfectly aligned with the Source of life and peace. Therefore, nothing in life could rob them of what was inside them and manifested itself outwardly. Paul says, "Those who live according to the sinful nature have their minds set on what that nature desires; but those who live in accordance with the Spirit have their minds set on what the Spirit desires. The mind of sinful man is death, but the mind controlled by the Spirit is life and peace" (Romans 8:5-6). We all would do well to spend a lot of time meditating on that verse!

As long as we are determined to live our lives on the physical level (which Paul describes as the "lower nature"), we will experience turmoil and fear in a hostile world. Find a good modern translation, and read the eighth chapter of Romans. Pray over it, meditate upon it and allow it to settle down into the deepest part of your inner being. Here, my friends, is the key to what you have been searching for—peace and happiness. I've shown you the doorway; now, by God's grace, be willing to enter it.

Living in Hope

9 The season of Advent should be a contemplative time—a time in which we think deep thoughts about the joy of our salvation. The joy of our salvation is Jesus, our Lord and Savior. Two millennia ago, the world was forever changed by the angel's announcement: "Do not be afraid. I bring you good news of great joy that will be for all the people. Today in the town of David a Savior has been born to you; he is Christ the Lord." (Luke 2: 10-11). It was a message of eternal hope, for the message came to a world that sat in darkness and the darkness was shattered forever with the light of God's hope.

Brennan Manning writes in *Lion and Lamb* (p. 160), "There are three ways of committing suicide—taking my own life, letting myself die, *and letting myself live without hope.*" There are many people in this world who are living without hope. Perhaps they have lost a loved

December

one, are terminally ill, have been forsaken by loved ones, grown old and feel lonely; or maybe they have lost a job, experienced a terrible crisis, feel no one cares about them. It is a terrible thing to live without hope, for it really isn't living at all—it is death by a thousand cuts. God does not want us to slowly die in the dungeon of hopelessness.

The message of the angel began with a phrase that Jesus often repeated when He walked this earth— "Do not be afraid!" The reason He could make such a statement was because within Him was the power to remove those things that can cause us to fear. Even when things in life go wrong, there is far more around and within us that is right. God saw that what the world needed was a Savior (someone to save us). The thing we need to be saved from the most is that which is within ourselves. As Franklin Roosevelt once said, "The only thing we have to fear is fear itself!" When Jesus spoke to the sea and commanded it to be calm, He was revealing more than His power over a body of water, He was revealing that He has the power to calm the storms of our lives. "Peace, be still," are words that all of us need to hear and absorb in our lives from time to time.

We serve a wonderful, magnificent Lord, one that has far greater power than our minds can imagine. Brennan Manning recounts the story about Arnold Palmer when he played a series of golf matches in Saudi Arabia. The king was so impressed with Palmer that he wanted to give him a gift. But Palmer politely demurred. "It really isn't necessary, your Highness. I'm honored to have been invited." But the king told him he would be greatly upset if Palmer refused to allow him to give a gift. So Palmer thought for a moment and said, "All right. How about a golf club?" The next day, delivered to Palmer's hotel, was the title to a golf club. Thousands of acres, trees, lakes, clubhouse, and so forth. . . . The moral of this story is: In the presence of a King, don't ask for small gifts. (*Lion and Lamb*, p. 165).

Hope is about trust. Christ is our hope and we do Him a disservice when we refuse to trust in His power to heal our brokenness and restore hope in life. As Christmas approaches, remember: God has sent us a Savior. Discover the joy of living in hope with Him.

December

Sound and Sight

10

In meditating on the Christmas narratives in Scripture, I am always drawn more powerfully to John's prologue to his Gospel (1:1-14) than to the accounts of Matthew and Luke. Beautiful though Matthew and Luke's birth stories may be, I think I am drawn to John because metaphorically he wraps the Incarnation in the language of the mystical. Not content to simply give similar descriptions of Jesus' physical conception and birth, he portrays Him in the majesty of symbols that transcend simple human flesh and blood—to John, He is "Word" and "Light"! He begins his Gospel, as does the writer of Genesis, in describing creation—"In the beginning God . . ." (John, of course, uses the noun "Word" as the verbal symbol to denote Jesus.)

The Genesis account of creation depicts God speaking everything into existence (e.g., "God said, 'Let there be light: and there was light"). John starts his Gospel by telling us Jesus is the Word. He is that eternal voice in which life originates and is maintained. Life is conceived by the spoken word, when that Word is God. The first thing God spoke into being (in Genesis) was "light." Now we have the two essential elements for all revelation, sound and sight. These two elements of revelation John uses to mystically describe Jesus, who is transcendent. Jesus is Word and Light—sound and sight, the essential qualities necessary for there to be revelation. "In him was life, and the life was the light of men." John is telling us that God came in order to reveal to us the essence of Himself and in that essence we discover the purpose and meaning of our very existence.

If Light is the metaphor for God in Christ, then darkness becomes the metaphor which describes our state of existence apart from Christ. "The light shines in the darkness; and the darkness comprehended it not." Jesus lived among us, and because of our blindness, we have not comprehended the greatness of His nature and the purpose of His coming. Thus, life apart from Christ is life lived in darkness. As long as we are content to live in darkness we will never behold the glory of God's presence. Julius Charles Hare wrote: "In darkness there is no choice. It is light that enables us to see the difference between things; and it is Christ that gives us light." Light

December

illuminates and reveals the truth of what is present. If we stood in a pitch-dark room and could not see the dozens of obstacles that lay in our path, we would constantly stumble and fall until the light came on and revealed their presence and position.

We live in a world of darkness filled with obstacles over which we will surely stumble unless the light of God in Christ reveals to us, by His life and teaching, how to recognize and avoid the things that would make us stumble. "And the Word was made flesh and dwelt among us, (and we beheld his glory, the glory as of the only begotten of the Father), full of grace and truth." God came that first Christmas not in ear-splitting thunder, not in dazzling, blinding flashes of lightning, but in the soft sound of a baby's crying and the radiance of a newborn child lying in a manger. Word and Light, nonetheless—Eternal God!

Darkness and Light

11 Three of the four Gospel writers record their understanding of the birth of Jesus. From the very beginning, Matthew, the Jew, weaves the story of Jesus' life in and out of the Old Testament prophecies. The focal point is Joseph and the choices he had to make concerning Mary's shocking pregnancy. We are told of an angelic visitor, Wise men and priests; of Herod's treachery and the slaughter of the innocents, and of a sudden flight to Egypt. In Matthew's account, Mary utters not a word!

Luke, the Gentile, gently unfolds his story with emphasis on Mary and her reaction to the angel's prophetic message. He ties in the story of Zacharias and Elizabeth and the birth of John the Baptist. He paints a portrait of a long journey from Nazareth to Bethlehem and of taxes and a census. There's an inn that is full, a cattle stall for a birthing room; and a baby in swaddling cloths. Luke rounds out the story not with the arrival of distant kings, but nearby shepherds, and angelic multitudes singing in the star-lit sky. In Luke's account, Joseph speaks not a word!

The previous devotional message spoke of John's point of view concerning Jesus' entrance into our world. It was filled with the mystical language of the Word made flesh, of the Creator of life taking

December

upon Himself the robe of human life. He talks of darkness that is shattered by light and of life contained in that light. There is glory, grace, and truth wrapped up in the being called "Word"—the One who is the only begotten of the Father and who would reveal to the world what God is like. Put all three accounts together and we have what we've all come to recognize as the revelation of the ancient Christmas story.

I reread the stories again and I was cognizant of the contrast in all three of the glory of Jesus' coming and the darkness into which He came—literal darkness and spiritual darkness. Aptly does Matthew define it when he writes (quoting Isaiah the prophet), "the people living in darkness have seen a great light; on those living in the land of the shadow of death a light has dawned." What's so interesting about that quotation is that Matthew doesn't include it in the events of Jesus' birth but records it after Jesus' return from the wilderness temptations at the beginning of His ministry. (Mt. 4:16) Yet when we turn back to Luke, the essence of Isaiah's words are found on the lips of Zecharias as he prophesies about his own son, John, and the role of the coming Messiah (Luke 1:76-79).

Instinctively, we realize that Jesus did enter a world of darkness. We assume (perhaps from paintings) that it was night when He arrived at the over-crowded inn, that it was surely dark when the shepherds left their flocks by night, and that wise men would have needed darkness to see a bright star. But the most significant truth was that the Lord came to a world of spiritual darkness, a world in which people huddled in fear. Christmas is about the Light shattering that darkness and bringing the peace of God. Darkness still seeks to enshroud our lives. This Christmas let the light of the Christ child banish your darkness forever. Come, worship Him who is born to be the Savior of the world!

The Fullness of Time

12 There is in Paul's letter to the Galatians a verse of scripture that is profoundly meaningful in describing the sovereignty of God as His will is carried out in our world. It says, "But when **the fullness of time** had come, God sent his Son,

December

born of a woman, born under the law, in order to redeem those who were under the law, so that we might receive adoption as children" (4:4-5, NRSV). Paul is saying that it was not by chance, not coincidental, not accidental that Jesus was born at the time He was. The "fullness of time" means at that exact moment in history that God chose for it to happen. The most significant event in human history happened according to God's time, not by chance.

From the Jewish perspective, there had been centuries of silence from the time the last Old Testament prophet (Malachi) spoke. Imagine, centuries pass and no profound word from God. Then suddenly John the Baptist appears, and most importantly, Jesus. The time was ripe for the birth of Christianity. The tremendous influence of the Greek culture and language had spread throughout Asia-Minor and the areas surrounding the Mediterranean. The Roman dynasty was at its zenith and with it there was a connectedness to the world that made the spread of the gospel more conducive to success. Highways had been built which allowed missionaries to travel more freely, and the expanded use of writing materials was beginning to become more prominent. For the most part, the known world was at peace. Into this moment in human history, God sent forth His son.

We will never fully know why God chose the exact time in history that He did to bring forth His Son. Jesus' conception by the Holy Spirit proclaims that God chose the moment for Jesus to be born in a way that is unique to the world—a child that was to be both human and divine. Events happen within the context of time. I believe that some events happen by chance and some are a result of God's sovereign power. I am not a Calvinist, one who believes every tiny thing that happens in life is dictatorially directed by God. In His divine wisdom, God chose to include in humanity the freedom to choose; freewill, John Wesley and others call it. If we have freewill, then that means God chooses not to manipulate every single event in our life.

God does have a plan for humanity. The plan is that every human being will have a chance to experience salvation and come to a saving knowledge of His Son. But God places limitations upon Himself. He allows each of us to make up our own mind. God's role is to provide the means for salvation; our role is to embrace it (or not).

December

Throughout our lives God either causes or allows events to take place that provide us with the opportunity to acknowledge Him as Lord and surrender to His desire to give us eternal life. Ultimately, the choice is left to us. Will we accept His grace or will we brush it aside? This year will soon end and a new one will begin. It would do each of us good to pause and ask ourselves the question, "Has the fullness of God's time come for me?" If it has, did I recognize it, or did I put it off? Is today, in God's time, my time, or is it yet to be? You do have a time. Just don't let it pass you by.

What Will You Bring?

13 At the birth of Jesus, only a few people came to celebrate His coming. Even they could not begin to imagine the significance of His life. The Christmas stories from the Bible tell us of shepherds and Wise Men who took time to visit; each one brought something special to the manger. It wasn't the gold, frankincense, and myrrh that are often sung about—it was the gift of their presence. The value of the Wise Men's gifts to Jesus was not found in the going price for gold, frankincense, and myrrh; the preciousness of their gift was revealed in their willingness to make a long and arduous journey of faith in order to find a child they would never see become King.

How many millions of gifts are exchanged at Christmas that quickly fade into the sea of obscurity in terms of their lasting value?

In the comic strip *For Better or For Worse*, (by Canadian Lynn Johnson), a seven year-old Lizzie cracks open her piggy bank. "Look!" she says, "I got nine dollars and 'leven cents to spend on Christmas."

Her thirteen year old brother, Michael, is not impressed. "You can't buy something for everyone with nine dollars and eleven cents, Lizzie."

"I'm gonna try," Lizzie says.

"Well," says Michael, "they're sure gonna be cheap presents."

But Lizzie responds, with absolute conviction, "Nothing is cheap, Michael, if it costs all the money you have."

December

The value of Lizzie's gift was not nine dollars and eleven cents, but the love in her heart that made her willing to sacrifice what she had. The value of the widow's mite was not in its monetary worth, but in the love for God in her heart which would cause her to put in all that she possessed. This year as you ponder what you will give others for Christmas, why not seek ways to give them a gift that somehow reveals the love in your heart?

If Christmas is truly the celebration of our Lord's birth, how can Christians celebrate it with alcohol and raucous behavior? Getting intoxicated for Jesus is hardly a spiritual gift. How much more fitting to approach it with awe and with joy; and with thoughtful acts of love and kindness. Surely there must be a way to celebrate Jesus' birth that does not involve having our minds impaired or our lives endangered.

Trees, ribbon, tinsel, paper, and frivolous gifts will all disappear soon after Christmas. What will be left besides the credit card debt incurred? What did you give your loved ones last year? I doubt any of us can remember. But we all know what God gave to the world on a dark Christmas night over 2,000 years ago! God waits for your gift. What will you bring? All He really wants is your heart!

That First Christmas

14 There must have been a time in which the first human to walk upon this earth marveled as his eyes watched the eastern sky grow lighter and the first light of dawn slowly drifted across the landscape, driving away the darkness as it overwhelmed the flickering light of a million stars. What once was only the faint whisper of light began to take on the brilliant glow of blinding radiance. I don't know if the word "Wow" was in Adam's vocabulary but there must at least have been a close equivalent. Imagine, beholding the light of your first dawn! That was a unique and special moment.

It must have been somewhat like that when a gentle and exhausted young woman looked quietly into the face of a tiny baby snuggled in her arms and was struck with the realization that the radiance she was gazing into was the very face of God! Was the face

December

of divinity more soft and delicate than the face of other newborn children? Probably not! Was the infant Jesus less likely to cry or wet than the "normal" one day old? Most likely, not! How soon did the Son of God reach out to His mother's breast for the nourishment that would sustain His life? What joy it must have brought the infinite heart of God to feel for the first time the love and warmth of a mother's arms cradling Him softly near her heart! Only a few minutes old, and already humanity and divinity shared an eternal moment that had never been known before.

I wonder what thoughts danced across the heart and mind of God as He watched His only begotten Son entrusted into the care of the very beings He had created. Perhaps a soft whisper reverberated across the heavens, "Please be gentle with Him!" Could already the heart of God have wondered if He could bear the unquenchable pain that lay ahead? Why do we suppose that it was easier for the divine heart to endure the suffering of His Son than it was for that of a human heart? Do we imagine because He could see beyond the rejection, the beating, and the crucifixion to the resurrection and ascension that God's heart would hurt less? Does just knowing that glory lies beyond death's door make one's heart invincible to pain and loss? If so, then why do we hurt when those we love pass from this life into what we proclaim we believe is an eternal life of peace and glory?

Maybe God wanted to whisper to Mary, "Cherish every happy moment, Mary; drink in every unique moment of feeling His softness in your arms and His tiny fingers clinging to yours. Bask in every gleaming smile and every moment your life touches His in gentle joy, for the time is coming when, as my messenger told you, a sword will pierce your soul. I know, Mary, for already it has plunged through Mine!" Might it be that the first Christmas Day was a difficult one for God because He already knew what awaited His precious Son in the future?

This Christmas, take the time to recognize the blessings of joy you have in this life. Cherish every moment you have with a parent, a spouse, a child, for it is an unrepeatable moment that can never be reclaimed. This Christmas, pause and gaze into the face of God's love and grace and marvel at the greatness of His gift!

December

15 The Fullness of Grace

"Grace and truth came through Jesus Christ." So writes John at the beginning of his Gospel (John 1:17). He also said, "We have seen his glory, the glory of the One and Only, who came from the Father, full of grace and truth. . . . From His fullness we have all received, grace upon grace." Would you believe that John does not use the word "grace" again in his Gospel after these brief references in Chapter One? The beginning of John's Gospel is his version of Christ's birth. Clearly, John intends for us to see that God's grace took on human flesh.

What is this grace of God which Jesus entered our world filled with? This mysterious, mystical, almost indefinable quality and power? Paul was so impressed with it that every single one of his letters refers to it—altogether 91 times. We struggle to put it into words because it contains so many concepts: undeserved love, love expressed in forgiveness, acceptance of the unacceptable sinner, infinite seeking of the unredeemed, divine strength, healing and power poured into individual lives, erasure of the memory of wrongs committed, good returned for evil, ultimate self-sacrifice, compassion to the greatest degree for human pain, holiness wedded to that which is unholy.

The Greek word for grace is *cháris*; the Greek word for joy is *chará*. It could not be otherwise, for it seems to me that to experience grace without joy would be impossible. The two are more closely connected than just a letter or two in a Greek word. How many times did Jesus tell stories about rejoicing (*chaírō*) in heaven over sinners who repent? Sinners repent when they have encountered grace. Where grace is encountered, joy and rejoicing are certain to follow! The father of the prodigal rejoiced when the wayward son turned home—he threw a big party! But the elder son did not rejoice because he could not comprehend nor condone the reality of grace. Grace brings joy to both the person extending it and the one receiving it. Therein lies its healing power. Guilt is dissolved in the sinner, and anger and vengeance is absent in the giver of grace.

Jesus brought grace because embodied in Jesus is God's grace that can be seen, touched, experienced, and understood. Grace could

December

not be more powerfully revealed than that which was nailed on a cross. And it all began gently packaged in a tiny little baby, born in a stable, cradled in the arms of a mother's love. Blessed indeed above all women was Mary, for she was chosen to be the one whose womb would give birth to God's grace! To look into the face of any newborn baby is to behold the pure glow of innocence; but to have looked into the face of the Christ-child was to have seen pure innocence merged with grace.

A parting thought—those who are the recipients of grace are expected to become the extensions of grace. Like manna, grace that is horded is grace that will dissolve. If we have received God's grace then we are obliged to share it. All around us there are people who hurt, who despair, who labor under the burden of guilt. Will you give them grace? Without it, they may never know joy.

Christmas and a Hummingbird

16 It was the summer of 1983 and I had been appointed as pastor to Glendale Heights United Methodist Church in Durham, N.C. Following the Sunday morning worship service, as was my custom, I went to the door to shake hands with my congregation as they were leaving. I immediately noticed a tiny hummingbird that was trapped inside the lobby, hovering above the stairwell. The ceiling was about twenty feet high and there were tall, sealed windows on both sides. Apparently, the tiny bird had flown in when the door had been left open before church. Unfortunately, the hummingbird could not figure out how to get out and kept flying into the windows and wall.

Everyone had left except for our youth minister. We tried everything we knew to rescue the bird, fearing that it would fly so hard into the wall that it would injure itself. We opened the doors wide, clapped our hands, shouted, even tried to shoo the bird toward the door with a long-handled broom—all to no avail. The bird was frightened and was quickly exhausting itself in its frantic effort to escape. A feeling of deep compassion came over me as I watched a terrified little creature, totally incapable of finding its way, refuse to descend

December

to the level where the door to freedom stood open. Nothing I could say or do from my vantage point made any difference, because the bird could not understand me; and even if it had been able to, there was nothing it shared with me on a level of trust.

Strange though it may seem, I began to pray for the bird. It seemed so unnecessary for it to die when freedom was only a few feet away. I told God that if I could communicate with this little creature I could show him the way to escape. But I couldn't speak his language! So in my prayer I asked God to show the bird the way out. No sooner had I ended my prayer than the hummingbird flew right above me, about 15 feet high. Slowly it began to descend like a miniature helicopter; beating its tiny little wings, it came straight down. Startled, I cupped my hands and held them straight out in front of me. The little bird gently sat down in them and stopped beating its wings. It looked at me and I looked at it—amazed at what I was seeing. Slowly I made my way to the door and carried it outside. It continued to sit on my hand until finally, I gently but quickly lifted my hand, causing it to fly off.

I recall this story now because it's Christmas and it reminds me that we are like the little hummingbird—trapped, frantic, on a course of self-destruction. The only way God could communicate with us and show us the way to freedom and life was to descend and become like us—robed in human flesh. He had compassion on us and loved us, and in the face of that love we learned to trust Him. He hears our prayers and no matter what the circumstances of life, He opens the door to Life and gently ushers us to freedom. If I, a mere human being, can have compassion on a little bird, and if God can use me to help one of His tiniest creatures to find life, how much more willing is God to show us the way to Life through His Son, who loves us eternally!

It's the season of Christmas—a reminder that God heard the cry of humanity and sent his Son to save us. He sent Him as a tiny little creature entrusted into the hands of humanity. The difference is, He showed us the way to life and freedom by giving His life for our sins! Remember that, on Christmas morning!

December

No Room in the Living Room

17

Have you ever felt like an "outsider?" Been someplace, stood alone in the midst of a crowd and felt like you didn't belong? Even worse, have you been somewhere and were blatantly rejected? Children often do that to other children who want to fit in. Unfortunately, even adults do it too when they form tight little cliques and don't allow strangers to join their group. I wonder how Joseph and Mary felt that night when they arrived in Bethlehem and stood shivering at the innkeeper's door, only to be told there was no room for them. No need to condemn the innkeeper—if there were no rooms, then there just weren't any rooms! After all, he wasn't running a 200-room Holiday Inn. Still, how fitting, that even while Jesus was at the very doorway of His mother's womb, the world had no room for Him! It was the forerunner of events yet to come.

I used to imagine that Isaiah's words, "He is despised and rejected by men, a Man of sorrows and acquainted with grief. And we hid, as it were, our faces from Him; He was despised, and we did not esteem Him" (53:3, NKJV), were words spoken only about Jesus' crucifixion. Now I begin to ponder if it wasn't descriptive of His life from the very beginning, even to the present day. No room for an expectant mother and a child on the threshold of birth. No room for a Savior; this heavenly being who chose to enter the world He created. No room for love compressed into the small body of a tiny baby. No room for One who lived that He might die—die for you and me. How those words should haunt us: No room! No room! No room!

Is there room in your heart for Jesus? Have you become such a packrat with the things of this world that every little corner of your heart has been filled with some meaningless treasure that denies Him a place to reside? Jesus can't sleep in the guest bedroom of our house. He never sleeps! He longs to take up residence in the living room, and the living room of our being is our heart, which beats twenty-four hours a day. Have you ever stopped long enough to look at what fills your heart? Devotion to material things, obsession with sports, longing for unexplored adventures, the daily cares of living in a world with expenses and taxes, keeping up with the Joneses, trying to impress our friends and neighbors, a daily To Do List that never

December

includes time with God, and a hundred other "before Jesus" priorities. "I'd really like to chat with you Lord, but my calendar's full!"

I wonder how it would feel to build a beautiful house, magnificently landscape it, plant all sorts of beautiful trees and flowers around it, and then, when you tried to enter, hear a voice on the other side say, "Sorry, no room for you here!" " That's nonsense," you say, "that couldn't happen." Well, it happened to Jesus, and it keeps on happening. "All things were made through Him, and without Him nothing was made that was made" (John 1:3, NKJV). "He came to His own, and His own did not receive Him." (John 1:11, NRSV). But now for the Good News. "But as many as received Him, to them He gave the right to become children of God, to those who believe in His name" (John 3:12, NRSV). Imagine, no room in our heart for Jesus, but room in Jesus' heart for us! He said He went away to prepare a place for us. I wonder—are we doing anything to prepare a place for Him? I bet He'd love to hear, "Come in today, Jesus, there's room in my heart for you.

Journey toward Destiny

18 Seventy miles is a long way to walk, especially in cold weather when the terrain is mountainous, rocky, and uneven. There was wilderness to pass through and the area was notorious for marauding bands of robbers. Under normal circumstances, a strong person could probably make the journey in four or five days, but when you are nine months pregnant the task would seem overwhelming. Only someone who has carried a baby to full-term could begin to imagine the discomfort and strain it would put on the human body to make such a journey. Yet this was the reality for Mary as she and Joseph made their way south from Nazareth toward the tiny village of Bethlehem. Even if she had ridden a donkey, I can't imagine that would have been any less uncomfortable than walking, and sleeping, who knows where, along the way.

Undoubtedly, the trip would have been divided into segments as they made their way from village to village. Approximately ten miles southeast of Nazareth lay the little town of Nain. Here they probably spent the first night. As they came into the village I wonder if she was there walking along the street—the widow of Nain, the woman who in

December

a little over thirty years would watch her only son being carried on a bier toward an early grave. There she would weep and wail as she said farewell to her only son. She could not have known that the child inside the pregnant maiden passing by would one day restore breath to her son's lifeless body with the words, "Young man, I say to you rise." Yes, thirty years later, the widow of Nain would know joy because of the son of Joseph and Mary (Luke 7:11ff).

Much farther south, about twenty-five miles, stood the ancient city of Sychar. Here Jacob had dug a well that for centuries had supplied water not only to residents but travelers passing through. Was the woman at the well there that day when destiny caused the pregnant Mary to intersect her path? Maybe she was a small child herself, perhaps playing in the street with her home-made doll as she gave a fleeting glance to the weary couple seeking out shelter for the night. But she could not have known that thirty years later she would meet the fruit of Mary's womb at this same well and be offered water that He called "living water." From that day on, her life of ostracism would be changed forever (John 4:4ff).

There was a barren wilderness that had to be traversed as they made their way through Samaria. Along this road, years later, Jesus would meet ten lepers and heal them all (Luke 17:11ff). Could it be that Mary and Joseph passed at least one of them on their journey to Bethlehem? Even if they did not, it is highly probable that there were many people whom they did pass that would one day behold the child of this young woman who was about to give birth to God's Son. How strange that even in the womb, Jesus passed through a wilderness—perhaps the very same one He would spend forty days and nights in, following His baptism.

The journey from Nazareth to Bethlehem was difficult. But joy waited in a cattle stall—the lowliest of places for anyone, much less the Son of God, to be born But then, God often meets us in the most unexpected places.

Christmas Reminds Us We're Not Alone

19 Life always seems different at Christmas time. It's true that people's schedules become full, shopping trips abound,

December

special worship services fill the calendar, and decorations brighten dreary skies and shops. But beyond all these obvious things, there seems to be a noticeable change in the way most people approach life. There is an unexplainable expectation that becomes evident in many people; smiles appear more frequently and generosity begins to increase. For many there will be a mixture of joy and sorrow as we share Christmas celebrations with family and deeply miss those who won't be there to share it with us. Perhaps for a few moments we will ponder the unanswerable questions of life that often bewilder and torment us. Why must there be sickness and death? Why do nations seek to destroy one another? Why do people hate, and act so intolerantly toward one another? Why do we allow our life to so quickly slip away without treasuring its significance, until too much of it is behind us?

We ponder our mortality and wonder about the meaning of life and the possibility of life to come. And what is God's answer to all these musings? In the quietness of a cold dark night, God slipped into our world and the soft cry of an infant forever changed the way the world would view God. Our vision of God was expanded beyond the omnipotent sovereign Being who reigned in majesty in the heavens, sometimes seeming to rule with divine indifference to the plight of His lowly creation. This magnificent Creator gently touched earth with His infant Son and forever banished the notion that God was not here with us.

One of the miracles of Christmas is that it is not confined to the past. The Spirit of the Christ-child did not vanish from the earth when Christ ascended. The presence of Jesus remains with us and once more becomes incarnated in the heart and soul of every person who will receive Him. In receiving Him we become His child ("He came to that which was his own, but his own did not receive him. Yet to all who received him, to those who believed in his name, he gave the right to become children of God.") What a powerful, transforming thought! We have been given the grace to become God's sons and daughters.

Before Christ came, the world had been touched by God's love, but now the world is immersed in it. The Incarnation is the indwelling power of the love of God in a loveless world. It is the outpouring of

December

hope in a civilization that too long has lived with hopelessness. It is the mighty rushing in of peace where conflict and turmoil have too long been in control.

The birth of the world's Savior transcends time. It is more than an event which occurred twenty centuries ago; it is an event which is as new as tomorrow's sunrise and as powerful as God Himself. Christ's birth is no religious fairy tale that is kept alive by human memory; Christ's birth is a dynamic event which occurs again and again as human beings claim Him anew as their Lord.

Life does seem different at Christmas, because life is different. Perhaps it's different because at this time of year, more than any other, we stop and remember that we are not alone—God dwells with us! Alleluia!

When Fear Gives Way to Joy

20 She was afraid—this young teen-age girl who was still in the midst of her adolescence, but was being rushed into adulthood. No doubt the upcoming wedding was an arranged marriage. She a child bride and her husband-to-be a much older man. Life is hard when you grow up in poverty and your very survival is dependent upon another person to look after you. In obedience to her parents she was willing to be given into the care of another, even if love had not yet sunk its roots into her heart. The only security she had ever known was about to be snatched from her. The humble little house, deplete of any luxuries, had at least allowed her to live peacefully in the womb of its secure enclosure.

She had no dreams or hopes beyond living her life routinely until old age or death claimed her body. The outlook for one so young was not appealing; but the uncertainty of the future and the fearful reservations she felt about her wedding were small in comparison to the anxiety that must have filled her soul when the angel of God stood before her to deliver the most unique message ever given to a human being. The startling appearance of a being of purity, radiating a dazzling light—the light that comes only from one having been in the presence of the Holy—overwhelmed her tender heart, and fear sprang up and wrote its unsettling effect across the lines of her face.

"Do not be afraid," were his words; but who would not have been? Would it thrill you with joy to suddenly be told that the Holy Spirit of God was to come over you and in your body would be conceived the very Son of God? Or would anyone's reaction not be one of fear? This was not a mature woman who was being told this news, but a young girl in the process of becoming a woman. How truly unique she must have been to have "found favor with God." For even out of the normalcy of her fear she was able to utter uncommon words of courage and trust: "Here am I, the servant of the Lord; let it be with me according to your word."

Somewhere between announcement and surrender Mary's heart gave birth to belief, even before her body yielded itself to conception. Later, when she visited her cousin Elizabeth, she was greeted with the words, "Blessed is she that believed that there would be a fulfillment of what was spoken to her by the Lord." Mary believed; then she conceived! True to the gentle nature of God's grace, He would not impose on Mary that which she would not accept in obedient surrender. It was in the act of surrender that Mary's fear was transformed into joy. When she responded to Elizabeth's greeting, she did so with words that are mingled with faith and joy: "My soul glorifies the Lord and my spirit rejoices in God my Savior," (Luke 1:46-47).

Mary's spirit found joy in God her Savior. Joseph was not to be her Savior, only her husband. Her Savior was to be the very One to whom she was to give birth. Because of her faithfulness a Savior was born. And that same Savior has the power to transform any fear you have into an experience of joy if, like Mary, we will believe that God loves us and wishes only to bring grace into our lives.

What About Joseph?

21 The earthly father of Jesus is almost a postscript in history. Little is known or said about him in scripture. Certainly the church has never given him the place of honor that has been granted to Mary. Yet somehow I think Joseph must have been a uniquely loving and honorable man. After all, he would have had the responsibility of taking care of both Mary and Jesus. He must

December

have loved them both very much, even though he knew that Jesus was more like an adopted son since he had not been responsible for His conception.

Matthew says that Joseph was "a righteous man and unwilling to expose her (Mary) to public disgrace." And so he married her, a woman who was pregnant, knowing that the child wasn't biologically his own. When trouble came and Herod intended to snuff out the life of this newborn child, Joseph took Mary and Jesus, left behind his carpentry shop and fled to Egypt in order to protect them.

Like Mary, he was undoubtedly a person of deep faith and one who was willing to surrender himself to the will of God. Like Mary, he could have said no to the angel's request to become the parent to our Lord, but he set aside his own comfort, indeed his own safety, in order to provide the loving, protective environment which Jesus would need. It would have been Joseph who was responsible for the religious training of his son, as well as teaching him the craft of carpentry. There must have been many days when Jesus was growing up that he sat at the feet of Joseph and learned about life, about goodness, about His heritage as a Jew and about how following the will of God often requires great sacrifice and trust.

The calloused, strong hands of Joseph must have enclosed the small, soft hands of Jesus many times within his own, as he showed Him how to saw boards and hammer nails. I imagine that he must have been a man of great patience, for the skill of carpentry requires patience, especially in a day in which there were no power saws and cordless drills—hand saws, chisels, and hammers were the tools that Jesus would have known. How fitting that the boy named Jesus, who according to John's Gospel (1:1-3) and Paul's epistle (Colossians 1:15-17) was responsible for shaping and creating the very world in which He lived, now in the form of human flesh, learned how to create something beautiful with human hands, under the guidance of a man called Joseph.

Unlike Mary, no one has ever called Joseph "Blessed." But in a real sense he was. In his own way he contributed immeasurably to the life of the One who is Savior of the world. He willingly accepted the special responsibility of nurturing the life of the One who would have

December

greater impact on the world than any person who ever lived. Joseph and Mary are the hidden threads woven throughout the life of Jesus. Like the unseen threads that shape a garment into the beautiful creation it becomes, so these two parents left the stamp of their own lives inextricably woven into the fabric of all that Jesus is.

This Christmas season, as we give thanks to God for the gift of our Savior, let us also pause and thank Him for the strength, nobleness, and character in Joseph's and Mary's lives, that gave us our Lord.

When Christmas Really Comes

22 Luke tells us about Elizabeth and Zechariah and about a taxation decree by the Emperor Augustus that required the parents of Jesus to be in Bethlehem. He also tells about shepherds and angels, and about Jesus being presented for circumcision in the Temple at eight days old. Matthew begins with Jesus' genealogy and tells us about the coming of Wise Men, the flight to Egypt, and the slaughter of the infants in Bethlehem by a jealous King Herod. When these two accounts are woven together we are given a picture of the first Christmas which reveals that it took place over weeks and months, not just in a few hours on a bright Christmas morn. The characters didn't just line up on cue around a hastily constructed manger wearing makeshift bathrobes and paper wings. This was real history in the making, a history unlike the birth of any other child.

Whether we realize it or not, we too stretch Christmas beyond just a couple of hours of gift opening on Christmas morning. We decorate weeks in advance, shop for gifts, go to dinners and parties, perhaps even concerts such as Handle's Messiah. We listen to Christmas music on the radio and TV and join in for several Sundays at church in the singing of carols and the lighting of Advent candles. Some even take time to attend Christmas Eve Communion and unknowingly present themselves at the altar as humble shepherds and inquiring wise men and women who have come to pay homage to the Lord of life.

Christmas has a way of grabbing hold of you and not letting go. It demands that your mind be drawn to it whether you like it or not.

December

Towns and cities decorate their light poles and the business world joins in with holly, poinsettias, tinsel, and blinking colored lights. Unlike any other time of the year, our hearts are turned toward the value of family. People all over the world write, call, or journey to the places of treasured memories where families once more are reunited. It's as if the whole world is saying there is a center to life and like metal particles drawn to a powerful magnet, the world is drawn once more to the mystical setting of Bethlehem.

When all the food is eaten and all the gifts unwrapped and stacked, when all the parties are over and the early hours of Christmas morn give way to the lingering hours of Christmas Day, we are finally left with God and ourselves. Somehow the Spirit of our Lord finds a way to gently enter our hearts and souls and reminds us ever so sweetly that this special birthday was God's gift to the whole world. When all the bows are pulled loose and all the bright paper is torn away, what is finally left in full view is the precious, innocent face of a Child. All our lives that face will draw us again and again to Himself, and the stories of Matthew and Luke will once more have far more impact on our lives than we ever thought possible.

The spirit of Christmas is in reality the Spirit of God once more sweeping over the confusion of our lives, seeking to bring order out of chaos. And God said, "Let there be light!" And the Light of the world shone forever through the face of a Child. And neither Satan, nor Herod, nor the powerful darkness of our sin had the power to snuff it out!

The Shrinking of God

23 One day long ago, God reduced Himself into a tiny imperceptible speck of matter and impregnated Himself into the life-bearing womb of a young woman named Mary. That which was purely spirit, that whose creative power lay entrenched in the marvel of the spoken Word, clothed Himself in human flesh and descended to our plane of existence. He came not with the spectacle of dazzling fireworks, not with universal proclamations, trumpets blaring, and masses waiting anxiously for His arrival; but quietly, on a dark and lonely night the God of all life slipped almost silently into the midst of human history.

December

Who were those invited to His birth? Not kings, governors, princes, rulers, politicians or emperors, but ordinary common people called shepherds. Should not this tell us something about His mission?—to touch the lives of humanity beginning at the level that those with power considered to be the least and most irrelevant among us.

God invited to His birth the shepherds of sheep! Those whose lives were lived not only in utter simplicity, but whose natural instincts were to be compassionate and concerned about something other than themselves. Shepherds are intimately acquainted with the fragileness and brevity of life and of the created order's dependence upon something beyond itself for life. Jesus would later honor them, when He claimed for Himself the title, "I am the Good Shepherd."

It was not the powerful and mighty alone that God came to save, but the most poor and humble that inhabit the earth. In a human world where wealth and power are elevated to places of honor and privilege, where many immerse themselves in luxury and extravagance—often at the expense of the most poverty-ridden among them—God entered history and challenged the order of things.

The wealthy and elite of the world often feel threatened by anyone who detracts from their power and glory. Herod sought Jesus not to honor Him but to destroy Him. But shepherds are not threatened by God's glory: they are comforted by it. They find joy in bending their knees and bowing their heads before the simplicity of His majesty.

Later on, wise men would come bearing expensive gifts; but the only gift the shepherds brought was themselves. They brought to the Child their hearts and souls and laid them at His feet. When the angel announced the good news to them, they did not mutter, "Why should we have to go?" Nor did they seek Jesus for personal gain. No, they left their sheep in the fields and they sought the one who would become the Good Shepherd in order to worship Him.

Christmas is approaching again. The announcement of His birth fills the air once more. Where will you go to worship the Child? Will you praise Him with carols of adoration? Will you receive His grace at the Blessed Sacrament? Will you discover Him in the comforting fellowship of shared faith in church? Or will you just ignore Him? Into

December

the darkness of our lives Christ wants to be born again. But will our darkness embrace His light or will we run from it?

It's a Celebration

24 For weeks now, millions in our world have had Christmas on their minds. Streets and homes have been lit up in bright, cheerful lights. Christmas trees adorn living rooms and malls. Shopping centers are crowded with patrons doing their annual chore of trying to find the right gift for a friend or loved one. Santa's helpers spread out across the country and listen to child after child express their secret hopes for Christmas morn. Stockings and stomachs will get stuffed, and diets and discipline get shelved—at least for a few days. In most places winter winds nip at the nose and ears, and love and compassion get challenged as frustrated shoppers look anxiously for that scarcest of commodities—the empty parking space near the store!

On the religious scene, churches join the festivities with Sunday School class Christmas parties; circles have luncheons, choirs sing cantatas, some observe Love Feasts, and let us not forget the annual bathrobe and towel nativity play, happily portrayed by excited children who jostle for the roles of shepherds, angels, wise men, and of course the starring roles of Joseph and Mary. Parental pride once more splashes itself on the smiling faces of parents and grandparents, oohing and aahing at their little offspring as they waddle across the stage in their assigned Nativity role with drooping see-through wings and tilted haloes made from coat hangers and silver tinsel, convinced that their child is the best little actor on stage.

Chrismon trees and Advent wreaths suddenly appear in their familiar spot off to the side of church chancels. Everywhere you look there are candles, garland, holly, poinsettias and all the trappings that unequivocally proclaim "It's that time of year again!" Congregations' hearts are warmed as once more they hear the words and melodies of "old familiar carols"; most of which were learned while we were children. Even the grumpy non-singer finds it difficult not to join in. Even if the preachers did not read Matthew or Luke's Christmas narratives, still the message would be proclaimed in the musical

December

sermonettes found in familiar hymns like: Silent Night, Joy to the World, Hark, the Herald Angels Sing, The First Noel, Away in a Manger and a dozen other songs that some inspired composer penned years ago. And oh, how beautifully did the writer draw us into holiness with the immortal words of O Holy Night!

Why all this familiar and prolonged celebration? In our hearts and souls we know the answer. It's in celebration of the event of our Lord's birth which is etched indelibly in the heart and mind of every true Christian. Rest assured, somewhere there will be grumpy ol' angry preachers who will waste the better part of their Christmas sermons bemoaning how we've commercialized Christmas and left Christ out of it—somewhat reminiscent of the elder brother who refused to join in the party at the return of his prodigal sibling. But you know what? Christmas is about a birthday and birthdays are about festive celebration—in this case joined together with holy celebration. Birthdays should be happy and joyful; surely it should be so as we remember our Lord's. Somehow I don't think God is upset with our decorations and our happy times together. After all, it ALL has to do with being happy that God loved us enough to send us His Son as the greatest birthday gift of all. Do get rid of that frown and grumpy disposition—come and celebrate!

The Christmas Baby

25 I wonder—how could it be that God would give the world a baby? Is there anything more precious or fragile, more defenseless or innocent? Perhaps God thought that surely our world would not want to harm or reject a baby. Yet Mary and Joseph had to flee to Egypt because, even at birth, Jesus was viewed as a threat to human power and institutions. What if Jesus had been conceived in our century? Would the narrative be changed from "no room in the inn" to "no room in the womb?" Millions of babies have been swept away by the edict of abortion. I guess the world has never fully loved, accepted, or wanted babies.

Babies represent responsibility, self-sacrifice, rearrangement of priorities, and the need to learn how to love. They can't harm you and they can't make you do anything against your will. But they can worm

December

their way into your heart and make you discover the best in yourself (and sometimes the worst). They can make you look at the world differently and become re-acquainted with a tenderness within yourself that you might have left behind at childhood.

In a real sense, Christmas is about babies. Yes, one baby in particular, but others as well. Even for the God/Man the entrance to life was the human womb. The Spirit of God is the creative force and energy of all life, including human life, and if Jesus was pre-existent, as our faith declares Him to be, then why is it so strange to us that God would shrink Him down to the microscopic size of a one day old embryo and gently place Him in the womb of a tender young woman?

I wonder if Mary had any regrets those nine months she carried Jesus? Somehow, I don't believe she did. Even if He had been just a "normal" baby, I imagine she would have found joy in carrying Him, because God would not have chosen a woman to bear Jesus who did not want to give Him birth. God does not force Jesus to be born in any heart that is unwilling to allow His conception within. Babies are gentle, you see, as is the full-grown Jesus who longs to be born again and again in human hearts. But alas, there are still too many heart-inns that can find no room—too many cares and concerns that fill each vacancy and turn aside anew the Child who longs to be born within.

For many, Christmas will come and go with nothing more significant occurring than the opening of presents, the eating of too much food, and for some, the ingestion of too much alcohol. There will be those who will be tending flocks elsewhere and not take time to "Come and see this thing which the Lord has done." Christmas day will be spent with little thought about whose birthday is being celebrated; indigestion that is inevitable; disappointment with gifts one didn't want or can't use; and hangovers, for many. Somewhere along the way the Baby will have gotten discarded and the meaning of Christmas will be lost.

But thanks be unto God, there will also be some individuals and families who will take time for a Baby, who will rejoice in His birth and touch others with His love. They will discover anew the indescribable joy of the Savior's birth. Yes, Christmas is about babies—a Divine Baby and human babies, and how their lives relate.

December

All that remains to be asked is: "How will you celebrate Christmas? With the Christ-child or without Him?"

Grace Brings Peace

26 On Christmas Eve night in 1996, Gaye and I served Holy Communion to 146 people who braved the bitterly cold weather and left the last minute rush of shopping and eating to come and kneel at an altar in honor of Jesus. It might have seemed strange to some to celebrate our Lord's birth by sharing in a sacrament that is oriented toward reminding us of His death. And yet, even when the angel announced to Mary that she would give birth to Jesus, he also informed her that her heart would eventually be pierced with pain because of what the world would do to her son.

We in the church tend to divide Jesus' life up into neat little compartments of time and events. In so doing, we overlook the fact that before He was even born God knew all that would take place and still loved us enough to send us His Son. The demented threats of Herod, which eventually led to the slaughter of the innocents in Bethlehem, were a precursor to how the world would treat Jesus. The Wise Men had to secretly visit Him and slip out of town silently in order to keep the demonic plan of Satan from attempting to circumvent the holy purpose of God.

The world has never loved Jesus and has always sought to eliminate Him. Sometimes overtly, at other times in hidden and secretive ways. What sad biblical words are these that allude to His birth: "He came unto His own and His own received Him not . . ." or "Light has come into the world and the world loved darkness rather than light because their deeds were evil."

Humanity was created by God for the purpose of bringing honor and glory to God. Yet like wayward children we not only lack the desire to bring Him honor and glory, we choose to ignore the reality of His presence in our very midst. Someone once said, "If Jesus was to come today in human flesh, we wouldn't crucify Him, we would simply ignore Him." We ignore God when we seek to live our lives apart from a conscious desire to accept Him as Lord. There rises up within us an inexplicable hunger for something and we attempt to

December

quench it by flooding our bodies and minds with "temporary" fixes; not realizing that what we are hungering for is the restoration of that union with the God from whom we are estranged.

In Holy Communion God offers us His grace—unmerited love, freely given. In receiving Communion at Christmastime, we are bearing witness to God's gift to the world. A gift that from the very beginning that anticipated a cross. Through Jesus' life and death we have been given the opportunity to discover the restoration of a lost relationship. In love God comes to meet us, in faith we receive His coming. In receiving we are restored and in restoration we find peace. Little wonder the angel announced, "Behold, I bring you good tidings of great joy. . . . Glory to God in the highest, and on earth peace good will toward men!"

When the Guests Have Gone Home

27 It was a strange sight, that first Christmas. The eyes of unkempt shepherds and foreign magi gazing down into the face of one of earth's newest arrivals. So much like all births and yet so different, for these were not the eyes of immediate family and friends looking into a baby boy's face, but the eyes of unfamiliar men who didn't even know the names of His mother and father. And yet in a real sense they were family because the whole world belonged to this child. All babies are innocent and have a look about their face which has not been marred by mistakes in judgment, outright sinfulness, or the toll of seeing too much sadness. But the innocent face of Jesus was somehow different.

As Mary watched the strangers arrive one by one she must have thought back to how it had all begun. First had come the angel's message: "Your child will be holy; He will be called Son of God." Then Elizabeth's remarkable greeting: "Blessed are you among women, and blessed is the fruit of your womb. And why has the mother of my Lord come to me?" The shepherds must have told her and Joseph what the angelic host had told them, that "A Savior, the Messiah was born in the city of David." And then the eastern magi came bearing gifts and proclaimed that He was the King of the Jews. Into the face of divine innocence the stranger/guests gazed for a few

December

minutes, perhaps even a few hours, and then they were gone. "And Mary treasured their words and pondered them in her heart" (Luke. 2:19).

When everyone had gone Mary must have struggled to understand it all and regain some sense of equilibrium from the events of the previous nine months. One more prophetic message was yet to be delivered. When she carried her Son to the Temple to be presented to the Lord (40 days after his birth), Simeon would deliver a troubling prophecy. "This child is destined to cause the falling and rising of many in Israel, and to be a sign that will be spoken against, so that the thoughts of many hearts will be revealed. And a sword will pierce your own soul too." Inner thoughts revealed, a soul-piercing sword? What could this possibly mean? So when the guests had finally gone home Mary was left with unanswered questions and prophecies to be pondered.

He was her child, and yet, He was the world's child—He was our child. When all our Christmas meals have been eaten, when all the parties have been attended, when all the gifts have been unwrapped and neatly put away, when all the decorations have come down and life resumes its normal routine, what are we left with from Christmas—indigestion, indebtedness, hangovers, happy memories, lonely memories? Or maybe we are left, like Mary, with words to treasure and prophecies to ponder.

Is this child our King? Savior? Son of God? A certain number of shepherds and wise men returned to their homes after the first Christmas not just pondering, but believing. How do I know? Because they believed the message enough to go and see for themselves; and when you come to God with a seeking heart, you never go away empty. You leave with a heart that is full of the glory that comes from looking into the face of God. Have you seen God's child? With what now is your heart filled?

Inner Thoughts Revealed

28 Simeon had told Mary that because of Jesus, opposition would arise and the inner thoughts of many would be revealed. We live and die with our inner thoughts. No one

December

can look into our hearts and minds and see what images dance across the hidden stage of our consciousness—some good and noble, others ugly and sinful. Each of us is the only person on earth who lives each waking moment with knowledge of what secret thoughts dwell within us. And yet how often our inner thoughts are revealed by the way we outwardly live our lives—sometimes unaware that people are reading our lives as if they were seeing a book come alive. All the plots and subplots that we think are so cleverly hidden are written boldly before the penetrating eyes of those who take the time to observe us.

The dark side of our humanity often reveals itself in angry words unleashed, cutting remarks thrown like poison-tipped arrows, disparaging statements heaped upon those we say we love; filthy language manifesting the soiled thoughts from which they arose; off-color comments and out of place deeds that rise from the cellar of our worst selves. We bring all of these things into the glorious light of the Son of God and their darkness becomes intensified, and we feel welling up within us that all-pervasive emotion called guilt. Along with it comes its twin companion called shame, and that center within us that we sometimes call "heart" begins to experience such heaviness that we feel quite clearly the first tear as it begins to form within us.

The consciousness of that tear is not a bad thing because it is first-hand evidence that the Spirit of God is sweeping across the darkness of our chaos and is attempting to breathe into us the breath of redeeming life. And if we allow that life-giving breath to take hold, it will lead us to a place called "repentance"; and from that repentance comes new life with its roots grounded in God.

Jesus did not come into the world to condemn the world but to save the world. He did not come to reveal the dark, hidden inner thoughts of our souls in order to destroy us, but to redeem us. When the dark side of us falls, the redeemed side of us rises. Furthermore, when Jesus looks within us He also sees the good that is within us. A goodness, I trust, that has come from previous moments in our lives in which we allowed the goodness of God to become our own. Good thoughts, noble thoughts, kind words and thoughtful acts—these He smiles upon; and as He pours out His grace upon them they grow deeper and stronger within us.

December

When the Lord of life was born in Bethlehem, He was declared to be Emmanuel—God with us. His coming has benefited the world and each person who willingly is embraced by Him. What a joy, what a blessing! And at what cost to his mother Mary— "a sword shall pierce your very soul." And it did; the day she stood and watched Emmanuel, her son, our Savior, die on a cross. No longer the face of a baby, but the face of a man torn asunder by the product of our inner thoughts. No shepherds, no wise men now, but Mary alone with her son. Yet, not really alone, because I was there, you were there, indeed, the whole world was there!

Something to Ponder

29 A week had passed since Mary gave birth to Jesus. Her body needed rest from the trauma of childbirth. There was in those days, of course, no anesthetic for pain, no transfusion for blood loss, no sterile environment to protect from infection, no medical professional to ensure the safety of mother and child. A long way from home, Mary could not even seek the help and counsel of her own mother to guide her into this strange new world of motherhood.

No doubt Mary thought about the unusual events surrounding her recent experience: The shepherds who appeared with news of angels singing on the hillside. The angelic visitor that had come to her nine months earlier. The strange dream that Joseph had which convinced him to marry her in spite of her pregnancy. Then there was the surprising reaction of the baby in her cousin Elizabeth's womb when she had visited her a few months earlier. Somehow Elizabeth knew that the child Mary was carrying was to be forever unique, for she said the baby "leaped in her womb" (Luke 1:41).

It's amazing how quickly parental skills develop. Like all mothers, Mary must have pondered her child's future as she looked down at her nursing child. Nothing the angel had said to her had forewarned her about the pain that lay ahead. The first hint that trouble awaited her and her child would come from a priest named Simeon when she and Joseph took Jesus to the Temple in a few weeks to present Him to the Lord. He uttered words that would haunt her all

December

the days of her life: "This child is destined to cause the falling and rising of many in Israel, and to be a sign that will be spoken against, so that the thoughts of many hearts will be revealed. And a sword will pierce your own soul too." (Luke 2:34). What did he mean, "a sword will pierce your soul?"

It would not be long after she heard those words that the first indication of the future would begin to unfold. Immediately after the wise men had left, an angel appeared once again to Joseph in a dream and told him to take Mary and the child and flee to Egypt, for Herod was seeking the child to kill Him (Matthew 2:13). From that moment on Mary's heart would live in fear for the safety of her child. Not a day would pass that she wouldn't reflect on those disturbing words. As she watched Him grow she must always have felt suspicious toward strangers and uneasy when soldiers suddenly appeared in her village. Even after Herod died a year or so later, Mary still lived with the knowledge that his heirs would always be a threat to Jesus.

And so almost a week has passed since we celebrated the birth of our Lord. Have you returned to life as usual or does the celebration of His birth and the commitment to His life still linger in your consciousness? With the putting away of ornaments and decorations have you also put away the Christ child? Stashed away in boxes, will Jesus now be secluded in the darkness of a closet or attic; or is it just possible that you have chosen to let Him live and be celebrated in your heart each day of the year? Only you can make that choice, but this I know for sure: God longs to commune with you every moment you live, even into eternal life.

Fear Not!

30 In 1999, at midnight on the last day of the month, we experienced something that had never been seen before—we watched history pass out of a millennium that ended with 1999 into the beginning of another thousand years that began with a "2" (2000). It was the simple changing of a number on a page and yet many throughout the world were filled with fear and apprehension. Some feared the coming new year because of the much ballyhooed talk surrounding what was commonly referred to then, as "Y2K"

December

(which stood for "Year 2000"—Y = year and K is the mathematical letter indicating thousand). Our world had become so intertwined and dependent upon computers that there was great fear that everything would crash or break down. Never mind that for months experts had been telling us that there would be no "major" problems. Clearly, nothing drives fear with greater intensity than does not knowing.

Here's a thought I asked my congregation to ponder: regardless of what does or doesn't happen on January 1, 2000, is God less God? When the clock strikes midnight will God's love and care diminish? Are you any less His child, any less saved by His grace? Someone said that there are 365 references in scripture in which we are told "Fear not!" If that is true, then that's one for each day of the year. Think of the number of times in Scripture that angels told people, "Fear not!" Jesus also told those around Him to fear not.

To live in fear is to deny one's self the serenity and benefit of God's comforting grace. When the apostle Paul was imprisoned in chains in Philippi, the scripture tells us at midnight he was singing hymns. Hardly the behavior of a person who was worried about what human beings could do to him! To live in fear is to focus one's attention on that which is less than God. Can you remember a time when you were a child and you felt frightened, so you ran to the arms of your mother or father and felt the strong, secure feeling of love encircling your tiny body? Suddenly everything seemed safe and secure again, not just because you were being held by a "big person" but because you instinctively knew you were being held by one who loved you. So it is with God: We are grown up now, and yet we can have the same secure feeling we had as a child, if we will pause and realize that the God of grace and mercy has embraced us with the strength of His love. Ultimately, nothing can harm us.

The Bible says: "There is no fear in love. But perfect love drives out fear, because fear has to do with punishment. The one who fears is not made perfect in love" (I John 4:18). There is but One whose love is perfect. Wonder of wonders, He hungers to give you that love. All that will prevent you from receiving it and living in it is your own desire. Most of us discovered as children growing up that our parents loved us. We also discovered as we grew that we had the choice to live

December

in or outside the power of that love. Whenever we chose to live outside it, our lives were diminished and our sense of self-worth decreased. There is a need within each human being to be loved by someone greater than him or herself. The ultimate need is to be loved by the Creator who is greatest of all—and you are! Come midnight December 31 or any other day of any year, lay your head on your pillow in peace and accept the fact that God's love has not changed! I think I hear an angel saying once more, "Fear not!"

A Day with God

31 One year ends and another begins. In reality the only thing that really changes is a date on a piece of paper. Rest assured, God doesn't flip a page in heaven and say, "Yesterday was December 31 and today is January 1, therefore the world is suddenly different." What changes, or at least has the opportunity to change, is people's perception, their mental outlook. Some view the beginning of the new year as a fresh start, an opportunity to put behind them the failures of the past and the unwanted bad experiences they may have encountered. Many who had invested heavily in the stock market in the past year are looking for a turnaround, the opportunity to recoup some of their losses. Others hope to put behind them the sad memory of a relationship gone sour and the inner pain that came with it.

Some people will take stock of the years they have lived and then make themselves depressed by complaining because they are another year older; thus in their minds somehow less alive. They construct mental walls that block future happiness and swing wide the doors of the past, thinking they can somehow take refuge in memories that are always steadily retreating into the distant "has been". While it is certainly okay to remember the past, one cannot live there. If one tries to do that, then one only succeeds in living an illusion, a mirage, something that no longer exists.

It seems to me that the apostle Paul had some good advice for all of us. He writes in Philippians 4:6-7:

Do not be anxious about anything, but in everything, by prayer and petition, with thanksgiving, present your requests to

December

God. And the peace of God, which transcends all understanding, will guard your hearts and your minds in Christ Jesus.

I take that to mean that Paul is saying you can quit worrying about things by taking them to God in prayer; and not just any kind of prayer but prayer that both states the need and at the same time offers thanksgiving. Crazy though it may sound, when the apostles Peter and James were dragged before the synagogue and were beaten for being Christians, they left rejoicing that they had been counted worthy to suffer for Jesus.

Are you going through something bad right now? Rather than complain and tell God how unfair He and life are, why not say, "Lord, I wouldn't have chosen this thing that's happening to me, but I surrender it to you and ask that you might teach me something valuable and in the process bring yourself glory." Maybe you're thinking, "That's easy for you to say; what have you gone through?" Well, in a few days I will have my fifth major operation—the third one for cancer. I didn't ask for cancer; it certainly isn't a pleasant experience, but I have discovered in all that I have been through because of it, I have grown closer to God and I believe have been able to be more useful to Him. So, I thank God for the opportunity to bear witness to His glory, even in pain and suffering.

And what does Paul say we can expect with such an attitude? "The peace of God which passes all understanding will keep your hearts and your minds in Christ Jesus." Hey, it works! I know, because I live in that peace! I am in Christ Jesus. No place on earth I'd rather be!